AF659796

XII
CBSE

micro

Introductory Microeconomics

T. R. Jain
Former Principal
S.A. Jain College
Ambala City

Dr. V. K. Ohri
Associate Professor(Retd.)
Shyam Lal College
(Delhi University), Delhi

VK Global Publications Pvt. Ltd.

Printing History: Edition: 2016-17

Syllabus Covered: Central Board of Secondary Education, Delhi

Medium: ENGLISH (Hindi medium is also available)

Price: Six Hundred Twelve Rupees (₹ 612/-)
(Set of Two Books)

ISBN: 978-81-909864-2-7

Published By: **VK Global Publications Pvt. Ltd.**

Regd. Office:
4323/3, Ansari Road, Darya Ganj, New Delhi-110002
Ph: 91-11-23250105, 23250106 Fax: 91-11-23250141

Corporate Office:
15/1, Main Mathura Road, Faridabad (NCR)
Haryana-121003
Phone: 0129-7117719 (30 lines) Fax: 0129-2250322

Email: mail@vkpublications.com
www.vkpublications.com

Printed At: Prince Print Process, Delhi

Contents

Introductory Microeconomics

Syllabus

Central Board of Secondary Education, Delhi

Economics **Class XII**

Paper One 1½ Hours Marks: 50

Units	Periods	Marks
Part–A: Introductory Microeconomics		
1. Introduction	11	06
2. Consumer's Equilibrium and Demand	34	16
3. Producer Behaviour and Supply	34	16
4. Forms of Market and Price Determination under Perfect Competition with Simple Applications	31	12
Total	110	50

PART–A: Introductory Microeconomics

Unit–1: Introduction (Periods 11)

Meaning of Microeconomics and Macroeconomics.

What is an economy? Central problems of an economy: what, how and for whom to produce; concepts of production possibility frontier and opportunity cost.

Unit–2: Consumer's Equilibrium and Demand (Periods 34)

Consumer's equilibrium—meaning of utility, marginal utility, law of diminishing marginal utility, conditions of consumer's equilibrium using marginal utility analysis.

Indifference curve analysis of consumer's equilibrium—the consumer's budget (budget set and budget line), preferences of the consumer (indifference curve, indifference map) and conditions of consumer's equilibrium.

Demand, market demand, determinants of demand, demand schedule, demand curve and its slope, movement along and shifts in the demand curve; price elasticity of demand—factors affecting price elasticity of demand; measurement of price elasticity of demand—(a) percentage-change method, and (b) geometric method (linear demand curve); relationship between price elasticity of demand and total expenditure.

Unit–3: Producer Behaviour and Supply (Periods 34)

Production function—Short Run and Long Run.
Total Product, Average Product and Marginal Product.
Returns to a Factor.

Cost: Short run costs—total cost, total fixed cost, total variable cost; Average cost; Average fixed cost, average variable cost and marginal cost—meaning and their relationships.

Revenue—total, average and marginal revenue—meaning and their relationships.

Producer's equilibrium—meaning and its conditions in terms of marginal revenue-marginal cost.

Supply, market supply, determinants of supply, supply schedule, supply curve and its slope, movements along and shifts in supply curve, price elasticity of supply; measurement of price elasticity of supply—(a) percentage-change method, and (b) geometric method.

Unit–4: Forms of Market and Price Determination under Perfect Competition with Simple Applications (Periods 31)

Perfect competition—features; determination of market equilibrium and effects of shifts in demand and supply.

Other market forms—monopoly, monopolistic competition, oligopoly—their meaning and features.

Simple applications of demand and supply: Price ceiling, price floor.

Design of Question Paper

Central Board of Secondary Education, Delhi

Economics

Class XII

Duration: 3 Hours

Marks: 100

S. No.	Typology of Questions	Very Short Answer MCQ 1 Mark	Short Answer I 3 Marks	Short Answer II 4 Marks	Long Answer 6 Marks	Marks	%
1.	**Remembering:** (Knowledge based simple recall questions, to know specific facts, terms, concepts, principles, or theories; identify, define, or recite, information)	2	1	2	2	25	25%
2.	**Understanding:** (Comprehension to be familiar with meaning and to understand conceptually, interpret, compare, contrast, explain, paraphrase, or interpret information)	3	2	1	2	25	25%
3.	**Application:** (Use abstract information in concrete situation, to apply knowledge to new situations; Use given content to interpret a situation, provide an example, or solve a problem)	3	1	2	1	20	20%
4.	**High Order Thinking Skills:** (Analysis and Synthesis– Classify, compare, contrast, or differentiate between different pieces of information, organise and/or integrate unique pieces of information from a variety of sources)	1	1	1	2	20	20%
5.	**Evaluation:** (Appraise, judge, and/or justify the value or worth of a decision or outcome, or to predict outcomes based on values)	1	1	—	1	10	10%
	Total	**10 × 1 = 10**	**6 × 3 = 18**	**6 × 4 = 24**	**8 × 6 = 48**	**100 (30)**	**100%**

Note: There will be internal choice in questions of 3 marks, 4 marks and 6 marks in both sections (A and B). (Total 3 internal choices in section A and total 3 internal choices in section B.)

Introductory Microeconomics

Economics, Economy and Central Problems of an Economy

CHAPTER 1

TODO

- Introduction
- Defining Economics
- Microeconomics and Macroeconomics
- Economy and its Central Problems
- Solution of Central Problems in Different Economies
- Production Possibility Curve (PPC)/Production Possibility Frontier
- Concept of Opportunity Cost

1. Introduction

Scarcity of resources is a universal problem: our needs are always ahead of our means (resources). It exists both at the micro level (at the level of an individual) and at the macro level (at the level of the economy as a whole). No matter how rich you are as an individual, resources at your command are always scarce to satisfy all your wants. Likewise, no matter how rich you are as a nation, planners and politicians will never find enough resources to achieve what they wish to achieve for the country. Scarcity is a hard fact of life. It is an unavoidable problem. It can only be managed; it can never be solved.

Resources are not only scarce, but have alternative uses as well. At the micro level, a farmer may decide to use his land for the production of rice, wheat or sugarcane. At the macro level, the government of a country may decide to use tax revenue for the purchase of defence goods or for the construction of night shelters for the homeless people.

Scarcity of resources and the fact that the resources have alternative uses lead to the problem of rational management of resources. It is the problem of allocation of resources to alternative uses. It is economic problem, often called the 'problem of choice.'

The subject matter of Economics revolves around the core problem of rational management of resources.

It is concerned with how limited resources are rationally managed (or optimally allocated to alternative uses) so that (i) at the micro level, an individual maximises his satisfaction as a consumer, and maximises his profit as a producer, and (ii) at the macro level, the economy is able to maximise social welfare along with the rapid pace of economic growth. [Pace of economic growth refers to the rate at which production of goods and services increases per unit of time period.]

2. Defining Economics

Economics is the study of economic issues (or economic problems) arising out of the fact that resources are scarce in relation to our needs/desires and the scarce resources have alternative uses. It focuses on the rational management of scarce resources in a manner such that our economic gains are maximised. At the micro level, an individual maximises his economic gain when he maximises his satisfaction as a consumer, and maximises his profit as a producer (from the given resources). At the macro level, a country maximises its economic gains when social welfare is maximised along with the rapid pace of economic growth.

Economics

Economics is a subject matter that focuses on the rational management of scarce resources in a manner such that our economic gains are maximised at the micro as well as the macro level.

HOTS

Q.1. State the fundamental economic problem that has led to the emergence of Economics as a subject matter of study.

Ans. It is the problem of scarcity of resources in relation to our needs/desires. It involves the problem of rational management of the scarce resources.

Q.2. Why does an economic problem arise?

Ans. An economic problem arises because

(i) resources are scarce in relation to our needs, and

(ii) resources have alternative uses.

Emergence of Economics as a Study of Rational Management of Resources

The fundamental fact:		**The fundamental problem:**
Resources are scarce & Resources have alternative uses	⇒	The Problem of Rational Management of Resources

⇓

The Concept of Economics

Economics is the study of rational management of the scarce resources in a manner such that the economic gains are maximised at the micro as well as the macro level.

Or

Economics is the study of optimum utilisation of the scarce resources in a manner such that the economic gains are maximised at the micro as well as the macro level.

3. Microeconomics and Macroeconomics

Economics is broadly divided into two parts: (i) Microeconomics, and (ii) Macroeconomics. Following is a brief description of micro and macro concepts of Economics.

Microeconomics

When economic problems or economic issues are studied considering small economic units like an individual consumer, or an individual producer, we are referring to microeconomics. At the level of an individual economic unit (producer or a consumer), the basic economic problem is the problem of choice related to allocation of scarce resources to alternative uses.

A consumer is to allocate his given income to the purchase of different goods and services. He is to maximise his satisfaction. **How does he do it? Can we as economists study and find some basic principles regarding consumer behaviour?** Yes, we have done it. We have formulated theories or a set of principles describing consumer behaviour (called Theory of Consumer Behaviour or Theory of Demand). Demand for goods and services and consumer's choice on the allocation of his income to different uses are the principal issues we study in the theory of consumer behaviour. It is an important component of microeconomics.

A producer is another small economic unit. He is also confronted with the problem of choice. He is to choose: (i) combination of inputs he should use in production, and (ii) the commodity he should produce. He is to allocate his resources in a manner that maximises his profits.

Studying producer's behaviour on the allocation of resources takes us to the area of production theory and the Theory of Supply. Theory of Producer Behaviour or the Theory of Supply is another important component of microeconomics.

When we are studying the theory of demand (relating to consumer's behaviour) and the theory of supply (relating to producer's behaviour) we cannot ignore the study of the market for goods and services (called commodity market) and market for factors of production, like labour and capital (called factor market). Microeconomics studies how prices of goods and services are determined in the commodity market and how prices of factors of production are determined in the factor market. Theories that explain market price determination are called Price Theories. These are other vital components of microeconomics.

Vital Components of Microeconomics

These are:

(i) Theory of Consumer Behaviour: It analysis how a consumer allocates his income to different uses so that he maximises his satisfaction.

(ii) Theory of Producer Behaviour: It analysis how a producer exercises his choice on the use of different inputs and how he decides what to produce and how much. The producer focuses on the maximisation of profit.

(iii) Theory of Price: It studies how prices of goods are determined in the commodity market and how prices of factors of production are determined in the factor market.

Macroeconomics

Macroeconomics refers to the study of economic problems or economic issues at the level of an economy as a whole. The basic problem continues to be the problem of rational management of scarce resources, as in microeconomics. But, unlike microeconomics, the focus shifts from maximisation of individuals' gain to the maximisation of social welfare. The central issues in macroeconomics relate to the overall level of employment, growth rate of national output, the general price level, and stability of the economy.

Macroeconomics begins with the study of macroeconomic variables such as AD (Aggregate Demand) and AS (Aggregate Supply). It analyses how equilibrium level of output is struck (where aggregate demand = aggregate supply). Departure from the full employment equilibrium level of output is analysed as the problem of inflationary gap or deflationary gap in the economy. Fiscal and monetary policies are studied as measures to combat/correct the situations of inflation and deflation. Also, issues related to exchange rate and BoP (Balance of Payments) are studied with a view to analysing their impact on the domestic economy.

Vital Components of Macroeconomics

These are:

(i) Theory related to Equilibrium Level of Output and Employment: It studies how equilibrium is struck when AS = AD.

(ii) Theory related to Inflationary and Deflationary Gap in the Economy: It studies how departure from full employment equilibrium output causes inflationary gap or deflationary gap.

(iii) Theory of Multiplier: It analysis the process of income generation owing to investment expenditure in the economy.

(iv) Fiscal and Monetary Policies: These relate to budgetary measures and monetary measures, respectively, to correct the situations of inflationary and deflationary gap.

(v) Money Supply and Credit Creation: It studies the components of money supply and how commercial banks add to money supply through credit creation.

(vi) Government Budget: It focuses on the measurement and impact of budgetary deficits in the economy.

(vii) Exchange Rate and BoP (Balance of Payments): It analyses how exchange rate is determined in the international money market and how BoP impacts the level of economic activity in the domestic economy.

Microeconomics and Macroeconomics: The Difference

Microeconomics	Macroeconomics
(i) Microeconomics studies economic relationships or economic problems at the level of an individual—an individual firm, an individual household or an individual consumer.	(i) Macroeconomics studies economic relationships or economic problems at the level of the economy as a whole.
(ii) Microeconomics is basically concerned with determination of output and price for an individual firm or industry.	(ii) Macroeconomics is basically concerned with determination of aggregate output and general price level in the economy as a whole.
(iii) Study of microeconomics assumes that macro variables remain constant, *e.g.* it is assumed that aggregate output is given while we are studying determination of output and price of an individual firm or industry.	(iii) Study of macroeconomics assumes that micro variables remain constant, *e.g.* it is assumed that distribution of income remains constant when we are studying the level of output in the economy.

4. Economy and its Central Problems

Basic Economic Activities

These are:
(i) Production
(ii) Consumption
(iii) Investment, and
(iv) Exchange (sale and purchase of goods and services).

'Economy' is a widely used concept in Economics. It refers to the nature and level of economic activities in an area, which may be a village, a city, a district, a state or a country as a whole. Economic activities include production, consumption, investment, and exchange. When we talk of the Indian economy we are referring to the nature and level of production, consumption, investment, and exchange in India. At the time of Independence, agriculture was the principal production activity in our country. Accordingly, Indian economy was described as agricultural economy. After Independence, we are gradually shifting from agriculture to industry. Accordingly, Indian economy may now be called as an emerging industrial economy.

Economy

Economy is a system spread over a particular area that reveals the nature and level of economic activities in that area. It shows how people of the concerned area earn their living.

Because resources are scarce, every economy faces the Problem of Choice. It is the basic economic problem. It relates to the allocation of resources to alternative uses. It is commonly known as the Problem of Resource Allocation.

It has three aspects, as these:

(i) What to produce?

(ii) How to produce? and

(iii) For whom to produce?

These are popularly known as Central Problems of an Economy. In what follows we attempt a brief description of these problems.

What to Produce?

This problem has two dimensions:

(i) What goods and services are to be produced, and

(ii) In what quantity goods and services are to be produced.

Owing to the fact that the resources are limited, every society must find an answer to these questions. But finding an answer is not so easy. The problem becomes complex when the choice is to be made across consumer goods and capital goods.

It cannot be an 'either-or' choice. Because, both consumer and capital goods are of significance. Consumer goods are essential to promote quality of life. Capital goods are essential to increase production capacity.

When 'either-or' choice is not possible, the economists must struggle with the other aspect of the problem: how much of consumer goods and how much of producer goods. Here again, the answer is not so simple. It has led to lot of debate amongst economists, planners and the politicians. Because, if you decide to produce more of consumer goods, the present generation enjoys good quality of life. But less production of capital goods would mean that you are reducing production capacity for the future generations.

How to Produce?

'How to produce' refers to the technique of production. The problem of choice emerges because there are more than one way of producing goods and services.

Broadly, there are two techniques of production: (i) labour-intensive technique, and (ii) capital-intensive technique. Labour-intensive technique implies greater use of labour than capital, while capital-intensive technique implies greater use of capital (machines, etc.) than labour. While capital-intensive technique promotes efficiency, labour-intensive technique promotes employment. Also, labour-intensive technique is less expensive, particularly in countries like India where labour is abundant in relation to capital. The choice between the labour-intensive and capital-intensive techniques becomes a problem because the producers need to minimise their costs, and at the same time, maximise their efficiency. At the level of the economy, labour-intensive technique helps reduce unemployment, while capital-intensive technique accelerates the pace of growth.

For Whom to Produce?

The problem relates to the distribution of output (or income) in the economy. **Who gets how much?** It has two aspects: (i) Factoral distribution of income, and (ii) Inter-personal distribution of income. Factoral distribution of income relates to income-share of different factors of production, *viz.*, wages for labour, interest for capital, and rent for land. Inter-personal distribution refers to income-share of individuals and households in the society. Whether, it is factoral distribution or inter-personal distribution, the basic question revolves around equality (or inequality) in the society. The problem is whether allocation of resources is promoting equality or inequality. Equality is a social virtue, of course. But inequality may induce higher saving, higher investment and therefore, higher rate of growth.

HOTS

Q. **For whom are the MNCs (Multinational Corporations) producing in India and why?**

Ans. Production by MNCs in India is driven by the profit motive. Accordingly, these corporations are producing goods for the relatively richer section of the society. As a result, the gulf between the quality of life of rich and the poor (briefly called Economic Divide) is widening.

5. Solution of Central Problems in Different Economies

Different economies solve the central problems differently, as under:

Market Economy

Market economy is a free economy. It means that producers are free to decide 'what, how and for whom to produce'. On what basis do they take their decisions? It is on the basis of supply and demand forces in the market.

What to Produce? The producers will produce those goods which are more in demand and less in supply. Such goods offer high price and high profit to the producers.

How to Produce? The producers will use those inputs which keep their cost of production as low as possible. So that their profits are maximised.

For Whom to Produce? In a free economy, the producers will produce goods for those people who can afford to pay high price. Poorer sections of the society are often ignored. It causes the problem of Economic Divide, as noted above.

Centrally Planned Economy

In a centrally planned economy, decisions relating to 'what, how and for whom to produce' are taken by some central authority of the government.

All decisions are taken with a view to maximising social welfare. Unlike the market economy, profit maximisation is not the consideration. Those goods and services will be produced which the central authority (or the government) finds as most useful for the society. That technique of production will be adopted which is socially most desirable . In a situation of mass unemployment, for example, labour-intensive technology will be preferred (rather than capital-intensive technology) so that unemployment is reduced. Enough goods will be produced for poorer sections of the society even when production of such goods does not yield profit. Social justice is given higher priority than profit maximisation.

Mixed Economy

Mixed economy shares the merits of market economies as well as centrally planned economies. Decisions regarding 'what, how and for whom to produce' are taken on the basis of market forces as well as on the basis of social considerations. In certain areas of production, producers are free to take their decisions with a view to maximising profits. In certain other areas, decisions are taken entirely on the basis of social considerations. **Example:** In India producers are free to produce cloth or steel to maximise their profits. But 'railways' are the monopoly of the government. The government provides transport services at nominal rates so that poorer sections of the society can avail them.

6. Production Possibility Curve (PPC)/Production Possibility Frontier

PPC is a curve showing alternative production possibilities of two goods with the given resources and technique of production. It is also called production possibility boundary or production possibility frontier.

Economists also call it Transformation Line or Transformation Curve.

> Production possibility curve shows different combinations of two goods which can be produced with the given resources on the assumptions that (i) resources are fully and efficiently utilised, and (ii) technique of production remains constant.

Illustration

A producer with the given resources (and given technology) may have the choice to produce rice or wheat. If all the resources are used for the production of wheat *alone* then 100 lakh tonnes of wheat can be produced. And, if all the resources are used for the production of rice alone then 40 lakh tonnes of rice can be produced. If he decides to produce both wheat and rice, then various combinations of the two goods can be produced, as shown in Table 1.

The table showing different possibilities of production of wheat and rice is called production possibility schedule.

Table 1. Production Possibility Schedule

Goods	Production Possibilities				
	A	B	C	D	E
Wheat (lakh tonnes)	100	90	70	40	0
Rice (lakh tonnes)	0	10	20	30	40

Combination A shows that 100 lakh tonnes of wheat can be produced without any production of rice. Likewise, combination E shows that 40 lakh tonnes of rice can be produced without any production of wheat. Besides these extreme limits, there are many alternative possibilities of production of wheat and rice. Combination B shows that 90 lakh tonnes of wheat and 10 lakh tonnes of rice can be produced with the given resources and technology. Likewise combination C shows that 70 lakh tonnes of wheat and 20 lakh tonnes of rice can be produced with the given resources and technology. Combination D shows that 40 lakh tonnes of wheat and 30 lakh tonnes of rice can be produced with the given resources and technology. Representing these various production possibilities on a graph, we get production possibility curve as in Fig. 1. Here, quantity of rice is shown on X-axis (horizontal axis) and quantity of wheat is shown on Y-axis (vertical axis). Points A, B, C, D and E show different possibilities of production, with the given resources and technology. Joining all these points we get AE curve. It is the production possibility curve or transformation curve.

FIGURE 1

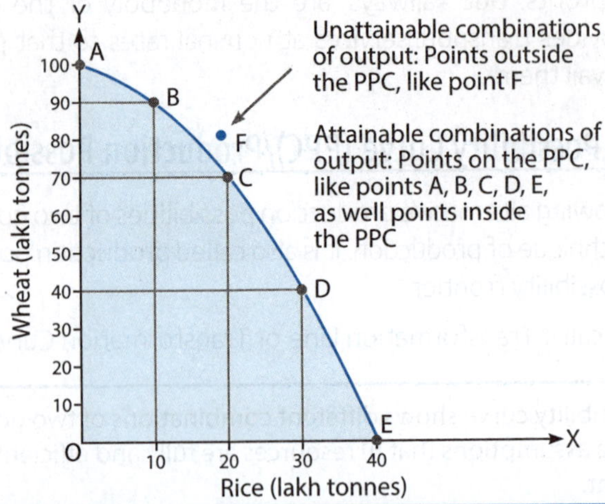

AE: Production Possibility Curve
Or
Transformation Curve
Or
Production Possibility Line/Frontier

AE curve (which is production possibility curve) is drawn on the assumptions that:

(i) the given resources are fully and efficiently utilised, and

(ii) technology remains constant.

Attainable and Unattainable Combinations of Output

All points on the PPC or inside the PPC are attainable combinations of output, with the given resources and technology. Thus, any point on the boundary line or within the boundary line (in Fig. 1) of production (within the shaded area) is a point that shows 'attainable combination' of output of two goods. Any point outside the boundary line of production (like point F in Fig. 1) shows 'unattainable combination' of output of two goods.

Assumptions of PPC

Two basic assumptions of PPC are as these:

(i) the given resources are fully and efficiently utilised, and

(ii) there is no change in technology.

Observe carefully, these assumptions include four points: (i) there is a given quantum of resources, (ii) the given resources are fully utilised, (iii) the given resources are efficiently utilised, and (iv) the state of technology does not change.

Once these assumptions are satisfied, we get PPC as concave to the origin. Why is PPC concave to the origin is a question being addressed in the next section.

A Note

The authors would like to draw attention of the readers to yet another assumption which is sometimes made with reference to PPC. It is assumed that "the resources are not equally efficient in production of all products" (Supplementary Reading Material in Economics, CBSE, issued 2015; Effective for March 2015 Examination). The authors feel that this simply is an uncontroversial fact and need not be converted into an assumption. The resources are indeed NOT equally efficient in production of all products. Certainly, land used for the production of wheat cannot be equally efficient for the production of apples or apricots. Likewise, engineers specialised in information technology and employed in Microsoft Corporation cannot be equally efficient in Garment factories. And, so on.

Shifting/Rotation of Production Possibility Curve

The production possibility curve will shift/rotate under the following conditions:

(i) Change in Resources

(a) Resources are Increased: If resources are increased, we can produce more of both the goods. Accordingly, PPC shifts to the right, as shown in Fig. 2 (from *ab* to a_1b_1):

FIGURE 2

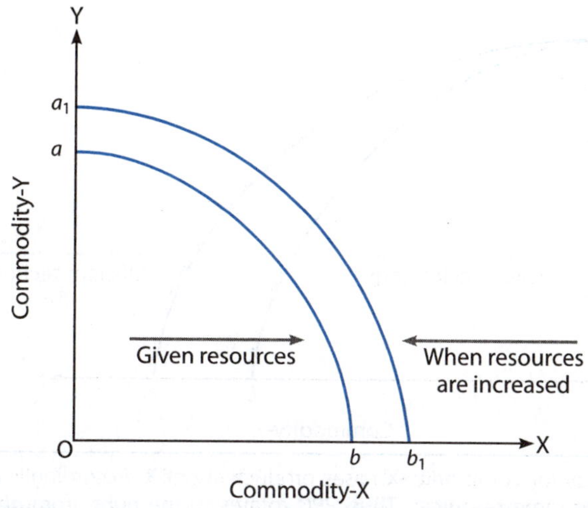

Over time, an entrepreneur may acquire more resources, (say) in the form of capital stock. This enhances his production capacity. Accordingly, PPC expands or shifts to the right, from *ab* to a_1b_1.

(b) Resources are Reduced: If resources are reduced, we can produce less of both the goods. Accordingly, PPC shifts to the left, as shown in Fig. 3 (from *ab* to a_1b_1):

FIGURE 3

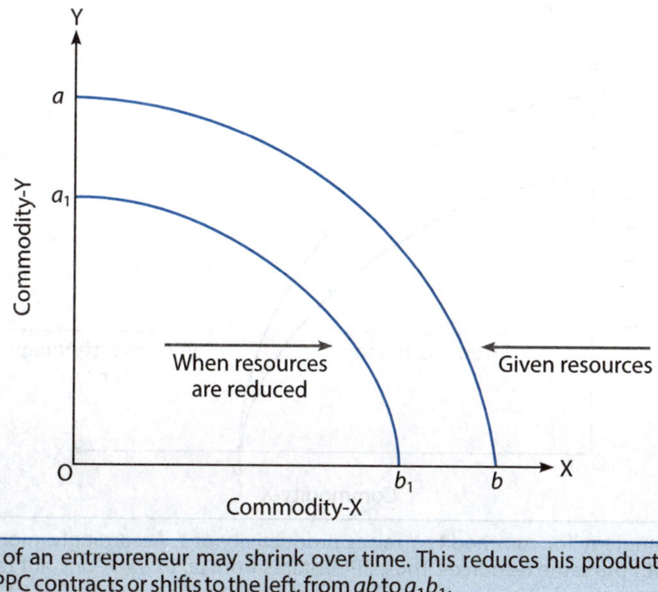

Capital stock of an entrepreneur may shrink over time. This reduces his production capacity. Accordingly, PPC contracts or shifts to the left, from *ab* to a_1b_1.

(ii) Change in Technology

(a) Efficient Technology for the Production of Commodity-X: Efficient technology for the production of commodity-X would mean more production of X with the same resources. Accordingly, PPC would rotate (NOT SHIFT) as shown in Fig. 4 (from *ab* to ab_1):

FIGURE 4

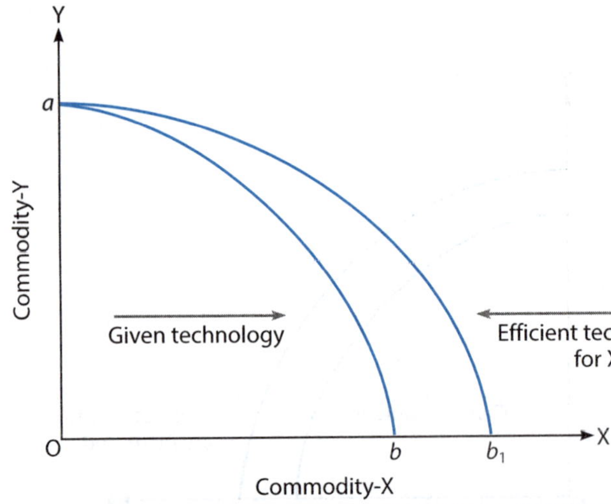

Efficient technology for commodity-X raises productivity of X. Accordingly, more of X can be produced with the same resources. Thus, PPC rotates to the right, from *ab* to ab_1. Constant technology for commodity-Y implies that maximum production of Y remains constant and equal to O*a*.

(b) Efficient Technology for the Production of Commodity-Y: Efficient technology for the production of commodity-Y would mean more production of Y with the same resources. Accordingly, PPC would rotate (NOT SHIFT) as shown in Fig. 5 (from *ab* to a_1b):

FIGURE 5

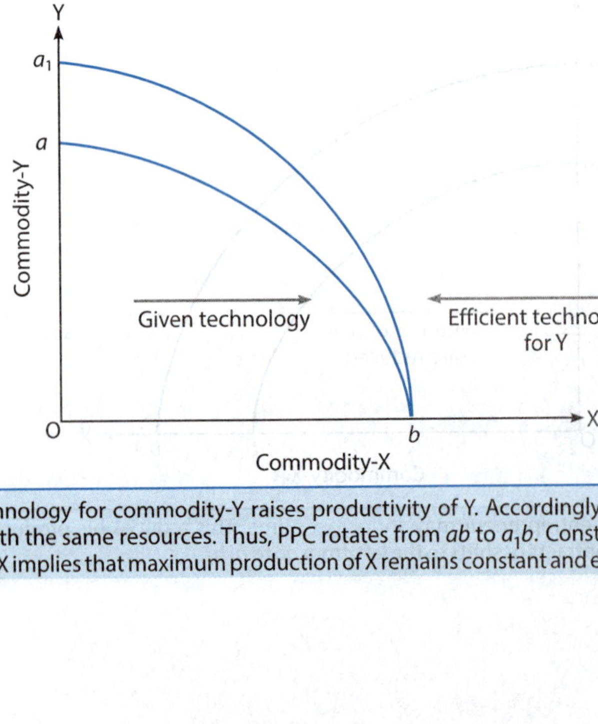

Efficient technology for commodity-Y raises productivity of Y. Accordingly, more of Y can be produced with the same resources. Thus, PPC rotates from *ab* to a_1b. Constant technology for commodity-X implies that maximum production of X remains constant and equal to O*b*.

(c) Efficient Technology for the Production of both X and Y: Efficient technology for the production of both X and Y would mean greater production of both X and Y with the same resources. Accordingly, PPC would shift to the right as shown in Fig. 6 (from *ab* to a_1b_1):

FIGURE 6

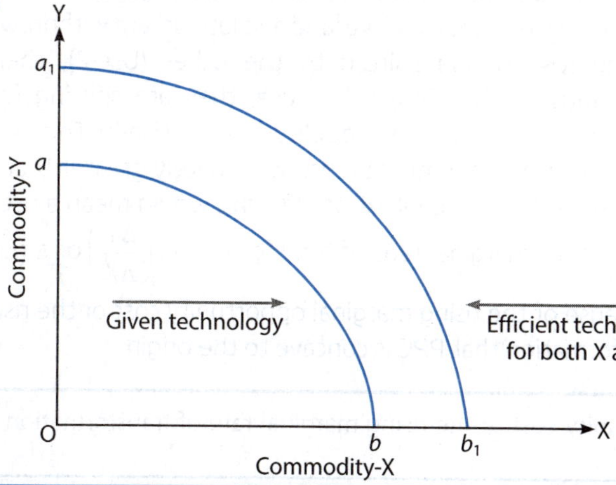

Efficient technology for commodity-X as well as for commodity-Y raises productivity of both X and Y. Accordingly, more of X as well as of Y can be produced with the same resources. Thus, PPC shifts to the right from *ab* to a_1b_1.

HOTS

Q. What is the slope of PPC? What does it show?

Ans. Slope of PPC refers to MRT (marginal rate of transformation). It shows the amount of Good-Y that needs to be sacrificed for producing every additional unit of Good-X. Slope of PPC = $\frac{\Delta Y}{\Delta X}$.
It is also called marginal opportunity cost.

[Note: There is no difference between marginal opportunity cost and marginal rate of transformation. Both are indicated by the slope of PPC.]

Two Basic Properties of PPC

Production possibility curve has two basic properties:

(1) Production Possibility Curve Slopes Downward: Production possibility curve slopes downward from left to right. It is because in a situation of fuller and efficient utilisation of the given resources, production of both the goods cannot be increased. More of Good-X can be produced only with less of Good-Y.

(2) Production Possibility Curve is Concave to the Point of Origin:

Here, 2 questions need to be answered:

(i) What does concavity of PPC mean?

(ii) Why PPC is concave to the origin?

Answer-(i)

Concavity of PPC means that for every additional unit of Good-X produced, more and more of Good-Y is to be sacrificed. It means that the opportunity cost of producing every additional unit of Good-X tends to rise in terms of the loss of output of Good-Y. In other words, concavity of PPC implies that the marginal opportunity cost tends to rise as resources are shifted from the production of Good-Y to the production of Good-X. Technically, it means that the slope of PPC (as indicated by marginal opportunity cost or marginal rate of transformation) tends to rise.

Answer-(ii)

Resources are use-specific. Thus, Ph.D in Economics is best suited to teach Economics rather than Physics or Chemistry. Likewise, soils with high water retention capacity are best suited to the production of rice rather than maize or *bajra*. And, so on. Also, most resources are already engaged in their specialised usage. Now, when the resources (like land and labour) are withdrawn from their existing usage (Use-1) and shifted to the other (Use-2), their efficiency (productivity) must suffer. Simply because, they are shifting from a more specialised usage (Use-1) to a less specialised usage (Use-2). This means that the loss of output in Use-1 (ΔY) must be proportionately greater than the gain of output in Use-2 (ΔX). In the context of PPC, this would mean a rise in marginal opportunity cost or marginal rate of transformation $\left(\frac{\Delta Y}{\Delta X}\right)$ or a rising slope of PPC. It is because of the rising marginal opportunity cost or the rising marginal rate of transformation that PPC is concave to the origin.

It is because of the rising marginal opportunity cost or the rising marginal rate of transformation that PPC is concave to the origin.

HOTS

Q. 1. When can PPC be a straight line?

Ans. When marginal opportunity cost or marginal rate of transformation is constant.

[**Note:** Constant marginal rate of transformation implies that the ratio between the loss of output in Use-2 and the gain of output in Use-1 remains constant whenever some resources are shifted from Use-2 to Use-1. It can happen only when:

(i) resources are equally efficient across their different uses.

or

(ii) differential in efficiency of resources across Use-1 and Use-2 remains constant whenever resources are shifted from Use-1 to Use-2.

These situations are seldom found in real life.]

Q. 2. Comment on the shape of PPC when resources are equally efficient across Use-1 and Use-2.

Ans. PPC will be a straight line (sloping downward). When resources are equally efficient across Use-1 and Use-2, 1 unit of Good-Y needs to be sacrificed for every additional unit of Good-X. Accordingly, MRT (or marginal opportunity cost) is constant and equal to one (Fig. 7).

FIGURE 7

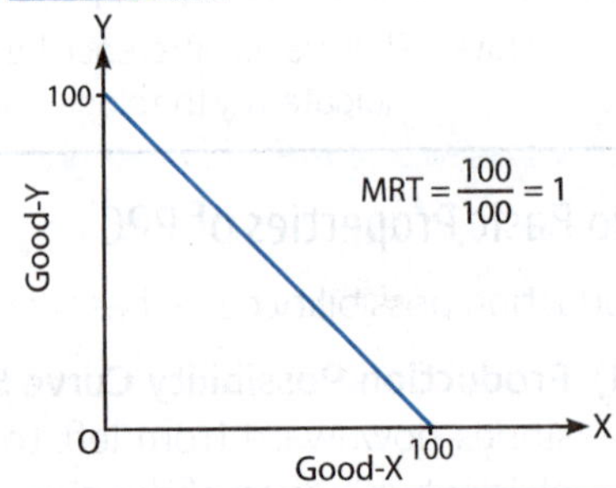

Q. 3. Comment on the shape of PPC when resources are differently efficient across Use-1 and Use-2, but the difference in efficiency remains constant whenever resources are shifted from Use-1 to Use-2.

Ans. PPC will be a straight line (sloping downward) but MRT will not be equal to one. It will be a straight line because the difference in efficiency is constant. In Fig. 8, 0.5 unit of Good-Y is lost for every additional unit of Good-X (so that $\Delta Y/\Delta X$ or MRT is constant). But, MRT is not equal to one, because resources are not equally efficient across Use-1 and Use-2.

FIGURE 8

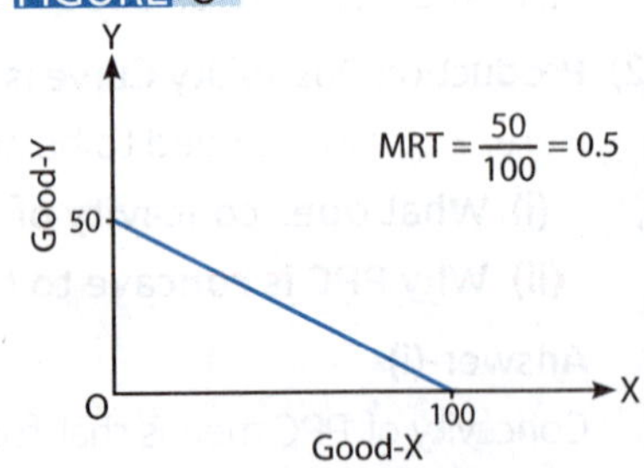

Actual and Potential Level of Output

It is with reference to PPC that we can draw the distinction between 'actual' and 'potential' level of output in the economy. Production Possibility Frontier indicates the potential level of output. It is the maximum level of output that we can achieve through efficient and fuller utilisation of the given resources, along with the given technology. Actual level of output, on the other hand, refers to that level of output which we are actually able to achieve. What we are able to achieve (actual level of output) can at its best be equal to the potential level of output. Often, actual output is less than the potential output. This is particularly true of less developed economies of the world. This is because, underutilisation of resources as well as inefficient utilisation of resources are the common features of these economies.

Actual output < Potential output, owing to underutilisation of resources or inefficient utilisation of resources.

Accordingly, the producers often operate at a point inside the PPC, rather than on the PPC. Underutilisation and/or inefficient utilisation of resources is a serious problem in less developed economies like India. It is an important factor contributing to backwardness of these economies. Fig. 9 illustrates the concept of actual and potential level of output.

FIGURE 9

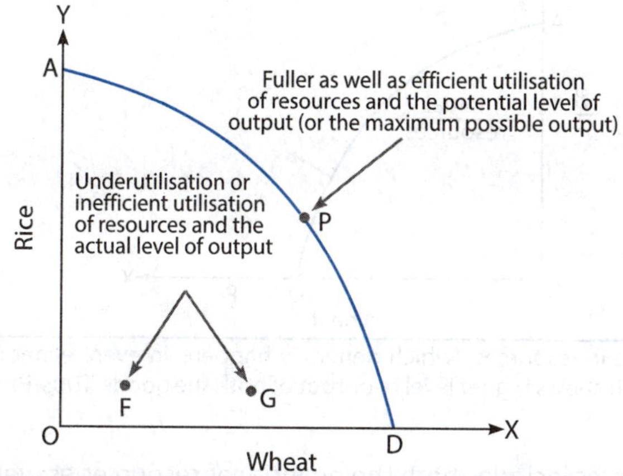

- Any point on AD (like point P) corresponds to:
  - (i) fuller utilisation of resources, and
  - (ii) efficient utilisation of resources.

  It shows the potential level of output in the economy.
- Any point inside AD (like point F or G) corresponds to:
  - (i) underutilisation of resources, or
  - (ii) inefficient utilisation of resources.

  It shows that the actual level of output is less than the potential level of output.

Example of Underutilisation of Resources: Labour is underutilised (or less than fully employed) in India: Mass unemployment in India proves this point. Accordingly, in India:

Actual output < Potential output

Example of Inefficient Utilisation of Resources: Lack of cleanliness (or lack of hygienic environment) impairs efficiency of the workers in India. Accordingly,

Actual output < Potential output

In this context, it may be useful to mention that 'Clean India Mission' by the Government of India is expected to improve hygienic enviornment. Accordingly, work-efficiency is expected to improve. When utilisation of the given resources increases or when the work-efficiency increases, actual level of output would get closer to the potential level of output. The economy would move closer to the PPC. However, PPC would not shift, as the level of resources and technology are constant.

HOTS

Q. Do all attainable combinations point to the same level of output?

Ans. No. Attainable combinations of output may broadly be split as: (i) attainable combinations on the PPC, and (ii) attainable combinations within the PPC. Those within the PPC point to underutilisation or inefficient utilisation of resources. Those on the PPC point to fuller and efficient utilisation of resources. Obviously, therefore, output level corresponding to attainable combinations on the PPC must be higher than the output level corresponding to attainable combinations within the PPC.

Growth of Resources: Over time an economy may generate or acquire more resources. Gulf countries, for example, have explored additional sources of oil. By selling oil these countries have acquired more capital goods. They have enhanced their production capacity. Accordingly, their PPC has shifted to the right. Fig. 10 shows shift in PPC to the right when availability of resources increases.

FIGURE 10

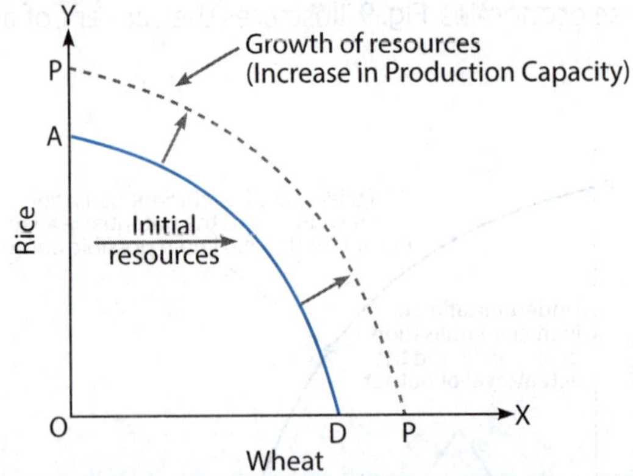

Owing to increase in resources, (which generally happens in every economy over time) PPC shifts to the right. It shows higher level of output of both the goods. Thus, PP shows higher level of output than AD.

Growth of resources includes both the quantity of resources as well as the quality of resources. Quantity of resources increases when, for example, mining of minerals is increased. On the other hand, quality of resources improves when, for example, skill-education is spread in the country so that the percentage of skilled workforce (in the total workforce) tends to rise. Production possibility curve tends to shift to the right both when the quantity of resources increases and when the quality of resources increases. Thus, emphasis on 'skill development' by the Government of India is expected to improve the quality of human resources in the country. Accordingly, PPC is expected to shift to the right.

A Note of Caution

A situation of unemployment of resources should not be confused as a situation of loss of resources or a situation of decrease in the stock of resources. It simply is a situation of underutilisation of resources. Thus, when unemployment occurs (owing to one reason or the other) it should NOT be reflected by a shift in PPC to the left. It should only be reflected as a situation of underutilisation of resources, as indicated by a point somewhere inside the existing PPC (Fig. 9).

7. Concept of Opportunity Cost

We know, resources can be put to different uses. These uses may be taken as different opportunities. When one opportunity is availed, the other is lost. Opportunity cost is the cost of availing one opportunity in terms of the loss of the other opportunity. Let us take an illustration: A given piece of land may be used to grow wheat (opportunity-1) or rice (opportunity-2). Assume that the output of wheat is 20 tonnes and that of rice is 15 tonnes. If land is actually used for the production of wheat (opportunity-1), we get 20 tonnes of wheat. But, what we lose is 15 tonnes of rice (opportunity-2). Accordingly, opportunity cost of using land for the production of 20 tonnes of wheat is equal to the loss of output of 15 tonnes of rice.

Using this illustration, we may also define opportunity cost as the value of a factor in its next best alternative use.

> Opportunity cost is the cost of availing one opportunity in terms of the loss of the other opportunity.
>
> Or
>
> Opportunity cost is the value of a factor in its next best alternative use.

HOTS

Q. What is the opportunity cost of opting for higher studies rather than a job?

Ans. It is the amount of wage/salary the person would have earned in a job.

It needs to be noted that a factor may have more than two uses. In any such situation, opportunity cost is to be taken as the value of the factor in its next best (or second best) use only. Take the following illustration to understand this point further:

Available Resources	One hectare of land and a given package of other inputs
Possible uses of land along with the package of other inputs	Use-1: Production of wheat Use-2: Production of rice Use-3: Production of maize Use-4: Production of sugarcane
Market Value of Production	Use-1: ₹ 5,000 Use-2: ₹ 4,000 Use-3: ₹ 3,500 Use-4: ₹ 6,000
Assumption	Technique of production is constant and resources are fully utilised.

Obviously, resources will be employed in Use-4 where the value of output is maximum, *viz.*, ₹ 6,000.

Opportunity cost of employing resources in Use-4 = loss of output in next best alternative use of the given resources which is ₹ 5,000 in Use-1.

Diagrammatic Illustration

Fig. 11 shows production possibility curve AB. X-axis shows Use-1 and Y-axis shows Use-2 of a given set of resources.

FIGURE 11

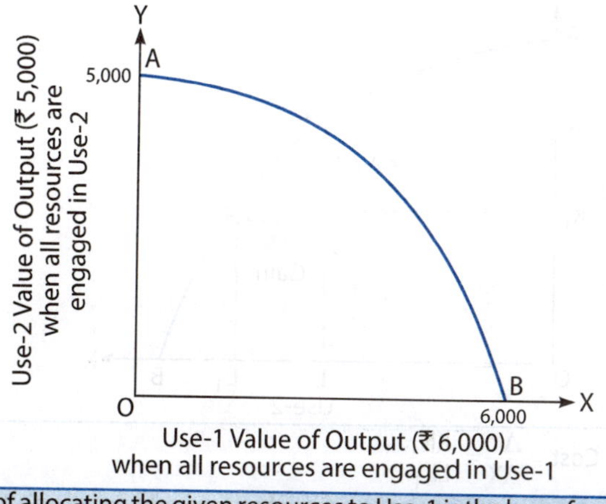

Opportunity cost of allocating the given resources to Use-1 is the loss of output in Use-2. Loss of output in Use-2 is worth ₹ 5,000 which is the opportunity cost.

The diagram (Fig. 11) is drawn on the assumptions that technology remains constant and that the resources are fully and efficiently utilised. Value of output in Use-1 is assumed as ₹ 6,000, and in Use-2 as ₹ 5,000. If resources are employed in Use-1 (as it should be) the opportunity cost = ₹ 5,000 [the value of the factor(s) in its next best alternative use].

Marginal Opportunity Cost

Marginal opportunity cost refers to additional opportunity cost when a unit more of Good-X is produced by withdrawing some resources from the production of Good-Y. It is measured in terms of the loss of output of Good-Y for a unit more of Good-X. Algebraically, marginal opportunity cost is expressed as:

$$\frac{\Delta Y}{\Delta X} = \text{loss of output of Good-Y for an additional unit of Good-X}$$

Marginal opportunity cost is also described as a rate at which output of Good-Y is to be sacrificed for every additional unit of Good-X. In this sense, it refers to the slope of PPC. Study the following illustration carefully for a precise comprehension of the concept.

Estimating Marginal Opportunity Cost–An Illustration

Production of X	Production of Y	Marginal Opportunity Cost
0	10,000	—
1	9,000	To produce 1 unit of X, 1,000 units of Y are to be given up. Marginal Opportunity Cost = 10,000 – 9,000 = 1,000
2	7,500	To produce another unit of X, 1,500 units of Y are to be given up. Marginal Opportunity Cost = 9,000 – 7,500 = 1,500
3	5,500	To produce still another unit of X, 2,000 units of Y are to be given up. Marginal Opportunity Cost = 7,500 – 5,500 = 2,000

Thus, marginal opportunity cost is calculated in terms of the loss of output of Y for every additional unit of X produced when resources are shifted from Y to X.

Or, Marginal Opportunity Cost = $\left(\frac{\Delta Y}{\Delta X}\right)$.

Diagrammatic Illustration

Fig. 12 illustrates the concept of marginal opportunity cost. It is assumed that initially resources are employed such that: output in Use-1 (Good-Y) = OK and output in Use-2 (Good-X) = OL.

FIGURE 12

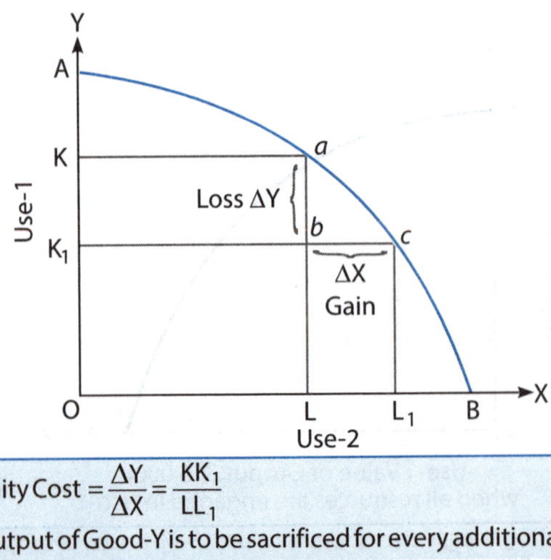

Marginal Opportunity Cost = $\frac{\Delta Y}{\Delta X} = \frac{KK_1}{LL_1}$

⇒ Rate at which output of Good-Y is to be sacrificed for every additional unit of Good-X.

Now, some resources are shifted from Use-1 to Use-2. Consequently, loss of output in Use-1 = KK_1, and gain of output in Use-2 = LL_1.

Marginal Opportunity Cost (MOC)

$$= \frac{\Delta Y \text{ (loss of output)}}{\Delta X \text{ (gain of output)}}$$

$$= \frac{KK_1}{LL_1} = \frac{ab}{bc}$$

= rate at which output of Good-Y is to be sacrificed for every additional unit of Good-X

= Slope of production possibility curve

(also called Marginal Rate of Transformation)

Example

An economy produces two goods: wheat and cloth. The following table summarises its production possibilities. Calculate the marginal opportunity cost of producing more cloth in place of wheat at various combinations. What does it indicate? Draw the Production Possibility Curve. What is the shape of the curve?

Wheat (kg)	100	90	70	40	10	0
Cloth (metres)	0	25	50	75	85	87

Solution:

Marginal Opportunity Cost of producing more cloth

$$= \frac{\Delta Y \text{(loss of output of wheat)}}{\Delta X \text{(gain of output of cloth)}}$$

= Opportunity cost of producing an additional unit of cloth when some resources are shifted from the production of wheat to the production of cloth

Wheat (kg)	**Cloth (metres)**	**Marginal Opportunity Cost**
100	0	—
90	25	$\frac{10}{25} = 0.4$
70	50	$\frac{20}{25} = 0.8$
40	75	$\frac{30}{25} = 1.2$
10	85	$\frac{30}{10} = 3$
0	87	$\frac{10}{2} = 5$

FIGURE 13

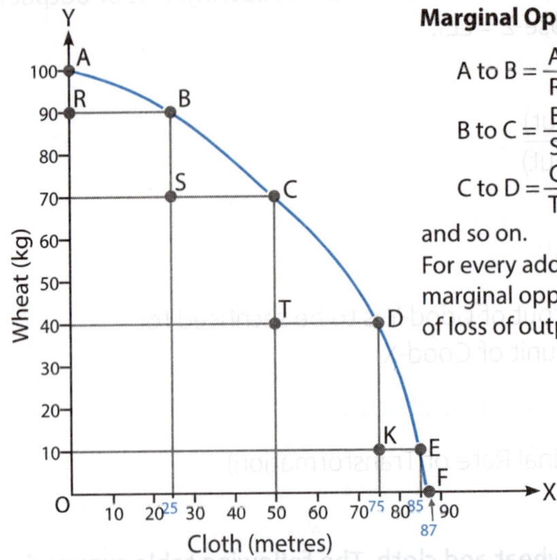

Marginal Opportunity Cost when we shift from:

$$\text{A to B} = \frac{AR}{RB} = \frac{100-90}{25-0} = \frac{10}{25} = 0.4$$

$$\text{B to C} = \frac{BS}{SC} = \frac{90-70}{50-25} = \frac{20}{25} = 0.8$$

$$\text{C to D} = \frac{CT}{TD} = \frac{70-40}{75-50} = \frac{30}{25} = 1.2$$

and so on.

For every additional unit of cloth, marginal opportunity cost (in terms of loss of output of wheat) tends to rise.

Marginal opportunity cost tends to rise as resources are shifted from wheat to cloth. Initially when 25 metres of cloth is produced 10 kg of wheat is to be sacrificed. For the next 25 metres of cloth, 20 kg of wheat is to be sacrificed and so on.

The curve is downward sloping and concave to the origin. The rising opportunity cost reflects that as more and more wheat (kg) is sacrificed for additional cloth, the cost in terms of wheat (kg) per unit of cloth (in metres) produced, rises.

POWER POINTS

- **Economics** is a subject matter that focuses on rational management of scarce resources in a manner such that the individuals maximise their economic gain at the micro level and the society maximises its welfare at the macro level.
- **Economic Problem** is the problem of choice or the problem of allocation of resources. It arises because: (i) resources are scarce, and (ii) resources have alternative uses.
- **Economic Activities** are those activities which are related to the use of scarce resources. Examples: Production, consumption, investment, and exchange.
- **Microeconomics** is that branch of Economics which studies economic problems (or economic issues) relating to individual economic units like a consumer, or a producer. Problem of resource allocation is the principal microeconomic issue.
- **Macroeconomics** is that branch of Economics which studies economic problems (or economic issues) relating to economy as a whole. Level of output and employment is the principal macroeconomic issue.
- **Market Economy** is a free economy in which central problems (what, how and for whom to produce) are solved by the market forces of supply and demand.
- **Centrally Planned Economy** is the one in which the central problems (what, how and for whom to produce) are addressed by some central authority of the government.
- **Mixed Economy** is the one which shares the characteristic features of a free economy as well as a planned economy. The central problems (what, how and for whom to produce) are not entirely left to the free play of market forces. Goal of profit maximisation is allowed to be pursued, but not at the cost of social justice.
- **Production Possibility Curve (PPC)** shows different combinations of two goods which can be produced when: (i) technology remains constant, and (ii) the given resources are fully and efficiently utilised.
- **Two Basic Assumptions of PPC** are that: (i) given resources are fully and efficiently utilised, and (ii) there is no change in technology.
- **Two Basic Characteristics of PPC** are that: (i) PPC always slopes downward from left to right, and (ii) PPC is always concave to the origin.
- **Opportunity Cost** is the value of a factor in its next best alternative use.

- Marginal Opportunity Cost/Marginal Rate of Transformation is the rate at which output of Good-Y is to be sacrificed for every additional unit of Good-X. It refers to the slope of PPC.
- Attainable and Unattainable Combinations of Output: Attainable combinations are those combinations of output which are indicated by the points on the PPC or inside the PPC. Unattainable combinations are those combinations which are indicated by the points outside the PPC.
- Potential and Actual Level of Output: Potential level of output refers to the maximum level of output which can be achieved through fuller utilisation of the resources, along with the given technology. Actual level of output is that level of output which we are actually able to achieve, using the given resources and the given technology.

EXERCISE

1. Very Short Questions (Remembering & Understanding) (1 mark each)

A. Multiple Choice Questions: Choose the Correct Answer

1. **Which of the following is not concerned with the problem of choice?**
   (a) Excessive income (b) Alternative use of resources
   (c) Unlimited wants (d) Limited (scarce) resources
2. **Principal characteristics of resources are:**
   (a) they are scarce in relation to our needs (b) they have alternative uses
   (c) both (a) and (b) (d) none of these
3. **In which of the following situations, does scarcity arise?**
   (a) Supply of resources > Demand for resources (b) Supply of resources < Demand for resources
   (c) Supply of resources = Demand for resources (d) None of these
4. **Economic problem arises due to the fact that:**
   (a) resources are scarce (b) human wants are unlimited
   (c) resources have alternative uses (d) all of these
5. **The resources for satisfying human wants are:**
   (a) limited (b) unlimited
   (c) available at zero price (d) none of these
6. **Example of micro economic variable is:**
   (a) wholesale price index (b) national income
   (c) market demand (d) aggregate demand
7. **Issues related to unemployment are studied at the:**
   (a) micro level (b) macro level
   (c) micro as well as macro level (d) none of these
8. **Who controls economic activities under centrally planned economies?**
   (a) Industrialists (b) Private firms
   (c) Government (d) Consumers
9. **Slope of production possibility curve is:**
   (a) a straight line (b) convex to the point of origin
   (c) concave to the point of origin (d) none of these
10. **The problem of 'what to produce' relates to:**
    (a) the choice of technique (b) distribution of income
    (c) market value of the goods and services (d) the choice of goods and services

11. Which of the following is related to the problem 'how to produce'?

(a) Factoral distribution of income
(b) The choice of technique
(c) The choice of product
(d) None of these

12. In the diagram alongside (Fig. 14), inefficient use of resources is shown by:

(a) points 'A' and 'B'
(b) point 'D'
(c) point 'C'
(d) points 'C' and 'D'

FIGURE 14

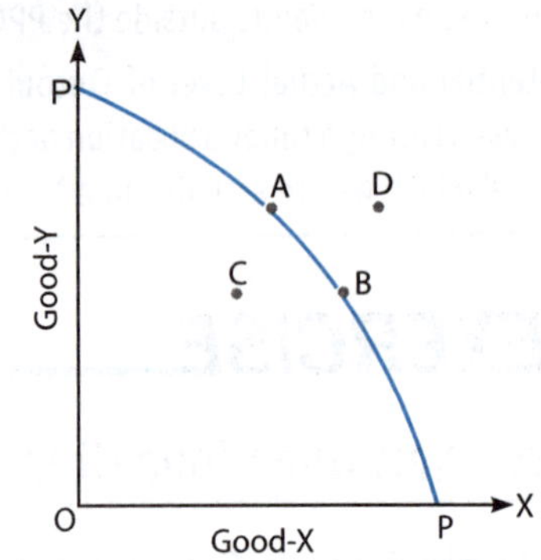

13. When an economy is operating on the PPC, it indicates:

(a) potential output > actual output
(b) potential output = actual output
(c) potential output < actual output
(d) none of these

14. In Fig. 14, the attainable combinations of output is shown by:

(a) point 'A' and 'C'
(b) point 'B' and 'C'
(c) point 'A', 'B' and 'C'
(d) point 'D'

15. Increase (growth) of resources implies that production possibility curve:

(a) shifts to the right
(b) shifts to the left
(c) rotates to the right
(d) none of these

16. The opportunity cost of 100 kg of rice produced on a land which can also produce 80 tonnes of wheat is:

(a) 100 kg of wheat
(b) 80 tonnes of wheat
(c) 8,000 tonnes of wheat
(d) none of these

17. In the diagram alongside (Fig. 15), marginal opportunity cost at point '*a*' is:

(a) $\frac{ab}{bc}$

(b) $\frac{bc}{ab}$

(c) $\frac{OP_1}{OL_1}$

(d) none of these

FIGURE 15

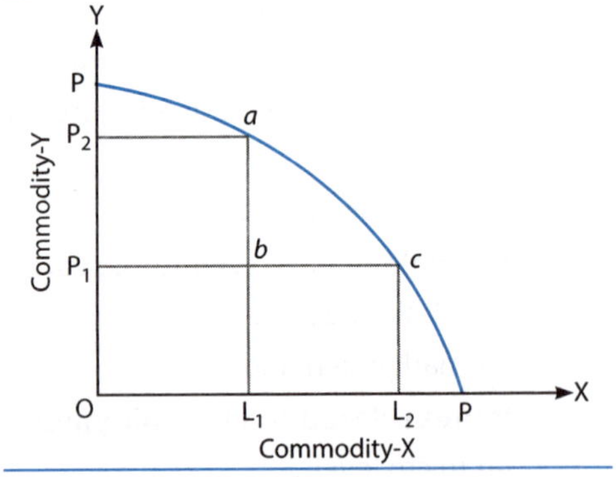

18. PPC is a straight line in case of:

(a) rising marginal opportunity cost
(b) falling marginal opportunity cost
(c) constant marginal opportunity cost
(d) none of these

19. The following table shows the production possibility of cricket bats and sarees of an imaginary economy:

Production of Cricket Bats (in thousand)	0	1	2	3	4	5
Production of Sarees (in lakh)	75	70	62	50	30	0

If the production of cricket bats is increased from 3 thousand to 4 thousand, what is the opportunity cost that the economy has to bear?

(a) Zero
(b) 8 lakh sarees
(c) 30 lakh sarees
(d) 20 lakh sarees

20. Concavity of PPC implies:

(a) increasing slope (b) decreasing slope

(c) constant slope (d) none of these

21. In Fig. 16, rotation of the PPC from *ab* to *ab*$_1$ shows:

(a) increase in resources

(b) decrease in resources

(c) improvement in technology of Good-A

(d) improvement in technology of Good-B

FIGURE 16

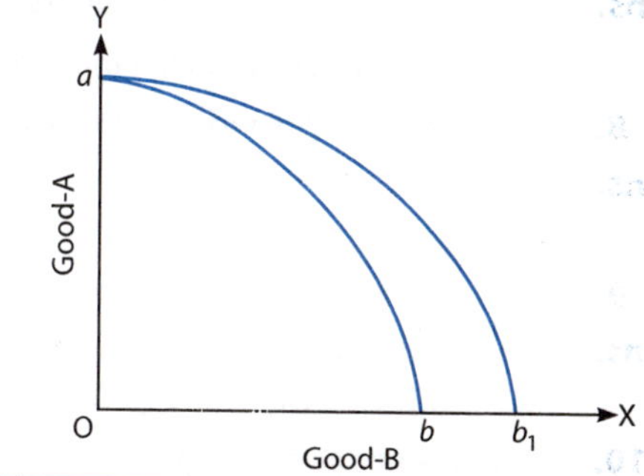

22. The shape of transformation curve is changed by:

(a) opportunity cost

(b) total cost

(c) marginal opportunity cost

(d) none of these

23. When some resources are shifted from Use-1 to Use-2 (given technology), the marginal rate of transformation:

(a) increases (b) decreases

(c) remains constant (d) is zero

24. Output of Good-X decreases by 500 units and output of Good-Y increases by 500 units, and some resources are shifted from the production of X to the production of Y, the marginal opportunity cost is:

(a) 0.2 (b) 0.75

(c) 0.8 (d) 1.0

25. When MRT is constant and equal to one, the PPC will be:

(a) a convex curve sloping downward

(b) a horizontal straight line

(c) a straight line sloping downward, cutting both X-axis and Y-axis at equal distance from the point of origin

(d) a concave curve sloping downward

Answers

1. (a) **2.** (c) **3.** (b) **4.** (d) **5.** (a) **6.** (c) **7.** (b) **8.** (c) **9.** (c) **10.** (d) **11.** (b) **12.** (c)
13. (b) **14.** (c) **15.** (a) **16.** (b) **17.** (a) **18.** (c) **19.** (d) **20.** (a) **21.** (d) **22.** (c) **23.** (a) **24.** (d)
25. (c)

B. Information & Concept-based Questions

1. Define Economics.

Ans. Economics is the study of rational management of the scarce resources in a manner such that the economic gains are maximised at the micro as well as the macro level.

2. Define scarcity.

Ans. Scarcity is a situation when demand for a good exceeds its supply even at a zero price.

3. What is meant by an economic problem?

Ans. Economic problem is a problem related to the allocation of resources (or problem of choice) arising due to limited means in relation to unlimited wants.

4. What is meant by an economy?

Ans. Economy is the sum total of economic activities directed towards the satisfaction of unlimited wants using the scarce means.

5. Define microeconomics.

Ans. Microeconomics is that branch of Economics which studies economic problems (or economic issues) at the level of an individual like a consumer, or a producer.

6. Define macroeconomics.

Ans. Macroeconomics is that branch of Economics which studies economic problems (or economic issues) at the level of economy as a whole.

7. Give two examples of microeconomic studies.

Ans. (i) Study of consumer behaviour: consumer equilibrium & law of demand, and

(ii) Study of cotton textile industry.

8. Give two examples of macroeconomic variables.

Ans. (i) General price level, and

(ii) Aggregate demand.

9. Give two examples of macroeconomic studies.

Ans. (i) Study of balance of payments, and

(ii) Study of national income and related aggregates.

10. What are economic agents?

Ans. Economic agents are the producers, households (consumers) and the government who take economic decisions in the economy.

11. State one principal difference between microeconomics and macroeconomics.

Ans. Microeconomics studies economic relationships or economic problems or economic issues at the level of an individual—an individual firm, an individual household or an individual consumer. Macroeconomics, on the other hand, studies economic relationships or economic problems or economic issues at the level of the economy as a whole.

12. State the two characteristics of resources.

Ans. (i) Resources are scarce in relation to the goods we wish to produce for the satisfaction of human wants.

(ii) Resources have alternative uses.

13. What is the problem of choice?

Ans. Problem of choice is the problem of allocating scarce resources to alternative uses.

14. Why does the problem of choice arise?

Ans. Problem of choice arises because:

(i) resources are limited in relation to our wants, and

(ii) resources have alternative uses.

15. What is the problem of resource allocation?

Ans. Problem of resource allocation is the problem related to the allocation of resources to alternative uses in a manner such that scarce resources are optimally utilised.

16. What are the central problems of an economy?

Ans. Central problems are those problems which arise in every economy. At the micro level, these problems are: (i) What to produce? (ii) How to produce? and (iii) For whom to produce?

At the macro level, these are (i) problem of fuller utilisation of resources, and (ii) problem of growth of resources.

17. Why do central problems arise? State the principal reason.

Ans. The central problems arise basically because of the fact that the resources are scarce and have alternative uses.

18. What is meant by production possibility curve?

Ans. Production possibility curve (or transformation curve) is a curve showing different possible combinations of a set of two goods which can be produced with the given resources and given technology.

19. Write the assumptions of production possibility curve.

Ans. The basic assumptions of production possibility curve are:

(i) Resources are given. These are fully and efficiently utilised.

(ii) No change in technique of production.

20. What does slope of PPC show?

Ans. Slope of PPC shows marginal opportunity cost.

21. Give one reason for a rightward shift of the production possibility curve.

Ans. Increase in the resources leads to rightward shift of the production possibility curve.

22. Define opportunity cost.

Ans. Opportunity cost is the value of a factor in its next best (or second best) alternative use.

23. Define marginal rate of transformation.

Ans. Marginal rate of transformation (or marginal opportunity cost) is the ratio between loss of output of Good-Y and gain of output of Good-X when some resources are shifted from Good-Y to Good-X.

2. Reason-based Questions (Comprehension of the Subject-matter)

Read the following statements carefully. Write 'True' or 'False' with a reason.

1. Economic problem and scarcity of resources are not related to each other.

Ans. False. Economic problem arises because of scarcity of resources. Hence, the two are related to each other.

2. Scarcity exists even when certain goods are available at zero price.

Ans. True. Scarcity is a situation when demand for a good exceeds its supply even at a zero price.

3. A free medicine given to the patients in hospitals is not a scarce commodity.

Ans. False. Although medicine is available at zero price, yet it is a scarce commodity. Because, it involves some opportunity cost.

[**Note:** A good is not scarce only when: (i) it is available at zero price, and (ii) it involves no opportunity cost.]

4. Lack of scarcity implies lack of economic problem.

Ans. True. Scarcity is the root cause of economic problem. Lack of scarcity definitely implies lack of economic problem.

5. If there were no choices in resource allocation, microeconomics would not have existed.

Ans. True. If there were no alternative choices in resource allocation, there would be no economic problem. Accordingly, microeconomics would not have existed.

6. All resources are not equally scarce all the time.

Ans. True. It is possible that some resources are more scarce than the others at a point of time. In India, for example, labour is certainly less scarce than capital.

7. Economising the use of resources means saving the resources for future use.

Ans. False. Economising the use of resources means that resources are to be used in a manner such that maximum output is realised per unit of input. It also means optimum utilisation of resources.

8. Problem of resource allocation would not arise if resources had not alternative uses.

Ans. True. Problem of resource allocation arises because resources have alternative uses. Where is the problem if a piece of land can only be used for the production of rice? Grow rice and relax!

9. Central problems of an economy are found only in those economies which are not governed or regulated by the government.

Ans. False. Every economy faces the central problems, though these are solved differently in different economies. Because, scarcity is the root cause of central problems, and scarcity of resources is common to all economies.

10. Problem of resource allocation is automatically solved in a free economy (capitalist economy).

Ans. True. In a free economy, problem of resource allocation finds its solution through the market forces of supply and demand.

11. Microeconomics does not deal with the aggregates.

Ans. False. Microeconomics deals with the aggregates of economic issues relating to small economic units. For example, market demand is the aggregation of individual demand.

12. Choice between 'production for the poor' and 'production for the rich' refers to the problem of what to produce.

Ans. False. Choice between 'production for the poor' and 'production for the rich' refers to the problem of 'for whom to produce'. It is a problem relating to choice of users of goods and services.

13. In a free economy, decision relating 'for whom to produce' enhances the gulf between rich and the poor.

Ans. True. In a free economy, the producers will produce goods for those who can afford to pay high price. Poorer sections of the society are often ignored. As a result, the gulf between rich and the poor enhances.

14. An economy produces goods and services in a manner such that it always operates on the PPC.

Ans. False. If resources are not fully utilised (or are underutilised), an economy may as well be inside the PPC.

15. A point below PPC points to underutilisation of resources.

Ans. True. A point below PPC points to underutilisation of resources. In such a situation actual output is less than potential output.

16. With fuller utilisation of resources, an economy can shift to point beyond PPC.

Ans. False. When an economy moves from a situation of underemployment to full employment, the economy is on the PPC, not beyond it.

17. Even when resources and technology are constant, an economy may not operate on the PPC.

Ans. True. Because resources may not be efficiently utilised.

18. PPC shows increasing slope.

Ans. True. PPC shows increasing slope because marginal opportunity cost tends to rise as resources are shifted from Use-1 to Use-2. [Slope of PPC = Marginal opportunity cost.]

19. Slope of PPC shows the ratio between the loss of output and gain of output.

Ans. True. Slope of PPC shows marginal opportunity cost. It is estimated as the ratio between loss of output and gain of output when some resources are shifted from Use-1 to Use-2.

20. If an economy is operating inside the PPC, it is possible to increase the production of Good-1 without any decrease in the production of Good-2.

Ans. True. It is possible to increase the production of Good-1 without any decrease in the production of Good-2. Because, being inside the PPC points to a situation when resources are not fully utilised (or are not efficiently utilised).

21. Marginal opportunity cost falls as resources are shifted from Use-1 to Use-2.

Ans. False. Marginal opportunity cost increases as resources are shifted from Use-1 to Use-2. Because resources are use-specific. Efficiency must suffer (leading to increase in marginal opportunity cost) when resources are shifted from one use to the other.

22. Opportunity cost is an avoidable cost.

Ans. False. Opportunity cost is the cost of a factor in its best alternative use. Accordingly, it is the minimum cost of a factor, and therefore, unavoidable.

23. When output of Good-1 increases from 100 units to 110 units and output of Good-2 decreases from 400 units to 350 units, marginal opportunity cost = 50 units.

Ans. False. Marginal opportunity cost = 5. Because,

$$\text{Marginal opportunity cost } = \frac{\text{Loss of output of Good-2}}{\text{Gain of output of Good-1}}\left[=\frac{50}{10}=5\right]$$

when some resources are shifted from Good-2 to Good-1.

3. HOTS & Applications

1. Explain how scarcity and choice go together.

Ans. Resources are not only scarce but also have alternative uses. Thus, land can be used for producing wheat or for constructing warehouses or factories. Hence, the problem of choice is the essence of any economic problem. However, if resources were not scarce, one could have anything any time and there would be no problem of choice.

2. "Economics is about making choices in the presence of scarcity." Explain.

Ans. If there were no scarcity, there would not have been any economic problem, or the problem related to 'choices'. In the absence of scarcity (of resources) the concept of unlimited wants does not exist. When resources are not limited and wants are no longer unlimited, where is the problem of choice? The problem of choice then ceases to exist; accordingly, there should not be any economic problem, and no Economics as such.

3. How to produce is a complex problem for less developed countries like India. Explain how.

Ans. 'How to produce' is a problem concerned with the choice of technique. Broadly, one is to choose between 'labour-intensive technique' and 'capital-intensive technique'. Labour-intensive technique uses more of labour per unit of capital whereas capital-intensive technique uses more of capital per unit of labour. In India, labour is abundant in relation to capital. While focusing on an ideal ratio between labour and capital, so as to obtain the maximum output per unit of input, labour would remain unutilised or unemployed. Thus, less developed countries like India often face the problem of unemployment while tackling the problem of 'how to produce'.

4. Why should there be huge unemployment in India when scarcity of resources is a universal fact?

Ans. Factors of production (labour and capital) are always jointly used: Labour is combined with capital (say plant, machinery, etc.). In India, there is severe shortage of capital. In the absence of capital, labour cannot be used. Hence, there is huge unemployment of labour although scarcity of resources is a universal fact.

5. Does production possibility frontier indicate the actual level of output or potential level of output?

Ans. Production possibility frontier indicates potential level of output. However, if resources are actually utilised fully as well as efficiently, the actual level of output coincides with the potential level of output.

6. (i) Do you think the actual level of output in the Indian economy is less than its potential level?
(ii) Does it mean that the level of our PPC could be higher than what it is now?

Ans. (i) Yes, the actual level of output in the Indian economy is far less than its potential level. This is because: (a) resources are not fully utilised. Mass unemployment in India points to this fact, and (b) resources are not efficiently utilised in India. Low level of productivity is a well known feature of the Indian economy.

(ii) No. Owing to underutilisation of resources as well as inefficient utilisation of resources we are operating somewhere within the PPC.

7. "Massive unemployment shifts the PPC to the left." Defend or refute.

Ans. PPC is drawn on the assumption that the given resources are fully as well as efficiently utilised. Unemployment is a situation when resources are not fully utilised. Or, it is a situation of underutilisation of resources. It would mean that the economy is not operating on the PPC but somewhere inside the PPC. PPC would not shift.

8. Why marginal opportunity cost must rise as resources are shifted from Use-1 to Use-2, even when given resources are fully and efficiently utilised?

Ans. When resources are shifted from Use-1 to Use-2, marginal opportunity cost must rise. This is because resources are use-specific. When these are shifted from their specialised use, efficiency must suffer. Loss of output of Good-Y (for every additional unit of Good-X) must rise.

9. How is production possibility frontier affected when resources are inefficiently employed in an economy?

Ans. Production possibility frontier is drawn on the assumption that the given resources are fully as well as efficiently utilised, along with the given technology. If resources are inefficiently employed in an economy, it implies that the economy is not maximising its output with the given resources. It is a situation when the concerned economy is NOT operating on the production possibility curve, but is somewhere within the production possibility frontier. So that, it is possible to increase the level of output of Good-X, or Good-Y, or both X and Y. Fig. 17 illustrates this situation.

FIGURE 17

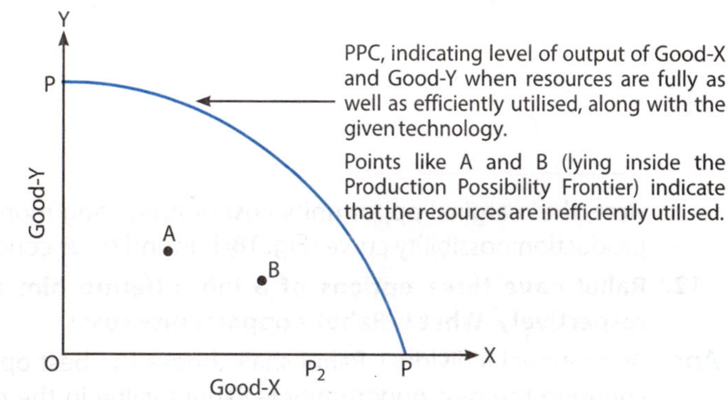

10. Giving reason, comment on the shape of production possibility frontier based on the following schedule. Also, find the marginal opportunity cost of producing Good-A.

Good-A (Units)	0	1	2	3	4	5
Good-B (Units)	65	52	39	26	13	0

Ans.

Good-A (Units)	Good-B (Units)	Marginal Opportunity Cost
0	65	—
1	52	$\frac{13}{1}=13$
2	39	$\frac{13}{1}=13$
3	26	$\frac{13}{1}=13$
4	13	$\frac{13}{1}=13$
5	0	$\frac{13}{1}=13$

The above schedule shows that the marginal opportunity cost of producing more of Good-A in place of Good-B is constant (=13). Accordingly, production possibility frontier should be a downward sloping straight line.

11. Draw a transformation curve, given the following possibilities of production (resources and technology remaining constant). Also, find the marginal opportunity cost when more and more guns are produced in place of bread.

Guns (Units)	0	1	2	3	4	5
Bread (Units)	30	28	24	18	10	0

Ans.

Guns (Units)	Bread (Units)	Marginal Opportunity Cost
0	30	—
1	28	$\frac{2}{1}=2$
2	24	$\frac{4}{1}=4$
3	18	$\frac{6}{1}=6$
4	10	$\frac{8}{1}=8$
5	0	$\frac{10}{1}=10$

FIGURE 18

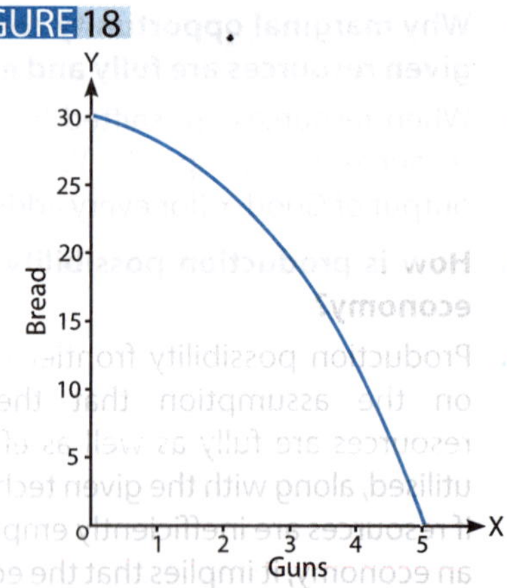

Here, the marginal opportunity cost of producing more of Guns in place of Bread is rising. Accordingly, production possibility curve (Fig. 18) is found to be concave to the origin.

12. Rahul have three options of a job, offering him a salary of ₹ 20,000, ₹ 25,000 and ₹ 30,000 respectively. What is Rahul's opportunity cost?

Ans. As a rational individual, Rahul shall choose the best opportunity, which is a job of ₹ 30,000. The cost of choosing the best opportunity is Rahul's value in the next best opportunity which is a job of ₹ 25,000. Opportunity cost is the value of a factor in its next best alternative use. Accordingly opportunity cost of Rahul = ₹ 25,000.

13. Your friend's and your birthday is on the same day. On the occasion, both of you exchange gifts. Each of you spends ₹ 200 on buying a gift. Both of you also spend ₹ 400 on your party and share the expenses equally. Did both of you incur any opportunity cost of celebrating the birthday? If so, what is it?

Ans. Yes, both of us incur opportunity cost. Individually we are spending ₹ 400 on the purchase of gift and on the party. Therefore, opportunity cost to each of us is ₹ 400.

Individual opportunity cost = ₹ 400.

14. You plan to attend the NCC Camp for two months. If you do, you won't be able to take your usual part time job that pays ₹ 10,000 for two months and you won't be able to live at home for free. The cost of your NCC Camp includes:

Living expenses ₹ 2,000, costume and stationery expenses ₹ 3,000 and study materials ₹ 1,000. Calculate the marginal opportunity cost of joining the NCC Camp.

Ans. Marginal opportunity cost

= Loss of your two months pay + Cost of your attending the NCC Camp (Living expenses + Expenses on costume and stationery + Expenses on study materials)

= ₹ 10,000 + (₹ 2,000 + ₹ 3,000 + ₹ 1,000)

= ₹ 10,000 + ₹ 6,000 = ₹ 16,000

Here, marginal opportunity cost of your joining the NCC Camp is ₹ 16,000, because opportunity cost is equal to the loss incurred (or sacrifice made) when the existing opportunity is foregone in favour of the other.

15. A shift from steam engines to diesel and electric engines has increased carrying capacity of the Indian Railways both for the passenger traffic and the goods traffic. How would you reflect this change using the concept of PPC?

Ans. Increase in carrying capacity of the Indian Railways (both for the passenger traffic and goods traffic) implies a shift in its potential level of output due to better technology. Diagrammatically, it is to be indicated by a shift in PPC to the right from *ab* to *cd*, as shown in Fig. 19.

FIGURE 19

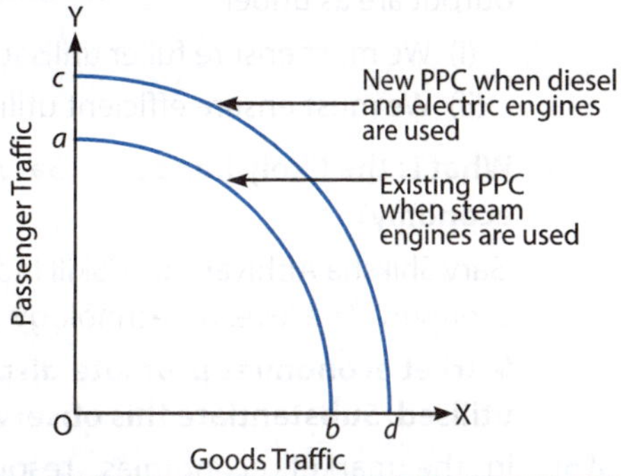

16. Using a diagram explain what happens to the PPC of Kashmir if the widespread floods have led to the destruction of human lives?

Ans. Production possibility curve (or PPC) is drawn on the assumption that the given resources are fully as well as efficiently utilised. If the widespread floods in Kashmir have led to the destruction of human lives, it implies the loss of manpower. This will shift the PPC leftward from *ab* to a_1b_1, as shown in Fig. 20.

FIGURE 20

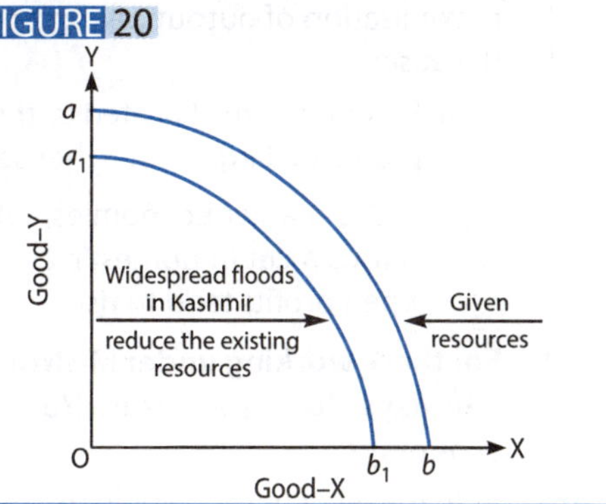

17. Apply the concept of PPC to explain the problem of scarcity.

Ans. PPC (production possibility curve) reveals scarcity of resources in two ways as in Fig. 21.

(i) PPC is a production possibility boundary, indicating maximum output of Good-X or Good-Y (or in combinations of X and Y) which can be produced. The boundary line points to the scarcity of resources.

(ii) 'Scarcity' is revealed by the fact that any movement along the PPC (like moving from point D to F), while it increases the output of Good-X (from OR to OS) must decrease the output of Good-Y (from OC to OE).

FIGURE 21

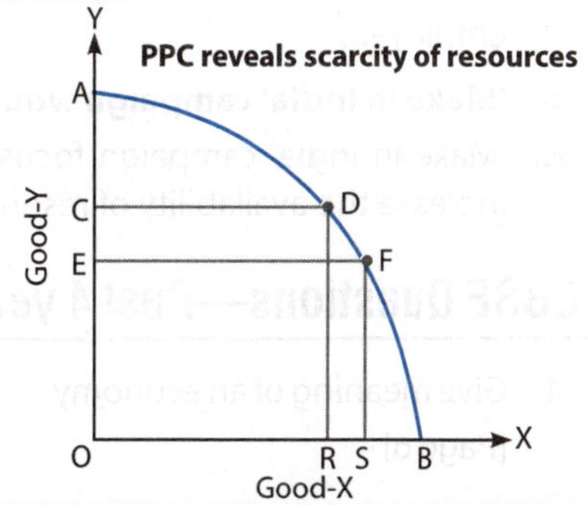

18. Apply the concept of PPC to explain the central problem of 'what to produce'.

Ans. 'What to produce' is essentially the problem of choice: what quantity of Good-X and Good-Y is to be produced. More of Good-X must lead to lesser production of Good-Y. Because, resources are assumed to fully and efficiently utilised, and technology is assumed to be constant. Fig. 21 illustrates this situation. It shows that if production of Good-X is increased from OR to OS, the production of Good-Y must reduce from OC to OE. Because, some resources must be shifted from Y to X.

4. Evaluation (Value-based Questions)

1. If more & more resources are constantly explored and new & new techniques of production are constantly discovered, don't you think a day will come when our central problems will be solved once for all?

Ans. When more & more resources are explored and new technology is discovered, PPC would expand, indicating larger & larger flow of goods and services in the economy. But the scarcity of resources in relation to human wants will always exist. Because, human wants are infinite while the resources are not. Accordingly, central problems can never be solved once for all.

2. How can we achieve the parity between the actual level of output and the potential level of output in the Indian economy? State two possible steps.

Ans. Two possible steps to achieve the parity between the actual level of output and the potential level of output are as under:

(i) We must ensure fuller utilisation of resources, and

(ii) We must ensure efficient utilisation of resources.

3. What is the likely impact of 'Sarv Shiksha Abhiyan' and 'Skill India Campaign' on PPC of the Indian economy?

Ans. 'Sarv Shiksha Abhiyan' and 'Skill India Campaign' are expected to improve the quality of labour force in the economy. The level of technology would rise. Accordingly, PPC is expected to shift to the right.

4. Market economies promote disparities in income distribution even when resources are optimally utilised. Substantiate this observation.

Ans. In the market economies, resources are optimally utilised because every producer focuses on maximisation of output per unit of input. But, disparities in income distribution are highly pronounced. Because:

(i) Resources are allocated to the production of those goods which yield high profits. So that goods are produced largely for richer sections of the society. The poor suffer deprivation.

(ii) In the market economies, jobs are outsourced to those economies where labour cost is low. This causes a cut in domestic employment. Accordingly, wage component of GDP tends to shrink even when profits tend to rise.

5. For those working under MGNREGA, the government has raised minimum employment from 100 to 150 days during an year. How would it impact the actual and potential level of output in the economy?

Ans. Actual level of output would rise, because of a rise in employment. Potential level of output would not rise (or PPC would not shift). Because, PPC is drawn on the assumption that the existing resources are fully employed.

6. 'Make in India' campaign would shift the PPC to the right. How?

Ans. 'Make in India' campaign focuses on the inflow of foreign capital in the domestic economy. It would increase the availability of resources in the domestic economy. Accordingly, PPC would shift to the right.

5. CBSE Questions—Past 4 years (With Answers or Reference to the Text for Answers)

1. Give meaning of an economy. *[CBSE Delhi 2012]*

[Page 6]

2. State reasons why does an economic problem arise. [CBSE Delhi 2012]

Or

Why does an economic problem arise? Explain. [CBSE (F) 2013]

[Page 4]

3. What is opportunity cost? Explain with the help of a numerical example. [CBSE Delhi 2012; (AI) 2012]

[Page 16, 17]

4. What is 'marginal rate of transformation'? Explain with the help of an example. [CBSE Delhi 2012]

Or

Explain the concept of marginal rate of transformation with the help of an example. [CBSE (F) 2012]

[Page 18]

5. Define microeconomics. [CBSE (AI) 2012]

[Page 4]

6. Explain the central problem of 'how to produce'. [CBSE (AI) 2012]

[Page 7]

7. Define production possibilities curve. Explain why it is downward sloping from left to right.

Or [CBSE (AI) 2012; (F) 2012]

Why is a production possibilities curve downward sloping? Explain. [CBSE (F) 2014]

[Page 9, 13]

8. Define macroeconomics. [CBSE (F) 2012]

[Page 5]

9. Explain, giving reason, why production possibilities curve is concave. [CBSE (F) 2012]

Or

Why is production possibilities curve concave? Explain. [CBSE (AI) 2014]

[Page 13, 14]

10. Production in an economy is below its potential due to unemployment. Government starts employment generation schemes. Explain its effect using production possibilities curve. [CBSE Delhi 2013]

[PPC (Production Possibility Curve) is drawn on the assumption that the given resources are fully as well as efficiently utilised. When production is below its potential due to unemployment, it would mean that the concerned economy is not operating on the PPC but is somewhere inside the PPC. This is indicated by point 'B' in the digram (Fig. 22). Since, our resources and technology remain the same, PPC would not shift. With the commencement of employment generation schemes, employment level will rise. Consequently, point B will shift closer to the PP line. Once full employment is achieved (other things remaining constant), the point B will finally be located somewhere on the PP line.]

FIGURE 22

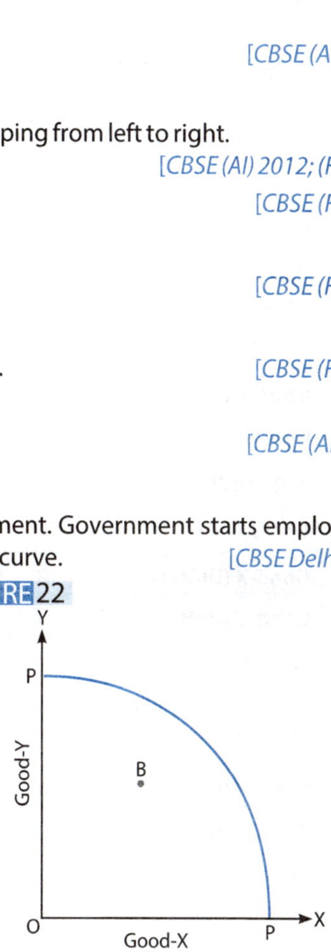

11. Explain the meaning of opportunity cost with the help of production possibility schedule. [CBSE (AI) 2013]

[Page 9, 16, 17]

12. With the help of suitable example explain the problem of 'for whom to produce'. [CBSE (AI) 2013]

Or

Explain the central problem 'for whom to produce'. [CBSE Delhi 2014]

[Page 7, 8]

13. Define opportunity cost. [CBSE (F) 2013]

[Page 16, 17]

14. Explain the problem of 'what to produce'. *[CBSE (F) 2013]*

[Page 7]

15. Unemployment is reduced due to the measures taken by the government. State its economic value in the context of production possibilities frontier. *[CBSE Delhi 2014]*

[Reduction of unemployment will make the economy move closer to the production possibility frontier, implying higher level of output.]

16. The government has started promoting foreign capital. What is its economic value in the context of production possibilities frontier? *[CBSE (AI) 2014]*

[The inflow of foreign capital is expected to increase the availability of the resources. Consequently, production possibility frontier will shift to the right.]

17. Large number of technical training institutions have been started by the government. State its economic value in the context of production possibilities frontier. *[CBSE (F) 2014]*

[This would lead to technological innovations in the economy. When the level of technology improves, production possibility frontier is expected to shift to the right.]

18. What will be the impact of recently launched 'Clean India Mission' (Swachh Bharat Mission) on the production possibilities curve of the economy and why? *[CBSE Delhi 2015]*

[Page 15]

19. What will likely be the impact of large scale outflow of foreign capital on production possibilities curve of the economy and why? *[CBSE Delhi 2015]*

[Page 30]

20. Giving reason comment on the shape of production possibilities curve based on the following schedule:

Good-X (Units)	0	1	2	3	4
Good-Y (Units)	10	9	7	4	0

[Page 359] *[CBSE Delhi 2015; (AI) 2015; (F) 2015]*

21. Giving reason comment on the shape of production possibilities curve based on the following schedule:

Good-X (Units)	0	1	2	3	4
Good-Y (Units)	8	6	4	2	0

[Page 359, 360] *[CBSE Delhi 2015]*

22. Giving reason comment on the shape of production possibilities curve based on the following schedule:

Good-X (Units)	0	1	2	3	4
Good-Y (Units)	20	18	14	8	0

[Page 360] *[CBSE Delhi 2015; (F) 2015]*

23. What is likely to be the impact of "Make in India" appeal to the foreign investors by the Prime Minister of India, on the production possibilities frontier of India? Explain. *[CBSE (AI) 2015]*

[Page 30]

24. What is likely to be the impact of efforts towards reducing unemployment on the production potential of the economy? Explain. *[CBSE (AI) 2015]*

[Page 31, Q. 10]

25. Giving reason comment on the shape of production possibilities curve based on the following schedule:

Good-X (Units)	0	1	2	3	4
Good-Y (Units)	30	27	21	12	0

[Page 360] *[CBSE (AI) 2015]*

26. Giving reason comment on the shape of production possibilities curve based on the following schedule:

Good-X (Units)	0	1	2	3	4
Good-Y (Units)	16	12	8	4	0

[Page 360] *[CBSE (AI) 2015]*

27. What will be the impact of "Education for All Campaign" (Sarv Shiksha Abhiyan) on the production possibilities curve of the Indian economy and why? *[CBSE (F) 2015]*

[Page 30]

28. What will likely be the impact of large scale inflow of foreign capital in India on production possibilities curve and why? *[CBSE (F) 2015]*

[Page 32, Q. 16]

29. Giving reasons comment on the shape of production possibilities curve based on the following table:

Good-X (Units)	0	1	2	3	4
Good-Y (Units)	4	3	2	1	0

[Page 361] *[CBSE (F) 2015]*

6. NCERT Questions (With Hints to Answers)

1. Discuss the central problems of an economy.

[**Hint:** Central problems of an economy are: What to produce, How to produce, and For whom to produce. 'What to produce' relates to the problem of choice of goods and services to be produced. 'How to produce' relates to the choice of technique of production. It involves a choice between labour-intensive technique and capital-intensive technique. 'For whom to produce' relates to the distribution of goods and services across different sections of the society. It focuses on the issue of Economic Equality.]

2. What do you mean by the production possibilities of an economy?

[**Hint:** Production possibilities of an economy are the different combinations of output that an economy can produce with the given resources and given technology.]

3. What is a production possibility frontier?

[**Hint:** It is a curve showing different combinations of output of a set of two goods. It is drawn on the assumptions of constant technology and constant resources to be fully and efficiently utilised.]

4. Define the subject matter of Economics.

[**Hint:** Economics is a subject matter that focuses on the rational management of scarce resources in a manner that our economic welfare is maximised.]

5. Distinguish between a centrally planned economy and a market economy.

[**Hint:** A centrally planned economy is the one in which decisions relating to 'what, how and for whom to produce' are taken by some central authority appointed by the government. Market economy is the one in which decisions regarding 'what, how and for whom to produce' are governed by the market forces of supply and demand.]

6. Distinguish between microeconomics and macroeconomics.

[**Hint:** Microeconomics studies economic relationships or economic problems or economic issues at the level of an individual—an individual firm, an individual household or an individual consumer. Macroeconomics studies economic relationships or economic problems or economic issues at the level of the economy as a whole.]

7. Miscellaneous Questions and Reference to the Text for Answers

A. Questions of 3 & 4 marks each

1. How is 'choice' a core parameter in the study of Economics?
   [Page 3, 6]
2. What are the components of microeconomics and macroeconomics?
   [Page 5, 6]
3. State in brief the problem of fuller utilisation of resources.
   [Page 14, 15]
4. What are the three central problems of an economy?
   [Page 7, 8]
5. Explain the central problem of 'what to produce'.
   [Page 7]
6. What does a production possibility curve show? When will it shift to the right?
   [Page 9, 11]
7. Why is production possibility curve concave?
   [Page 13, 14]
8. Discuss the concept of opportunity cost with an example.
   [Page 16, 17]
9. Define marginal opportunity cost along a PPC.
   [Page 18, 19]
10. "An economy always produces on but not inside a PPC." Defend or refute.
    [Page 14, 15]
11. Which factors lead to a shift of the PPC?
    [Page 11, 13]
12. Explain the central problem of 'choice of technique'.
    [Page 7]
13. Explain the central problem of 'distribution of income'.
    [Page 7, 8]

B. Questions of 6 marks each

1. State the central problems of an economy. Why do they arise?
   [Page 6–8]
2. Why do central problems arise? Explain the problem of allocation of resources.
   [Page 4, 6]
3. How are central problems solved in different economies?
   [Page 8, 9]
4. What is meant by production possibility curve? Illustrate with the help of a table and diagram.
   [Page 9, 10]
5. What is meant by production possibility curve? Illustrate the central problem of 'what to produce' using this curve.
   [Page 7, 9, 30]

6. Draw a production possibility curve and indicate the following situations on the diagram:
   (i) Fuller and efficient utilisation of resources,
   (ii) Underutilisation of resources, and
   (iii) Growth of resources.

   [Page 9, 10, 15, 16]

7. Draw a production possibility curve. What do the points inside and outside this curve indicate? Explain.
   [Page 9, 10]

DOs and DON'Ts

1. Never draw PPC as convex to the origin. PPC is always concave to the origin. Because, it is drawn on the assumption that the available resources are fully and efficiently utilised along with the given technology. We know, resources are use-specific. So that, when the use-specific resources are already efficiently utilised, their efficiency must suffer when they are shifted from Use-1 to Use-2. It implies that marginal opportunity cost must rise when resources are shifted from Use-1 to Use-2. Rising marginal opportunity cost implies rising slope of PPC (because slope of PPC = marginal opportunity cost). And, rising slope of PPC implies that PPC must be concave to the origin.
2. Never consider Production Possibility Frontier as indicative of the actual level of output. It only indicates the potential level (or the maximum level) of output which is achievable when the given resources are fully and efficiently utilised, along with the given technology. Actual level of output can coincide with the potential level of output only when the given resources are actually utilised fully as well as efficiently, along with the given technology.
3. Don't ignore the difference between opportunity cost and marginal opportunity cost.

   Opportunity cost refers to the loss of output of Good-Y when resources are shifted from the production of Good-Y to the production of Good-X.

   Marginal opportunity cost refers to the loss of output of Good-Y per unit of additional output of Good-X (when some resources are shifted from the production of Good-Y to Good-X).

ability ZONE

❑ Scarcity

In Economics, scarcity is defined as a situation when demand for goods exceeds their supply even at a zero price.

❑ Full Employment of Resources does not mean that the Economy is operating on PPC

This is because resources may not be optimally/efficiently utilised, even when they are fully utilised. In such a situation the economy may be operating somewhere inside the PPC.

❑ PPC (Production Possibility Curve) and Transformation Curve

PPC (Production Possibility Curve) and transformation curve are identical concepts. Likewise, marginal opportunity cost and marginal rate of transformation are identical concepts.

❑ Over Time PPC for a Nation is likely to Shift to the Right

This is because of (i) discovery of new resources, and (ii) discovery of new technology.

❑ Increase in Labour Productivity Shifts PPC to the Right

This is when productivity increases, owing to improvement in technology.

❑ Increase in the Level of Unemployment does not Shift PPC to the Left

This is because PPC is drawn on the assumption that the given resources are fully and efficiently utilised. Increase in unemployment only implies a situation when the economy is actually operating somewhere inside the PPC, so that actual output is less than the potential output.

❑ Micro-Macro Paradox

What is logical at the micro level may not be logical at the macro level.

Illustration

—If an individual saves more, he adds to his future prosperity.

If all the people in an economy save more (and spend less), demand for goods and services may decline. Consequently, investment may decline; production and employment level may fall. It may cause poverty rather than prosperity.

❑ Economic Agents and Economic Decisions

Economic agents are the individuals or institutions who take economic decisions. They are the producers, households (consumers), and the government. Consumers decide how much to buy of different goods and services; producers decide how much to produce of different goods and services; and the government decides about the reallocation of the resources with a view to ensuring growth with stability and equality.

Appendix

❑ Market Economies, Centrally Planned Economies, and Mixed Economies: Some Notable Characteristics

Market Economy	Centrally Planned Economy	Mixed Economy
(i) There is a market mechanism (market system) that connects buyers and sellers.	(i) There is almost a complete lack of market mechanism or the free play of the forces of demand and supply.	(i) Market mechanism operates to connect buyers and sellers. But, not without 'checks and balances' by the government.
(ii) Prices of goods and services are settled through the market forces of demand and supply.	(ii) Prices of goods and services are largely settled by the 'Central Authority' appointed by the government of the country.	(ii) Prices of goods and services are largely settled through the market forces of demand and supply. But, policies like of 'Floor Price', 'Price Ceiling', 'Support Price' are often pursued to promote equality and social justice.
(iii) The consumers (households) are sovereign. They buy according to their tastes and preferences, and maximise their satisfaction. The producers maximise their profits by producing goods and services as demanded by the consumers.	(iii) Consumer's sovereignty is ruled out. Instead, the central authority decides what goods and services the consumers would need for their livelihood.	(iii) Consumer is sovereign. But resources are not allowed to be used in the production of such goods which are socially harmful (like narcotics).
(iv) The government does not interfere with the decisions of the households and the producers. Or, we can say that the government does not interfere with the free play of the market forces of demand and supply. It focuses largely on the maintenance of law & order and defence of the country.	(iv) The government takes upon itself the responsibility of growth and development of the country.	(iv) The government plays a key role in the process of growth and development, but focuses largely on fighting drawbacks of the market economy.
(v) Accumulation of capital is allowed as a matter of right. Capital emerges as the principal means of production.	(v) There is a state ownership or collective ownership of the means of production.	(v) There is a private as well as public (collective) ownership of the means of production.

Consumer's Equilibrium —Utility Analysis

CHAPTER 2

TODO

- Concept of Utility
- Total Utility and Marginal Utility
- Law of Diminishing Marginal Utility
- Concept of Consumer's Equilibrium
- Marginal Utility Analysis and Consumer's Equilibrium: (i) One Commodity Case, (ii) Two Commodity Case
- Conditions of Consumer's Equilibrium using Marginal Utility Analysis
- The Basic Limitation of Utility Analysis

1. Concept of Utility

In Economics, the term 'utility' refers to the quality of a commodity by virtue of which it satisfies our wants. In other words, want-satisfying power of a good is called utility. The present chapter is based on the assumption that utility can be measured in terms of cardinal numbers, such as 1, 2, 3, 4, etc. These numbers are called utils or units of utility. Thus, 4 utils of utility are greater than 3 utils of utility, 3 utils are greater than 2, and so on. The reader must note that there is no standard yardstick of a 'util' or of a unit of utility. It is something that a consumer is expected to define himself while he is buying a commodity for his consumption. A glass of milk must yield some satisfaction and we expect the consumer to express it in terms of cardinal numbers like 2, 3 or 4. We call it as utils or units of utility. This is called cardinal measurement of utility.

2. Total Utility and Marginal Utility

Total Utility (TU): It is the sum total of utility derived from the consumption of all the units of a commodity. To illustrate, if 2 units of a commodity are consumed and 1st unit yields satisfaction of 10 utils, while the 2nd unit yields satisfaction of 9 utils, then total utility = 10 utils + 9 utils = 19 utils (or 19 units of utility).

Marginal Utility (MU): It refers to additional utility on account of the consumption of an additional unit of a commodity. If 10 units of a commodity yield satisfaction of 100 utils, and 11 units of a commodity yield satisfaction of 105 utils, then additional utility on account of the consumption of 11th unit of the commodity is 105 utils – 100 utils = 5 utils. This is called marginal utility. Thus, marginal utility (MU) is measured as under:

$$MU_{nth} = TU_n - TU_{n-1}$$

Referring to the above example

MU (when 11 units of a commodity are consumed)

$= TU_{11} - TU_{10}$

= 105 utils – 100 utils

= 5 utils

Table 1 illustrates the estimation of TU and MU.

Table 1. Estimation of TU and MU

Consumption of Commodity-X [Units]	TU_X	MU_X
1	100	100 [$TU_1 - TU_0 = 100 - 0 = 100$]
2	190	90 [$TU_2 - TU_1 = 190 - 100 = 90$]
3	270	80 [$TU_3 - TU_2 = 270 - 190 = 80$]
4	340	70 [$TU_4 - TU_3 = 340 - 270 = 70$]
5	400	60 [$TU_5 - TU_4 = 400 - 340 = 60$]

The Table shows:

(i) $MU_{nth} = TU_n - TU_{n-1}$

[Marginal utility of nth unit of a commodity

= Total utility from n units – Total utility from (n – 1) units]

(ii) TU $= \Sigma MU$

$= [100 + 90 + 80 + 70 + 60]$

$= 400$

[Total Utility = Sum total of marginal utility from all units of consumption of a commodity.]

Converting Table 1 into a diagram, we get the following picture:

FIGURE 1

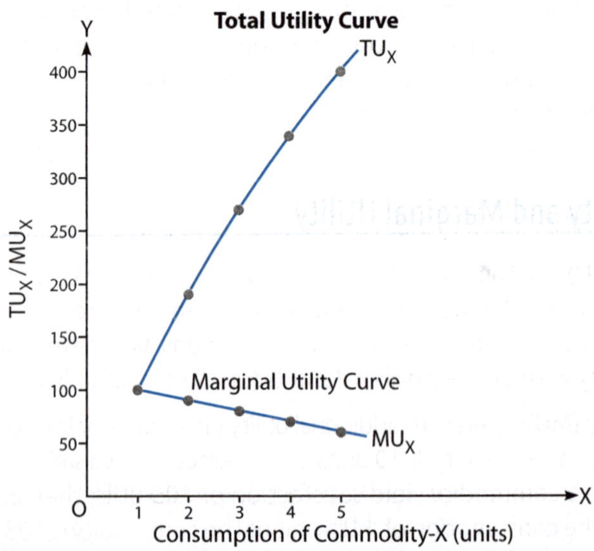

$MU_{nth} = TU_n - TU_{n-1}$

$TU = \Sigma MU$

When only 1 unit of the commodity-X is consumed

$TU_X = MU_X = 100.$

Relation between Total Utility and Marginal Utility

Table 2 explains the relationship between TU and MU.

Table 2. Relation between Total Utility and Marginal Utility

Quantity (Units)	Total Utility	Marginal Utility
0	0	—
1	8	8 – 0 = 8
2	14	14 – 8 = 6
3	18	18 – 14 = 4
4	20	20 – 18 = 2
5	20	20 – 20 = 0
6	18	18 – 20 = –2

Table 2 offers the following observations on the relation between total utility and marginal utility:

(i) As more and more units of a commodity are consumed, marginal utility derived from each successive unit tends to diminish. It may even become zero or negative.

(ii) So long as MU is positive, TU increases.

(iii) TU is maximum when MU = 0.

(iv) TU starts decreasing when MU is negative.

(v) Decreasing MU implies that TU increases at a decreasing rate.

Thus, 8 utils of MU are added to TU when one unit is consumed, 6 utils of MU are added to TU when 2 units are consumed, 4 utils of MU are added to TU when 3 units are consumed, and so on. Each successive unit of consumption adds increasingly less utils to TU. Implying that TU increases at a decreasing rate when MU is decreasing.

Diagrammatic Illustration of the Relation between TU and MU

Fig. 2 offers a diagrammatic illustration of the relation between TU and MU. It is drawn on hypothetical data. It just focuses on the shapes of TU and MU curves.

Fig. 2 shows that

(i) TU continues to rise so long as MU is positive. It happens up to 5 units of consumption.

(ii) TU is maximum when MU = 0. It happens when exactly 5 units of the commodity are consumed.

(iii) TU starts declining when MU is negative. It happens after 5 units of consumption.

(iv) Decreasing MU implies that TU is increasing at a decreasing rate.

FIGURE 2

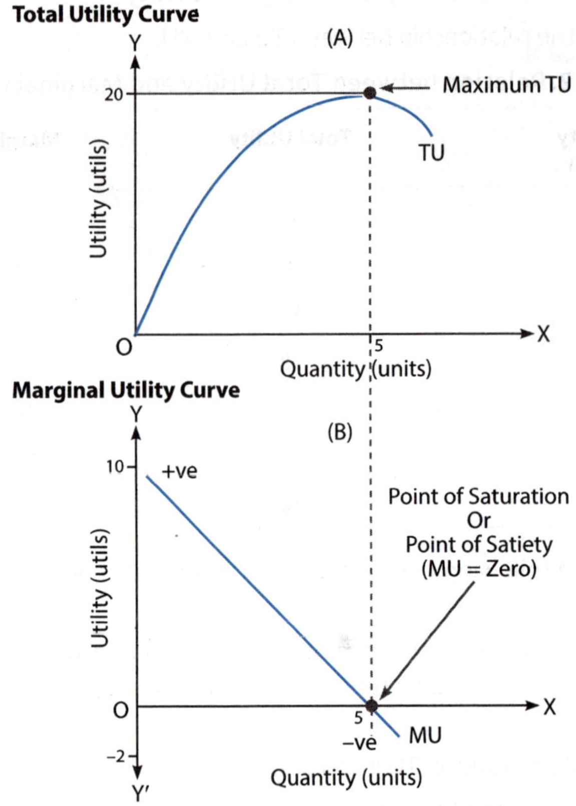

- TU increases so long as MU is +ve.
- TU is maximum when MU = 0.
- TU starts declining when MU is –ve.
- Decreasing MU implies that TU increases at a decreasing rate (MU is the rate of TU).

Relation between TU and MU

(i) TU = ΣMU.

(ii) TU increases so long as MU is positive.

(iii) When MU is zero, TU is maximum.

(iv) When MU is negative, TU starts diminishing.

(v) Decreasing MU implies that TU is increasing at a decreasing rate.

HOTS

Q. At which rate TU increases when MU is diminishing?

Ans. When MU is diminishing, TU increases at a diminishing rate.

EXAMPLES

Example 1.

The total utility schedule of individual 'A' is given below. Derive his marginal utility schedule.

Units Consumed	Total Utility
0	0
1	15
2	28
3	40
4	51
5	61

Solution:

Units Consumed	TU	MU
0	0	—
1	15	15
2	28	13
3	40	12
4	51	11
5	61	10

Example 2.

Marginal utility schedule of individual 'A' is given below. Derive his total utility schedule. (Assume that total utility of consuming zero unit is zero.)

Units Consumed	Marginal Utility
1	10
2	8
3	7
4	6
5	3
6	0

Solution:

Units Consumed	MU	TU
1	10	10
2	8	18
3	7	25
4	6	31
5	3	34
6	0	34

3. Law of Diminishing Marginal Utility

Psychologically, intensity of desire for a commodity tends to decrease as more and more units of a commodity are consumed. Accordingly, every successive unit of the commodity offers less and less satisfaction. It means MU tends to decline as consumption of the commodity increases. This is called law of diminishing marginal utility.

Table 1 and Fig. 1 illustrate this law. The Table and the figure show that MU tends to diminish as consumption increases. Because MU is diminishing (as from 100 to 90, 80, 70, 60), TU increases only at the diminishing rate. As noted earlier, MU is the rate of TU.

Law of Diminishing Marginal Utility is a Fundamental Law

Law of diminishing marginal utility states that as more and more **units** of a commodity are **consumed**, marginal utility derived from every additional unit must decline. It happens in respect of all goods and services. It is, therefore, called 'Fundamental Law of Satisfaction' or 'Fundamental Psychological Law'.

Two Basic Assumptions

Basic assumptions of the law are as under:

(i) Only standard units of the commodity are consumed. Like, a cup of tea, not a spoon of tea.

(ii) Consumption of the commodity is continuous. Not that one unit of the commodity is consumed now, and the other tomorrow.

4. Concept of Consumer's Equilibrium

Consumer's equilibrium refers to a situation of maximum satisfaction while he is spending his given income across different goods. In other words, a consumer is in equilibrium when he allocates his given income to the purchase of different goods in a manner such that his total satisfaction is maximised. Any change in the allocation of income (under the given circumstances) will only lead to a fall in total satisfaction or total utility.

Consumer's Equilibrium

The consumer is in equilibrium when, given his income and market prices, he plans his expenditure (on different goods and services) in such a manner that he maximises his total satisfaction.

5. Marginal Utility Analysis and Consumer's Equilibrium

Now we are addressing the basic question of this chapter: **How much of a commodity a consumer buys so that he maximises his satisfaction and attains the point of equilibrium?** This is discussed with reference to two different situations:

(i) when only one commodity is consumed, and

(ii) when two or more commodities are consumed.

Following is brief description of both the situations.

Consumer's Equilibrium: One Commodity Case

Purchase of a commodity by a consumer depends on three factors:

(i) Price of the commodity.

(ii) Marginal (and total) utility of the commodity.

(iii) Marginal utility of money.

What is Marginal Utility of Money?

Marginal utility of money refers to **'worth of a rupee'** to a consumer. **What is worth of a rupee?** The consumer is expected to define it himself. It is assumed that he defines it in terms of utility that he derives from a standard basket of goods he can buy with a rupee. **Example:** If a rupee can buy 100g of sugar, 500g of rice and 500g of salt (which represent a standard basket of goods to the consumer), and if total utility from these goods is (say) 4 utils, then 4 is to be taken as marginal utility of money. This becomes his 'standard reference' whenever he is buying any commodity. Buying a unit of commodity-X for a rupee would mean the consumer expects 4 units of utility from the consumption of commodity-X. Thus, MU_M (marginal utility of money) becomes a measuring rod for a rupee worth of satisfaction.

Important: It is assumed that MU_M is constant. Simply because, it is a measuring rod for a rupee worth of satisfaction.

Let marginal utility of money for the consumer = 4 utils (referring to the utility he expects to receive when he spends ₹ 1).

Let X be the commodity he intends to buy.

Let P_X (Price of X) = ₹ 4 per unit.

Marginal Utility Schedule of X is taken to be as follows:

Table 3. Marginal Utility Schedule of Commodity-X

Units of Commodity-X	MU_X (Utils)
1	20
2	18
3	16
4	10
5	0
6	–5

Using the scale that 4 utils = ₹ 1, he can express MU_X in terms of rupees, as in Table 4.

Table 4. Conversion of MU_X into Rupees

Units of Commodity-X	MU_X (Utils)	MU in terms of Rupees when 4 utils = ₹ 1
1	20	20 ÷ 4 = 5.0
2	18	18 ÷ 4 = 4.5
3	16	16 ÷ 4 = 4.0
4	10	10 ÷ 4 = 2.5
5	0	0 ÷ 4 = 0
6	–5	–5 ÷ 4 = –1.25

Now comes the basic question: **How many units of X the consumer will purchase to be in a state of equilibrium?** To answer this question, let us proceed step by step:

- **Will he buy 1st unit of X?**

Yes. Because:

MU_X = 20 utils = worth ₹ 5, while P_X = ₹ 4

What he pays (₹ 4) is less than what he gets (worth ₹ 5). Hence, he must buy the 1st unit of X.

- **Will he buy 2nd unit of X?**

Yes. Again, because:

MU_X = 18 utils = worth ₹ 4.5, while P_X = ₹ 4

What he pays (₹ 4) is less than what he gets (worth ₹ 4.5). Hence, he must buy the 2nd unit of X.

Continuing like this, he will stop buying X, only when:

MU_X (in terms of rupees) = P_X

It occurs when the consumer buys 3 units of commodity-X. Here,

MU_X (in terms of rupees) = P_X = ₹ 4

Diagrammatic Illustration

Fig. 3 shows consumer equilibrium when only one commodity is purchased.

FIGURE 3

Consumer Equilibrium: One Commodity Case

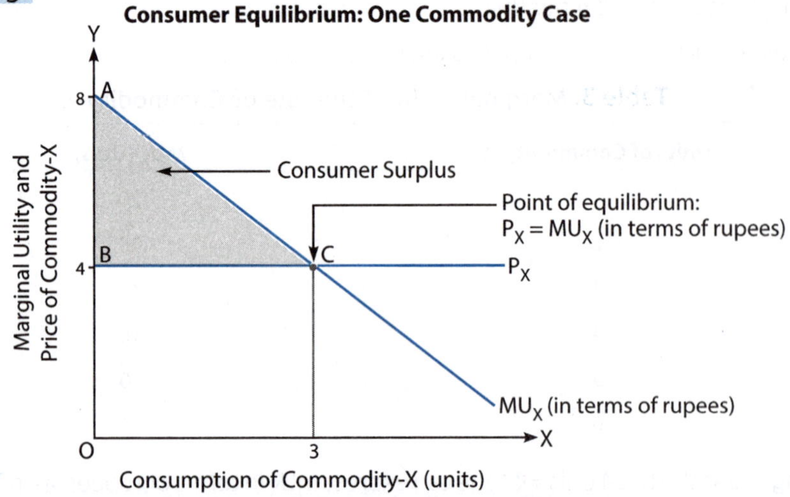

- Equilibrium is struck at point C when 3 units of commodity-X are purchased.
- Corresponding to point C, the price that the consumer is willing to pay for a unit of the commodity exactly matches with the price that he actually pays (= ₹ 4).
- Area ABC reflects consumer surplus. It is maximum in a state of consumer equilibrium.

[Note: Fig. 3 is NOT based on the data in Table 4. We have drawn a smoothed MU_X curve to keep the diagram simple.]

Note the following observations carefully with reference to Fig. 3:

(i) MU_X is a downward sloping curve showing that MU_X declines as consumption of X increases. (This is in accordance with the law of diminishing marginal utility.)

(ii) P_X indicates market price of commodity-X. It is fixed for the consumer and is taken to be equal to ₹ 4.

(iii) Each point on MU_X curve shows the MU_X in terms of money. It indicates the price that the consumer is willing to pay for each successive unit of the commodity.

(iv) Equilibrium is struck at point C when the price he is willing to pay is exactly equal the price he actually pays. In a state of equilibrium, the consumer buys 3 units of commodity-X.

(v) So long as the price he is willing to pay is greater than the price he actually pays, the consumer makes a gain which is called consumer surplus.

(vi) In a state of equilibrium, consumer surplus is maximum. It is equal to area ABC in Fig. 3.

Alternative Presentation of Consumer Equilibrium: One Commodity Case

Let: X be the commodity that the consumer buys

MU_M (rupee worth of satisfaction) = 4 utils

P_X (price of commodity-X) = ₹ 4

Marginal Utility Schedule be as under:

Units of Commodity-X	MU_X (Utils)
1	20
2	18
3	16
4	10

The equilibrium is struck when rupee worth of satisfaction that the consumer expects to get (MU_M) is equal to rupee worth of satisfaction that he actually gets $\left(=\frac{MU_X}{P_X}\right)$.

Thus, equilibrium is struck when:

$$\frac{MU_X}{P_X} = MU_M$$

↑ $\frac{MU_X}{P_X}$: rupee worth of satisfaction that the consumer actually gets

↑ MU_M: rupee worth of satisfaction that the consumer expects to get

With reference to the above schedule, the consumer strikes his equilibrium when:

$$\frac{MU_X}{P_X} = MU_M$$

$$\Rightarrow \quad \frac{MU_X}{4} = 4 \quad \Rightarrow \quad MU_X = 16$$

The schedule shows that $MU_X = 16$, when 3 units of the Good-X are consumed. Hence, equilibrium is struck when 3 units of Good-X are consumed.

HOTS

Q.1. What price the consumer is ready to pay for a commodity in a state of his equilibrium?

Ans. In a state of equilibrium, the price that the consumer is ready to pay for a commodity is the marginal utility of the commodity (estimated in terms of money). Because, in a state of equilibrium: $P_X = MU_X$ (in terms of money).

Q.2. How will you, as a consumer, react to the situation when P_X falls and your state of equilibrium is disturbed for the consumption of Good-X?

Ans. As a consumer, I strike my equilibrium when:

$$P_X = MU_X \text{ (in terms of money)}$$

In case P_X falls, my gain in terms of MU_X becomes greater than my sacrifice in terms of P_X. Thus,

$$MU_X > P_X$$

This induces me to buy more of Good-X. As consumption of X increases, MU_X will decline, in accordance with the law of diminishing marginal utility. I shall stop at a point when:

$$MU_X = P_X$$

Briefly, **a fall in P_X will induce me to buy more of Good-X.**

Q.3. **Ice cream sells for ₹20. Mohini who likes ice cream, has already consumed 4. Her marginal utility of one rupee is 4. Should she consume more ice cream or stop the consumption?**

Ans. A consumer attains equilibrium when:

$$\frac{MU_X}{P_X} = MU_M$$

Substituting the given values, we get $\frac{MU_X}{20} = 4$ implying that, in a state of equilibrium, Mohini's MU_X must be equal to 80 utils. If, having consumed 4 ice creams, Mohini's $MU_X = 80$ utils she must stop consuming more. However, if $MU_X > 80$ she should consume more ice creams till MU_X reduces to 80 and in terms of its money worth is equal to ₹20.

Consumer's Equilibrium: Two Commodities (or Several Commodities) Case

Consider a situation when a consumer is buying commodities X and Y with his given income. **How will he strike his equilibrium?** In case of any one commodity, say commodity-X, a consumer strikes his equilibrium when:

$$\frac{MU_X}{P_X} = MU_M \qquad \text{...(i)}$$

Likewise, for commodity-Y, consumer will strike equilibrium when:

$$\frac{MU_Y}{P_Y} = MU_M \qquad \text{...(ii)}$$

Relating equations (i) and (ii) and considering a situation when a consumer buys both commodities X and Y, we can state his equilibrium as in the following equation:

$$\frac{MU_X}{P_X} = \frac{MU_Y}{P_Y} = MU_M \qquad \text{...(iii)}$$

It implies that a consumer is maximising his satisfaction from commodities X and Y when a rupee worth of marginal utility $\left(\frac{MU_X}{P_X} \text{ or } \frac{MU_Y}{P_Y}\right)$ is the same for commodities X and Y. It is also equal to the marginal utility of money (which is rupee worth of satisfaction as defined by the consumer himself). In other words, we can write that a consumer strikes his equilibrium when MU derived from the last rupee is the same whether spent on 'X' or 'Y'.

The equilibrium equation $\frac{MU_X}{P_X} = \frac{MU_Y}{P_Y}$ can also be written as $\frac{MU_X}{MU_Y} = \frac{P_X}{P_Y}$. Implying that for any set of two commodities, a consumer strikes his equilibrium when ratio of their marginal utilities $\left(\frac{MU_X}{MU_Y}\right)$ is equal to the ratio of their prices $\left(\frac{P_X}{P_Y}\right)$.

Equilibrium Equation for 'n' Number of Commodities

The logic that a consumer strikes his equilibrium for a set of two commodities X and Y when $\frac{MU_X}{P_X} = \frac{MU_Y}{P_Y}$ can be extended to any number of commodities. The equilibrium equation for 'n' number of commodities would be as under:

$$\frac{MU_1}{P_1} = \frac{MU_2}{P_2} = \frac{MU_3}{P_3} = \ldots = \frac{MU_{nth}}{P_{nth}} = MU_M$$

Thus, **Lipsey** and **Chrystal** state "Each consumer demands each good up to the point at which the marginal utility per pound spent on it is the same as the marginal utility of a pound spent on each other good."

Simplified Tabular Illustration

We now present a simplified tabular illustration of consumer's equilibrium, considering Good-X and Good-Y. Table 5 is based on the assumption that $P_X = P_Y = ₹ 1$. With this assumption equilibrium equation changes.

$$\frac{MU_X}{P_X} = \frac{MU_Y}{P_Y} = MU_M$$

The equation now becomes:

$$MU_X = MU_Y = MU_M$$

Note that MU_X now shows marginal utility of commodity-X when another unit of X is purchased or when another rupee is spent on X. Likewise, MU_Y shows marginal utility of commodity-Y when another unit of Y is purchased or when another rupee is spent on Y. Now refer to Table 5 showing MU_X and MU_Y when successive units of X and Y are purchased.

Table 5. Schedule showing MU_X and MU_Y

Units of Commodity-X	MU_X (Utils)	MU_Y (Utils)	
1	25	30	Assumption: $P_X = P_Y$ = ₹1 per unit
2	20	26	
3	15	15	
4	10	2	
5	0	0	

Let us assume that the consumer has six rupees to spend across goods X and Y. He will spend 1st rupee on Good-Y, getting 30 utils of utility, 2nd rupee again on Good-Y, getting 26 utils of utility, 3rd rupee on Good-X, getting 25 utils of utility, 4th rupee again on Good-X, getting 20 utils of utility, 5th rupee on Good-X or Good-Y, getting 15 utils of utility, and finally 6th rupee on Good-X or Good-Y, again getting 15 utils of utility. Thus, total utility is maximised (= 30 + 26 + 25 + 20 + 15 + 15 = 131). No other combination of X and Y will offer the consumer higher than 131 utils of utility, while he is spending 6 rupees on the purchase of Good-X and Good-Y.

Thus, consumer strikes his equilibrium when total satisfaction is maximised. It occurs when $MU_X = MU_Y$ (on the assumption that $P_X = P_Y$). This means that the consumer strikes his equilibrium when the last rupee spent on X or Y yields the same level of satisfaction. This condition of equilibrium is popularly known as law of equi-marginal utility.

Example

Satish has ₹ 88 with him. He intended to purchase good X and Y with his money. The market price of X and Y per unit is ₹ 8. The marginal utility schedule of good X and Y is given below. Find out how many units of X and Y should Satish purchase so that he will get maximum satisfaction.

Units of Commodity-X	MU_X	MU_Y
1	88	40
2	72	36
3	64	24
4	56	20
5	48	16
6	40	12
7	32	8
8	24	4
9	16	0
10	8	0

Solution:

We know, in case of two commodities, a consumer strikes equilibrium when:

$$\frac{MU_X}{P_X} = \frac{MU_Y}{P_Y} \quad \text{...(i)}$$

Or

$$\frac{MU_X}{MU_Y} = \frac{P_X}{P_Y} \quad \text{...(ii)}$$

In the present case, $P_X = P_Y =$ ₹ 8 per unit so that, equilibrium would be struck when:

$MU_X = MU_Y$, according to equation (i)

Or, when $\frac{MU_X}{MU_Y} = \frac{P_X}{P_Y} = \frac{8}{8} = 1$, according to equation (ii)

It occurs when Satish purchases 8 units of X (spending 8 × ₹ 8 = ₹ 64) and 3 units of Y (spending 3 × ₹ 8 = ₹ 24).

[**Note:** It is only corresponding to this combination of X and Y that the consumer is maximising his satisfaction, spending his given money income (₹ 88), and given the price of X and Y.]

Consider combination X = 6 and Y = 1, here also $MU_X = MU_Y$. But it is not an equilibrium point because here all income is not spent, *i.e.*,

₹ 48 (= 6 × ₹ 8) + ₹ 8 (= 1 × ₹ 8) = ₹ 56.

Further, when X = 9 and Y = 5, again $MU_X = MU_Y$. But this is not affordable, as it exceeds consumer's budget. [Because, ₹ 72 (= 9 × ₹ 8) + ₹ 40 (= 5 × ₹ 8) = ₹ 112 > ₹ 88.]

6. Conditions of Consumer's Equilibrium using Marginal Utility Analysis

Conditions of consumer's equilibrium are specified separately for one commodity case and two commodity case, as under:

One Commodity Case

1. Rupee worth of marginal utility actually received by the consumer is equal to marginal utility of money as specified by the consumer himself.

$$\frac{MU_X}{P_X} = MU_M$$

Or

$P_X = MU_X$ (in terms of money)

Rationale: It simply means that the rupee worth of MU actually received is exactly equal to the rupee worth of satisfaction as desired by the consumer.

Or

Price paid by the consumer should be exactly equal to the money value of MU that he derives. In case of $P_X < MU_X$ (in terms of money), he should be prompted to buy more of Good-X. Higher consumption will lead to a fall in MU. The consumption of X would stop only when $P_X = MU_X$ (in terms of money). Likewise, if $P_X > MU_X$ (in terms of money), the consumer will be prompted to buy less of X, leading to a fall in MU_X. The cut in consumption would stop only when $P_X = MU_X$ (in terms of money).

2. Marginal utility of money (MU_M) remains constant.

Rationale: Since utility is measured in terms of money, it is essential that MU_M (the measuring rod) should not change.

3. Law of diminishing marginal utility holds good.

Rationale: MU must diminish as more and more units of a commodity are consumed. In case MU tends to rise, consumption of a commodity will never reach an end. Equilibrium will never be struck.

Two Commodity Case

1. Rupee worth of marginal utility should be the same across Good-X and Good-Y, and equal to marginal utility of money.

$$\frac{MU_X}{P_X} = \frac{MU_Y}{P_Y} = MU_M$$

Rationale: This simply means that the rupee worth of MU derived from either commodity is the same (and equal to marginal utility of money). In case rupee worth of satisfaction $\left(\frac{MU_X}{P_X}\right)$ is greater for Good-X than Good-Y, the consumer will be prompted to shift some expenditure from Y to X. This would lead to a fall in MU_X and a rise in MU_Y. This process would continue till $\frac{MU_X}{P_X} = \frac{MU_Y}{P_Y}$. Likewise, if $\frac{MU_X}{P_X} < \frac{MU_Y}{P_Y}$, the consumer would be prompted to shift some expenditure from X to Y. This would lead to a fall in MU_Y and a rise in MU_X. The process would continue till $\frac{MU_X}{P_X} = \frac{MU_Y}{P_Y}$.

2. Marginal utility of money remains constant.

Rationale: Since utility is measured in terms of money, it is essential that MU_M (the measuring rod) remains constant.

3. Law of diminishing marginal utility holds good.

Rationale: MU must fall as more and more units of a commodity is consumed. In case MU is rising for a commodity, the consumer will never stop the consumption of that commodity. The equilibrium for two goods would never be achieved.

Conditions should not be Confused with the Assumptions

Conditions of consumer's equilibrium (using utility approach) as stated above should not be confused with the assumptions which are as under:

(i) That utility can be expressed in cardinal numbers, like 1, 2, 3,...

(ii) That marginal utility of money remains constant.

(iii) That the law of diminishing marginal utility holds good.

(iv) That the consumer behaves rationally, and aims at the maximisation of his satisfaction.

HOTS

Q.1. What happens when: $\frac{MU_X}{P_X} > \frac{MU_Y}{P_Y}$?

Ans. This situation implies that by spending a rupee on Good-X, the consumer gets greater marginal utility than in case of Good-Y. Accordingly, he will spend more on X than Y. As consumption of X rises, MU_X will fall. On the other hand, as consumption of Y falls, MU_Y will rise. The consumer will stop buying more of X in place of Y only when $\frac{MU_X}{P_X} = \frac{MU_Y}{P_Y}$.

It is here only that the equilibrium is struck.

Q.2. How is equilibrium of the consumer affected when MU_M happens to rise, and P_X is constant?

Ans. Equilibrium is struck when: $\frac{MU_X}{P_X} = MU_M$.

If MU_M rises and P_X is constant, the consumer will be off the point of equilibrium. Because $\frac{MU_X}{P_X}$ would then be less than MU_M. The consumer will reach back his equilibrium only if MU_X rises, as P_X is given to be constant. This will happen only when consumption of commodity-X is decreased (in accordance with the law of diminishing marginal utility).

Q.3. Price of coffee rises, while price of tea remains constant. How would the consumer react to this situation to restore his equilibrium? Use the law of equi-marginal utility.

Ans. According to the law of equi-marginal utility, a consumer strikes his equilibrium when:

$$\frac{MU_X}{P_X} = \frac{MU_Y}{P_Y} = MU_M$$

Let X be coffee and Y be tea.

When P_X rises,

$$\frac{MU_X}{P_X} < \frac{MU_Y}{P_Y} \qquad \text{[The equilibrium is disturbed]}$$

Rise in the price of X in relation to Y will induce the buyer to buy less of X and more of Y. When less of X is purchased/consumed, MU_X will rise. When more of Y is purchased, MU_Y will fall. The switch-over from X to Y will continue till $\frac{MU_X}{P_X} = \frac{MU_Y}{P_Y}$.

Briefly, when P_X rises, less of X and more of Y will be purchased.

7. The Basic Limitation of Utility Analysis

The basic limitation of utility analysis relates to the basic assumption of this analysis: that utility can be expressed in cardinal numbers. Implying that utility can be measured in units like 1, 2 and 3. Is it really possible? Do you, as a consumer, ever express your satisfaction in terms of units like 1, 2 and 3? Perhaps never. Satisfaction at best can be compared (as less or more) when two goods are simultaneously consumed. It is hard to express it in figures.

It is owing to this limitation of utility analysis, that it is found to of little practical relevance in explaining consumer's equilibrium.

POWER POINTS

- Marginal Utility is additional utility when a unit more of a commodity is consumed.

$$MU_{nth} = TU_n - TU_{n-1}$$

- $TU = \Sigma MU$.
- As MU decreases, TU increases only at a decreasing rate.
- TU is maximum when MU = 0.
- TU starts declining only when MU is negative.
- Law of Diminishing Marginal Utility states that marginal utility tends to diminish as more and more (standard) units of a commodity are (continuously) consumed by a consumer.
- Consumer's Equilibrium refers to a situation when a consumer maximises his satisfaction, spending his given income across different goods and services.
- Equilibrium in case of one commodity (say commodity-X) is struck when

$$MU_X \text{ (in terms of money)} = P_X$$

Or,
$$\frac{MU_X}{P_X} = MU_M$$

- Equilibrium in case of two commodities (say X and Y) is struck when

$$\frac{MU_X}{P_X} = \frac{MU_Y}{P_Y} = MU_M$$

Or,
$$\frac{MU_X}{MU_Y} = \frac{P_X}{P_Y} = MU_M$$

- Conditions of Consumer's Equilibrium are:
  (i) Rupee worth of satisfaction should be the same across all goods purchased by the consumer and equal to marginal utility of money.
  (ii) Marginal utility of money remains constant.
  (iii) Law of diminishing marginal utility holds good.
- Principal Limitation of Utility Analysis relates to its basic assumption that utility can be expressed in terms of cardinal numbers like 1, 2 and 3.

EXERCISE

1. Very Short Questions (Remembering & Understanding) (1 mark each)

A. Multiple Choice Questions: Choose the Correct Answer

1. Want satisfying power of a commodity is called:

(a) consumption (b) utility
(c) production (d) value addition

2. Formula for calculation of total utility is:

(a) $TU = \Sigma MU$ (b) $TU = MU_1 + MU_2 + MU_3 + \ldots + MU_n$
(c) both (a) and (b) (d) none of these

3. Formula for calculation of marginal utility is:

(a) $MU_n = TU_n - TU_{n+1}$ (b) $MU_n = TU_{n+1} - TU_{n-1}$
(c) $MU_n = TU_n - TU_{n-1}$ (d) none of these

4. When only 1 unit of the commodity is consumed:

(a) MU = TU (b) MU > TU

(c) MU < TU (d) none of these

5. If the consumer consumes only one commodity 'X', he will be in equilibrium when:

(a) $MU_X < P_X$ (b) $MU_X = P_X$

(c) $MU_X > P_X$ (d) none of these

[Here, MU_X = Marginal utility of the Good-X (in terms of money); P_X = Price of Good-X.]

6. When marginal utility is negative, total utility is:

(a) zero (b) diminishing

(c) maximum (d) minimum

7. Law of Diminishing Marginal Utility states that when more and more units of a commodity are consumed, marginal utility:

(a) begins to increase (b) remains constant

(c) begins to decrease (d) becomes zero

8. When total utility is maximum, marginal utility becomes:

(a) zero (b) unity

(c) positive (d) negative

9. What will be the condition of total utility, when marginal utility stays positive?

(a) Maximum (b) Diminishing

(c) Increasing (d) Minimum

10. When TU is increasing at a diminishing rate, MU must be:

(a) increasing (b) decreasing

(c) constant (d) negative

11. Marginal utility of a particular commodity at the point of saturation is:

(a) zero (b) unity

(c) greater than unity (d) less than unity

12. Which of the following equations is incorrect?

(a) $MU = TU_{n+2} - TU_{n+1}$ (b) $MU = \frac{TU}{Q}$

(c) $MU = TU_n - TU_{n-1}$ (d) $TU = \sum MU$

13. Consuming two goods, a consumer attains equilibrium when:

(a) $\frac{MU_1}{P_1} > \frac{MU_2}{P_2}$ (b) $\frac{MU_2}{P_2} > \frac{MU_1}{P_1}$

(c) $\frac{MU_1}{P_1} = \frac{MU_2}{P_2}$ (d) $\frac{TU_1}{P_1} = \frac{TU_2}{P_2}$

14. The rate at which TU changes is indicated by:

(a) MU (b) TU

(c) both (a) and (b) (d) none of these

15. Initially $\frac{MU_X}{P_X} = \frac{MU_Y}{P_Y}$. With a fall in the price of Y, the consumption of the commodity-Y:

(a) diminishes (b) increases

(c) remains constant (d) becomes zero

16. **With the increase in consumption by one unit of the commodity, TU increases from 150 to 180, then marginal utility is:**
(a) 50 (b) 1.2
(c) 30 (d) 0.833

17. **The consumer is in equilibrium and is consuming commodity-X only. The marginal utility from last unit consumed of commodity-X = 50 utils and MU_M = 10. Find the price of the commodity-X.**
(a) ₹ 5 (b) ₹ 40
(c) ₹ 10 (d) ₹ 4

18. **When price of both the commodities is same, the consumer attains maximum satisfaction where:**
(a) $\frac{MU_X}{MU_Y} > \frac{P_X}{P_Y}$ (b) $\frac{MU_X}{P_X} < \frac{MU_Y}{P_Y}$
(c) $\frac{MU_X}{P_X} > \frac{MU_Y}{P_Y}$ (d) $MU_X = MU_Y$

19. **The shape of MU curve is:**
(a) upward sloping (b) downward sloping
(c) concave to origin (d) straight line

20. **A consumer will purchase more of Good-X than Good-Y, only when:**
(a) $\frac{MU_X}{P_X} = MU_M$ (b) $\frac{MU_X}{P_X} < \frac{MU_Y}{P_Y}$
(c) $\frac{MU_Y}{P_Y} = MU_M$ (d) $\frac{MU_X}{P_X} > \frac{MU_Y}{P_Y}$

21. **The principal limitation of utility analysis relates to the basic assumption that utility can be expressed in terms of:**
(a) cardinal numbers (b) ordinal numbers
(c) both (a) and (b) (d) none of these

Answers

1. (b) **2.** (c) **3.** (c) **4.** (a) **5.** (b) **6.** (b) **7.** (c) **8.** (a) **9.** (c) **10.** (b) **11.** (a) **12.** (b)
13. (c) **14.** (a) **15.** (b) **16.** (c) **17.** (a) **18.** (d) **19.** (b) **20.** (d) **21.** (a)

B. Information & Concept-based Questions

1. **What is meant by utility?**

Ans. Utility refers to the want satisfying capacity of a commodity.

2. **Define total utility.**

Ans. Total utility is the sum total of utility derived from the consumption of all units of a commodity.

3. **Define marginal utility.**

Ans. Marginal utility refers to the additional utility due to the consumption of an additional unit of a commodity.

4. **State the law of diminishing marginal utility.**

Ans. Law of diminishing marginal utility states that as more and more units of a commodity are consumed, marginal utility derived from every additional unit must decline.

5. **What is the meaning of consumer's equilibrium?**

Ans. A consumer is in a state of equilibrium when he maximises his satisfaction by spending his given income on different goods and services.

6. **What is meant by marginal utility of money?**

Ans. Marginal utility of money refers to utility that the consumer expects to obtain from a standard basket of goods which he or she can buy for a rupee.

2. Reason-based Questions (Comprehension of the Subject-matter)

Read the following statements carefully. Write 'True' or 'False' with a reason.

1. TU is the sum total of MU from all units of consumption of a commodity.

Ans. True. Because marginal unit starts from the 1st unit and ends with the nth unit (last unit) consumed by the consumer. So that, $TU = \Sigma MU$.

2. Total utility will increase even when marginal utility decreases.

Ans. True. We know $TU = \Sigma MU$. Accordingly, TU will increase so long as MU is positive, even when it is decreasing.

3. Total utility is maximum when marginal utility starts declining.

Ans. False. When marginal utility starts declining, total utility increases at a diminishing rate. Total utility is maximum when marginal utility is zero.

4. Total utility starts diminishing when marginal utility begins to diminish.

Ans. False. Total utility diminishes only when marginal utility is negative.

5. MU must diminish as more and more standard units of a commodity are continuously consumed.

Ans. True. MU must diminish as more and more standard units of a commodity are continuously consumed. This is in accordance with the law of diminishing marginal utility.

6. Marginal utility analysis of consumer equilibrium assumes that utility can be expressed in terms of cardinal numbers which is a serious limitation of utility analysis.

Ans. True. It is assumed that consumer expresses utility in terms of cardinal numbers like 2, 3 or 4. This is a serious limitation of utility analysis, because this assumption is wide away from the real life situation.

7. Consumer equilibrium can be determined only if the law of diminishing marginal utility holds good.

Ans. True. Because, if the law of diminishing marginal utility does not hold good (or if MU tends to increase) why should the consumer ever stop or reduce the consumption of any commodity.

8. A consumer strikes his equilibrium when: $\frac{MU_X}{P_X} = MU_M$ in case of two commodities.

Ans. False. A consumer strikes his equilibrium when: $\frac{MU_X}{P_X} = MU_M$ in case of single commodity only.

9. A consumer strikes his equilibrium when $MU_X = MU_Y = MU_M$, in case of two commodities, and when P_X and P_Y are not equal.

Ans. False. In case P_X and P_Y are not equal, a consumer strikes his equilibrium when: $\frac{MU_X}{P_X} = \frac{MU_Y}{P_Y} = MU_M$.

10. Unless MU_M is assumed to be constant, equilibrium of the consumer cannot be specified.

Ans. True. It must be assumed that marginal utility of money (MU_M) is constant. [Marginal utility of money refers to 'worth of a rupee' to a consumer. It is a measuring rod (of utility) which must remain constant.] In case it is not constant, money value of utility cannot be determined and the equilibrium equation ($MU_X = P_X$) becomes meaningless.

11. If $\frac{MU_X}{P_X} > \frac{MU_Y}{P_Y}$, the consumer should buy more of commodity-Y and less of commodity-X.

Ans. False. Consumer should buy more of commodity-X in place of commodity-Y. Only then the equality between commodity-X and commodity-Y can be restored, and the equilibrium is attained.

12. A situation when $\frac{P_X}{P_Y} > \frac{MU_X}{MU_Y}$ is better than when $\frac{P_X}{P_Y} = \frac{MU_X}{MU_Y}$.

Ans. False. A consumer attains his equilibrium only when: $\frac{P_X}{P_Y} = \frac{MU_X}{MU_Y}$. It is a situation of maximum satisfaction. Any other situation will not yield maximum satisfaction.

13. A consumer is in equilibrium and buys commodities X and Y. When price of X falls, he starts buying more of X than Y.

Ans. True. When P_X falls, $\frac{MU_X}{P_X} > \frac{MU_Y}{P_Y}$ implying that rupee worth of satisfaction is greater for commodity-X than commodity-Y. Accordingly, the consumer starts buying more of X than Y.

3. HOTS & Applications

1. In case of a normal good, MU must decline as more and more standard units of it are consumed continuously. Comment.

Ans. Yes. Increase in the consumption of a commodity leads to decrease in intensity of desire to have more of it. Thus, every additional unit offers lesser satisfaction to the consumer.

2. Once a consumer reaches the point of equilibrium (which is the point of maximum satisfaction) he would not like to change his allocation of expenditure (to goods X and Y) even if price of one commodity changes. Do you agree?

Ans. No. Equilibrium is struck when:

$$\frac{MU_X}{P_X} = \frac{MU_Y}{P_Y} = MU_M$$

Or,

$$\frac{MU_X}{MU_Y} = \frac{P_X}{P_Y} = MU_M$$

Now, if P_X changes, the equation of equilibrium is disturbed.

In case P_X increases,

$\frac{MU_X}{P_X} < \frac{MU_Y}{P_Y}$. This would prompt the consumer to buy more of Y in place of X.

In case P_X decreases,

$\frac{MU_X}{P_X} > \frac{MU_Y}{P_Y}$. This would prompt the consumer to buy more of X in place of Y.

3. On the consumption of 10 units of a commodity, a consumer finds that rupee worth of MU_X has exceeded the marginal utility of money. Should he not reduce the consumption of X so that he strikes an equilibrium? Give reason in support of your answer.

Ans. Given, $\frac{MU_X}{P_X} > MU_M$ when 10 units of a commodity are consumed.

The consumer should not reduce but increase the consumption of X in order to achieve equilibrium. Only when the consumption of X is increased that MU_X will reduce, so that $\frac{MU_X}{P_X}$ becomes equal to MU_M.

4. Higher consumption of a commodity may mean lower and lower marginal utility, but it never implies negative utility. Do you agree?

Ans. Yes. As the consumer increases the consumption, the marginal utility derived from the consumption of a commodity must diminish as more units of that commodity are consumed at a point of time, and even can be negative. But the total utility or total satisfaction derived from that commodity can never be negative. A rational consumer would never buy a commodity which offers only negative satisfaction.

5. Why should a consumer purchase more of a commodity when MU must decline as consumption of the commodity increases?

Ans. We know, in equilibrium, $P_X = MU_X$ (in terms of money). The consumer will continue purchasing more of a commodity so long as $MU_X > P_X$ even when MU_X is decreasing.

6. When MU of the commodity declines demand for the commodity must be rising consequent upon a fall in its price. Explain it with reference to consumer's equilibrium equation for a single commodity.

Ans. The consumer strikes his equilibrium when:

$$\frac{MU_X}{P_X} = MU_M \quad \text{...(i)}$$

When MU_X declines, it must be associated with rising consumption of X. Implying a rising demand for X. Demand for X would rise only when price of X reduces. Thus, when MU_X falls, equation (i) changes as under:

$$\frac{MU_X}{P_X} > MU_M$$

Now, the equilibrium will be restored only when P_X falls, because MU_M is assumed as constant. In case P_X falls, demand for the commodity must be rising.

7. Mr. X consumes two commodities A and B whose prices are ₹ 6 and ₹ 8 per unit respectively. Does the Mr. X strikes his equilibrium when he is getting marginal utility of A equal to 7 and that of B also equal to 7?

Ans. We know that, Mr. X strikes his equilibrium when:

$$\frac{MU_A}{P_A} = \frac{MU_B}{P_B}$$

$$\frac{MU_A}{P_A} = \frac{7}{6}$$

and

$$\frac{MU_B}{P_B} = \frac{7}{8}$$

Here, $\frac{7}{6} > \frac{7}{8}$ or $\frac{MU_A}{P_A} \neq \frac{MU_B}{P_B}$. Therefore, Mr. X does not strike his equilibrium.

8. Given below is the utility schedule of a consumer for commodity-X. The price of the commodity is ₹ 6 per unit. How many units should the consumer purchase to maximise satisfaction? (Assume that utility is expressed in utils and 1 util = ₹ 1). Give reasons for your answer.

Consumption (Units)	Total Utility (Utils)	Marginal Utility (Utils)
1	10	10
2	18	8
3	25	7
4	31	6
5	34	3
6	34	0

Ans. Consumer attains equilibrium when:

$$\frac{MU_X}{P_X} = \text{MU of Money}$$

[Here, MU_X = Marginal utility of X; P_X = Price of X.]

Or, when: $MU_X = P_X \cdot \text{MU of Money}$

When X = 4, $MU_X = P_X \times MU_M = 6$ $[MU_M = 1]$

The consumer should purchases 4 units in order to get maximum satisfaction.

4. Evaluation (Value-based Questions)

1. As a consumer, would you equate price of a commodity with total utility or marginal utility? Give reason in support of your answer.

Ans. A consumer would equate price (P) of the commodity with its marginal utility (MU), not total utility (TU).
Reason: The consumer, while buying a unit of a commodity, compares additional benefit and additional cost related to that unit. Additional benefit is MU, while additional cost is price of the commodity. He will buy a particular unit only when MU is at least equal to price. And, **he strikes his equilibrium when MU (in terms of money) = Price.**

The consumer does not compare price with TU. Because, TU is the sum total of utility resulting from **all** the units of a commodity he is buying. It cannot be compared with price which is always related to **one** unit (or is always expressed as 'per unit').

2. Explain the economic value of the following equation, $\frac{MU_X}{P_X} = MU_M$ when X happens to be a domestic fuel (LPG) and P_X is lowered by way of subsidy by the government.

Ans. Taking MU_M as constant, a fall in P_X (by way of subsidy) would mean that $\frac{MU_X}{P_X} > MU_M$. The consumer's equilibrium is disturbed. But the change is good for the consumer. Induced by lower P_X, the consumer increase the consumption of LPG. A rise in the consumption of LPG leads to a fall in MU_X. The equilibrium $\left(\frac{MU_X}{P_X} = MU_M\right)$ is now established at a higher level of consumption of LPG. **The subsidy plays its role by increasing the consumption of LPG, as desired by the government. Consumer's equilibrium is shifted to a higher level of satisfaction, even when his income remains constant.**

3. When onion price hits hard, the poor man simply stops buying it. Explain the Economics of it, using utility analysis.

Ans. A consumer buys a commodity only when a rupee spent on it yields rupee worth of satisfaction (MU_M). A poor man stops the consumption of onion when he finds that a rupee spent on it does not yield rupee worth of satisfaction (no matter what quantity of onions is purchased), so that, $\frac{MU_X}{P_X} < MU_M$.

5. CBSE Questions—Past 4 years (With Answers or Reference to the Text for Answers)

1. Given price of a good, how does a consumer decide as to how much of that good to buy? *[CBSE Delhi 2012]*

   Or

   Given the price of a good, how will a consumer decide as to how much quantity of that good to buy? Use utility analysis. *[CBSE (AI) 2014]*

   [Page 43–45]

2. A consumer consumes only two goods X and Y and is in equilibrium. Price of X falls. Explain the reaction of the consumer through the utility analysis. *[CBSE (AI) 2012]*

   [Page 50]

3. A consumer consumes only two goods X and Y and is in equilibrium. Price of X rises. Explain the reaction of the consumer with the help of utility analysis. *[CBSE (F) 2012]*

   [Page 50]

4. Explain the law of diminishing marginal utility with the help of a total utility schedule. *[CBSE Delhi 2013]*

   [Page 38, 41, 42]

5. Explain the conditions of consumer's equilibrium with the help of utility analysis. *[CBSE Delhi 2013]*

   Or

   Explain the conditions of consumer's equilibrium under utility analysis. *[CBSE (AI) 2013]*

   [Page 48, 49]

6. What is meant by consumer's equilibrium? *[CBSE (F) 2013]*

   [Page 42]

7. By spending his entire income only on two goods X and Y a consumer finds that

   $$\frac{\text{Marginal Utility of X}}{\text{Price of X}} > \frac{\text{Marginal Utility of Y}}{\text{Price of Y}}$$

   Explain how will the consumer react. *[CBSE (F) 2013]*

   [Page 50]

8. By spending his entire income only on two goods X and Y a consumer finds that

$$\frac{\text{Marginal Utility of X}}{\text{Price of X}} < \frac{\text{Marginal Utility of Y}}{\text{Price of Y}}$$

Explain how will the consumer react. *[CBSE (F) 2013]*

[Page 50]

9. A consumer consumes only two goods. Explain consumer's equilibrium with the help of utility analysis. *[CBSE Delhi 2014]*

[Page 46, 47]

10. A consumer consumes only two goods A and B and is in equilibrium. Show that when price of Good-B falls, demand for B rises. Answer this question with the help of utility analysis. *[CBSE Delhi 2014]*

Or

A consumer consumes only two goods X and Y and is in equilibrium. Show that when price of Good-X falls, demand for Good-X rises. Use utility analysis. *[CBSE (F) 2014]*

[Page 50]

11. A consumer consumes only two goods X and Y and is in equilibrium. Show that when the price of Good-X rises, the consumer buys less of Good-X. Use utility analysis. *[CBSE (AI) 2014]*

[Page 50]

12. Define utility. *[CBSE (F) 2014; 2015]*

[Page 37]

13. What is law of diminishing marginal utility? *[CBSE (F) 2014]*

[Page 41, 42]

14. Assuming that a consumer consumes only two goods, explain the conditions of consumer's equilibrium with the help of utility analysis. *[CBSE (F) 2014]*

[Page 48, 49]

15. A consumer consumes only two goods X and Y whose prices are ₹ 4 and ₹ 5 per unit respectively. If the consumer chooses a combination of the two goods with marginal utility of X equal to 5 and that of Y equal to 4, is the consumer in equilibrium? Give reasons. What will a rational consumer do in this situation? Use utility analysis. *[CBSE Delhi 2015]*

[Page 46, 50, 56]

16. A consumer consumes only two goods X and Y whose prices are ₹ 5 and ₹ 4 respectively. If the consumer chooses a combination of the two goods with marginal utility of X equal to 4 and that of Y equal to 5, is the consumer in equilibrium? Why or why not? What will a rational consumer do in this situation? Use utility analysis. *[CBSE (AI) 2015]*

[Page 46, 50, 56]

17. A consumer consumes only two goods X and Y whose prices are ₹ 2 and ₹ 1 per unit respectively. If the consumer chooses a combination of the two goods with marginal utility of X being 4 and that of Y also being 4, is the consumer in equilibrium? Give reasons. Explain what will a rational consumer do in this situation. Use marginal utility analysis. *[CBSE (F) 2015]*

[Page 46, 50, 56]

6. NCERT Questions (With Hints to Answers)

1. State the condition of consumer's equilibrium.

[**Hint:** A consumer strikes his equilibrium when rupee worth of marginal utility actually received by the consumer is equal to marginal utility of money (rupee worth of satisfaction that the consumer wishes to get).

$$\frac{MU_X}{P_X} = MU_M$$]

2. Starting from the initial situation of consumer's equilibrium, suppose that the marginal utility of a rupee increases. Will it increase or decrease the quantity demanded of a product?

   [**Hint:** Consumer's equilibrium is struck when:

$$\frac{MU_X}{P_X} = MU_M$$

   A rise in MU_M implies that $\frac{MU_X}{P_X} < MU_M$.

   If P_X is constant, MU_X must rise for the equilibrium to be restored. MU_X will rise only if quantity demanded of X decreases (in accordance with the law of diminishing marginal utility).]

3. Ice creams sell for ₹ 30. Lakshmi who loves ice cream, has already eaten 3. Her MU from eating 3 ice creams is 90. Suppose further that, for her, the MU of one rupee is 3. Should she eat more ice cream or should she stop?

   [**Hint:** Consumer's equilibrium is struck when:

$$\frac{MU_X}{P_X} = MU_M$$

   Substituting the values, we find that, $\frac{90}{30} = 3$.

   It shows that Lakshmi has already reached the point of equilibrium by consuming 3 ice creams. She should stop eating any more.]

7. Miscellaneous Questions and Reference to the Text for Answers

A. Questions of 3 & 4 marks each

1. What is the relation between total utility and marginal utility?

   [Page 39, 40]

2. Define marginal utility. State the law of diminishing marginal utility.

   [Page 37, 41, 42]

3. Distinguish between marginal utility and total utility.

   [Page 37]

4. What is meant by consumer's equilibrium? State its condition in case of a single commodity.

   [Page 42, 48, 49]

5. How does a consumer reach equilibrium position when he is buying only one commodity? Explain with the help of marginal utility schedule.

   [Page 43–45]

6. What change does it make to the equation of consumer's equilibrium when he decides to spend his income on two commodities rather than one?

   [Page 46, 47]

7. Given the market price of a good, how does a consumer decide as to how many units of that good to buy? Explain.

   [Page 43–45]

B. Questions of 6 marks each

1. Explain the meaning of consumer's equilibrium with the help of a table and diagram.

   [Page 42–45]

2. What do you understand by consumer's equilibrium? Give logical reasoning as to how he reaches his state of equilibrium.

   [Page 42–47]

3. What do you understand by consumer's equilibrium? Explain consumer's equilibrium in case of a single commodity.
   [Page 42–45]
4. A consumer consumes only two goods. Explain his equilibrium with the help of utility approach.
   [Page 46, 47]
5. Explain the conditions of consumer's equilibrium with the help of marginal utility analysis.
   [Page 48, 49]

DOs and DON'Ts

1. **Never miss this fact:** Higher consumption of a good may lead to higher total utility. But, if total utility is rising, it does not mean that the consumer should keep on increasing the consumption of the concerned good. The consumption of the commodity must stop when $\frac{MU_X}{P_X} = MU_M$ (rupee worth of utility derived by the consumer is equal to rupee worth of satisfaction as defined or desired by the consumer).
2. **Equilibrium equation is common to all consumers. But not the equilibrium quantity.** Equilibrium equation $\left(\frac{MU_X}{P_X} = MU_M\right)$ is of universal relevance. Every consumer strikes his equilibrium according to this equation. But, no way should it be interpreted to mean that (given a particular price of the commodity), each consumer will strike his equilibrium by buying the same amount of the commodity. Because: (i) each consumer has his own MU_M (marginal utility of money, or rupee worth of satisfaction), and (ii) each consumer has his own scale of marginal utilities from the consumption of a commodity. For some consumers, MU of a commodity may decline faster than others. It all depends on tastes and preferences of the individual consumer.

ability ZONE

❑ Marginal Utility of Money

Marginal utility of money is assumed to be constant because it is like a measuring rod of utility when a unit of money is spent on the purchase of a commodity. A measuring rod must remain constant. However, it is not like a standard yardstick (like a metre of a cloth or a litre of milk) which is uniformly accepted by one and all. It is a measuring rod of utility as specified by each individual according to his own tastes and preferences.

❑ Algebraically

$$TU = \sum MU$$

Geometrically, TU = area under MU curve corresponding to a given level of consumption of a commodity.

Fig. 4 illustrates this point.

When OL units of commodity-X are consumed, TU = area OLST, which is area under MU curve corresponding to a given level of consumption.

FIGURE 4

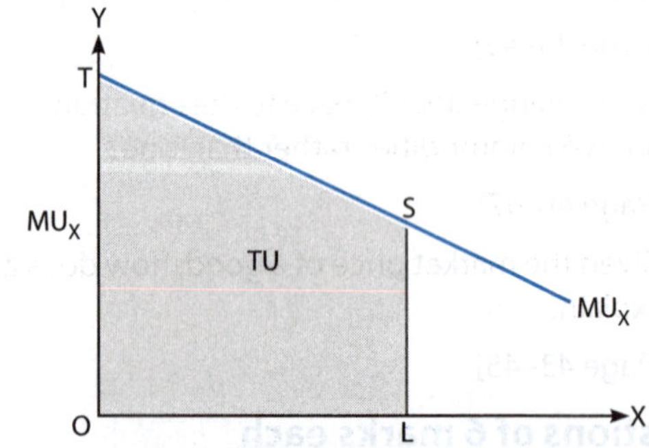

Units of Consumption of Commodity-X

$TU = \Sigma MU$
$= \text{Area } OLST$
when consumption = OL.

Consumer's Equilibrium —Indifference Curve Analysis

CHAPTER 3

TODO

- Introduction: Cardinal and Ordinal Concepts of Utility
- Concept of Indifference Set and Indifference Curve
- Monotonic Preferences of the Consumer and Downward Sloping IC
- Consumer's Budget (Budget Set and Budget Line)
- Consumer's Equilibrium using Indifference Curve Analysis

1. Introduction: Cardinal and Ordinal Concepts of Utility

We have already discussed consumer's equilibrium in chapter 2. But, the discussion in chapter 2 is based on the assumption that utility can be expressed in cardinal numbers, like 2, 4, 6, and 8, or it can be measured in terms of units. **Prof. Hicks** challenges the relevance of this assumption. He is of the opinion that measurement of utility in terms of units like 2, 4, 6, and 8 is not realistic. Do you ever do it in your daily life? Do you ever say that a cup of tea gives you 5 units of utility or that a cup of coffee gives you 6 units of utility? Perhaps never. At best, what you say is that a cup of tea offers you greater satisfaction than a cup of coffee, or *vice versa* (depending on your preferences). This exactly is the opinion of Prof. Hicks. He says that utility can at best be compared, depending on your tastes and preferences. Comparison of utility (in terms of higher or lower level of satisfaction) refers to ordinal concept of utility. It differs from the cardinal concept where utility is measured in terms of units like 2, 4, 6, and 8. Prof. Hicks has developed a theory of consumer's equilibrium based on ordinal concept of utility. This theory is popularly known as 'Indifference Curve Analysis'. The present chapter focuses on indifference curve analysis of consumer's equilibrium. You will see that throughout this analysis, we shall never express utility in terms of cardinal numbers or never measure utility in terms of units like 2, 4, 6 and 8; we shall only compare utility (or the level of satisfaction) as 'equal, less or more' in different situations.

Cardinal and Ordinal Concepts of Utility

Cardinal concept of utility suggests that utility (satisfaction from the consumption of a commodity) can be measured in terms of units like 2, 4, 6, and 8.

Ordinal concept of utility, on the other hand, suggests that utility cannot be measured in terms of units. It can at best be **ranked** or compared as high or low.

2. Concept of Indifference Set and Indifference Curve

Consider a situation when a consumer is spending his given income across goods A and B. Let Good-A be apples, and Good-B be oranges. Consider these goods as substitutes of each other.

Consider Table 1, showing different combinations of apples and oranges.

Table 1. Different Combinations of Apples and Oranges

Combination	Number of Apples	Number of Oranges
A	1	10
B	2	7
C	3	5
D	4	4

Note the following observations relating to Table 1:

(i) Combinations A, B, C and D are specified by the consumer according to his tastes and preferences.

(ii) Each combination offers the same level of satisfaction to the consumer. So that (in terms of the level of satisfaction), Combination A = Combination B = Combination C = Combination D.

(iii) As there is no difference among combinations A, B, C and D, we may say that the consumer is indifferent across these combinations. Accordingly, these combinations together form an 'Indifference Set' of the consumer.

Indifference Set

It is a set of those combinations of two goods which offer the consumer the same level of satisfaction. So that, the consumer is indifferent across all combinations in his indifference set.

Diagrammatic presentation of Table 1 gives the following curve.

FIGURE 1

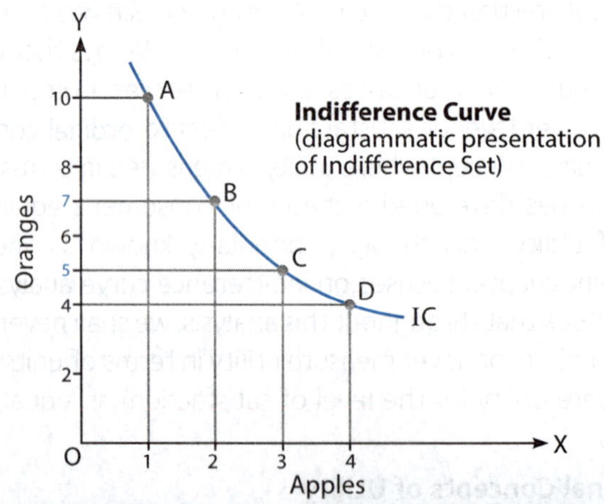

IC is an indifference curve. Each point on the curve shows a combination of two goods, offering the same level of satisfaction to the consumer. Thus, level of satisfaction of the consumer at point A is the same as at points B, C or D.

Each point on the curve (like A, B, C, ...) shows one combination of apples and oranges. Since each combination offers the same level of satisfaction to a consumer, this curve is called indifference curve.

Indifference Curve

Indifference curve is a diagrammatic presentation of an indifference set of a consumer. It is a locus of all such points which show different combinations of two commodities (like apples and oranges) yielding the same level of satisfaction to the consumer. Each point on the indifference curve indicates one combination of two goods. Each combination yields the same level of satisfaction.

3. Monotonic Preferences of the Consumer and Downward Sloping IC

Monotonic preferences of the consumer is the basic assumption of IC analysis. It means, the consumer preferences are such that greater consumption of a commodity always offers him a higher level of satisfaction. Implying that the consumer is never over supplied with a commodity. Or that, he never finds himself in a situation of negative marginal utility. Here is an illustration:

Let us assume that initially the consumer is buying 2 apples and 5 oranges. Now, his income level (or purchasing power) rises. Now he buys 3 apples and 5 oranges. So that he has one more apple than before, while the number of oranges is the same as before. According to monotonic preferences, 3 apples and 5 oranges must yield higher satisfaction than 2 apples and 5 oranges. The satisfaction level can remain constant only if the consumption of oranges is reduced from 5 when the consumption of apples is increased from 2 to 3. Equal satisfaction level from different combinations of two goods is the basic characteristics of indifference curve. Thus, Fig. 2 shows that on the indifference curve (IC) when the consumption of apples increases from 2 to 3, that of oranges decreases from 5 to 3. Gain of utility owing to increase in consumption of apples from 2 to 3 is exactly offset by the loss of utility owing to decrease in consumption of oranges from 5 to 3. Consumption of Good-X is negatively related to consumption of Good-Y (increase in one implies decrease in the other). This imparts negative slope to IC curve. Accordingly, IC slopes downward. Briefly, it is because of monotonic preferences of the consumer that IC slopes downward, indicating negative slope.

FIGURE 2

IC slopes downward, or it shows a negative slope

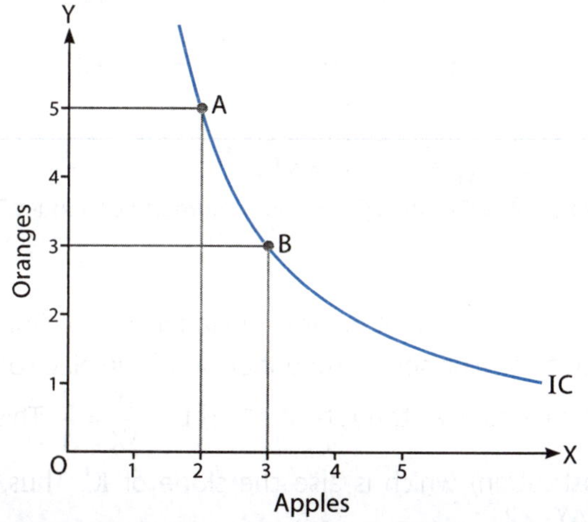

- Satisfaction level at A = Satisfaction level at B.
- Between A to B, consumption of oranges must reduce when the consumption of apples is increasing.
- Since consumption of two goods on the IC is negatively (or inversely) related, IC tends to slope downward.

Slope of IC: Algebraic Expression

$$\text{Slope of IC} = \frac{\Delta Y}{\Delta X}$$

$$= \frac{AB}{BC} = (-)\frac{2}{1}$$

$$= (-)\ 2$$

[consumption of one additional unit of Good-X involves a sacrifice of 2 units of Good-Y]

Negative slope of IC implies that it slopes downward from left to right.

FIGURE 3

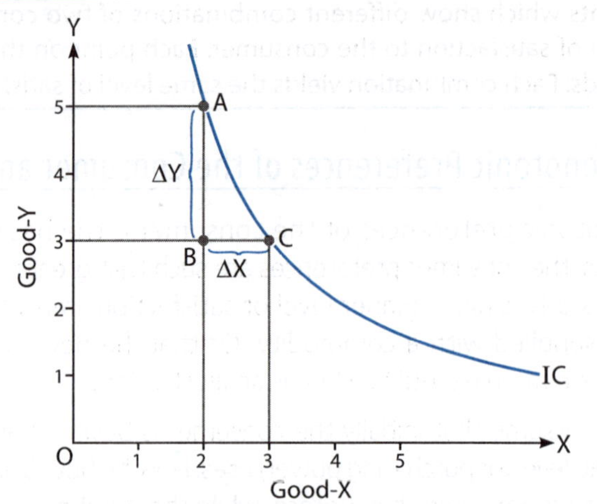

Slope of IC shows MRS (Marginal Rate of Substitution)

Let us discuss this point with reference to Fig. 4.

FIGURE 4

Slope of IC = MRS

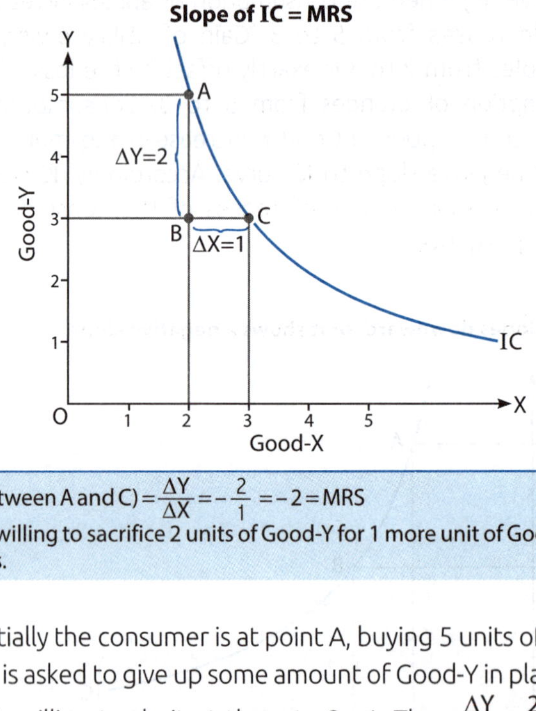

Slope of IC (between A and C) $= \frac{\Delta Y}{\Delta X} = -\frac{2}{1} = -2 = \text{MRS}$

The consumer is willing to sacrifice 2 units of Good-Y for 1 more unit of Good-X. This is according to his preferences.

Assume that initially the consumer is at point A, buying 5 units of Good-Y and 2 units of Good-X. If he is asked to give up some amount of Good-Y in place of one more unit of Good-X, he is willing to do it at the rate 2 : 1. Thus, $\frac{\Delta Y}{\Delta X} = \frac{2}{1}$. This is called MRS (marginal rate of substitution) which is also the slope of IC. Thus, in Fig. 4 MRS (between A and C) $= \frac{\Delta Y}{\Delta X} = \frac{2}{1} = 2$. [Often '–' sign is prescribed as a prefix before the value of MRS. Thus, we write MRS : –2, to indicate that IC curve tends to slope downward.]

MRS

> MRS is the same as slope of IC. It shows the amount of Good-Y that the consumer is willing to give up for one more unit of Good-X. It is measured as: $\frac{\Delta Y}{\Delta X}$ between any two points on IC. It is determined by the consumer himself, according to his preferences.

Slope of IC (or MRS) tends to Decline: IC is Convex to the Origin

As we move down the IC, we find that its slope tends to decline. Implying that MRS tends to decline. Which is why IC is convex to the origin. Fig. 5 illustrates this point.

Between points A and B, the consumer is willing to give up 1.5 units of Good-Y for 1 more unit of Good-X. So that, MRS $= -\frac{\Delta Y}{\Delta X} = -\frac{1.5}{1} = -1.5$. But, as we move down the curve, we find that between points B and C, the consumer is willing to give up 1.5 units of Good-Y for 2 more units of Good-X or 0.75 units of Good-Y for 1 more unit of Good-X. So that, MRS $= -\frac{\Delta Y}{\Delta X} = -\frac{1.5}{2} = -0.75$. Likewise, between points C and D, $\Delta Y = 0.5$ and $\Delta X = 2$, so that MRS $= -\frac{\Delta Y}{\Delta X} = -\frac{0.5}{2} = -0.25$. It is because of the declining slope of IC (or diminishing MRS) that IC is convex to the origin.

FIGURE 5

Slope of IC (or MRS) declines, and IC is convex to the origin

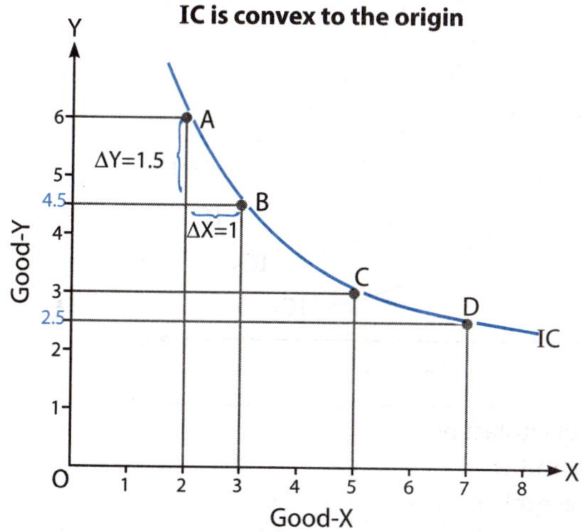

Diminishing MRS

X	Y	MRS $\left(\frac{\Delta Y}{\Delta X}\right)$
2	6	–
3	4.5	$-\frac{1.5}{1} = -1.5$
5	3	$-\frac{1.5}{2} = -0.75$
7	2.5	$-\frac{0.5}{2} = -0.25$

- Between points A–B, slope of IC $= -\frac{\Delta Y}{\Delta X} = -\frac{1.5}{1} = -1.5$ (or MRS $= -1.5$)
- Between points B–C, slope of IC $= -\frac{\Delta Y}{\Delta X} = -\frac{1.5}{2} = -0.75$ (or MRS $= -0.75$)
- Between points C–D, slope of IC $= -\frac{\Delta Y}{\Delta X} = -\frac{0.5}{2} = -0.25$ (or MRS $= -0.25$)

MRS tends to decline as we move down the IC. So that IC is convex to origin.

But, a question needs to be answered at this point:

Why should the consumer be willing to sacrifice less and less amount of Good-Y for every successive unit of Good-X?

Answer is as follows:

As more and more units of Good-X are obtained by the consumer, his intensity of desire for Good-X tends to decline. Implying that marginal utility of Good-X tends to fall (in accordance with the law of diminishing marginal utility). On the other hand, as more and more units of Good-Y are given up, his intensity of desire for Good-Y tends to rise. Implying that marginal utility of Good-Y tends to rise with every additional unit of it being sacrificed. It is because of this that for every successive unit of Good-X, the consumer is willing to give up less and less amount of Good-Y. Accordingly, $\frac{\Delta Y}{\Delta X}$ (sacrificing Y per unit of X) tends to fall as we move down the IC. Falling $\frac{\Delta Y}{\Delta X}$ implies falling MRS, and it is because of falling MRS that IC is convex to the origin.

IC is Convex to the Origin

Yes, IC is normally convex to the origin. It is because the slope of IC $\left(=\frac{\Delta Y}{\Delta X}\right)$ tends to decline, or because MRS tends to decline as we move along the curve, left to right.

Indifference Map

Fig. 6 shows a set of indifference curves one above the other. A set of ICs drawn in a graph is called Indifference Map.

FIGURE 6

Indifference Map

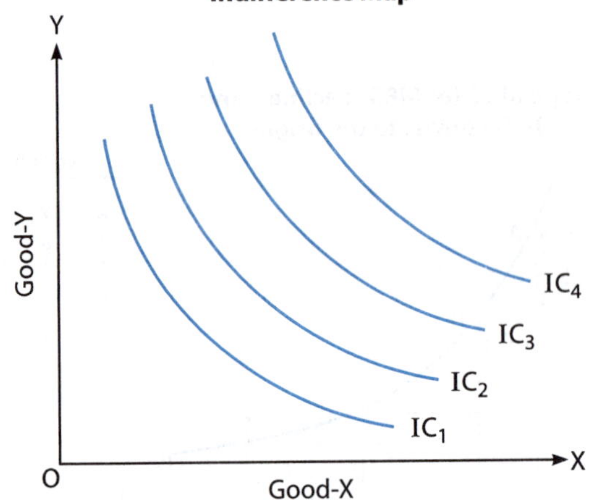

- Higher IC shows higher level of satisfaction.
- ICs need not be parallel to each other.
- ICs never touch or intersect each other.

With reference to Fig. 6, following observations need to be carefully noted:

- Higher IC (to the right and above another IC) indicates higher level of satisfaction. Thus, IC_4 indicates higher level of satisfaction than IC_3; IC_3 indicates higher level of satisfaction than IC_2, and IC_2 indicates higher level of satisfaction than IC_1.
- Each IC in the indifference map indicates a different preference set of the consumer, and it corresponds to a different level of consumer's income.
- ICs need not be parallel to each other.
- ICs do not touch or intersect each other.

Higher IC indicates Higher Level of Satisfaction

Fig. 7 illustrates this point.

FIGURE 7

Higher IC indicates higher level of satisfaction

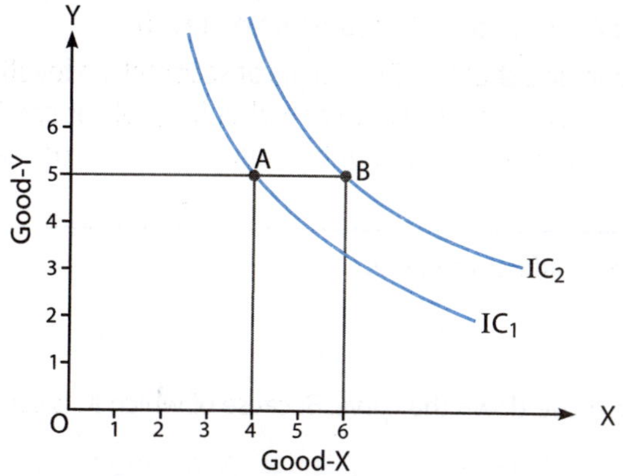

- Point B offers 5 units of Good-Y, and 6 units of Good-X.
- Point A offers 5 units of Good-Y, and 4 units of Good-X.
- Since point B offers greater amount of Good-X (even when the amount of Good-Y is the same), it must yield higher level of satisfaction than point A.

Apparently IC_2 is higher than IC_1. Consider point 'A' on IC_1 and point 'B' on IC_2. At point A, the consumer gets 4 units of Good-X and 5 units of Good-Y. At point B, the consumer gets 6 units of Good-X and 5 units of Good-Y. Thus, the consumer gets 2 more units of Good-X at point B even when the amount of Good-Y is the same as point A. The assumption of monotonic preferences of the consumer permits us to conclude that greater the consumption, higher must be the level of satisfaction. Implying that point 'B' (or for that matter, any point on IC_2) must yield higher level of satisfaction than point A (or any point on IC_1).

ICs do not Cross or Intersect each other

Yes, ICs do not cross or intersect each other. What, if they do? Well, we get inconsistent results. Fig. 8 illustrates how.

FIGURE 8

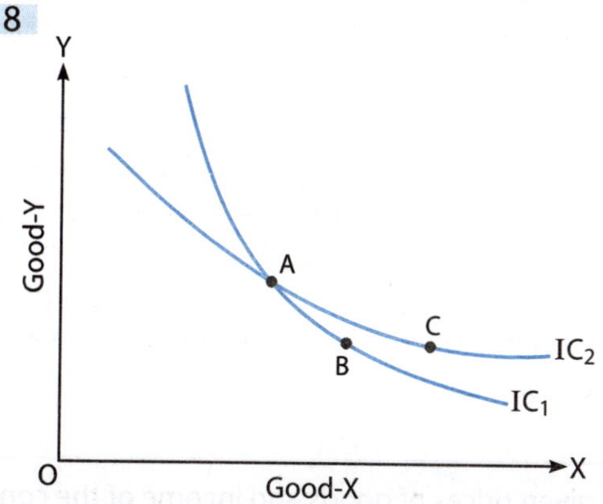

A = B
A = C
∴ B = C (A Contradictory Result)

- A and C are on the same IC, and therefore, should be offering equal satisfaction.
- A and B are on the same IC, and therefore, should be offering equal satisfaction.
- If A and C are equal, & A and B are equal, B and C should also be equal (in terms of satisfaction level). But this is wrong, because C is to the right and above B, and therefore, must offer higher level of satisfaction.

Point C is to the right and above point B. Implying that point C must yield higher level of satisfaction than point B. But, because IC_1 and IC_2 are intersecting, we get inconsistent results as under:

A and B are on IC_1, implying A = B (in terms of satisfaction level)

A and C are on IC_2, implying A = C (in terms of satisfaction level)

If A = B, and A = C, we can conclude that B = C (in terms of satisfaction level). But this is NOT true. We have already noted that C must offer higher level of satisfaction, as it is to the right and above B. Thus, we get inconsistent result in case ICs cross each other.

Properties/Characteristics of ICs

The above discussion reveals following characteristics of indifference curve:

(i) IC slopes downward, left to right.

(ii) Slope of IC indicates MRS.

(iii) The slope of IC (or MRS) tends to diminish as we move down the curve. Because of which IC is convex to the origin.

(iv) In an indifference map, higher IC indicates higher level of satisfaction.

(v) ICs do not cross or intersect each other.

(vi) When two commodities are consumed, IC neither touches X-axis nor Y-axis.

4. Consumer's Budget (Budget Set and Budget Line)

Let us assume that a consumer has a budget of ₹ 60 to be spent on Good-1 and Good-2. Also, assume that price of Good-1 is ₹ 2 per unit and price of Good-2 is ₹ 1 per unit. Accordingly, we find the following budget set of the consumer. This set shows consumption possibilities for the consumer, given his income and prices of Good-1 and Good-2.

Table 2. Budget Set of the Consumer

Units of Good-1	Units of Good-2
0	60
10	40
20	20
30	0

[**Note:** This budget set is drawn on the assumptions that consumer's income/budget = ₹ 60, $P_{Good\text{-}1}$ = ₹ 2 per unit and $P_{Good\text{-}2}$ = ₹ 1 per unit.]

If a consumer spends his entire income on Good-1, he can buy 30 units of it. On the other hand, if he spends his entire money on Good-2, he gets 60 units of it. Alternatively, a consumer can buy 10 units of Good-1 (spending 10 × ₹ 2 = ₹ 20 on it) and 40 units of Good-2 (spending 40 × ₹ 1 = ₹ 40 on it). Also, he can buy 20 units of Good-1 (spending 20 × ₹ 2 = ₹ 40 on it) and 20 units of Good-2 (spending 20 × ₹ 1 = ₹ 20 on it). Likewise, you can think of various other combinations that a consumer can buy, given his income and prices of Good-1 and Good-2.

Budget Set

It refers to attainable combinations of a set of two goods, given prices of goods and income of the consumer.

The budget set equation (briefly called 'Budget Equation'): $P_1X_1 + P_2X_2 \leq Y$

Here, P_1 = Price of Good-1; X_1 = Quantity of Good-1; P_2 = Price of Good-2; X_2 = Quantity of Good-2; Y = Total expenditure or total budget.

What can lead to a change in Budget Set?

Budget set depends on P_1, P_2 and Y. Change in any of these variables will lead to a change in budget set.

Diagrammatic presentation of the budget set (as in Table 2) offers a budget line, as in Fig. 9.

FIGURE 9

Budget Line of the Consumer

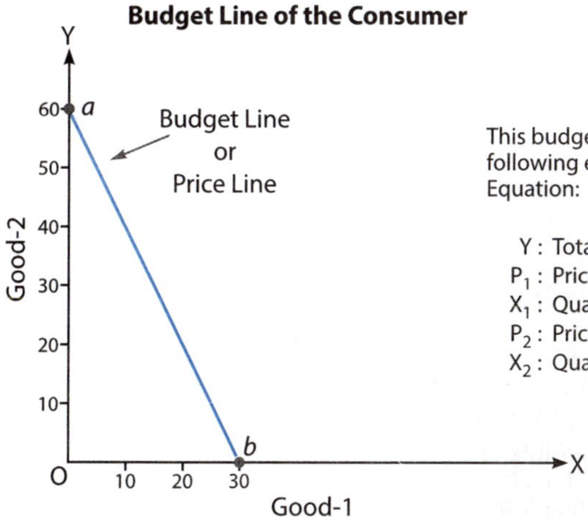

This budget line corresponds to the following equation, called Budget Line Equation:

$$P_1X_1 + P_2X_2 = Y$$

Y : Total expenditure or total budget.
P_1 : Price of Good-1.
X_1 : Quantity of Good-1.
P_2 : Price of Good-2.
X_2 : Quantity of Good-2.

This budget line is drawn on the assumptions that price of Good-1 is ₹ 2 per unit, price of Good-2 is ₹ 1 per unit, and the consumer has ₹ 60 to spend. Accordingly, maximum 30 units of Good-1 are purchased when entire budget is spent on Good-1 and maximum 60 units of Good-2 can be purchased when entire budget is spent on Good-2.

Line *ab* (in Fig. 9) is called Budget Line. Why?

Because, a consumer with his given income of ₹ 60 can buy 30 units of Good-1 or 60 units of Good-2, or other possible combinations on the line *ab*. Each point on the line *ab* indicates one combination of Good-1 and Good-2 which a consumer can buy with his given income, and given the prices of Good-1 and Good-2.

Budget Line

It is a line showing different possible combinations of Good-1 and Good-2, which a consumer can buy, given his budget and the prices of Good-1 and Good-2. Anywhere, on the budget line, a consumer is spending his entire income either on Good-1 or on Good-2 or on both Good-1 and Good-2.

Line *ab* (in Fig. 9) is called Price Line. Why?

Because line *ab* shows that 30 units of Good-1 are equal to 60 units of Good-2 in the market. So that,

Price of 1 unit of Good-1 = Price of 2 units of Good-2.

Thus, $$\frac{P_1}{P_2} = \frac{60}{30} = \frac{2}{1}$$

Thus, price line shows price ratio between Good-1 and Good-2. It shows that '2' units of Good-2 are to be sacrificed for getting '1' unit of Good-1.

Budget Line and Attainable & Non-attainable Combinations

Budget line is a line that separates attainable combinations (also called feasible combinations) from the non-attainable (non-feasible) combinations. **Can a consumer go beyond the budget line?** Certainly not, given his budget and the prices of Good-1 and Good-2. Thus, any point beyond the budget line shows a non-attainable combination or a non- feasible combination. Fig. 10 illustrates this point.

[**Note:** The diagram shows budget line when: Consumer's budget = ₹ 60; price of Good-1 = ₹ 2 per unit; price of Good-2 = ₹ 1 per unit.]

A consumer can only afford to buy combinations that fall along his budget line (*ab* in Fig. 10) or inside it. This region is known as feasible region. A consumer cannot afford to buy combinations that are beyond his budget line. This region is called non-feasible region.

FIGURE 10

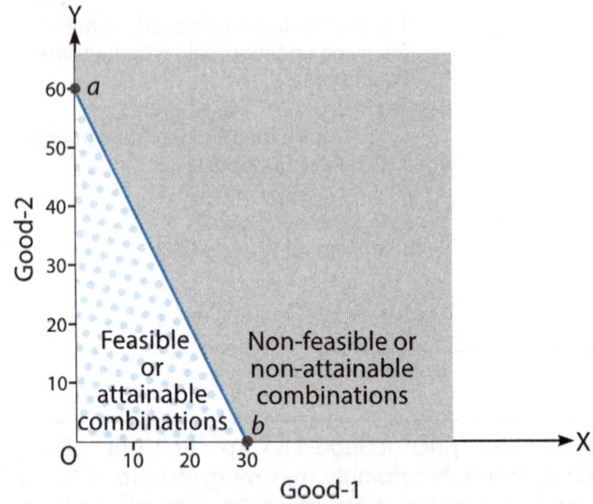

- Feasible or attainable combinations: along the line *ab* or inside it.
- Non-feasible or non-attainable combinations: outside the line *ab*.

Slope of Budget Line/Price Line

Slope of budget line/price line = $\frac{\Delta Y}{\Delta X}$, as in Fig. 11.

FIGURE 11 **Slope of Budget Line/Price Line**

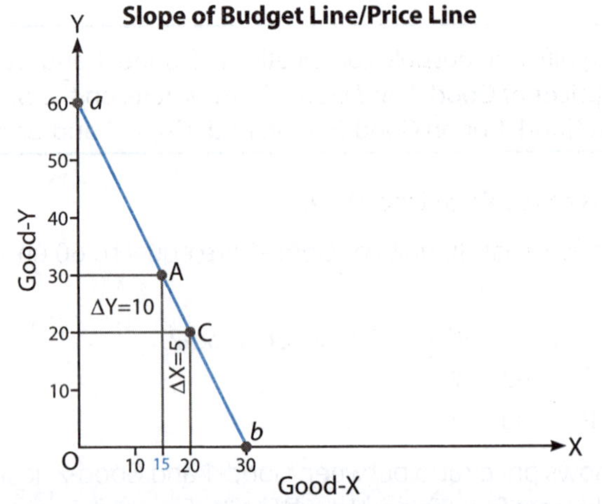

- Slope of price line = $\frac{\Delta Y}{\Delta X} = \frac{10}{5} = 2$.
- It is constant throughout the price line, simply because this is a straight line.
- Price line is drawn as a straight line, because P_X and P_Y are taken as given in the market.

The figure shows that $\Delta Y = 10$ when $\Delta X = 5$.

So that the slope of price line = $\frac{\Delta Y}{\Delta X} = \frac{10}{5} = 2$.

It shows that to obtain 1 more unit of Good-X, the consumer must sacrifice 2 units of Good-Y. Thus, the price of Good-X is expressed in terms of the sacrifice of Good-Y for obtaining every additional unit of Good-X. So that:

$$\frac{P_X}{P_Y} = \frac{\Delta Y}{\Delta X}$$

showing how much of Good-Y is to be sacrificed for obtaining one more unit of Good-X.

It must be noted that the slope of price line is constant, simply because price line is a straight line (we know, a straight line has a constant slope). Further, price line is drawn as a straight line, because prices of Good-X and Good-Y are taken as given in the market.

Budget Line Slopes Downward

Budget line slopes downward. Because, given consumers' income and prices of goods X and Y, the consumer can buy more of Good-X only when he buys less of Good-Y (Refer to Table 2 for details).

Budget Line can Shift

Budget line shifts forward (without changing its slope) when income of the consumer increases. Prices are assumed as constant.

Budget line shifts backward (without changing its slope) when income of the consumer decreases. Prices are assumed as constant.

Illustration

Existing Budget Set when Income (Y) = ₹ 60, P_1 = ₹ 2, P_2 = ₹ 1		**New Budget Set when Income (Y) = ₹120**	
Good-1	**Good-2**	**Good-1**	**Good-2**
0	60	0	120
10	40	20	80
20	20	40	40
30	0	60	0

Consequent upon increase in consumers' income, his budget line shifts to the right as shown in Fig. 12.

FIGURE 12

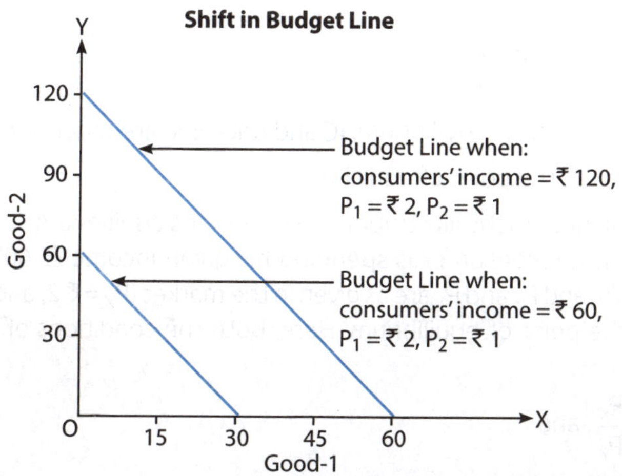

- Budget line shifts to the right, and the shift is parallel when: (i) P_X and P_Y are constant, and (ii) income of the consumer increases.
- Budget line shifts to the left, and the shift is parallel when: (i) P_X and P_Y are constant, and (ii) income of the consumer decreases.

Budget Line can Rotate

Budget line can rotate to the right or to the left.

It rotates to the right when P_X (and Good-X shown on the X-axis) falls. It rotates to the left when P_X (and Good-X shown on the X-axis) rises. Fig. 13 illustrates these situations:

FIGURE 13

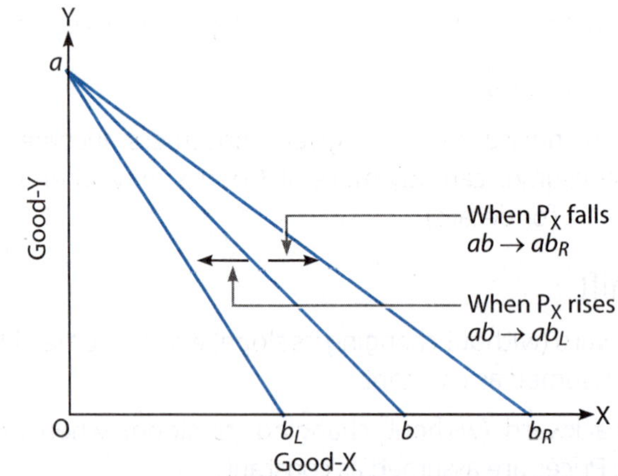

- *ab* rotates to the right (to become ab_R) when P_X falls. It shows that more of Good-X can now be purchased with the given income.
- *ab* rotates to the left (to become ab_L) when P_X rises. It shows that less of Good-X can now be purchased with the given income.

5. Consumer's Equilibrium using Indifference Curve Analysis

Consumer's equilibrium refers to optimum choice of the consumer. It is reached when he maximises his satisfaction. In terms of indifference curve analysis, the consumer reaches his optimum choice when two conditions are satisfied:

(i) $MRS = \frac{P_X}{P_Y}$

↑ Slope of IC ↑ Slope of Price Line

So that, in a state of equilibrium, IC and price line are tangent to each other.

(ii) IC is convex at the point of equilibrium.

Fig. 14 offers diagrammatic illustration of consumer's equilibrium. It is drawn on the assumption that the consumer is spending his given income (₹ 60) across Good-X and Good-Y only, and P_X and P_Y are as given in the market (P_X = ₹ 2, and P_Y = ₹ 1). In the diagram, E is the point of equilibrium. Here, both the conditions of equilibrium are satisfied:

(i) $MRS_{XY} = \frac{P_X}{P_Y}$, and

(ii) IC is convex to the origin.

In a state of equilibrium, the consumer is buying 15 units of Good-X and 30 units of Good-Y. He is maximising his satisfaction.

FIGURE 14

Consumer's Equilibrium: Diagrammatic Presentation

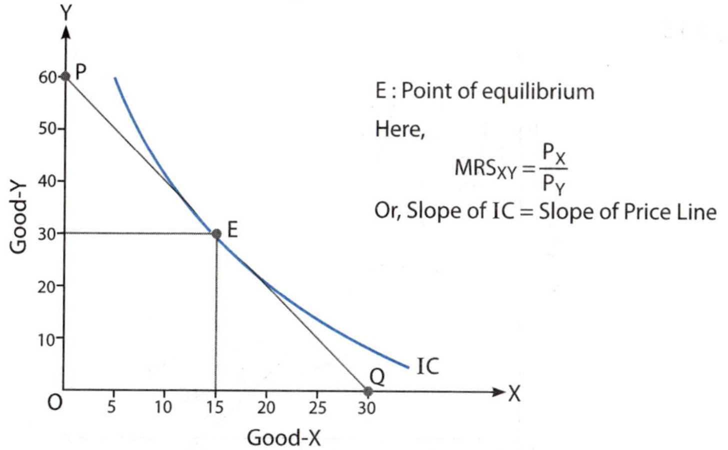

- E : Point of equilibrium. It is here only that $MRS_{XY} = \frac{P_X}{P_Y}$ or Slope of IC = Slope of price line, or IC and price line are tangent to each other.
- Given his income (₹ 60), he is buying 15 units of Good-X (at the price of ₹ 2 per unit) and 30 units of Good-Y (at the price of ₹ 1 per unit).

In Fig. 14, PQ is the budget line. It sets a budget constraint for the consumer. The consumer cannot go beyond this line given his income (₹ 60) and price of Good-X (₹ 2 per unit) and of Good-Y (₹ 1 per unit). The budget line also reflects how much of Good-Y is to be sacrificed for an additional unit of Good-X, given the prices of X and Y. IC is the indifference curve. It shows consumer's preferences for Good-X and Good-Y. It reflects how much the consumer is willing to sacrifice of Good-Y for an additional unit of Good-X.

The equilibrium is struck at point E where $MRS_{XY} = \frac{P_X}{P_Y}$. The rate at which the consumer is willing to substitute X for Y (given his tastes and preferences) coincides with the rate at which the market allows the consumer to substitute X for Y (given his income and prices of X and Y). At point E, the consumer is willing to sacrifice 2 units of Y for 1 unit of X (= MRS). This is exactly equal to the rate at which the market allows him to substitute X for Y $\left(\frac{P_X}{P_Y} = \frac{2}{1}\right)$. At the point of equilibrium, the consumer is buying 15 units of Good-X (at the price of ₹ 2 per unit) and 30 units of Good-Y (at the price of ₹ 1 per unit). He is spending his given income (₹ 60) on Good-X and Good-Y and maximising his satisfaction. This is the optimum allocation of his expenditure. Any departure from this would only lower the level of his satisfaction.

Rationale Behind Conditions of Equilibrium

Let us understand the rationale behind the conditions of equilibrium in detail.

Condition–1: $MRS = \frac{P_X}{P_Y}\left[\begin{array}{l}\text{Slope of IC} = \text{Slope of price line} \\ \text{Or, IC and price line are tangent to each other}\end{array}\right]$

The consumer will strike his equilibrium only when $MRS_{XY} = \frac{P_X}{P_Y}$. Because, at no other point (within the range of available/feasible combinations of Good-X and Good-Y) can he maximise his satisfaction.

Fig. 15 illustrates this fact.

FIGURE 15

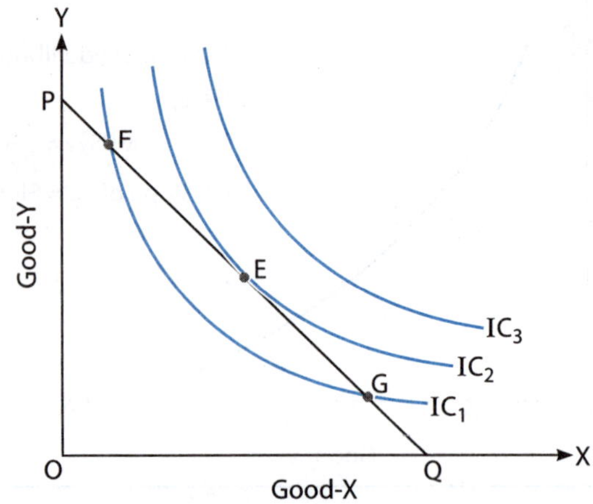

E is the point of equilibrium. Points like F and G (or any other to the left or right of E) falls on a lower indifference curve. Therefore, E is the only point of equilibrium where satisfaction is maximised.

PQ is the budget line. It shows the budget constraint. The consumer cannot go beyond this line. IC_1, IC_2 and IC_3 indicate indifference map of the consumer. The consumer will try to reach the highest possible IC, because higher IC reflects higher level of satisfaction.

Equilibrium on IC_3 is ruled out, because it is beyond the budget line (PQ).

Any point on the budget line to the left of E (like F) or to the right of E (like G) falls on a lower IC. Both F and G are on IC_1 which offers lower satisfaction than IC_2.

Hence, the consumer would prefer to stick to point E and E alone, given his income and prices of goods X and Y.

Condition– 2: IC is Convex at the point of Equilibrium

At the point of equilibrium, IC must be convex to the origin. Why? The reason as under:

Convexity of IC indicates that MRS is declining. Or, that the consumer is willing to sacrifice less and less amount of Good-Y for every successive unit of Good-X. This is in accordance with the law of diminishing marginal utility. If MRS is not declining then the law of diminishing marginal utility is not in operation. In which situation the consumer will continue to consume more and more of one commodity, getting higher marginal utility from its every successive unit. We cannot even imagine that the consumer can strike any stable equilibrium in such a situation.

Fig. 16 illustrates that equilibrium will not be stable in case IC is not convex but concave at the point of equilibrium.

FIGURE 16

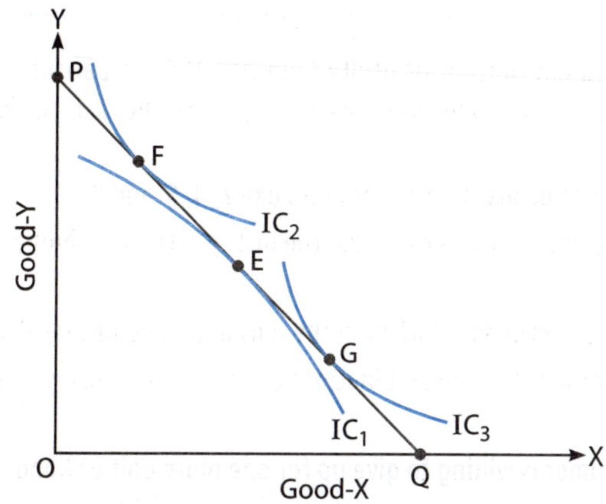

- E : Point of equilibrium where, $MRS_{XY} = \frac{P_X}{P_Y}$.

  But IC is concave and therefore, equilibrium is NOT stable.
- The consumer can move to IC_2, striking equilibrium at F.

  Or

  The consumer can move to IC_3, striking equilibrium at G.
- IC_2 and IC_3 are higher indifference curves than IC_1.

Let us assume that the consumer strikes his equilibrium at point E where $MRS_{XY} = \frac{P_X}{P_Y}$.

But IC is NOT convex but concave. This cannot be a point of stable equilibrium. Because (given his income and prices), the consumer can move to point F on IC_2 or point G on IC_3. Both points F and G fall on the budget line (within the range of affordable combinations). But F or G is offering higher level of satisfaction compared to E, as these are on higher indifference curves (IC_2 and IC_3) compared to IC_1.

Hence, the conclusion that only convexity of IC allows stable equilibrium, NOT the concavity.

Assumptions of IC Analysis of Consumer's Equilibrium

The IC analysis of consumer's equilibrium is based on four principal assumptions:

(i) The consumer is driven by monotonic preferences.

(ii) The consumer's scale of preference for the two goods does not change.

(iii) Prices of the two goods are given and remain constant.

(iv) Money income of the consumer is given and does not change.

HOTS

Q.1. How will the consumer move along his IC in a situation when $MRS_{XY} > \frac{P_X}{P_Y}$?

Ans. The consumer should move downward to the right along the IC. Convexity of the IC ensures that as the consumer moves downward to the right along his IC, MRS_{XY} tends to fall. Implying that the consumer should start consuming more of X in place of Y.

Q.2. How will a consumer adjust his consumption of goods X and Y in a situation when $MRS_{XY} < \frac{P_X}{P_Y}$?

Ans. The consumer should starts consuming more of Y in place of X. That is, he should move upward to the left along the IC. Convexity of the IC ensures that as the consumer moves upward to the left along his IC, MRS_{XY} tends to rise. He should stop at a point when $MRS_{XY} = \frac{P_X}{P_Y}$

POWER POINTS

- IC Analysis of Consumer's Equilibrium is based on ordinal concept of utility (allowing the comparison of utility), while utility analysis of demand is based on cardinal concept of utility (allowing measurement of utility in terms of units like 2, 4, 6, and 8).
- Cardinal Concept of utility refers to the measurement of utility in terms of units like 2, 4, 6, and 8.
- Ordinal Concept of utility refers to ranking of utility: comparing or expressing the utility in terms of higher, lower or equal level of satisfaction across different situations.
- Indifference Set refers to a set of different combinations of two goods which offer the consumer the same level of satisfaction.
- Indifference Curve is a locus of all such points which show different combinations offering the same level of satisfaction to the consumer.
- Slope of IC shows the amount of Good-Y which a consumer is willing to give up for one more unit of Good-X. It is known as MRS, and is expressed as $\frac{\Delta Y}{\Delta X}$. This is determined by the consumer, depending on his tastes and preferences.
- Indifference Map refers to a set of indifference curves placed together in a diagram. An IC which is to the right and above another IC corresponds to higher level of income and therefore, represents higher level of satisfaction.
- Budget Set refers to a set of attainable combinations of two goods, given market price of the goods and income of the consumer.
- Budget Line (or Price Line) is a line showing different combinations of two goods which a consumer can attain, given his income and market price of the goods.
- Slope of Budget Line/Price Line shows the rate at which market price allows the consumer to substitute Good-X for Good-Y. It is expressed as $\frac{P_X}{P_Y}$.
- The Consumer reaches his Optimum Choice when: (i) MRS = $\frac{P_X}{P_Y}$, and (ii) IC is convex to the origin.

EXERCISE

1. Very Short Questions (Remembering & Understanding) (1 mark each)

A. Multiple Choice Questions: Choose the Correct Answer

1. **In which analysis can utility be measured in definite numbers such as 1, 2, 3, 4, etc.?**

   (a) Cardinal utility analysis (b) Ordinal utility analysis

   (c) Both (a) and (b) (d) None of these

2. **Ordinal concept of utility expresses utility in terms of:**

   (a) units (b) level of satisfaction

   (c) constants (d) none of these

3. **Diagrammatic presentation of consumer's indifference set is called:**

   (a) indifference curve (b) utility curve

   (c) budget line (d) transformation curve

4. **Given the money income and the price, the line which shows all different combinations of two goods that a consumer can buy by spending all his income is called:**

   (a) production line (b) budget line

   (c) iso-cost line (d) none of these

5. **Attainable combinations of X and Y are drawn on the assumption that P_X and P_Y are:**

   (a) constant (b) variable

   (c) change in the same ratio (d) equal to each other

6. **According to IC analysis, a consumer attains equilibrium when:**

(a) $MRS_{XY} = \frac{P_X}{P_Y}$ (b) $MRS_{XY} > \frac{P_X}{P_Y}$

(c) $MRS_{XY} < \frac{P_X}{P_Y}$ (d) none of these

7. **An indifference curve is related to:**

(a) consumer's income (b) prices of goods X and Y

(c) total utility from goods X and Y (d) choice and preferences of the consumer

8. **Given the fact that MRS between goods X and Y is diminishing, IC is:**

(a) convex to the origin (b) concave to the origin

(c) straight line (d) none of these

9. **Marginal rate of substitution indicates:**

(a) slope of production possibility curve (b) slope of indifference curve

(c) slope of budget line (d) slope of income line

10. **Budget line indicates:**

(a) price ratio (b) income ratio

(c) cost ratio (d) none of these

11. **As we move down the indifference curve left to right, the slope of IC tends to:**

(a) unity (b) rise

(c) zero (d) decline

12. **A shift in the budget line, when prices are constant, is due to:**

(a) change in demand (b) change in income

(c) change in preferences (d) change in utility

13. **The slope of indifference curve is measured by:**

(a) marginal rate of transformation (b) marginal rate of substitution

(c) marginal rate of technical substitution (d) none of these

14. **Marginal rate of substitution of X for Y is calculated as:**

(a) $\frac{P_X}{P_Y}$ (b) $\frac{P_Y}{P_X}$

(c) $\frac{\Delta Y}{\Delta X}$ (d) $\frac{\Delta X}{\Delta Y}$

15. **Slope of budget line is indicated by:**

(a) $\frac{P_X}{P_Y}$ (b) $\frac{P_Y}{P_X}$

(c) $P_X = P_Y$ (d) all of these

16. **A set of ICs drawn in a graph is called:**

(a) indifference curve (b) indifference map

(c) budget line (d) budget set

17. **In an indifference map, higher IC indicates:**

(a) lower level of satisfaction (b) same level of satisfaction

(c) higher level of satisfaction (d) either same or higher level of satisfaction

18. **MRS is determined by:**

(a) satisfaction level of the consumer (b) income of the consumer

(c) tastes of the consumer (d) preferences of the consumer

19. At the point of equilibrium:

(a) MRS $> \frac{P_X}{P_Y}$ and IC is convex at the point of equilibrium

(b) MRS $< \frac{P_X}{P_Y}$ and IC is convex at the point of equilibrium

(c) MRS $= \frac{P_X}{P_Y}$

(d) MRS $= \frac{P_X}{P_Y}$ and IC is convex at the point of equilibrium

20. In a situation when MRS $> \frac{P_X}{P_Y}$, the consumer would react by:

(a) diminishing the consumption of commodity-X (b) increasing the consumption of commodity-Y

(c) increasing the consumption of commodity-X (d) none of these

Answers

1. (a) **2.** (b) **3.** (a) **4.** (b) **5.** (a) **6.** (a) **7.** (d) **8.** (a) **9.** (b) **10.** (a) **11.** (d) **12.** (b)
13. (b) **14.** (c) **15.** (a) **16.** (b) **17.** (c) **18.** (d) **19.** (d) **20.** (c)

B. Information & Concept-based Questions

1. What is meant by an indifference curve?

Ans. Indifference curve is a curve showing different combinations of a set of 2-Goods, each combination offering the same level of satisfaction to the consumer.

2. What is meant by indifference set?

Ans. Indifference set refers to those combinations of two goods which offer the consumer the same level of satisfaction.

3. Define monotonic preferences of the consumer.

Ans. Monotonic preferences means the consumer preferences are such that greater consumption of a commodity always offers him a higher level of satisfaction.

4. Define indifference map.

Ans. A set of indifference curves placed together in a diagram is known as indifference map.

5. What is consumer's equilibrium?

Ans. Consumer equilibrium refers to that situation in which he maximises his satisfaction by spending his given income on different goods and services, with a given set of prices.

6. Define marginal rate of substitution.

Ans. Marginal rate of substitution refers to the rate at which the consumer is willing to sacrifice Good-Y for a unit more of Good-X.

7. Define price line.

Ans. Price line is a line showing different combinations of two goods which a consumer can attain, given his income and market price of the goods.

8. What is meant by budget set?

Ans. Budget set refers to a set of attainable combinations of two goods, given market price of the goods and income of the consumer.

2. Reason-based Questions (Comprehension of the Subject-matter)

Read the following statements carefully. Write 'True' or 'False' with a reason.

1. Indifference curve is not convex to the origin in case of two normal goods.

Ans. False. Indifference curve is convex to the origin in case of two normal goods. This is because MRS tends to diminish. And, MRS must diminish in accordance with the law of diminishing marginal utility.

2. **Slope of indifference curve shows MRS.**

Ans. True. The slope of an indifference curve shows the rate at which the consumer is willing to substitute one commodity for the other. Or, it shows the MRS.

3. **If IC is convex to the origin, MRS should not be diminishing.**

Ans. False. If IC is convex to the origin, MRS should be diminishing. Because, the consumer is willing to sacrifice less and less amount of Good-Y for every additional unit of Good-X.

4. **A consumer strikes his equilibrium when: $MRS = \frac{P_X}{P_Y}$.**

Ans. True. In terms of indifference curve approach, a consumer strikes his equilibrium when:

Slope of IC = Slope of Price Line

Or

$$MRS = \frac{P_X}{P_Y}$$

It is here only that the consumer maximises his satisfaction (given P_X, P_Y and income of the consumer).

5. **All attainable combinations of Good-X and Good-Y are below the budget line of a consumer.**

Ans. False. All attainable combinations of Good-X and Good-Y are below as well as along the budget line.

6. **Feasible combinations of goods are those combinations which a consumer can always buy, no matter what his income is.**

Ans. False. Feasible combinations of goods are those combinations which a consumer can buy, given his income and the prices of Good-1 and Good-2.

7. **The rate at which the consumer can substitute Good-X for Good-Y tends to decline as we move downward along the price line.**

Ans. False. The rate at which the consumer can substitute Good-X for Good-Y remains constant throughout the price line. Because, P_X and P_Y are assumed to be constant.

8. **A situation when $MRS > \frac{P_X}{P_Y}$ is better than when $MRS = \frac{P_X}{P_Y}$.**

Ans. False. A consumer attains his equilibrium only when: $MRS = \frac{P_X}{P_Y}$ given the constraint of his budget, as well as the prices of Goods X and Y. It is a point of maximum satisfaction. No other situation offers as much satisfaction as this.

9. **In an indifference map, higher IC always points to higher level of satisfaction.**

Ans. True. Higher indifference curve shows higher level of satisfaction. Because, higher IC corresponds to higher level of income of the consumer.

10. **Increase in income of the consumer is the only cause that leads to a parallel shift of budget line to the right.**

Ans. False. Budget line shifts to the right (i) when income of consumer increases assuming price of two goods remains unchanged, and (ii) when there is proportionate fall in the prices of two goods, income of the consumer remaining unchanged.

11. **When $MRS_{XY} < \frac{P_X}{P_Y}$, in order to reach at equilibrium point, the consumption of X increases and of Y decreases.**

Ans. False. When $MRS_{XY} < \frac{P_X}{P_Y}$, the consumer consuming more of Y in place of X or the consumption of X decreases and of Y increases. It is only then that MRS_{XY} increases and becomes equal to price ratio.

3. HOTS & Applications

1. **If IC is not convex at the point of equilibrium, the consumer cannot reach the point of stable equilibrium. Comment.**

Ans. True. If IC is not convex at the point of equilibrium (or MRS_{XY} is not diminishing), the consumer cannot reach the point of stable equilibrium. In case IC is concave, it implies that marginal utility tends to rise as more of a commodity is consumed. Why should a consumer stop the consumption of that commodity, at all? In such a situation any equilibrium (when two goods are consumed) will never be a stable equilibrium.

2. **MRS (marginal rate of substitution) along an indifference curve tends to diminish. Comment.**

Ans. True. As we move along the indifference curve, marginal rate of substitution (MRS) tends to diminish. Because when we have less of a commodity, intensity of its desire increases. Accordingly, less and less of it is sacrificed for every additional unit of the other commodity.

3. **MRS tends to diminish because of the law of diminishing marginal utility. Comment.**

Ans. True. Diminishing MRS suggests that the consumer sacrifices less and less quantity of Good-Y for every additional unit of Good-X. Why does he do it? It is because the rising consumption of Good-X leads to a fall in its MU, while the falling consumption of Good-Y leads to a rise in its MU. This is in accordance with the law of diminishing marginal utility.

4. **It is because of monotonic preferences of the consumer that IC slopes downward. Comment.**

Ans. True. An IC slopes downward because of monotonic preferences of the consumer. According to this, more of one commodity implies less of the other, so that total satisfaction remains the same. An IC, therefore, must slope downward.

5. **MRS between goods X and Y is determined by the prices of these goods in the market. Is it true?**

Ans. No. MRS between goods X and Y is determined as the rate at which a consumer is willing to give up Good-Y for a unit more of Good-X. It depends on choice and preferences of the consumer.

6. **In a situation when P_X and P_Y are constant, and $MRS_{XY} > \frac{P_X}{P_Y}$, the consumer will get greater satisfaction than when $MRS_{XY} = \frac{P_X}{P_Y}$?**

Ans. False. In a situation when P_X and P_Y are constant, and $MRS_{XY} > \frac{P_X}{P_Y}$, the satisfaction level of the consumer will be less than when $MRS_{XY} = \frac{P_X}{P_Y}$. Provided, of course, that the consumer does not cross his budgetary constraint. In other words, along with constant P_X and P_Y, income of the consumer must also remain constant.

7. **On what factors, position of budget line depend?**

Ans. Position of the budget line depends on two factors namely, income of the consumer and prices of the two goods. If prices of two goods remain unchanged, then with an increase in income, budget line of the consumer shifts to the right and *vice versa*. Similarly, if income of the consumer remains unchanged, the budget line will shift to the right when there is a proportionate fall in the prices of both goods X and Y and *vice versa*. Thus, if the prices of both goods X and Y are reduced to half, the budget line will shift to the right showing twice the possible purchase of X and Y than before.

8. **Mr. X consumes two commodities X and Y whose prices are ₹ 4 and ₹ 2 per unit respectively. What will be the value of marginal rate of substitution if the consumer is in the state of equilibrium?**

Ans. Given, P_X = ₹ 4; P_Y = ₹ 2

We know, at the point of equilibrium:

$$\text{MRS (marginal rate of substitution)} = \frac{P_X}{P_Y}$$

According to the given question, $\frac{P_X}{P_Y}$ is equal to $\frac{4}{2} = 2$. Therefore, value of marginal rate of substitution is equal to 2 in the state of equilibrium.

9. **Explain the equation of budget line with the help of a hypothetical numerical example.**

Ans. The budget line shows all the different combinations of the two commodities that a consumer can purchase, given his money income and the price of two commodities.

The equation of a budget line is given by

$$M = P_X . Q_X + P_Y . Q_Y$$

Where, M = Money income of the consumer; P_X = Price of Good-X; P_Y = Price of Good-Y; Q_X = Quantity of Good-X; Q_Y = Quantity of Good-Y.

Supposing a consumer has an income of ₹40 to be spent on apples and oranges. Price of an orange is ₹5 and an apple is ₹10. With his given income and given prices of apples and oranges, the different combinations that a consumer can get of these two goods are shown in the given table.

Combination	Income (M)	Oranges	Apples
A	40	8	0
B	40	6	1
C	40	4	2
D	40	2	3
E	40	0	4

A consumer can purchase any of the above combinations in accordance with the budget line equation.

10. Marginal rate of substitution of X for Y is higher than the ratio of prices. Explain the reaction of the consumer in this situation.

Ans. A consumer strikes his equilibrium when $MRS_{XY} = \frac{P_X}{P_Y}$.

In a situation when $MRS_{XY} > \frac{P_X}{P_Y}$, equilibrium of the consumer is disturbed. On the assumption that $\frac{P_X}{P_Y}$ remains constant (and also, income of the consumer is constant) equilibrium can be struck only when MRS_{XY} starts falling and becomes equal to $\frac{P_X}{P_Y}$. This happens only when the consumer starts consuming more of X in place of Y. That is, he moves downward to the right along the IC. Convexity of the IC ensures that as the consumer moves downward to the right along his IC, MRS_{XY} tends to fall.

Briefly, when $MRS_{XY} > \frac{P_X}{P_Y}$, the consumer would react to this situation by substituting X for Y so that MRS_{XY} declines and becomes equal to price ratio.

11. How is the equation indicating budget line different from the equation indicating budget set?

Ans. The budget line equation shows different combinations of Good-1 and Good-2 that the consumer **can** buy spending his entire income across the two goods.

The budget set equation shows all **attainable** combinations of Good-1 and Good-2 when the consumer spends his entire income or a part of it on the purchase of two goods. It is indicated by the shaded area under the budget line in Fig. 17.

FIGURE 17

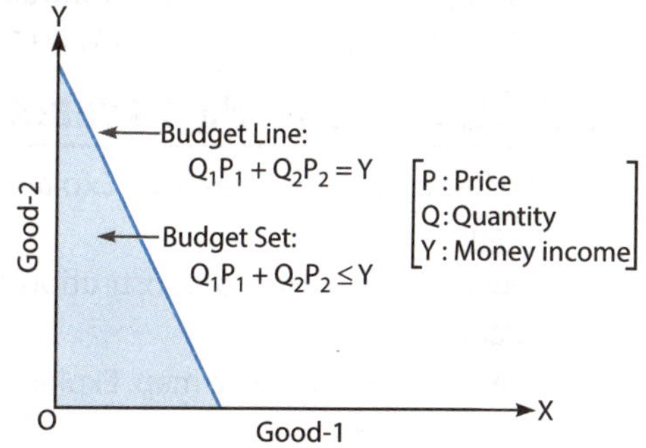

12. A consumer's budget is ₹ 40. He is buying Good-1 and Good-2. Price of Good-1 is ₹ 8 per unit, and of Good-2 is ₹ 10 per unit. Draw a budget line on the basis of these figures.

Ans. Let X_1 denotes quantity of Good-1 and X_2 denotes quantity of Good-2.

Given, consumer's budget, *i.e.*, consumer's income (Y) = ₹ 40

Price of Good-1 (P_1) = ₹ 8 per unit

Price of Good-2 (P_2) = ₹ 10 per unit

We know equation of the budget line is:

$$P_1X_1 + P_2X_2 = Y$$

$$8X_1 + 10X_2 = 40$$

When $X_2 = 0$

$\Rightarrow \quad 8X_1 = 40 \quad \Rightarrow \quad X_1 = 5$

Thus, when the entire income of the consumer is spent on Good-1, he can buy 5 units of Good-1.

When $X_1 = 0$

$\Rightarrow \quad 10X_2 = 40 \quad \Rightarrow \quad X_2 = 4$

FIGURE 18

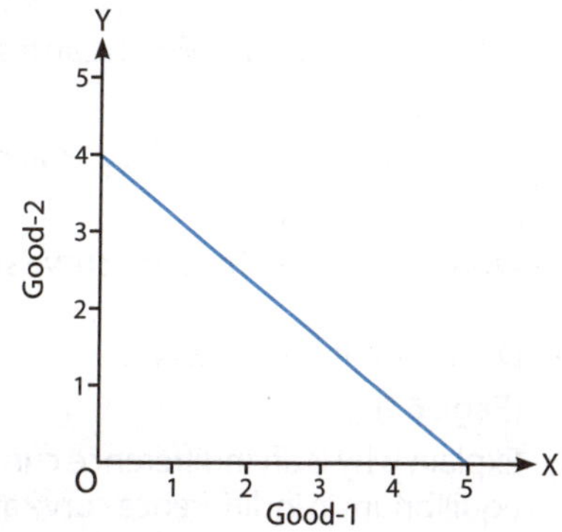

Thus, when the entire income of the consumer is spent on Good-2, he can buy 4 units of Good-2. Accordingly, the budget line touches 4 units on Y-axis and 5 units on X-axis, as in Fig. 18. Since price ratio remains constant, budget line is a straight line.

4. Evaluation (Value-based Questions)

1. **How would you as a consumer change your consumption basket when the rate at which you are willing to substitute Good-X for Good-Y is higher than the rate at which the market allows you to do it?**

Ans. It is a situation when:

$$MRS_{XY} > \frac{P_X}{P_Y}$$

Or, it is a situation when:

$$\text{Desired } \frac{\Delta Y}{\Delta X} \text{ (as indicated by MRS)} > \text{Feasible } \frac{\Delta Y}{\Delta X} \text{ (as allowed by the market prices of X and Y)}$$

The consumer should be prompted to buy more of X in place of Y. So that when the stock of Good-Y is reduced he is willing to sacrifice less and less of it for every additional unit of Good-X. He will continue this substitution (X for Y) till 'desired' $\frac{\Delta Y}{\Delta X}$ is reduced to become exactly equal to the 'feasible' $\frac{\Delta Y}{\Delta X}$, and he is in a state of equilibrium.

2. **Utility Analysis studies consumer's equilibrium on the assumption that utility can be expressed in terms of units like 2, 4, 6. Indifference Curve Analysis, on the other hand, assumes that utility cannot be expressed in terms of units; it can at best be compared. Does it mean that consumer's equilibrium (in terms of the consumption of goods X and Y) should be different, using different assumptions?**

Ans. 'No' is the answer.

Utility analysis and IC analysis are simply the two techniques of analysing consumer's behaviour. A rational consumer always maximises his satisfaction, spending his given income across goods X and Y. The maximum level of satisfaction should be the same level of satisfaction, and it must mean the same level of consumption of goods X and Y, no matter by which technique we study his behaviour.

5. CBSE Questions—Past 4 years (With Answers or Reference to the Text for Answers)

1. Define an indifference curve. Explain why an indifference curve is downward sloping from left to right. *[CBSE Delhi 2012]*
   [Page 62, 63]
2. Define marginal rate of substitution. Explain why is an indifference curve convex. *[CBSE Delhi 2012]*
   [Page 65, 66]
3. Define an indifference map. Explain why an indifference curve to the right shows higher utility level.
   Or *[CBSE Delhi 2012]*
   Define an indifference map. Why does an indifference curve to the right show more utility? Explain. *[CBSE (AI) 2012]*
   [Page 66, 67]
4. Explain the difference between cardinal utility and ordinal utility. Give example in each case. *[CBSE (AI) 2012]*
   [Page 61]
5. Define a budget line. When can it shift to the right? *[CBSE (AI) 2012]*
   [Page 69, 71]
6. What is budget set? Explain what can lead to change in budget set. *[CBSE (AI) 2012]*
   [Page 68]
7. What does an indifference curve show? *[CBSE (F) 2012]*
   Or
   Define indifference curve. *[CBSE (AI) 2014, 2015]*
   [Page 63]
8. Explain why is an indifference curve downward sloping from left to right. State the conditions of consumer's equilibrium in indifference curve analysis. *[CBSE (F) 2012]*
   [Page 63, 72]
9. Explain the concept of marginal rate of substitution with the help of a numerical example. *[CBSE (F) 2012]*
   Or
   Explain the concept of 'Marginal Rate of Substitution' with the help of a numerical example. Also explain its behaviour along an indifference curve. *[CBSE (AI) 2014]*
   [Page 64–66]

10. Explain the distinction between budget set and budget line. [CBSE (F) 2012]
[Page 68, 69]

11. What are monotonic preferences? Explain why an indifference curve to the right shows higher utility.
[Page 63, 67] [CBSE (F) 2012]

12. Explain consumer's equilibrium with the help of indifference curve analysis. [CBSE Delhi 2013]
[Page 72, 73]

13. Explain the meaning of diminishing marginal rate of substitution with the help of a numerical example.
Or [CBSE (AI) 2013]
Explain the meaning of diminishing marginal rate of substitution. [CBSE (F) 2013]
[Page 64-66]

14. What is a budget line? Why is it downward sloping? [CBSE (AI) 2013]
[Page 69, 71]

15. Explain the three properties of indifference curves. [CBSE Delhi 2014; (AI) 2013; (F) 2014]
[Page 68]

16. Explain the conditions of consumer's equilibrium under indifference curve approach.
Or [CBSE (AI) 2013; (F) 2013]
Explain the conditions of consumer's equilibrium with the help of the indifference curve analysis.
[Page 72–73] [CBSE Delhi 2014]

17. What is a budget line? [CBSE (F) 2013]
Or
Define budget line. [CBSE (AI) 2015]
[Page 69]

18. Define indifference map. [CBSE Delhi 2014; (AI) 2015]
[Page 66]

19. Define budget set. [CBSE Delhi 2014; 2015]
[Page 68]

20. What is meant by monotonic preferences? [CBSE (AI) 2014]
Or
What are monotonic preferences? [CBSE (F) 2015]
[Page 63]

21. Explain why is an indifference curve (a) downward sloping, and (b) convex. [CBSE (AI) 2014]
[Page 63, 65, 66]

22. State the conditions of consumer's equilibrium in the indifference curve analysis and explain the rationale behind these conditions. [CBSE (F) 2014]
[Page 72–75]

23. Give equation of budget line. [CBSE Delhi 2015]
[Page 69]

24. Give equation of budget set. [CBSE Delhi 2015]
[Page 68]

25. If marginal rate of substitution is constant throughout, the indifference curve will be: (choose the correct alternative) [CBSE Delhi 2015]

(a) parallel to the X-axis
(b) downward sloping concave
(c) downward sloping convex
(d) downward sloping straight line

[(d)]

26. A consumer consumes only two goods X and Y, both priced at ₹ 3 per unit. If the consumer chooses a combination of these two goods with marginal rate of substitution equal to 3, is the consumer in equilibrium? Give reasons. What will a rational consumer do in this situation? Explain. [CBSE Delhi 2015]
[Page 72, 75, 80]

27. If marginal rate of substitution is increasing throughout, the indifference curve will be: (choose the correct alternative) [CBSE (AI) 2015]

(a) downward sloping convex (b) downward sloping concave

(c) downward sloping straight line (d) upward sloping convex

[(b)]

28. A consumer consumes only two goods X and Y, both priced at ₹ 2 per unit. If the consumer chooses a combination of the two goods with marginal rate of substitution equal to 2, is the consumer in equilibrium? Why or why not? What will a rational consumer do in this situation? Explain. [CBSE (AI) 2015]

[Page 72, 75, 80]

29. What is 'ordinal' utility? [CBSE (F) 2015]

[Page 61]

30. A consumer consumes only two goods. If price of one of the goods falls, the indifference curve: (choose the correct alternative) [CBSE (F) 2015]

(a) shifts upwards (b) shifts downwards

(c) can shift both upwards or downwards (d) does not shift

[(d)

Note: When P_X falls (Good-X on the X-axis), price line rotates to the right. It indicates a rise in real income of the consumer, allowing him to shift to a higher IC.

Thus, change in price directly impacts the price line/budget line, NOT the IC.]

31. A consumer consumes only two goods, each priced at rupee one per unit. If the consumer chooses a combination of the two goods with marginal rate of substitution equal to 2, is the consumer in equilibrium? Give reasons. Explain what will a rational consumer do in this situation. [CBSE (F) 2015]

[Page 72, 75, 80]

6. NCERT Questions (With Hints to Answers)

1. What do you mean by budget set of a consumer?

[**Hint:** It refers to attainable combinations of a set of two goods, given prices of the goods and income of the consumer.]

2. What is budget line?

[**Hint:** It is a line showing different combinations of a set of two goods that the consumer can buy, given his income and price of the goods.]

3. Explain why the budget line is downward sloping.

[**Hint:** Budget line is a downward sloping line because given the prices of goods X and Y, and income of the consumer, more of Good-X (on X-axis) can be purchased only when less of Good-Y (on Y-axis) is purchased.]

4. A consumer wants to consume two goods. The prices of the goods are ₹ 4 and ₹ 5 respectively. The consumer's income is ₹ 20.

(i) Write down the equation of the budget line.

(ii) How much of Good-1 can the consumer consume if she spends her entire income on that good?

(iii) How much of Good-2 can she consume if she spends her entire income on that good?

(iv) What is the slope of the budget line?

[**Hint:** Let X_1 denote Good-1 and X_2 denote Good-2.

$P_1 = ₹4, P_2 = ₹5, Y = ₹20$

(i) $P_1X_1 + P_2X_2 = Y$

$4X_1 + 5X_2 = 20$

Thus, the equation of the budget line is $4X_1 + 5X_2 = 20$.

(ii) We know equation of the budget line is:

$P_1X_1 + P_2X_2 = Y$

If the consumer spends her entire income on Good-1, then

$$X_2 = 0$$

$\therefore$ $P_1X_1 = Y \Rightarrow 4X_1 = 20$

$\Rightarrow$ $X_1 = 5$

Thus, the consumer can buy 5 units of Good-1 if she spends her entire income on that good.

(iii) If the consumer spends her entire income on Good-2, then

$$X_1 = 0$$

$\therefore$ $P_2X_2 = Y \Rightarrow 5X_2 = 20$

$\Rightarrow$ $X_2 = 4$

Thus, the consumer can buy 4 units of Good-2 if she spends her entire income on that good.

(iv) Slope of budget line $= \frac{P_X}{P_Y} = \frac{4}{5}$.]

5. How does the budget line change if the consumer's income increases to ₹ 40 but the prices remain unchanged [as in Q. 4]?

[**Hint:** If the consumer's income increases to ₹ 40, the new budget line would be $4X_1 + 5X_2 = 40$.]

6. How does the budget line change if the price of Good-2 decreases by a rupee but the price of Good-1 and the consumer's income remains unchanged [as in Q. 4]?

[**Hint:** If the price of Good-2 decreases by a rupee, *i.e.*, P_2 = ₹ 4, other things remaining constant, the new budget line would become $4X_1 + 4X_2 = 20$.]

7. What happens to the budget set if both the prices as well as the income double [as in Q. 4]?

[**Hint:** If both the prices as well as the income doubles, the budget set would remain the same as before, since the attainable combinations would not change for the consumer.]

8. Suppose a consumer can afford to buy 6 units of Good-1 and 8 units of Good-2, if she spends her entire income. The prices of the two goods are ₹ 6 and ₹ 8 respectively. How much is the consumer's income?

[**Hint:** Given, quantity of Good-1 = 6 units

Quantity of Good-2 = 8 units

Price of Good-1 = ₹ 6

Price of Good-2 = ₹ 8

We know that,

$$P_1X_1 + P_2X_2 = Y \Rightarrow 6 \times 6 + 8 \times 8 = Y$$

$$36 + 64 = Y \Rightarrow 100 = Y$$

Thus, consumer's income is ₹ 100.]

9. What do you mean by 'monotonic preferences'?

[**Hint:** It means that a rational consumer always prefers more of a commodity as it offers him a higher level of satisfaction.]

10. If a consumer has monotonic preferences, can she be indifferent between the bundles (10, 8) and (8, 6)?

[**Hint:** No. If the consumer's preferences are monotonic, she cannot be indifferent between the combinations (10, 8) and (8, 6). Because, the first combination (10, 8) allows more of both the goods as compared to the second combination (8, 6). Implying that first combination offers higher level of satisfaction, and the consumer must prefer it to the other.]

11. Suppose a consumer's preferences are monotonic. What can you say about her preference ranking over the bundles (10, 10), (10, 9) and (9, 9)?

[**Hint:** If the consumer's preferences are monotonic, his most preferred bundle would be (10, 10). His second preferred bundle would be (10, 9) and his third preferred bundle would be (9, 9).]

12. Suppose your friend is indifferent to the bundles (5, 6) and (6, 6). Are the preferences of your friend monotonic?

[**Hint:** No. These preferences are not monotonic. If a consumer has monotonic preferences, he would prefer the bundle (6, 6) to the bundle (5, 6) because the bundle (6, 6) has more of Good-1 as compared to the bundle (5, 6).]

7. Miscellaneous Questions and Reference to the Text for Answers

A. Questions of 3 & 4 marks each

1. Distinguish between cardinal and ordinal measurement of utility.
   [Page 61]
2. State briefly the concept of indifference curve.
   [Page 62, 63]
3. State the properties of indifference curves.
   [Page 68]
4. Explain briefly the concept of consumer budget.
   [Page 68, 69]
5. Why should consumer's equilibrium point be located on the budget line?
   [Page 72, 73]
6. Distinguish between attainable (or feasible) and non-attainable (or non-feasible) combinations of a set of two goods. Draw a suitable diagram.
   [Page 69, 70]

B. Questions of 6 marks each

1. What do you understand by consumer's equilibrium? Show consumer's equilibrium with the help of indifference curve analysis.
   [Page 72, 73]
2. Show diagrammatically consumer's equilibrium using indifference curve analysis. Also, analysis the conditions of consumer's equilibrium.
   [Page 72–75]
3. Explain the reaction of the consumer when (i) price ratio is higher than the marginal rate of substitution, and (ii) price ratio is lower than the marginal rate of substitution.
   [Page 75]

DOs and DON'Ts

1. Never believe that different IC_S in an Indifference Map should be parallel to each other. They should simply be not touching each other, or cutting each other. They need not be parallel to each other. IC_S are parallel to each other only when MRS tends to change at the same rate for all the IC_S corresponding to different levels of income.
2. Remember that IC Analysis and Utility Analysis yield the same results in terms of equilibrium of the consumer. Never expect them to yield different results. Check the following equations for clarification:
   $\frac{MU_X}{P_X} = \frac{MU_Y}{P_Y}$ indicates consumer's equilibrium, according to utility analysis. This can be written as:
   $$\frac{MU_X}{MU_Y} = \frac{P_X}{P_Y}$$
   We know, $MU_X = \frac{\Delta TU}{\Delta X}$, and $MU_Y = \frac{\Delta TU}{\Delta Y}$. So that, in equilibrium:
   $$\frac{\frac{\Delta TU}{\Delta X}}{\frac{\Delta TU}{\Delta Y}} = \frac{P_X}{P_Y} \text{ or } \frac{\Delta TU}{\Delta X} \times \frac{\Delta Y}{\Delta TU} = \frac{P_X}{P_Y} \text{ or } \frac{\Delta Y}{\Delta X} = \frac{P_X}{P_Y} \text{ or MRS} = \frac{P_X}{P_Y}$$ (equilibrium according to IC analysis).
3. Remember that a change in price of the commodity directly impacts the price line, not the IC. However, a fall in price allows the consumer to shift to a higher IC because real income of the consumer tends to rise. Likewise, a rise in price forces the consumer to shift to a lower IC, because real income of the consumer tends to fall (Real income refers to the amount of goods the consumer can buy with his given money income.)

Theory of Demand

CHAPTER 4

TODO

- Concept of Demand—
  Difference between Demand and Quantity Demanded
- Demand Schedule—
  Individual Demand Schedule and Market Demand Schedule
- Demand Curve and its Slope
- Demand Function, showing relationship between Demand and its various Determinants
- Law of Demand—How Quantity Demanded of a Commodity responds to Changes in its own Price
- Movements along a Demand Curve and Shifts in Demand Curve
- Cross Price Effects, showing how Prices of Related Goods affect Demand for a Commodity
- Relationship between Income and Demand
- Impact of Tastes and Preferences on Demand for a Commodity

1. Concept of Demand

Ordinarily, the terms desire and demand are used inter-changeably. But in Economics, demand has a distinct meaning. Supposing, you desire to have a LED TV, but you do not have enough money to buy it. Then, this desire will remain just a wishful thinking; it will not be called demand. And, if in spite of having enough money, you are not willing to spend it on LED TV, demand does not emerge. The desire becomes demand only when you are ready to spend money to buy LED TV. Thus, demand for a commodity is the desire to buy a commodity backed with sufficient purchasing power and the willingness to spend.

Demand and Quantity Demanded

Demand for a commodity is always expressed with reference to price. Ask anybody how much of Good-X he will buy. 'It depends upon price of Good-X', is likely to be the obvious answer. At higher price quantity demanded will be low, and at lower price quantity demanded will be high. Here, comes the distinction between demand and quantity demanded. Demand refers to different possible quantities to be purchased at different possible prices of a commodity. On the other hand, quantity demanded refers to a specific quantity to be purchased against a specific price of the commodity.

Illustration

Demand for commodity-X refers to (say) 10 units of X if P_X (price of X) = ₹ 5 per unit, 8 units of X if P_X = ₹ 6 per unit, 6 units of X if P_X = ₹ 7 per unit, and so on.

Quantity demanded of commodity-X refers to (say) 8 units of X if P_X happens to be ₹ 6 per unit.

Demand refers to different possible quantities of a commodity that the consumer is ready to buy at different possible prices of that commodity.

Quantity demanded refers to a specific quantity to be purchased against a specific price of the commodity.

2. Demand Schedule

Demand schedule is a table showing the relation between different quantities of a commodity to be purchased at different prices of that commodity. According to **Samuelson,** *"The table relating to price and quantity demanded is called the demand schedule."* Concept of demand schedule includes:

(i) Individual Demand Schedule, and

(ii) Market Demand Schedule.

(i) Individual Demand Schedule

Individual demand schedule refers to demand schedule of an individual buyer (of a commodity) in the market. It shows quantities of a commodity which an individual buyer will buy at different possible prices of that commodity, at a point of time. Table 1 is an individual demand schedule. It shows different quantities of Good-X to be bought by a consumer at different prices of Good-X, at a given time.

Table 1. Individual Demand Schedule

P_X (Price of Good-X) (₹)	Q_X (Quantity Demanded of Good-X) (Units)	Inverse relationship between P_X and Q_X:
1	4	$P_X \uparrow \longrightarrow Q_X \downarrow$
2	3	**Or**
3	2	$P_X \downarrow \longrightarrow Q_X \uparrow$
4	1	

Table 1 shows that as the price of Good-X increases, quantity demanded tends to decrease. When price is ₹ 1 per unit, the consumer demands 4 units; when price rises to ₹ 4 per unit, the quantity demanded decreases to 1 unit. Thus, there is an inverse relationship between own price of the commodity and its quantity demanded.

(ii) Market Demand Schedule

In every market, there are several consumers of a commodity. Market demand schedule represents demand for a commodity by all the consumers in the market. It shows different quantities of a commodity which the consumers intend to buy at different possible prices of that commodity, at a point of time. On the assumption that there are only 2 consumers/buyers in the market, market demand schedule for (say) Good-X may be drawn as in Table 2.

Table 2. Market Demand Schedule

P_X (Price of Good-X) (₹)	Q_X (Consumer A) (Units) (1)	Q_X (Consumer B) (Units) (2)	Q_X (Consumer A + Consumer B = Market Demand) (Units) (3) = (1+2)
1	4	5	4 + 5 = 9
2	3	4	3 + 4 = 7
3	2	3	2 + 3 = 5
4	1	2	1 + 2 = 3

(**Assumption:** There are only 2 consumers/buyers in the market.)

Table 2 shows that when price of Good-X rises, its market demand falls. For example, when price is ₹ 1 per unit, A's demand = 4 units and B's demand = 5 units. Thus, the total market demand at ₹ 1 is 9 units. But when price rises to ₹ 2 per unit, then market demand falls to 7 units. Thus, the inverse relationship between own price of the commodity and its quantity demanded is established in case of market demand as well.

Individual Demand Schedule and Market Demand Schedule

Individual demand or individual demand schedule is a table showing different quantities of **a commodity** that **one particular buyer** in the market is ready to buy at different possible prices of the commodity at a point of time.

Market demand or market demand schedule is a table showing different quantities of **a commodity** that **all the buyers** in the market are ready to buy at different possible prices of the commodity at a point of time.

The inverse relationship between own price of the commodity and its quantity demanded holds good both in case of individual demand schedule and market demand schedule.

3. Demand Curve and its Slope

Demand curve is simply a graphic representation of demand schedule showing how quantity demanded of a commodity is related to its own price. Like demand schedule, concept of demand curve includes:

(i) Individual Demand Curve, and

(ii) Market Demand Curve.

(i) Individual Demand Curve

Individual demand curve is a curve showing different quantities of a commodity that one particular buyer is ready to buy at different possible prices of the commodity at a point of time. Fig. 1 shows individual demand curve. In this diagram, quantity of the commodity is shown on X-axis and price on Y-axis. DD is the demand curve. It is a graphic presentation of individual demand schedule, as in Table 1.

FIGURE 1 **Individual Demand Curve**

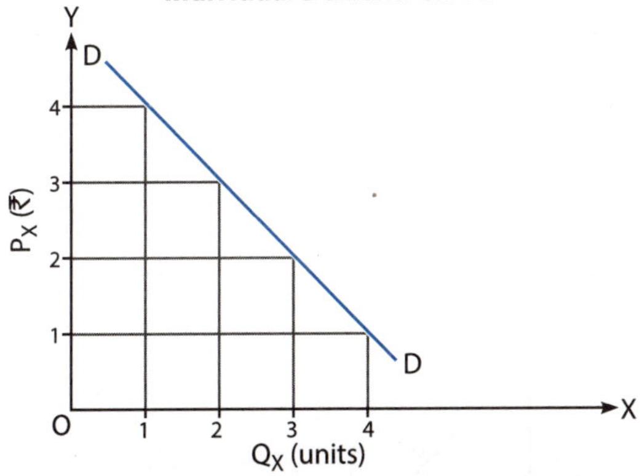

Demand curve slopes downward. It shows inverse relation between price and quantity demanded. Thus, 4 units of the commodity are demanded when price is ₹ 1 per unit while only 1 unit is demanded when the price is ₹ 4 per unit.

Demand curve slopes downward from left to right indicating inverse relationship between own price of the commodity and its quantity demanded. Higher price leads to a fall in quantity demanded; lower price leads to a rise in quantity demanded of a commodity.

(ii) Market Demand Curve

Market demand curve is the horizontal summation of the individual demand curves. It shows various quantities of a commodity that all the buyers in the market are ready to buy at different possible prices of the commodity at a point of time. Fig. 2 shows market demand curve. It is a graphic presentation of market demand schedule, as in Table 2.

FIGURE 2

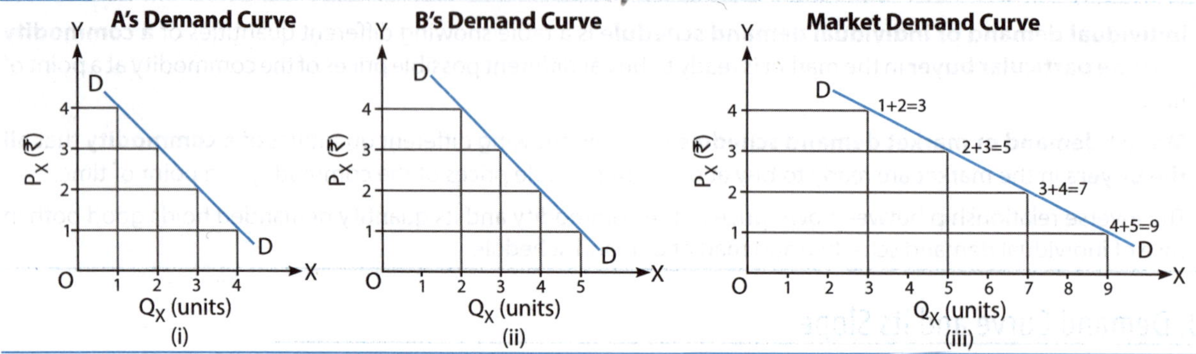

A and B are two buyers in the market. Fig. 2(i) is A's demand curve. Fig. 2(ii) is B's demand curve. Fig. 2(iii) is the market demand curve. When price is ₹ 1 per unit, A's demand = 4 units and B's demand = 5 units. Accordingly, market demand is 4 + 5 = 9 units when the price is ₹ 1 per unit. Likewise, when price is ₹ 4 per unit, market demand is 1 + 2 = 3 units. Market demand curve also slopes downward showing inverse relationship between own price of the commodity and its quantity demanded.

Note

Though demand and quantity demanded are two different concepts, for all practical purposes the difference between the two is ignored. It is almost-customary to write that there is an inverse relationship between price and demand. However, when demand for a commodity is related to its own price, it should always be understood as 'quantity demanded'.]

Slope of Demand Curve

Demand curve normally slopes downward, indicating negative (or inverse) relationship between price of a commodity and its quantity demanded.

Slope of demand curve is estimated as $(-)\frac{\Delta P}{\Delta Q}$. It shows the ratio between change in price corresponding to a unit change in quantity demanded of a commodity. Negative sign indicates the inverse relationship between price and quantity demanded of a commodity.

In Fig. 3, a straight line demand curve (*dd'*) is drawn, indicating a linear demand function.

FIGURE 3

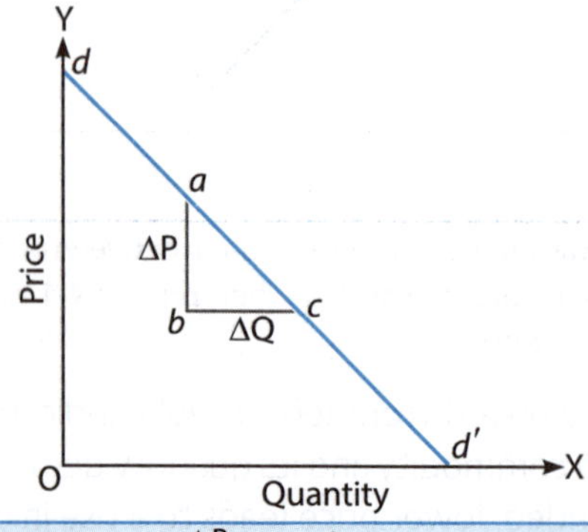

Slope of Demand Curve $= (-)\frac{\Delta P}{\Delta Q} = (-)\frac{ab}{bc}$

It is constant, because demand curve is a straight line.

Slope of a demand curve = $(-)\frac{\Delta P}{\Delta Q} = (-)\frac{ab}{bc}$. It is constant at all points on the demand line *dd'*. Because, *dd'* is a linear straight line and slope of a straight line is constant.

4. Demand Function or Determinants of Demand

Demand function shows the relationship between demand for a commodity and its various determinants. It shows how demand for a commodity is related to, say, own price of the commodity or income of the consumer or other determinants.

Corresponding to two aspects of demand, *viz.*, individual demand and market demand, we have two types of demand function:

(i) Individual Demand Function, and

(ii) Market Demand Function.

Individual Demand Function

Individual demand function shows how demand for a commodity, by an individual consumer in the market, is related to its various determinants. It is expressed as under:

$$D_X = f(P_X, P_r, Y, T, E)$$

(Here, D_X = Quantity demanded of commodity-X; P_X = Own price of commodity-X; P_r = Price of related goods; Y = Consumer's income; T = Consumer's tastes and preferences; E = Consumer's expectations.)

(1) Own Price of Commodity: Other things being equal, with a rise in own price of the commodity, its demand contracts, and with a fall in price, its demand extends. This inverse relationship between own price of the commodity and its demand is called Law of Demand.

(2) Price of Related Goods: Demand for a commodity is also influenced by change in price of related goods. These are of two types:

(i) Substitute Goods: These are the goods which can be substituted for each other, such as tea and coffee, or ball-pen and ink-pen. In case of such goods, increase in the price of one causes increase in demand for the other and decrease in the price of one causes decrease in the demand for the other. Increase in the price of coffee, for example, will increase the demand for tea–the consumers will shift from the consumption of coffee to the consumption of tea.

(ii) Complementary Goods: Complementary goods are those goods which complete the demand for each other, and are, therefore, demanded together. Pen and ink, or bread and butter may be cited as examples. In case of complementary goods, a fall in the price of one causes increase in the demand of the other and a rise in the price of one causes decrease in the demand for the other. For example, when the price of fountain pen rises, its demand will fall; as a result demand for ink will also fall. Conversely, if the price of fountain pen falls, its demand will rise; also will rise the demand for ink.

(3) Income of the Consumer: Change in the income of the consumer also influences his demand for different goods. The demand for normal goods tends to increase with increase in income, and *vice versa.* On the other hand, the demand for inferior goods like coarse grain tends to decrease with increase in income, and *vice versa.*

How do we distinguish between Related Goods and Unrelated Goods?

Goods are said to be related when demand for one changes in response to change in price of the other. For example, increase in the price of coffee is expected to cause increase in demand for tea. So, tea and coffee are related goods.

Goods are unrelated when demand for one is independent of any change in price of the other. Demand for shoes, for example, is not affected by change in price of sugar. Shoes and sugar are thus unrelated goods.

Briefly, while related goods show **cross-price effect** (change in the price of one causing a change in demand for the other) unrelated goods do not.

Normal Goods and Inferior Goods

Normal goods are those in case of which there is a positive relationship between income and quantity demanded. Other things remaining constant, quantity demanded increases in response to increase in consumer's income and *vice versa*.

Inferior goods are those in case of which there is negative (or inverse) relationship between income and quantity demanded. Other things remaining constant, quantity demanded decreases in response to increase in consumer's income and *vice versa*.

Briefly, in case of normal goods income effect is positive, while in case of inferior goods income effect is negative.

(4) Tastes and Preferences: The demand for goods and services also depends on individual's tastes and preferences. Tastes and preferences of the consumers are influenced by advertisement, change in fashion, climate, new inventions, etc. Other things being equal, demand for those goods increases for which consumers develop strong tastes and preferences. Contrary to it, if taste or preference for a product is fading (decreasing), its demand will decrease.

(5) Expectations: If the consumer expects a significant change in the availability of the concerned commodity in the near future, he may decide to change his present demand for the commodity. Particularly, if the consumer fears acute shortage of the commodity in the near future, he may raise his present demand for the commodity at its existing price.

Market Demand Function

Market demand function shows how market demand for a commodity (or aggregate demand for a commodity in the market) is related to its various determinants. Or, it shows the relationship between market demand for a commodity and its various determinants. It is expressed as under:

$$\text{Mkt. } D_X = f(P_X, P_r, Y, T, E, N, Y_d)$$

Here, Mkt. D_X = Market demand for commodity-X

P_X = Own price of commodity-X

P_r = Price of related goods

Y = Income of the consumers

T = Tastes and preferences of consumers

E = Expectations of consumers

N = Population size/Number of buyers

Y_d = Distribution of income.

P_X, P_r, Y, T, E have already been discussed in case of individual demand function. We discuss the remaining factors (N and Y_d) as under:

(1) Population Size: Demand increases with increase in the number of buyers for a commodity. **Example:** Owing to a substantial increase in the number of buyers, the demand for cars has substantially risen in India.

(2) Distribution of Income: Market demand is also influenced by the distribution of income in the society. If redistribution of income increases inequality (rich becoming richer, and poor becoming poorer), the demand for luxury goods (like big cars) is expected to rise. Also, a fall in the income of the poor people may compel them to shift from normal to inferior goods. Implying a rise in the demand for inferior goods, like coarse grain.

5. Law of Demand

The law of demand states that, other things being equal, quantity demanded increases with a decrease in own price of the commodity, and *vice versa*. In other words, there is an inverse relationship between quantity demanded of a commodity and its own price, other things remaining constant. The term 'other things being equal' implies that all other determinants of demand, other than own price of the commodity, remain constant.

Why are Goods Demanded?

We demand goods and services because these have the capacity to satisfy our wants. The capacity to satisfy human wants is called 'Utility'. Thus, we can state that goods are demanded because these possess utility.

The Law of Demand states that other things remaining constant, there is an inverse relationship between quantity demanded and own price of the commodity.

Explanation

Law of demand may be explained with the help of demand schedule:

Table 3. Demand Schedule

P_X (₹)	Q_X (Units)
10	100
9	150
8	200

The schedule shows that quantity demanded increases from 100 to 150 units when own price of the commodity reduces from ₹ 10 to ₹ 9 per unit. Likewise, quantity demanded increases from 150 to 200 units when own price of the commodity reduces from ₹ 9 to ₹ 8 per unit. It may be further illustrated with the help of a demand curve, as in Fig 4.

FIGURE 4

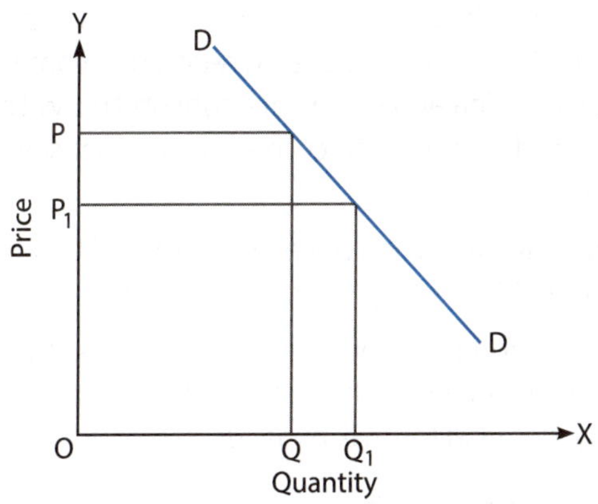

DD slopes downward. It shows inverse relationship between price and quantity demanded. This is universally true in case of normal goods. It is, therefore, called the law of demand.

In Fig. 4, demand curve DD shows that demand for commodity-X extends from OQ to OQ_1 when its price falls from OP to OP_1. In fact, downward slope of demand curve itself is an expression of the law of demand.

Assumptions of the Law of Demand

Law of demand holds good when "other things remain the same". It means factors influencing demand other than own price of the commodity are assumed to be constant. Thus,

(i) Tastes and preferences of the consumers are assumed to remain constant.

(ii) There is no change in income of the buyers.

(iii) Prices of the related goods do not change.

(iv) Consumers do not expect any significant change in the availability of the commodity in the near future.

Important

It is important to note that the assumptions of the law of demand refer to all other determinants of demand, other than own price of the commodity. Law of demand studies the relationship between demand for a commodity and own price of the commodity on the assumption that all other determinants of demand remain constant.

Why More of a Good is Purchased When its Price Fall?
Or
Why does Demand Curve Slope Downward?

Downward slope of demand curve indicates that more is purchased in response to fall in price. Thus, there is inverse relationship between own price of a commodity and its quantity demanded. This may be explained in terms of the following factors:

(1) Law of Diminishing Marginal Utility: According to this law, as consumption of a commodity increases, marginal utility of each successive unit goes on diminishing to a consumer. Accordingly, for every additional unit to be purchased, the consumer is willing to pay less and less price.

(2) Income Effect: *Income effect refers to change in quantity demanded when real income of the buyer changes owing to change in price of the commodity.* With a fall in price, real income increases. Accordingly, demand for the commodity expands.

(3) Substitution Effect: *Substitution effect refers to substitution of one commodity for the other when it becomes relatively cheaper.* Thus, when own price of commodity-X falls, it becomes cheaper in relation to commodity-Y. Accordingly, X is substituted for Y. Tea and coffee are substitutes. With a fall in the price of tea, it is substituted in place of coffee. It is expansion of demand due to *substitution effect.*

(4) Size of Consumer Group: When price of a commodity falls, many more buyers can afford to buy it. Accordingly, demand expands.

(5) Different Uses: A good may have several uses. Milk, for example, is used for making curd, cheese and butter. If price of milk reduces it will be put to different uses. Accordingly, demand for milk expands.

Exceptions should not be confused with Assumptions

It is important not to confuse exceptions with assumptions of the law of demand. Exceptions refer only to those rare situations when law of demand fails even when assumptions of the law are maintained. Do not convert assumptions into exceptions.

Exceptions to the Law of Demand

Law of demand has some exceptions as well. There are some commodities whose demand expands when their price rises and contracts when their price falls. In such situations, the demand curve slopes upward from left to right. Following are some notable exceptions to the law of demand:

(1) Articles of Distinction: According to **Prof. Veblen**, there are certain goods which command social distinction. Veblen calls them as 'articles of social distinction'. These articles are demanded only because their prices are very high. If their prices fall, they will no longer be considered as articles of distinction and their demand will shrink. Thus, these goods defy the law of demand. Precious diamonds and vintage cars may be cited as examples.

(2) Giffen Goods: Giffen goods are highly inferior goods, showing a very high negative income effect. As a result, when price of such commodities falls, their demand also falls, even when they happen to be relatively cheaper than other goods. This is popularly known as 'Giffen Paradox'.

(3) When Consumers Judge Quality of a Commodity by its Price: Law of demand is violated when consumers judge the quality of a commodity by its price. The emerging trend to buy 'organic' farm products explains this phenomenon. Perhaps it is owing to a huge price difference between 'organic' and non-organic products in the market, that richer sections of the society consider organic products as of very high quality. Accordingly, quantity demanded of these products has tended to rise even when their prices are extremely high.

Demand Curve Slopes Upward when Law of Demand Fails

When law of demand fails, the demand curve does not slope downward. Instead, it slopes upward, as in Fig. 5.

When price increases from OP_1 to OP_2, demand extends from OQ_1 to OQ_2. Conversely, when price decreases from OP_2 to OP_1, demand shrinks from OQ_2 to OQ_1. As already stated, positive relationship between demand and price of the commodity is established in case of Giffen goods or when goods are demanded simply because of their high price, or when consumers judge the quality of a commodity by its price.

FIGURE 5

When Law of Demand Fails

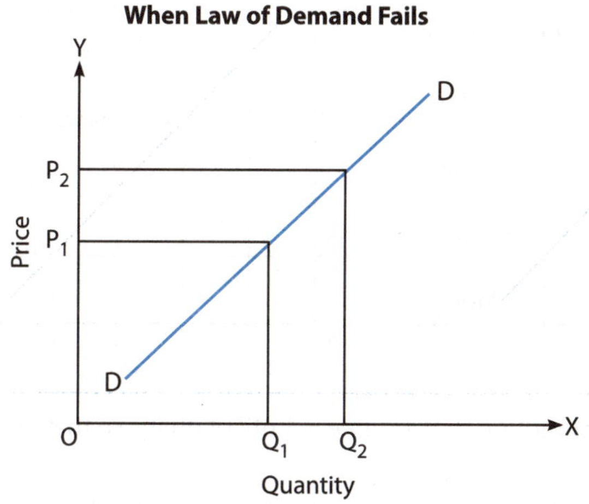

When P_X rises from OP_1 to OP_2, quantity demanded increases from OQ_1 to OQ_2 : A case of positive relationship between quantity demanded and own price of the commodity.

Utility Analysis and Law of Demand

(i) Derivation of Law of Demand from the Consumer's Equilibrium Equation—One Commodity Case

The consumer strikes his equilibrium when:

$$\frac{MU_X}{P_X} = MU_M$$

$\frac{MU_X}{P_X}$ ↑ rupee worth of satisfaction that the consumer actually receives

MU_M ↑ rupee worth of satisfaction that the consumer expects to receive (assumed to be constant)

Suppose P_X falls, as a result,

$$\frac{MU_X}{P_X} > MU_M$$

This induces the consumer to buy more of commodity-X. Higher consumption of commodity-X will lead to a fall in MU_X (according to the law of diminishing marginal utility). Increase in purchase of commodity-X would continue till the equilibrium is restored. Thus, we find that a fall in P_X leads to a rise in quantity demanded, which is what the law of demand states.

(ii) Derivation of Law of Demand from the Consumer's Equilibrium Equation—Two Commodity Case

The consumer strikes his equilibrium when:

$$\frac{MU_X}{P_X} = \frac{MU_Y}{P_Y} = MU_M$$

In case P_X falls,

$$\frac{MU_X}{P_X} > \frac{MU_Y}{P_Y}$$

This implies that 'a rupee worth of satisfaction' in case of commodity-X is greater than the rupee worth of satisfaction in case of commodity-Y. Accordingly, the consumer should be prompted to spend more on X and less on Y (his money income remaining constant). Thus, quantity demanded of commodity-X would increase in response to a fall in the price of X. This is what the law of demand states.

(iii) Derivation of Law of Demand from the Law of Diminishing Marginal Utility

Derivation of the law of demand from the law of diminishing marginal utility is explained with reference to Fig. 6 (A, B).

FIGURE 6 **Law of Diminishing Marginal Utility and Law of Demand**

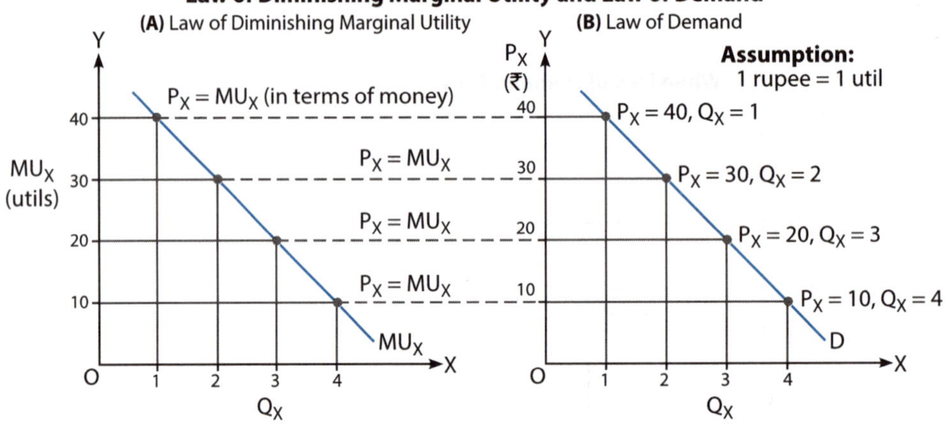

The explanation is based on the assumption that 1 rupee = 1 util of utility, so that, in equilibrium:

$$MU_X = P_X$$

MU_X curve demonstrates the law of diminishing marginal utility. When 1 unit is consumed/purchased, MU = 40. It continues to diminish as more and more units of commodity-X are consumed/purchased.

Since we have assumed 1 util of utility = 1 rupee, 40 utils can be taken as equal to 40 rupees, 30 utils as equal to 30 rupees, and so on. Thus, Fig. 6(B) demonstrates that when $P_X = 40, Q_X = 1$; when $P_X = 30, Q_X = 2$ and so on. Implying that Q_X increases in response to a fall in P_X.

Thus, the law of demand is derived from the law of diminishing marginal utility: **more is purchased in response to a fall in own price of the commodity. Because, fall in price is proportionately linked with the fall in marginal utility.**

6. Movements along a Demand Curve and Shifts in Demand Curve

Movements along a demand curve refer to moving 'up or down' the demand curve. When we move down the curve, it is a situation of extension of demand: buying more in response to decrease in own price of the commodity. When we move up the curve, it is a situation of contraction of demand: buying less in response to increase in own price of the commodity. Thus, movements along the demand curve refer to extension or contraction of demand.

> Movements along the demand curve refer to **extension** or **contraction** of demand.
>
> **Extension of demand** occurs when quantity demanded increases in response to a fall in own price of the commodity.
>
> **Contraction of demand** occurs when quantity demanded decreases in response to a rise in own price of the commodity.

Shifts in demand curve refer to all such situations when demand for a commodity increases or decreases due to changes in other determinants of demand, other than own price of the commodity. In such situations, quantity demanded of a commodity increases or decreases even when own price of the commodity remains constant. **Example:** A consumer may buy more T-shirts when his income rises, price of a T-shirt remaining the same. A consumer now draws his fresh demand schedule, showing higher number of T-shirts against each possible price than before. Accordingly, his demand curve (for T-shirts) shifts to the right. Likewise, when income of a consumer decreases, he may decide to buy less number of T-shirts, price of a T-shirt remaining constant. A fresh demand schedule is again drawn, but showing lower number of T-shirts against each possible price than before. So that, his demand curve (for T-shirts) would shift to the left. Thus, owing to a change in factors (other than own price of the commodity) consumers demand curve may shift to the right or to the left. A situation when demand curve shifts to the right is described as a situation of increase in demand (when more is purchased at the same price of the commodity). On the other hand, a situation when demand curve shifts to the left is described as a situation of decrease in demand (when less is purchased at the same price of the commodity).

Check the following flow chart for a complete picture:

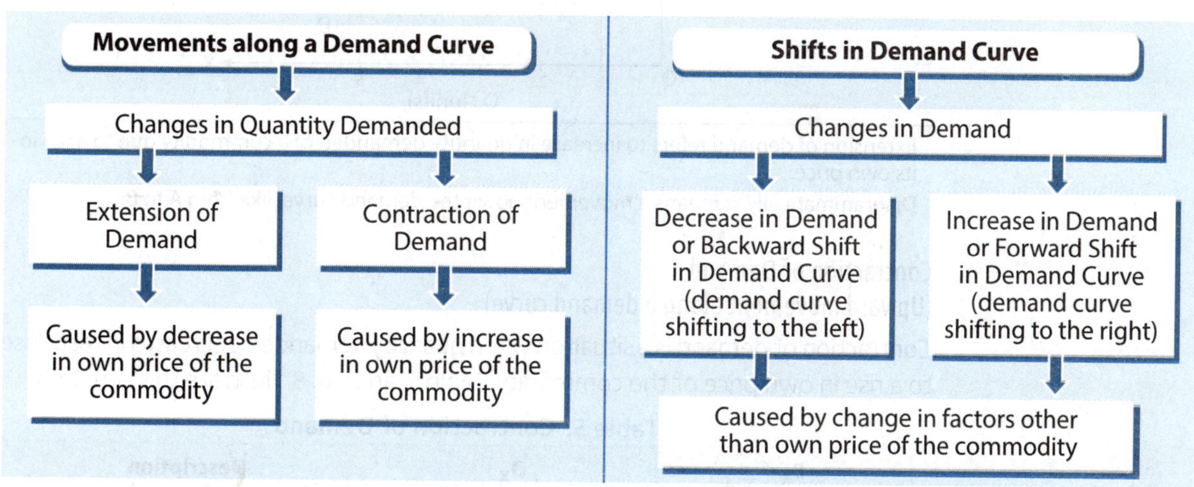

Tabular and Diagrammatic Illustrations

Following are the tabular and diagrammatic illustrations of different situations relating to movements along a demand curve and shifts in demand curve.

Movements along a Demand Curve

Movements along a demand curve refer to extension and contraction of demand. These are caused by changes in own price of the commodity.

Extension of Demand
(Downward movement along a demand curve)

Extension of demand (also called expansion of demand) is a situation when quantity demanded increases in response to a fall in own price of the commodity. Table 4 and Fig. 7 illustrate this situation.

Table 4. Extension of Demand

P_X (₹)	Q_X (Units)	Description
5	1	Fall in Own Price of the Commodity ↓
1	5	Rise in Quantity Demanded

When the price of Good-X is ₹ 5 per unit, 1 unit is demanded. When price reduces to ₹ 1 per unit, demand extends to 5 units.

Extension of demand is indicated by a downward movement along the demand curve, as from point A to B in Fig. 7.

FIGURE 7

Extension of Demand

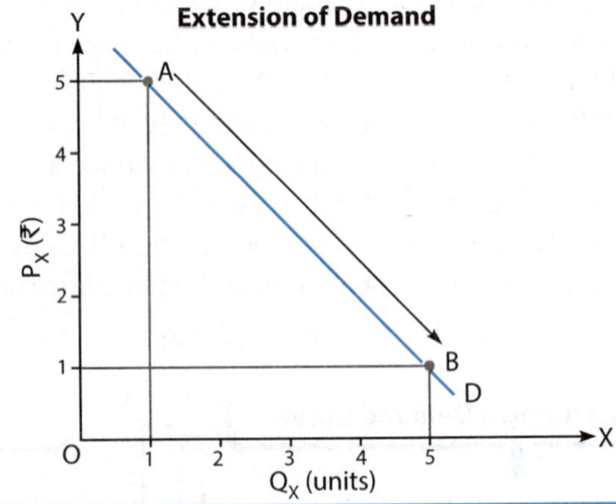

Extension of demand refers to increase in quantity demanded of a commodity due to a fall in its own price.
Diagrammatically, it means a movement down the demand curve, like from A to B.

Contraction of Demand
(Upward movement along a demand curve)

Contraction of demand is a situation when quantity demanded decreases in response to a rise in own price of the commodity. Table 5 and Fig. 8 illustrate this situation.

Table 5. Contraction of Demand

P_X (₹)	Q_X (Units)	Description
1	5	Rise in Own Price of the Commodity ↓
5	1	Fall in Quantity Demanded

When the price of Good-X is ₹ 1 per unit, 5 units are demanded. When price rises to ₹ 5 per unit, demand contracts to 1 unit only.

Like extension of demand, contraction of demand is indicated by an upward movement along the demand curve, as from point B to A in Fig. 8.

FIGURE 8

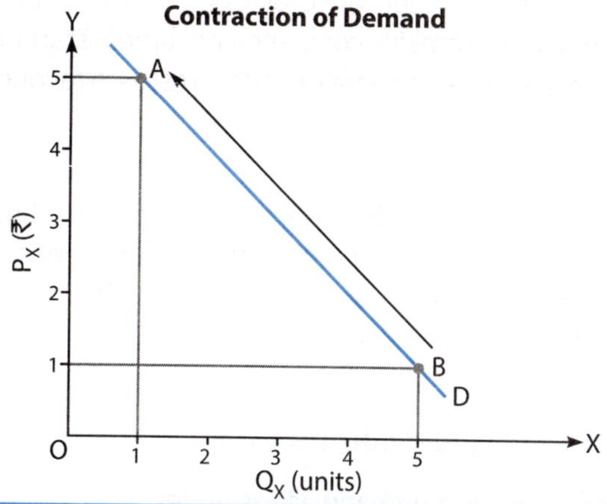

Contraction of demand refers to decrease in quantity demanded of a commodity due to a rise in its own price.
Diagrammatically, it means a movement up the demand curve, like from B to A.

Shifts in Demand Curve

Shifts in demand curve include (i) forward shift, and (ii) backward shift. Forward shift in demand curve refers to increase in demand. While backward shift in demand curve refers to decrease in demand. Shifts in demand curve occur due to change in other factors, other than own price of the commodity.

Forward Shift in Demand Curve—Increase in Demand

Forward shift in demand curve (increase in demand) refers to a situation when quantity demanded of a commodity increases, even when own price of the commodity is constant. In other words, increase in demand occurs when quantity demanded of a commodity increases because of the factors, other than 'own price of the commodity'. It is illustrated by Table 6 and Fig. 9.

Table 6. Increase in Demand

P_X (₹)	Q_X (Units)
10	20
10	30

FIGURE 9

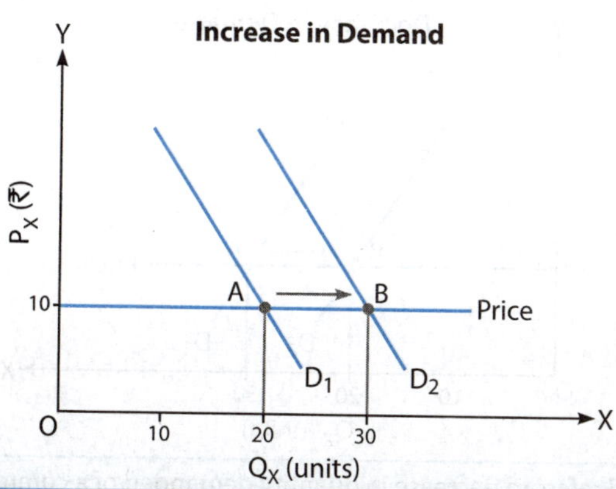

Increase in demand refers to increase in quantity demanded of a commodity at its existing price. It is caused by factors other than 'own price of the commodity'.
Diagrammatically, it means a forward shift in demand curve, as from D_1 to D_2.

Table 6 and Fig. 9 show that when price of Good-X is ₹ 10 per unit, 20 units are demanded. Even when price remains constant, consumers start demanding 30 units. It may be due to increase in their income or shift in tastes in favour of the commodity, or other such factors.

It is important to note that increase in demand is indicated by a shift in demand curve to the right, also called forward shift in demand curve. Fig. 9 shows demand curve shifting from D_1 to D_2 when the consumers decide to buy 30 units (instead of 20) even when own price of the commodity remains constant at ₹ 10 per unit. The consumer shifts from point A on D_1 to point B on D_2.

Causes of Increase in Demand [Situations when Demand Curve Shifts Forward]

Important causes of increase in demand are as under:

(i) When income of the consumer increases.

(ii) When price of substitute good increases.

(iii) When price of complementary good falls.

(iv) When taste of the consumer shifts in favour of the commodity due to change in fashion or climate.

(v) When availability of the commodity is expected to reduce in the near future.

Backward Shift in Demand Curve—Decrease in Demand

Backward shift in demand curve (decrease in demand) refers to a situation when quantity demanded of a commodity decreases, even when own price of the commodity is constant. In other words, decrease in demand occurs when quantity demanded of a commodity decreases because of the factors, other than 'own price of the commodity'. It is illustrated by Table 7 and Fig. 10.

Table 7. Decrease in Demand

P_X (₹)	Q_X (Units)
10	30
10	20

FIGURE 10

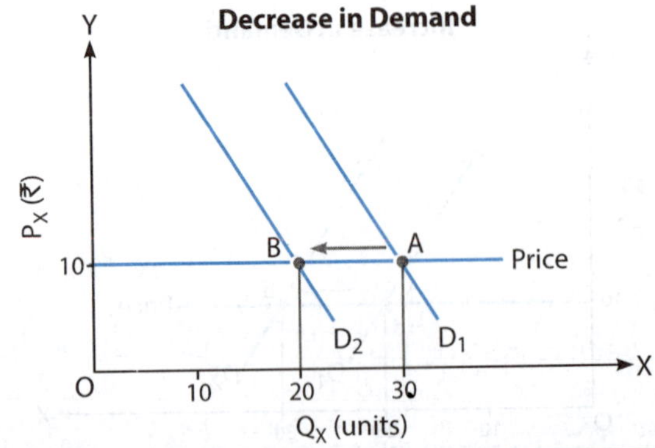

Decrease in demand refers to decrease in quantity demanded of a commodity at its existing price. It is caused by factors other than 'own price of the commodity'. Diagrammatically, it means a backward shift in demand curve, as from D_1 to D_2.

Table 7 and Fig. 10 show that when price of Good-X is ₹ 10 per unit, 30 units are demanded. Even when price remains constant, consumers decide to buy 20 units rather than 30 units of the commodity. It may be due to decrease in their income or loss of taste for the commodity, or other such factors.

Decrease in demand is indicated by a shift in demand curve to the left, also called backward shift in demand curve. Fig. 10 shows demand curve shifting from D_1 to D_2 when the consumers decide to buy only 20 units (instead of 30) even when own price of the commodity remains constant at ₹ 10 per unit. The consumer shifts from point A on D_1 to point B on D_2.

Causes of Decrease in Demand [Situations when Demand Curve Shifts Backward]

Important causes of decrease in demand are as under:

(i) When income of the consumer falls.

(ii) When price of the substitute good decreases.

(iii) When price of the complementary good increases.

(iv) When taste of the consumer shifts against the commodity due to change in fashion or climate.

(v) When availability of the commodity is expected to rise in the near future.

Difference between Extension and Increase in Demand

Extension of Demand	Increase in Demand
(i) This is caused by change in own price of the commodity.	(i) This is caused by change in determinants, other than own price of the commodity.
(ii) Decrease in own price of the commodity is the only cause.	(ii) Several Causes: These include increase in income, increase in price of the substitute good, decrease in price of the complementary good, and change in tastes and preferences in favour of the commodity.
(iii) Diagrammatically, this is shown as a downward movement (left to right) on the same demand curve (refer Fig. 7).	(iii) Diagrammatically, this is shown as a forward shift in demand curve (refer Fig. 9).

Difference between Contraction and Decrease in Demand

Contraction of Demand	Decrease in Demand
(i) This is caused by change in own price of the commodity.	(i) This is caused by change in determinants, other than own price of the commodity.
(ii) Increase in own price of the commodity is the only cause.	(ii) Several Causes: These include decrease in income, decrease in price of the substitute good, increase in price of the complementary good, and change in tastes and preferences against the commodity.
(iii) Diagrammatically, this is shown as an upward movement (right to left) on the same demand curve (refer Fig. 8).	(iii) Diagrammatically, this is shown as a backward shift in demand curve (refer Fig. 10).

HOTS

Q.1. Answer in one sentence the assumptions on which a demand curve is constructed.

Ans. That all other determinants (other than own price of the commodity) are constant.

Q.2. Give one reason, why more of a commodity is demanded even when own price of the commodity happens to rise. Support your answer with an example.

Ans. More of a commodity may be demanded even when own price of the commodity happens to rise, due to expectations of the buyers that the concerned commodity (which happens to be a necessity of life) may not be easily available in the near future.

Example: In curfew bound areas, demand for salt and cereals often shoots up even when prices of these goods tend to rise.

7. Cross Price Effects: How Price of Related Goods (Substitute/Complementary) affects Demand for a Commodity?

Effect of change in price of a related good on the demand for a commodity is called cross price effect.

We know related goods are:

(i) substitute goods, and

(ii) complementary goods.

Accordingly, we can split our discussion into two parts, as under:

(i) Demand for a Commodity in relation to Price of the Substitute Good: Let us consider tea and coffee as two substitute goods. Let tea be the commodity demanded of which demand curve is D_1 as shown in Fig. 11.

FIGURE 11

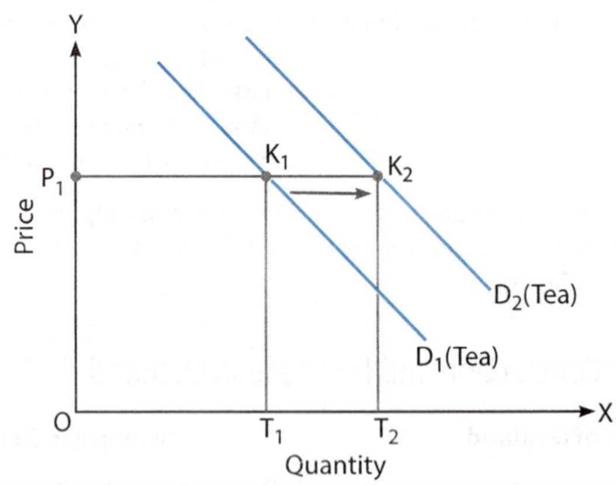

Demand curve for tea shifts to the right when price of the substitute commodity (coffee) increases. Thus, the consumer shifts from D_1 to D_2, buying more of tea even when its price is constant.

(a) Increase in Price of Substitute Good: Initially, if price of tea is OP_1, quantity purchased is OT_1. Now, suppose the price of tea remains constant but the price of coffee increases. **How would you react as a consumer?**

As a rational consumer, you may decide to substitute some tea in place of coffee. Or, you are expected to buy more of tea even when its price is constant (Fig. 11).

Initially you were buying P_1K_1 quantity of tea (which is equal to OT_1). Now you are willing to buy P_1K_2. Greater purchase of a commodity at its constant price points to a situation of increase in demand, or forward shift in demand curve. Accordingly, demand curve for tea shifts to the right, from D_1 to D_2.

(b) Decrease in Price of Substitute Good: If price of coffee decreases, you will tend to substitute some coffee in place of tea. Or, you will demand less tea even when its price is constant. Fig. 12 illustrates this situation. Initially you were buying OT_1 (= P_1K_1) of tea. Now, you are buying OT_2 (= P_1K_2) of tea even when price of tea is constant (= OP_1). This is a situation of backward shift in demand curve.

FIGURE 12

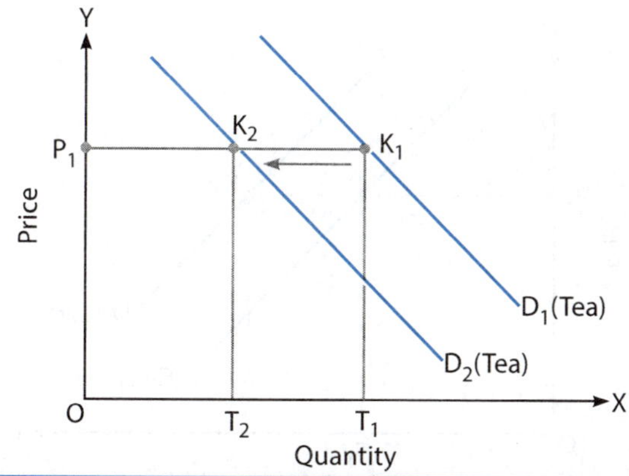

Demand curve for tea shifts to the left when price of the substitute commodity (coffee) decreases. Thus, the consumer shifts from D_1 to D_2, buying less of tea even when price of tea is constant.

If X and Y are substitutes and price of X remains constant:
—demand curve for X would shift to the right if price of Y increases.
—demand curve for X would shift to the left if price of Y decreases.

(ii) Demand for a Commodity in relation to Price of the Complementary Good: Let us consider car and petrol as complementary goods. Let cars be the commodity demanded of which the demand curve is D_1 as shown in Fig. 13.

FIGURE 13

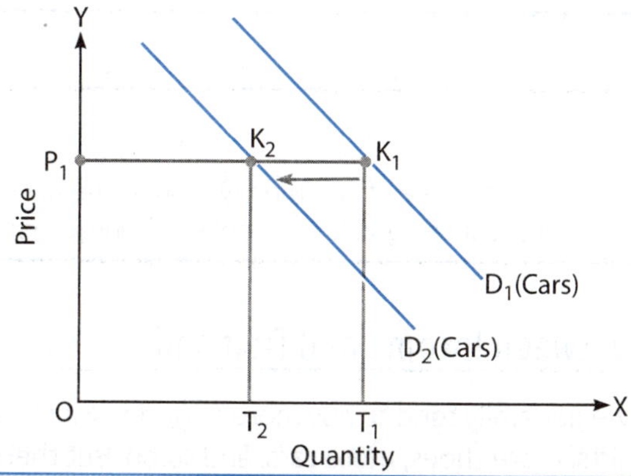

Demand curve for cars shifts to the left when price of the complementary good (petrol) increases. Thus, the consumers shift from D_1 to D_2, buying less of cars even when their price is constant.

(a) Increase in Price of Complementary Good: Initially, if price of cars (say Swift) is OP_1, number of cars purchased is OT_1 (= P_1K_1).

Now, suppose this price remains constant but the price of petrol increases.

How would the consumers react to such a situation? They would tend to buy less cars, even when price of the cars is constant (Fig. 13).

Now, even when price of cars is constant, P_1K_2 cars are purchased, because price of petrol has increased. This is a situation of decrease in demand or backward shift in demand curve. Accordingly, demand curve shifts from D_1 to D_2.

(b) Decrease in Price of Complementary Good: If price of petrol decreases, people will have the tendency to buy more cars, even when price of cars is constant. This is a situation of increase in demand, or forward shift in demand curve, as illustrated in Fig. 14.

FIGURE 14

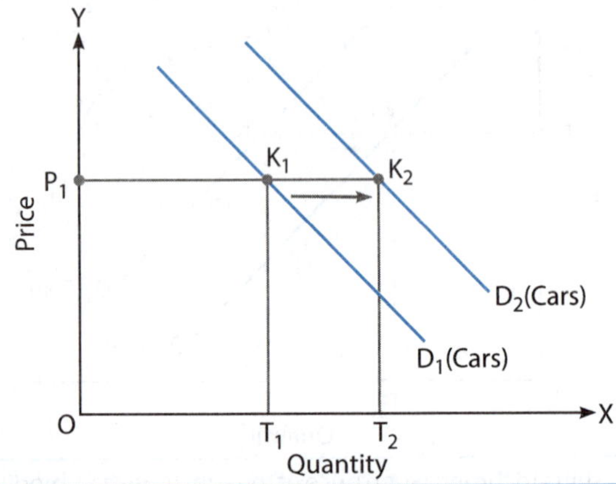

Demand curve for cars shifts to the right when price of the complementary good (petrol) decreases. Thus, the consumers shift from D_1 to D_2, buying more of cars even when their price is constant.

Initially P_1K_1 (= OT_1) cars were purchased. As price of petrol decreases, P_1K_2 cars are purchased even when price of cars is constant. Accordingly, demand curve shifts forward from D_1 to D_2.

If X and Y are complementary goods and price of X remains constant:

—demand curve for X would shift forward if price of Y reduces.

—demand curve for X would shift backward if price of Y increases.

HOTS

Q. What is cross price effect?

Ans. Cross price effect refers to the effect of change in the price of commodity-X on the demand for commodity-Y when X and Y are related goods (X and Y are either substitute goods or complementary goods).

8. Relationship between Income and Demand

If our income rises, we generally tend to buy more of goods. More income would mean more pens, more shirts, more shoes, more cars, and so on. But there are exceptions. If initially you are buying coarse grain (simply because you cannot afford to buy a finer grain), how would you take your increase in income now? Perhaps, as a first step, you would discard the consumption of inferiors: you will reduce (or give up) the consumption of coarse grains and shift to the consumption of superior grains. Surely, this happens in the deserts of Rajasthan where, the rich minority eats wheat while the poor majority eats *bajra* as their staple food. This suggests division of goods into two categories: (i) normal goods, and (ii) inferior goods.

(i) Normal Goods

These are the goods the demand for which increases as income of the buyers rises. There is a positive relationship between income and demand. Or, in case of normal goods, income effect is positive.

How Demand Curve of a Normal Good changes when Income of the Buyers changes?

In a situation of increase in income, more of a (normal) good is purchased even when its price is constant. This refers to a situation of increase in demand or forward shift in demand curve. On the other hand, in a situation of decrease in income, less of a (normal) good is purchased even when its price is constant. This refers to a situation of decrease in demand or backward shift in demand curve.

Diagram (Fig. 15) illustrates these situations.

FIGURE 15

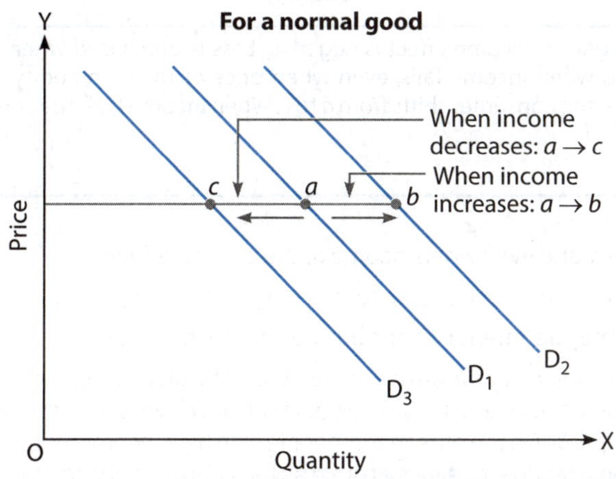

In case of normal goods, income effect is positive. More is purchased when income rises, and less is purchased when income falls, even when price of the commodity is constant. When income rises, the consumer shifts from *a* to *b*. When income falls, the consumer shifts from *a* to *c*.

(ii) Inferior Goods

These are the goods the demand for which decreases as income of buyers rises. Thus, there is negative relationship between income and demand. Or, in case of inferior goods, income effect is negative.

How Demand Curve of an Inferior Good changes when Income of the Buyers changes?

In a situation of increase in income, less of the (inferior) good is purchased. The consumer prefers to shift on to superior substitutes, because now he can afford them.

Buying less of a commodity at its existing price implies a backward shift in demand curve, or decrease in demand. On the other hand, if income decreases, the consumer, already consuming an inferior good, is further compelled to depend on it. May be he has to further cut his consumption of superior substitute and buy more of the inferior goods. It implies a situation of forward shift in demand curve or increase in demand for inferior goods.

Diagram (Fig. 16) illustrates these situations.

FIGURE 16

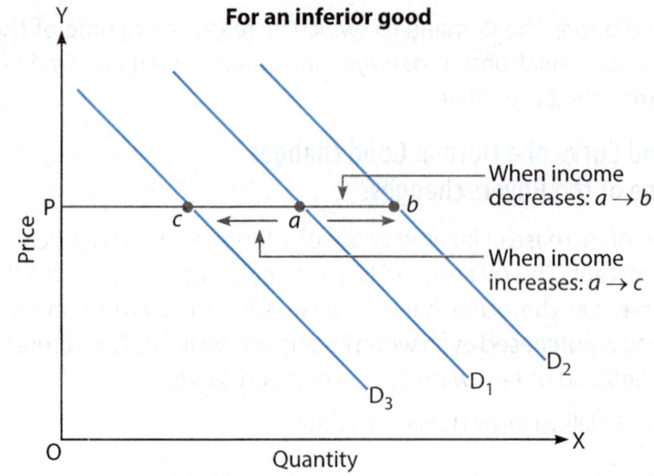

In case of inferior goods, income effect is negative. Less is purchased when income rises, and more is purchased when income falls, even when price of the commodity remains constant. When income rises, the consumer shifts from *a* to *c*. When income falls, the consumer shifts from *a* to *b*.

HOTS

Q.1. What type of goods find a rise in their demand even when income of the buyers reduces?

Ans. Inferior goods. When income of the buyers reduces they tend to increase the consumption of inferior goods.

Q.2. Do you agree with the view that a good may be 'inferior' to one but 'normal' to the other?

Ans. Yes. It is true that a good may be 'inferior' to one and 'normal' to the other. The distinction between inferior good and normal good is drawn with reference to the level of income. People with low level of income would find coarse grain as a normal good for their consumption. On the other hand, people with high income would consider coarse grain as an inferior good. They would consider finer qualities of grain as their normal good for consumption.

9. Impact of Tastes and Preferences on Demand for a Commodity

Tastes and preferences of the buyers are determined by three factors, as under:

(1) Individual's Likes and Dislikes: You tend to buy more or less of a commodity simply because your likes and dislikes tend to change.

(2) Trends and Fashions: You are influenced by the emerging trends and fashions. You simply want to be 'trendy'; accordingly, you prefer to buy more of a commodity.

(3) Climatic Environment: Your tastes and preferences tend to change with change in climatic environment. Winter season induces you to goods like, tea and coffee while summer induces you to goods like, cold drink and ice cream.

Favourable and Unfavourable Change in Tastes and Preferences

Favourable change in tastes and preferences induces the buyers to buy more of a commodity even when its price continues to be the same. This is a situation of increase in demand, implying a forward shift in demand curve. On the other hand, an unfavourable change in tastes and preferences causes lesser purchase of the commodity at its existing price—a situation of decrease in demand or backward shift in demand curve.

Fig. 17 illustrates these situations.

FIGURE 17

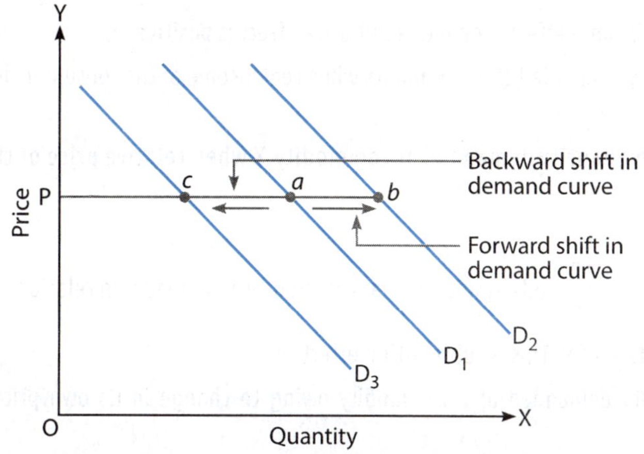

✦ Backward shift in demand curve ($a \rightarrow c$) owing to unfavourable shift in tastes and preferences for a commodity.

✦ Forward shift in demand curve ($a \rightarrow b$) owing to favourable shift in tastes and preferences for a commodity.

A favourable change in tastes and preferences causes a forward shift in demand curve from D_1 to D_2 (or from '*a*' to '*b*').

An unfavourable change in tastes and preferences causes a backward shift in demand curve from D_1 to D_3 (or from '*a*' to '*c*').

POWER POINTS

- **Quantity Demanded** refers to a specific quantity of a commodity to be purchased against a specific price of that commodity at a point of time.
- **Demand** refers to various amounts of a commodity that a consumer is ready to buy at different possible prices of the commodity at a point of time.
- **Individual Demand Schedule** is a table showing various quantities of a commodity which an individual buyer is ready to buy at different possible prices of the commodity at a point of time.
- **Market Demand Schedule** is a schedule showing various quantities of a commodity which all the buyers in the market are ready to buy at different possible prices of the commodity at a point of time.
- **Demand Curve** is a graphic presentation of demand schedule.
- **Market Demand Curve** is a horizontal summation of individual demand curves.
- **Law of Demand** expresses inverse relationship between own price of a commodity and its quantity demanded. It means that, other things being equal, quantity demanded decreases with a rise in own price of the commodity, and vice versa. Geometrically, it is represented by a downward sloping demand curve.
- **Exceptions to the Law of Demand** occur in case of: (i) Articles of distinction, (ii) Giffen goods, and (iii) When consumers judge quality of a commodity by its price.
- **Movements along a Demand Curve** occur when changes in quantity demanded are related to changes in own price of the commodity. When quantity demanded decreases in response to increase in price, it is called contraction of demand. When quantity demanded increases in response to decrease in price, it is called extension of demand.
- **Shifts in Demand Curve** occur when demand for a commodity is related to factors other than own price of the commodity. When more is demanded at the same price, there is forward shift in demand curve; when less is demanded at the same price, there is backward shift in demand curve. Forward shift in demand curve is a situation of increase in demand. Backward shift in demand curve is a situation of decrease in demand.

- **Normal Good** is that good whose income effect is positive and price effect is negative.
- **Inferior Good** is that good whose income effect is negative.
- **Giffen Good** is that inferior good whose income effect is negative but price effect is positive.
- **Income Effect** refers to change in quantity demanded of a commodity when real income of the consumer changes owing to change in own price of the commodity.
- **Substitution Effect** refers to change in quantity demanded of commodity-X when relative price of the commodity $\left(\frac{P_X}{P_Y}\right)$ changes owing to change in P_X.

  Illustration: If P_X falls and P_Y is constant, then $\frac{P_X}{P_Y}$ falls. It implies that commodity-X is cheaper in relation to commodity-Y. Accordingly, more of X is purchased in place of Y. This is substitution effect.
- **Price Effect** refers to change in quantity demanded of a commodity owing to change in its own price, other things remaining constant.
- **Cross Price Effect** refers to effect of a change in price of commodity-X on demand for commodity-Y when X and Y are related goods (X and Y are either substitute goods or complementary goods).

EXERCISE

1. Very Short Questions (Remembering & Understanding) (1 mark each)

A. Multiple Choice Questions: Choose the Correct Answer

1. **Specific quantity to be purchased against a specific price of the commodity is called:**
   (a) demand (b) quantity demanded
   (c) movement along the demand curve (d) shift in demand curve
2. **The graphic presentation of a table showing price and demand relationship for a commodity in the market is called:**
   (a) individual demand curve (b) producer's demand curve
   (c) market demand curve (d) consumer's demand curve
3. **When at the price of ₹ 5 per unit of a commodity, A's demand is for 11 units, B's demand is for 14 units and C's demand is for 8 units, then market demand will be:**
   (a) 11 units (b) 14 units
   (c) 17 units (d) 33 units
4. **Downward slope of the demand curve shows:**
   (a) positive relationship between price and quantity demanded
   (b) inverse relationship between price and quantity demanded
   (c) no relationship between price and quantity demanded
   (d) none of these
5. **How are the two goods (apple and orange) related when, as a result of rise in the price of apples, demand for oranges increases?**
   (a) Substitute goods (b) Complementary goods
   (c) Normal goods (d) Inferior goods
6. **In case of normal goods, demand curve shows:**
   (a) a negative slope (b) a positive slope
   (c) zero slope (d) none of these

7. Law of demand must fail in case of:

(a) normal goods (b) Giffen goods

(c) inferior goods (d) none of these

8. Inferior goods are those whose income effect is:

(a) negative (b) positive

(c) zero (d) none of these

9. Which of the following pairs represents substitute goods?

(a) Car and petrol (b) Juice and cold drink

(c) Bread and butter (d) All of these

10. In case of Giffen's Paradox, the slope of demand curve is:

(a) negative (b) positive

(c) parallel to X-axis (d) parallel to Y-axis

11. As a result of rise in consumer's income, demand curve for coarse grain (inferior good):

(a) becomes a horizontal straight line (b) becomes a vertical straight line

(c) shifts to the right (d) shifts to the left

12. If two goods are complementary then rise in the price of one results in:

(a) rise in demand for the other (b) fall in demand for the other

(c) rise in demand for both (d) none of these

13. Demand curve is upward sloping for:

(a) normal goods (b) inferior goods

(c) Giffen goods (d) none of these

14. Movement along the demand curve occurs due to change in:

(a) own price of the commodity

(b) determinants of demand, other than own price of the commodity

(c) both (a) and (b)

(d) none of these

15. An increase in the price of electricity will cause the demand for electric appliances to:

(a) rise (b) fall

(c) remain the same (d) none of these

16. Shift in demand curve means:

(a) fall in demand due to rise in own price of the commodity

(b) rise in demand due to fall in own price of the commodity

(c) change in demand due to factors other than own price of the commodity

(d) none of these

17. A fall in income of the consumer (in case of normal goods) will cause:

(a) upward movement on the demand curve (b) downward movement on the demand curve

(c) rightward shift of the demand curve (d) leftward shift of the demand curve

18. Change in quantity demanded of a commodity due to change in its own price, other things remaining constant, is called:

(a) cross price effect (b) price effect

(c) income effect (d) substitution effect

19. In case of contraction of demand, we move:

(a) from lower point to upper point on the same demand curve

(b) to right on the another demand curve

(c) from upper point to lower point on the same demand curve

(d) to left on the another demand curve

20. Increase in demand occurs due to:

(a) decrease in price of the complementary good (b) increase in income of the consumer

(c) increase in price of the substitutes (d) all of these

21. Assumptions of the law of demand refer to:

(a) constant own price of the commodity

(b) determinants of demand, other than own price of the commodity

(c) constant cost of production

(d) none of these

22. Law of demand is violated when:

(a) income effect is negative

(b) substitution effect is negative

(c) negative income effect is greater than substitution effect

(d) negative income effect is less than substitution effect

23. A fall in own price of the commodity leads to:

(a) increase in real income of the consumer

(b) decrease in real income of the consumer

(c) increase in purchasing power of the consumer

(d) both (a) and (c)

24. Substitution effect takes place when price of the commodity becomes:

(a) relatively cheaper (b) relatively dearer

(c) stable (d) both (a) and (b)

25. In Fig. 18, the slope of the demand curve is:

(a) negative

(b) positive

(c) constant

(d) both (a) and (c)

FIGURE 18

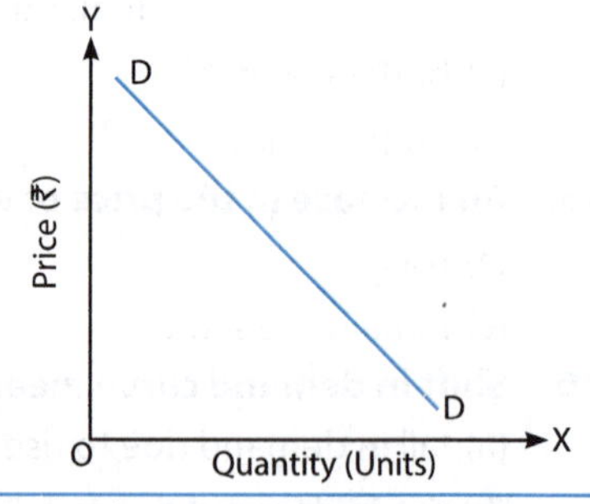

26. Find the missing entries from the following:

Price (₹)	Demand for A (Units)	Demand for B (Units)	Market Demand (Units)
1	18	14	32
2	15	10	25
3	—	9	22
4	10	—	17
5	6	4	—

(a) 13, 7, 10 (b) 31, 27, 2

(c) 27, 40, 2 (d) none of these

Answers

1. (b) **2.** (c) **3.** (d) **4.** (b) **5.** (a) **6.** (a) **7.** (b) **8.** (a) **9.** (b) **10.** (b) **11.** (d) **12.** (b) **13.** (c)
14. (a) **15.** (b) **16.** (c) **17.** (d) **18.** (b) **19.** (a) **20.** (d) **21.** (b) **22.** (c) **23.** (d) **24.** (d) **25.** (d) **26.** (a)

B. Information & Concept-based Questions

1. **Define demand.**

Ans. Demand refers to the desire to have a commodity backed by willingness and ability to purchase that commodity at given price during a period of time.

2. **What is meant by quantity demanded?**

Ans. Quantity demanded refers to a specific quantity to be purchased against a specific price of the commodity.

3. **What is a demand schedule?**

Ans. Demand schedule is a table which shows the relationship between price and quantity demanded of a commodity.

4. **What is a demand curve?**

Ans. Demand curve is a graphic presentation of demand schedule showing inverse relationship between price and quantity demanded of a commodity.

5. **Name two determinants of consumer's demand for a commodity.**

Ans. Two determinants of consumer's demand for a commodity are:

(i) Own price of the commodity, and

(ii) Income of the consumer.

6. **What is the slope of demand curve like?**

Ans. Demand curve slopes downward from left to right, indicating inverse relationship between price and quantity demanded of a commodity.

7. **What is the slope of demand curve for Giffen goods?**

Ans. Slope of demand curve for Giffen goods is upward sloping, indicating positive relationship between price and quantity demanded of a commodity.

8. **Define normal goods.**

Ans. Normal goods are those goods in case of which there is a positive relationship between consumer's income and quantity demanded. Implying that income effect is positive.

9. **Define inferior goods.**

Ans. Inferior goods are those goods in case of which there is a negative relationship between consumer's income and quantity demanded. Implying that income effect is negative.

10. **Define Giffen goods.**

Ans. Giffen goods are those inferior goods in the case of which there is a positive relationship between price and quantity demanded.

11. **What is meant by extension of demand?**

Ans. When quantity demanded of a commodity increases due to decrease in own price of the commodity, other factors remain constant, it is a situation of extension of demand.

12. **What is meant by contraction of demand?**

Ans. When quantity demanded of a commodity decreases due to increase in own price of the commodity, other factors remain constant, it is a situation of contraction of demand.

13. **What do you understand by substitutes?**

Ans. Substitute goods are those goods which can be substituted for each other.

14. **What is meant by complementary goods?**

Ans. Complementary goods are those goods which complete the demand for each other.

15. **If the quantity demanded of Good-X decreases as the household income increases, what type of good is X?**

Ans. Good-X is an inferior good.

16. If the demand for Good-Y increases as price of another Good-X rises, how are the two goods related?

Ans. The two goods (X and Y) are substitute goods.

17. What happens to the demand for a complementary good of a commodity when the price of the commodity rises?

Ans. Demand for a complementary good decreases when the price of the commodity rises. Demand curve will shift to the left.

18. Why does the demand for coffee increase when the price of tea increases?

Ans. Because tea and coffee are substitute goods.

19. What does the movement on the same demand curve show?

Ans. Movement on the same demand curve shows extension or contraction of demand.

20. What does the shifting of a demand curve show?

Ans. Shifting of a demand curve shows increase or decrease in demand.

21. If the demand for CNG increases as price of petrol increases, how are these two goods related?

Ans. CNG and petrol are substitute goods.

22. How is the demand for a good affected by a change in tastes and preferences of the consumers in favour of the commodity?

Ans. Change in tastes and preferences of the consumers in favour of the commodity will shift the demand curve of the commodity to the right.

2. Reason-based Questions (Comprehension of the Subject-matter)

Read the following statements carefully. Write 'True' or 'False' with a reason.

1. Demand for a commodity can exist independent of its price.

Ans. False. Demand for a commodity is always expressed with reference to price.

2. **Quantity demanded is a specific amount of a commodity that the consumer is ready to buy against a specific price, while demand is not.**

Ans. True. Because demand refers to various quantities of a commodity that the consumer is ready to buy against different possible prices.

3. **For a family of four, demand schedule for rice should be the same for each member.**

Ans. False. Each member's demand for rice depends on his or her preference and taste for rice.

4. **Demand for a commodity refers to the entire demand schedule.**

Ans. True. Demand for a commodity refers to the entire demand schedule showing various quantities of the commodity that the buyers in the market are ready to buy at different possible prices at a point of time.

5. **Even when P_X remains constant, Q_X may increase or decrease.**

Ans. True. Q_X may increase or decrease due to change in other determinants of demand even when P_X remains constant.

6. **Individual demand is a concept related to microeconomics, while market demand is a concept related to macroeconomics.**

Ans. False. Both individual demand and market demand are related to microeconomics. Market demand is a micro concept because it refers to demand for one commodity.

7. **Law of demand must fail if less of a commodity is demanded even when income of the buyer rises.**

Ans. False. Law of demand does not fail when less of a commodity is demanded while income of the buyer rises. A cut in demand with a rise in income is simply a case of inferior good. A rise in income will shift the demand curve to the left.

8. If disposable income of the people rises, their demand curve for butter may not obey the law of demand.

Ans. True. Because law of demand shows the relationship between price of commodity and its demand on the assumption that disposable income remains constant.

9. In case of substitute goods, a fall in price of Good-X causes a fall in demand for Good-Y.

Ans. True. Because, cheaper good replaces the one which is more expensive.

10. In case of complementary goods, a rise in price of Good-X causes a rise in demand for Good-Y.

Ans. False. In case of complementary goods, a rise in price of Good-X causes a fall in demand for Good-Y. Because consumption of both goods X and Y goes together.

11. It is quantity demanded (and not demand for a commodity) that changes with respect to its own price.

Ans. True. It is quantity demanded of a commodity that changes in response to change in its own price. Change in demand occurs even when own price of the commodity remains constant.

12. Changes in income cause a shift in demand curve, while change in own price of the commodity does not.

Ans. True. Shift in demand curve occurs due to change in factors other than own price of the commodity such as change in income of the consumer, tastes or preferences.

13. Shift in demand curve does not occur so long as own price of the commodity is constant.

Ans. False. Shift in demand curve occurs due to change in other factors, other than own price of the commodity.

14. Forward shift in demand curve occurs when own price of the commodity rises, and consumer's income remains constant.

Ans. False. Forward shift in demand curve occurs when own price of the commodity remains constant and consumer's income rises.

15. Increase in demand refers to extension of demand.

Ans. False. Increase in demand refers to increase in quantity demanded of a commodity at its existing price. It is a situation of forward shift in demand curve, not of extension of demand.

16. Decrease in demand refers to contraction of demand.

Ans. False. Decrease in demand refers to decrease in quantity demanded of a commodity at its existing price. It is a situation of backward shift in demand curve, not of contraction of demand.

17. In case of normal goods, income effect is positive, while in case of inferior goods, it is negative.

Ans. True. Income effect is positive when increase in income causes increase in demand, as in case of normal goods. It is negative when increase in income causes decrease in demand, as in case of inferior goods.

18. In case of inferior goods, law of demand fails.

Ans. False. In case of inferior goods, law of demand fails only when negative income effect is greater than substitution effect. When negative income effect is less than substitution effect law of demand does not fail.

19. An individual can shift from the consumption of a normal good to the consumption of an inferior good.

Ans. True. It happens when the income of the consumer happens to fall.

20. Cross price effect occurs in case of substitute goods, and not in case of complementary goods.

Ans. False. Cross price effect occurs both in case of substitute goods and complementary goods. Because both substitute goods and complementary goods are related to each other.

21. In case of Giffen goods, income effect is higher than the substitution effect.

Ans. True. In case of Giffen goods, income effect is higher than the substitution effect. Implying law of demand fails in case of Giffen goods.

22. A consumer buy more of a commodity even when MU of every successive unit tends to decrease.

Ans. True. Even when MU_X is decreasing, the consumer will continue to buy more of commodity-X so long as $P_X < MU_X$ (in terms of money). The consumer stops buying a good only when its money worth of MU is equal to its price.

3. HOTS & Applications

1. The price of eggs rises and yet it is observed that the demand for eggs is rising. Does it mean that the demand curve for eggs is upward sloping?

Ans. No. Increase in demand for eggs may not be related to increase in price of eggs, instead it may be related to income or expectations or seasonal change. When any of other determinant of demand (other than own price of the concerned commodity) changes, there is a shift in demand curve which has nothing to do with the law of demand.

2. What is the relation between Good-X and Good-Y, if with rise in the price of Good-X, demand for Good-Y rises? Give an example.

Ans. These are substitute goods. When price of Good-X rises, consumers switch over from X to Y and therefore, demand for Good-Y rises. **Example:** If price of Pepsi rises, consumers are prompted to shift to Coke. Accordingly, demand for Coke rises.

3. If demand curve is found to be positively sloped, what it could be due to? Give your answer in terms of nature of the commodity, income effect and substitution effect.

Ans. Positively sloped demand curve violates the law of demand. It is found in case of Giffen goods. These are those inferior goods in case of which income effect is negative and greater than substitution effect, so that net effect (or price effect) points to a positive relation between price and quantity demanded of the commodity.

4. Fall in price of a commodity always leads to expansion of its demand. Comment.

Ans. Fall in price of a commodity lead to expansion of its demand but not always. There are situations of 'exceptions' to the inverse relationship between P_X and Q_X. These exceptions are: (i) cases of Giffen goods, (ii) articles of social distinction, and (iii) judgement of the consumers (when the consumers are driven by the idea 'costlier the better').

5. Giffen goods must be inferior goods, while inferior goods, may or may not be Giffen goods. Comment.

Ans. Yes. Because Giffen goods, by definition, are those inferior goods in case of which two conditions are satisfied: (i) income effect is negative, and (ii) income effect is greater than substitution effect. In case of inferior goods, on the other hand, only one condition needs to be satisfied: that income effect is negative.

6. Do you agree with the view that law of demand need not necessarily fail in case of inferior goods?

Ans. Yes, it is true that law of demand need not necessarily fail in case of inferior goods. Inferior goods are those goods in case of which we find inverse relation between income and quantity demanded. Even when inverse relation between income and quantity demanded is established (implying a situation of negative income effect), law of demand will not fail in case negative income effect is less than the substitution effect. Law of demand fails only when negative income effect is greater than the substitution effect.

7. Law of demand is derived from the law of diminishing marginal utility. Explain how. Give an illustration using single commodity equilibrium condition.

Ans. Consider Fig. 19. Part (A) shows the law of diminishing marginal utility. MU_X curve shows that marginal utility diminishes with the consumption of every additional unit of the commodity-X. First unit offers the consumer satisfaction worth ₹ 30 (= 30 utils). Accordingly, for the first unit purchased, the consumer is willing to pay ₹ 30. The second unit offers utility worth ₹ 20 (= 20 utils). Accordingly, the consumer is willing to pay ₹ 20 as the price for it. Likewise, third unit offers utility worth ₹ 10 (= 10 utils), and the price offered is ₹ 10. The fourth unit offers zero satisfaction. Accordingly, the consumer is not willing to pay any price for it.

FIGURE 19

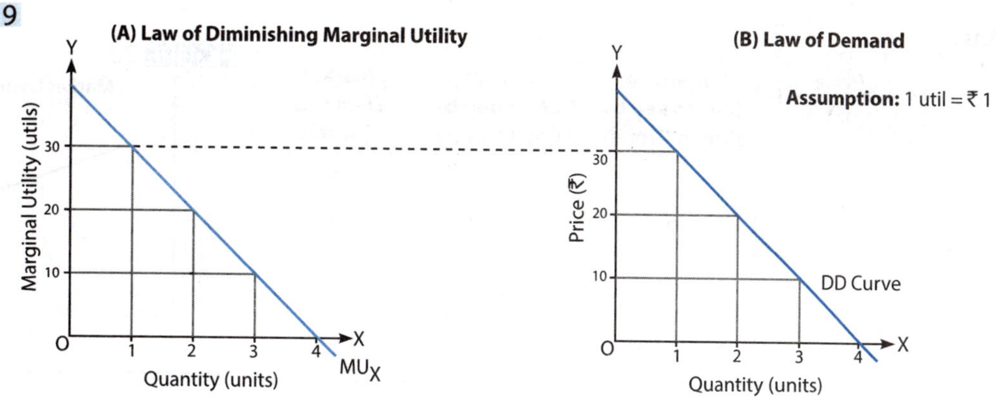

Thus, the consumer, while buying commodity-X sees to it that corresponding to every additional unit purchased, $P_X = MU_X$ (in terms of money value).

As he buys more of X, MU_X falls. Accordingly, as he buys more of X, price of X must fall. Because P_X must be equal to MU_X. Thus, law of demand is derived from the equation $MU_X = P_X$. Part (B) of the diagram shows that demand curve is just a shadow of MU curve for a commodity.

8. Derive market demand schedule of the individuals A, B and C.

Price (₹)	Demand of A (Units)	Demand of B (Units)	Demand of C (Units)
1	7	10	12
2	6	8	9
3	5	6	7
4	4	4	5
5	3	2	3

Ans. **Market Demand Schedule**

Price (₹)	Demand of A (Units)	Demand of B (Units)	Demand of C (Units)	Market Demand (Units)
1	7	10	12	7 + 10 + 12 = 29
2	6	8	9	6 + 8 + 9 = 23
3	5	6	7	5 + 6 + 7 = 18
4	4	4	5	4 + 4 + 5 = 13
5	3	2	3	3 + 2 + 3 = 8

9. Complete the following table and also draw the market demand curve.

Price (₹)	Quantity Demanded by Rohan (Units)	Quantity Demanded by Sohan (Units)	Market Demand (Units)
10	3	—	8
9	—	8	15
8	11	—	22
7	—	14	30
6	20	22	—

Ans.

Price (₹)	Quantity Demanded by Rohan (Units)	Quantity Demanded by Sohan (Units)	Market Demand (Units)
10	3	5	8
9	7	8	15
8	11	11	22
7	16	14	30
6	20	22	42

FIGURE 20

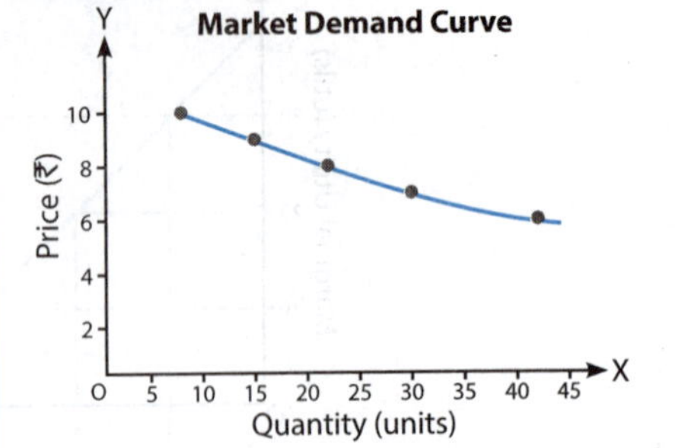

10. Suggest two policy initiatives to curb the consumption of narcotics in the country.

Ans. Two possible policy initiatives to curb the consumption of narcotics in the country are:

(i) Make it unlawful for the individuals and households to possess narcotics even in a small quantity.

(ii) Undertake awareness campaigns highlighting the fatal effects of the consumption of narcotics.

11. Suggest any two policy initiatives that the government can take through the market to decrease the consumption of diesel in the country, so that the environmental pollution is arrested.

Ans. Demand for diesel can be decreased in two ways, as under:

(i) Use of Substitute Fuel (CNG): The CNG (Compressed Natural Gas) is a substitute of petrol. It is much more environment-friendly than the diesel. The government should encourage the use of CNG through subsidy.

(ii) High Taxation on Diesel Vehicles: Excise duty on the production of diesel vehicles may be raised. So that, their market price rises to curb their demand.

12. On 16th December 2014, the following news was printed in the *Economic Times*:

"Petrol and diesel prices were cut by ₹ 2 per litre each as international oil prices slumped to a five-year low."

Use a diagram and economic theory to analyse the impact on the demand for cars in India.

Ans. When the prices of petrol and diesel are cut, the demand for cars is expected to rise. Because car and petrol are complementary goods. It implies that demand curve for cars will shift to the right. More cars are demanded at their existing price. Fig. 21 illustrates this situation.

Initially PK cars were purchased. As price of petrol and diesel decreases, PS cars are purchased even when price of cars is constant. Accordingly, demand curve for cars shifts forward from DD to D_1D_1.

FIGURE 21

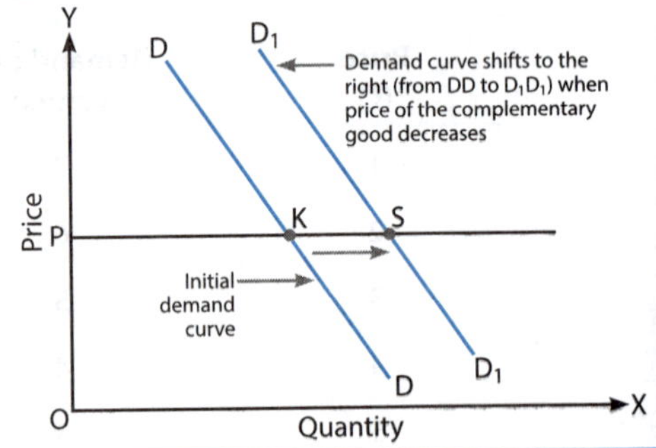

13. *"Petrol is becoming cheaper, yet the demand for cars is not rising."*

Does it mean that the law of demand is not operative?

Ans. Price of petrol and its impact on the demand for cars has nothing to do with the law of demand. Law of demand studies how quantity demanded of a commodity responds to changes in own price of the commodity. Change in price of petrol would lead to a shift in demand curve for the cars.

4. Evaluation (Value-based Questions)

1. Certain goods are demanded even when their price is zero. Does it mean that we are demanding even those goods which are not scarce?

Ans. Only scarce goods are demanded. Goods which are not scarce are available to us in plenty and they need not be demanded (though these may be needed, like sun and air). But, when goods are available to us at a zero price, we should not jump to the conclusion that these are not scarce. Goods are not scarce when two conditions are satisfied: (i) goods do not have price, and (ii) goods do not have any opportunity cost. Thus, medicines available in government hospitals at zero price are demanded. And these are scarce because these do have an opportunity cost, even when these are available at zero price.

2. Why should diamonds be priced so high and water be priced so low even when water is essential to sustain life while diamonds are not?

Ans. One should distinguish between 'value-in-use' and 'market value' of a commodity. Water has high 'value-in-use', of course. But its market value (price) is low (compared with diamonds) because it is available in plenty. In terms of its market supply, water is scarce, but not as scarce as diamonds. Therefore, market price of water is much lower than of the diamonds.

Imagine a situation when you are in a desert and you are dieing to quench your thirst. You are then ready to pay any amount for a glass of water. You might even be ready to forego a diamond in your possession just for a glass of water.

3. How do you account for a rise in demand for rice even when own price of rice was rising in the flood-ravaged Jammu & Kashmir state of India?

Ans. A rise in demand for rice (even when its price was rising) is to be ascribed to expectations of the people in flood-ravaged Jammu & Kashmir. They are crazy to buy more of rice even at a higher price fearing that rice may not be available in the near future as most stocks of it in the state had been washed away.

4. Why do people buy inferior goods at the first instance, even when their consumption is phased out as income rises?

Ans. Because inferior goods are essentials of life.

5. CBSE Questions—Past 4 years (With Answers or Reference to the Text for Answers)

1. What is market demand? *[CBSE Delhi 2012]*

   Or

   Give the meaning of market demand. *[CBSE Delhi 2013]*

   [Page 89]

2. Explain how do the following influence demand for a good:

   (i) Rise in income of the consumer.

   (ii) Fall in prices of the related goods. *[CBSE Delhi 2012]*

   [Page (i) 105, 106 (ii) 103, 104]

3. Give one reason for a shift in demand curve. *[CBSE (AI) 2012]*

   [Page 100, 101]

4. Explain the difference between inferior goods and normal goods. Give example in each case. *[CBSE (AI) 2012]*

   Or

   Explain the difference between an inferior good and a normal good. *[CBSE Delhi 2013]*

   [Page 92]

5. Explain the distinction between 'change in demand' and 'change in quantity demanded'. *[CBSE (F) 2012]*

   [Page 96, 97]

6. Explain the relationship between

   (i) Prices of other goods and demand for the given good.

   (ii) Income of the buyers and demand for a good. *[CBSE Delhi 2013]*

   [Page 91]

7. What does a rightward shift of demand curve indicate? *[CBSE (AI) 2013]*

   [Page 99]

8. How is the demand for a good affected by a rise in the prices of other goods? Explain. [CBSE (AI) 2013]

Or

How is the demand for a good affected by the rise in prices of related goods? Explain. [CBSE (F) 2013]
[Page 102–104]

9. What is a normal good? [CBSE (F) 2013]
[Page 92]

10. Give one reason for a rightward shift of demand curve. [CBSE (F) 2013]
[Page 100]

11. Give one reason for a leftward shift in demand curve. [CBSE (F) 2013]
[Page 101]

12. What is market demand for a good? Name the factors determining market demand. [CBSE Delhi 2014]
[Page 89, 91, 92]

13. Explain the change in demand for a good on account of change in prices of related goods.
[Page 102–104] [CBSE Delhi 2014; (F) 2014]

14. What happens to the demand for a good when consumer's income changes? Explain. [CBSE Delhi 2014]
[Page 104–106]

15. Give the meaning of "inferior" good and explain the same with the help of an example. [CBSE (AI) 2014]
[Page 92, 105, 106]

16. How does change in price of a substitute good affect the demand of the given good? Explain with the help of an example. [CBSE (AI) 2014]
[Page 102–104]

17. How does change in price of a complementary good affect the demand of the given good? Explain with the help of an example. [CBSE (AI) 2014]
[Page 103, 104]

18. Distinguish between an inferior good and a normal good. Is a good which is inferior for one consumer also inferior for all the consumers? Explain. [CBSE (F) 2014]
[Page 92, 106]

19. Distinguish between demand by an individual consumer and market demand of a good. Also state the factors leading to fall in demand by an individual consumer. [CBSE (F) 2014]
[Page 89, 91, 92]

20. When income of the consumer falls the impact on price-demand curve of an inferior good is: (choose the correct alternative) [CBSE Delhi 2015]
(a) shifts to the right
(b) shifts to the left
(c) there is upward movement along the curve
(d) there is downward movement along the curve
[(a)]

21. If due to fall in the price of Good-X, demand for Good-Y rises, the two goods are: (choose the correct alternative) [CBSE (AI) 2015]
(a) substitutes
(b) complements
(c) not related
(d) competitive
[(b)]

22. If with the rise in price of Good-Y, demand for Good-X rises, the two goods are: (choose the correct alternative) [CBSE (F) 2015]
(a) substitutes
(b) complements
(c) not related
(d) jointly demanded
[(a)]

6. NCERT Questions (With Hints to Answers)

1. Consider a market where there are just two consumers and suppose their demands for the good are given as follows:

p	d_1	d_2
1	9	24
2	8	20
3	7	18
4	6	16
5	5	14
6	4	12

Calculate market demand for the good.

[**Hint:**

p	d_1	d_2	Market Demand ($= d_1+d_2$)
1	9	24	$9 + 24 = 33$
2	8	20	$8 + 20 = 28$
3	7	18	$7 + 18 = 25$
4	6	16	$6 + 16 = 22$
5	5	14	$5 + 14 = 19$
6	4	12	$4 + 12 = 16$

2. What do you mean by a normal good?

   [**Hint:** It is a good whose demand increases with rise in income and decreases with fall in income of the consumer. So that, there is a positive relation between income and quantity demanded.]

3. What do you mean by an 'inferior good'? Give some examples.

   [**Hint:** It is a good whose demand decreases with rise in income and increases with fall in income of the consumer. So that, there is inverse (or negative) relation between income and quantity demanded. **Examples:** Coarse cloth, coarse grain.]

4. What do you mean by substitutes? Give examples of two goods which are substitutes of each other.

   [**Hint:** These are those goods which can be used in place of each other to satisfy a consumer's want. **Example:** Tea and coffee.]

5. What do you mean by complements? Give examples of two goods which are complements of each other.

   [**Hint:** These are those goods which complete the demand for each other. Two together satisfy a consumer's want. **Example:** Fountain pen and ink.]

7. Miscellaneous Questions and Reference to the Text for Answers

A. Questions of 3 & 4 marks each

1. Define demand. State the factors affecting demand for a commodity by a consumer.
   [Page 87, 91, 92]
2. Explain the law of demand with the help of a demand schedule.
   [Page 93]
3. Why does demand curve of a normal good slope downward from left to right?
   [Page 94]
4. Define increase in demand. What causes increase in demand?
   [Page 99, 100]

5. Define decrease in demand. What causes decrease in demand?
   [Page 100, 101]
6. State the determinants of the market demand curve.
   [Page 91, 92]
7. Distinguish between normal good and inferior good.
   [Page 92]
8. Distinguish between complementary good and substitute good.
   [Page 91]
9. Distinguish between 'change in demand' and 'change in quantity demanded'.

   Or

   Distinguish between 'movement along a demand curve' and 'shift in demand curve '.
   [Page 96, 97]
10. Distinguish between extension of demand and contraction of demand.
    [Page 101]
11. Distinguish between individual demand and market demand.
    [Page 89]
12. Distinguish between individual demand schedule and market demand schedule.
    [Page 89]
13. How is the market demand curve derived from the individual demand curves?
    [Page 90]
14. Define market demand. State the law of demand and the assumption behind it.
    [Page 89, 93, 94]
15. Explain the effect of increase in income of the consumer on the demand for a good.
    [Page 104–106]
16. Explain the effect of rise in the prices of related goods on the demand for a good.
    [Page 102–104]
17. What is the relation between Good-X and Good-Y in each case, if with fall in the price of Good-X demand for Good-Y (i) rises, and (ii) falls? Give reason.
    [Page 103, 104]

B. Questions of 6 marks each

1. Define market demand. Explain the factors that affect it.
   [Page 89, 91, 92]
2. Explain the factors that shift the demand curve to the right.
   [Page 100]
3. Explain the causes for a leftward shift of demand curve.
   [Page 101]
4. How is the demand of a commodity affected by changes in the price of related goods? Explain with the help of diagrams.
   [Page 102–104]
5. Explain the effect of the following on demand for a good:
   (i) Rise in income of its buyers.
   (ii) Fall in income of its buyers.
   [Page 104–106]

6. Explain with the help of diagrams, the effect of the following changes on the demand for a commodity:

(i) A rise in the price of substitute good.

(ii) A rise in the price of complementary good.

[Page 102–104]

7. Explain with the help of diagrams, the effect of the following changes on the demand for a commodity:

(i) Fall in the price of substitute good.

(ii) Fall in the price of complementary good.

[Page 102–104]

DOs and DON'Ts

1. Do not define inferior goods as those goods in case of which the law of demand fails. Inferior goods are those goods in the case of which income effect is negative or these are the goods, the demand for which decreases when income (NOT PRICE) increases. To repeat, **inferior goods have inverse relationship between income and demand, but not necessarily the positive relationship between price and demand.**

Yes, law of demand fails in case of **Giffen goods**. It is in the case of these goods that there is:

(i) inverse relationship between income and demand, and

(ii) positive relationship between price and demand.

Thus, while all Giffen goods are inferior goods (because of the inverse relationship between income and demand), all inferior goods are not Giffen goods (because they may not show inverse relationship between price and demand).

2. If the question relates to consumer's demand function, do not specify such determinants of demand as 'population size' and 'distribution of income'.

Consumer's demand refers to demand for a commodity by an individual consumer in the market. It has nothing to do with population size or distribution of income. Such determinants of demand are relevant only when the question relates to market demand function (referring to demand for a commodity by all the buyers in the market).

abilityZONE

❑ Price Effect (PE) = Substitution Effect (SE) + Income Effect (YE)

PE: It refers to change in Q_X owing to change in P_X. Often it is negative because P_X and Q_X are inversely related.

SE: It refers to change in Q_X owing to change in $\frac{P_X}{P_Y}$, when P_X changes. When P_X reduces, X becomes cheaper in relation to Y. Accordingly, more of X is purchased in place of Y. In case of all goods (normal or inferior) SE always subscribes to the inverse relation between P_X and Q_X.

YE: It refers to change in Q_X owing to change in real income/purchasing power of the consumer, when P_X changes. In case of normal goods, YE subscribes to the inverse relation between P_X and Q_X. In case of inferior goods, it does not.

PE is the combined effect of SE and YE.

Law of Demand and Inferior Goods

It is wrong to presume that law of demand fails in case of inferior goods. It may or may not. We know,

$$PE = SE + YE$$

SE always subscribes to the inverse relation between P_X and Q_X, no matter goods are normal or inferior.

YE does not subscribe to the inverse relation between P_X and Q_X in case of inferior goods. It defies this relationship.

But, in case of inferior goods, law of demand will fail only if YE is stronger than SE. It will not fail in case YE is weaker than SE.

> In case of inferior goods, law of demand will fail only if SE < YE. Not, if SE > YE.

Law of Demand and Giffen Goods

Giffen goods, by definition, are those goods in case of which there is a positive relation between P_X and Q_X. The law of demand must fail. These goods are so strongly inferior that the negative income effect exceeds the substitution effect. So that (instead of the inverse relation between P_X and Q_X), there is a positive relationship between P_X and Q_X.

Algebraic Expression of Demand Function and Some Related Questions

Algebraically, demand function is often studied as a functional relationship between price and quantity demanded of a commodity. This is expressed as:

$$Q_d = a - bP$$

Here,

Q_d = Quantity demanded of a commodity.

P = Own price of the commodity.

a = Constant, indicating quantity demanded even at zero price.

b = $\frac{\Delta Q}{\Delta P}$: ratio between change in quantity demanded and change in price. It indicates change in quantity for a unit change in price.

The actual equation could be:

$$Q_d = 1{,}000 - 20P$$

This equation allows us to estimate quantity demanded corresponding to different values of P. In other words, it allows us to draw a demand schedule or a demand curve.

Illustration

Let us assume that different values of P as: 10, 20, 30, 40, 50 (rupees).

The demand schedule

P	**Q_d**
10	1,000 – 20 × 10 = 1,000 – 200 = 800
20	1,000 – 20 × 20 = 1,000 – 400 = 600
30	1,000 – 20 × 30 = 1,000 – 600 = 400
40	1,000 – 20 × 40 = 1,000 – 800 = 200
50	1,000 – 20 × 50 = 1,000 – 1,000 = 0

[**Note:** The equation tells us that a = 1,000 which is constant, and the value of Q_d when P = 0.]

Diagrammatic presentation of the demand schedule yields the following demand curve:

FIGURE 22

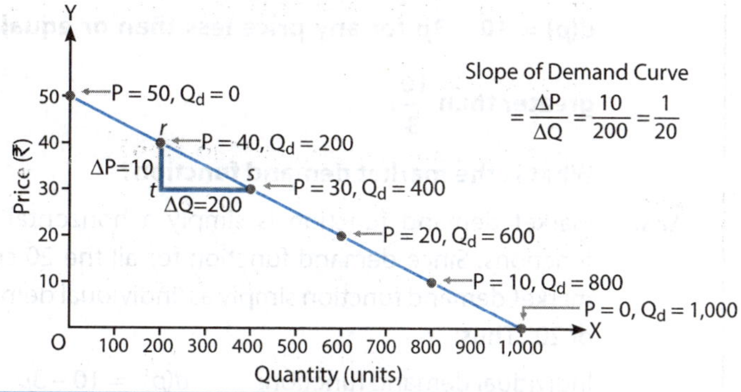

The table and the diagram tell us that every time P changes by 10 units and Q_d changes by 200 units. So that,

$$b = \frac{\Delta Q}{\Delta P} = \frac{200}{10} = 20$$

Or, Slope of demand curve $= \frac{\Delta P}{\Delta Q} = \frac{10}{200} = \frac{1}{20}$

Questions

1. Demand equation is given as:

$$\mathbf{Q_d = a - bP}$$

(i) What is there in this equation that makes the demand curve a straight line?

(ii) What happens to demand curve in case '*a*' increases?

(iii) What makes the demand curve slope downward?

Ans. (i) It is the constant value of *b* which makes the demand curve a straight line. (*b* indicates the rate at which Q_d changes in response to a change in P.)

(ii) In case *a* increases the demand curve will take a parallel shift to the right.

(iii) It is the inverse relationship between P and Q_d, as indicated by the '–' sign as a prefix to *b*.

2. Suppose there are two consumers in the market for a good and their demand functions are as follows:

$d_1(p) = 20 - p$ for any price less than or equal to 20, and $d_1(p) = 0$ at any price greater than 20.

$d_2(p) = 30 - 2p$ for any price less than or equal to 15 and $d_1(p) = 0$ at any price greater than 15.

Find out the market demand function. *[NCERT]*

Ans. Market demand function is simply a horizontal summation of individual demand functions. Since demand functions of two consumers are given, we can write market demand function simply as total of the 'individual demand functions of the two consumers'. Thus:

$$\text{Market demand function} = d_1(p) + d_2(p)$$

$$M_d(p) = 20 - p + 30 - 2p$$

$$= 50 - 3p$$

Hence, market demand function is $50 - 3p$ for any price greater than 15 and less than or equal to 20.

3. Suppose there are 20 consumers for a good and they have identical demand functions:

$d(p) = 10 - 3p$ for any price less than or equal to $\frac{10}{3}$ and $d_1(p) = 0$ at any price greater than $\frac{10}{3}$.

What is the market demand function? [*NCERT*]

Ans. Market demand function is simply a horizontal summation of individual demand functions. Since demand function for all the 20 consumers is identical, we can write market demand function simply as 'individual demand function multiplying by a factor of 20'. Thus:

Individual demand function: $d(p) = 10 - 3p$

Market demand function: $M_d(p) = 10 \times 20 - 3(20)\,p$

$= 200 - 60p$

Market demand function is $200 - 60p$ for any price less than or equal to $\frac{10}{3}$.

CHAPTER 5

Price Elasticity of Demand

TO DO

- Concept of Price Elasticity of Demand
- Measurement of Price Elasticity of Demand:
  (i) Percentage Change Method, and
  (ii) Geometric Method
- Relationship between Price Elasticity of Demand and Total Expenditure
- Factors Affecting Price Elasticity of Demand

1. Concept of Price Elasticity of Demand

In the previous chapter we learnt how quantity demanded is related to own price of the commodity. We learnt that decrease in own price of the commodity causes extension of demand, while increase in own price of the commodity causes contraction of demand. It is important to note that while discussing the concepts of extension and contraction of demand, we do not talk of the degree of change in quantity demanded; we only talk of the direction of change. Degree of change in quantity demanded (or the degree of extension and contraction) in response to change in own price of the commodity is the subject matter of elasticity of demand. In fact elasticity of demand is a measurement of the degree of change in demand in response to a given change in own price of the commodity. However, a notable point here is that while measuring the degree of change in demand (in response to change in own price of the commodity) we always consider percentage values, not the absolute values. Thus, we relate percentage change in quantity demanded to percentage change in own price of the commodity. Accordingly, price elasticity of demand (E_d) may be defined as a measurement of percentage change in quantity demanded in response to a given percentage change in own price of the commodity.

Price elasticity of demand is defined as a measurement of percentage change in quantity demanded in response to a given percentage change in own price of the commodity.

2. Measurement of Price Elasticity of Demand

There are two important methods of measuring price elasticity of demand:

(1) Proportionate or Percentage Method, and

(2) Geometric Method.

Following is a detailed description of these methods.

Elasticity of Demand always measures Percentage Change

It must be noted that elasticity of demand always measures percentage change in price of the commodity and its quantity demanded.

Reason: If percentage change is not taken or if absolute change is taken then unit of the commodity continues to exist in the estimation, and comparison of elasticity of two goods is ruled out in such a situation.

Example: Price of X (chairs) decreases from ₹ 10 to ₹ 5. Demand for X increases from 5 chairs to 10 chairs. If absolute change is taken then we can only say that 5 more chairs are demanded when price per chair is lowered to half. Likewise, one will say that 4 more buffaloes are purchased when price per buffalo is lowered to half. It hardly makes any sense, particularly when comparison of elasticity across goods X (chairs) and Y (buffaloes) is to be studied. Take a percentage change in P_X and D_X or P_Y and D_Y, unit of the commodity disappears and comparison of the elasticity is facilitated.

(1) Proportionate or Percentage Method

This is the most popular method of measuring price elasticity of demand. Under this method, elasticity of demand is measured by the ratio of the proportionate (percentage) change in quantity demanded to the proportionate (percentage) change in price. It is worked out as under:

$$E_d = (-)\frac{\text{Proportionate Change in Quantity Demanded}}{\text{Proportionate Change in Price}}$$

$$= (-)\frac{\dfrac{\text{Change in Demand}}{\text{Initial Demand}} \times 100}{\dfrac{\text{Change in Price}}{\text{Initial Price}} \times 100}$$

$$= (-)\frac{\dfrac{Q_1 - Q}{Q}}{\dfrac{P_1 - P}{P}} = (-)\frac{\dfrac{\Delta Q}{Q}}{\dfrac{\Delta P}{P}}$$

Or, $$E_d = (-)\frac{\Delta Q}{Q} \div \frac{\Delta P}{P} = (-)\frac{\Delta Q}{Q} \times \frac{P}{\Delta P}$$

Or, $$E_d = (-)\frac{P}{Q} \times \frac{\Delta Q}{\Delta P}$$

Here, E_d = Price elasticity of demand;

Q = Initial demand; Q_1 = New demand;

P = Initial price; P_1 = New price;

ΔQ = Change in demand; ΔP = Change in price.

EXAMPLES

Example 1.

Supposing the price of ice cream is ₹ 4 per cup and demand is for 1 cup. If the price of ice cream falls to ₹ 2 per cup demand increases to 4 cups. Find elasticity of demand, using proportionate method.

Solution:

$P = ₹\,4;\ P_1 = ₹\,2;\ \Delta P = P_1 - P = ₹\,2 - ₹\,4 = (-)\,₹\,2$

$Q = 1$ cup; $Q_1 = 4$ cups; $\Delta Q = Q_1 - Q = (4 - 1)$ cups $= 3$ cups

$$\text{Elasticity of demand } (E_d) = (-)\frac{P}{Q} \times \frac{\Delta Q}{\Delta P}$$

$$= (-)\frac{4}{1} \times \frac{3}{-2}$$

$$= 6$$

Ans. Elasticity of demand = 6.

It implies that 1 per cent fall in own price of the commodity causes 6 per cent rise in its quantity demanded.

Example 2.

When price of a good is ₹ 5, the consumer buys 20 units of that good. When price changes to ₹ 7, the quantity purchased changes to 12 units. Calculate the price elasticity of demand, using proportionate method.

Solution:

P = ₹ 5; P_1 = ₹ 7; $\Delta P = P_1 - P$ = ₹ 7 − ₹ 5 = ₹ 2

Q = 20 units; Q_1 = 12 units; $\Delta Q = Q_1 - Q$ = (12 − 20) units = (–) 8 units

$$\text{Price elasticity of demand } (E_d) = (-)\frac{P}{Q} \times \frac{\Delta Q}{\Delta P}$$

$$= (-)\frac{5}{20} \times \frac{-8}{2}$$

$$= 1$$

Ans. Price elasticity of demand = 1.

(2) Geometric Method

Geometric method measures price elasticity of demand at different points on the demand curve. It is also called 'point method of measuring elasticity of demand'. As specified in the syllabus, we are to use this method only with reference to a linear demand curve, which is a straight line demand curve, as in Fig. 1.

FIGURE 1

Estimation of Price Elasticity of Demand using Point Method

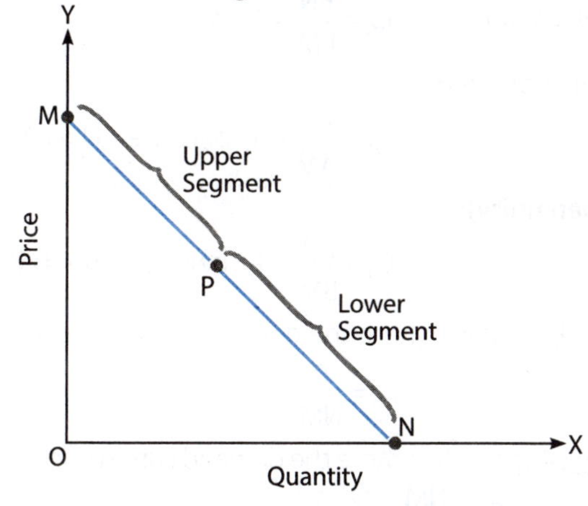

MN is a straight line demand curve sloping downward. A point (like P) can be taken anywhere on the demand curve. It divides the demand curve into two segments, lower segment (PN) and upper segment (PM).

$$E_d \text{ (at point P)} = \frac{\text{Lower Segment}}{\text{Upper Segment}} = \frac{PN}{PM}$$

In this figure, MN is a straight line demand curve. P is a specific point on the demand curve. The point P divides the demand curve into two segments, *viz.*, lower segment PN and upper segment PM. Elasticity of demand at point P is estimated as the ratio between lower segment (PN) and upper segment (PM).

$$E_d \text{(at P)} = \frac{\text{PN (Lower Segment from P)}}{\text{PM (Upper Segment from P)}}$$

Fig. 2 illustrates this point further. It shows elasticity of demand at different points of a straight line demand curve.

FIGURE 2 Price Elasticity of Demand at Different Points on Straight Line Demand Curve

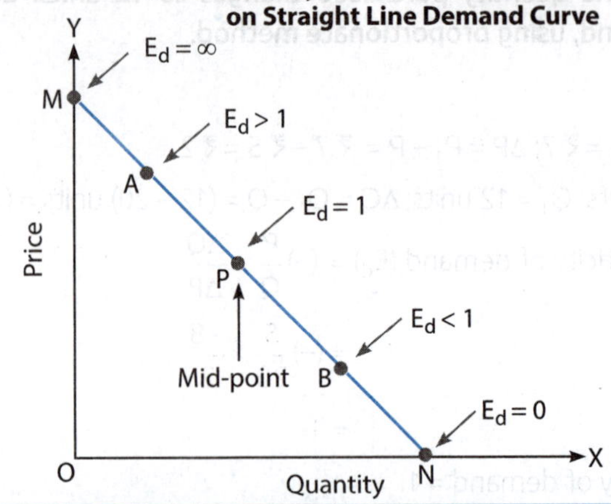

P is mid-point on the demand curve.

- At point P — $E_d = 1$ (∵ lower segment = upper segment)
- Between M and P — $E_d > 1$ (∵ lower segment > upper segment)
- Between P and N — $E_d < 1$ (∵ lower segment < upper segment)
- At point M — $E_d = \infty$ (because upper segment = 0)
- At point N — $E_d = 0$ (because lower segment = 0)

Following situations are evident from Fig. 2.

(i) $E_d = 1$ (unity): If point P is at the middle of the demand curve, then, lower segment = upper segment.

Accordingly, at point P $E_d = \frac{PN}{PM} = 1.$

(ii) $E_d > 1$ (greater than unity):

At point A $E_d = \frac{AN}{AM} > 1,$ because AN > AM.

(iii) $E_d < 1$ (less than unity):

At point B $E_d = \frac{BN}{BM} < 1,$ because BN < BM.

(iv) $E_d = 0$ (zero): At point N (where the demand curve touches the X-axis)

$$E_d = \frac{0}{NM} = 0.$$

(v) $E_d = \infty$ (infinity): At point M (where the demand curve touches the Y-axis)

$$E_d = \frac{NM}{0} = \infty.$$

[**Note:** Any real number divided by zero tends towards infinity.]

3. Relationship between Price Elasticity of Demand and Total Expenditure

Prof. Marshall works out a relationship between price elasticity of demand and total expenditure. He estimates the degree of price elasticity of demand depending on the change in total expenditure following a change in own price of the commodity. He observes three different situations, as under:

Situation 1: E_d = Unitary or $E_d = 1$

If rise or fall in own price of a commodity causes no change in total expenditure on the commodity, then elasticity of demand is unitary.

Example:

P_X		Q_X		Total Expenditure	
2 1	falls ↓	4 8	rises ↑	8 8	constant

Or

P_X		Q_X		Total Expenditure	
1 2	rises ↑	8 4	falls ↓	8 8	constant

E_d = Unitary **Or** $E_d = 1$ — No matter P_X increases or decreases, total expenditure remains constant.

Situation 2: E_d > Unitary or $E_d > 1$

If a fall in own price of a commodity causes a rise in total expenditure and a rise in price causes a fall in total expenditure on the commodity, then elasticity of demand is greater than unitary.

Example:

P_X		Q_X		Total Expenditure	
2 1	falls ↓	4 10	rises ↑	8 10	increases ↑

Or

P_X		Q_X		Total Expenditure	
1 2	rises ↑	10 4	falls ↓	10 8	decreases ↓

E_d > Unitary **Or** $E_d > 1$ — When P_X falls, total expenditure increases, and when P_X rises, total expenditure decreases. **P_X and total expenditure are inversely related.**

Situation 3: E_d < Unitary or $E_d < 1$

If a fall in own price of a commodity causes a fall in total expenditure and a rise in price causes a rise in total expenditure on the commodity, then elasticity of demand is less than unitary.

Example:

P_X		Q_X		Total Expenditure	
2 1	falls ↓	3 4	rises ↑	6 4	falls ↓

Or

P_X		Q_X		Total Expenditure	
1 2	rises ↑	4 3	falls ↓	4 6	rises ↑

E_d < Unitary **Or** $E_d < 1$ — When P_X falls, total expenditure also falls, and when P_X rises, total expenditure also rises. **P_X and total expenditure are positively related.**

These situations are further illustrated through Table 1.

Table 1. Relationship between Price Elasticity of Demand and Total Expenditure

Total Expenditure in response to a Fall in Price of the Commodity	Elasticity of Demand
Constant	Unitary Elastic $E_d = 1$
Increases	Greater than Unitary $E_d > 1$
Decreases	Less than Unitary $E_d < 1$

Diagrammatic Illustration

Diagrammatically, the relationship between price elasticity of demand and total expenditure is illustrated through Fig. 3.

FIGURE 3 **Relationship between Price Elasticity of Demand and Total Expenditure**

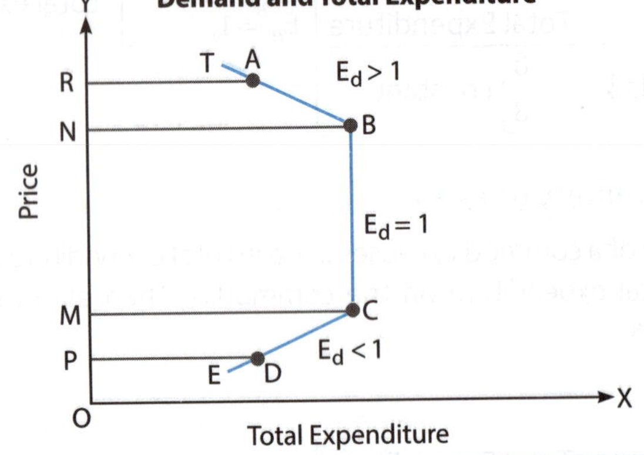

- TB shows inverse relationship between price and total expenditure. It is a situation when $E_d > 1$.
- EC shows positive relationship between price and total expenditure. It is a situation when $E_d < 1$.
- BC shows total expenditure as constant in response to increase or decrease in price. It is a situation when $E_d = 1$.

In this figure (Fig. 3), price is shown on Y-axis and total expenditure on X-axis. TE is total expenditure curve. BC part of TE curve represents unitary elastic demand. It shows that when price is OM, total expenditure is MC, as price rises to ON, total expenditure remains NB (= MC), *i.e.*, same as before. It corresponds to the situation when $E_d = 1$.

TB part of TE curve corresponds to the situation when $E_d > 1$. It shows that when price rises from ON to OR, total expenditure falls from NB to RA. Likewise, EC part of TE curve corresponds to the situation when $E_d < 1$. It shows that when price falls from OM to OP, total expenditure also falls from MC to PD.

Note

(i) Total expenditure method does not give us any exact value of elasticity. It only indicates three situations:

$E_d > 1$, $E_d < 1$ or $E_d = 1$.

—If $E_d > 1$, it is a situation of elastic demand.

—If $E_d < 1$, it is a situation of inelastic demand.

—If $E_d = 1$, it is a situation of unitary elastic demand.

(ii) TE in Fig. 3 is a total expenditure curve, not a demand curve.

(iii) **The relationship between 'change in price' and 'total expenditure' indicating different degrees of elasticity of demand is valid only on the assumption that there is inverse relationship between own price of a commodity and its quantity demanded.**

Example.

Find the degree of price elasticity of demand in the following cases, using total expenditure approach.

(1) Price (₹)	Quantity Demanded (Units)
8	100
10	90
(2) Price (₹)	**Quantity Demanded (Units)**
8	100
10	80

(3) Price (₹)	Quantity Demanded (Units)
8	100
10	70

Solution:

Case 1:

Price (₹)	Quantity Demanded (Units)	Total Expenditure (₹)
8	100	800
10	90	900

Ans. Elasticity of demand is less than unity. Because, in response to an increase in price, total expenditure has also risen even when quantity demanded has reduced.

Case 2:

Price (₹)	Quantity Demanded (Units)	Total Expenditure (₹)
8	100	800
10	80	800

Ans. Elasticity of demand is equal to unity. Because, in response to a change in price, total expenditure has not changed even when quantity demanded has reduced.

Case 3:

Price (₹)	Quantity Demanded (Units)	Total Expenditure (₹)
8	100	800
10	70	700

Ans. Elasticity of demand is more than unity. Because, in response to an increase in price, total expenditure has fallen even when quantity demanded has also reduced.

HOTS

Q.1. Given the fact that the slope of a straight line demand curve = $\frac{\Delta P}{\Delta Q}$, how do you relate it to own price elasticity of demand?

Ans. We know, E_d (own price elasticity of demand) = $\frac{\Delta Q}{\Delta P} \times \frac{P}{Q}$.

Given the fact that slope of demand curve = $\frac{\Delta P}{\Delta Q}$,

we can write that $E_d = \frac{1}{\text{Slope of demand curve}} \times \frac{P}{Q}$.

Q.2. The demand curve of a commodity is a straight line sloping downward as in the diagram. Write true or false against the following statements:

(i) Elasticity of demand is low corresponding to lower level of price of the commodity.

(ii) Elasticity of demand = 0, when price = 0.

(iii) Elasticity of demand at point 'D' < Elasticity of demand at point 'C'.

FIGURE 4

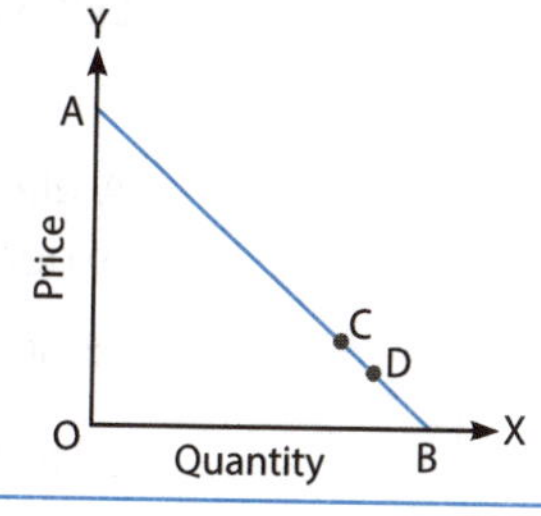

Ans. (i) The statement is true.

We know, $E_d = \frac{\text{Lower segment from a given point on demand curve}}{\text{Upper segment from a given point on demand curve}}$

At a lower level of price, lower segment tends to decrease while upper segment tends to increase. Implying that elasticity of demand reduces as price tends to be lower than before.

(ii) The statement is true.

Price = 0, at point B.

E_d at point B = $\frac{0}{AB} = 0$

∴ Elasticity of demand = 0, when price = 0.

(iii) The statement is true. Because $\frac{DB}{AD} < \frac{CB}{AC}$

∴ Elasticity of demand at point D is less than elasticity of demand at point C.

Demand Curves indicating $E_d > 1$, $E_d < 1$ and $E_d = 1$

We now present diagrammatic illustration of different degrees of elasticities of demand.

Situation 1: $E_d > 1$ (Greater than Unitary Elastic Demand)

Demand is greater than unitary elastic when change in quantity demanded in response to change in own price of the commodity is such that total expenditure on the commodity increases when price decreases, and total expenditure decreases when price increases.

FIGURE 5 **Greater than Unitary Elastic Demand [$E_d > 1$]**

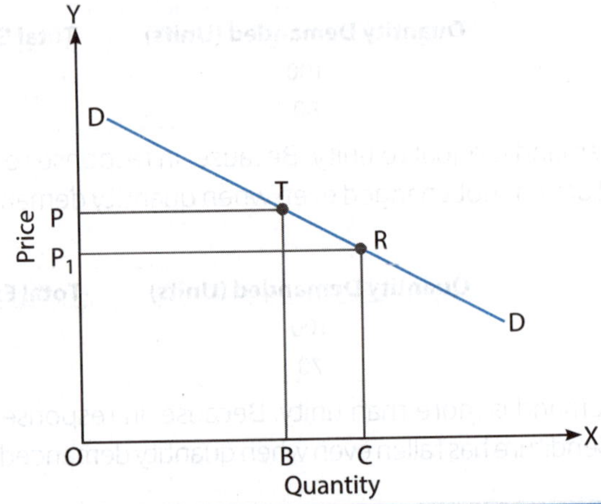

When price falls from OP to OP_1, total expenditure on the commodity increases (area $OCRP_1$ > area OBTP). Accordingly, elasticity at point T > 1.

$$\text{Total expenditure} = \text{Quantity purchased} \times \text{Price}$$

In Fig. 5, when price is OP, quantity demanded is OB, total expenditure is

OB (Quantity) × OP (Price) = area OBTP.

Likewise, when price falls to OP_1, quantity demanded is OC, total expenditure is

OC (Quantity) × OP_1 (Price) = area $OCRP_1$.

A glance at the diagram shows that area $OCRP_1$ > area OBTP. It implies that total expenditure increases in response to decrease in price of the commodity.

Hence, elasticity of demand is greater than unity (or $E_d > 1$).

Situation 2: $E_d < 1$ (Less than Unitary Elastic Demand)

Demand is less than unitary elastic when change in quantity demanded in response to change in own price of the commodity is such that total expenditure on the commodity decreases when price falls, and total expenditure increases when price rises.

In Fig. 6, at price OP, quantity demanded is OB, total expenditure is OB × OP = area OBTP. Likewise, when price is OP_1 and quantity demanded is OC, total expenditure is OC × OP_1 = area $OCRP_1$. Clearly, area $OCRP_1$ is smaller than area OBTP. It implies that total expenditure is reduced in response to fall in price of the commodity.

Hence, elasticity of demand is less than unity (or $E_d < 1$).

FIGURE 6

Less than Unitary Elastic Demand [$E_d < 1$]

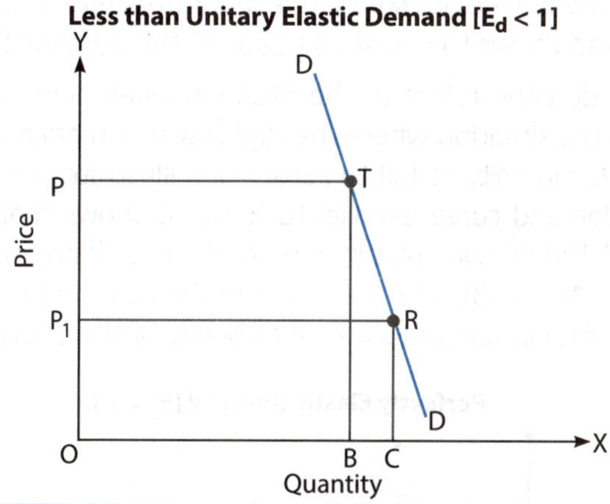

When price falls from OP to OP_1, total expenditure on the commodity also falls (area $OCRP_1$ < area OBTP). Accordingly, elasticity at point T < 1.

Situation3: $E_d = 1$ (Unitary Elastic Demand)

It is a situation when change in quantity demanded in response to change in own price of the commodity is such that total expenditure on the commodity remains constant.

FIGURE 7

Unitary Elastic Demand [$E_d = 1$]

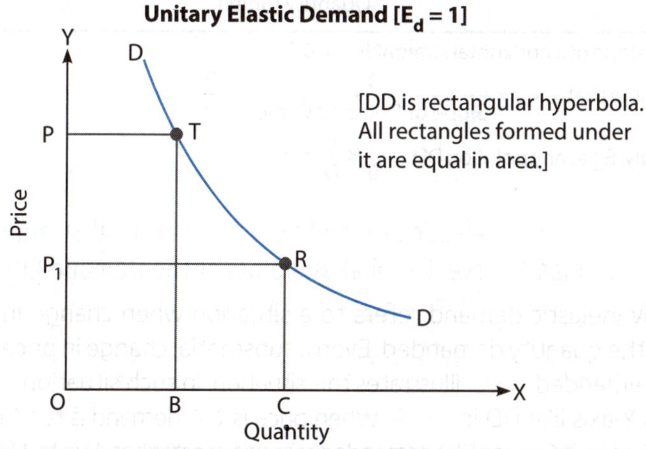

When price falls from OP to OP_1, total expenditure on the commodity remains constant (area OBTP = area $OCRP_1$). Accordingly, elasticity at point T = 1.

In Fig. 7, demand curve is drawn as a rectangular hyperbola. Its basic property is that all rectangles formed under this curve are equal in area. So that, area OBTP = area $OCRP_1$. Area OBTP indicates total expenditure when price is OP. Area $OCRP_1$ indicates total expenditure when price is OP_1. Since, area OBTP = area $OCRP_1$, it implies that total expenditure remains constant even after change in price of the commodity.

Hence, elasticity of demand is unity (or $E_d = 1$).

Three Distinct Situations:
Demand Curve indicating Same Elasticity of Demand at all its Points

We have learnt so far that a straight line downward sloping demand curve shows different elasticity at its different points. Because, as we move along the demand curve, the ratio between lower segment and upper segment tends to change. However, there are three distinct situations (or three distinct shapes of demand curve) when elasticity of demand is found to be the same at all points. These are as under:

Situation 1: Perfectly Elastic Demand Curve or a Horizontal Straight Line Demand Curve: $E_d = \infty$ at all points of the Demand Curve

A perfectly elastic demand refers to the situation when demand is infinite at the prevailing price. It is a situation where the slightest rise in price causes the quantity demanded of the commodity to fall to zero. Fig. 8 illustrates this situation. DD is a perfectly elastic demand curve, parallel to X-axis. It shows that if price is slightly increased from ₹ 4, the demand falls to zero. At the prevailing price of ₹ 4, quantity demanded may be 10, 20, 30 or any amount of the commodity. In such a situation, elasticity of demand is infinite (or $E_d = \infty$) at all points of the demand curve.

FIGURE 8

Perfectly Elastic Demand [$E_d = \infty$]

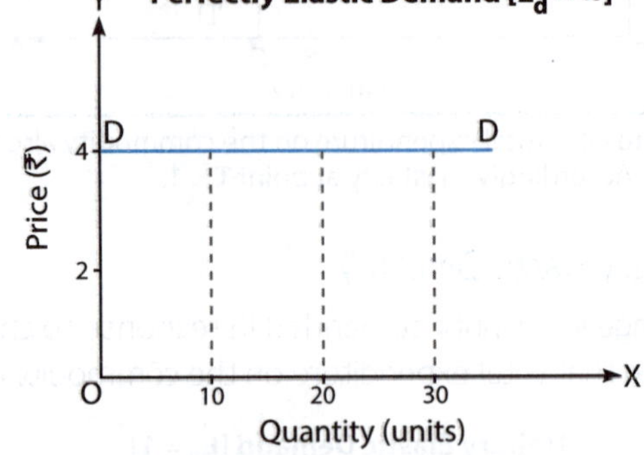

We know, slope of a horizontal straight line = 0.

We also know that, $E_d = \dfrac{1}{\text{Slope of Demand Curve}} \times \dfrac{P}{Q}$

Accordingly, E_d at any point on DD $= \dfrac{1}{0} \times \dfrac{P}{Q} = \infty$.

Situation 2: Perfectly Inelastic Demand Curve or a Vertical Straight Line Demand Curve: $E_d = 0$ at all points of the Demand Curve

A perfectly inelastic demand refers to a situation when change in price causes no change in the quantity demanded. Even a substantial change in price does not impact quantity demanded. Fig. 9 illustrates this situation. In such situations, demand curve is parallel to Y-axis like DD in Fig. 9. When price is ₹ 2, demand is for 4 units. When price rises to ₹ 4 or to ₹ 6, quantity demanded remains constant at 4 units. Hence, elasticity of demand is zero (or $E_d = 0$).

FIGURE 9

Perfectly Inelastic Demand [$E_d = 0$]

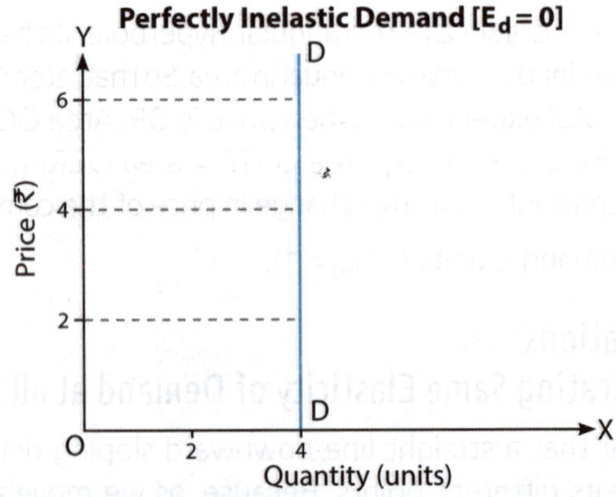

We know, slope of a vertical straight line = ∞.

We also know that, $E_d = \dfrac{1}{\text{Slope of Demand Curve}} \times \dfrac{P}{Q}$

Accordingly, E_d at any point on DD $= \dfrac{1}{\infty} \times \dfrac{P}{Q} = 0$.

Situation 3: Rectangular Hyperbola: $E_d = 1$ at all points of the Demand Curve

Elasticity of demand happens to be equal to unity (or equal to one) at all points of demand curve when demand curve is rectangular hyperbola. We have already noted that rectangular hyperbola is a curve under which all rectangular areas are equal. Because each rectangular area shows total expenditure on the commodity, it implies that total expenditure on the commodity remains constant, no matter what the price of the commodity is. Hence, elasticity of demand is unity (or $E_d = 1$) at all points of the demand curve as shown in Fig. 10.

FIGURE 10

Unitary Elastic Demand Corresponding to all points of the Demand Curve [$E_d = 1$ at all points of the Demand Curve]

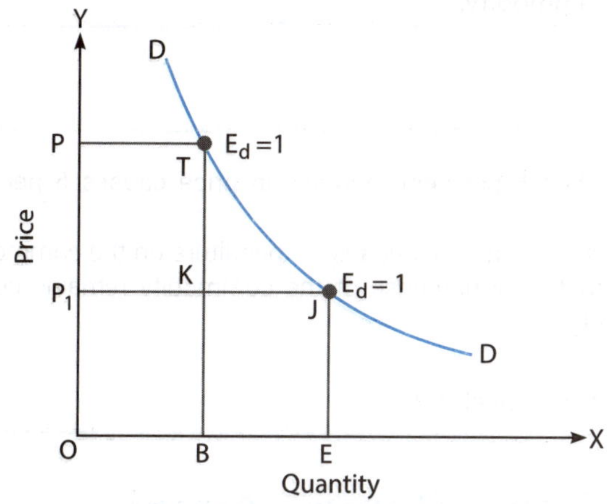

Demand curve is rectangular hyperbola. At any point on this demand curve, $E_d = 1$. Because total expenditure remains constant in response to increase or decrease in price of the commodity.

Flatter the Curve, Greater the Elasticity

Remember, if two demand curves are shooting from the same point, then flatter the curve, greater the elasticity of demand. Fig. 11 illustrates this situation.

FIGURE 11

Flatter Curve shows Higher Elasticity of Demand

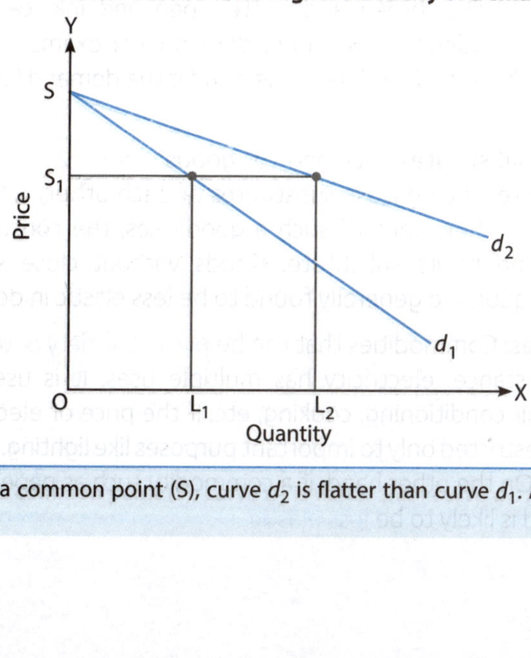

Shooting from a common point (S), curve d_2 is flatter than curve d_1. Accordingly, d_2 is more elastic than d_1.

Shooting from the common point S, demand curve d_2 is flatter and therefore, more elastic than demand curve d_1. This is how it happens:

If price of the commodity falls from OS to OS_1, demand curve d_1 shows a rise in quantity demanded from zero to OL_1, while demand curve d_2 shows a rise in quantity demanded from zero to OL_2. Implying that, for a given change in price, change in quantity is greater corresponding to d_2 than d_1. Hence, d_2 is more elastic than d_1.

Elastic and Inelastic Demand

Demand for a commodity is often categorised as 'elastic' or 'inelastic'. It is a standard practice to treat demand for a commodity as 'elastic' if $E_d > 1$ (elasticity of demand is greater than unity). Implying that percentage change in quantity demanded is greater than percentage change in price of the commodity. Demand is treated as 'inelastic' if $E_d < 1$ (elasticity of demand is less than unity). Implying that percentage change in quantity demanded is less than the percentage change in price of the commodity.

HOTS

Q.1. Find own price elasticity of demand when 5 per cent increase in price causes 5 per cent increase in expenditure on the commodity.

Ans. It is a situation of zero own price elasticity of demand. Because expenditure on the commodity is increasing proportionate to increase in price, so that total purchase of the commodity remains constant. Constant purchase means zero elasticity of demand.

Q.2. Why is demand for water inelastic?

Ans. Demand for water is inelastic, as water is an essential of life.

4. Factors Affecting Price Elasticity of Demand

Price elasticity of demand is high or low, depending on various factors. Some of the important determinants of price elasticity of demand are as under:

(1) Nature of Commodity: Ordinarily, necessaries like salt, kerosene oil, matchboxes, textbooks, seasonal vegetables, etc., have less than unitary elastic (inelastic) demand. Luxuries, like air-conditioner, costly furniture, fashionable garments, etc., have greater than unitary elastic demand. Comforts like milk, transistor, cooler, fans, etc., have neither very elastic nor very inelastic demand. Jointly demanded goods, like, bread and butter, pen and ink, camera and film, ordinarily show a moderate elasticity of demand. For example, rise in price of butter will not substantially reduce its demand if the demand for bread has not decreased.

(2) Availability of Substitutes: Demand for goods which have close substitutes (like, tea and coffee, being close substitutes of each other) is relatively more elastic. Because, when price of such a good rises, the consumers have the option of shifting to its substitute. Goods without close substitutes like cigarettes and liquor, are generally found to be less elastic in demand.

(3) Diversity of Uses: Commodities that can be put to a variety of uses have elastic demand. For instance, electricity has multiple uses. It is used for lighting, room-heating, air conditioning, cooking, etc. If the price of electricity increase, its use may be restricted only to important purposes like lighting. Other uses may be abandoned. On the other hand, if a commodity such as paper has only a few uses, its demand is likely to be less elastic.

(4) Postponement of Use: Demand will be elastic for goods, the consumption of which can be postponed. Demand for residential houses may be cited as an example. People often defer their demand for residential houses when interest rates on the loans are high.

(5) Income Level of the Buyers: Elasticity of demand for a good also depends on the income level of its buyers. If the buyers of a good are high-end consumers (with high level of income) they will not be bothered by a rise in its price. Accordingly, elasticity of demand is expected to be low. **Example:** Demand for luxury cars by the multi-billionaires. On the other hand, if income level of the buyers of a good is low, elasticity of demand is expected to be high. **Example:** Demand for small cars by the middle class people in India.

(6) Habit of Consumers: Goods to which consumers become accustomed or habitual will have inelastic demand like cigarette and tobacco. It is because of this factor that the demand for cigarettes and liquor does not reduce even when these goods are highly taxed.

(7) Proportion of Income Spent on a Commodity: Goods on which consumers spend a small proportion of their income (toothpaste, boot-polish, newspaper, needles, etc.), will have an inelastic demand. On the other hand, goods on which the consumers spend a large proportion of their income (cloth, scooter, etc.), tend to have elastic demand.

(8) Price Level: Elasticity of demand also depends on the level of price of the concerned commodity. Elasticity of demand will be high at higher level of the price of the commodity and low at the lower level of the price.

(9) Time Period: Demand is inelastic in short period but elastic in long period. It is because, in the long run, a consumer can change his consumption habits more conveniently than in the short period.

Briefly, goods with multiple uses, carrying a high price tag, and having a large number of close substitutes tend to show higher elasticity of demand than the goods which are low priced, are essentials of life and do not have close substitutes.

POWER POINTS

- Price Elasticity of Demand is a ratio between percentage change in quantity demanded and percentage change in own price of the commodity.
- Methods of Measurement of Price Elasticity of Demand are:
  (i) Proportionate Method, (ii) Geometric Method or Point Method.
- Proportionate or Percentage Method: $E_d = (-)\frac{P}{Q} \times \frac{\Delta Q}{\Delta P}$.
- Geometric Method: $E_d = \frac{\text{Lower Segment of the Demand Curve}}{\text{Upper Segment of the Demand Curve}}$ [Corresponding to a given point on the demand curve]
- Relation between Price Elasticity of Demand and Total Expenditure: Price elasticity of demand is said to be unity ($E_d = 1$) when total expenditure on the commodity remains constant, no matter price of the commodity increases or decreases.

  Price Elasticity of Demand is said to be greater than unity ($E_d > 1$) when total expenditure on the commodity increases in response to decrease in its price, and when total expenditure on the commodity decreases in response to increase in its price.

Price Elasticity of Demand is said to be less than unity ($E_d < 1$) when total expenditure on the commodity increases in response to increase in its price, and when total expenditure on the commodity decreases in response to decrease in its price.

- Elastic Demand is a situation when $E_d > 1$. Diagrammatically, it is indicated by a point on the upper segment (upper-half) of the straight line demand curve.
- Inelastic Demand is a situation when $E_d < 1$. Diagrammatically, it is indicated by a point on the lower segment (lower-half) of the straight line demand curve.
- Unitary Elastic Demand is a situation when $E_d = 1$. Diagrammatically, it is indicated by a mid-point on the straight line demand curve.
- Perfectly Elastic Demand Curve is a horizontal straight line, parallel to X-axis. It shows $E_d = \infty$ at all points of the demand curve.
- Perfectly Inelastic Demand Curve is a vertical straight line, parallel to Y-axis. It shows $E_d = 0$ at all points of the demand curve.
- Rectangular Hyperbola Demand Curve shows $E_d = 1$ at all points of the demand curve.
- Factors Affecting Elasticity of Demand are:
  (i) Nature of commodity,
  (ii) Availability of substitutes,
  (iii) Diversity of uses,
  (iv) Postponement of use,
  (v) Income level of the buyers,
  (vi) Habit of consumers,
  (vii) Proportion of income spent on a commodity,
  (viii) Price level,
  (ix) Time period.

EXERCISE

1. Very Short Questions (Remembering & Understanding) (1 mark each)

A. Multiple Choice Questions: Choose the Correct Answer

1. The subject matter of elasticity of demand is:

(a) direction of change in response to change in own price of the commodity

(b) degree of change in response to change in own price of the commodity

(c) absolute change in response to change in own price of the commodity

(d) none of these

2. $(-)\frac{P}{Q} \times \frac{\Delta Q}{\Delta P}$ **is the formula of measuring price elasticity of demand through:**

(a) proportionate method
(b) percentage method
(c) geometric method
(d) both (a) and (b)

3. When there is no change in quantity demanded in response to any change in price, it is a situation of:

(a) zero price elasticity
(b) infinite price elasticity
(c) unitary price elasticity
(d) none of these

4. When demand curve is parallel to X-axis, elasticity of demand is:

(a) unity
(b) zero
(c) greater than unity
(d) infinity

5. On all points of a rectangular hyperbola demand curve, elasticity of demand is:

(a) equal to unity
(b) zero
(c) greater than unity
(d) less than unity

6. **$E_d > 1$ represents:**
(a) elastic demand
(b) inelastic demand
(c) unitary elastic demand
(d) none of these

7. **When percentage change in demand is less than percentage change in price, demand is:**
(a) perfectly inelastic
(b) perfectly elastic
(c) more than unitary elastic
(d) less than unitary elastic

8. **At the mid-point of a straight line downward sloping demand curve, elasticity of demand (E_d) is:**
(a) 2
(b) 0.5
(c) 1
(d) 4

9. **When total expenditure increases in response to decrease in the price of the commodity, the elasticity of demand is:**
(a) greater than unity
(b) less than unity
(c) unity
(d) infinity

10. **When percentage change in demand is more than percentage change in price, demand is:**
(a) inelastic
(b) elastic
(c) perfectly inelastic
(d) perfectly elastic

11. **What will be the elasticity of demand when demand curve is parallel to Y-axis?**
(a) Unity
(b) Zero
(c) Less than unity
(d) More than unity

12. **If due to fall in price, total expenditure on the commodity falls, it indicates:**
(a) a case of inferior good
(b) price elasticity of demand is less than unity
(c) price elasticity of demand is greater than unity
(d) price elasticity of demand is infinity

13. **A consumer demands 5 units of a commodity at the price of ₹ 4 per unit. He demands 10 units when the price falls to ₹ 3 per unit. Price elasticity of demand is equal to:**
(a) 3
(b) 4
(c) 2
(d) 1.5

14. **Using total expenditure approach, find E_d when price and demand are as under:**

Price	10	15
Demand	40	20

(a) $E_d = 1$
(b) $E_d < 1$
(c) $E_d > 1$
(d) $E_d = 0$

15. **As the flatness of the demand curve increases, the elasticity of demand becomes:**
(a) higher
(b) lower
(c) equal to infinity
(d) equal to zero

16. **The demand for sugar and tea is usually:**
(a) elastic
(b) inelastic
(c) perfectly elastic
(d) perfectly inelastic

17. **Availability of close substitutes makes the demand:**
(a) less elastic
(b) more elastic
(c) parallel to X-axis
(d) parallel to Y-axis

18. In case of $E_d = \infty$, demand curve is:

(a) parallel to X-axis
(b) a straight line
(c) parallel to Y-axis
(d) none of these

19. When 8% decrease in price of a commodity causes 2% increase in expenditure of the commodity, the elasticity of demand is:

(a) zero
(b) greater than one
(c) less than one
(d) unity

20. Elasticity is greater than unity for:

(a) necessaries
(b) luxuries
(c) complementary goods
(d) comforts

21. When slope of demand curve = 0, the elasticity of demand is:

(a) 0
(b) 1
(c) ∞
(d) none of these

22. For a commodity, $\frac{\Delta P}{P} = (-)\ 0.2$ and elasticity of demand $= (-)\ 0.3$, the percentage change in quantity demanded is:

(a) 6
(b) 40
(c) (–) 6
(d) 10

Answers

1. (b) **2.** (d) **3.** (a) **4.** (d) **5.** (a) **6.** (a) **7.** (d) **8.** (c) **9.** (a) **10.** (b) **11.** (b) **12.** (b)
13. (b) **14.** (c) **15.** (a) **16.** (b) **17.** (b) **18.** (a) **19.** (b) **20.** (b) **21.** (c) **22.** (a)

B. Information & Concept-based Questions

1. What is meant by price elasticity of demand?

Ans. Price elasticity of demand is a measurement of the percentage change in demand in response to a given percentage change in own price of the commodity $\left[E_d = (-)\frac{\Delta Q}{\Delta P} \times \frac{P}{Q}\right]$.

2. What is meant by perfectly elastic demand?

Ans. Perfectly elastic demand implies infinite change in quantity demanded as a result of a slight change in price.

3. What is meant by perfectly inelastic demand?

Ans. Perfectly inelastic demand refers to a situation in which any percentage change in price causes no change in quantity demanded. In other words, change in price causes no change in demand.

4. When is elasticity of demand called unitary?

Ans. When the proportionate change in quantity demanded is same as the proportionate change in price, elasticity of demand is called unitary.

5. What will be the elasticity of demand for goods to which the consumer is habituated?

Ans. Elasticity of demand will be less than unity or inelastic for the goods to which the consumer is habituated.

6. What will be the elasticity of demand in terms of the relationship between price and total expenditure, given the following information?

Price (₹)	Quantity Demanded (Units)
5	4
4	5

Ans.

Price (₹)	Quantity Demanded (Units)	Total Expenditure (₹)
5	4	20
4	5	20

Demand will be unitary elastic, because total expenditure remains the same despite fall in price.

7. Give the formula of graphic method to find out elasticity of demand.

Ans. $E_d = \frac{\text{Lower Segment of the Demand Curve}}{\text{Upper Segment of the Demand Curve}}$

8. Give the formula to find out elasticity of demand by percentage method.

Ans. $E_d = (-)\frac{\Delta Q}{\Delta P} \times \frac{P}{Q}$

9. The demand for a commodity does not change with the increase in its price from ₹ 5 to ₹ 10. What is its elasticity of demand?

Ans. The elasticity of demand is zero (or $E_d = 0$) because change in price causes no change in demand.

10. Why is perfectly elastic demand curve parallel to X-axis?

Ans. Perfectly elastic demand curve is a horizontal straight line, parallel to X-axis because it is a situation where the slightest change in price causes an infinite change in demand.

11. Give the formula to measure elasticity of demand on a straight line demand curve.

Ans. $E_d = \frac{\text{Lower Segment of the Demand Curve}}{\text{Upper Segment of the Demand Curve}}$ (at a particular point on a straight line demand curve)

2. Reason-based Questions (Comprehension of the Subject-matter)

Read the following statements carefully. Write 'True' or 'False' with a reason.

1. Elasticity of demand refers to change in quantity consequent upon change in price of the commodity.

Ans. False. Elasticity of demand is always measured as a percentage change in quantity demanded in response to a percentage change in price.

2. If 2% increase in P_X is accompanied with constant expenditure on the commodity, elasticity of demand = 1.

Ans. True. Because increase in price is not causing any change in expenditure on the commodity.

3. Price elasticity of demand is identical with slope of demand curve.

Ans. False. We know, $E_d = \frac{\Delta Q}{\Delta P} \times \frac{P}{Q}$

Slope of the demand curve $= \frac{\Delta P}{\Delta Q}$

So that, $E_d = \frac{1}{\text{Slope of demand curve}} \times \frac{P}{Q}$

4. When total expenditure on the commodity remains constant, price elasticity of demand also remains constant, no matter price of the commodity increases or decreases.

Ans. True. When total expenditure on the commodity remains constant, price elasticity of demand also remains constant (which is equal to one), no matter price of the commodity increases or decreases. Because there is proportionate opposite change in quantity in response to a given change in own price of the commodity (such that the total expenditure does not change).

5. If price elasticity of demand is zero, it means expenditure on the commodity does not change with change in price of the commodity.

Ans. False. When $E_d = 0$, demand remains constant, no matter what the price is. Implying that total expenditure may increase/decrease, but not the quantity demanded.

6. Elasticity of demand (with respect to price of the commodity) is constant along a straight line demand curve.

Ans. False. Price elasticity of demand along a straight line demand curve is different at different points on the demand curve. Because, at a particular point on the demand curve, $E_d = \frac{\text{Lower segment}}{\text{Upper segment}}$, which tends to change from point to point.

7. A horizontal straight line demand curve shows zero elasticity of demand.

Ans. False. A horizontal straight line demand curve parallel to X-axis shows infinite elasticity of demand ($E_d = \infty$). Because, slope of a horizontal straight line = 0.

So that,
$$E_d = \frac{1}{\text{Slope of demand curve}} \times \frac{P}{Q}$$
$$= \frac{1}{0} \times \frac{P}{Q} = \infty$$

8. A vertical straight line demand curve shows that demand rises to infinity even when price remains constant.

Ans. False. A vertical straight line demand curve parallel to Y-axis shows no change in the demand irrespective of change in price. So that, $E_d = 0$.

9. If slope of two demand curves is the same, they show the same elasticity of demand.

Ans. False. Because, $E_d = \frac{1}{\text{Slope of demand curve}} \times \frac{P}{Q}$

When slope of two demand curves is the same, elasticity of demand depends on the initial price and initial quantity of the commodity.

10. When slope of demand curve = 0, price elasticity of demand = ∞.

Ans. True. We know

$$E_d = \frac{1}{\text{Slope of demand curve}} \times \frac{P}{Q}$$
$$= \frac{1}{0} \times \frac{P}{Q} = \infty$$

11. When slope of demand curve = ∞, price elasticity of demand = 0.

Ans. True. We know

$$E_d = \frac{1}{\text{Slope of demand curve}} \times \frac{P}{Q}$$
$$= \frac{1}{\infty} \times \frac{P}{Q} = 0$$

12. From a point of intersection of the two demand curves, a flatter demand curve shows higher elasticity of demand.

Ans. True. Because, at the point of intersection:

— percentage change in price is the same for both the demand curves.

— initial quantity demanded is the same for both the demand curves. Change in quantity demanded is higher in case of flatter demand curve. Implying that percentage change in quantity demanded in response to a given percentage change in price is higher corresponding to the flatter demand curve. See Fig. 11 of this chapter.

13. Complementary goods often exhibit low elasticity of demand.

Ans. True. Complementary goods often exhibit low elasticity of demand. Because, increase or decrease in the demand for Good-1 causes a simultaneous increase or decrease in the demand for Good-2 even when price of Good-2 has not changed.

14. Luxuries of life often exhibit low elasticity of demand.

Ans. False. Luxuries of life have greater elasticity of demand. Change in their prices has a great effect on their demand. Because, these goods are not essentials of life and their purchase requires high percentage of income.

15. Greater the alternative uses of a commodity, lesser is the elasticity of demand.

Ans. False. Commodities having variety of uses have elastic demand. Because, at lower price, the commodity can be put to several uses.

16. Higher the price level, higher should be the elasticity of demand.

Ans. True. Elasticity of demand will be high at higher level of price of the commodity. Because corresponding to higher level of P_X, the ratio $\left(\frac{\text{lower segment}}{\text{upper segment}}\right)$ tends to be high.

3. HOTS & Applications

1. If 7% increase in P_X causes 7% increase in expenditure on Good-X, elasticity of demand = 1. Comment.

Ans. No. It is a situation of zero price elasticity of demand. Because, when expenditure on the commodity is increasing proportionate to increase in price, total purchase of the commodity remains constant. Constant purchase means zero elasticity of demand.

2. Price of the commodity increases from ₹ 10 to ₹ 12 per unit and expenditure on the commodity increases by 20%. Give a logical support to your answer.

Ans. It is a situation when 20% increase in price leads to 20% increase in expenditure on the commodity. It implies that quantity demanded remains constant. Accordingly, $E_d = 0$.

3. In a situation when price of the commodity falls, and elasticity of demand is greater than unity, should total expenditure on the commodity be increasing, decreasing or remain constant. Give reason.

Ans. Total expenditure on the commodity should increase in a situation when price of the commodity falls and elasticity of demand is greater than unity.

Increase in total expenditure on the commodity (despite the fact that price of the commodity has fallen) suggests a substantial (or more than proportionate) increase in demand for the commodity in response to a fall in its price. Hence, elasticity of demand should be greater than one or greater than unity.

4. Elasticity of demand is different at different points of a demand curve, unless demand curve is a rectangular hyperbola. Comment.

Ans. Yes. Elasticity of demand happens to be equal to one at all points of demand curve when demand curve is a rectangular hyperbola. In case, demand curve is a straight line sloping downward, elasticity must be different at its different points. Because, $E_d = \frac{\text{lower segment}}{\text{upper segment}}$. This ratio change as we move from one point to the other.

5. A commodity showing high elasticity of demand often has a large number of close substitutes in the market. Do you agree?

Ans. Yes, we agree with the give statement. Elasticity of demand is high in case of goods with close substitutes (for example, tea has its substitute in coffee). Availability of close substitutes makes it possible for the consumer to switch from one commodity (like tea) to the other (like coffee) in response to change in the relative price structure. Accordingly, elasticity of demand is high.

6. Elasticity of demand is generally high during the long period compared to the short period. Why?

Ans. Elasticity of demand is generally high during the long period. Because, during the short period, full adjustment in demand (to a change in price) may not be possible owing to rigid consumption habits of the consumers. For example, in response to a substantial increase in price of wine, the consumers may not immediately reduce the consumption of wine. However, they may plan to give up or reduce the consumption of wine gradually over a long period of time.

7. At ₹ 26 per unit, the demand for a commodity is 30 units. If the price increases from ₹ 26 to ₹ 30 per unit, the demand decreases to 15 units. Calculate the price elasticity of demand.

Ans. Given, $P = ₹\ 26; P_1 = ₹\ 30; \Delta P = P_1 - P = ₹\ 30 - ₹\ 26 = ₹\ 4$

$Q = 30$ units; $Q_1 = 15$ units; $\Delta Q = Q_1 - Q = (15 - 30)$ units $= (-)\ 15$ units

$$\text{Price elasticity of demand } (E_d) = (-)\frac{P}{Q} \times \frac{\Delta Q}{\Delta P} = (-)\frac{26}{30} \times \frac{-15}{4} = 3.25$$

Price elasticity of demand = 3.25.

8. Price elasticity of demand is found to be (–) 2. Price falls from ₹ 10 per unit to ₹ 8 per unit. Find the percentage increase in quantity demanded.

Ans. Given, $P = ₹\ 10; P_1 = ₹\ 8; \Delta P = P_1 - P = ₹\ 8 - ₹\ 10 = (-)\ ₹\ 2$

$E_d = (-)\ 2$

$$\text{Percentage change in price} = \frac{\Delta P}{P} \times 100$$

$$= \frac{-2}{10} \times 100 = (-)\ 20 \text{ per cent}$$

$$\text{Price elasticity of demand } (E_d) = \frac{\text{Percentage change in quantity demanded}}{\text{Percentage change in price}}$$

$$-2 = \frac{\text{Percentage change in quantity demanded}}{-20\%}$$

Percentage change in quantity demanded = (–) 2 × (–) 20 per cent = 40 per cent

Percentage increase in quantity demanded = 40%.

9. When price of a good rises from ₹ 20 per unit to ₹ 23 per unit, its demand falls by 30 per cent. Calculate price elasticity of demand.

Ans. Given, $P = ₹\ 20; P_1 = ₹\ 23; \Delta P = P_1 - P = ₹\ 23 - ₹\ 20 = ₹\ 3$

$$\text{Percentage change in price} = \frac{\Delta P}{P} \times 100 = \frac{3}{20} \times 100 = 15 \text{ per cent}$$

Percentage change in quantity demanded = (–) 30 per cent

$$\text{Price elasticity of demand } (E_d) = (-)\frac{\text{Percentage change in quantity demanded}}{\text{Percentage change in price}}$$

$$= (-)\frac{-30\%}{15\%} = 2$$

Price elasticity of demand = 2.

10. For a commodity, $\frac{\Delta P}{P} = -0.2$, and elasticity of demand = –0.6. Find percentage change in quantity demanded.

Ans. $$\text{Percentage change in price} = \frac{\Delta P}{P} \times 100$$

$$= -0.2 \times 100 = (-)\ 20 \text{ per cent}$$

$$\text{Elasticity of demand } (E_d) = \frac{\text{Percentage change in quantity demanded}}{\text{Percentage change in price}}$$

$$-0.6 = \frac{\text{Percentage change in quantity demanded}}{-20\%}$$

Percentage change in quantity demanded = (–) 0.6 × (–) 20 per cent = 12 per cent

Percentage change in quantity demanded = 12%.

11. From the following table, calculate price elasticity of demand by the percentage method.

Price of X (₹ per unit)	Total Expenditure (₹)
4	600
5	525

Ans.

Price of X (₹ per unit)	Total Expenditure (₹)	Demand (Units)
4	600	$\frac{600}{4} = 150$
5	525	$\frac{525}{5} = 105$

Here, P = ₹ 4; P_1 = ₹ 5; $\Delta P = P_1 - P$ = ₹ 5 – ₹ 4 = ₹ 1

Q = 150 units; Q_1 = 105 units; $\Delta Q = Q_1 - Q$ = (105 – 150) units = (–) 45 units

$$\text{Price elasticity of demand } (E_d) = (-)\frac{P}{Q} \times \frac{\Delta Q}{\Delta P}$$

$$= (-)\frac{4}{150} \times \frac{-45}{1} = 1.2$$

Price elasticity of demand = 1.2.

12. Price of the commodity increases from ₹ 50 to ₹ 60 per unit. Quantity demanded initially was 200 units. What should be the new quantity so that elasticity of demand is established to be unitary?

Ans. P = ₹ 50; P_1 = ₹ 60; $\Delta P = P_1 - P$ = ₹ 60 – ₹ 50 = ₹ 10; Q = 200 units; $E_d = 1$

We know,

$$\text{Price elasticity of demand } (E_d) = (-)\frac{P}{Q} \times \frac{\Delta Q}{\Delta P}$$

$$1 = (-)\frac{50}{200} \times \frac{\Delta Q}{10}$$

$$1 = (-)\frac{\Delta Q}{40}$$

$$\Delta Q = (-)\,40$$

$$Q_1 = Q + \Delta Q$$

$$\text{New quantity} = 200 + (-)\,40$$

$$= 200 - 40 = 160$$

In order to get unitary elasticity, new quantity should be 160 units.

13. When the price of a good changes to ₹ 3 per unit, the consumer's demand rises from 18 units to 30 units. The price elasticity of demand is 1. What was the price before change? Use expenditure approach of price elasticity of demand to answer this question.

Ans.

Price (₹)	Demand (Units)	Total Expenditure (₹)
5	18	90
3	30	90

Given the fact that, price elasticity of demand is 1, total expenditure should remain constant even after the change in price. Total expenditure remaining constant at ₹ 90, the initial quantity (18 units) implies that the initial price should be:

$$= \frac{\text{Initial expenditure}}{\text{Initial quantity}}$$

$$= \frac{₹\,90}{18} = ₹\,5.$$

Price before change = ₹ 5.

14. A consumer spends ₹ 1,500 on a good priced at ₹ 10 per unit. When price rises by 20 per cent, the consumer continues to spend ₹ 1,500 on the good. Calculate price elasticity of demand by percentage method.

Ans. Initial price (P) = ₹ 10

Rise in price by 20 per cent $= 10 \times \frac{20}{100} = ₹\,2$

New price (P_1) = ₹ 10 + ₹ 2 = ₹ 12

Given, P = ₹ 10; P_1 = ₹ 12; $\Delta P = P_1 - P$ = ₹ 12 – ₹ 10 = ₹ 2

$$Q = \frac{1{,}500}{10} = 150 \text{ units}; \; Q_1 = \frac{1{,}500}{12} = 125 \text{ units}; \; \Delta Q = Q_1 - Q = (125 - 150) \text{ units} = (-)\,25 \text{ units}$$

$$\text{Price elasticity of demand } (E_d) = (-)\frac{P}{Q} \times \frac{\Delta Q}{\Delta P}$$

$$= (-)\frac{10}{150} \times \frac{-25}{2}$$

$$= \frac{5}{6} = 0.83$$

Price elasticity of demand = 0.83.

15. Given E_d = –0.2 and percentage increase in quantity demanded = 20 per cent, find the percentage change in expenditure.

Ans. $E_d = -0.2$

$$\text{Elasticity of demand } (E_d) = \frac{\text{Percentage change in quantity demanded}}{\text{Percentage change in price}}$$

$$-0.2 = \frac{20\%}{\text{Percentage change in price}}$$

$$\text{Percentage change in price} = \frac{20\%}{-0.2} = (-)\,100 \text{ per cent}$$

Let the initial price be ₹ 200 and quantity = 100 units.

Q = 100;	Q_1 = 120
P = 200;	P_1 = 100
TE = P × Q	$TE_1 = P_1 \times Q_1$
= 200 × 100	= 120 × 100
= 20,000	= 12,000

$$\text{Percentage change in TE} = \frac{\Delta TE}{TE} \times 100$$

$$= \frac{12{,}000 - 20{,}000}{20{,}000} \times 100$$

$$= \frac{-8{,}000}{20{,}000} \times 100 = (-)\,40 \text{ per cent}$$

Total expenditure reduces by 40 per cent.

16. If $E_d = -0.4$ and $\frac{\Delta Q}{Q} = -0.5$, find new expenditure on the commodity if initial expenditure is ₹ 1,500.

Ans. Given, $E_d = -0.4$

$$\frac{\Delta Q}{Q} = -0.5$$

$$\text{Percentage change in quantity demanded} = \frac{\Delta Q}{Q} \times 100 = -0.5 \times 100 = (-)\ 50 \text{ per cent}$$

$$\text{Elasticity of demand } (E_d) = \frac{\text{Percentage change in quantity demanded}}{\text{Percentage change in price}}$$

$$-0.4 = \frac{-50\%}{\text{Percentage change in price}}$$

$$\text{Percentage change in price} = \frac{-50\%}{-0.4} = 125\%$$

$$\text{New expenditure} = P(1 + 1.25) \times Q(1 - 0.5)$$

$$= P(2.25) \times Q(0.5)$$

$$\text{Percentage change in expenditure} = \frac{\text{New expenditure} - \text{Old expenditure}}{\text{Old expenditure}} \times 100$$

$$= \frac{P(2.25) \times Q\,(0.5) - P \times Q}{P \times Q} \times 100$$

$$= \frac{PQ(1.125) - PQ}{PQ} \times 100$$

$$= \frac{PQ(1.125 - 1)}{PQ} \times 100$$

$$= (1.125 - 1) \times 100$$

$$= 0.125 \times 100 = 12.5 \text{ per cent}$$

Total expenditure increases by 12.5 per cent.

$$\text{New expenditure} = 1{,}500 + 12.5\% \text{ of } 1{,}500$$

$$= 1{,}500 + 187.50$$

$$= 1{,}687.50$$

New expenditure = ₹ 1,687.50

17. If $E_d = -0.4$ and $\frac{\Delta Q}{Q} = 0.2$, find new expenditure on the commodity if initially expenditure is ₹ 2,000.

Ans. Given, $E_d = -0.4$

$$\frac{\Delta Q}{Q} = 0.2$$

$$\text{Percentage change in quantity demanded} = \frac{\Delta Q}{Q} \times 100$$

$$= 0.2 \times 100 = 20 \text{ per cent}$$

$$\text{Elasticity of demand } (E_d) = \frac{\text{Percentage change in quantity demanded}}{\text{Percentage change in price}}$$

$$-0.4 = \frac{20\%}{\text{Percentage change in price}}$$

$$\text{Percentage change in price} = \frac{20\%}{-0.4} = (-)\ 50 \text{ per cent}$$

$$\text{New expenditure} = P\,(1 - 0.5) \times Q\,(1 + 0.2)$$

$$= P\,(0.5) \times Q\,(1.2)$$

$$\text{Percentage change in expenditure} = \frac{\text{New expenditure} - \text{Old expenditure}}{\text{Old expenditure}} \times 100$$

$$= \frac{P(0.5) \times Q\,(1.2) - P \times Q}{P \times Q} \times 100$$

$$= \frac{PQ(0.6) - PQ}{PQ} \times 100$$

$$= \frac{PQ(0.6 - 1)}{PQ} \times 100$$

$$= (0.6 - 1) \times 100$$

$$= -0.4 \times 100$$

$$= (-)\ 40 \text{ per cent}$$

Total expenditure reduces by 40 per cent.

$$\text{New expenditure} = 2{,}000 - 40\% \text{ of } 2{,}000$$

$$= 2{,}000 - 800$$

$$= 1{,}200$$

New expenditure = ₹ 1,200.

18. On 22nd December 2014, the following news was printed in the *Economic Times*:

"Narrow petrol-diesel price gap and higher price of diesel cars alter buyer preference."

Explain this statement linking it to the concept of elasticity of demand.

Ans. Buyer's preferences between diesel and petrol cars is significantly influenced by the relative prices of these fuels. In India, people have high preference for diesel cars, despite their higher price compared with petrol cars. Because, diesel has been much cheaper than petrol. So that elasticity of demand for diesel cars has been low. However, in the recent past the gap between diesel and petrol price has tended to shrink. Accordingly, buyer's preferences are likely to change. Low price differential between petrol and diesel (along with the fact that the diesel cars are more expensive) is expected to induce the buyers to shift from diesel cars to petrol cars. It implies a situation when elasticity of demand for diesel cars is expected to rise. A rise in price of diesel cars will prompt many buyers to shift from diesel to petrol cars.

4. Evaluation (Value-based Questions)

1. The government in India keeps raising taxes on cigarettes leading to a rise in price of this commodity. But the fall in demand is insignificant. How do you explain this phenomenon?

Ans. This is a situation of low elasticity of demand for cigarettes. This is owing to the fact that: (i) there are no close substitutes of this commodity in the market, and (ii) it is a habit-forming commodity.

2. If power tariff is lowered during off-peak hours, do you think the problem of load-shedding for household consumption can be solved to some extent? Use the concept of elasticity of demand.

Ans. Power (electricity) is put to several uses by the households. It involves the use of several appliances. Some appliances (like washing machines, dish-washers) can be used during off-peak hours if the households have to pay lower tariff. Accordingly, it is expected that the peak-hour demand would reduce in response to high tariff rates. As a result, load-shedding is expected to reduce.

3. Explain how, in any two ways, demand for electricity can be decreased when price elasticity of demand is extremely low.

Ans. Demand for electricity can be reduced in following ways:

(i) Using Energy Efficient Electric Appliances: Air conditioners, washing machines, refrigerators and water heaters are biggest electricity using appliances at home. These appliances have efficiency rating ranging from 1 to 5 stars. The government should make it mandatory to fix efficiency labels on the appliances. This will prompt the buyers to buy efficient appliances. Accordingly, demand for electricity is expected to reduce. The appliances having higher number of stars are considered more efficient. They consume two to ten times less electricity. Thus, using these efficient electric appliances, we can reduce our demand for electricity.

(ii) Subsidy on Solar Energy: The government can give subsidy on the purchase of solar energy equipment. So that, the people are induced to shift from electricity to solar energy. Accordingly, demand for electricity will reduce. States like Haryana are already pursuing this policy.

5. CBSE Questions—Past 4 years (With Answers or Reference to the Text for Answers)

1. When price of a good is ₹ 7 per unit a consumer buys 12 units. When price falls to ₹ 6 per unit he spends ₹ 72 on the good. Calculate price elasticity of demand by using the percentage method. Comment on the likely shape of demand curve based on this measure of elasticity. *[CBSE Delhi 2012]*

   [Page 369]

2. A consumer buys 10 units of a good at a price of ₹ 9 per unit. At price ₹ 10 per unit he buys 9 units. What is price elasticity of demand? Use expenditure approach. Comment on the likely shape of demand curve on the basis of this measure of elasticity. *[CBSE Delhi 2012]*

   [Page 369]

3. A consumer buys 20 units of a good at a price of ₹ 5 per unit. He incurs an expenditure of ₹ 120 when he buys 24 units. Calculate price elasticity of demand using the percentage method. Comment upon the likely shape of demand curve based on this information. *[CBSE Delhi 2012]*

   [Page 369, 370]

4. A consumer buys 10 units of a commodity at a price of ₹ 10 per unit. He incurs an expenditure of ₹ 200 on buying 20 units. Calculate price elasticity of demand by the percentage method. Comment upon the shape of demand curve based on this information. *[CBSE (AI) 2012]*

   [Page 370]

5. A consumer buys 14 units of a good at a price of ₹ 8 per unit. At price ₹ 7 per unit he spends ₹ 98 on the good. Calculate price elasticity of demand by the percentage method. Comment upon the shape of demand curve based on this information. *[CBSE (AI) 2012]*

   [Page 370]

6. A consumer buys 8 units of a good at a price of ₹ 7 per unit. When price rises to ₹ 8 per unit he buys 7 units. Calculate price elasticity of demand through the expenditure approach. Comment upon the shape of demand curve based on this information. *[CBSE (AI) 2012]*

   [Page 370]

7. A consumer buys 13 units of a good at a price of ₹ 11 per unit. When price rises to ₹ 13 per unit he buys 11 units. Use expenditure approach to find price elasticity of demand. Also comment on the shape of the demand curve based on this information. *[CBSE (F) 2012]*

   [Page 370, 371]

8. A consumer buys 11 units of a good at a price of ₹ 10 per unit. He can buy 13 units of the same by incurring an expenditure of ₹ 130. Calculate price elasticity of demand by the percentage method. Also comment on the shape of the demand curve based on this information. *[CBSE (F) 2012]*

   [Page 371]

9. A consumer buys 10 units of a good at a price of ₹ 11 per unit. When the price falls to ₹ 9 per unit, he spends ₹ 90 on the good. Calculate price elasticity of demand using the percentage method. Also comment upon the shape of demand curve based on this information. *[CBSE (F) 2012]*

   [Page 371]

10. When is the demand for a good said to be inelastic? *[CBSE Delhi 2013]*

    Or

    Give the meaning of 'inelastic demand'. *[CBSE (AI) 2014]*

    [Page 136]

11. Explain any two factors that affect the price elasticity of demand. Give suitable examples. [CBSE Delhi 2013]

Or

Explain any two factors that affect the price elasticity of demand. [CBSE (F) 2013]

[Page 136, 137]

12. How is price elasticity of demand affected by:

    (i) Number of substitutes available for the good.

    (ii) Nature of the good. [CBSE Delhi 2013]

[Page 136]

13. The price elasticity of demand for a good is –0.4. If its price increases by 5 per cent, by what percentage will its demand fall? Calculate. [CBSE Delhi 2013]

[Page 371]

14. The demand for good rises by 20 per cent as a result of fall in its price. Its price elasticity of demand is (–) 0.8. Calculate the percentage fall in price. [CBSE Delhi 2013]

[Page 371, 372]

15. When is the demand for a good said to be perfectly inelastic? [CBSE (AI) 2013]

Or

When is demand called perfectly inelastic? [CBSE (F) 2014]

[Page 134]

16. A 5 per cent fall in the price of a good raises its demand from 300 units to 318 units. Calculate its price elasticity of demand. [CBSE (AI) 2013]

[Page 372]

17. When the price of a commodity falls by 20 per cent, its demand rises from 400 units to 500 units. Calculate its price elasticity of demand. [CBSE (AI) 2013]

[Page 372]

18. Price elasticity of demand of a good is –0.75. Calculate the percentage fall in its price that will result in 15 per cent rise in its demand. [CBSE (AI) 2013]

[Page 372]

19. What is meant by price elasticity of demand? [CBSE (F) 2013]

[Page 125]

20. A 20 per cent fall in the price of a good, raises its demand from 600 units to 750 units. Calculate its price elasticity of demand. [CBSE (F) 2013]

[Page 372, 373]

21. A consumer buys 18 units of a good at a price of ₹ 9 per unit. The price elasticity of demand for the good is (–) 1. How many units the consumer will buy at a price of ₹ 10 per unit? Calculate. [CBSE Delhi 2014]

[Page 373]

22. Price elasticity of demand of a good is (–) 1. When its price per unit falls by one rupee, its demand rises from 16 to 18 units. Calculate the price before change. [CBSE Delhi 2014]

[Page 373]

23. A consumer buys 30 units of a good at a price of ₹ 10 per unit. Price elasticity of demand for the good is (–) 1. How many units the consumer will buy at a price of ₹ 9 per unit? Calculate. [CBSE Delhi 2014]

[Page 373]

24. When the price of a good falls from ₹ 10 to ₹ 8 per unit, its demand rises from 20 units to 24 units. What can you say about price elasticity of demand of the good through the 'expenditure approach'? [CBSE (AI) 2014]

[Page 374]

25. When the price of a good rises from ₹ 10 to ₹12 per unit, its demand falls from 25 units to 20 units. What can you say about price elasticity of demand of the good through the 'expenditure approach'? [CBSE (AI) 2014]

[Page 374]

26. A consumer buys 27 units of a good at a price of ₹ 10 per unit. When the price falls to ₹ 9 per unit, the demand rises to 30 units. What can you say about price elasticity of demand of the good through the 'expenditure approach'? *[CBSE (AI) 2014]*

[Page 374]

27. When price of a good falls from ₹ 15 per unit to ₹ 12 per unit, its demand rises by 25 per cent. Calculate price elasticity of demand. *[CBSE (F) 2014]*

[Page 374]

28. Price elasticity of demand of a good is (–) 1. Calculate the percentage change in price that will raise the demand from 20 units to 30 units. *[CBSE (F) 2014]*

[Page 374, 375]

29. Price elasticity of demand of two goods A and B is (–) 3 and (–) 4 respectively. Which of the two goods has higher elasticity and why? *[CBSE (F) 2014]*

[Page 375]

30. A consumer spends ₹ 1,000 on a good priced at ₹ 8 per unit. When price rises by 25 per cent, the consumer continues to spend ₹ 1,000 on the good. Calculate price elasticity of demand by percentage method.

[Page 375] *[CBSE Delhi 2015]*

31. A consumer spends ₹ 60 on a good priced at ₹ 5 per unit. When price falls by 20 per cent, the consumer continues to spend ₹ 60 on the good. Calculate price elasticity of demand by percentage method.

[Page 375, 376] *[CBSE Delhi 2015]*

32. A consumer spends ₹ 100 on a good priced at ₹ 4 per unit. When price falls by 50 per cent, the consumer continues to spend ₹ 100 on the good. Calculate price elasticity of demand by percentage method.

[Page 376] *[CBSE Delhi 2015]*

33. A consumer spends ₹ 1,000 on a good priced at ₹ 10 per unit. When its price falls by 20 per cent, the consumer spends ₹ 800 on the good. Calculate the price elasticity of demand by the percentage method.

[Page 376] *[CBSE (AI) 2015]*

34. A consumer spends ₹ 100 on a good priced at ₹ 4 per unit. When its price falls by 25 per cent, the consumer spends ₹ 75 on the good. Calculate the price elasticity of demand by the percentage method.

[Page 376, 377] *[CBSE (AI) 2015]*

35. A consumer spends ₹ 400 on a good priced at ₹ 8 per unit. When its price rises by 25 per cent, the consumer spends ₹ 500 on the good. Calculate the price elasticity of demand by the percentage method.

[Page 377] *[CBSE (AI) 2015]*

36. A consumer spends ₹ 400 on a good priced at ₹ 4 per unit. When the price rises by 25 per cent, the consumer continues to spend ₹ 400. Calculate the price elasticity of demand by percentage method.

[Page 377, 378] *[CBSE (F) 2015]*

37. A consumer spends ₹ 200 on a good priced at ₹ 5 per unit. When the price falls by 20 per cent, he continues to spend ₹ 200. Find the price elasticity of demand by percentage method.

[Page 378] *[CBSE (F) 2015]*

38. A consumer spends ₹ 60 on a good priced at ₹ 1 per unit. When the price rises by 100 per cent, he continues to spend ₹ 60 on the good. Calculate the price elasticity of demand by percentage method.

[Page 378] *[CBSE (F) 2015]*

6. NCERT Questions (With Hints to Answers)

1. Explain price elasticity of demand.

[**Hint:** Price elasticity of demand is a measure showing percentage change in quantity demanded with respect to some percentage change in own price of the commodity.

Price elasticity of demand $(E_d) = (-)\frac{P}{Q} \times \frac{\Delta Q}{\Delta P}$

Here, ΔQ = Change in quantity demanded; ΔP = Change in price; Q = Initial quantity; P = Initial price.]

2. Consider the demand for a good. At price ₹ 4, the demand for the good is 25 units. Suppose price of the good increases to ₹ 5, and as a result, the demand for the good falls to 20 units. Calculate the price elasticity.

[**Hint:** Price elasticity of demand $(E_d) = (-)\frac{P}{Q} \times \frac{\Delta Q}{\Delta P}$

Here, $P = ₹\,4; P_1 = ₹\,5; \Delta P = P_1 - P = ₹\,5 - ₹\,4 = ₹\,1$

$Q = 25$ units; $Q_1 = 20$ units; $\Delta Q = Q_1 - Q = (20 - 25)$ units $= (-)\,5$ units

$$E_d = (-)\frac{4}{25} \times \frac{-5}{1}$$

$= 0.8.$]

3. Consider the demand curve $D(p) = 10 - 3p$. What is the elasticity at price $\frac{5}{3}$?

[**Hint:** Given, demand curve $D(p) = 10 - 3p$

$$\text{Price} = \frac{5}{3}$$

$$D = 10 - 3 \times \frac{5}{3} = 10 - 5 = 5$$

$\Rightarrow$ $D = 5$ units

$$D(p) = 10 - 3p$$

$$\frac{\Delta D}{\Delta p} = -3 \quad \text{or} \quad \frac{\Delta q}{\Delta p} = -3$$

$$\text{Elasticity of demand } (E_d) = (-)\frac{p}{q} \times \frac{\Delta q}{\Delta p} = (-)\frac{\frac{5}{3}}{5} \times -3$$

$$E_d = (-)\frac{5}{3} \times \frac{1}{5} \times -3$$

$\Rightarrow$ $E_d = 1$

$\therefore$ Elasticity of demand = 1.]

4. Suppose the price elasticity of demand for a good is –0.2. If there is a 5 per cent increase in the price of the good, by what percentage will the demand for the good go down?

[**Hint:** Price elasticity of demand $(E_d) = \frac{\text{Percentage change in quantity demanded}}{\text{Percentage change in price}}$

Price elasticity of demand = –0.2

Percentage change in price = 5 per cent

$$-0.2 = \frac{\text{Percentage change in quantity demanded}}{5}$$

$\Rightarrow$ Percentage change in quantity demanded = (–) 1 per cent

$\therefore$ Demand for the good goes down by 1 per cent.]

5. Suppose the price elasticity of demand for a good is –0.2. How will the expenditure on the good be affected if there is a 10 per cent increase in the price of the good?

[**Hint:** Given, price elasticity of demand = –0.2. Price elasticity of demand in this case is less than unitary elastic, therefore, expenditure on the good will increase with increase in price of the commodity.]

6. Suppose there was a 4 per cent decrease in the price of a good, and as a result, the expenditure on the good increased by 2 per cent. What can you say about the elasticity of demand?

[**Hint:** Elasticity of demand of the commodity in this case will be greater than unitary elastic because with fall in price of the commodity, total expenditure increases.]

7. Miscellaneous Questions and Reference to the Text for Answers

A. Questions of 3 & 4 marks each

1. What is meant by price elasticity of demand? How is it measured? Name the methods of measuring it.
[Page 125, 126]
2. Define elasticity of demand. Explain any one method of measuring it.
[Page 125–128]
3. Show the different degrees of elasticity of demand with the help of a diagram.
[Page 132–134]
4. Explain the relation between price elasticity of demand and total expenditure.
[Page 128–130]
5. Show the points illustrating all types of elasticity of demand on a straight line demand curve which touches both the axes.
[Page 128]
6. What is the degree of elasticity of demand in case of the following demand curves:
   (i) Straight line parallel to X-axis?
   (ii) Straight line parallel to Y-axis?
   (iii) At mid-point of a downward sloping straight line curve?
[Page 128, 134]
7. Draw a straight line demand curve. Choose any three points on it and compare the point elasticities at those three points.
[Page 128]
8. What do you understand by price elasticity of demand? State the factors which influence it.
[Page 125, 136, 137]
9. Explain the measurement of price elasticity of demand with the help of percentage or proportionate method.
[Page 126]
10. How is price elasticity of demand measured with the help of the point method?
Or
Explain with the help of a diagram, the geometric method of measuring price elasticity of demand.
[Page 127, 128]
11. "Flatter the curve, greater the elasticity of demand." Comment.
[Page 135, 136]
12. How does the level of price of a good affect the price elasticity of demand? Explain.
[Page 137]
13. If a product price increases, a family's spending on the product has to increase. Defend or refute.
[Page 128, 129]

B. Questions of 6 marks each

1. What do you understand by price elasticity of demand? How is it measured?
[Page 125–128]
2. Explain any six factors determining price elasticity of demand.
[Page 136, 137]
3. Define price elasticity of demand for a commodity. What would be the shape of a demand curve of a commodity when its price elasticity of demand is:
(i) zero? (ii) infinite?
[Page 125, 134]
4. Draw a downward sloping straight line demand curve touching both the axes. Mark the price elasticity at different points of this demand curve. Also explain briefly any three factors affecting price elasticity of demand.
[Page 127, 128, 136, 137]

5. Explain by giving examples, how do the following determine price elasticity of demand:
   (i) Nature of the good, and
   (ii) Availability of substitutes.
   [Page 136]

DOs and DON'Ts

1. Never measure elasticity of demand in terms of an absolute change in quantity in response to a given change in price of the commodity. Always consider, percentage change in quantity in relation to a percentage change in price of the commodity. Thus, in the adjoining figure (Fig. 12), measuring elasticity at point R, students are often inclined to conclude that $E_d < 1$, because change in quantity is less than the change in price.

   This is a wrong conclusion. Because, you are simply relating change in quantity to change in price. The fact is that we should relate percentage change in quantity to percentage change in price. If we follow the correct procedure, we shall find that elasticity of demand at point R is greater than unity ($E_d > 1$).

FIGURE 12

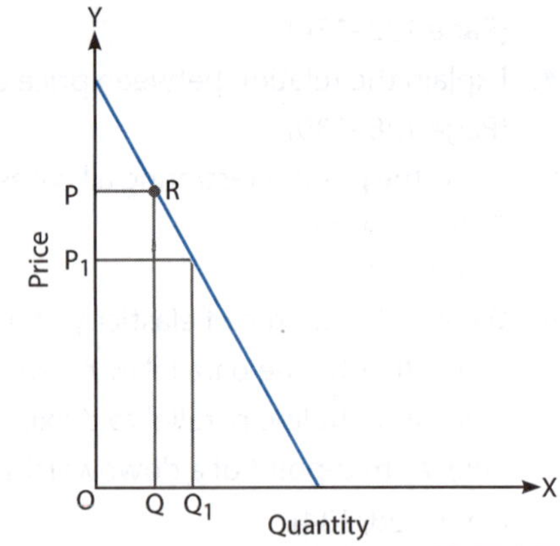

The point R lies at the upper-half segment of the demand curve. Accordingly, elasticity of demand at point R is bound to be greater than one.

2. Keep in mind that expenditure approach and percentage method of measuring elasticity are not comparable. Because, expenditure approach does not measure elasticity in terms of any precise number, while the percentage method does. The expenditure approach just gives three broad categories of elasticity of demand. These are that $E_d = 1$, $E_d < 1$, $E_d > 1$. Precise coefficients are not estimated.

   Any comparison using the expenditure approach and percentage method might lead us to contradictory results, as in the following illustration:

P_X	Q_X	Total Expenditure	Percentage Change in Price	Percentage Change in Quantity
10	100	1,000	50% (fall)	100% (rise)
5	200	1,000		

   $E_d = 1$ according to expenditure approach (because total expenditure remains constant).

   $E_d = 2$ according to percentage method (because $E_d = \frac{100}{50} = 2$).

   [**Note:** Percentage method of measuring elasticity of demand should be used only when changes in price and demand are very small.]

3. You must understand that the slope of demand curve is different from elasticity of demand.

   Elasticity of demand (E_d) is estimated as under:

$$E_d = \frac{\Delta Q}{\Delta P} \times \frac{P}{Q} \qquad \begin{bmatrix} \text{Here, P: Price of the commodity} \\ \text{Q: Quantity demanded.} \end{bmatrix}$$

$$\text{Slope of demand curve} = \frac{\Delta P}{\Delta Q}$$

   Accordingly, elasticity of demand may be expressed as under:

$$E_d = \frac{1}{\text{Slope of demand curve}} \times \frac{P}{Q}$$

ability ZONE

❑ Geometric Method—An Alternative Approach

Let us consider a linear demand curve, as in Fig. 13.

ab is a linear demand curve.

A notable property of a linear demand curve is that it has a constant slope. We know,

$$\textbf{Slope of demand curve} = \frac{\Delta P}{\Delta Q}$$

This is equal to

$$\frac{20}{40} = \frac{1}{2} \text{ in Fig. 13.}$$

FIGURE 13

Estimation of Price Elasticity of Demand considering a Linear Demand Curve

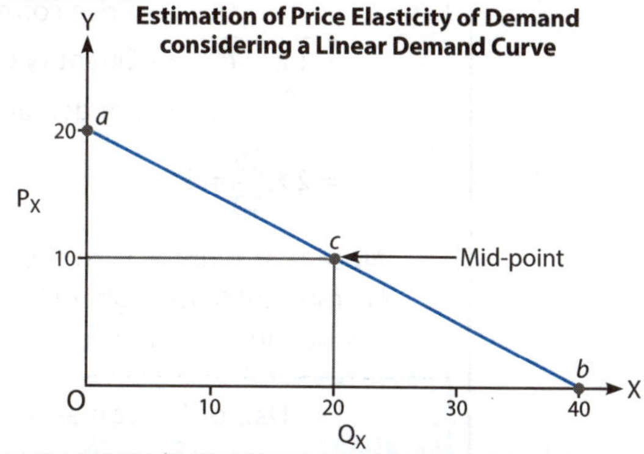

ab is a straight line demand curve, called linear demand curve. *c* is a mid-point on the demand curve.
Price elasticity of demand at point c is equal to

$$= \frac{1}{\text{Slope of Demand Curve at point } c} \times \frac{P}{Q}$$

$$= \frac{1}{1/2} \times \frac{10}{20} = 1$$

This is exactly equal to the ratio between lower segment and upper segment $= \frac{cb}{ac}$.

According to percentage method, price elasticity of demand is estimated using the following formula:

$$E_d = \frac{\Delta Q}{\Delta P} \times \frac{P}{Q}$$

Since slope of demand curve $= \frac{\Delta P}{\Delta Q}$, we can rewrite the above formula as under:

$$E_d = \frac{1}{\text{Slope of demand curve}} \times \frac{P}{Q}$$

Using this formula, let us estimate price elasticity of demand at point *c* which is a mid-point on the demand curve:

$$\text{At point } c, \quad E_d = \frac{1}{\text{Slope of demand curve at point } c} \times \frac{P}{Q}$$

$$= \frac{1}{1/2} \times \frac{10}{20} \quad \begin{matrix} \leftarrow \text{Price corresponding to point } c \\ \leftarrow \text{Quantity corresponding to point } c \end{matrix}$$

↑ $\frac{1}{2}$ is slope of demand curve

$$= 2 \times \frac{10}{20} = 1$$

Thus, for a straight line demand curve (linear demand curve) E_d at point *c* (mid-point on the demand curve) = 1.

Let us refer to Fig. 14 for another illustration.

At point K (which is away from the mid-point) on the demand curve, price elasticity of demand (E_d) is estimated as under:

FIGURE 14

Estimation of Price Elasticity of Demand at a Specific Point on a Linear Demand Curve

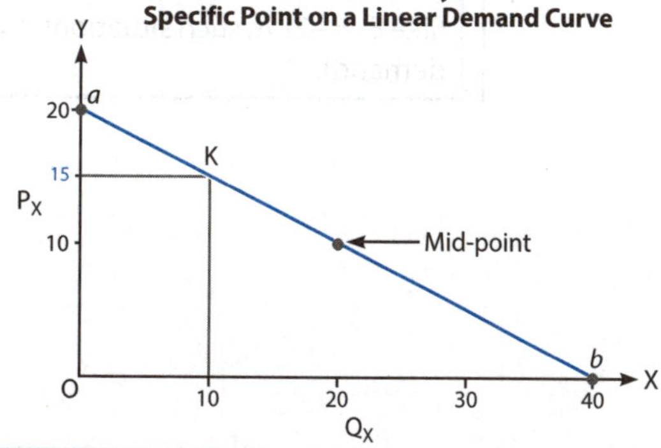

$$E_d = \frac{1}{\text{Slope of demand curve at point K}} \times \frac{P}{Q}$$

$$= \frac{1}{1/2} \times \frac{15}{10} \quad \begin{array}{l} \leftarrow \text{Price corresponding to point K} \\ \leftarrow \text{Quantity corresponding to point K} \end{array}$$

$\uparrow$ $\frac{1}{2}$ is slope of demand curve

$$= 2 \times \frac{15}{10} = 3$$

[**Note** that point K is to the left of mid-point of the demand curve. Accordingly, $E_d > 1$. At any point to the right of the mid-point of the demand curve, you will find $E_d < 1$. At point *a*, $E_d = \infty$, and at point *b*, $E_d = 0$.]

Use of '–' sign as a prefix to the formula of Elasticity of Demand

A careful reader should observe that we have prefixed '–' sign to the formula of elasticity of demand. We have written that:

$$E_d = (-)\frac{\Delta Q}{\Delta P} \times \frac{P}{Q}$$

$\uparrow$ '–' Sign is prefixed to the formula

Why should it be done? Following is the reason:

Owing to inverse relationship between price and quantity demanded, elasticity of demand ought to be negative, like – 1, – 2, – 3, etc. Thus, if price of the commodity reduces from ₹ 10 to ₹ 5 per unit and quantity demanded increases from 50 to 100 units of the commodity, elasticity of demand (in terms of the ratio between percentage change in quantity demanded and percentage change in price) would be –2 $\left[E_d = \frac{\Delta Q}{\Delta P} \times \frac{P}{Q} = \frac{50}{-5} \times \frac{10}{50} = -2\right]$.

However, it is conventional to ignore the '–' sign and treat elasticity of demand just as 2 rather than –2. The rationale behind this convention is that mathematically –3 is lesser than –2 while in the context of elasticity of demand –3 shows higher elasticity of demand compared to –2. An alternative to ignoring the '–' sign is to prefix '–' sign to the formula of estimation of elasticity of demand. Accordingly, coefficient of E_d would always be found as positive.

Continuing with the same illustration (where $\Delta Q = 50$; $\Delta P = -5$; $P = 10$; $Q = 50$) elasticity of demand (when '–' sign is prefixed to the formula) would be worked out as under:

$$E_d = (-)\frac{\Delta Q}{\Delta P} \times \frac{P}{Q} = (-)\frac{50}{-5} \times \frac{10}{50} = 2$$

Thus, prefixing '–' sign to the formula avoids the hassle of ignoring the '–' sign while making comparisons of the coefficients of elasticity of demand.

However, it is important to note here that the students may get a numerical problem where the examiner himself specifies the coefficient of elasticity of demand with a negative sign (like $E_d = -2$). In such situations make it a point not to prefix '–' sign to the formula (of elasticity of demand).

Production Function and Returns to a Factor

CHAPTER 6

TODO

- Concept of Production Function: Short Run and Long Run
- Concepts of TP (Total Product), MP (Marginal Product) and AP (Average Product)
- Returns to a Factor: Law of Diminishing Returns or the Law of Variable Proportions
- Relation between: (i) TP & MP, (ii) AP & MP, and Shapes of TP, MP and AP Curves

1. Concept of Production Function: Short Run and Long Run

Output needs inputs. Land, labour and capital are the common inputs for the production of goods and services. As a producer, you would always be interested to know how much labour and capital (and other inputs) are required to produce a given quantity of a commodity. You may find, for example, that 10 units of capital and 5 units of labour are required to produce 100 units of the commodity. It is this relationship between physical inputs (*i.e.*, 10 units of capital and 5 units of labour) and physical output (100 units of the commodity produced) which is known as Production Function.

Production function, thus, studies the functional relationship between physical inputs and physical output of a commodity. It is purely a technical relationship between material output on the one hand and material inputs on the other. Usually, it is expressed in terms of the following equation:

$$Q_X = f(L, K)$$

it says that Q_X (production of commodity-X) is the function of L (labour) and K (capital). Using some arbitrary values, we may write that,

$$40_X = f(5L, 4K) \quad ...(i)$$

it says that maximum of 40 units of commodity-X can be produced using 5 units of labour and 4 units of capital.

Or, $$45_X = f(6L, 4K) \quad ...(ii)$$

Implying that maximum of 45 units of commodity-X can be produced using 6 units of labour and 4 units of capital.

Or, $$80_X = f(10L, 8K) \quad ...(iii)$$

Implying that maximum of 80 units of commodity-X can be produced using 10 units of labour and 8 units of capital.

A Caution

In the context of production function, only material inputs or physical inputs are considered in relation to the material or physical output. We do not consider the market value of inputs or output.

In the words of **Watson,** "Production function is the relation between a firm's production (output) and the material factors of production (input)."

It is important to note that production function does not establish any economic relation between inputs and output. It only establishes a technical relation between inputs and output. It is the engineers (not the economists) who tell us that 10 workers working on 2 machines will yield the maximum output of (say) 100 units of commodity-X. Thus, writes **Koutsoyiannis,** *"The production function is purely a technical relation which connects factor inputs and output."*

It is equally important to note that a production function is always defined with respect to a given technology or a given technical know-how. Over time, technical know-how may improve; accordingly, it may become possible to produce 110 units of commodity-X (instead of 100 units) with the same inputs. It is a situation of shift (or change) in production function.

Fixed and Variable Factors

Factors of production are classified as:

(i) fixed factors, and (ii) variable factors.

Fixed factors are those the application of which does not change with the change in output. In fact, fixed factors (like machines) are installed before output actually commences. Thus, a machine is there even when output is zero. Let us assume that machine can produce maximum 1,000 units of commodity-X. It means that for any change in output ranging between 0–1,000 units; input of machine (fixed factor) remains constant.

Variable factors are those the application of which varies (or changes) with the change in output. Labour is an example of a variable factor. You need more labour to produce more units of a commodity, other things remaining constant. Thus, use of a variable factor is zero when output is zero; it increases as output increases.

Short Run Production Function

Short run is a period of time when production can be increased only by increasing the application of variable factor(s). Fixed factor, by definition, remains constant. To elaborate further, once a plant (of a particular production capacity) is installed, it cannot be changed during the short period. Short period is too short to change it. Thus, production capacity (as indicated by the plant size, or the fixed factor) remains constant during the short period.

When one factor is a fixed factor and the other is a variable factor, production function may be specified as under:

$$Q_X = f(L, \bar{K})$$

Here, Q_X = Output of Good-X.

L = Labour, a variable factor.

$\bar{K}$ = Capital, a fixed factor.

In this type of production function, output can be increased only by increasing the application of L (the variable factor). The following equations illustrate this point further:

$$40_X = f(5L, 4\bar{K}) \qquad \text{...(i)}$$

$$45_X = f(6L, 4\bar{K}) \qquad \text{...(ii)}$$

We find that K is constant at 4 units. Output increases from 40 to 45 units of commodity-X because input of L has increased from 5 to 6 units. Since **K** is constant and only **L** changes, the ratio (or proportion) between L and K tends to change. This generates the law of variable proportions which is discussed in Section 3 of the chapter.

Long Run Production Function

Long run is a period of time when the distinction between 'fixed factor' and 'variable factor' vanishes. All factors are variable factors. Long period is long enough to increase production capacity of a firm: plant size can be changed, or more and more plants can be installed. Thus, what is fixed factor during the short period ($\overline{K}$) becomes the variable factor.

When both the factors are variable factors, the long period production function is expressed as under:

$$Q_X = f(L, K) \quad \left[\textbf{Note} \text{ that K is not indicated by } \overline{K}. \text{ Like L, it is a variable factor.}\right]$$

Illustration

$$40_X = f(5L, 4K) \qquad \text{...(i)}$$

$$80_X = f(10L, 8K) \qquad \text{...(ii)}$$

Both L and K are variable factors. Output is increased by increasing the application of both the factors.

Vital Difference 1: Short period production function is 'variable proportions type production function' while the long period production function is 'constant proportions type production function'

In the short period production function, factor ratio (L : K) must change at different levels of output. This is because one factor is constant all through the production process. Thus, $\overline{K} = 4$ when 5 units of labour are applied to produce 40 units of output or when 6 units of labour are applied to produce 45 units of output. Accordingly, factor ratio shifts from 5 : 4 to 6 : 4 as the level of output is raised from 40 to 45 units of commodity-X. In the long period production function, on the other hand, factor ratio remains constant. It is 5 : 4 when output = 40 units, and 10 : 8 (the same as 5 : 4) when output = 80 units. Thus, while short period production function is called 'variable proportions type production function', the long period production function is called 'constant proportions type production function'. Fig. 1 (A & B) is a diagrammatic illustration of constant factor ratio (in case of long period production function) and variable factor ratio (in case of short period production function).

FIGURE 1

(A) Constant Factor Ratio (relevant to long period production function)

(B) Variable Factor Ratio (relevant to short period production function)

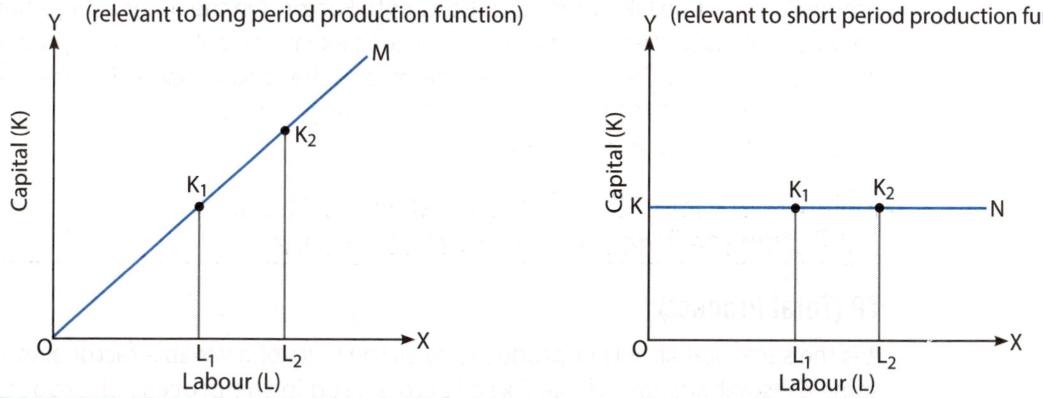

In Fig. 1(A), $\frac{K_1L_1}{OL_1} = \frac{K_2L_2}{OL_2}$ (because ΔOL_1K_1 and ΔOL_2K_2 are similar to each other).

K_1L_1 : Units of capital for a lower level of output.

K_2L_2 : Units of capital for a higher level of output.

OL_1 : Units of labour for a lower level of output.

OL_2 : Units of labour for a higher level of output.

In Fig. 1(B), a horizontal straight line (KN) starting from point K on Y-axis shows that OK units of capital remain fixed, and the higher level of output is achieved only by increasing the inputs of labour from OL_1 to OL_2.

Thus,

$$\frac{K_1L_1}{OL_1} \neq \frac{K_2L_2}{OL_2}$$

Instead

$$\frac{K_1L_1}{OL_1} > \frac{K_2L_2}{OL_2}$$

as,

$$K_1L_1 = K_2L_2, \text{ while } OL_1 < OL_2.$$

Implying that the factor ratio tends to change as the level of output changes.

Vital Difference 2: Short period production function exhibits constant scale of output, while long period production function exhibits change in the scale of output

Fixed factor (capital) often refers to the scale of output of a firm. It is like a plant (of a given production capacity) installed by the producer when the firm is being established (and the output is yet to start). By definition short period is too short for the firm to change scale of output.

Thus, in the short period, the producer increases the level of his output only by increasing the application of the variable factor, sticking to the same scale of output (or the same plant of production). In the long period, on the other hand, the producer increases the level of output by increasing the scale of production (by increasing number of plants or by shifting from a smaller to a bigger plant of production). Thus, the short period production function exhibits constant scale of output, while the long period production function exhibits change in the scale of output.

Here comes the point of central significance. When the behaviour of output is studied with reference to increasing application of the variable factor (short period production function), it is termed as 'Returns to Factor'. On the other hand, when the behaviour of output is studied with reference to expansion of the scale of production (long period production function), it is termed as 'Returns to Scale'. In other words, short period production function exhibits Returns to a Factor; long period production function exhibits Returns to Scale.

2. TP (Total Product), MP (Marginal Product) and AP (Average Product) of the Variable Factor

TP (Total Product)

It is the sum total of output produced by all the units of a variable factor along with some constant amount of the fixed factors used in the process of production. Let us consider L (Labour) as the variable factor and K (Capital) as the fixed factor. Assume also that along with some constant application of the fixed factor (say one machine), the producer is using 1 through 6 units of the variable factor. The resultant output is 10, 12, 15, 12, 10, 6 units of the commodity corresponding to each unit of labour used. In such a situation,

$$TP = 10 + 12 + 15 + 12 + 10 + 6$$
$$= 65 \text{ units of the commodity.}$$

> TP is the sum total of output of each unit of the variable factor used in the process of production. This is also called total return of the variable factor.

MP (Marginal Product)

MP refers to change in TP when one more unit of the variable factor is used (fixed factor remaining constant). **Example:** If output increases from 40 to 45 units when the input of labour is increased from 5 to 6 units (input of capital remaining constant), then

$$MP = \underset{\substack{\uparrow \\ \text{TP when 6 units of} \\ \text{labour are used}}}{45} - \underset{\substack{\uparrow \\ \text{TP when 5 units of} \\ \text{labour are used}}}{40} = \underset{\substack{\uparrow \\ \text{Increase in TP when 1 more} \\ \text{unit of labour is used}}}{5}$$

MP = 5 is related to the 6th unit of labour. Likewise,

MP of 10th unit of L = TP of 10 units of L – TP of 9 (or 10 – 1) units of L

Or

MP of 1st unit of L = TP of 1 unit of L – TP of 0 (or 1 – 1) unit of L

Generalising it we can say that:

$$MP_n = TP_n - TP_{n-1}$$

If you have understood the technique of estimating MP, you should also understand the fact that by adding up MP of all the units of a variable factor, we get TP.

Thus,

$$TP = \sum_{i=1}^{n} MP_i$$

Note the Synonyms

- MP (marginal product) is also called MPP (marginal physical product).
- AP (average product) is also called APP (average physical product).
- TP (total product) is also called TPP (total physical product).

Physical product refers to production as measured in terms of physical units of the commodity.

Example: 1,000 shirts is physical product. Production of shirts worth ₹ 10,000 is NOT physical product. It is called revenue product.

> MP refers to change in TP when one more unit of the variable factor is used, fixed factor remaining constant.
> TP is the sum total of MP corresponding to each unit of the variable factor.

AP (Average Product)

AP is output per unit of the variable factor.

It is estimated as under:

$$AP = \frac{TP}{L} \quad \begin{matrix} \leftarrow \text{Total product/output} \\ \leftarrow \text{Units of the variable factor} \end{matrix}$$

Example: If TP = 40 when 5 units of L (Labour) are used, then

$$AP = \frac{TP}{L}$$
$$= \frac{40}{5} = 8 \text{ units of output}$$

> AP refers to physical output per unit of the variable factor used in the process of production.

Illustration (Estimation of AP, MP and TP)

Following table illustrates the estimation of AP, MP and TP, using hypothetical figures. The table is based on the assumption that L (Labour) is the variable factor, and that some constant amount of fixed factor is used in the process of production.

L (Units of Labour)	TP (Total Product)	AP (Average Product)	MP (Marginal Product)
1	50	$50 \div 1 = 50$	$TP_1 - TP_0 = 50 - 0 = 50$
2	90	$90 \div 2 = 45$	$TP_2 - TP_1 = 90 - 50 = 40$
3	120	$120 \div 3 = 40$	$TP_3 - TP_2 = 120 - 90 = 30$
4	140	$140 \div 4 = 35$	$TP_4 - TP_3 = 140 - 120 = 20$
5	150	$150 \div 5 = 30$	$TP_5 - TP_4 = 150 - 140 = 10$
6	150	$150 \div 6 = 25$	$TP_6 - TP_5 = 150 - 150 = 0$
7	147	$147 \div 7 = 21$	$TP_7 - TP_6 = 147 - 150 = -3$

When 6 units of labour (or variable factor) are employed:

$$TP = AP \times L = 25 \times 6 = 150$$

Also,

$$TP = \Sigma MP = 50 + 40 + 30 + 20 + 10 + 0 = 150$$

$$AP = \frac{TP}{L} = \frac{150}{6} = 25$$

$$MP_{\text{of 6th unit}} = TP_n - TP_{n-1} = TP_6 - TP_5 = 150 - 150 = 0$$

Likewise, when 7 units of labour are employed:

$$TP = AP \times L = 21 \times 7 = 147$$

Also,

$$TP = \Sigma MP = 50 + 40 + 30 + 20 + 10 + 0 - 3 = 147$$

$$AP = \frac{TP}{L} = \frac{147}{7} = 21$$

$$MP_{\text{of 7th unit}} = TP_n - TP_{n-1} = TP_7 - TP_6 = 147 - 150 = -3$$

Negative MP

Yes, MP can be negative in certain situations. Particularly when there is excessive employment (or disguised unemployment) as in some public sector undertakings in India. Excessive employment (employment of workers more than required) reduces overall efficiency of the workers, because of which MP may be negative. In such situations, TP increases when some workers are withdrawn.

3. Returns to a Factor: The Law of Variable Proportions

Consider a situation when land is a fixed factor and labour is a variable factor, and the farmer is producing wheat. Since land is a fixed factor, he can produce more of wheat only by using more and more of labour. Here comes an important question: **Will every additional unit of labour employed on the given land yield the same amount of additional output of wheat?** In other words, will MP of the labour remain constant for each and every additional unit of labour employed? Don't say 'may be'. It can never happen. If MP of labour was to remain constant (no matter how much of labour is employed), then a country like India would have produced more and more of wheat using more and more of labour on the same piece of land. It would have never faced any food problem. The fact of the matter is that MP must eventually diminish. The logic is simple: Always there is some ideal ratio of factors of production. If L and K are the two factors and if K is constant, the ideal ratio is struck by varying the use of L. Corresponding to the ideal ratio between L and K, MP_L should be at its maximum. But once the ideal ratio is reached, any increase in L would mean excessive employment of the variable factor. Or, it would mean lesser and lesser availability of the fixed factor per unit of the variable factor. Or, it would mean over-exploitation of the fixed factor. Accordingly, MP_L must start declining. We may ultimately reach a point when another additional unit of labour (on the same land) adds nothing to total output. Implying that MP_L becomes zero. In exceptional situations, MP may even become negative, as noted earlier. This is the essence of the law of variable proportions or the law of diminishing returns (also called law of diminishing marginal product).

Law of Variable Proportions states that as more and more of the variable factor is combined with the fixed factor, marginal product of the variable factor may initially rise, but eventually a situation must come when marginal product of the variable factor starts declining. Marginal product may ultimately become zero or even negative.

CAN MP EVER RISE? Yes, MP of the variable factor can rise, but only in a situation when the fixed factor is not fully utilised. If ideally, 4 full time workers are needed to cultivate 2 hectares of land, MP_L may increase when initially less than 4 workers are employed. MP should be maximum when 4 workers are employed, and must start diminishing when more than 4 workers are employed.

Thus, the law of variable proportions may be defined, as under.

Tabular and Diagrammatic Presentation of the Law

The law of variable proportions is explained with the help of Table 1 and Fig. 2.

You must note important observations as these

- When MP is increasing (from 2 to 3 to 4), TP is increasing at increasing rate: first 2 units are added to TP, then 3 and then 4 units of output.
- When MP is decreasing (from 4 to 3 to 2 to 1), TP is increasing at a diminishing rate: addition to TP reduces from 4 to 3 to 2 to 1 unit.
- When MP is zero, there is no addition to TP. Hence, TP is maximum when MP = 0.
- When MP is negative, TP starts declining.

Table 1. Law of Variable Proportions— Increasing Returns, Diminishing Returns and Negative Returns

Units of Land	Units of Labour	Total Product	Marginal Product	
1	1	2	2	Increasing MP implying increasing returns to a factor
1	2	5	3	
1	3	9	4	
1	4	12	3	Diminishing MP implying diminishing returns to a factor
1	5	14	2	
1	6	15	1	
1	7	15	0	Negative MP implying negative returns to a factor
1	8	14	–1	

[**Note:** Where MP stops increasing, from that very point it starts diminishing. Thus, overlapping is indicated in the above Table when MP = 4.]

FIGURE 2

Law of Variable Proportions—Increasing Returns, Diminishing Returns and Negative Returns

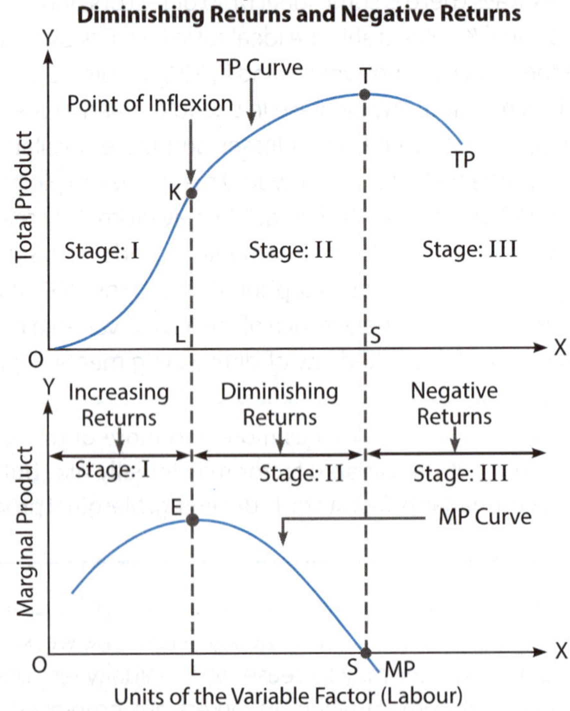

- Stage I is between O to K on the curve TP. In this zone, MP is increasing and TP is increasing at the increasing rate.
- Stage II is between K to T. In this zone, MP is decreasing and TP is increasing at the decreasing rate.
- Stage III is beyond point T. Now TP starts declining because MP is negative.
- K is the point of inflexion where TP stops increasing at the increasing rate and instead, starts increasing at the decreasing rate.

Point of Inflexion

It is a point from where slope of TP changes. Up to this point, TP has been increasing at the increasing rate. From this point onwards TP increases, but only at the diminishing rate.

It is a point which coincides with the end of stage I of production (as MP stops increasing at this point) or this is a point which marks the beginning of stage II of production (as MP starts diminishing from this point).

In Fig. 2, K is the point of inflexion.

Table 1 shows that as more and more units of labour (Variable Factor) are used, MP (Marginal Product) tends to rise till 3 units of labour are employed. In this situation, TP (Total Product) increases at the increasing rate. This is a situation of increasing returns to the factor. But, with the application of 4th unit of labour, situation of diminishing returns sets in: MP starts decreasing and TP increases only at the decreasing rate.

Diminishing MP reduces to zero. Total output is maximum (= 15), when marginal output is zero.

Eventually, MP may be negative. Now output (TP) starts declining (as from 15 to 14) when 8th unit of labour is employed.

Fig. 2 shows that:

(i) MP tends to rise till OL units of labour are used. This corresponds to point E on the MP curve. This is a situation of increasing returns to a factor.

(ii) When MP is rising, TP tends to rise at an increasing rate. This occurs till point K on the TP curve. This corresponds to the situation of increasing returns to a factor.

(iii) Beyond OL units of labour, MP tends to decline, and TP increases only at diminishing rate. This occurs between E and S on MP curve, and between K and T on TP curve. This corresponds to a situation of diminishing returns to a factor.

(iv) When employment of labour exceeds OS units, MP becomes negative. Accordingly, TP starts declining. This is a situation of negative returns to a factor, occurring beyond point T on TP curve and beyond point S on MP curve.

Causes of Increasing Returns to a Factor

Increasing returns to a factor occur because of the following factors:

(1) Fuller Utilisation of the Fixed Factor: In the initial stages, fixed factor (such as machine) remains underutilised. Its fuller utilisation calls for greater application of the variable factor (Labour). Hence, initially (so long as fixed factor remains underutilised) additional units of the variable factor add more and more to total output, or marginal product of the variable factor tends to increase.

(2) Division of Labour and Increase in Efficiency: Additional application of the variable factor (Labour) enables *process based division of labour*. Specialised workers may be used for different processes of production. This increases efficiency or productivity of the variable factor. Accordingly, marginal productivity tends to rise.

(3) Better Coordination between the Factors: So long as fixed factor remains underutilised, additional application of the variable factor tends to improve the degree of coordination between the fixed and variable factors. As a result, marginal product (MP) increases and total product (TP) increases at the increasing rate.

HOTS

Q.1. Do you agree with the view that TP increases even when MP is decreasing?

Ans. Yes, TP increases even when MP is decreasing. Because MP is an addition to TP. When MP is decreasing, only an addition to TP is decreasing, not the TP as such. TP continues to increase, though at a diminishing rate. TP starts declining only when MP is negative.

Q.2. Can TP ever fall when more and more of the variable factor is combined with the fixed factor?

Ans. Yes, TP will fall when MP of the variable factor becomes negative. It is a situation of excessive employment of the variable factor, or a situation of disguised unemployment of the variable factor like labour.

Causes of Diminishing Returns to a Factor

Diminishing returns to a factor or the law of diminishing returns may be explained in terms of the following factors:

(1) Fixity of the Factor: Fixity of the factor(s) is the principal cause behind the law of diminishing returns. As more and more units of the variable factor are combined with the fixed factor, the latter gets excessively utilised. It suffers greater wear and tear and loses its efficiency. Hence, the diminishing returns.

(2) Imperfect Factor Substitutability: Factors of production are imperfect substitutes of each other. More and more of labour cannot be continuously used in place of capital. Accordingly, diminishing returns are bound to set in if only the variable factor is increased to increase output.

(3) Poor Coordination between the Factors: Increasing application of the variable factor (along with the fixed factor) eventually disturbs the ideal factor ratio. This results in poor coordination between the fixed and variable factors. Hence, the diminishing returns.

Assumptions of the Law

The law of variable proportions is based on certain assumptions. These are as follows:

(i) Ratio in which factors of production are combined can be changed.

(ii) Units of the variable factor are homogeneous or equally efficient, and are increased one by one. Thus, the law of diminishing returns sets in not because latter units of the variable factors are less efficient than the former ones. It sets in because the ideal factor ratio is disturbed or because the availability of the fixed factor (like machines) reduces per unit of the variable factor.

(iii) State of technology does not change.

Three Stages of Production

Law of variable proportions suggests three stages of production (also called three phases of production):

(i) Stage I, when MP is increasing, called the **stage of increasing returns,**

(ii) Stage II, when MP is diminishing, called the **stage of diminishing returns**, and

(iii) Stage III, when MP is negative, called the **stage of negative returns.**

Significance of the Stages of Production

Will you as a producer stop in stage I of production?

No. Because in **stage I,** employment of every additional unit of the variable factor (other things remaining constant) is giving more and more marginal output **(rising MP).**

Will you as a producer enter in stage III of production?

No. Because in **stage III,** employment of every additional unit of the variable factor (other things remaining constant) is causing loss of total output **(because, MP is negative).** In fact, it is foolish to get into a situation when total output declines even when the cost of production is rising on account of additional employment of the variable factor.

This brings us to the conclusion that you, as a producer will stop only in **stage II**. Technically, it means that a producer will find his equilibrium (where he maximises his profits) **only in stage II of production when MP is declining but remains positive.**

HOTS

Q. There is always an ideal factor ratio. What happens if this ideal ratio is crossed?

Ans. If the ideal factor ratio is crossed, diminishing returns to a factor set in. MP of the variable factor starts declining. TP increases only at a decreasing rate.

A Situation of Constant Returns to a Factor

Between the situations of 'increasing returns to a factor' and 'diminishing returns to a factor', a firm may have a situation of constant returns to a factor. It is a situation when MP of the variable factor tends to remain constant even when more and more of the variable factor is combined with the fixed factor(s). When MP is constant (say = 10), TP will increase only at a constant rate: every time it will increase by 10 units of output.

Postponement of the Law

Postponement of the law of variable proportions (the situation of diminishing MP) is possible under two situations, as under:

(i) When there is improvement in technology used in the process of production. So that greater output is achieved with the same inputs.

(ii) When some substitute of the fixed factor is discovered. So that the constraint of fixity of the factor is removed. However, such a situation is very rare, if not impossible.

Postponement of the law should not be interpreted to mean that the law can be avoided. Ultimately, the law must set in when factor ratio does not remain optimum.

4. Relation between: (i) TP & MP, and (ii) AP & MP

Table 2 and Fig. 3 illustrate how TP, MP and AP are related to each other.

Table 2. TP, MP, and AP

Units of Land (Hectares)– Fixed Factor	Units of Variable Factor (L) (No. of workers employed)	MP (Output of rice in tonnes)	TP (=ΣMP) (Output of rice in tonnes)	AP $\left(=\frac{TP}{L}\right)$ (Output of rice in tonnes)
1	0	—	0	—
1	1	6	6	6
1	2	14	20	10
1	3	28	48	16
1	4	24	72	18
1	5	8	80	16
1	6	4	84	14
1	7	0	84	12
1	8	–4	80	10

FIGURE 3

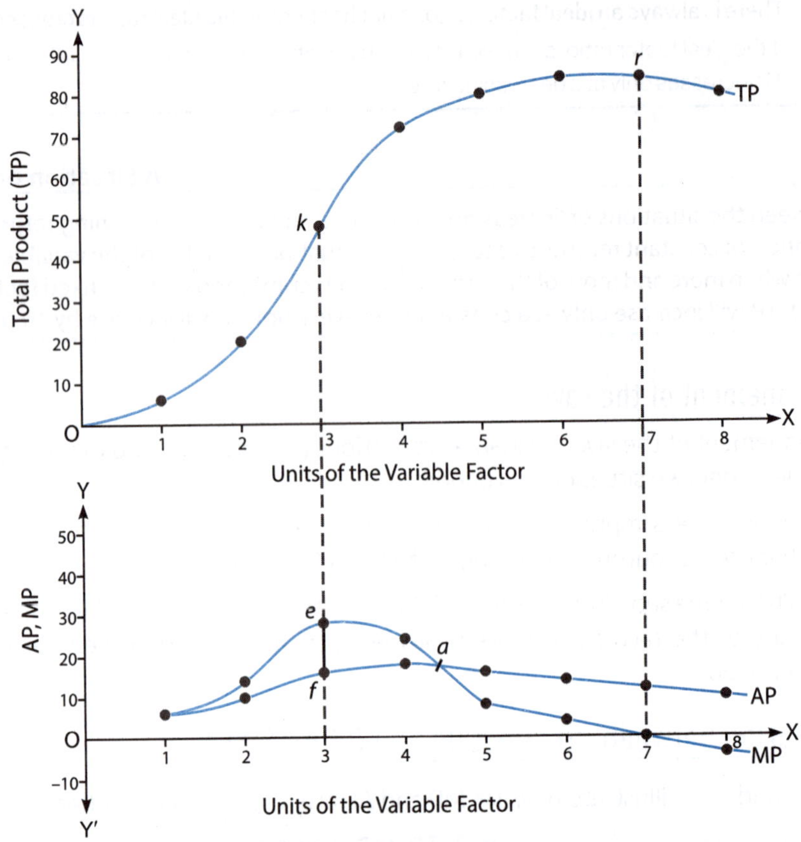

- MP is increasing till 3 units of labour are employed. Accordingly, between O to *k*, TP is increasing at an increasing rate.
- Between 3 to 7 units of labour, MP is declining. Accordingly, between *k* to *r*, TP is increasing at diminishing rate.
- When 7 units of labour are employed, MP = 0. Accordingly, at point *r*, TP is maximum.
- Beyond 7 units of labour, MP becomes negative. Accordingly beyond *r*, TP starts declining.

Observations: Relation between TP and MP

Table 2 and Fig. 3 offer following observations on the relation between TP and MP:

(i) So long as MP is increasing, TP is increasing at increasing rate. Table 2 and Fig. 3 show that till the 3rd unit of variable factor, MP is increasing from 6 to 14 to 28 tonnes of rice. Accordingly, while the 1st unit of labour contributes 6 tonnes of rice to total output, 2nd unit contributes 14 tonnes and the 3rd unit contributes 28 tonnes. Implying that TP is increasing at increasing rate.

(ii) When MP starts diminishing, TP increases only at a diminishing rate. It starts happening when 4th unit of labour is used. MP of the 4th unit is 24 tonnes of rice, of the 5th unit it is 8 tonnes of rice, and of the 6th unit it is just 4 tonnes of rice. Accordingly, when 4th unit of labour is used, TP increases by 24 tonnes; when 5th unit of labour is used, TP increases by 8 units, and when 6th unit of labour is used, TP increases only by 4 tonnes. Implying that TP is increasing only at decreasing rate.

(iii) When MP = 0, there is no addition to TP. It happens when 7th unit of labour is used. Corresponding to zero MP, TP is maximum.

(iv) When MP is negative, TP starts declining. It happens when 8th unit of labour is employed. TP diminishes from 84 to 80, and MP is 80 – 84 = –4.

MP is the rate of TP

Increasing MP implies TP is increasing at increasing rate. Diminishing MP implies that TP is increasing at diminishing rate. Zero MP implies that TP stops increasing. Negative MP implies reduction in TP.

Observations: Relation between AP and MP

(i) AP increases so long as MP > AP. It happens in Fig. 3 till point '*d*' where AP is at its top.

(ii) AP decreases when MP < AP. It happens in Fig. 3 beyond point '*d*' where AP is at its top.

(iii) AP is at its maximum when AP = MP. It is exactly at point '*d*' in Fig. 3. Thus, MP curve cuts AP curve from its top.

(iv) MP may be zero or negative, but AP continues to be positive.

HOTS

Q.1. Why MP curve cuts AP curve from its top?

Ans. This is because, when AP rises, MP > AP; when AP falls, MP < AP. Accordingly, it is only when AP is constant at its top, that AP = MP. Implying that MP curve cuts AP curve from its top.

Q.2. AP may continue to rise even when MP starts declining. Why?

Ans. This happens so long as declining MP is greater than the existing AP. **Example:** In Table 2, MP declines from 28 to 24 when 4th unit of labour is employed. Yet the corresponding AP increases from 16 to 18. Simply because, even when MP declines to 24 it still is greater than the existing average product which is 16 (when 3 units of labour are employed). In Fig. 3, this happens corresponding to the stretch '*ea*' on MP curve and the stretch '*fa*' on AP curve.

Q.3. Do you agree that TP must decrease in a situation of diminishing returns?

Ans. No. TP should not be decreasing in a situation of diminishing returns. In a situation of diminishing returns, MP decreases (like from 10 to 9 to 8). It means less and less units of output are added to TP. Nevertheless, TP must be rising. TP decreases only in a situation of negative returns.

Q.4. Should both TP and MP be declining in a situation of diminishing returns?

Ans. No. In a situation of diminishing returns, only MP should be declining. And, when MP is decreasing, TP should be increasing, though at a diminishing rate.

Geometrically, MP and TP show the following relationships:

FIGURE 4

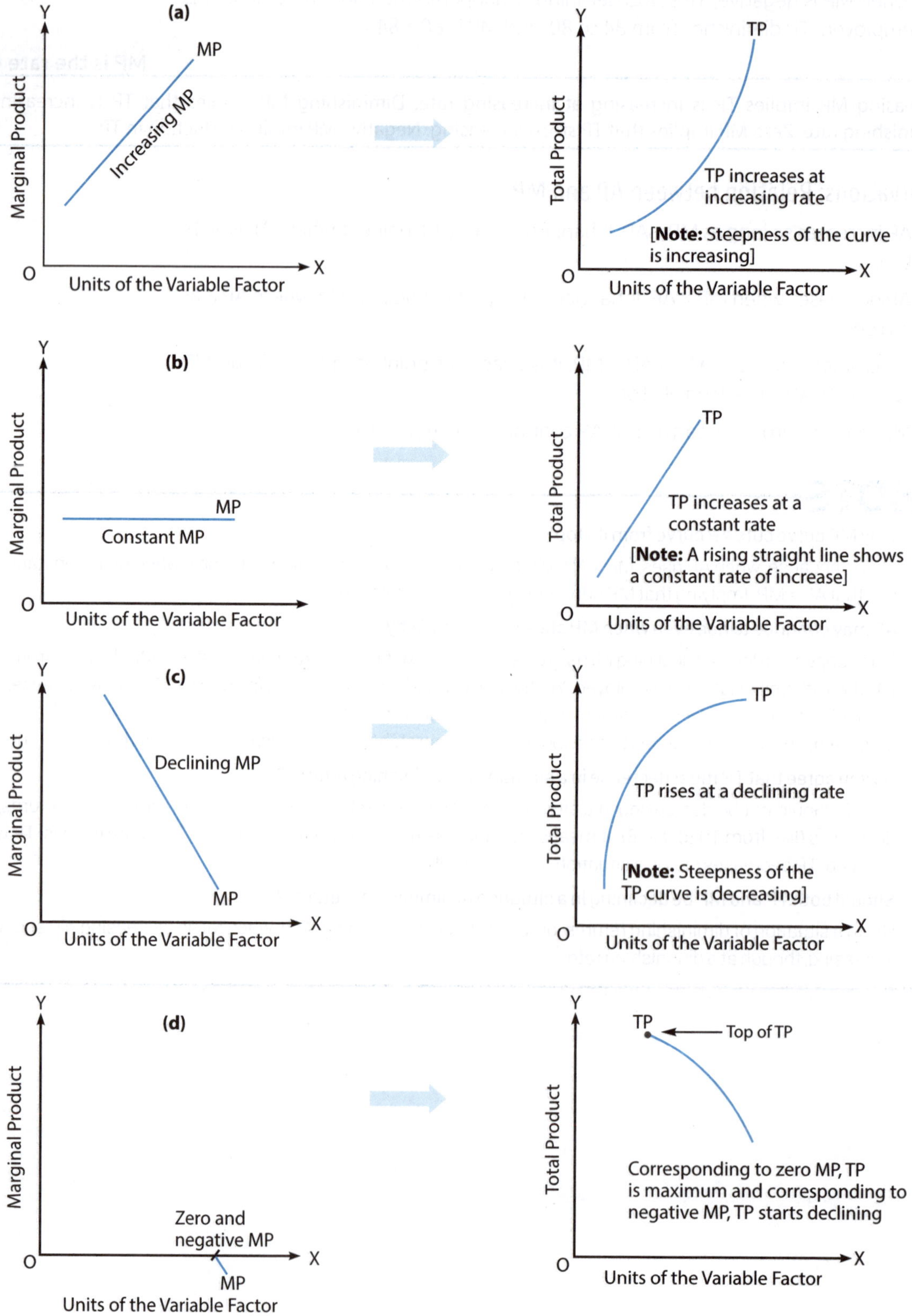

POWER POINTS

- **Production Function** studies the functional relationship between physical inputs and physical output.
- **Short Period Production Function** is a variable proportions type production function. It studies the behaviour of output in response to a change in variable factor only.
- **Long Period Production Function** is a constant proportions type production function. It studies the behaviour of output in response to a change in 'all factors in a constant ratio'.
- **Total Product (TP)** is the sum total of output corresponding to each unit of the variable factor used in the process of production.

$$TP = \Sigma MP$$

Or, $TP = AP \times L$ (units of the variable factor)

- **Marginal Product (MP)** is additional output when one more unit of the variable factor is used, fixed factor remaining constant.

$$MP_{nth} = TP_n - TP_{n-1}$$

- **Average Product (AP)** is per unit output of the variable factor.

$$AP = \frac{TP}{L}$$

- **Law of Variable Proportions** states that as more and more of the variable factor is used (along with the fixed factor), marginal product of the variable factor may initially rise, but eventually a situation must come when marginal product of the variable factor starts declining.
- **Causes of Law of Variable Proportions** are: (i) Fixity of the factor, (ii) Imperfect factor substitutability, (iii) Poor coordination between the factors.
- **Postponement of the Law of Variable Proportions** is possible only through new technology, or when some substitute of the fixed factor is discovered. In no situation, occurrence of the law can be avoided for all time to come.
- **Three Stages of Production:**
  - (i) Stage of increasing returns to a factor (when MP is increasing).
  - (ii) Stage of diminishing returns to a factor (when MP is decreasing).
  - (iii) Stage of negative returns to a factor (when MP is negative).

EXERCISE

1. Very Short Questions (Remembering & Understanding) (1 mark each)

A. Multiple Choice Questions: Choose the Correct Answer

1. Short run production function is related to:

(a) the law of variable proportions (b) returns to scale

(c) both (a) and (b) (d) none of these

2. In the context of long run production function, factor ratio is:

(a) variable (b) constant

(c) variable as well as constant (d) none of these

3. Per unit production of the variable factor is called:

(a) total product (b) average product

(c) marginal product (d) none of these

4. Which of the following equations is correct?

(a) $AP = \frac{Q}{L}$ (b) $MP = \frac{Q}{\Delta L}$

(c) $MP = \frac{\Delta Q}{L}$ (d) none of these

[AP = Average product; Q = Output; L = Variable factor; MP = Marginal product]

5. Which of the following equations is correct?

(a) $MP = TP_n - TP_{n-2}$
(b) $AP = TP \times L$
(c) $TP = \frac{AP}{L}$
(d) $MP = \frac{\Delta TP}{\Delta L}$

6. Variable proportions type production function exists:

(a) when with change in the level of output there is change in factor ratio
(b) when it is possible to increase output by increasing the application of the variable factor
(c) when scale of production changes with change in the level of output
(d) both (a) and (b)

7. What will be the state of total output when marginal product turns negative?

(a) Total output will begin to fall
(b) Total output will begin to rise
(c) Total output will remain constant
(d) None of these

8. When average product (output) increases, marginal product is:

(a) equal to average product
(b) greater than average product
(c) less than average product
(d) zero

9. Which one of the following leads to the law of variable proportions?

(a) Some factors are constant
(b) Some factors are more efficient than others
(c) Specialisation of factors
(d) None of these

10. In case of diminishing returns to a factor:

(a) total product increases at diminishing rate
(b) total product increases at increasing rate
(c) marginal product diminishes
(d) both (a) and (c)

11. When more and more units of a variable factor are combined with the fixed factor, the resulting law is called:

(a) Law of Variable Proportions
(b) Law of Increasing Returns to Scale
(c) Law of Decreasing Returns to Scale
(d) Law of Constant Returns to Scale

12. Stage of negative returns sets in when:

(a) MP is diminishing
(b) MP is rising
(c) MP is negative
(d) none of these

13. When MP cuts AP at its highest point:

(a) $MP > AP$
(b) $MP < AP$
(c) $MP = AP$
(d) all of these

14. When MP is decreasing, TP increases:

(a) at an increasing rate
(b) at a decreasing rate
(c) at a constant rate
(d) none of these

15. Physical product refers to production as measured in terms of:

(a) physical units
(b) monetary units
(c) utility
(d) value

16. When total product is maximum then marginal product:

(a) decreases
(b) increases
(c) is also maximum
(d) is zero

17. When MP is constant:

(a) TP is also constant
(b) TP is zero
(c) TP is increasing at a constant rate
(d) TP is decreasing at a constant rate

18. Point of inflexion refers to that point from where:

(a) slope of TP changes
(b) TP stops increasing at an increasing rate
(c) slope of AP changes
(d) both (a) and (b)

19. **Marginal product curve is a:**
   (a) U-shaped curve (b) inverse U-shaped curve
   (c) rectangular hyperbola (d) none of these
20. **When total product is 100 units and units of variable factor are 4, average product will be:**
   (a) 25 (b) 400
   (c) 96 (d) 104
21. **During short period, production can be increased through:**
   (a) greater application of fixed factors (b) greater application of variable factors
   (c) greater application of all the factors of production (d) none of these
22. **Stages of production are the consequences of:**
   (a) Law of Diminishing Marginal Rate of Transformation
   (b) Law of Diminishing Marginal Utility
   (c) Law of Variable Proportions
   (d) Law of Diminishing Returns to Scale

Answers

1. (a) **2.** (b) **3.** (b) **4.** (a) **5.** (d) **6.** (d) **7.** (a) **8.** (b) **9.** (a) **10.** (d) **11.** (a) **12.** (c)
13. (c) **14.** (b) **15.** (a) **16.** (d) **17.** (c) **18.** (d) **19.** (b) **20.** (a) **21.** (b) **22.** (c)

B. Information & Concept-based Questions

1. **What is meant by production function?**

Ans. Production function refers to the functional relationship between (physical) inputs and (physical) output.

2. **What is the basic difference between short run production function and long run production function?**

Ans. Short run production function is variable proportions type production function. Long run production function, on the other hand, is constant proportions type production function.

3. **What are the fixed and variable factors of production?**

Ans. Fixed factors of production are those factors of production the application of which does not change with the change in output.

Variable factors of production are those factors of production the application of which changes with the change in output.

4. **What is meant by returns to a factor?**

Ans. Returns to a factor refers to the behaviour of physical output owing to change in physical input of a variable factor, fixed factors remaining constant.

5. **Spell out the basic difference between the 'law of variable proportions', and 'returns to scale'.**

Ans. Law of variable proportions is a short period concept when output can be increased only by increasing the application of the variable factor. Fixed factor (indicating scale of output) remains constant. Returns to scale is a long period concept when output can be increased by increasing the scale of output. Increasing returns, constant returns and diminishing returns tend to operate when the scale of output is expanded, even when all the factors are variable factors.

6. **When is TP maximum in relation to MP?**

Ans. TP is maximum when MP is zero.

7. **When TP increases at an increasing rate, what happens to MP?**

Ans. When TP increases at an increasing rate, MP should be increasing.

8. **When TP increases at a diminishing rate, what happens to MP?**

Ans. When TP increases at a diminishing rate, MP should be decreasing.

9. **When TP becomes constant at its maximum, what happens to MP?**

Ans. When TP becomes constant at its maximum, MP should be zero.

2. Reason-based Questions (Comprehension of the Subject-matter)

Read the following statements carefully. Write 'True' or 'False' with a reason.

1. Production function is only a technical relationship between physical inputs and physical output.

Ans. True. Production function is only a technical relationship between physical inputs and physical output. This tells us how best resources can be utilised for maximising output.

2. TP is obtained when MP of different units of output is added.

Ans. True. $TP = \sum_{i=1}^{n} MP_i$ or TP is the summation of MP corresponding to each unit of the variable factor employed in production.

3. In the short period, production is done only by using the variable factors.

Ans. False. In the short period, production is done by using the both fixed and variable factors of production. In fact, short period is a period of time when some factors are fixed.

4. Law of variable proportions must operate, even when all factors of production are variable.

Ans. False. Law of variable proportions operates basically because of the fixity of some factors.

5. Diminishing returns to a variable factor occur because the producer fails to buy the variable factor in the required quantity.

Ans. False. Diminishing returns to a variable factor occur because the producer fails to maintain the ideal ratio between the factors, as the use of fixed factors cannot be changed during the short period.

6. Increasing returns to a factor occur because the fixed factor is excessively used in production.

Ans. False. Increasing returns to a factor occur because the fixed factor remains under-utilised.

7. Diminishing returns to a factor occur simply because supply of all factors cannot be increased.

Ans. True. It is because some factors are fixed that output is increased by using more and more units of the variable factor. It disturbs the ideal factor ratio and diminishing returns set in.

8. Law of variable proportions operates only if factor ratio happens to change.

Ans. True. Factor ratio ought to change in case of law of variable proportions. It is precisely because the proportion of factors varies that the law is named as the law of variable proportions.

9. Diminishing returns to a factor occurs because fixed factor cannot be used as much as the variable factor.

Ans. True. As more and more units of a variable factor are combined with the fixed factor, the latter gets over utilised. Hence, the diminishing returns.

10. It is because of the law of variable proportions that MP curve makes an inverted-U.

Ans. True. In accordance with the law of variable proportions, MP of the variable factor (combined with the fixed factor) initially tends to rise, subsequently stabilises and finally must fall. Hence, MP curve forms an inverted-U.

11. TP must rise as more and more units of a variable factor are combined with the fixed factor.

Ans. False. As more and more units of the variable factor are combined with the fixed factor, TP will rise only so long as MP is positive. Once MP becomes negative, TP will start falling.

12. When MP is declining, TP must also decline.

Ans. False. When MP is declining TP should increasing, though at a diminishing rate. It is only when MP is negative that TP must decline.

13. AP can rise even when MP is falling.

Ans. True. AP can rise even when MP is falling. This happens in a situation when falling MP is greater than the existing AP.

14. MP = AP when AP is maximum.

Ans. True. AP is at its maximum when MP = AP. In this case, MP curve cuts AP curve from its top.

15. If AP is falling, MP must also fall.

Ans. True. If AP is falling, MP must also fall. Because, unless MP (showing additions to TP) is falling, AP (showing average output) will not fall.

16. MP is the rate of TP.

Ans. True. MP is the rate of TP. Increasing MP implies that TP is increasing at increasing rate. Diminishing MP implies that TP is increasing at diminishing rate.

17. It is more profitable for the producer to be in a stage of increasing returns than the stage of diminishing returns.

Ans. False. A producer would maximise his profits only in the stage of diminishing returns when MP is declining but is still positive.

18. Diminishing returns to a factor always lead to fall in total product.

Ans. False. This is because in a situation of diminishing returns to a factor marginal product tends to fall. Falling marginal product implies that total product should be increasing, though at a diminishing rate. It simply implies diminishing slope of TP (total product) curve, NOT diminishing TP.

19. Increase in total product always follows the increase in marginal product.

Ans. False. Total product will also increase when marginal product decreases. In that case, total product increases at diminishing rate. However, MP should not be negative.

20. Increasing returns to a factor are indicated whenever there is increase in total product.

Ans. False. Total product increases even when there are diminishing returns to a factor, even though it (TP) increases at a diminishing rate.

21. Diminishing returns to a factor must lead to a fall in marginal product as well as total product.

Ans. False. Diminishing returns to a factor lead to a fall in marginal product only. Total product increases (at the diminishing rate).

22. Fall in marginal product must lead to a fall in average product as well.

Ans. False. Average product can rise even when marginal product falls. See AP and MP corresponding to output range MQ in Fig. 5. AP rises corresponding to falling MP so long as falling MP is greater than the existing AP.

FIGURE 5

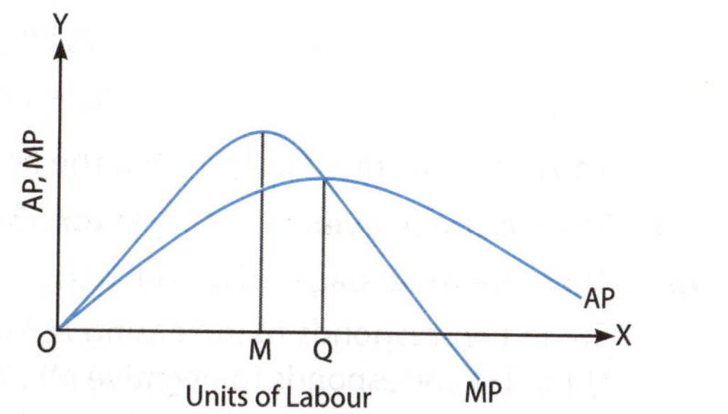

23. Initially total product increases but ultimately falls when there are diminishing returns to a factor.

Ans. False. In a situation of diminishing returns to a factor marginal product tends to fall. Falling marginal product implies that total product should be increasing, though at a diminishing rate. It simply implies diminishing slope of TP (total product) curve, NOT diminishing TP.

24. Total product must increase no matter there are increasing or diminishing returns to a factor.

Ans. True. In a situation of increasing returns to a factor, marginal product tends to rise. Accordingly, total product should be increasing at an increasing rate. In a situation of diminishing returns to a factor, marginal product tends to fall. Accordingly, total product should be increasing at a decreasing rate.

3. HOTS & Applications

1. Why should TP be maximum when MP = 0?

Ans. MP is the rate of TP (*i.e.*, it measures the change in TP). When MP = 0, there is no change (or addition) in TP. Implying that TP should be maximum when MP = 0.

2. Find TP when 5 units of the variable factor are combined with 5 units of the fixed factor and MP remains constant at 10 units.

Ans. When MP remains constant at 10 units, and 5 units of the variable factor are used,

TP = 10 + 10 + 10 + 10 + 10 = 50. $(\because TP = \Sigma MP)$

3. MP can be negative, but not the AP. Comment.

Ans. Yes. MP can be zero or negative but AP is never. Because, AP is the ratio between TP and units of the variable factor (which is always positive) while MP is change in TP (owing to an additional unit of the variable factor) which can be zero or negative.

4. Stage of increasing returns (when MP is increasing) is economically redundant, because the producer will not strike his equilibrium in this stage. Comment.

Ans. Yes. Because in a stage of increasing returns, cost of producing every additional unit of output tends to fall. Accordingly, it would be irrational for the producer to stop production in this stage.

5. At the existing level of output, MP = AP = 10 units. Would AP be equal to MP when production is increased and law of variable proportions is in operation?

Ans. No. When production is increased beyond a point where MP = AP (implying AP is at its top), MP and AP should start declining. Fall in MP should be faster than the fall in AP. So that AP > MP.

6. Do you agree that an intelligent producer can avoid the occurrence of diminishing returns to a factor even with the existing technology?

Ans. No. Diminishing returns to a factor cannot be avoided with the constant technology. Because diminishing returns occur as a matter of law when the producer drifts from the ideal factor ratio owing to the fixity of the factor(s).

7. Let us take a production function $Q = 3L^{1/3}K^{1/3}$. Find out the maximum possible output that the firm can produce with125 units of L and 125 units of K.

Ans. Given,

$$Q = 3L^{1/3}K^{1/3}$$

$$Q = 3(125)^{1/3}(125)^{1/3}$$

$$= 3(5^3)^{1/3}(5^3)^{1/3}$$

$$= 3 \times 5 \times 5 = 75$$

Thus, the maximum output that the firm can produce with125 units of L and 125 units of K is 75.

8. What is the relevance of stages (or phases) of production to the producer?

Ans. There are three stages of production:

Stage I corresponds to increasing MP (marginal product), stage II corresponds to decreasing MP, and stage III corresponds to negative MP. We know, cost is the reciprocal of productivity so that we can say that stage I corresponds to decreasing MC, stage II corresponds to increasing MC, and stage III corresponds to a situation when total product starts declining. No firm will ever like to enter stage III when with greater application of a factor, total product starts declining.

Also, other things remaining constant, no firm will ever like to strike its equilibrium in stage I when its MC is falling. Thus, from the producer's equilibrium point of view, the only relevant stage is stage II when MC tends to rise; stages I and III are redundant.

9. Do the terms 'diminishing' or 'constant' mean that the output decreases or remains constant in the context of the law of variable proportions?

Ans. No, the terms 'diminishing' or 'constant' do not mean that the output decreases or remains constant. Output always increases when an input is increased. This holds as long as marginal product of each factor is positive, *i.e.*, the firm is not operating in stage III of negative returns to a factor. 'Diminishing' or 'constant' only refer to marginal product of the output. It is marginal product which tends to diminish when diminishing returns are in operation. Again, it is marginal product which tends to remain constant when constant returns are operative.

10. Complete the following table:

Units of Labour	Average Product	Marginal Product
1	4	—
2	5	—
3	5	—
4	4	—
5	3	—

Ans.

Units of Labour	Average Product	Total Product	Marginal Product
1	4	4	4
2	5	10	6
3	5	15	5
4	4	16	1
5	3	15	–1

11. Complete the following table, on the assumption that for each additional unit of the variable factor, marginal product decreases by 5 units of output.

Units of Labour	TP	AP	MP
—	—	—	—
—	—	—	—
—	—	—	—
—	—	—	–5

Ans.

Units of Labour	TP	AP	MP
1	10	10	10
2	15	7.5	5
3	15	5	0
4	10	2.5	–5

12. From the following table, find TP and MP of labour assuming that TP of labour is zero at zero level of employment of labour.

Units of Labour	1	2	3	4	5
AP	15	14	13	12	11

Ans.

Units of Labour	AP	TP	MP
1	15	15	15
2	14	28	13
3	13	39	11
4	12	48	9
5	11	55	7

13. Fill in the blanks:

Units of Fixed Factor (Land)	Units of Variable Factor (Labour)	TP_L	AP_L	MP_L
10	0	0	—	—
10	1	60	—	—
10	2	—	85	—
10	3	—	—	100
10	4	300	—	—
10	5	—	—	50
10	6	—	75	—

Ans.

Units of Fixed Factor (Land)	Units of Variable Factor (Labour)	TP_L	AP_L	MP_L
10	0	0	—	—
10	1	60	60	60
10	2	170	85	110
10	3	270	90	100
10	4	300	75	30
10	5	350	70	50
10	6	450	75	100

14. Complete the following table:

Labour (Units)	Total Product	Average Product	Marginal Product
1	40	—	—
2	—	—	60
3	—	—	50
4	180	—	—
5	—	36	—
6	—	—	–18

Ans.

Labour (Units)	Total Product	Average Product	Marginal Product
1	40	40	40
2	100	50	60
3	150	50	50
4	180	45	30
5	180	36	0
6	162	27	–18

15. Complete the following table. Identify the point where TP tends to increase at the diminishing rate.

Units of Labour	TP	AP	MP
1	—	—	100
2	—	—	120
3	—	—	80
4	—	—	60
5	—	—	0
6	—	—	–60

Ans.

Units of Labour	TP	AP	MP
1	100	100	100
2	220	110	120
3	300	100	80
4	360	90	60
5	360	72	0
6	300	50	–60

It is when 3rd unit of the variable factor is applied that TP tends to increase at the diminishing rate.

4. Evaluation (Value-based Questions)

1. Output of food grain in India at one stage was less than its domestic demand. Now it is not. Does it mean that the law of diminishing returns has failed in Indian agriculture?

Ans. Rise in output of food grain in India is owing to the use of new technology (related to High-Yielding Variety Seeds). When there is an improvement in technology, the occurrence of the law of diminishing returns is deferred for some time. It does not mean that the law of diminishing returns has failed. It only means postponement of the law. The law is bound to set-in again once the effect of new technology is exhausted.

2. When law of diminishing returns is a universal law, why is AP found to be much higher in developed countries like USA than in less developed countries like India? Give two reasons.

Ans. It is a fact that the law of diminishing returns is a universal law. It operates in all economies, more developed or less developed. However, AP is much higher in developed countries, because:

(i) Developed countries use a much more advanced technology than the less developed economies.

(ii) Developed countries are rich economies. Labour in these countries is aided with capital, much more than in poor countries. Accordingly, efficiency of labour (implying productivity of labour) is much higher in countries like USA than India.

3. When diminishing returns are reversed through mechanisation in agriculture, how does it impact the employment of labour?

Ans. Mechanisation implies the use of capital (machinery) in place of labour. It raises productivity of labour, of course. But, leads to the emergence of surplus labour in agriculture.

4. FDI not only brings investment in the domestic economy, it also brings new technology. How would the availability of new technology (relating to auto industry) impact the short period production function of a car manufacturer in India?

Ans. Short period production function of a firm is drawn on the assumption of a given technology. When new technology is available, the whole production function would shift: more output would be available from the same quantum of inputs. In terms of costs, firm's AC curve would shift downward. Thus, the availability of new technology (relating to auto industry) would shift the AC curve (of a car manufacturer) downward. It would prompt him to produce more at the going price.

5. CBSE Questions—Past 4 years (With Answers or Reference to the Text for Answers)

1. What does the law of variable proportions show? State the behaviour of total product according to this law. *[CBSE Delhi 2012]*
[Page 163–165]

2. What does the law of variable proportions show? State the behaviour of marginal product according to this law. *[CBSE (AI) 2012]*
[Page 163–165]

3. State the phases of changes in total product in the law of variable proportions. Also explain the reason behind each phase. Use diagram. *[CBSE (F) 2012]*

Or

State the different phases of change in total product according to the law of variable proportions. Use diagram. *[CBSE (F) 2014]*

Or

What are the different phases in the law of variable proportions in terms of total product? Give reasons behind each phase. Use diagram. *[CBSE (F) 2015]*
[Page 164–166]

4. Explain the law of variable proportions with the help of total product and marginal product curves. *[CBSE Delhi 2013]*

Or

Explain the law of variable proportions. Use diagram. *[CBSE (F) 2013]*
[Page 163–165]

5. Complete the following table: [CBSE Delhi 2013]

Units of Labour	Average Product (Units)	Marginal Product (Units)
1	8	—
2	10	—
3	—	10
4	9	—
5	—	4
6	7	—

[Page 381]

6. Complete the following table: [CBSE Delhi 2013]

Units of Labour	Average Product (Units)	Marginal Product (Units)
1	16	—
2	20	—
3	—	20
4	18	—
5	—	8
6	14	—

[Page 382]

7. Give reasons, state whether the following statements are true or false:
   (i) Average product will increase only when marginal product increases.
   (ii) Under diminishing returns to a factor, total product continues to increase till marginal product reaches zero. [CBSE (AI) 2013]

   [(i) False. Average product can rise even when marginal product falls. See AP and MP corresponding to output range MQ in Fig. 5.
   (ii) True. Under diminishing returns to a factor, marginal product tends to fall. Falling marginal product implies that total product increases at a diminishing rate. TP is maximum when MP = 0.]

8. Define production function. [CBSE (F) 2013, 2014]
   [Page 157]

9. How is marginal product calculated? [CBSE (F) 2013]
   [Page 161]

10. Give meaning of 'returns to a factor'. [CBSE Delhi 2014]
    [Page 163]

11. State the behaviour of marginal product in the law of variable proportions. Explain the causes of this behaviour. [CBSE Delhi 2014]
    [Page 163–166]

12. Define marginal product. [CBSE (AI) 2014]
    [Page 161]

13. Giving reasons, explain the 'Law of Variable Proportions'. [CBSE (AI) 2014]
    [Page 163–166]

14. State the different phases of changes in total product and marginal product in the law of variable proportions. Also show the same in a single diagram. [CBSE Delhi 2015]
    [Page 164, 165]

15. What are the different phases in the law of variable proportions in terms of marginal product? Give reason behind each phase. Use diagram. [CBSE (AI) 2015]
    [Page 164–166]

6. NCERT Questions (With Hints to Answers)

1. Explain the concept of a production function.

   [**Hint:** Production function studies the functional relationship between physical inputs and physical output. It is expressed as under:

   $$Q_X = f(L, K)$$

   Here, Q = Production of the commodity-X; L = Units of labour; K = Units of capital.]

2. What is the total product of an input?

   [**Hint:** It is the sum total of output produced by all units of the input. Or, it is the sum total of marginal product corresponding to each unit of the input.]

3. What is the average product of an input?

   [**Hint:** It is output per unit of the input.]

4. What is the marginal product of an input?

   [**Hint:** It is the additional output as a result of a unit change in the input.]

5. Explain the relationship between the marginal product and the total product of an input.

   [**Hint:** (i) When MP increases, TP increases at increasing rate.
   (ii) When MP decreases, TP increases at a diminishing rate.
   (iii) When MP is constant, TP increases at constant rate.
   (iv) When MP = 0, TP is maximum.
   (v) When MP is negative, TP declines.]

6. Explain the concepts of the short run and the long run.

   [**Hint:** Short run is a period of time when some factors of production are fixed and some are variable. So that, output can be increased only by increasing the application of variable factor. In the short run, scale of production remains constant. Long run is a period of time when all factors of production are variable. So that, output can be increased by increasing the application of all factors of production. In the long run, scale of output can be changed.]

7. What is the law of diminishing marginal product?

   [**Hint:** Law of diminishing marginal product refers to a situation in which total output increases at the diminishing rate when more of the variable factor is combined with the fixed factor(s) of production.]

8. What is the law of variable proportions?

   [**Hint:** The law states that as more and more of the variable factor is combined with the fixed factor, marginal product of the variable factor may initially increase and subsequently stabilise, but must finally decrease.]

9. The following table gives the total product schedule of labour. Find the corresponding average product and marginal product schedules of labour.

L	0	1	2	3	4	5
TP_L	0	15	35	50	40	48

[**Hint:**

L	TP_L	AP_L	MP_L
0	0	—	—
1	15	15	15
2	35	17.5	20
3	50	16.67	15
4	40	10	-10
5	48	9.6	8

10. The following table gives the average product schedule of labour. Find the total product and marginal product schedules. It is given that the total product is zero at zero level of labour employment.

L	1	2	3	4	5	6
AP_L	2	3	4	4.25	4	3.5

[**Hint:**

L	**AP_L**	**TP_L**	**MP_L**
1	2	2	2
2	3	6	4
3	4	12	6
4	4.25	17	5
5	4	20	3
6	3.5	21	1

11. The following table gives the marginal product schedule of labour. It is also given that total product of labour is zero at zero level of employment. Calculate the total and average product schedules of labour.

L	1	2	3	4	5	6
MP_L	3	5	7	5	3	1

[**Hint:**

L	**MP_L**	**TP_L**	**AP_L**
1	3	3	3
2	5	8	4
3	7	15	5
4	5	20	5
5	3	23	4.6
6	1	24	4

12. Let the production function of a firm be:

$$Q = 5L^{1/2}K^{1/2}$$

Find out the maximum possible output that the firm can produce with 100 units of L and 100 units of K.

[**Hint:** Given,

$$Q = 5L^{1/2}K^{1/2}$$
$$Q = 5(100)^{1/2}(100)^{1/2}$$
$$= 5(10^2)^{1/2}(10^2)^{1/2}$$
$$= 5 \times 10 \times 10 = 500$$

The maximum output the firm can produce with 100 units of L and 100 units of K is 500.]

13. Let the production function of a firm be:

$$Q = 2L^2K^2$$

Find out the maximum possible output that the firm can produce with 5 units of L and 2 units of K.

[**Hint:** Given,

$$Q = 2L^2K^2$$
$$Q = 2(5)^2(2)^2$$
$$= 2 \times 25 \times 4$$
$$= 200$$

The maximum possible output that the firm can produce with 5 units of L and 2 units of K is 200.]

14. Find out the maximum possible output for a firm with 10 units of L and 10 units of K when its production function is: Q = 5L + 2K

[**Hint:** Given, Q = 5L + 2K

Q = 5(10) + 2(10)

= 50 + 20 = 70

The maximum possible output that the firm can produce with 10 units of L and 10 units of K is 70.]

7. Miscellaneous Questions and Reference to the Text for Answers

A. Questions of 3 & 4 marks each

1. Explain the concepts of total, average and marginal product with the help of a table.
[Page 160–162]
2. What is the relation of TP with MP in different stages of the operation of the law of variable proportions?
[Page 164, 165]
3. What is meant by returns to a factor? Explain.
[Page 163]
4. What is meant by increasing returns to a factor? What leads to increasing returns to a factor?
[Page 164, 165]
5. What is meant by diminishing returns to a factor? Explain its causes.
[Page 164–166]

B. Questions of 6 marks each

1. Explain the law of variable proportions in terms of the behaviour of total physical product with the help of a diagram.
[Page 163–165]
2. State the phases of the law of variable proportions in terms of total physical product. Use diagram.
[Page 164, 165]
3. Explain the relationship between marginal product and total product, using a suitable diagram.
[Page 168, 169]
4. Explain the relationship between AP and MP, using a suitable diagram.
[Page 168,169]

DOs and DON'Ts

1. Students are often found to be talking of three laws: (i) Law of increasing returns, (ii) Law of constant returns, and (iii) Law of diminishing returns. It is wrong Economics. There is nothing like law of increasing returns, and there is nothing like the law of constant returns. Increasing returns and constant returns are just the possibilities which a producer may encounter during the course of his production process. A possibility is not a law. A law refers to a situation which must occur. Situation of diminishing returns must occur. Increasing application of the variable factor along with the fixed factor must eventually lead to diminishing returns. Hence, it is a law.
2. Never think that good economists can avoid the occurrence of the law of variable proportions through good planning. As noted in the text, occurrence of the law is a universal phenomenon. It is not formulated by the economists. It is formulated by the technocrats. It is the technocrats who tell us that the application of the variable factor beyond a specified limit must lead to a fall in marginal product of the factor. Again, it is the technocrats who tell us how the use of more efficient technology leads to higher level of 'potential output', a situation when more is produced with the given resources, and the law (of diminishing returns) is deferred.

abilityZONE

Returns to a Factor and Behaviour of TP

Should TP always increase in a situation of increasing returns?

Yes. Because increasing returns occur when MP is increasing. Increasing MP implies a situation when TP should be increasing at an increasing rate.

Should TP ever decrease in a situation of diminishing returns?

No. Diminishing returns occur when MP is diminishing. Diminishing MP does not imply a fall in TP. It only implies a situation when TP is increasing at a diminishing rate. TP decreases only in a situation of negative returns.

Does rising TP always point to increasing returns?

No. Rising TP does not always point to increasing returns. TP rises even when MP is decreasing, as in a situation of diminishing returns. The difference is that in a situation of increasing returns, TP rises at an increasing rate while in a situation of diminishing returns, TP rises at a diminishing rate.

A Shift in Approach with Regard to Stages of Production

Earlier, stages of production were explained largely with reference to the behaviour of AP. Thus, stage I coincided with rising AP and stage II coincided with falling AP. Now there is a shift in approach. These stages are now explained with reference to the behaviour of MP. While stage I is taken to coincide with rising MP, stage II is taken to coincide with falling MP. The readers should note that this shift in approach is not due to any error in the conventional approach. It is entirely due to an emerging belief that relating stages of production to the behaviour of MP should make the subject matter simpler for the +2 students. Particularly, the current approach is in sync with the discussion in later chapters where students are told that a producer would strike his equilibrium only when MP is falling (or when MC—which is the reciprocal of MP—is rising).

Long Period Production Function and Returns to Scale

When, in the long run, the scale of production is increased (factor ratio remaining constant), the behaviour of output indicates three distinct phases, as under:

Phase-1: Increasing Returns to Scale

This is a situation when a given percentage increase in all factor inputs causes a higher percentage increase in output. **Example:** 10% increase in both L and K leads to more than 10% increase in output. Thus, the unit cost of production (AC) tends to decline.

Phase-2: Constant Returns to Scale

This is a situation when a given percentage increase in all factor inputs causes the same percentage increase in output. **Example:** 10% increase in both L and K leads to 10% increase in output. Here, the unit cost of production (AC) remains constant.

Phase-3: Diminishing Returns to Scale

This is a situation when a given percentage increase in all factor inputs causes a lower percentage increase in output. **Example:** 10% increase in both L and K leads to less than 10% increase in output. Now, the unit cost of production (AC) tends to rise.

It is owing to these phases of output behaviour (or owing to the returns to scale) that the long run average cost curve becomes U-shaped.

However, long run average cost curve is flatter than the short run average cost curve. **Reason:** Short run average cost is related to one plant (or constant scale of output). Long run average cost, on the other hand, is related to several plants (or shifting scale of output).

Concepts of Cost

CHAPTER 7

TODO

- Concept of Cost
- Short Run Costs of Production:
  - (i) Fixed and Variable Costs—Behaviour of Fixed Cost, Variable Cost and Total Cost
  - (ii) Average Cost—Fixed and Variable Components of Average Cost
  - (iii) Marginal Cost—Estimation and Behaviour of MC
- Relation between Average, Marginal and Total Cost

1. Concept of Cost

Output needs inputs. Broadly, there are two types of inputs (i) factor inputs (land, labour, capital & entrepreneurship, called factors of production), and (ii) non-factor inputs (raw material). Cost refers to the expenditure incurred by a producer on the factor as well as non-factor inputs for a given amount of output of a commodity.

Cost

Cost refers to the expenditure incurred by a producer (explicitly or implicitly) on the factor as well as non-factor inputs for a given amount of output of a commodity.

Explicit and Implicit Cost

All inputs may not be purchased from the market. A producer may use some self-owned inputs. **Example:** Instead of hired workers from the market, producer may use his family labour. Likewise, a producer may use his own land instead of taking it on lease. Expenditure incurred by the producer on the purchase of inputs from the market is called explicit cost. Estimated expenditure on the use of self-owned inputs is called implicit cost. In Economics, total cost is estimated considering both its elements, *viz.*, explicit cost and implicit cost.

It is significant to note that in Economics, cost is always measured as opportunity cost. And, we know that opportunity cost of an activity is measured in terms of the total sacrifice involved in undertaking that activity. Thus, cost of producing a given amount of output always implies opportunity cost of producing that output, and is to be measured in terms of the sacrifice involved in producing that output. From the producer's point of view (or the firm's point of view), the sacrifice involved in producing a given amount of output includes:

(i) explicit cost, and

(ii) implicit cost of production.

A glance at the following flow chart should bring further clarity on this point.

Flow Chart : Measurement of Cost

Cost = Opportunity Cost

- **Explicit Cost**
  - ↓ Opportunity cost of hiring/purchasing inputs from the market
  - ↓ Payments made by a firm to others for hiring/purchasing inputs from the market
- **Implicit Cost**
  - ↓ Opportunity cost of using self-owned inputs
  - ↓ Market value of self-owned inputs in their next best alternative use

Example

Leaving a job of ₹ 40,000 per month and evicting his tenant who was paying ₹ 50,000 per month for the factory premises, an entrepreneur undertakes production of garments. He pays ₹ 10,00,000 for the purchase of inputs. Find cost of production in terms of explicit cost and implicit cost.

Solution:

Total Cost = Opportunity Cost
= Explicit Cost + Implicit Cost

Explicit Cost ↓	Implicit Cost ↓
Payments to others for the purchase of inputs	Value of self-owned inputs in their next best alternative use
= ₹10,00,000	= ₹ 40,000 (entrepreneur's own services) + ₹ 50,000 (imputed rent)

Total Cost = ₹ 10,00,000 + ₹ 90,000
= ₹ 10,90,000

Opportunity Cost

It refers to the total sacrifice made (explicitly or implicitly) for availing an opportunity (or producing a given level of output).

Selling Cost and Production Cost

Selling costs are different from production costs. Selling costs refer to the expenditure incurred by the producer to promote sale of the commodity. **Example:** Expenditure on advertisement. Production costs refer to the expenditure incurred by a producer (explicitly or implicitly) on the inputs for producing a given level of output.

In the present chapter, we are focusing only on production cost, as prescribed in the syllabus.

2. Short Run Costs

Short run is a period of time during which some factors are fixed and some are variable. Accordingly, short run costs have two components, *viz.*, (i) fixed costs, referring to expenditure on fixed factors, and (ii) variable costs, referring to expenditure on variable factors. Thus,

$$TC = TFC + TVC$$

[Here, TC = Total cost
TFC = Total fixed cost
TVC = Total variable cost.]

Let us discuss the details of fixed costs and variable costs.

(i) Fixed Costs

Costs related to the use of fixed factors are known as fixed costs.

> Fixed costs are the costs related to the use of fixed factors of production.

These are also called *supplementary costs*, or *overhead costs* or *indirect costs*. These costs do not change with the change in output. Even when output is zero, fixed costs remain the same. Let us take an illustration. In a carpet manufacturing firm, a machine is installed as a fixed factor. Let us assume that it can make 6 carpets a day and that the cost of hiring the machine is ₹100 per day. Obviously, ₹100 per day is the fixed cost that the producer has to incur even when no carpet is made in a day. Between 0–6 carpets in a day, the fixed cost would remain ₹100.

Besides expenditure on machine and plant, fixed costs also include expenses like: (i) Rent, (ii) Wages of permanent employees, (iii) Licence fees, etc.

Important Components of Fixed Cost

- Expenditure on machine and plant
- Expenditure on land and building
- Licence fee and related expenses
- Wages and salaries of permanent staff.

Table 1 and Fig. 1 illustrate the concept of fixed costs.

Table 1. Total Fixed Cost

Units of Output	Total Fixed Cost (₹)
0	10
1	10
2	10
3	10
4	10
5	10
6	10

Table 1 indicates that fixed costs remain constant at all levels of output. When output is zero unit, fixed cost is ₹10. When it increases to two or four or six units, even then, total fixed cost is ₹10.

FIGURE 1

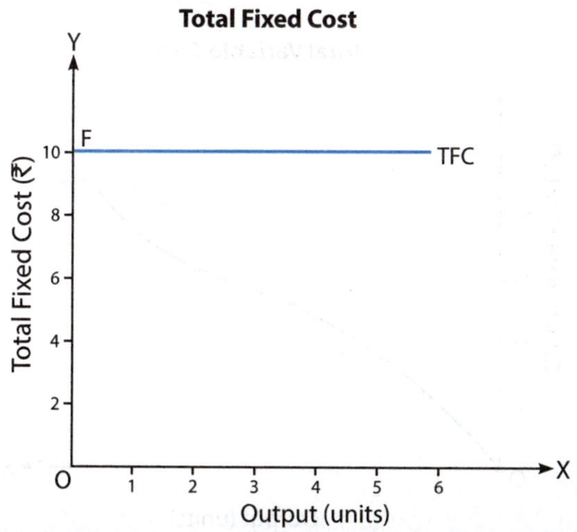

TFC is a horizontal straight line parallel to X-axis, showing that total fixed cost is constant at all levels of output. It is = ₹10, even when output is zero.

In Fig. 1, units of output are shown on X-axis and total fixed cost on Y-axis. TFC curve represents total fixed cost. This curve is parallel to X-axis, implying that cost is constant at all levels of output. TFC curve touches Y-axis at point 'F' which means that fixed cost remains ₹10 even when output is zero.

Fixed Costs and Fixed Factors of Production

Fixed costs refer to the expenditure incurred by the producer on the fixed factors of production like plant and machinery. The application of these factors cannot be changed during short period. Therefore, fixed costs are constant costs of the short period.
Further, fixed factors are purchased before production actually starts. Therefore, fixed costs are incurred even when output is zero.

(ii) Variable Costs

Variable costs are those costs which are related to the use of variable factors.

Variable costs refer to the expenditure incurred by the producer on the use of variable factors of production.

Variable costs change with a change in the volume of output. As output increases, these costs also increase and as the output decreases, these costs also decrease. When output is zero, these costs are also zero. These costs are called *Prime Costs* or *Direct Costs*. Variable costs include expenses like: (i) Purchases of raw material, (ii) Wages of casual labour, (iii) Expenses on electricity, (iv) Wear and tear expenses.

What is Short Period?

Short period is a period of time during which the application of fixed factors (plant and machinery) cannot be increased or decreased. It is because the time is too short for any such change.

Table 2 and Fig. 2 illustrate the concept of variable costs.

Table 2. Total Variable Cost

Units of Output	Total Variable Cost (₹)
0	0
1	10
2	18
3	24
4	28
5	32
6	38

Table 2 shows that as output increases, total variable cost also increases. When output is zero, total variable cost is also zero. When output is one unit, total variable cost = ₹10 and when output is six units, total variable cost = ₹38.

FIGURE 2

Total Variable Cost

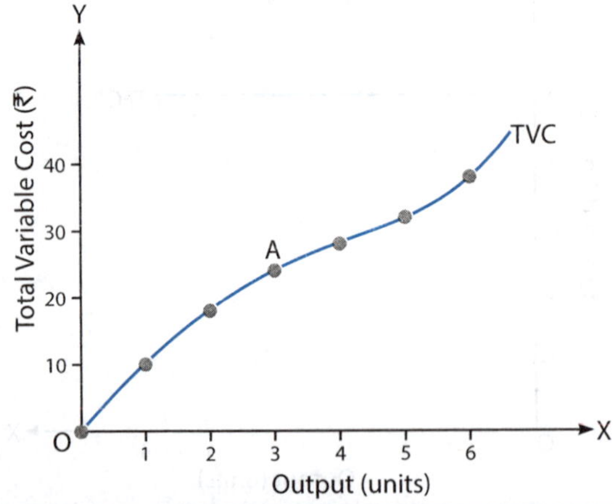

TVC increases with increase in output. It is = ₹ 10, when output = 1 unit, and is = ₹ 38, when output = 6 units. Between 0-A, TVC increases at a decreasing rate. Beyond point A, TVC increases at an increasing rate.

In Fig. 2, X-axis shows units of output and Y-axis shows total variable cost. TVC is an upward sloping curve implying that total variable cost tends to increase with increase in output.

Fixed Costs and Variable Costs—A Contrast

Fixed Costs	Variable Costs
(i) Fixed costs do not change with change in quantity of output. (ii) Fixed costs remain the same whether output is zero or maximum. **Examples:** (a) Rent, (b) Wages of permanent staff, (c) Licence fee, (d) Cost of plant and machinery.	(i) Variable costs change with change in quantity of output. (ii) Variable costs are zero when output is zero. These costs increase when output increases and decrease when output decreases. **Examples:** (a) Cost of raw material, (b) Wages of casual labour, (c) Expenses on electricity.

Initially TVC Increases at a Diminishing Rate

Initially TVC tends to increase at a diminishing rate. Implying that less and less of additional cost (marginal cost) is incurred for every additional unit of output. Table 2 shows that when output is increased from 1 to 2 units, TVC increases by ₹ 8, and when output is increased from 2 to 3 units, TVC increases by ₹ 6. This is because of increasing returns to a factor. It is a situation when: MP of the variable factor tends to rise; MC of the variable factor tends to fall; less and less of additional cost is incurred for producing every additional unit of ouput. (**Note** that MC is the reciprocal of MP.) It is between 0-A in Fig. 2 that TVC is increasing at a decreasing rate, because additional cost of producing every successive unit tends to fall.

Eventually TVC Increases at an Increasing Rate

Eventually, the law of diminishing returns sets in. Accordingly, MP of the variable factor tends to fall. Implying that MC tends to rise. TVC tends to increase at an increasing rate. So that, more and more of additional cost (MC) is incurred for every additional unit of output. Table 2 shows that when output is increased from 3 to 4 units, TVC increases by ₹ 4, and when output is increased from 4 to 5 units, TVC increases by ₹ 4. In Fig. 2, it is beyond point A, that TVC increases at an increasing rate. This is a situation of diminishing returns to a factor when: MP of the variable factor is falling; MC of the variable factor is rising; more and more of additional cost is incurred for producing every additional unit of output.

(iii) Behaviour of Fixed Cost, Variable Cost and Total Cost

Behaviour of fixed cost, variable cost and total cost is explained with the help of Table 3 and Fig. 3.

Table 3. Fixed Cost, Variable Cost and Total Cost

Output (Units)	Fixed Cost (₹)	Variable Cost (₹)	Total Cost (₹)
0	10	0	10
1	10	10	20
2	10	18	28
3	10	24	34
4	10	28	38
5	10	32	42
6	10	38	48

In Table 3, total cost is found as the sum total of fixed cost and variable cost. With increase in output, total cost is also increasing. When output is zero, total cost is ₹ 10, because fixed cost is ₹10, although variable cost is zero. When output increases to 6 units, total cost goes up to ₹48 (= ₹38 + ₹10).

FIGURE 3

Total Cost

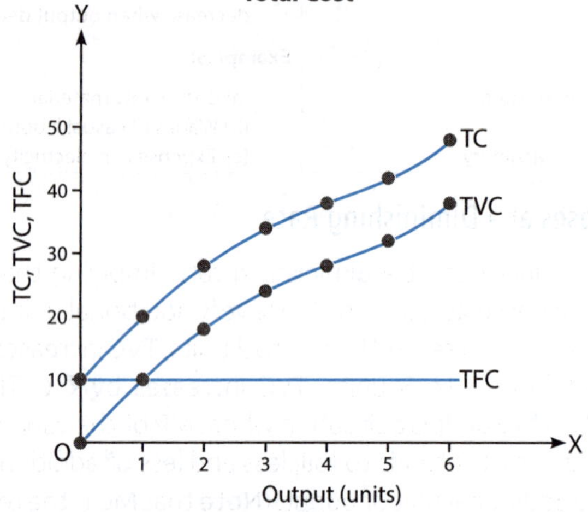

TC = TFC + TVC

- TFC is constant at all levels of output.
- TVC increases as output increases.
- TC is parallel to TVC. It shows that the difference between TC and TVC (= TFC) is constant.

In Fig. 3, units of output are shown on X-axis and costs on Y-axis. TFC shows total fixed cost. TVC shows total variable cost and TC shows total cost. TC is the aggregate of TFC and TVC curves. TC curve begins from 10 (on the Y-axis). This is because at zero level of output, TFC = 10 while TVC = 0; so that TFC + TVC = 10. Note that the difference between TC and TVC is constant, because of which TC and TVC are parallel to each other. And we know, the difference between TC and TVC is equal to TFC which is constant.

Average Cost (AC)

Cost per unit of output is called average cost.

$$AC = \frac{TC}{Q}$$

[Here, AC = Average cost
TC = Total cost
Q = Quantity of output.]

In Table 3, total cost of producing 6 units of a commodity is ₹48. Accordingly, cost per unit or average cost will be $= \frac{₹\,48}{6} = ₹8$.

Average cost is the cost per unit of output produced. It is also called unit cost of production.

Table 4 illustrates the estimation of AC when TC is given.

Table 4. Total Cost and Average Cost

Output (Units)	Total Cost (₹)	Average Cost (₹)
0	10	$\frac{10}{0} = \infty$
1	20	$\frac{20}{1} = 20$
2	28	$\frac{28}{2} = 14$
3	34	$\frac{34}{3} = 11.3$
4	38	$\frac{38}{4} = 9.5$
5	42	$\frac{42}{5} = 8.4$
6	48	$\frac{48}{6} = 8$

Fixed and Variable Components of AC

Average cost is the sum total of average fixed cost and average variable cost, *i.e.*,

$$AC = AFC + AVC$$

[Here, AC = Average cost
AFC = Average fixed cost
AVC = Average variable cost.]

(i) Average Fixed Cost: Average fixed cost is the fixed cost per unit of output.

$$AFC = \frac{TFC}{Q}$$

[Here, AFC = Average fixed cost
TFC = Total fixed cost
Q = Quantity of output.]

Table 5 and Fig. 4 illustrate the behaviour of AFC.

Table 5. Average Fixed Cost

Output (Units)	Fixed Cost (₹)	Average Fixed Cost (₹)
1	10	10
2	10	5
3	10	3.3
4	10	2.5
5	10	2
6	10	1.67
7	10	1.42
8	10	1.25

Table 5 shows that when 1 unit is produced, the average fixed cost is ₹10. When 5 units are produced then average fixed cost is ₹2. Average fixed cost goes on diminishing as output increases.

FIGURE 4

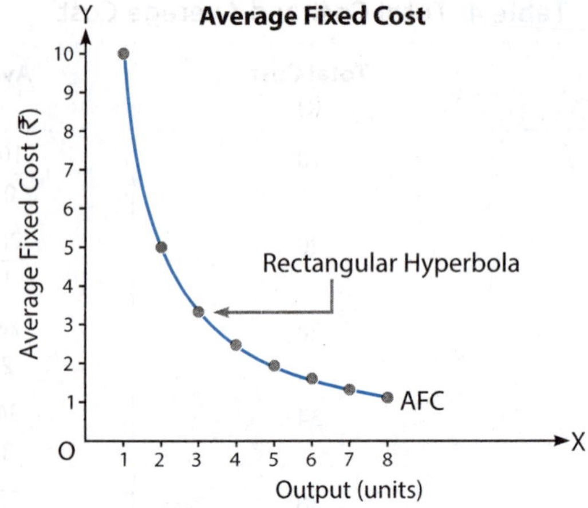

AFC is rectangular hyperbola. It shows:

(i) that AFC decreases as output increases.

(ii) AFC × Q at any level of output is the same. Because,

$$AFC \times Q = TFC$$

which is constant at all levels of output.

Thus: $4 \times 2.5 = 10$

$8 \times 1.25 = 10$

In Fig. 4, AFC shows average fixed cost. This curve slopes downward to the right. Downward slope of AFC shows that AFC decreases as output increases. It is important to note that AFC curve is a rectangular hyperbola. It means that AFC × Q (which is equal to TFC) is constant at all levels of output.

AFC Curve is Rectangular Hyperbola

If we take any point on AFC curve and multiply AFC at that point with the corresponding level of output, the product (AFC × Output = TFC) shall always be the same. This shows that total fixed cost remains constant at all levels of output.

(ii) Average Variable Cost: Average variable cost is the variable cost per unit of output.

$$AVC = \frac{TVC}{Q}$$

[Here, AVC = Average variable cost
TVC = Total variable cost
Q = Quantity of output.]

Table 6 and Fig. 5 illustrate the estimation (and behaviour) of AVC.

Table 6. Average Variable Cost

Output (Units)	Variable Cost (₹)	Average Variable Cost (₹)
1	10	10
2	18	9
3	24	8
4	28	7
5	32	6.4
6	38	6.3
7	46	6.6
8	62	7.7

Table 6 shows that up to sixth unit of output, average variable cost falls but from 7th unit it begins to rise. Falling AVC is in accordance with increasing returns to a factor, while rising AVC is in accordance with diminishing returns to a factor. (We know, as output expands, initially increasing returns to a factor may operate.

But, eventually, diminishing returns to a factor must prevail. This is what law of variable proportions tells us.)

FIGURE 5

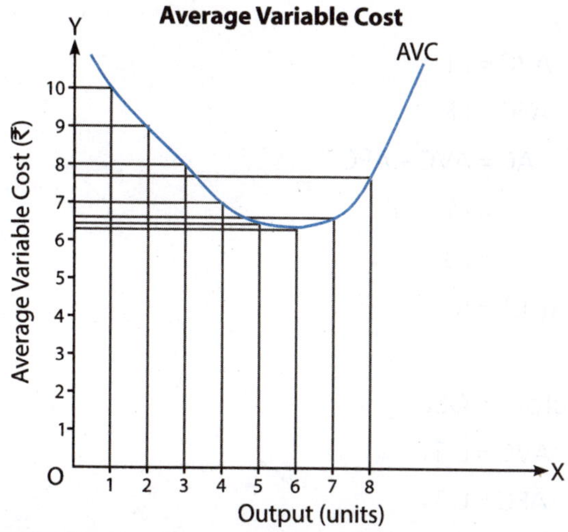

AVC curve is U-shaped. This is in accordance with the law of variable proportions. It falls so long as returns to a factor are increasing. It rises when returns to a factor are decreasing.

In Fig. 5, output is shown on X-axis and AVC on Y-axis. The shape of AVC is like 'U'. Up to the sixth unit of output, it is falling. It means, as output increases, average variable cost tends to fall. The curve starts rising from seventh unit; which means that AVC begins to rise. The AVC curve makes a 'U' because of the operation of law of variable proportions. In the early stages of production of a commodity, the AVC tends to fall, then gradually it tends to rise.

(iii) AC as the Summation of AFC and AVC: AC curve is a vertical summation of AFC and AVC curves, as in Fig. 6.

FIGURE 6

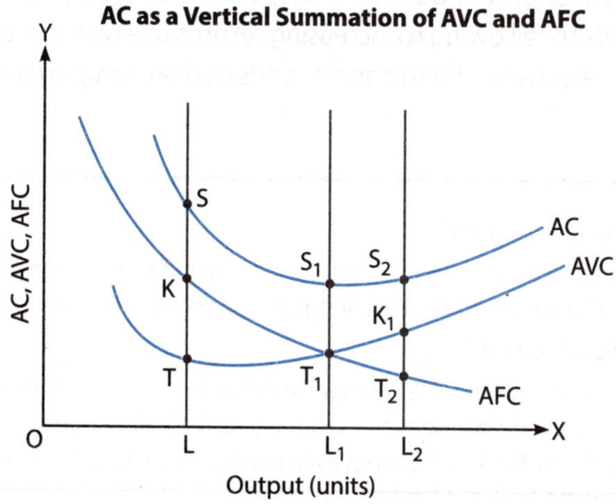

$[LT = KS; L_1T_1 = T_1S_1; L_2T_2 = K_1S_2]$

AC is the vertical summation of AVC and AFC at different levels of output.

Thus: LS = LT + LK

↑ ↑ ↑

AC AVC AFC

This is when output = OL.

AC is similarly estimated for other levels of output.

What is Vertical Summation?

It is vertically adding up the values of AFC and AVC at different levels of output. Thus, when output = OL:

$$AVC = LT$$
$$AFC = LK$$
$$AC = AVC + AFC$$
$$= LT + LK$$
$$= LS$$

[See Fig. 6: LT = KS]

Likewise,

when output = OL_1:

$$AVC = L_1T_1$$
$$AFC = L_1T_1$$
$$AC = L_1T_1 + L_1T_1$$
$$= L_1S_1$$

[See Fig. 6: $L_1T_1 = T_1S_1$]

When output = OL_2:

$$AVC = L_2K_1$$
$$AFC = L_2T_2$$
$$AC = L_2K_1 + L_2T_2$$
$$= L_2S_2$$

[See Fig. 6: $L_2T_2 = K_1S_2$]

As is clear from Fig. 6, short period AC is U-shaped. It is because of the law of variable proportions: it tends to fall owing to increasing returns to a factor; it tends to stabilise owing to constant returns to a factor; and it tends to rise owing to diminishing returns to a factor.

HOTS

Q.1. As output increases, AC tends to be closer to AVC. Why?

Ans. We know that AC = AFC + AVC. As output increases, AFC must continuously fall, because TFC is constant. Consequently, the component of AFC in AC tends to shrink. This brings AC closer to AVC (See Fig. 6).

Q.2. Can AC and AVC ever be equal for any level of output?

Ans. AC and AVC can never be equal for any level of output. This is because AC is the vertical summation of AVC and AFC. Being a vertical summation, AC must be vertically above AFC as well as AVC. Also, because TFC is fixed for all levels of output, AFC can never be zero. Accordingly, AC cannot even concide with AVC for any level of output.

Marginal Cost (MC)

Marginal cost is the change in total cost when an additional unit of output is produced.

According to **Ferguson,** "Marginal cost is the addition to total cost due to the addition of one unit of output."

$$MC_n = TC_n - TC_{n-1}$$
Or
$$MC = \frac{\Delta TC}{\Delta Q}$$

[Here, MC_n = Marginal cost of 'n' units of output
TC_n = Total cost of 'n' units of output
TC_{n-1} = Total cost of 'n−1' units of output
ΔTC = Change in total cost
ΔQ = Change in output.]

Supposing total cost of producing 5 units of a commodity is ₹135 and of 6 units it is ₹180. Marginal cost of sixth unit will be (₹ 180 – ₹135) = ₹45.

Estimation and Behaviour of MC

Table 7 and Fig. 7 illustrate the estimation and behaviour of MC.

Table 7. Marginal Cost

Output (Units) (1)	Total Fixed Cost (₹) (2)	Total Variable Cost (₹) (3)	Total Cost (₹) (2 + 3) (4)	Marginal Cost (₹) (5)
0	10	0	10	—
1	10	10	20	10
2	10	18	28	8
3	10	24	34	6
4	10	28	38	4
5	10	32	42	4
6	10	38	48	6
7	10	46	56	8
8	10	62	72	16

FIGURE 7

Marginal Cost

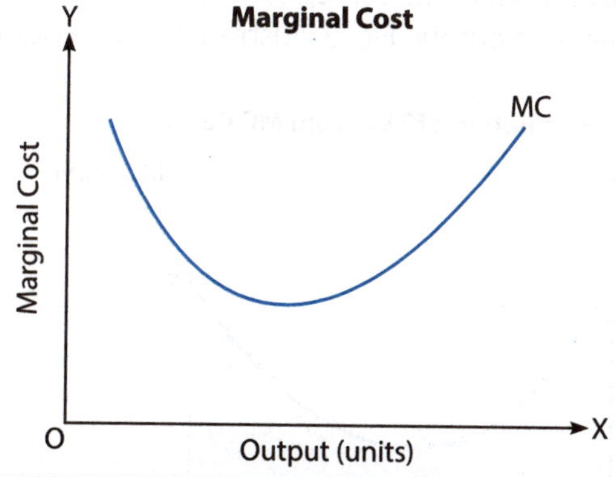

MC is U-shaped in accordance with the law of variable proportions. Initially, MC is falling. It is because MP tends to rise when there are increasing returns to a factor. Subsequently, MC tends to rise. It is because MP tends to fall when there are diminishing returns to a factor.
[**Note** that MC is the reciprocal of MP.]

Table 7 shows that $MC_n = TC_n - TC_{n-1}$.

When 4 units of output are produced,

$$MC = TC_4 - TC_3$$
$$= 38 - 34 = 4$$

When 8 units of output are produced,

$$MC = TC_8 - TC_7$$
$$= 72 - 56 = 16$$

When only 1 unit of output is produced,

$$MC = TC_1 - TC_0$$
$$= 20 - 10 = 10$$

It is evident from the Table 7 that initially MC tends to fall and eventually it tends to rise. Falling MC corresponds to rising MP (when there are increasing returns to a factor). Rising MC corresponds to falling MP (when there are diminishing returns to a factor). Accordingly, MC is U-shaped, as in Fig. 7.

MC is Variable Cost Only

It needs to be noted with emphasis that MC is an additional cost (corresponding to an additional unit of output). By definition, additional cost cannot be fixed cost; it can only be variable cost. Accordingly, the sum total of marginal cost corresponding to different units of output (1 to n units) becomes TVC. Thus,

$$\Sigma MC = TVC$$

Table 7 illustrates this point. Consider any level of output, say 8 units. Here, TVC = 62 which is equal to ΣMC for 1 to 8 units of output.

$$\Sigma MC \text{ (for 1 to 8 units)} = 10 + 8 + 6 + 4 + 4 + 6 + 8 + 16$$
$$= 62 = TVC.$$

Likewise, for 1 to 6 units of output,

$$TVC = 38$$
$$= \Sigma MC \text{ (for 1 to 6 units)}$$
$$= 10 + 8 + 6 + 4 + 4 + 6$$
$$= 38.$$

Geometrically, total area under MC curve, corresponding to any level of output, measures TVC of that level of output. Fig. 8 illustrates this situation.

FIGURE 8

Estimation of TVC from MC Curve

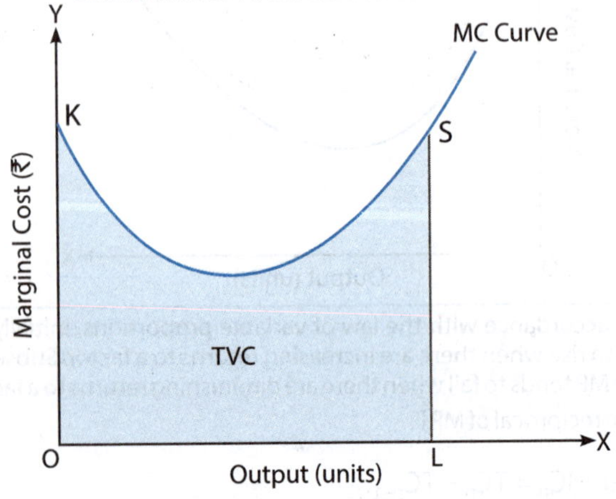

At OL level of output, area under MC Curve = OLSK.
This is equal to TVC (total variable cost).
This is because TVC = ΣMC. Total variable cost is the sum total of marginal cost for each unit of a given output.

Short Period MC can be estimated either from TVC or from TC

MC is an additional cost. Additional cost by definition cannot be fixed cost; it can only be variable cost. Therefore, MC can be estimated in either of the following ways:

$$MC_n = TC_n - TC_{n-1}$$

Or, $$MC_n = TVC_n - TVC_{n-1}$$

Proof: $$MC_n = TC_n - TC_{n-1}$$

$$= (TFC_n + TVC_n) - (TFC_{n-1} + TVC_{n-1}) \quad (\because TC = TFC + TVC)$$

$$= TFC_n + TVC_n - TFC_{n-1} - TVC_{n-1}$$

$$= TVC_n - TVC_{n-1}$$

[$TFC_n = TFC_{n-1}$, because TFC is constant.]

The figure (Fig. 8) shows that for OL level of output,

$$TVC = \text{area } OLSK$$
$$= \Sigma MC$$

for all units of output between O to L.

3. Relation between Average, Marginal and Total Cost

Having discussed the estimation and behaviour of average, marginal and total cost, we now proceed to discuss how these costs are related to each other. Basically, we are focusing on two relationships: (i) relation between average cost and marginal cost, and (ii) relation between total cost and marginal cost. Details are as under:

Relation between Average Cost and Marginal Cost

Relation between average cost and marginal cost is explained through Table 8 and Fig. 9.

Table 8. Relation between Average Cost and Marginal Cost

Output (Units)	Total Cost (₹)	Average Cost $AC = \frac{TC}{Q}$ (₹)	Marginal Cost $MC = TC_n - TC_{n-1}$ (₹)
0	10	∞	—
1	20	20	10
2	28	14	8
3	34	11.3	6
4	38	9.5	4
5	42	8.4	4
6	48	8	6
7	56	8	8
8	72	9	16

FIGURE 9

Relation between AC and MC

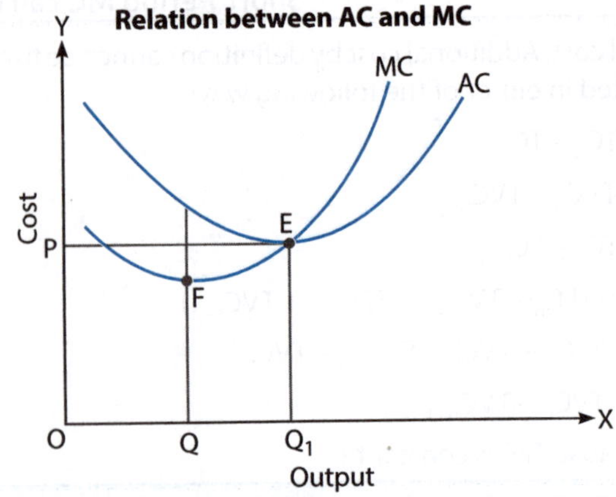

- When AC is falling, MC < AC.
- When AC is rising, MC > AC.
- When AC is constant (as at point E), MC = AC.
- MC is always to the left of AC, and cuts AC from its lowest point.

Table 8 and Fig. 9 offer the following observations with regard to the relation between average cost and marginal cost:

(1) When AC Falls, MC is Lower than AC: When average cost falls, marginal cost is less than AC. In Table 8, AC is falling till it becomes ₹ 8, and MC remains less than ₹ 8. In Fig. 9, AC is falling till point E, and MC continues to be lower than AC. In this case, marginal cost falls more rapidly than the average cost. That is why when marginal cost (MC) curve is falling, it is below the average cost (AC) curve. It is shown in Fig. 9.

(2) When AC Rises, MC is Greater than AC: When average cost starts rising, marginal cost is greater than average cost. In Table 8, when AC rises from ₹ 8 to ₹ 9, MC rises from ₹ 8 to ₹ 16. In Fig. 9, AC starts rising from point E. And, beyond E, MC is higher than AC.

(3) When AC does not change, MC is equal to AC: When average cost does not change, then MC = AC. It happens when falling AC reaches its lowest point. In Table 8, at the 7th unit, average cost does not change. It sticks to its minimum level of ₹ 8. Here, marginal cost is also ₹ 8. Thus, Fig. 9 shows that MC curve is intersecting AC curve at its minimum point E.

Relationship between AVC and MC

The relationship between AVC and MC is similar to the relationship between AC and MC.

Thus, Fig. 10 reveals:

(i) When AVC falls, MC < AVC.

(ii) When AVC rises, MC > AVC, and

(iii) When AVC is constant,
MC = AVC (it is the lowest point of AVC).

FIGURE 10

AVC and MC

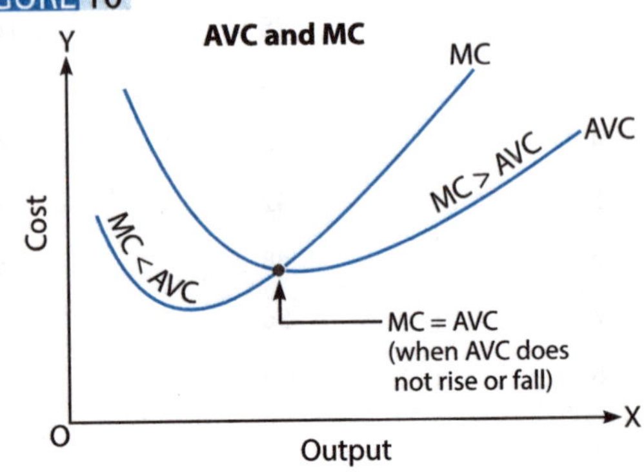

Relation between Total Cost and Marginal Cost

Table 8 and Fig. 11 offer the following observations with regard to the relation between total cost and marginal cost:

(i) Marginal cost is estimated as the difference between total cost of two successive units of output.

Thus, $MC_n = TC_n - TC_{n-1}$

(ii) When MC is diminishing, TC increases at a diminishing rate.

(iii) When MC is rising, TC increases at an increasing rate.

(iv) When MC reaches its lowest point (point Q in Fig. 11), TC stops increasing at a decreasing rate (point Q* in Fig. 11).

Briefly, MC is the rate of TC.

[**Note:** The relation between TVC and MC will be the same as between TC and MC, because the difference between TC and TVC is constant (equal to fixed cost).]

FIGURE 11

Relation between TC and MC

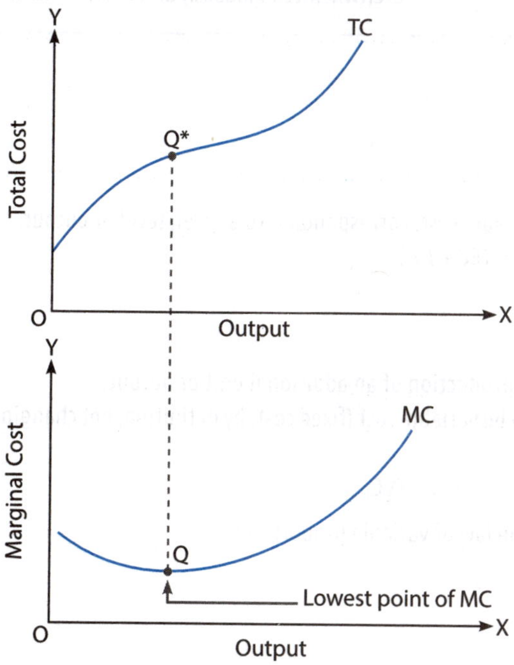

✦ Up to point Q*, TC is increasing at a decreasing rate, because MC is decreasing.
✦ Beyond point Q*, TC is increasing at an increasing rate, because MC is increasing.
✦ At point Q*, TC stops increasing at a decreasing rate, because MC touches its lowest point.

HOTS

Q.1. AC may continue to decline even when MC is rising. Why?

Ans. Even when MC is rising, AC will continue to fall so long as MC < AC.

Q.2. Is it true to say that AC falls only when MC falls?

Ans. No. AC may fall even when MC is rising, provided MC < AC.
[Refer to Fig. 9. Between points F and E, MC is rising, but AC is falling.]

AC, AVC, AFC and MC in one Diagram

Fig. 12 combines AC, AVC, AFC and MC.

The point to be specifically noted in this figure is that **MC curve should be shown cutting both AC and AVC at their lowest points.**

Also, note the following observations:

(i) When AC declines, MC declines faster than AC. So that MC curve remains below AC curve.

(ii) When AC increases, MC increases faster than AC. So that MC curve is above AC curve.

(iii) Since MC declines faster than AC, it reaches its lowest point earlier than AC. So that MC starts rising even when AC is falling.

(iv) MC must cut AC from its lowest point.

FIGURE 12

AC, AVC, AFC and MC

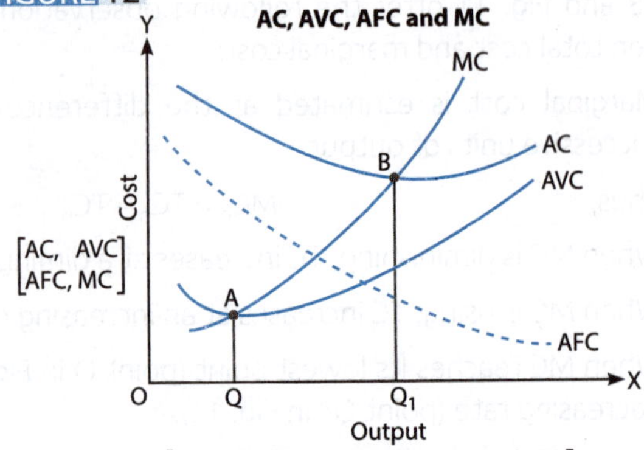

[**Note:** AC – AVC = Vertical Distance of AFC
AFC is Rectangular Hyperbola]

Note: AC and AVC get close to each other as output increases. On the other hand, AC and AFC get away from each other as output increases. This is because, as output increases, the component of AVC in AC tends to increase while the component of AFC in AC tends to decrease. However, at no stage AVC will touch AC because AFC can never be zero even when it continuously declines with increase in output.

POWER POINTS

- Total Cost is the sum total of fixed cost and variable cost, corresponding to a given level of output.

$$TC = TFC + TVC$$

- Average Cost (AC) $= \frac{TC}{Q} = \frac{TFC}{Q} + \frac{TVC}{Q}$

- Marginal Cost is 'additional cost' owing to the production of an additional unit of output.
$MC_n = TC_n - TC_{n-1}$. Since additional cost can only be variable cost (fixed cost, by definition, not changing with output), it can also be estimated as:

$$MC_n = TVC_n - TVC_{n-1}$$

- AC and MC are U-shaped, in accordance with the law of variable proportions.
- Relationship between AC and MC:
  — if average cost is falling, AC > MC.
  — if average cost is rising, AC < MC.
  — if average cost is constant, AC = MC.
- Relationship between TC and MC: MC is additional cost when output increases by a unit. It shows the rate at which TC increases. Accordingly, the following relationship emerges between TC and MC:
  — TC increases at an increasing rate when MC is increasing.
  — TC increases at a constant rate when MC is constant.
  — TC increases at a diminishing rate when MC is decreasing.
- Because MC is the reciprocal of MP:
  (i) falling MC corresponds to rising MP, a situation of increasing returns to a factor.
  (ii) rising MC corresponds to falling MP, a situation of diminishing returns to a factor.

EXERCISE

1. Very Short Questions (Remembering & Understanding) (1 mark each)

A. Multiple Choice Questions: Choose the Correct Answer

1. **Fixed costs are also known as:**
   (a) supplementary costs (b) overhead costs
   (c) indirect costs (d) all of these
2. **The costs which vary as the level of output varies are called:**
   (a) prime costs (b) indirect costs
   (c) real costs (d) none of these
3. **Which one of the following is correct?**
   (a) $TC = TFC \times TVC$ (b) $TC = TFC \div TVC$
   (c) $TC = TFC + TVC$ (d) $TC = TFC - TVC$
4. **Wages paid to labourers is an example of:**
   (a) explicit cost (b) implicit cost
   (c) opportunity cost (d) none of these
5. **When production level is zero, then fixed cost is:**
   (a) zero (b) negative
   (c) positive (d) equal to variable cost
6. **The costs which do not change with change in the quantity of output are called:**
   (a) supplementary costs (b) money costs
   (c) real costs (d) none of these
7. **Which of the following indicates fixed cost?**
   (a) Electricity bill (b) Expenses on raw material
   (c) Wages of daily workers (d) Interest on fixed capital
8. **When production is zero, total cost will be:**
   (a) zero (b) equal to variable cost
   (c) equal to fixed cost (d) equal to marginal cost
9. **TVC can be calculated as:**
   (a) $\frac{AVC}{Q}$ (b) ΣMC
   (c) $TC - TFC$ (d) both (b) and (c)
10. **Average fixed cost (AFC) is indicated by:**
    (a) a rectangular hyperbola (b) a straight line parallel to X-axis
    (c) a straight line parallel to Y-axis (d) a U-shaped curve
11. **When MC curve cuts AC curve:**
    (a) $AC = MC$ (b) $AC < MC$
    (c) $AC > MC$ (d) both AC and MC are falling
12. **Per unit cost of a good is called:**
    (a) fixed cost (b) variable cost
    (c) average cost (d) none of these

13. What happens to ATC when MC > ATC?

(a) ATC will rise
(b) ATC will fall
(c) ATC will remain constant
(d) None of these

14. TC increases at an increasing rate when MC is:

(a) constant
(b) increasing
(c) decreasing
(d) negative

15. Marginal cost of a good includes:

(a) only variable cost
(b) only fixed cost
(c) both (a) and (b)
(d) none of these

16. When average cost (AC) is falling:

(a) MC > AC
(b) MC < AC
(c) MC = AC
(d) none of these

17. Which of the following is correct?

(a) MC = TFC × TVC
(b) TC = TFC – TVC
(c) $MC = TC_{n-2} - TC_{n-1}$
(d) TC = TFC ÷ Q

18. Total cost is the vertical summation of:

(a) TFC and TVC
(b) AFC and AVC
(c) TVC and AVC
(d) none of these

19. What does shaded area show in the Fig. 13 alongside?

(a) TFC
(b) TVC
(c) TC
(d) ATC

FIGURE 13

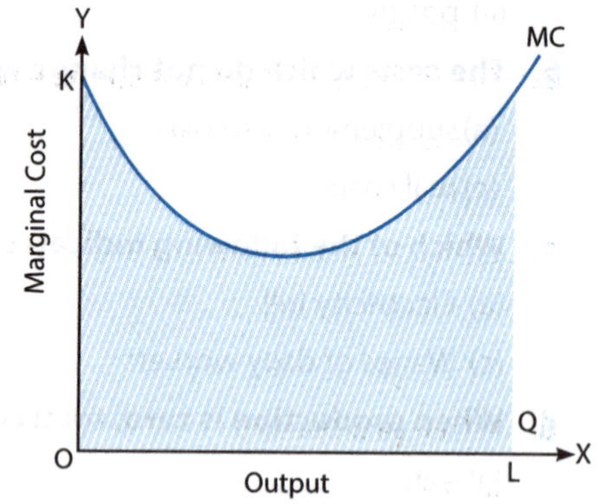

20. The average cost is ₹ 20 and it is minimum when 4 units are produced. The marginal cost of producing 4 units is:

(a) ₹ 20
(b) ₹ 80
(c) ₹ 24
(d) ₹ 5

21. If the marginal cost of producing 1 unit of a commodity is ₹ 15 and that of producing 2 units is ₹ 10, which of the following is correct?

(a) Total cost = ₹ 25
(b) Variable cost = ₹ 25
(c) Average cost = ₹ 25
(d) None of these

22. The total cost at 10 units of output is ₹ 55. The fixed cost is ₹ 5. The average variable cost at 10 units of output is:

(a) ₹ 25
(b) ₹ 6
(c) ₹ 5
(d) ₹ 1

Answers

1. (d) **2.** (a) **3.** (c) **4.** (a) **5.** (c) **6.** (a) **7.** (d) **8.** (c) **9.** (d) **10.** (a) **11.** (a) **12.** (c)
13. (a) **14.** (b) **15.** (a) **16.** (b) **17.** (c) **18.** (a) **19.** (b) **20.** (a) **21.** (b) **22.** (c)

B. Information & Concept-based Questions

1. **Give meaning of cost.**

Or

What does cost mean in Economics?

Ans. Cost is the expenditure incurred by the producer (explicitly or implicitly) on factor as well as non-factor inputs for a given amount of output of a commodity.

2. **What is meant by explicit and implicit costs?**

Ans. Explicit costs are those cash payments which a firm makes to others for the purchase of inputs. **Example:** (i) Wages paid to labourers, (ii) Payment made for the purchase of raw material.

Implicit costs are imputed (estimated) costs of self-owned and self-employed resources. **Example:** (i) Interest on entrepreneur's own capital, (ii) Rent on entrepreneur's own land used in business.

3. **Define opportunity cost.**

Ans. Opportunity cost is the total sacrifice made for availing an opportunity (or producing a given level of output).

4. **What are selling costs?**

Ans. Selling costs refer to the expenditure incurred by the producer in order to promote the sale of the commodity. **Example:** Expenditure on advertisement.

5. **Define production cost.**

Ans. Production cost refers to the expenditure incurred by the producer (explicitly or implicitly) on the inputs for producing a given level of output.

6. **What is meant by fixed cost?**

Ans. Fixed cost is the cost (or expenditure) incurred on the purchase (or hiring) of fixed inputs of production, like plant and machinery.

7. **What is meant by variable cost?**

Ans. Variable cost is the cost (or expenditure) incurred on the purchase of variable inputs of production like raw material.

8. **Define total cost.**

Ans. Total cost refers to all expenses incurred by the producer (explicitly or implicitly) to produce a given quantity of output.

9. **What is meant by average cost?**

Ans. Average cost is the expenditure incurred by the firm on the fixed factors, estimated per unit of output.

10. **What is marginal cost?**

Ans. Marginal cost is the change in total cost when an additional unit of output is produced.

11. **State the formula to determine average cost.**

Ans. $$\text{Average Cost} = \frac{\text{Total Cost}}{\text{Quantity of Output}}$$

Or

$$\text{Average Cost} = \text{Average Fixed Cost} + \text{Average Variable Cost}$$

12. **If the total cost of producing 5 units of a commodity is ₹ 20 and that of producing 4 units is ₹ 15, what will be the marginal cost?**

Ans. $MC = TC_5 - TC_4$

$= ₹\,20 - ₹\,15$

$= ₹\,5$

13. The cost of zero level of output is equal to which cost?

Ans. The cost of zero level of output is equal to fixed cost.

14. Why does variable cost curve originate from the point of origin?

Ans. Variable cost curve originates from the point of origin because when output is zero, variable cost is also zero.

15. In which cost will the expenditure on raw material and wages of casual labourers be included?

Ans. The expenditure on raw material and wages of casual labourers will be included in the variable cost.

16. Why is total fixed cost curve parallel to X-axis?

Ans. Total fixed cost remains constant at all levels of output. So, total fixed cost curve is parallel to X-axis.

17. Why are total cost curve and variable cost curve parallel to each other?

Ans. Total cost curve and variable cost curve are parallel to each other because the difference between TC and TVC is equal to TFC which is constant at all levels of output.

18. Does average fixed cost fall as output rises?

Ans. Yes, average fixed cost falls as output rises because total fixed cost is constant at all levels of output.

19. What is the general shape of AC curve?

Ans. AC curve is generally 'U' shaped.

20. What is the general shape of MC curve?

Ans. MC curve is generally 'U' shaped.

21. What would you say about the average cost of a firm if the marginal cost of production is less than the average cost?

Ans. If the marginal cost (MC) of production is less than the average cost (AC), AC would be falling.

22. Why does marginal cost curve cut average cost curve only at its minimum point?

Ans. Marginal cost curve cuts average cost curve only at its minimum point because it is only here that MC = AC.

2. Reason-based Questions (Comprehension of the Subject-matter)

Read the following statements carefully. Write 'True' or 'False' with a reason.

1. Fixed cost is constant even when output is zero.

Ans. True. Because fixed costs are incurred even before output actually starts.

2. Variable cost is incurred before production is started.

Ans. False. Variable costs are the expenditure incurred by the producer on the use of variable factors of production. These are incurred only after output actually starts.

3. Fixed cost must be greater than variable cost when output is zero.

Ans. True. Because fixed costs are incurred even when output is zero, while variable costs are incurred only after output actually starts (so that variable costs are zero when output is zero).

4. Variable cost reduces as output increases.

Ans. False. As the output increases, variable cost also increases. Because variable costs are largely the costs of raw material.

5. Total fixed cost is indicated by a vertical straight line.

Ans. False. Total fixed cost is indicated by a horizontal straight line parallel to X-axis.

6. Total cost is the sum total of marginal costs.

Ans. False. Sum total of marginal costs (MC) corresponding to different units of output become total variable cost (TVC). TVC = ΣMC. Because, marginal costs are variable costs only.

7. Average fixed cost curve is a rectangular hyperbola.

Ans. True. Average fixed cost (AFC) curve is a rectangular hyperbola. Because TFC does not change with output.

8. Average variable cost tends to fall, stabilise and rise as output increases.

Ans. True. Average variable cost tends to fall, stabilise and rise as output increase due to the law of variable proportions.

9. Average cost includes both fixed cost and variable cost.

Ans. True. AC = AFC + AVC.

10. AC curve tends to be U-shaped.

Ans. True. AC curve is U-shaped in accordance with the law of variable proportions: it tends to fall owing to increasing returns to a factor, it tends to stabilise owing to constant returns to a factor, and it tends to rise owing to diminishing returns to a factor.

11. MC is greater than AC when production is in a state of diminishing returns.

Ans. True. When the production is in a state of diminishing returns, MC will be rising in accordance with falling MP. AC is rising, with the rising MC but less than MC or MC > AC.

12. AC is greater than MC, so long as AC is falling.

Ans. True. AC is greater than MC or MC is less than AC when AC falls. See AC and MC till point E in the diagram (Fig. 14). In the diagram, AC is falling till point E and MC continues to be lower than AC.

FIGURE 14

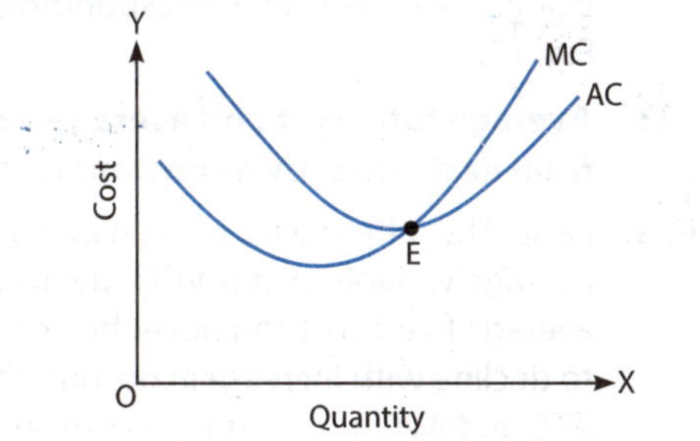

13. MC and AC are equal when AC tends to stabilise.

Ans. True. MC and AC are equal when AC tends to stabilise or when AC is constant, AC = MC. See AC and MC corresponding to point E in the diagram (Fig. 14) where AC = MC.

14. When MC > ATC, ATC must rise.

Ans. True. When MC > ATC, ATC rises. See AC and MC beyond point E in the diagram (Fig. 14). In the diagram, AC starts rising from point E and after that point E, MC > AC.

15. The distance between AC and AVC curves tends to increase at higher levels of output.

Ans. False. The distance between AC and AVC curves tends to reduce as output increases. This is because as output increases the component of AVC in AC tends to increase while the component of AFC in AC tends to decrease. See Fig. 15.

FIGURE 15

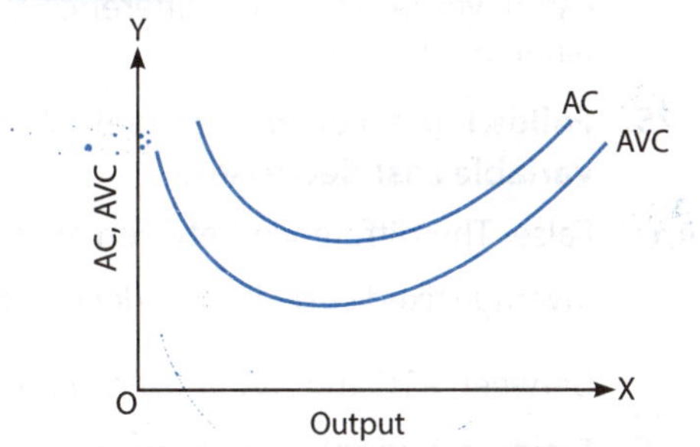

16. ATC and AVC tend to intersect at some level of output.

Ans. False. Because ATC is the sum of AFC and AVC. Since AFC can never be zero, AVC can never be equal or greater than ATC. Thus, ATC always remains above AVC.

17. Area under MC curve = TVC.

Ans. True. Total variable cost (TVC) is the area covered under MC curve corresponding to a given level of output. In Fig. 16, area OLKM is total variable cost when output is OL.

FIGURE 16

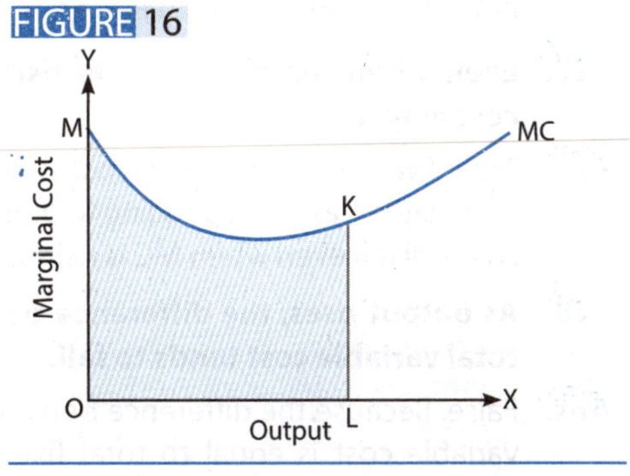

18. Short period TC curve starts from Y-axis.

Ans. True. TC = TFC + TVC and TFC remains constant even at zero level of output.

At zero level of output, TVC = 0. Therefore, TC = TFC.

Accordingly, TC curve starts from the Y-axis in the short period.

19. When a bus with a seating capacity of 35 passengers is carrying only 30 passengers, the MC of carrying an additional passenger would be equal to the cost of a passenger ticket.

Ans. False. MC of carrying an additional passenger should be zero, because there is excess seating capacity in the bus.

20. When MC of carrying an additional passenger in a coach is zero, more passengers should always be added to make more profits.

Ans. False. The capacity of coach is limited. Using an asset beyond its capacity would lead to higher wear & tear and greater chances of sudden damages. Accordingly, more passengers should not always mean more profit.

21. Should the difference between ATC and AVC be constant, because TFC is constant?

Ans. False. TFC is constant, therefore, AFC (difference between ATC and AVC) must decline with increase in output. [**Note:** At no point AVC and ATC will touch each other.

$\because$ ATC is always positive.]

22. Average cost does not fall unless marginal cost also falls.

Ans. False. Average cost can fall even when marginal cost is rising. See AC and MC corresponding to output range LQ in Fig. 17.

FIGURE 17

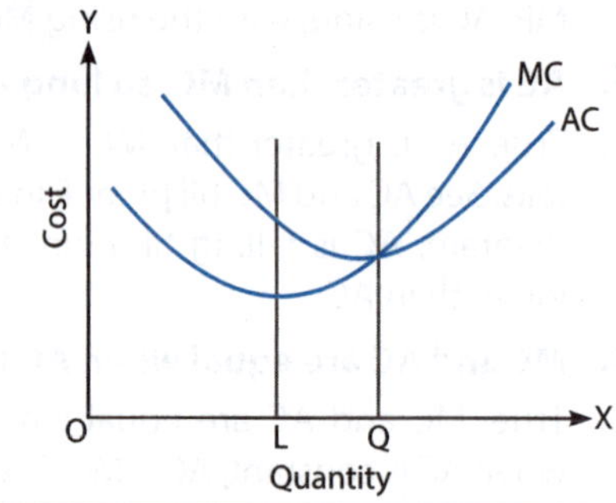

23. Average total cost and average variable cost are apart from each other by a constant factor.

Ans. False. The difference between average total cost (ATC) and average variable cost (AVC) is average fixed cost (AFC) and average fixed cost can never be constant. Since AFC tends to decline with increase in output, the difference between ATC and AVC must reduce as output increases.

24. Following increase in output, the reducing difference between average total cost and average variable cost ultimately becomes zero.

Ans. False. As output increases, the difference between average total cost and average variable cost reduces but can never be zero. The difference is equal to AFC (average fixed cost) which must remain positive, even when it is falling.

25. Following a cut in the level of output, the difference between average total cost and average variable cost decreases.

Ans. False. The difference between average total cost (ATC) and average variable cost (AVC) is equal to AFC (average fixed cost). It must decrease as output increases, because AFC $= \frac{TFC}{Q}$. Implying that the difference between ATC and AVC must rise following a cut in the level of output.

26. Rising marginal cost always implies a rising average cost.

Ans. False. Average cost can fall even when marginal cost is rising, as corresponding to output range LQ in Fig. 17. AC will fall even when MC is rising, so long as MC < AC.

27. Even when marginal cost is rising, average variable cost may fall.

Ans. True. Even when marginal cost is rising, average variable cost may fall, as corresponding to output range MQ in Fig. 18. AVC will fall even when MC is rising, so long as MC < AVC.

FIGURE 18

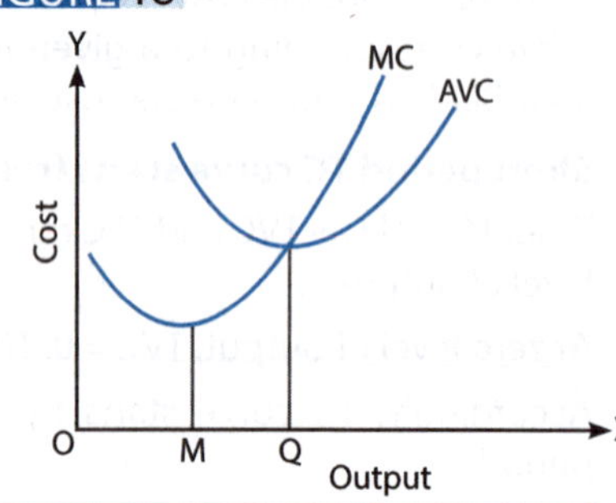

28. As output rises, the difference between total cost and total variable cost tends to fall.

Ans. False. Because the difference between total cost and total variable cost is equal to total fixed cost which remains constant at all levels of output.

29. As soon as marginal cost rises, average variable cost also rises.

Ans. False. Average variable cost can fall even when marginal cost starts rising, as corresponding to output range MQ in Fig. 18. AVC falls even when MC is rising, so long as MC < AVC.

30. Long run average cost curve is flatter than the short run average cost curve, even when both the curves are U-shaped.

Ans. True. Long run average cost curve is flatter than the short run average cost curve, because short run average cost curve relates to one plant, or the constant scale of output. Long run average cost curve, on the other hand, relates to several plants or the expanding scale of output.

3. HOTS & Applications

1. Does TC always shoot from Y-axis?

Ans. No. TC shoots from the Y-axis only when we are referring to the short period and are therefore, distinguishing between fixed costs and variable costs.

In the long period, all costs are variable costs. Accordingly, in the long period TC shoots from the origin.

2. Marginal cost includes both fixed cost and variable cost. Comment.

Ans. No. Marginal cost is only variable cost, it does not include fixed cost. Because, marginal cost is additional cost and additional cost cannot be fixed cost.

3. TC = ΣMC during the short period. Is it true?

Ans. No. In short period TC = TFC + TVC = TFC + ΣMC. Because, MC includes only variable costs, while TC include both variable and fixed costs.

4. Marginal cost is always variable cost. Why?

Ans. Marginal cost is an additional cost and additional cost cannot be fixed cost, it can be variable cost. Accordingly, the sum total of marginal costs corresponding to different units of output become TVC.

$$\Sigma MC = TVC$$

5. Why should TVC increase at a decreasing rate in the initial stages of production?

Ans. In the initial stages of production, a firm may be enjoying increasing returns to a factor (because of underutilisation of the fixed factor). It is a situation when MP (of the variable factor) tends to rise. Cost is just the opposite of productivity. Rising MP means falling cost. When the cost of producing an additional unit is falling, TVC should be increasing only at the decreasing rate.

6. Does long period TC curve starts from the origin?

Ans. Yes. Long period total cost (TC) curve starts from the origin (or zero) because in the long period, all costs are variable costs and variable costs always vary with output, so that when output is zero, variable costs are also zero.

7. ATC must fall simply because AFC always falls. Comment.

Ans. No. ATC = AFC + AVC. Being a component of ATC, falling AFC implies falling ATC. But this is true only in the initial stages of production when average fixed cost is a significant component of AC. In the later stages of production, average fixed cost (because it is continuously falling) reduces to an insignificant component of AC. Accordingly, AC tends to rise in assonance with rising AVC, even when AFC tends to fall.

8. The distance between AVC and AFC curves tends to reduce as output increases. Is it true?

Ans. No, it is not true. Initially as output increases the distance between AVC and AFC curves may tend to reduce but once the two curves cross each other (as in the diagram), the difference between the two tends to increase. Because, while AVC tends to rise after a certain level of output, AFC continuously falls (Fig. 19).

FIGURE 19

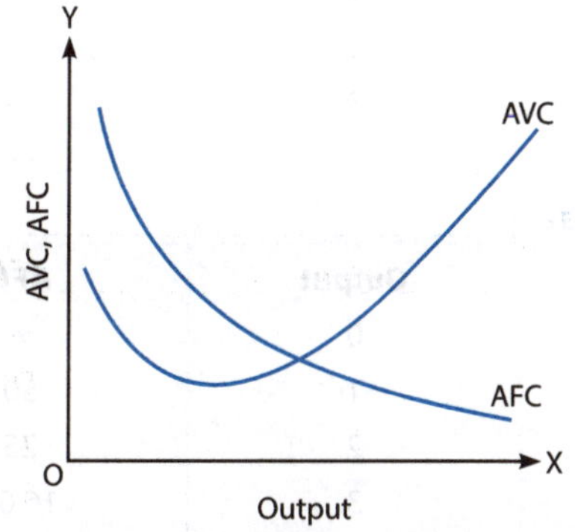

9. AC curve must eventually start rising during the short period. Do you agree?

Ans. Yes. Diminishing returns to a factor result in AVC to rise and hence AC curve must eventually start rising during the short period. This happens even when AFC is falling. Because, in the later stages of production, AFC (as it is continuously falling) reduces to an insignificant component of ATC.

10. Average cost of production must ultimately rise when the level of output continues to expand, no matter it is related to short period production function or long period production function. Then, where is the difference between the two types of production functions?

Ans. In the short period production function, rise in the average cost is related to the 'diminishing returns to a factor'. In the long period production function, on the other hand, rise in the average cost is related to diminishing returns to scale. In the short period, diminishing returns must set in when the ideal factor ratio is crossed because of the fixity of the factor. In the long period, diminishing returns must set in when diseconomies of scale start overshadowing the economies of scale.

11. Consider a situation when 10% increase in all inputs leads to 12% increase in output. How does it impact the average cost? Is it a short period phenomenon or a long period phenomenon?

Ans. When 10% increase in all inputs leads to 12% increase in output, unit cost of production $\left(\frac{TC}{Q}\right)$ must decline. Implying a fall in average cost.

It certainly is a long period phenomenon when all inputs are increased. Because, it is only in the long period that all factors are variable factors. In the short period, some factors must be fixed. Accordingly, the possibility of increasing all inputs is ruled out.

12. Find out TC, given the following information on MC for a firm which has spent ₹ 50 thousand on its establishment even when output was zero.

Output (Units)	1	2	3	4	5	6	7
MC (₹ thousand)	7	6	5	4	3	2	1

Ans.

Output (Units)	**MC (₹ thousand)**	**TVC (₹ thousand)**	**TC (= TFC + TVC) (TFC = ₹ 50 thousand)**
1	7	7	50 + 7 = 57
2	6	13	50 + 13 = 63
3	5	18	50 + 18 = 68
4	4	22	50 + 22 = 72
5	3	25	50 + 25 = 75
6	2	27	50 + 27 = 77
7	1	28	50 + 28 = 78

13. Complete the following table:

Output	**AFC**	**TFC**	**TVC**	**MC**
0	—	50	—	—
1	—	—	—	10
2	—	—	18	—
3	—	—	—	6
4	—	—	20	—

Ans.

Output	**AFC**	**TFC**	**TVC**	**MC**
0	∞	50	—	—
1	50	50	10	10
2	25	50	18	8
3	16.67	50	24	6
4	12.5	50	20	–4

14. From the following information, find average total cost when average fixed cost of producing 3 units of output is ₹ 6.

Output (Units)	0	1	2	3	4
MC (₹)	—	10	7	12	15

Ans.

Output (Units)	TFC (₹)	MC (₹)	TVC (₹)	TC (₹)	ATC (₹)
0	18	—	—	18	∞
1	18	10	10	28	28
2	18	7	17	35	17.5
3	18	12	29	47	15.67
4	18	15	44	62	15.5

When Output = 3 units, AFC = ₹ 6

TFC = AFC × Output

= ₹ 6 × 3

= ₹ 18.

15. Complete the following table:

Output (Units)	TVC (₹)	AVC (₹)	MC (₹)
1	20	—	—
—	—	16	12
3	54	—	—
—	—	20	26

Ans.

Output (Units)	TVC (₹)	AVC (₹)	MC (₹)
1	20	20	20
2	32	16	12
3	54	18	22
4	80	20	26

16. Complete the following table:

Output (Units)	ATC (₹)	AVC (₹)	MC (₹)
1	54	30	30
2	—	24	—
3	—	—	24
4	33	—	—

Ans.

Output (Units)	ATC (₹)	AVC (₹)	MC (₹)
1	54	30	30
2	36	24	18
3	32	24	24
4	33	27	36

ATC – AVC = AFC = 54 – 30 = 24 (when output = 1) = TFC.

17. A firm's average fixed cost of producing 2 units of a good is ₹ 9 and given below is its total cost schedule. Calculate its average variable cost and marginal cost for each of the given level of output.

Output (Units)	1	2	3
TC (₹)	23	27	30

Ans.

Output (Units)	TC (₹)	AFC (₹)	TFC (₹)	TVC (₹)	AVC (₹)	MC (₹)
1	23	18	18	23 – 18 = 5	$\frac{5}{1} = 5$	5
2	27	9	18	27 – 18 = 9	$\frac{9}{2} = 4.5$	4
3	30	6	18	30 – 18 = 12	$\frac{12}{3} = 4$	3

AFC (when output = 2) = ₹ 9

TFC = ₹ 9 × 2 = ₹ 18.

18. Find average cost, given the following information:

Output (Units)	0	1	2	3	4
Additional Variable Cost (₹)	—	10	11	12	13
Fixed Cost (₹)	20	—	—	—	—

Ans.

Output (Units)	Additional Variable Cost or MC (₹)	Fixed Cost (₹)	TVC (₹)	TC (₹)	AC (₹)
0	—	20	—	20	∞
1	10	20	10	30	30
2	11	20	21	41	20.5
3	12	20	33	53	17.67
4	13	20	46	66	16.5

19. Total product schedule of a firm at different levels of labour employment is given below. Calculate the firm's total variable cost, total cost, average cost, average variable cost and average fixed cost, if wage rate is ₹ 100 per day and total fixed cost is ₹ 1,000.

Labour Employment (Units)	1	2	3	4	5	6	7	8	9	10
Output (Units)	5	10	17	25	40	56	70	82	90	95

Ans.

Labour Employment (Units)	Output (Units)	TFC (₹)	TVC = Wage Rate × No. of Labours (₹)	TC (₹)	AC (₹)	AVC (₹)	AFC (₹)
1	5	1,000	100	1,100	220	20	200
2	10	1,000	200	1,200	120	20	100
3	17	1,000	300	1,300	76.4	17.6	58.8
4	25	1,000	400	1,400	56	16	40
5	40	1,000	500	1,500	37.5	12.5	25
6	56	1,000	600	1,600	28.5	10.7	17.8
7	70	1,000	700	1,700	24.2	10	14.2
8	82	1,000	800	1,800	21.9	9.7	12.2
9	90	1,000	900	1,900	21.1	10	11.1
10	95	1,000	1,000	2,000	21	10.5	10.5

4. Evaluation (Value-based Questions)

1. A firm withdraws ₹ 10,000 from its fixed deposits with the bank and uses the money for the purchase of factory equipment. Find the cost of this investment.

Or

An industrialist withdraws ₹ 10,000 from his term deposits and purchases a generation set. It involves an element both of explicit cost as well as implicit cost. Explain this fact with a reason.

Ans. Withdrawal of funds from the fixed deposits/term deposits, for the purchase of a factory equipment/generation set involves an element of explicit cost equal to the price of factory equipment/generation set paid by the industrialist.

It involves an element of **implicit cost equal to the loss of interest on the funds withdrawn from the bank.**

Cost of investment = Opportunity cost of investment

= Explicit Cost + Implicit Cost

↓ ↓

Expenditure of ₹ 10,000 for the purchase of factory equipment/ generation set + Interest amount that ₹ 10,000 would have earned if kept in the bank

2. As an owner of a firm, you find that your overhead cost per unit of output is continuously falling as output is increased. Does it mean a situation of ever rising profits for your firm?

Ans. No, falling overhead cost per unit of output does not imply a situation of ever rising profits. Because:

(i) Overhead costs are fixed costs. These costs are constant, no matter what the level of output is. Accordingly, per unit fixed cost is bound to fall as output increases.

(ii) Fixed cost is only a component of total cost. The other component is variable cost.

(iii) While estimating profits, we must account for both the fixed costs as well as variable costs.

(iv) It is only when the difference between total receipts from the sale of output (on the one hand) and total cost of production (on the other hand) is maximum that total profits are maximised.

3. Land Acquisition Act in India has led to a considerable rise in compensation to the farmers whose land is acquired for the establishment of industry.

(i) How is it going to impact the cost structure of new industry?

(ii) Will it work as an inducement or a deterrent for the new industry?

Ans. (i) Now, availability of land for the new industry will become more expensive. Accordingly, fixed cost of production is expected to rise considerably.

(ii) Fixed cost is incurred even before output actually starts. A rise in fixed cost, therefore, will definitely work as a deterrent for the new industry.

4. Electricity tariff is increased for the commercial use. Would it affect fixed cost or variable cost of the industry? Explain with a reason.

Ans. Electricity cost is a component of variable cost, not the fixed cost. Because, use of electricity varies with variation in output. Accordingly, increase in electricity tariff would increase variable cost of the industry.

5. How is the development of an SEZ (special economic zone) expected to influence the cost structure of a firm?

Ans. An SEZ offers multi-faceted infrastructural facility for the firms operating in the specified zone. It offers facilities of raw material, transportation, banking and insurance services. These facilities generate external economies for all the firms located in the SEZ. Because of the external economies, cost structure of an individual firm tends to be moderated. Unit cost of production is lowered.

5. CBSE Questions—Past 4 years (With Answers or Reference to the Text for Answers)

1. What is the behaviour of average fixed cost as output increases? [CBSE Delhi 2012]

   Or

   What is the behaviour of average fixed cost as output is increased? Why is it so? [CBSE Delhi 2014]

   [Page 191, 192]

2. Draw average variable cost, average total cost and marginal cost curves in a single diagram. [CBSE Delhi 2012]

   [Page 200]

3. An individual is both the owner and the manager of a shop taken on rent. Identify implicit cost and explicit cost from this information. Explain. [CBSE Delhi 2012]

   [Page 185, 186]

4. A producer borrows money and opens a shop. The shop premises is owned by him. Identify the implicit and explicit costs from this information. Explain. [CBSE Delhi 2012]

   [Page 185, 186]

5. A producer invests his own savings in starting a business and employs a manager to look after it. Identify the implicit and explicit costs from this information. Explain. [CBSE Delhi 2012]

   Or

   A producer starts a business by investing his own savings. He employs a manager to look after the business. Identify the explicit and implicit costs from this information. Explain. [CBSE (F) 2012]

   [Page 185, 186]

6. What is the behaviour of total variable cost as output increases? [CBSE (AI) 2012]

   [Page 188, 189]

7. Draw total variable cost, total cost, and total fixed cost curves in a single diagram. [CBSE (AI) 2012]

   [Page 190]

8. A producer starts a business by investing his own savings and hiring the labour. Identify implicit and explicit costs from this information. Explain. [CBSE (AI) 2012]

   [Page 185, 186]

9. A farmer takes a farm on rent and carries on farming with the help of family members. Identify explicit and implicit costs from this information. Explain. [CBSE (AI) 2012]

   [Page 185, 186]

10. A producer borrows money and starts a business. He himself looks after the business. Identify implicit and explicit costs from this information. Explain. [CBSE (AI) 2012]

    Or

    A producer borrows money to start a business and looks after the business himself. Identify the implicit and explicit costs from this information. Explain. [CBSE (F) 2012]

    [Page 185, 186]

11. Define marginal cost. [CBSE (F) 2012; Delhi 2013]

    [Page 194]

12. A producer takes a building on rent for carrying out business. He looks after the business himself. Identify the implicit and explicit costs from this information. Explain. [CBSE (F) 2012]

    [Page 185, 186]

13. Give two examples of fixed costs. [CBSE Delhi 2013]

    [Page 189]

14. Give two examples of variable costs. [CBSE Delhi 2013]

    [Page 189]

15. Give an example each of fixed cost and variable cost. [CBSE Delhi 2013]

[Page 189]

16. Complete the following table: [CBSE Delhi 2013]

Output (Units)	Average Cost (₹)	Marginal Cost (₹)
1	12	—
2	10	—
3	—	10
4	10.5	—
5	11	—
6	—	17

[Page 386]

17. With increase in level of output, average fixed cost goes on falling till it reaches zero. [CBSE (AI) 2013]

[False. Because as the level of output increases, average fixed cost falls but can never be zero, because average of any positive value (fixed cost) can never be zero.]

18. Explain the relationship between marginal cost and average variable cost. [CBSE (F) 2013]

Or

Define cost. State the relation between marginal cost and average variable cost. [CBSE Delhi 2015]

[Page 185, 198]

19. Explain the relationship between marginal cost and average cost. [CBSE (F) 2013]

[Page 197, 198]

20. Show with the help of a numerical example that average cost is constant when marginal cost is equal to it.

[Page 197, 198] [CBSE (F) 2013]

21. What is meant by cost in Economics? [CBSE Delhi 2014]

[Page 185, 186]

22. State the relation between total cost and marginal cost. [CBSE Delhi 2014]

[Page 199]

23. Define variable cost. [CBSE (AI) 2014]

Or

Give the meaning of variable cost. [CBSE (F) 2014]

[Page 188]

24. Define fixed cost. [CBSE (F) 2014]

[Page187]

25. What is the behaviour of (a) average fixed cost, and (b) average variable cost as more and more units of a good are produced? [CBSE (AI) 2015]

[Page 191–193]

6. NCERT Questions (With Hints to Answers)

1. Briefly explain the concept of the cost function.

[**Hint:** Cost function refers to the functional relationship between cost and output. It studies the behaviour of cost at different levels of output, when technology is assumed to be constant. It can be expressed as under:

$$C = f(Q)$$

Here, C = Cost of production; and Q = Quantum of output.]

2. What are the total fixed cost, total variable cost and total cost of a firm? How are they related?

   [**Hint:** Total fixed cost (TFC) is that cost which does not change with change in the level of output. Total variable cost (TVC) is that cost which changes as the level of output changes. Total cost (TC) is the sum of total fixed cost and total variable fixed cost. So that, TC curve is the vertical summation of TFC and TVC curves.]

3. What are the average fixed cost, average variable cost and average cost of a firm? How are they related?

   [**Hint:** Average fixed cost (AFC) is the fixed cost per unit of output produced. Average variable cost (AVC) is the variable cost per unit of output produced. Average cost (AC) is the sum of average fixed cost and average variable cost. So that, AC curve is the vertical summation of AFC and AVC curves.]

4. Can there be some fixed cost in the long run? If not, why.

   [**Hint:** No, because all costs are variable costs in the long run and no factor is a fixed factor in the long run.]

5. What does the average fixed cost curve look like? Why does it look so?

   [**Hint:** The average fixed cost (AFC) curve is a rectangular hyperbola. Because TFC is constant at all levels of output.]

6. What do the short run marginal cost, average variable cost and short run average cost curves look like?

   [**Hint:** Short run marginal cost (MC), average variable cost (AVC) and short run average cost (AC) curves are generally 'U' shaped in accordance with the law of variable proportions.]

7. Why does the SMC curve cut the AVC curve at the minimum point of the AVC curve?

   [**Hint:** SMC (short run marginal cost) curve cuts the AVC (average variable cost) curve at the minimum point of the AVC curve because it is only here that SMC = AVC.]

8. At which point does the SMC curve cut the SAC curve? Give reason in support of your answer.

   [**Hint:** SMC curve cuts the SAC curve only at its lowest (or minimum) point because it is only here that SMC = SAC.]

9. Why is the short run marginal cost curve 'U' shaped?

   [**Hint:** In the short run as the application of variable factor increases (fixed cost remaining constant) in the initial stage marginal cost decreases (owing to increasing returns), but eventually it tends to rise in accordance with the law of variable proportions. Hence, the 'U' shape of MC.]

10. How do the long run marginal cost and the average cost curves look like?

    [**Hint:** Long run marginal cost (LMC) and the average cost (LAC) curves are U-shaped in accordance with the returns to scale.]

11. The following table shows the total cost schedule of a firm. What is the total fixed cost schedule of this firm? Calculate the TVC, AFC, AVC, SAC and SMC schedules of the firm.

Q	0	1	2	3	4	5	6
TC	10	30	45	55	70	90	120

[**Hint:**

Q	**TC**	**TFC**	**TVC**	**AFC**	**AVC**	**SAC**	**SMC**
0	10	10	0	∞	—	—	—
1	30	10	20	10	20	30	20
2	45	10	35	5	17.5	22.5	15
3	55	10	45	3.33	15	18.33	10
4	70	10	60	2.5	15	17.5	15
5	90	10	80	2	16	18	20
6	120	10	110	1.67	18.33	20	30

12. The following table gives the total cost schedule of a firm. It is also given that the average fixed cost at 4 units of output is ₹5. Find the TVC, TFC, AVC, AFC, SAC and SMC schedules of the firm for the corresponding values of output.

Q	1	2	3	4	5	6
TC	50	65	75	95	130	185

[**Hint:**

Q	TC (₹)	TFC (4 × ₹5) (₹)	TVC (₹)	AFC (₹)	AVC (₹)	SAC (₹)	SMC (₹)	
1	50	20	30	20	30	50	30	
2	65	20	45	10	22.5	32.5	15	MC (when output is
3	75	20	55	6.67	18.33	25	10	1 unit)
4	95	20	75	5	18.75	23.75	20	$= TVC_n - TVC_{n-1}$
5	130	20	110	4	22	26	35	= 30 – 0
6	185	20	165	3.33	27.5	30.83	55	= 30

13. A firm's SMC schedule is shown in the following table. The total fixed cost of the firm is ₹100. Find the TVC, TC, AVC and SAC schedules of the firm.

Q	0	1	2	3	4	5	6
SMC	—	500	300	200	300	500	800

[**Hint:**

Q	SMC (₹)	TFC (₹)	TVC (₹)	TC (₹)	AVC (₹)	SAC (₹)
0	—	100	0	100	—	—
1	500	100	500	600	500	600
2	300	100	800	900	400	450
3	200	100	1,000	1,100	333.33	366.67
4	300	100	1,300	1,400	325	350
5	500	100	1,800	1,900	360	380
6	800	100	2,600	2,700	433.33	450

7. Miscellaneous Questions and Reference to the Text for Answers

A. Questions of 3 & 4 marks each

1. Explain the concept of fixed cost with the help of a table and diagram.
   [Page 187, 188]
2. Explain the concept of variable cost with the help of a table and diagram.
   [Page 188]
3. Distinguish between fixed costs and variable costs. Give two examples of each.
   [Page 189]
4. Explain average cost with the help of a table and diagram.
   [Page 190–194]
5. Explain marginal cost with the help of a table and diagram.
   [Page 194–196]

6. Why is short run average cost curve U-shaped?
   [Page 194, 217]
7. Explain the relation between marginal cost and average cost.

   Or

   Explain the relationship between marginal cost and average cost with the help of a cost schedule.
   [Page 197, 198]
8. Explain whether marginal cost can increase when average cost decreases.
   [Page 197, 198]
9. Draw one diagram showing average total cost curve, average variable cost curve and marginal cost curve.
   [Page 200]
10. Why does the difference between average cost curve and average variable cost curve gradually decline?
    [Page 200]
11. Draw a diagram showing TVC in terms of the area under MC curve.
    [Page 196]
12. MC is only a variable cost. Why?
    [Page 196, 197]

B. Questions of 6 marks each

1. Describe the various types of production costs. Explain the mutual relationship between average cost and marginal cost.
   [Page 187–194, 197, 198]
2. What is total cost, average cost and marginal cost? Explain the relationship between average cost and marginal cost with the help of a table and diagram.
   [Page 189, 190, 194, 197, 198]
3. What are fixed costs? Explain the nature and shape of the total fixed and average fixed cost curves.
   [Page 187, 191, 192]
4. Explain the relationship between (i) average cost curve and marginal cost curve, (ii) total cost curve and marginal cost curve.
   [Page 197–199]
5. Diagrammatically, explain the relationship between AVC and MC and between TC and MC.
   [Page 198, 199]
6. MC determines the shape of both TC and TVC curves. Explain how.
   [Page 189, 190, 196, 197]

DOs and DON'Ts

1. You should be absolutely clear about the behaviour of two components of AC: (i) AFC, and (ii) AVC.
   (i) AFC is always a falling component of AC. Because, TFC is constant for all levels of output, and AFC $\left(=\frac{TFC}{Q}\right)$ must fall as the level of output (Q) rises.
   (ii) Initially, AVC is a falling component of AC. This is because of increasing returns to a factor. Eventually, AVC becomes a rising component of AC, because of diminishing returns to a factor.

2. Never miss the point that, in Economics, total cost is always estimated as total opportunity cost. This is the total cost of availing an opportunity. This is estimated in terms of the total sacrifice involved in availing an opportunity. This has two elements: (i) explicit (opportunity) cost, referring to sacrifice involved in terms of payments to others, and (ii) implicit (opportunity) cost, referring to sacrifice involved in terms of the use of self-owned inputs, like the use of own premises or own labour for running a factory. Implicit cost does not involve payments to others. We have to find 'imputed value' of these costs. **Example:** Imputed cost of using self-owned premises for purpose of business is equal to the rental value of the premises if it were let out to others.

abilityZONE

❑ Cost Function

The functional relationship between cost and output is called cost function.

It may be specified as under:

$$C = f(Q)$$

[Here, C = Cost of production
Q = Quantum of output.]

For a producer, a cost function shows least cost combinations of inputs corresponding to different levels of output.

❑ Why is the Short Run Average Cost Curve U-Shaped?

Short run average cost curve is U-shaped. It means that at first, this curve tends to fall and after reaching the minimum point, it begins to rise. It finds its explanation in the law of variable proportions. As discussed in the previous chapter, the law of variable proportion states that initially (so long as fixed factor remains underutilised), MP (marginal product) of the variable factor tends to rise. And, eventually (after fixed factor and variable factor reach their ideal ratio or optimum ratio), MP of the variable factor tends to fall. Let variable factor be L (Labour) and fixed factor be K (Capital). When MP_L tends to rise it means more of output per every additional unit of L. Rising MP also implies an increase in AP. Looked from a different angle it means, requirement of L per unit of output tends to fall (in a state of increasing returns to a factor). Ultimately it means cost of the variable factor (L) per unit of output tends to fall. Or, that AVC tends to fall. Exactly opposite is the situation when diminishing returns are in operation. Thus, AVC assumes U-shape. AC = AVC + AFC. AFC must always fall as output increases, and its component (in AC) tends to gradually shrink with increase in output.

Thus, initially both AFC and AVC tend to fall. Accordingly, AC (which is the sum aggregate of AFC and AVC) also falls. Subsequently, AFC tends to be a very small component of AC. So that, even when it is falling, it causes little impact on the rising AC (owing to rising AVC). Hence, the final conclusion that AC (along with AVC) tends to be U-shaped in accordance with the law of variable proportions.

❑ Time Element and Cost

Time element has an important bearing on the cost and production of a commodity. This is discussed with reference to (1) Very short or market period, (2) Short period, and (3) Long period.

(1) **Very Short or Market Period:** Very short period is also referred to as market period. It is so short a period that production cannot be increased. Accordingly, it becomes immaterial whether the producer covers his cost of production or not at the prevailing price of the product.

(2) **Short Period:** It is the period of time during which production can be increased only by increasing the variable factors. Application of fixed factor (by definition) remains constant. The producer can control only the variable cost, not the fixed cost. Accordingly, the producer must cover at least variable costs of production during the short period.

(3) **Long Period:** It is the period of time during which production can be increased by way of additional application of all the factors of production. Accordingly, the producer must cover all costs of production. In fact all costs are of the nature of variable costs in the long run because no factor is a fixed factor in the long run. Accordingly, all costs are under the control of the producer, and therefore, must be covered.

In short, while during the market period, cost factor becomes irrelevant, the producer must cover at least variable costs during the short period, and all costs, during the long period.

Concept of Revenue

CHAPTER 8

TODO

- What is Revenue?
- Total Revenue, Marginal Revenue and Average Revenue
- Firm's Revenue Curve (or Demand Curve) in Different Markets

1. What is Revenue?

Suppose, you are running a factory producing ice cream. You produce 1,000 ice creams daily. By selling these ice creams you get ₹ 1,000. In Economics, this amount of ₹ 1,000 is called revenue. Thus, by selling a commodity whatever money a firm receives is called its revenue.

In the words of **Dooley**, "*The revenue of a firm is its sale receipts or money receipts from the sale of a product.*" It is also called sale proceeds.

Revenue and Profit are Different Concepts

The concept of revenue is different from the concept of profit. The following equation shows the difference:

Profit = Revenue – Costs

Revenue = Costs + Profit

2. Total Revenue, Marginal Revenue and Average Revenue

Revenue is estimated in three different ways, as under:

(1) Total Revenue,

(2) Marginal Revenue, and

(3) Average Revenue.

(1) Total Revenue (TR)

Total money receipts of a firm from the sale of a given output is called total revenue. If 100 ice cream slabs are sold at the rate of ₹ 50 per slab, total revenue (TR) of the firm will be:

$$\underset{\text{Output}}{100} \times \underset{\text{Price}}{₹50} = \underset{\text{Total Revenue}}{₹5{,}000}$$

Total revenue is money receipts of a firm from the sale of its total output.

Or, $TR = AR \times Q$ [Here, TR = Total revenue; AR = Revenue per unit of output; Q = Total output.]

(2) Marginal Revenue (MR)

Be Careful

Don't confuse marginal revenue as the price at which last unit of the commodity is sold. MR simply is the difference in TR when an additional unit of output is sold Thus:

$MR = TR_n - TR_{n-1}$

This difference may be zero (or even negative) even when price is some positive number.

Marginal revenue is the change in total revenue when one more unit of a commodity is sold.

In order to calculate marginal revenue, change in total revenue (ΔTR) is divided by change in quantity sold (ΔQ). Or, it is estimated as the difference between 'TR of n units of output' and 'TR of n–1 units of output'.

$$MR = \frac{\text{Change in Total Revenue}}{\text{Change in Quantity Sold}} = \frac{\Delta TR}{\Delta Q}$$

Example:

TR of 10 units = 1,000

TR of 15 units = 1,500

$\Delta TR = 1{,}500 - 1{,}000 = 500$

$\Delta Q = 15 - 10 = 5$

$$MR = \frac{\Delta TR}{\Delta Q} = \frac{500}{5} = 100$$

MR as the difference between TR of n units of output and TR of n–1 units of output is estimated as under:

$$MR = TR_n - TR_{n-1}$$

[Here, MR = Marginal revenue; Δ = Change in; TR = Total revenue; Q = Product; TR_n = Total revenue of 'n' units of output; TR_{n-1} = Total revenue of 'n – 1' units of output]

Example:

If TR = ₹ 1,000 when 10 units of a commodity are sold and it is ₹ 1,100 when 11 units of a commodity are sold, then additional revenue (on account of the sale of one more unit) is ₹ 100 which is marginal revenue.

$$MR = TR_{11} - TR_{10}$$

$$= ₹\,1{,}100 - ₹\,1{,}000 = ₹\,100$$

Marginal revenue is the change in total revenue on account of the sale of an additional unit of output.

Two ways of estimating MR:

(i) $MR = \frac{\Delta TR}{\Delta Q}$

(ii) $MR = TR_n - TR_{n-1}$

Since MR is additional revenue (from the sale of an additional unit of output), sum total of MR corresponding to each unit of output is equal to TR. Thus, if 5 units of output are produced, $MR_1 + MR_2 + MR_3 + MR_4 + MR_5 = TR$.

$$\sum MR = TR$$

Sum total of MR corresponding to every additional unit of output is equal to TR.

(3) Average Revenue (AR)

Average revenue refers to revenue per unit of output. If,

TR = ₹ 1,000, and Q = 100, then

$$AR = \frac{TR}{Q}$$

$$= \frac{1,000}{100} = ₹\ 10$$

Thus, AR refers to the rate at which output is sold. **What is rate?** It refers to price of the commodity. Thus, AR is nothing but price of the product.

Average revenue is the revenue per unit of output. It is the same as price of the commodity.

HOTS

Q. Show that AR = Price.

Ans. We know that,

$$AR = \frac{TR}{Q}$$

We also know that TR = P × Q (Where P = Price, Q = Quantity or output sold)
Relating the two equations, we can write that:

$$AR = \frac{P \times Q}{Q} = P$$

Thus, it is proved that AR = Price.

Let Us Be Practical

Let us take an example of a firm under perfect competition. A firm under perfect competition is a price taker. It is not a price maker. It takes market price as given. Since market price = AR of the firm, we can state that AR is given to a firm. Implying that it can sell any quantity at the given price or the given AR. Let us assume the price = ₹ 10, implying firm's AR = ₹ 10. It implies that the firm can sell 10, 20, 30, 40, 50 (or any quantity) at the existing price of ₹ 10. Thus, for a firm under perfect competition AR, TR and MR would be as in Table 1.

Table 1. Total Revenue, Marginal Revenue and Average Revenue, when AR is constant = ₹ 10

Output Q (Units)	Price P = AR (₹)	Total Revenue TR = AR × Q (₹)	Marginal Revenue $MR = TR_n - TR_{n-1}$ (₹)
1	10	10	10 – 0 = 10
2	10	20	20 – 10 = 10
3	10	30	30 – 20 = 10
4	10	40	40 – 30 = 10
5	10	50	50 – 40 = 10

Now, you can check the following relationships:

(i) TR = AR × Q = ₹ 10 × 5 = ₹ 50

Or, TR = Σ MR (sum total of MR corresponding to every additional unit of output)

= ₹ (10 + 10 + 10 + 10 + 10) = ₹ 50

(ii) $AR = \frac{TR}{Q} = \frac{50}{5}$ = ₹ 10 = Price

(iii) $MR = TR_n - TR_{n-1}$

= ₹ 50 – ₹ 40 = ₹ 10

= [TR of 5 units] – [TR of 4 units]

Also check:

That if AR is constant, then MR = AR.

A Few More Relationships

You can work out a few more relationships from this Table. Check the Table and see for yourself if the following observations are correct:

(i) MR is simply an addition to TR when one more unit of output is sold/produced.

(ii) In case price is constant (implying AR is constant), then MR should also be constant (AR being equal to MR).

(iii) Constant MR implies constant addition to TR when an additional unit of the commodity is sold/produced. This implies that TR will increase at a constant rate.

Diagrammatic Illustration: AR, MR and TR when Price is Constant

In case price (AR) is constant (as under perfect competition), MR is also constant. Implying that TR increases at a constant rate. Because, MR indicates the rate at which TR increases. Increasing at constant rate, TR forms a straight line sloping upward and starting from the origin as in Fig. 1.

Fig. 1 shows that if output level is OL, TR = OS = LT. Alternatively, TR can be estimated as the multiple of AR (= price) and output. So that TR = AR × output. It can also be estimated as the total area under MR curve, corresponding to a given level of output. Because, TR is the sum total of MR corresponding to each unit of output. Fig. 2 illustrates this situation.

FIGURE 1

TR when price is constant

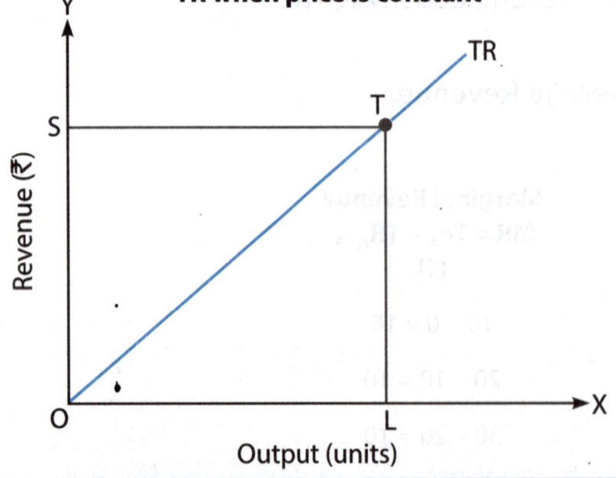

FIGURE 2

Estimation of TR through MR, when price is constant

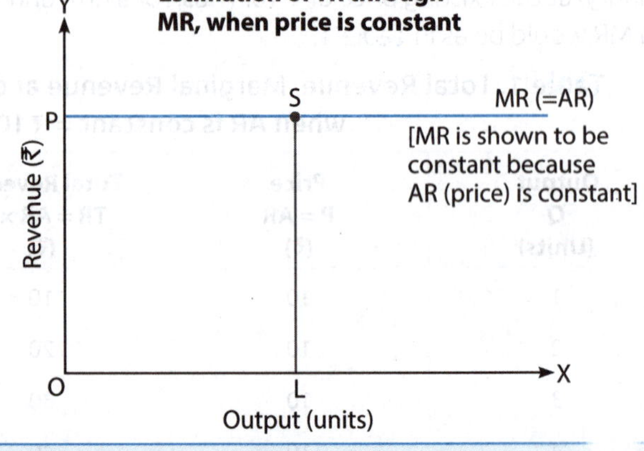

- Constant price (and therefore, constant MR) means TR increases at a constant rate. Therefore, TR is shown as a straight line moving upward. It shoots from the origin, because TR = 0 when output = 0 (Fig. 1).
- Both AR and MR are indicated by a horizontal straight line because price (AR) is constant. When AR is constant, MR is also constant, and AR = MR (Fig. 2).

Fig. 2 is drawn on the assumption that price is constant for a firm as under perfect competition. Implying AR = MR = OP in Fig 2. If output = OL, TR = OL × OP = area OLSP.

↑ ↑ ↑
Output × Price = Total Revenue

Or, TR = ΣMR = area OLSP.

[**Note:** Firm's Demand Curve or Price Line is the same as AR Curve Because, AR means price, and demand curve (or AR curve) shows the relationship between price and quantity demanded of firm's output.]

What happens if AR is not Constant?

Under monopoly and monopolistic competition, price (= AR) tends to decrease as more is sold. In such a situation, we will have a Table like the following:

Table 2. Total Revenue, Average Revenue, Marginal Revenue, when AR is not constant

Output Q (Units)	Price P = AR (₹)	Total Revenue TR = AR × Q (₹)	Marginal Revenue $MR = TR_n - TR_{n-1}$ (₹)
1	10	10	10 (= 10 – 0)
2	9.5	19	9 (= 19 – 10)
3	9	27	8 (= 27 –19)
4	8.5	34	7 (= 34 – 27)

Check Table 2 for the following relationships:

(i) In case AR is declining, MR is also declining.

(ii) When AR is declining by ₹ 0.5, MR is declining by ₹ 1. This proves that under monopoly and monopolistic competition, MR declines faster than AR. So that, AR > MR.

(iii) When MR is declining, we are adding less and less to TR for every additional unit of output. So that TR increases only at a decreasing rate.

Can MR be Zero or Negative?

Yes, MR can be zero or negative. It is clear from the following illustration:

Table 3. A Situation of Zero and Negative MR

Average Revenue or Price (₹)	Output (Units)	Total Revenue (₹)	Marginal Revenue (₹)
100	1	100	100 (= 100 – 0)
80	2	160	60 (= 160 – 100)
40	4	160	$0\left(=\frac{160-160}{2}\right)$
30	5	150	–10 (= 150 – 160)

Negative MR

Negative MR is possible only when price is declining as under monopoly or monopolistic competition. It is not possible in case of perfect competition where price is given to a firm, so that AR = MR and both are constant.

Check Table 3 for the following relationships:

(i) MR can be zero or even negative, when price is declining. Thus, MR = 0 when output = 4 units. MR is negative (–10) when output = 5 units.

(ii) TR stops increasing when MR = 0, so that TR is maximum when MR = 0.

(iii) TR starts declining when MR is negative.

(iv) When MR is declining, less and less is added to TR for every additional unit of output. Accordingly, TR increases only at a decreasing rate.

Diagrammatic Illustration: AR, MR and TR when Price is not Constant

Fig. 3 illustrates the relationship between TR, AR and MR, when price (AR) is not constant, as under monopoly and monopolistic competition.

FIGURE 3

TR, AR and MR, when price is not constant

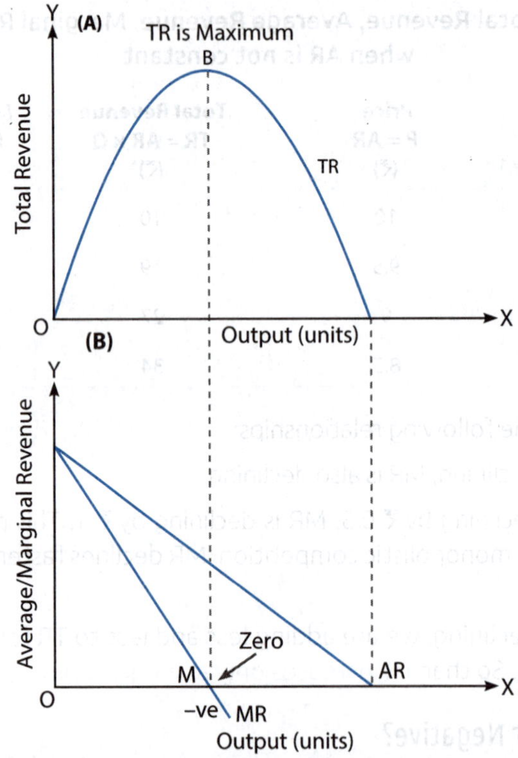

Up to point B, TR curve is increasing at a decreasing rate. This is because MR is decreasing. At point B, TR is maximum. This is because, MR = 0. Beyond point B, TR starts declining. This is because MR is negative. In a situation of zero price, AR touches X-axis. Accordingly, TR also touches X-axis.

Part (A) of the figure shows TR. Part (B) shows AR and MR.

Declining AR indicates that more of a commodity is sold only when price is lowered.

When AR is falling, MR falls faster than AR. Important it is to note that TR increases at a decreasing rate till point B, when MR is decreasing (MR is the rate of TR). TR is maximum at point B, because corresponding to point B, MR = 0. Beyond point B, TR starts declining. This is because MR turns negative. AR, of course, can never be negative. At most it can be zero (touching the X-axis). Zero price leads to zero TR. It happens when TR curve touches X-axis (corresponding to AR curve touching X-axis). However, it may be noted that zero AR and negative MR are more like theoretical possibilities.

Estimation of TR, AR & MR, and their Relationship

Estimation

(i) $TR = AR \times Q$ or ΣMR

(ii) $AR = \frac{TR}{Q}$

(iii) $MR = TR_n - TR_{n-1}$

Relationship between TR and MR

(i) When TR is increasing at constant rate, MR should be constant. It happens under perfect competition.

(ii) When TR is increasing at diminishing rate, MR should be diminishing [a situation of monopoly or monopolistic competition].

(iii) When TR is maximum, MR is zero.

(iv) When TR is diminishing, MR is negative.

Relationship between AR and MR

(i) When AR is decreasing, MR should be decreasing faster than AR. Thus, downward sloping MR curve is below the downward sloping AR curve [a situation of monopoly and monopolistic competition]. Accordingly, $MR < AR$.

(ii) If AR is constant, MR is equal to AR. Both are indicated by the same horizontal straight line [a situation of perfect competition].

(iii) MR can be negative, but not AR.

HOTS

Q.1. What is firm's demand curve?

Ans. **Firm's demand curve is a curve showing relationship between price of the product (that the firm is producing) and its quantity demanded in the market.** We know for a firm, price = AR. We also know that firm's AR curve shows the relationship between price (or AR) and output (or quantity demanded) in the market. Accordingly, we can state that firm's demand curve is the same as AR curve of the firm. It is also called firm's price line (see Fig. 2).

Q.2. What is firm's price line? What is its shape?

Ans. **Firm's price line is the same as firm's AR curve.** Under perfect competition, firm's price line is a horizontal straight line. Both AR and MR tend to coincide (AR = MR). Under monopoly or monopolistic competition, firm's price line slopes downward. When AR slopes downward, MR slopes downward faster than AR. So that, MR < AR (see Fig. 4 for a firm under perfect competition, Fig. 6 for a firm under monopoly, and Fig. 7 for a firm under monopolistic competition).

3. Firm's Revenue Curve in Different Markets

Broadly, markets are of three types:

(1) Perfectly Competitive market,

(2) Monopoly market, and

(3) Monopolistic Competitive market.

Firm's revenue curves are different in different markets. These are discussed as under:

(1) Revenue Curve Under Perfectly Competitive Market or Perfect Competition: Under perfect competition, a firm is a price taker. It cannot influence/change the market price. It can sell any quantity at the prevailing price. If a firm tries to sell its product at a price higher than the prevailing price, it will lose all its customers. Because there are so many other firms in the market, selling the same product at the prevailing price.

Identical Terms

The students should understand that

(i) firm's price line,

(ii) firm's revenue curve, and

(iii) firm's demand curve

are identical terms. There is no difference among these terms.

A firm under perfect competition has to accept the prevailing price. It means that AR (price) is constant for a firm. Its constant AR implies constant MR. It also means that AR = MR. Table 4 and Fig. 4 illustrate the behaviour of AR and MR for a firm under perfect competition.

Table 4. Firm's Revenue Under Perfect Competition

Output/Sales Q (Units)	Average Revenue = Price (₹)	Total Revenue TR = AR × Q (₹)	Marginal Revenue $MR = TR_n - TR_{n-1}$ (₹)
1	5	5	5
2	5	10	5
3	5	15	5
4	5	20	5

FIGURE 4

Firm's Revenue Curve Under Perfect Competition

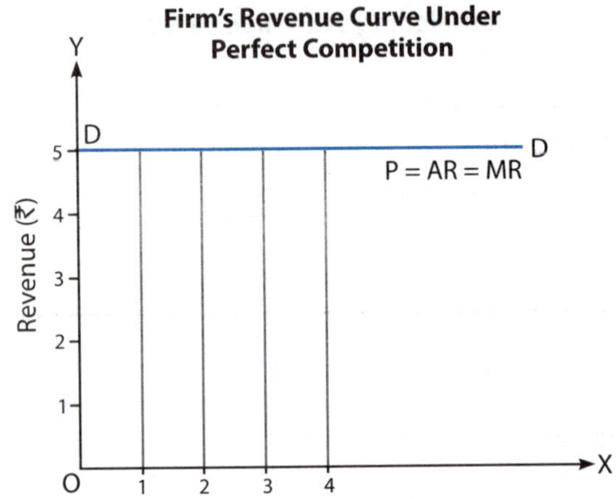

DD is the firm's revenue curve under perfect competition. It is a horizontal straight line. A firm can sell any quantity at the prevailling price (= ₹ 5). AR being constant: (i) MR is also constant, and (ii) AR = MR. Both AR and MR are indicated by the same horizontal straight line DD.

Table 4 shows that price (or AR) of the product = ₹ 5 per unit. It remains constant for a firm for all levels of output. Constant AR leads to: (i) constant MR, and (ii) AR = MR. Fig. 4 shows horizontal straight line DD indicating firm's revenue curve (or price line or demand curve). It shows that at a price of ₹ 5 per unit, a firm can sell any quantity. Thus, firm's AR curve is perfectly elastic under perfect competition.

HOTS

Q. Draw AR and MR curves for a firm when, in a perfectly competitive market, price of the product reduces from ₹ 12 to ₹ 10 per unit.

Ans. A perfectly competitive firm has to accept new market price (₹ 10) as given. Constant AR implies that AR = MR. Therefore, AR = MR = ₹ 10 are indicated by a horizontal straight line (Fig. 5).

Price of the product is given to a firm, or it is constant for a firm under perfect competition. It does not mean that the market price cannot change. It only means that the firm on its own cannot change the price. The market price can change depending on the change in market demand or market supply of the product.

FIGURE 5

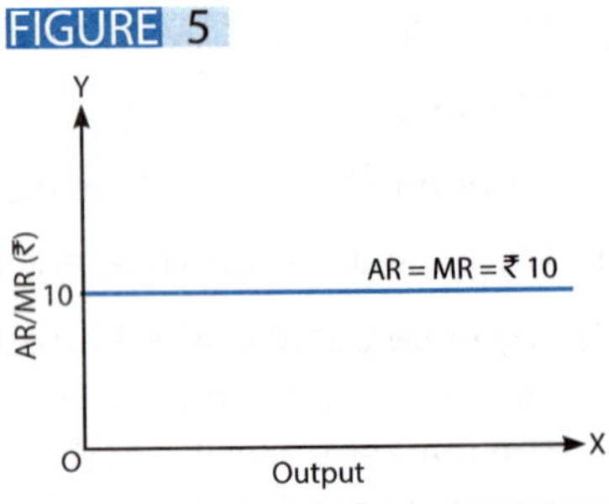

(2) Revenue Curve Under Monopoly: Under monopoly, the firm's average revenue curve slopes downward from left to right. It means that if a monopolist desires to sell more, he has to reduce price of the product. A monopolist is a price maker. Being a single seller of the product in the market, he can fix whatever price he wishes to. But, he can sell more only if he lowers the price of his product. Thus, there is negative relationship between price of the product and demand for the product in a monopoly market. Accordingly, firm's AR curve (or demand curve or price line) slopes downward. As noted earlier, if AR curve slopes downward, MR curve also slopes downward, and faster than AR curve. So that MR < AR. Table 5 and Fig. 6 illustrate the behaviour of AR (and MR) for a monopoly firm.

Table 5. Firm's Revenue Under Monopoly

Output/Sales Q (Units)	**Average Revenue $AR = \frac{TR}{Q}$ = Price (₹)**	**Total Revenue TR = AR × Q (₹)**	**Marginal Revenue $MR = TR_n - TR_{n-1}$ (₹)**
1	10	10	10
2	9	18	8
3	8	24	6
4	7	28	4

FIGURE 6

Firm's Revenue Curve Under Monopoly

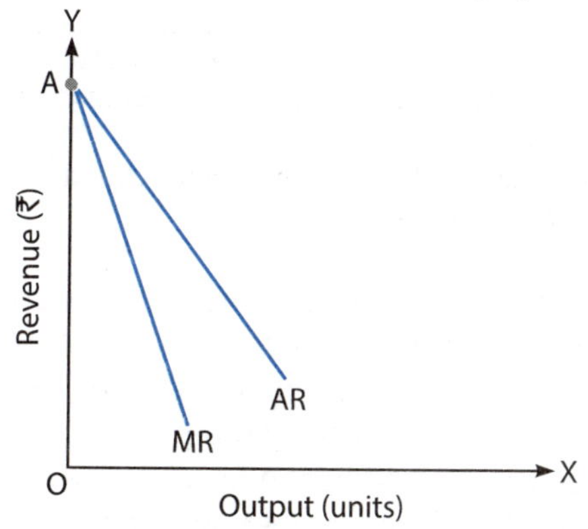

AR curve slopes downward. It shows that monopoly firm must lower price (AR) of the product in case it wants to sell more of it. If AR falls, MR also falls, and falls faster than AR. So that, MR < AR.

Table 5 shows that the monopolist sells 4 units when price of the product is ₹ 7 per unit. If he increases price to ₹ 8, he only sells 3 units. Fig. 6 also brings out the fact that a monopoly firm can sell more only by lowering price of the product. Downward sloping AR curve shows the inverse relationship between price (AR) and output.

(3) Revenue Curve Under Monopolistic Competition: Firm's revenue curve under monopolistic competition is similar to monopoly as illustrated by Table 6 and Fig. 7.

Table 6. Firm's Revenue Under Monopolistic Competition

Output/Sales Q (Units)	Average Revenue $AR = \frac{TR}{Q}$ = Price (₹)	Total Revenue TR = AR × Q (₹)	Marginal Revenue $MR = TR_n - TR_{n-1}$ (₹)
1	10	10	10
2	9.5	19	9
3	9	27	8
4	8.5	34	7

FIGURE 7

Firm's Revenue Curve Under Monopolistic Competition

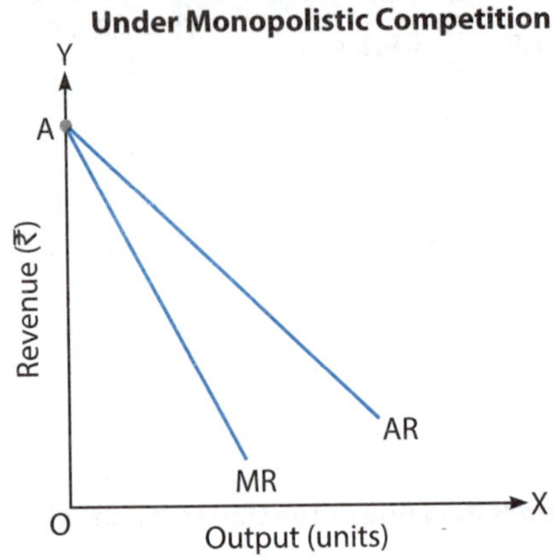

Like under monopoly, AR curve for a firm under monopolistic competition also slopes downward. However, the difference is that AR curve under monopolistic competition is more elastic than under monopoly.

Reason: Lack of close substitutes for the monopoly product, and availability of close substitutes for a firm under monopolistic competition.

As under monopoly, there is inverse relationship between AR (Price) and output. Accordingly, AR curve slopes downward. MR curve also slopes downward, and faster than AR curve. So that, MR < AR. The difference between monopoly and monopolistic competition is that under monopolistic competition, AR curve is more elastic. It means that in response to a given change in price, the change in demand will be relatively more for a monopolistic competitive firm than a monopoly firm. It is because in a monopolistic competitive market, goods have close substitutes; in a monopoly market, on the other hand, goods do not have close substitutes. (We know that goods with close substitutes show higher degree of elasticity of demand than those without close substitutes.)

Firm's Revenue Curve or Demand Curve in Different Market Situations—A Comparative Look

Fig. 8 offers a comparative glimpse of producer's revenue curve or demand curve under different market situations:

(i) D_P is firm's revenue curve or demand curve under perfect competition. It is perfectly elastic. It shows that elasticity of demand for the firm's product = ∞. It can sell any quantity at the prevailing price and no quantity if it raises the price.

FIGURE 8 Firm's Revenue Curve/Demand Curve in Different Market Situations

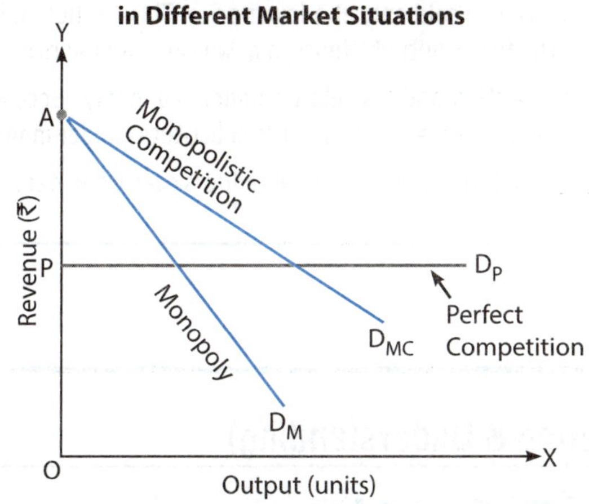

Note: Firm's demand curve is perfectly elastic under perfect competition, it is relatively less elastic under monopoly, and more elastic under monopolistic competition.

(ii) D_M is demand curve under monopoly. It is relatively less elastic. Because, monopolist is a single seller of the product, and there are no close substitutes of the product in the market.

(iii) D_{MC} is demand curve under monopolistic competition. It is relatively more elastic. Because, there is a large number of close substitutes of the product in the market.

POWER POINTS

- Revenue refers to money receipts of the producer from the sale of his output.
- Total Revenue (TR) is estimated as: TR = AR × Q.
- Average Revenue (AR) = $\frac{TR}{Q}$.
- Marginal Revenue (MR) = $TR_n - TR_{n-1}$ or MR = $\frac{\Delta TR}{\Delta Q}$.
- Relationship between TR (Total Revenue) and MR (Marginal Revenue):
  MR is additional revenue when an additional unit of output is sold. Sum total of MR of each unit of output is equal to TR. Thus,
  $$TR = \Sigma MR$$
  This relationship further tells us that MR is the rate at which TR increases:
  — TR increases at diminishing rate, if MR is diminishing.
  — TR increases at constant rate, when MR is constant.
- Relationship between AR and MR:
  — If AR is constant, AR = MR.
  — If AR is diminishing, AR > MR.
  — MR can be negative, but not AR. Average revenue refers to price per unit of the commodity which can never be negative.
- AR Curve is Firm's Demand Curve. The reason is this: We know that AR = price of the commodity. Thus, AR curve shows the relationship between price of the commodity on the Y-axis and quantity sold (= quantity demanded) on the X-axis.
- AR Curve is a Horizontal Straight Line under Perfect Competition because a firm under perfect competition is a price taker. Implying a constant AR for a firm at all levels of output. Given the price, a firm under perfect competition can sell any quantity at the prevailing price and no quantity if it raises the price.

- **AR Curve Slopes Downward under Monopoly and Monopolistic Competition.** The reason being, under monopoly or monopolistic competition, more of the commodity can be sold only at a lower price. This implies an inverse relationship between price of the commodity and demand for the firm's output. Hence, a downward sloping firm's demand curve.
- **AR Curve is more elastic under Monopolistic Competition and less elastic under Monopoly.** Because, there is a large number of close substitutes under monopolistic competition and lack of close substitutes under monopoly.
- **Negative MR.** It occurs when price of the commodity reduces so much that TR reduces even when demand tends to be more than before.

EXERCISE

1. Very Short Questions (Remembering & Understanding) (1 mark each)

A. Multiple Choice Questions: Choose the Correct Answer

1. **Revenue =**

   (a) Costs – Profit (b) Costs + Profit

   (c) Costs × Profit (d) Costs ÷ Profit

2. **For a perfectly competitive firm, price is:**

   (a) greater than MR (b) equal to AR

   (c) equal to MR (d) both (b) and (c)

3. **Select the correct equation:**

   (a) $TR = \Sigma AR$ (b) $MR = \frac{\Delta TR}{\Delta Q}$

   (c) $TR = \frac{AR}{\text{Total Output}}$ (d) $AR = TR \times \text{Total Output}$

4. **Average revenue:**

   (a) can be negative (b) cannot be negative

   (c) is zero when TR is zero (d) both (b) and (c)

5. **Under monopoly, MR can be negative only when:**

   (a) AR is increasing (b) AR is decreasing

   (c) AR is constant (d) AR is zero

6. **Which of the following equations is correct?**

   (a) $AR = \frac{P \times Q}{Q}$ (b) $AR = P + Q$

   (c) $AR = P - Q$ (d) $AR = P \div Q$

7. **When MR is zero, then:**

   (a) TR is minimum (b) TR is zero

   (c) TR is maximum (d) TR is equal to MR

8. **When TR increases at constant rate, MR should be:**

   (a) increasing (b) decreasing

   (c) constant (d) zero

9. **Which of the following statements is appropriate in case of monopoly?**

   (a) AR curve slopes upward while MR curve slopes downward

   (b) Slope of both AR and MR curves is upwards

   (c) Slope of both AR and MR curves is downwards and MR curve is below AR curve

   (d) Slope of both AR and MR curves is downwards and MR curve is above AR curve

10. Under perfect competition:

(a) MR curve is below AR curve
(b) price = AR = MR
(c) AR remains constant
(d) both (b) and (c)

11. What is the shape of the average revenue curve under perfect competition?

(a) Horizontal straight line
(b) Vertical straight line
(c) Rectangular hyperbola
(d) Downward to the right

12. MR is different from AR only under:

(a) perfect competition
(b) monopoly
(c) monopolistic competition
(d) both (b) and (c)

13. Price line is the same as:

(a) budget line
(b) firm's demand curve
(c) firm's AR curve
(d) both (b) and (c)

14. AR curve is more elastic under monopolistic competition than under monopoly due to:

(a) lack of close substitutes
(b) availability of close substitutes
(c) high degree of product differentiation
(d) both (b) and (c)

15. When a firm is able to sell more quantity of output at the same price, then:

(a) AR > MR
(b) AR = MR
(c) AR < MR
(d) none of these

16. When output increases from 8 units to 10 units and TR increases from ₹ 270 to ₹ 300 then, MR is:

(a) ₹ 30
(b) ₹ 20
(c) ₹ 15
(d) ₹ 40

17. Under perfect competition, 'Average Revenue' and 'Marginal Revenue' are indicated by:

(a) a common horizontal straight line
(b) a common vertical straight line
(c) a common rectagular hyperbola
(d) different lines sloping downward

18. Increase in MR is the rate at which TR:

(a) increases
(b) diminishes
(c) remains constant
(d) none of these

19. When owing to a unit change in output, total revenue increases by ₹ 100, then marginal revenue will be:

(a) greater than ₹ 100
(b) less than ₹ 100
(c) equal to ₹ 100
(d) equal to zero

20. When average revenue is ₹ 50 and output is equal to 15 units, total revenue will be:

(a) ₹ 735
(b) ₹ 750
(c) ₹ 765
(d) ₹ 770

Answers

1. (b) **2.** (d) **3.** (b) **4.** (d) **5.** (b) **6.** (a) **7.** (c) **8.** (c) **9.** (c) **10.** (d) **11.** (a) **12.** (d)
13. (d) **14.** (d) **15.** (b) **16.** (c) **17.** (a) **18.** (a) **19.** (c) **20.** (b)

B. Information & Concept-based Questions

1. Define revenue.

Ans. Revenue refers to the money receipts of a firm from the sale of its output.

2. Define total revenue.

Ans. Total revenue is the sum total of money receipts by a firm from the sale of its total output.

3. Define average revenue.

Ans. Average revenue is the per unit revenue corresponding to a given level of output of a firm (AR = P).

4. What is meant by marginal revenue?

Ans. Marginal revenue is the addition to total revenue on account of sale of one more unit of output.

5. Which concept of revenue is called price?

Ans. Average revenue is called price.

6. Define price line.

Ans. Price line or firm's demand curve is the same as firm's AR curve, because AR means price, and demand curve (or AR curve) shows the relationship between price and quantity demanded of firm's output.

7. What is the shape of total revenue curve under perfect competition?

Ans. Under perfect competition, total revenue curve is an upward sloping straight line starting from the origin.

8. What is the relation between marginal revenue and average revenue under perfect competition?

Ans. Under perfect competition, marginal revenue is equal to average revenue.

9. What are the shapes of marginal revenue curve and average revenue curve under perfect competition?

Ans. Under perfect competition, both marginal revenue curve and average revenue curve are equal and indicated by the same horizontal straight line parallel to X-axis.

10. What are the shapes of average revenue and marginal revenue curves under monopoly and monopolistic competition?

Ans. Average revenue and marginal revenue curves under monopoly and monopolistic competition slope downward from left to right. However, AR is more elastic under monopolistic competition than under monopoly.

11. Why do the marginal revenue and average revenue curves look alike under monopoly and monopolistic competition?

Ans. The marginal revenue and average revenue curves look alike under monopoly and monopolistic competition because in both the market situations, more can be sold only by lowering the price of the product.

12. When average revenue is constant, what is the shape of marginal revenue?

Ans. When average revenue is constant, marginal revenue = average revenue. Both AR and MR are indicated by the same horizontal straight line parallel to X-axis.

2. Reason-based Questions (Comprehension of the Subject-matter)

Read the following statements carefully. Write 'True' or 'False' with a reason.

1. Greater production always means greater revenue.

Ans. False. Greater production does not always mean greater revenue (TR). Price (AR) may fall so much that higher output yields lower TR.

2. Greater revenue always implies higher profit for a firm.

Ans. False. Profit = Total Revenue – Total Cost

Therefore, greater revenue would not mean higher profit when increase in TR is less than increase in TC.

3. Total revenue is the sum total of marginal revenues.

Ans. True. Sum total of marginal revenues for all the units of output is equal to total revenue.

$$TR = \Sigma MR$$

4. TR curve always shoots from the origin.

Ans. True. TR curve can shoots from the origin as TR = 0 when output is zero.

5. AR curve never shoots from the origin.

Ans True. AR (= price) curve never shoots from the origin because market price of a commodity is often not zero.

6. AR = 0, when TR is maximum.

Ans. False. When TR is maximum, MR = 0 even when AR is declining as under monopoly and monopolistic competition.

7. MR can never be negative as it implies a situation of zero price.

Ans. False. Zero price is a situation when AR = 0. Therefore, MR can be negative even when price is not.

8. TR must increase even when MR is falling.

Ans. False. TR will increase only when MR is positive. TR will start declining when MR is falling and is negative.

9. When price is constant, AR > MR.

Ans. False. When price is constant, AR is constant. Constant AR implies that MR is also constant. Thus, when price is constant, AR = MR.

10. When price reduces as output increases, AR = MR.

Ans. False. When price (= average revenue) reduces as output increases, MR declines faster than AR. So that AR > MR.

11. MR tends to fall even when AR is constant.

Ans. False. When AR is constant, MR is also constant and AR = MR.

12. When MR = 0, TR is maximum.

Ans. True. MR is addition to TR. When MR = 0, addition to TR is zero, implying that TR is maximum.

13. MR is the slope of TR.

Ans. True. Slope of TR $= \frac{\Delta TR}{\Delta Q} = MR$

14. Under perfect competition, AR and MR curves tends to slope downward.

Ans. False. Under perfect competition, AR and MR curves coincide and are a horizontal straight line parallel to X-axis.

15. Under monopoly, AR and MR curves are indicated by horizontal straight lines.

Ans. False. Under monopoly, AR and MR curves slope downward from left to right.

16. Under perfect competition, rate of TR never declines, but under monopoly and monopolistic competition, it does.

Ans. True. Because rate of TR is equal to MR which is constant under perfect competition, but tends to decline under monopoly and monopolistic competition.

17. AR is always greater than MR, under monopoly.

Ans. True. AR > MR under monopoly because AR tends to fall, and falling AR implies falling MR at a higher rate.

18. Under monopoly, TR curve increases only at a diminishing rate.

Ans True. TR curve increases only at a diminishing rate because a monopolist can sell more only if he lowers the price of his product. Accordingly, MR tends to decline following a decline in AR.

19. Average revenue is constant when marginal revenue is zero.

Ans. False. When marginal revenue is zero, average revenue should be diminishing, as in Fig. 9.

20. Marginal revenue refers to the price of the last unit of a commodity.

Ans. False. Marginal revenue simply refers to additional revenue when an additional unit of a commodity is sold. It happens to be equal to price under perfect competition. But, under monopoly and monopolistic competition MR and price are definitely different from each other.

FIGURE 9

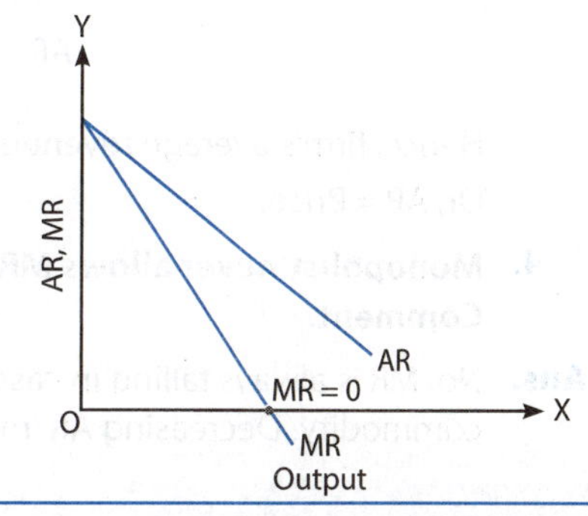

21. Maximum total revenue implies maximum marginal revenue.

Ans. False. Total revenue is maximum when marginal revenue is zero.

22. In response to constant and positive marginal revenue, both total revenue and average revenue tend to rise at a constant rate.

Ans. False. In response to constant and positive marginal revenue, total revenue increases at constant rate. AR will be constant and equal to MR. Fig. 10 illustrates it.

23. Constant total revenue implies constant average and marginal revenue.

Ans. False. When total revenue is constant, AR should be diminishing, and MR = 0. Fig. 11 illustrates it.

24. Average revenue is maximum when marginal revenue reduces to zero.

Ans. False. When marginal revenue reduces to zero, average revenue should be diminishing, as in Fig. 11(B).

25. Total revenue is constant when marginal revenue is constant.

Ans. False. When marginal revenue is constant, total revenue should be increasing at a constant rate.

FIGURE 10

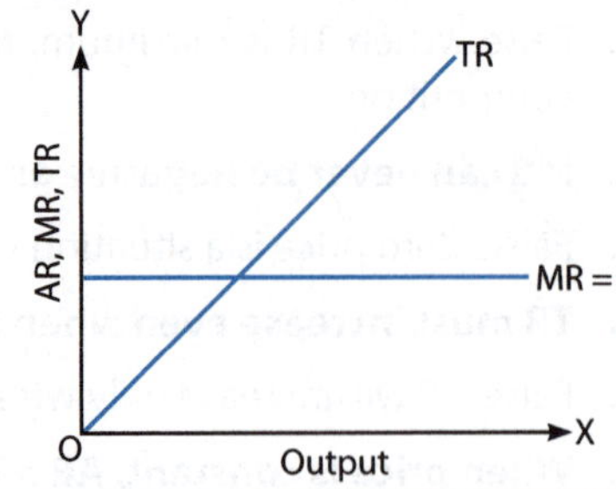

FIGURE 11

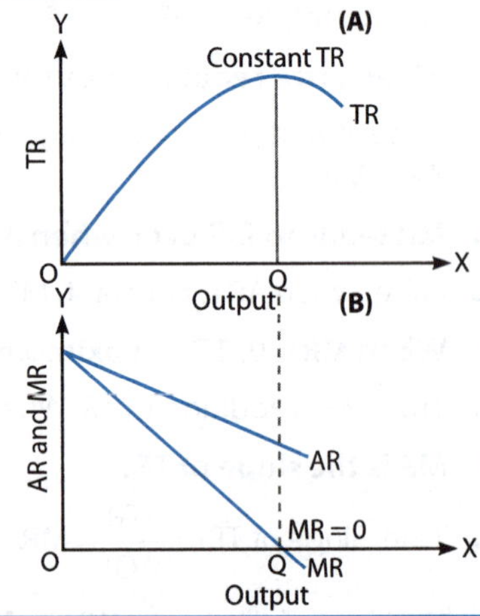

3. HOTS & Applications

1. TR curve under perfect competition is a straight line, sloping upward from the origin. Is it true?

Ans. Yes, it is true. Under perfect competition, AR and MR are constant. Constant MR implies TR increases at a constant rate. Therefore, TR is shown as a straight line sloping upward from the origin and it shoots from the origin. When output = 0, TR = 0.

2. Producer's price line shows highest price elasticity of demand in a state of perfect competition. Do you agree?

Ans. Yes. In perfect competition, producer's price line shows the highest price elasticity of demand which is infinity (∞). This is because producer's price line under perfect competition is a horizontal straight line.

3. Average revenue is the same as market price of the commodity. Comment.

Ans. Yes. We know that,

$$AR = \frac{TR}{Q}$$

We also know that, $TR = P \times Q$ (Where P = Price, and Q = Quantity or output sold.)

Relating the two equations, we can write that:

$$AR = \frac{TR}{Q} = \frac{P \times Q}{Q} = P$$

Hence, firm's average revenue means price of the product corresponding to a given level of output.

Or, AR = Price.

4. Monopolist never allows MR to fall because he is the only producer of a commodity in the market. Comment.

Ans. No. MR is always falling in case of monopoly because monopolist can sell more only at lower price of the commodity. Decreasing AR implies decreasing MR.

5. When output increases from 10 units to 15 units and TR increases from ₹100 to ₹150 then, MR is ₹50. Is it true?

Ans. No.

$$MR = \frac{\Delta TR}{\Delta Q}$$

$$= \frac{150 - 100}{15 - 10} = \frac{50}{5} = 10$$

MR refers to change in TR when output changes by one unit.

6. Under which condition marginal revenue can be negative? Explain with the help of an example.

Ans. MR can be negative, though only when average revenue is decreasing. Or, when price is declining as under monopoly and monopolistic competition. In case of perfect competition, it is not possible where price remains constant for a firm.

When price = ₹4, and output =10

$$TR_{10} = P \times Q$$

$$= 4 \times 10 = 40$$

When price falls to ₹ 3, and output = 11

$$TR_{11} = P \times Q$$

$$= 3 \times 11 = 33$$

Accordingly, $MR = TR_{11} - TR_{10}$

$$= 33 - 40 = -7$$

Implying that MR is negative.

7. MR of the firm falls from ₹ 20 to (–) ₹ 20. Find the corresponding TR, if AR = MR = ₹ 20 corresponding to a specific output of 5,000 units.

Ans. AR = MR = ₹ 20

$$AR = \frac{TR}{Q}$$

Or, $20 = \frac{TR}{5,000}$

∴ TR = ₹ 1,00,000 corresponding to output of 5,000 units.

When MR of the firm falls from ₹ 20 to (–) ₹ 20, it implies a change in TR by ₹ 40.

∴ TR = ₹ 1,00,000 – ₹ 40 = ₹ 99,960.

8. Complete the following table:

Price (₹)	Output (Units)	Total Revenue (₹)	Marginal Revenue (₹)
10	—	—	10
7	—	—	4
5	—	—	1
3	—	—	–3

Ans.

Price (₹)	Output (Units)	Total Revenue (₹)	Marginal Revenue (₹)
10	1	10	10
7	2	14	4
5	3	15	1
3	4	12	–3

9. Complete the following table:

Output (Units)	Average Revenue (₹)	Total Revenue (₹)	Marginal Revenue (₹)
1	—	—	15
2	—	24	—
3	10	—	—
4	—	28	—

Ans.

Output (Units)	Average Revenue (₹)	Total Revenue (₹)	Marginal Revenue (₹)
1	15	15	15
2	12	24	9
3	10	30	6
4	7	28	–2

10. Complete the following table:

Output (Units)	Price (₹)	Total Revenue (₹)	Marginal Revenue (₹)
1	—	18	—
—	16	—	14
3	—	42	—
4	12	—	—
—	10	—	2

Ans.

Output (Units)	Price (₹)	Total Revenue (₹)	Marginal Revenue (₹)
1	18	18	18
2	16	32	14
3	14	42	10
4	12	48	6
5	10	50	2

11. Find a fall in market demand for the commodity when TR of the monopoly firm reduces from ₹ 5,000 to ₹ 4,500, and AR increases from ₹ 50 to ₹ 90.

Ans. TR = ₹ 5,000, P (= AR) = ₹ 50

$$TR = P \times Q$$

$$\Rightarrow \quad Q = \frac{TR}{P} = \frac{5{,}000}{50} = 100$$

When TR = ₹ 4,500, P (= AR) = ₹ 90

$$Q = \frac{4{,}500}{90} = 50$$

Market demand falls by (50 – 100) units = 50 units.

12. Complete the following table:

Output (Units)	Price (₹)	Marginal Revenue (₹)	Total Revenue (₹)
1	—	10	—
2	9	—	—
3	—	—	24
4	—	4	—

Ans.

Output (Units)	Price (₹)	MR (₹)	TR (₹)
1	10	10	10
2	9	8	18
3	8	6	24
4	7	4	28

13. Complete the following table:

Output (Units)	Average Revenue (₹)	Total Revenue (₹)	Marginal Revenue (₹)
1	20	—	—
2	—	36	—
3	—	—	9
4	13	52	—
5	—	—	–2

Ans.

Output (Units)	Average Revenue (₹)	Total Revenue (₹)	Marginal Revenue (₹)
1	20	20	20
2	18	36	16
3	15	45	9
4	13	52	7
5	10	50	–2

14. If the average revenue is ₹ 15 per unit and demand curve is perfectly elastic and producer sells 10 units of output, find total revenue. At what rate TR of the producer will change?

Ans. In case of perfectly elastic demand curve, AR = MR = Price.

∴ Price = ₹ 15

Total Revenue = Price × Quantity

= ₹ 15 × 10 = ₹ 150

Rate of change in TR = MR = ₹ 15

For every additional unit sold, TR increases by ₹ 15.

15. The following headline appeared in the *Economic Times* on 20th December, 2014:

"Room Supply may Hit Hotel Revenues."

Explain the economic theory to analyse the impact of the statement.

Ans. With a increase in the number of Hotel rooms, supply of Hotels rooms increases. This must lead to increase to TC. However, demand has not responded. It remains constant. Accordingly, TR will remain constant.

16. A farmer's entire produce of potatoes is destroyed by the wild animals. What impact would it cause on the AR curve of the farmer? Assume perfect competition.

Ans. AR curve of the farmer would not be affected at all. Under perfect competition, AR curve is given to an individual producer. It is a horizontal straight line. It indicates constant price even when an individual producer brings no supplies in the market.

4. Evaluation (Value-based Questions)

1. Explain the economic value of a horizontal straight line price line for a firm.

Ans. Horizontal straight line price line/revenue curve indicates that price of the product is constant for a firm, or it is given to a firm. At the given price, a firm can sell any quantity. However, if the firm increases the price, it will sell nothing. It would lose all its buyers to other firms in the market. It implies that the elasticity of demand for the firm's product = infinity. It is a situation of perfect competition in the market.

2. A firm is facing a downward sloping price line (AR curve). Why should it produce more when it must lead to fall in price of the commodity?

Ans. A firm produces more of a commodity even when price is reducing only in a situation when it finds that the difference between TR and TC is increasing, so that its total profit (TR – TC) is rising. It will stop production when profit is maximum or when the difference between TR and TC is maximum.

5. CBSE Questions—Past 4 years (With Answers or Reference to the Text for Answers)

1. What is the behaviour of average revenue in a market in which a firm can sell more only by lowering the price? *[CBSE Delhi 2012]*

   [Page 227, 228]

2. What is the behaviour of marginal revenue in a market in which a firm can sell any quantity of the output it produces at a given price? *[CBSE (AI) 2012]*

   [Page 225, 226]

3. What is the behaviour of average revenue in a market in which a firm can sell any quantity of a good at a given price? *[CBSE (F) 2012]*

   [Page 225, 226]

4. What is revenue? Explain the relation between marginal revenue and average revenue. *[CBSE (F) 2012]*

   Or

   State the relation between marginal revenue and average revenue. *[CBSE Delhi 2014]*

   Or

   Define revenue. State the relation between marginal revenue and average revenue. *[CBSE Delhi 2015]*

   [Page 219, 225]

5. Under which market form a firm's marginal revenue is always equal to price? *[CBSE Delhi 2013]*

   [Page 225, 226]

6. Define marginal revenue. *[CBSE Delhi 2014; (AI) 2013, 2014]*

   [Page 220]

7. Give the meaning of total revenue. *[CBSE (F) 2013]*

   [Page 219]

8. When will marginal revenue be negative? *[CBSE (F) 2013]*

   [Page 223, 224]

9. What is meant by revenue in microeconomics? *[CBSE Delhi 2014]*

   [Page 219]

10. Why is average revenue always equal to price? *[CBSE (AI) 2014]*

    [Page 221]

11. Under what market condition does average revenue always equal marginal revenue? Explain.

    [Page 225, 226] *[CBSE (F) 2014]*

12. Define average revenue. Show that average revenue and price are same. *[CBSE (AI) 2015]*
[Page 221]

6. NCERT Questions (With Hints to Answers)

1. How are the total revenue of a firm, market price, and the quantity sold by the firm related to each other?
[**Hint:** Total revenue is the multiplication of quantity sold and market price whereas market price is the ratio of total revenue and quantity sold.

$$TR = P \times Q; P = \frac{TR}{Q}$$

Here, TR = Total revenue; P = Price; Q = Quantity sold.]

2. What is the 'price line'?
[**Hint:** Price line or firm's demand curve is the same as firm's AR curve, because AR means price, and demand curve (or AR curve) shows the relationship between price and quantity demanded of firm's output.]

3. Why is the total revenue curve of a price taking firm an upward sloping straight line? Why does the curve pass through the origin?
[**Hint:** For a price taking firm, AR is constant. In case AR is constant, MR is also constant. Implying that TR increases at a constant rate. Hence, TR forms a straight line sloping upward. It passes through the point of origin, simply because TR is zero when output is zero.]

4. What is the relation between market price and average revenue of a price taking firm?
[**Hint:** Market price and average revenue of a price taking firm are equal. Both are indicated by a horizontal straight line. Because market price is constant for a price taking firm.]

5. What is the relation between market price and marginal revenue of a price taking firm?
[**Hint:** For a price taking firm, market price is equal to marginal revenue. See Fig. 4 of this chapter.]

6. Compute the total revenue, marginal revenue and average revenue schedules in the following table. Market price of each unit of the good is ₹10.

Quantity Sold	TR	MR	AR
0			
1			
2			
3			
4			
5			
6			

[**Hint:**

Quantity Sold	AR (Market Price) (₹)	TR (₹)	MR (₹)
0	0	0	—
1	10	10	10
2	10	20	10
3	10	30	10
4	10	40	10
5	10	50	10
6	10	60	10

7. Miscellaneous Questions and Reference to the Text for Answers

A. Questions of 3 & 4 marks each

1. What are meant by total revenue, average revenue and marginal revenue?
[Page 219–221]
2. Explain diagrammatically that total revenue is maximum when marginal revenue is zero.
[Page 224]
3. What is marginal revenue? How is it related to average revenue?
[Page 220, 225]
4. Distinguish between average revenue and marginal revenue. Mention also the relation between them.
[Page 219, 220, 225]
5. Explain the nature of the shape of average revenue curve of a firm under perfect competition.
[Page 225, 226]
6. Draw the curves of AR and MR under perfect competition, monopoly and imperfect competition.
[Page 226–228]
7. How do changes in marginal revenue affect total revenue?
[Page 220, 225]
8. Explain the relationship between marginal revenue and total revenue.
[Page 225]
9. Explain the relationship between marginal revenue and average revenue. Use diagram.
[Page 222–225]
10. Draw a marginal revenue curve of a perfectly competitive firm and explain why the marginal revenue of a perfectly competitive firm is always equal to its average revenue.
[Page 225, 226]
11. What change in total revenue will result when:
(i) marginal revenue is constant? and
(ii) marginal revenue is decreasing?
[Page 225]
12. What will be the effect of the following changes in total revenue on marginal revenue?
(i) Total revenue increases at a decreasing rate.
(ii) Total revenue increases at a constant rate.
[Page 225]

B. Questions of 6 marks each

1. Derive average revenue and marginal revenue from total revenue with the help of a table.
[Page 221, 222]
2. Define TR, AR and MR. Discuss the relationship between AR and MR.
[Page 219–221, 225]
3. Distinguish among total, average and marginal revenue curves.
[Page 221–224]
4. Explain the average and marginal revenue curves of a firm under perfect competition.
[Page 225, 226]
5. Explain the average and marginal revenue curves of a firm under monopoly and monopolistic competition.
[Page 227, 228]

DOs and DON'Ts

1. If a firm can sell any quantity at the prevailing price, it should never be interpreted to mean that an individual firm can cater to entire demand for the product in the market. The reason is this: a situation when an individual firm can sell any quantity at the prevailing price exists only under perfect competition. And, it is a necessary condition of perfect competition that there is a large number of small firms (selling identical product) in the market. No firm is big enough to cater to the entire market demand.

2. Always be careful about the gap between AR and MR curve when these are straight lines sloping downward. Check Fig. 12 for clarity:

   Note that $ac = cb$.

   So that, MR passes through mid-point of any horizontal straight line like ab joining Y-axis and AR curve. It means that the slope of MR curve is twice the slope of AR curve.

FIGURE 12

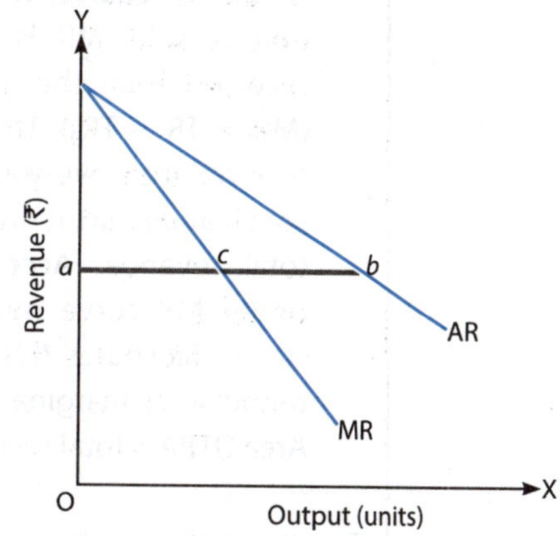

ability ZONE

❑ Slope of the Line (or the Ray) from the Origin to any Point on TR Curve shows AR (or Price)

In Fig. 13, Oa is the ray from the origin onto point a on TR curve.

Slope of $Oa = \dfrac{30}{5} = 6$ which is to be AR (or price).

FIGURE 13

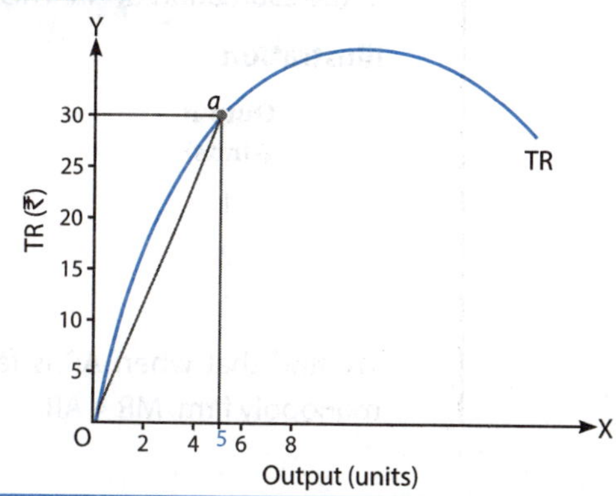

At point a, slope of the ray (from the origin) $= \frac{30}{5} = 6$. Implying that when 5 units of output are produced TR = 30, and price = 6.

❑ MR for any Level of Output is the Slope of TR Curve Corresponding to that Level of Output. It is obtained by Drawing a Tangent on the Specified Point on TR Curve

In Fig. 14, when output is 10 units, the slope of TR is equal to the slope of the tangent at point c. This is equal to zero. Because corresponding to point c, the tangent is a horizontal straight line. Thus, we find that when output is 10 units, MR = 0. Likewise, when output is 7 units, MR = slope of TR at point b. And, so on.

FIGURE 14

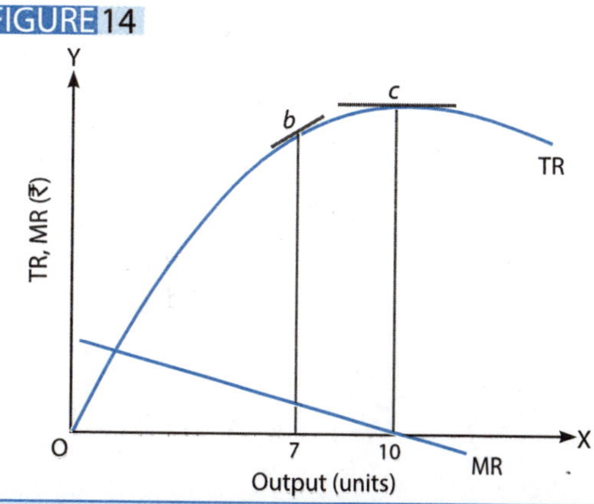

- c is at the top of TR curve. Implying that TR is maximum at point c.
- The tangent at c is a horizontal straight line. Implying that slope of TR at point c is zero.
- MR = 0, when TR is maximum, as at point c.

Area under MR Curve = TR for a Given Level of Output

We know MR is additional revenue when an additional unit of output is sold. Of course, when only one unit is sold, MR is the revenue received from the 1st unit itself ($MR_1 = TR_1 - TR_0$). Thus, if revenue received from every additional unit sold is added up, it must amount to total revenue. Accordingly, area under MR curve must show TR. Fig. 15 illustrates this point. When output = OT, marginal revenue = TP. Area OTPA = total revenue.

FIGURE 15

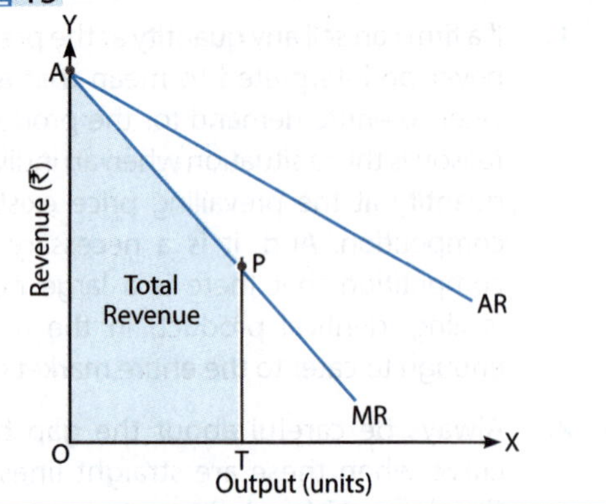

Area OTPA = TR
$= MR_1 + MR_2 + MR_3 + ... + MR_n$

Why MR < AR for a Monopoly Firm?

For a monopoly firm, MR < AR. This is because a monopolist can sell more only by lowering the price of his product. This implies a situation of falling AR (price) for a monopoly firm. In case AR is falling MR must be falling faster than AR. Because a given fall in MR is averaged out in the estimation of AR. This is borne out by the following illustration:

Illustration

Output (Units)	AR (₹)	TR (₹)	MR (₹)
1	10	10	10
2	9	18	8
3	8	24	6

We find that when AR is falling by ₹1 every time, MR is falling by ₹2. Thus, in case of a monopoly firm, MR < AR.

CHAPTER 9

Producer's Equilibrium

TODO

- What does Producer's Equilibrium mean?
- Conditions of Producer's Equilibrium in terms of Marginal Revenue and Marginal Cost Approach

1. What does Producer's Equilibrium mean?

Producer's equilibrium refers to a situation of 'profit maximisation'. A producer strikes his equilibrium at that level of output where profit is maximised. Any other level of output will yield lower profit (lower than the maximum).

Profit is generally calculated as the difference between TR (total revenue) and TC (total cost).

$$\pi = TR - TC \qquad \left[\begin{array}{ll}\text{Here,} & \pi = \text{Profit}\\ & TR = \text{Total revenue}\\ & TC = \text{Total cost.}\end{array}\right]$$

Producer's equilibrium is struck at that level of output where π is maximised.

We know,

$$TC = TVC + TFC$$

Since, TFC is constant, we can state that π is maximised when the difference between TR and TC is maximised or when the difference between TR and TVC is maximised. However, it must be noted that while the difference between TR and TC yields net profit, the difference between TR and TVC yields gross profit.

Gross and Net Profit

$$\text{Gross Profit} = TR - TVC$$

$$\text{Net Profit} = TR - (TVC + TFC)$$

$$= TR - TC$$

You must know it

In Economics, the concept of profit has three aspects, *viz.*

(i) abnormal profits or extra-normal profits, when:

$$TR > TC$$

Or, $$\frac{TR}{Q} > \frac{TC}{Q}$$

Or, $$AR > AC \qquad \left[\text{We know } \frac{TR}{Q} = AR, \frac{TC}{Q} = AC\right]$$

(ii) normal profits, when:

$$TR = TC$$

Or, $$\frac{TR}{Q} = \frac{TC}{Q}$$

Or, $$AR = AC$$

(iii) sub-normal profits (or losses) when:

$$TR < TC$$

Or, $$\frac{TR}{Q} < \frac{TC}{Q}$$

Or, $$AR < AC$$

A situation of normal profit (when TR = TC) needs to be properly understood. A doubt may come to your mind: **Where are profits when TR and TC are equal to each other? Where are profits when the producer is only covering his total cost of production?** The answer is this: In Economics, normal profits are a part of TC. Normal profits are defined as the minimum return that the producer expects from his capital invested in the business. If this minimum return is not available, he will withdraw his capital from the existing use and shift it to some different use.

Normal Profits

Normal profits are defined as the minimum return that the producer expects from his capital invested in the business. If this minimum return is not available, he will withdraw his capital from the existing use and shift it to some different use. Normal profits are a part of TC.

2. Conditions of Producer's Equilibrium in terms of Marginal Revenue and Marginal Cost Approach

Producer's equilibrium is often explained in terms of marginal revenue (MR) and marginal cost (MC) of production. Profit is maximised (or a producer strikes his equilibrium) when two conditions are satisfied: (i) MR = MC, and (ii) MC is rising (or MC is greater than MR beyond the point of equilibrium output). Let us understand the significance/rationale of these conditions with reference to Table 1.

Note

- Table 1 is drawn on the assumption that the product price is constant for a firm, as under perfect competition. It is assumed to be ₹ 12 per unit. Constant AR implies constant MR = ₹ 12.
- MC is shown as initially falling and subsequently rising. This is in accordance with the law of variable proportions. Falling MC is due to rising MP (a situation of increasing returns). Rising MC is due to falling MP (a situation of diminishing returns). We know, MC is the reciprocal of MP.

Table 1. MR, MC and Producer's Equilibrium

Q (Units of Output)	MR (₹)	MC (₹)
1	12	15
2	12	12
3	12	10
4	12	9
5	12	8
6	12	7
7	12	8
8	12	9
9	12	10
10	12	12
11	12	15

In Table 1, MR = MC in two situations: (i) when 2 units of output are produced, and (ii) when 10 units of output are produced. However, while in situation 1 (when output = 2 units) MC is falling, while in situation 2 (when output = 10 units) MC is rising. As noted earlier, a producer will strike his equilibrium only when MC is rising. Implying that the equilibrium will be struck when 10 units of output are produced, not when 2 units of output are produced. Reason is simple. Given the price, falling MC only increases the difference between TR and TVC (recall, ΣMC = TVC, and ΣMR = TR). So that TR – TVC tends to rise, or that profits tends to rise in a situation of falling MC. Accordingly, it would be an irrational decision for a producer to strike his equilibrium in a situation of falling MC. It is only when MC is rising that a producer would strike his equilibrium. Thus, equilibrium will be struck when MR = MC = 12, and MC is rising. The producer will maximise profits when10 units of output are produced. Let us illustrate this point further with reference to Table 1. Table 1 offers us two different situations when MR = MC, as under:

Situation 1: When output = 2 (and MR = MC, and MC is falling)

$$
\begin{aligned}
TR &= \Sigma MR \\
&= 12 + 12 = 24 \\
TVC &= \Sigma MC \\
&= 15 + 12 = 27 \\
\pi &= TR - TVC \\
&= 24 - 27 = -3
\end{aligned}
$$

Situation 2: When output = 10 (and MR = MC, and MC is rising)

$$
\begin{aligned}
TR &= \Sigma MR \\
&= 12 + 12 + 12 + 12 + 12 + 12 + 12 + 12 + 12 + 12 \\
&= 120 \\
TVC &= \Sigma MC \\
&= 15 + 12 + 10 + 9 + 8 + 7 + 8 + 9 + 10 + 12 \\
&= 100 \\
\pi &= TR - TVC \\
&= 120 - 100 \\
&= 20
\end{aligned}
$$

We find that the difference between TR and TVC tends to rise, as output is increased from 2 to 10. In fact, it is only when output = 10 units that the profit (π) is maximum. If output is increased beyond 10 units, π will reduce. Thus, if 11 units of output are produced, ΣMR = 132, while ΣMC = 115, so that π = TR – TVC = 132 – 115 = 17 (which is less than 20 when output = 10).

It is only when MR = MC, and when MC is rising that a producer will reach the point of equilibrium, where profit is maximised.

Diagrammatic Illustration

Fig. 1 illustrates producer's equilibrium in terms of MR and MC approach.

FIGURE 1

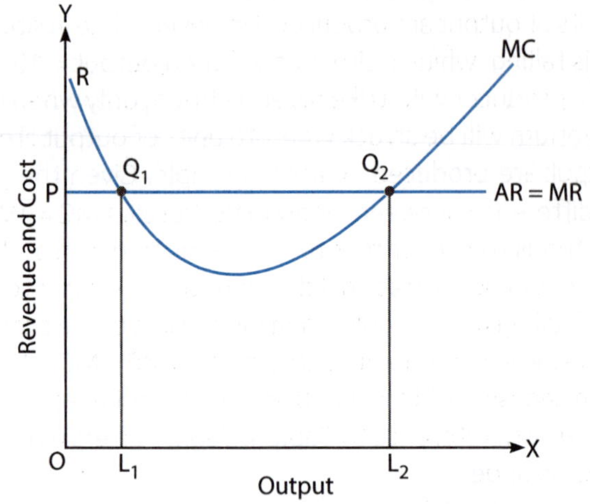

Note: Fig. 1 is drawn on the assumption that AR is constant for a firm and is equal to OP. It is as in a situation of perfect competition. Constant AR implies constant MR. Accordingly, AR = MR, and both are indicated by a horizontal straight line, parallel to X-axis.

In Fig. 1, AR is assumed to be constant as under perfect competition. Constant AR implies constant MR. Thus, both AR and MR are indicated by a horizontal straight line parallel to X-axis. MC curve is shown to be U-shaped, as usual. MR is equal to MC in two situations: (i) at point Q_1 when output = OL_1, and (ii) at point Q_2 when output = OL_2. In situation 1, MC is falling but in situation 2, MC is rising. Equilibrium of the producer will be struck at point Q_2 when: (i) MR = MC, and (ii) MC is rising.

It is at point Q_2 that the profit (= TR – TVC) is maximised, not at point Q_1. In fact, Q_2 is a situation of profit while Q_1 is a situation of loss. This is how we can prove it.

We know,

TR = Area under MR corresponding to a given level of output.

This is equal to OL_1Q_1P in situation 1.

Likewise, TVC = Area under MC corresponding to a given level of output.

This is equal to OL_1Q_1R in situation 1.

Evidently, area OL_1Q_1R > area OL_1Q_1P.

It is a situation of loss: the firm is not covering even its variable costs. In such a situation, it would not be wise for the producer to undertake production of the commodity.

Corresponding to situation 2, when MC is rising, at point Q_2, we find that:

$$TR = OL_2Q_2P, \text{ and}$$

$$TVC = OL_2Q_2R$$

Evidently, $TR > TVC$

This indicates the existence of profit. Accordingly, the producer will strike his equilibrium only in situation 2 when (i) MR = MC, and (ii) MC is rising.

What happens when a unit more or a unit less is produced than OL_2 units of output?

Answer is that in both the situations π will be less compared to the situation when OL_2 units of output are produced. Figs. 2 and 3 illustrate this situation.

In case OL_3 units of output are produced (as in Fig. 2):

Addition to TR = Area $L_2L_3TQ_2$

Addition to TVC = Area $L_2L_3Q_3Q_2$

Addition to TVC is greater than addition to TR. Additional TVC exceeds additional TR by the area Q_2TQ_3. So that TR – TVC will tend to shrink.

FIGURE 2

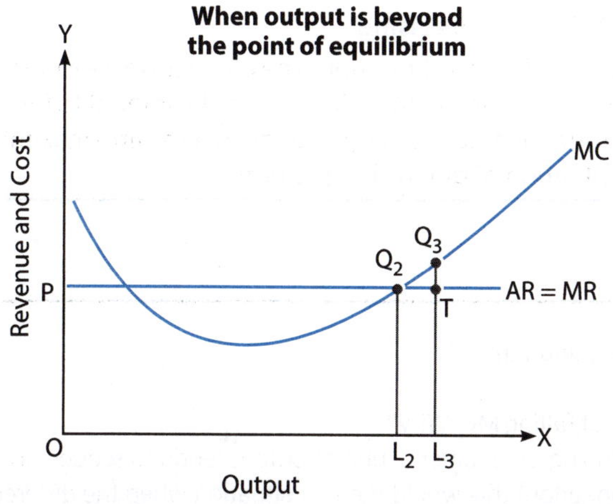

Area $L_2L_3TQ_2$ (additional revenue) < Area $L_2L_3Q_3Q_2$ (additional cost)

In case OL_1 units of output are produced (as in Fig. 3):

TR reduces by the area $L_1L_2Q_2Q_1$

TVC reduces by the area $L_1L_2Q_2T$

Thus, reduction in TVC is less than the reduction in TR. Or, the loss of TR is greater than the gain of TVC.

Accordingly, TR – TVC will tend to shrink.

Thus, any departure from the state of equilibrium (when MR = MC, and MC is rising) would only mean that the difference between TR and TVC will tend to shrink, or that the profits will not be maximised.

FIGURE 3

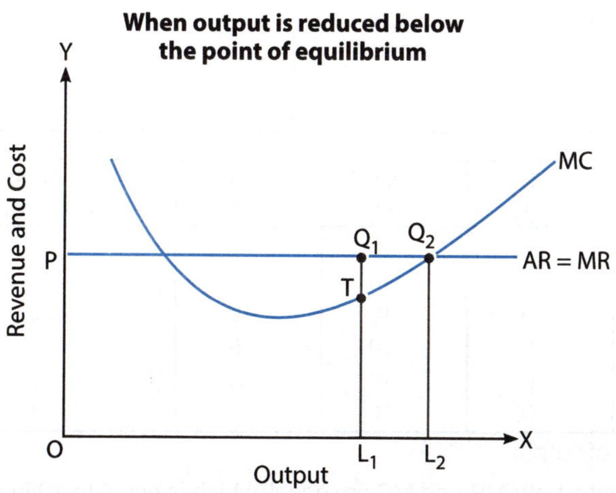

Area $L_1L_2Q_2Q_1$ (loss of TR) > Area $L_1L_2Q_2T$ (gain of TVC)

Rationale of the Conditions of Producer's Equilibrium

Condition 1 : MR = MC

In case MR and MC are not equal, it would mean there is a scope for the firm to increase the difference between TR and TC. Implying that there is a scope to increase profits. Thus:

(i) In case MR > MC, additional unit of output leads to greater revenue than the cost of production. By increasing output, profit would rise.

(ii) In case MR < MC, additional unit of output leads to greater cost than the revenue. By cutting output, profit would increase.

Condition 2 : At the point of equilibrium MC should be rising

If MC is not rising, but falling at the point of equilibrium, the firm should be enjoying increasing returns to a factor. Stopping output when returns are rising (MP is increasing or MC is falling) would amount to foregoing the profits which the firm can earn by increasing the output. It is a standard knowledge that the firm maximises its profits not in a situation of increasing returns, but in a situation of diminishing returns.

HOTS

Q.1. Why should MC be rising at the point of equilibrium?

Or

Equilibrium is never struck in a situation of falling MC. Why?

Ans. Falling MC means that the cost of producing an additional unit of output tends to reduce. In a situation when price is constant (as under perfect competition) this would mean a situation when the difference between the firm's TR and TVC (Note that TVC = ΣMC) tends to increase. This means a situation when firm's gross profit (TR – TVC) tends to rise. Why should a firm not increase output when its gross profits are rising? Certainly it will. Therefore, it is only when MC is rising that the firm will find its equilibrium output.

Q.2. What happens if the firm increases its output even when MR = MC?

Ans. In a situation when MR = MC, any increase in output would mean MC > MR. This is because MR is assumed to be constant (as under perfect competition) and (at the point of equilibrium) MC is rising. It would be a situation when the difference between TR (= ΣMR) and TVC (= ΣMC) tends to reduce. Or, that the firm's gross profits start reducing.

Q.3. Using marginal revenue and marginal cost approach, find out the level of output at which the producer is in equilibrium. Give reasons for your answer.

Output (Units)	Price (₹)	TC (₹)
1	10	11
2	10	21
3	10	30
4	10	38
5	10	48
6	10	59

Ans.

Output (Units)	Price (₹)	TC (₹)	TR (₹)	MR (₹)	MC (₹)	Profit (TR – TC) (₹)
1	10	11	10	10	11	–1
2	10	21	20	10	10	–1
3	10	30	30	10	9	0
4	10	38	40	10	8	2
5	10	48	50	10	10	2
6	10	59	60	10	11	1

The producer is in equilibrium at 5th unit of output.

Reason: At output levels 2nd and 5th units, both MR and MC are equal, which is equal to 10 in both the cases. But the producer is in equilibrium at 5th unit only where profit is maximum (= 2). Profit is maximised only when (i) MR = MC, and (ii) MC is rising.

Q.4. When price is constant for a firm (as under perfect competition) producer equilibrium is struck only when commodity price coincides with MC, and MC is rising. Do you agree?

Ans. Yes, it is true. In a situation when price is constant, AR = MR. So that conditions of producer's equilibrium may be written as:

(i) Price = MC, and (ii) MC is rising.

Do All Firms always Maximise their Profit?

'No' is the answer. Profit maximisation is only a goal. A firm may or may not achieve it. After all there are firms which close down, owing to their mounting losses. However, a notable point in this context is that a firm may suffer losses, and yet continue to stay in the market; it does not suspend its production activity. Yes, this happens in the short period. Because in the short period a firm is confronted with 2 sets of costs: (i) fixed cost, and (ii) variable cost. Fixed cost is incurred even when output is zero. A firm has to bear the loss of fixed cost even when production is stopped. Accordingly, a firm may decide to continue production so long as variable costs are covered. Thus, production may continue so long as TR ≥ TVC, even when a producer is in losses (as he is not covering his fixed costs).

Of course, in the long period, when all costs are variable costs, a firm will undertake production only when all costs are covered. Otherwise, it will quit the industry.

Firm's Equilibrium when Price (AR) is not Constant

When price is not constant, a firm can generally sell more of a commodity by lowering its price. Implying that AR curve slopes downward. In such a situation, MR curve also slopes downward and at a rate faster than AR. Even, in such situations, equilibrium of a firm is struck when two conditions are satisfied:

(i) MR = MC, and (ii) MC is rising.

This is illustrated through Fig. 4.

Both at points Q and Q*, MR = MC. But at point Q, MC is falling. It is only at point Q* that (i) MR = MC, and (ii) MC is rising.

Accordingly, a firm will strike its equilibrium only at point Q*.

FIGURE 4

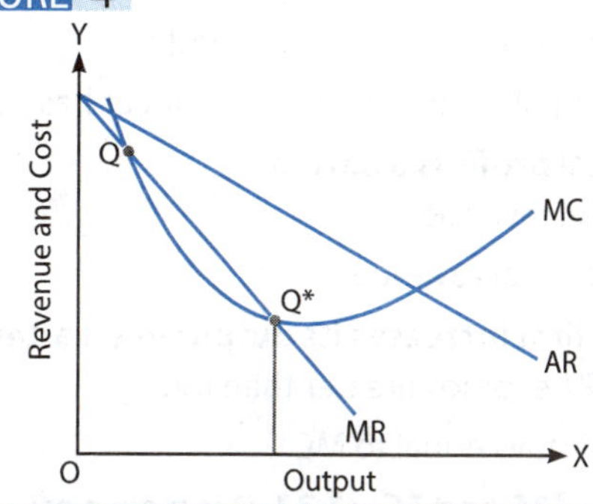

Q* is the point of equilibrium when: (i) MR = MC, and (ii) MC is rising.

POWER POINTS

- **Producer's Equilibrium** refers to the situation of profit maximisation.
- **Two Necessary Conditions of Producer's Equilibrium are:** (i) MR = MC, and (ii) MC is rising.
- **Profits are Maximised** only when MR = MC not when MR > MC or when MR < MC. Under perfect competition, price (AR) = MR. Accordingly, profits are maximised only when price = MC, not when price < MC or when price > MC.
- **Profits** are estimated as the difference between TR and TC, or the difference between TR and TVC.
- **Gross Profit** = TR – TVC.
  Net Profit = TR – TC.
- **Under Perfect Competition, equilibrium** is never struck when MC is falling. Because, given AR, falling MC increases the difference between TR and TVC.
- **Profit Maximisation is a goal.** It may not be achieved by all the firms and all the time. Some firms run into losses, and may quit the market. However, quitting is possible only in the long run.

EXERCISE

1. Very Short Questions (Remembering & Understanding) (1 mark each)

A. Multiple Choice Questions: Choose the Correct Answer

1. **Difference between TR and TC is maximum when:**
   (a) AR = MR (b) MR = MC
   (c) MR = AC (d) MC = AC
2. **TR > TC is a situation of:**
   (a) normal profits (b) normal losses
   (c) abnormal profits (d) abnormal losses
3. **Normal profits occur when:**
   (a) AR > AC (b) AR = AC
   (c) AR < AC (d) TR > TC
4. **Under perfect competition, for the producer to be in equilibrium:**
   (a) AR = MR = AC and AC must be rising (b) AR = MR = MC and MC must be falling
   (c) AR = MR = MC and MC must be rising (d) AR = MR = TC and TC must be rising
5. **In the context of producer's equilibrium which one is wrong?**
   (a) Minimum difference between TR and TC
   (b) MR = MC
   (c) Producer gets maximum profit
   (d) In equilibrium situation producer has no tendency to change his production
6. **Normal profit is a part of:**
   (a) total revenue (b) total cost
   (c) marginal revenue (d) average revenue
7. **If the firm increases its output even after MR = MC, then:**
   (a) MR becomes greater than MC (b) MC becomes greater than MR
   (c) MR stays equal to MC (d) none of these
8. **If TR = ₹25 and TC = ₹ 37, it is a case of:**
   (a) abnormal profits (b) normal profits
   (c) sub-normal profits (d) break-even point
9. **What does break-even point indicate?**
   (a) TR > TC (b) TR < TC
   (c) TR = TC (d) TC = 0
10. **MC = MR = AC = AR refers to long run equilibrium of a:**
    (a) competitive firm (b) oligopoly firm
    (c) monopoly firm (d) none of these
11. **A firm reaches shut-down point when:**
    (a) TR = TVC (b) TR = TC
    (c) TC = AVC (d) MC = AC
12. **In case of break-even point, a firm covers:**
    (a) variable cost only (b) average variable cost only
    (c) both fixed costs and variable costs (d) none of these
13. **TR – TVC =**
    (a) Gross profit (b) Net profit
    (c) Normal profit (d) none of these

14. AR < AVC is a point of:

(a) break-even (b) discontinuation of production

(c) continuation of production (d) none of these

15. When a firm is able to cover its variable costs only, it will be at:

(a) break-even point (b) equilibrium point

(c) shut-down point (d) none of these

16. At break-even point, a firm makes:

(a) normal profits (b) extra-normal profits

(c) extra-normal losses (d) none of these

17. Production may continue so long as:

(a) TR ≥ TC (b) TR ≥ TVC

(c) TR ≥ TFC (d) none of these

Answers

1. (b) **2.** (c) **3.** (b) **4.** (c) **5.** (a) **6.** (b) **7.** (b) **8.** (c) **9.** (c) **10.** (a) **11.** (a) **12.** (c) **13.** (a) **14.** (b) **15.** (c) **16.** (a) **17.** (b).

B. Information & Concept-based Questions

1. What is meant by producer's equilibrium?

Ans. Producer's equilibrium refers to a situation where profits are maximised, *i.e.,* the difference between total revenue and total cost is maximised or losses are minimised.

2. What are gross profits?

Ans. Gross profits are the difference between total revenue and total variable cost.

Gross Profits = TR – TVC

3. What are net profits?

Ans. Net profits are the difference between total revenue and total cost.

Net Profits = TR – TC

4. Define normal profits.

Ans. Profits are said to be normal when: TR = TC or AR = AC.

5. What are extra-normal profits?

Ans. Profits are said to be extra-normal or abnormal when: TR > TC or AR > AC.

6. Define sub-normal profits.

Ans. Sub-normal profits or losses occur when: TR < TC or AR < AC.

7. What are the conditions for the producer's equilibrium?

Ans. A producer is in a state of equilibrium, when following two conditions are satisfied:

(i) MR = MC, and (ii) MC is rising.

2. Reason-based Questions (Comprehension of the Subject-matter)

Read the following statements carefully. Write 'True' or 'False' with a reason.

1. Producer's equilibrium is a situation of 'revenue maximisation'.

Ans. False. A producer strikes his equilibrium at that level of output where profit is maximised. Hence, producer's equilibrium is a situation of 'profit maximisation'.

2. A producer strikes his equilibrium when the difference between TR and TC is maximised.

Ans. True. A producer strikes his equilibrium when he produces that amount of output at which the difference between total revenue and total cost is maximum. Because, net profit = TR – TC.

3. Gross profit is the difference between total revenue and total cost.

Ans. False. Gross profit is the difference between total revenue and total variable cost.

4. **Losses occur when average cost is equal to average revenue.**

Ans. False. Losses occur when average cost is greater than average revenue, *i.e.*, AC > AR.

5. **A firm maximises its profit when TR = TC.**

Ans. False. A firm maximises its profit when the difference between total revenue and total cost is maximum.

6. **If MR > MC, it is always a better situation than if MR = MC for profits to be maximised.**

Ans. False. MR = MC is a better situation as it coincides with producer's equilibrium where profits are maximised.

7. **Equality between MR and MC is a sufficient condition for profit maximisation.**

Ans. False. MR = MC is only a necessary condition for profit maximisation, the sufficient condition also requires that MC should be rising.

8. **The producer strikes his equilibrium only when MP is diminishing.**

Ans. True. A producer strikes his equilibrium only when MP is diminishing. Because, diminishing MP means rising MC. The producer stops production when rising MC matches with MR. Beyond this point, rising MC would exceed MR, causing loss of profit.

9. **When output is beyond the point of equilibrium, profits are maximised.**

Ans. False. Profits are less compared to equilibrium level. Because in such a situation, addition to TVC is greater than addition to TR. So that TR – TVC, *i.e.*, profits will tend to shrink.

10. **In the long run, a firm must cover all costs of production.**

Ans. True. In the long run, a firm must cover all costs of production. Because, in the long run, all costs are variable costs.

11. **In a state of perfect competition, commodity price should not exceed MC in case profits are to be maximised.**

Ans. True. In a state of perfect competition, commodity price should not exceed MC. It should be equal to MC if profits are to be maximised.

12. **Shut-down point occurs when a firm is just covering its fixed costs only.**

Ans. False. Shut-down point occurs when a firm is just covering its variable costs only. Or, it is a situation when: TR = TVC or AR = AVC.

13. **A firm can quit the industry in the short run also.**

Ans. False. Quitting is not possible in the short run because short run, by definition, is a period of time which is too short for the existing firms to quit the industry. Therefore, a firm can quit the industry only in the long run.

3. HOTS & Applications

1. **Normal profit is a part of total cost. Is it true?**

Ans. Yes. Normal profit is defined as the minimum return that the producer expects from his capital invested in the business. If this minimum return is not available, he will withdraw his capital from the existing use and shift it to the next best alternative use. Therefore, normal profit is a part of total cost.

2. **Why equilibrium is not struck when MR > MC?**

Ans. In a situation when MR > MC, the addition to revenue is greater than the addition to cost if a firm expands its production. Accordingly, expansion of production (when MR > MC) would take the firm to a higher level of profit. Implying that the firm will not be in a state of equilibrium so long as MR > MC. Equilibrium will be struck only when MR = MC.

3. **Shut-down point means shutting down the firm. Do you agree?**

Ans. No, shut-down point occurs when a firm just covers its variable cost. A firm may decide to suspend production of the commodity for the time being. No way, can it close down during the short period.

[**Note:** Shut-down point is a short period phenomenon.]

4. **Should production be discontinued when AR = AVC?**

Ans. Not necessarily. When AR = AVC the firm is incurring the loss of fixed costs. This loss is to be borne by the firm no matter it continues production or not. The producer, therefore, may or may not discontinue production when: AR = AVC.

5. A firm may undertake production even in a state of losses. Comment.

Ans. Yes. In state of losses, TR < TC or AR < AC. A firm may strike equilibrium even in this situation, because equilibrium is struck when MR = MC and MC is rising. Production continues and equilibrium is struck, so long as variable costs are covered. Total losses a firm can sustain is up to 'total fixed cost'.

6. Will a firm continue to produce even if it is incurring losses under perfect competition? Explain.

Ans. No, in the long run; Yes in the short run. In the long run, a firm will quit the industry in case it is incurring losses. In the short run, a firm continues to cope with losses so long as AR ≥ AVC. Because, by covering variable costs, the firm is incurring the loss of fixed cost only which it has to incur even when production is discontinued.

7. From the following information about a firm, find the firm's equilibrium output in terms of marginal cost and marginal revenue. Give reasons. Also find profit at this output.

Output (Units)	Total Revenue (₹)	Total Cost (₹)
1	6	7
2	12	13
3	18	18
4	24	22
5	30	28
6	36	35

Ans.

Output (Units)	Total Revenue (TR) (₹)	Total Cost (TC) (₹)	Marginal Revenue (MR) (₹)	Marginal Cost (MC) (₹)	Profit (= TR – TC) (₹)
1	6	7	6	7	–1
2	12	13	6	6	–1
3	18	18	6	5	0
4	24	22	6	4	2
5	30	28	6	6	2
6	36	35	6	7	1

Producer's equilibrium is struck when output level is 5 units.

Reason: At output levels 2nd and 5th units, MR and MC are equal (= 6). But the producer is in equilibrium when 5 units of output are produced. Because, it is here only that: (i) MR = MC, and (ii) MC is rising.

When 5 units of output are produced, TR = 30 and TC = 28

$$\text{Profit} = TR - TC$$

$$\text{Profit} = 30 - 28 = 2$$

∴ Profit = ₹ 2.

8. Find the producer's equilibrium from the following:

Output (Units)	Total Revenue (₹)	Marginal Cost (₹)
1	15	8
2	28	5
3	39	11
4	49	13

Ans.

Output (Units)	Total Revenue (TR) (₹)	Marginal Revenue (MR) (₹)	Marginal Cost (MC) (₹)
1	15	15	8
2	28	13	5
3	39	11	11
4	49	10	13

Profit is maximised when (i) MR = MC, and (ii) MC is rising. In this case, it is at 3rd unit. Hence, producer's equilibrium occurs at output level 3.

Producer is in equilibrium when the level of output = 3 units.

9. With the help of the table given below, find producer's equilibrium using MR and MC approach. Give reason for your answer.

Output (Units)	TR (₹)	AC (₹)
1	20	20
2	40	15
3	60	12
4	80	10
5	100	12
6	120	15

Ans.

Output (Units)	TR (₹)	MR (₹)	AC (₹)	TC (₹)	MC (₹)	Profit (₹) (π = TR – TC)
1	20	20	20	20	20	0
2	40	20	15	30	10	10
3	60	20	12	36	6	24
4	80	20	10	40	4	40
5	100	20	12	60	20	40
6	120	20	15	90	30	30

Producer's equilibrium is struck when output level = 5 units.

Reason: At output levels 1st and 5th units, both MR and MC are equal, which is equal to 20 in both the cases. But producer is in equilibrium at 5th unit only where profit is maximum (= 40).

The producer is in equilibrium when the level of output = 5 units.

10. From the table given below, determine the level of output at which the producer is in equilibrium. Use the marginal revenue and marginal cost approach. Given reasons for your answer.

Output (Units)	Price (₹)	Total Cost (₹)
1	5	7
2	5	12
3	5	16
4	5	18
5	5	23

Ans.

Output (Units)	Price (₹)	Total Revenue (TR) (₹)	Total Cost (TC) (₹)	Marginal Revenue (MR) (₹)	Marginal Cost (MC) (₹)	Profit (π = TR – TC) (₹)
1	5	5	7	5	7	–2
2	5	10	12	5	5	–2
3	5	15	16	5	4	–1
4	5	20	18	5	2	2
5	5	25	23	5	5	2

Producer's equilibrium is struck when output level is 5 units.

Reason: At output levels 2nd and 5th units, both MR and MC are equal, which is equal to 5 in both the cases. But the producer is in equilibrium at 5th unit only where profit is maximum (= 2).

The producer is in equilibrium when the level of output = 5 units.

11. *"Discovery of natural gas in the international market leads to a cut in the petrol and diesel prices."* Explain the economic theory to analyse the impact of the statement on the cost of production of the transport firms in India. Also analyse its impact on the cost of transportation.

Ans. India meets its domestic demand for petrol and diesel largely through imports. Accordingly, a cut in their price in the international market leads to cut in price in the domestic market as well.

Transport firms use petrol and diesel as a major input. A cut in their price is expected to lower their cost of production. Other things remaining constant, it would lead to lower cost for the transportation of goods across different places.

4. Evaluation (Value-based Questions)

1. As a producer, how would you adjust your level of output when MR and MC are not equal? Assume that, price of your product is constant for you, and the law of variable proportions is operative.

Ans. Constant price means, AR is constant. If AR is constant, AR = MR. Both AR and MR are, therefore, indicated by a horizontal straight line, parallel to X-axis. When the law of variable proportions is operative, MC curve tends to be U-shaped: MC tends to decline corresponding to increasing returns, and it tends to rise corresponding to diminishing returns.

I will strike my equilibrium at a point when:

(i) MR = MC, and (ii) MC is rising.

I may be confronted with two situations:

(i) MR > MC, and (ii) MR < MC.

How will I adjust my output?

For me, MR is constant in both the situations. So that the equality between MR and MC will be achieved only through changes in MC.

In **situation 1**, when MR > MC:

I would like to increase the level of output. This would cause increase in MC. The process of increasing output is to be continued till MR = MC.

In **situation 2**, when MR < MC:

I would like to decrease the level of output. This would cause decrease in MC. The process of decreasing output is to be continued till MR = MC.

2. Do you think it is rational for a producer to strike equilibrium when MC is rising, not when it is falling?

Ans. Yes, it is rational for a producer to strike equilibrium when MC is rising, not when it is falling. When MC is falling, cost of producing an additional unit tends to fall. Other things remaining constant, it would lead to a rise in total profits. Why should a producer stop production when total profits are rising? It would not be a rational decision. The equilibrium will, therefore, be struck only when MC is rising, and is equal to MR.

3. Imagine yourself a producer (in a perfectly competitive market structure), focusing on profit maximisation. Will you prefer striking an equilibrium in a state of increasing returns?

Ans. Striking an equilibrium in a state of increasing returns to a factor (when MP is rising or MC is falling) is absolutely ruled out. Because it is a situation when every additional unit of output adds more and more to total profits. **Reason:** While MR is constant (under perfect competition) MC is falling (owing to increasing returns), so that the difference between MR and MC tends to rise. It is only when the differential (MR – MC) starts shrinking, and is finally eliminated, that the profits are maximised. This happens only in a state of diminishing returns when MP is falling or MC is rising.

4. Using your judgement as an entrepreneur, would you agree with the following statement?

"Maximisation of profit implies equilibrium, but equilibrium does not always imply maximisation of profit."

Ans. Yes, we do agree with the statement that maximisation of profit implies equilibrium, but equilibrium does not always imply maximisation of profit. Profit is maximised when the difference between total revenue and total cost is maximum. But equilibrium can be struck even in the state of losses, when the two conditions are satisfied, *i.e.*, (i) MR = MC and (ii) MC is rising. Fig. 5 illustrates it.

Note: It is a situation of low price prevailing in the market when the firm is covering variable cost, but not the total cost.

FIGURE 5

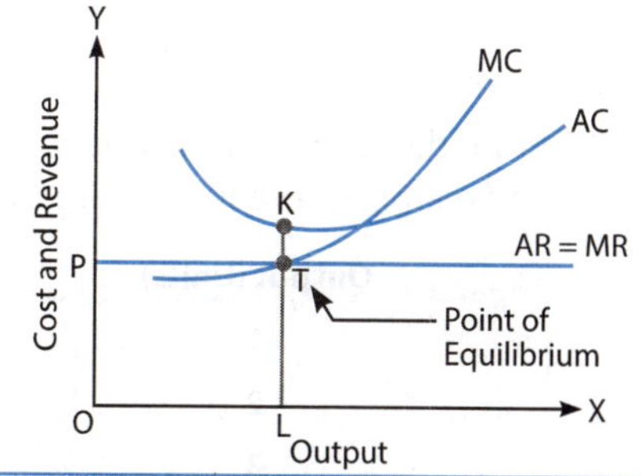

Equilibrium is struck at point T, as here:
(i) MR = MC, and (ii) MC is rising.
But at this level of output:
AR (= LT) < AC (= LK)
⇒ Loss = TK per unit of output

5. CBSE Questions—Past 4 years (With Answers or Reference to the Text for Answers)

1. Explain the conditions of a producer's equilibrium in terms of marginal cost and marginal revenue. Use diagram. [Page 244–246] *[CBSE Delhi 2012]*
2. Explain the conditions of producer's equilibrium with the help of a numerical example. *[CBSE Delhi 2013]* [Page 244, 245]
3. Give the meaning of producer's equilibrium. A producer produces that quantity of his product at which marginal cost and marginal revenue are equal. Is he earning maximum profits? Give reasons for your answer. [Page 243–247] *[CBSE Delhi 2013]*
4. From the following table, find out the level of output at which the producer will be in equilibrium. Give reasons for your answer. *[CBSE (AI) 2013]*

Output (Units)	Marginal Revenue (₹)	Marginal Cost (₹)
1	8	10
2	8	8
3	8	7
4	8	8
5	8	9

[Page 391, 392]

5. From the following table find out the level of output at which the producer is in equilibrium. Give reasons for your answer. (Use marginal cost–marginal revenue method.) *[CBSE (F) 2013]*

Output (Units)	Marginal Cost (₹)	Total Revenue (₹)
1	12	10
2	10	20
3	8	30
4	10	40
5	12	50

[Page 392]

6. From the following information about a firm, find the firm's equilibrium output in terms of marginal cost and marginal revenue. Give reasons. Also find profit at this output. *[CBSE Delhi 2014]*

Output (Units)	Total Revenue (₹)	Total Cost (₹)
1	7	8
2	14	15
3	21	21
4	28	28
5	35	36

[Page 392, 393]

7. From the following information about a firm, find the firm's equilibrium output in terms of marginal cost and marginal revenue. Give reasons. Also find profit at this output. *[CBSE (AI) 2014]*

Output (Units)	Total Revenue (₹)	Total Cost (₹)
1	6	7
2	12	13
3	18	17
4	24	23
5	30	31

[Page 393]

8. From the following information about a firm, find the firm's equilibrium output in terms of marginal cost and marginal revenue. Give reasons. Also calculate profit at this output. *[CBSE (F) 2014]*

Output (Units)	Total Revenue (₹)	Total Cost (₹)
1	8	10
2	16	18
3	24	23
4	32	31
5	40	41

[Page 393, 394]

9. Why is the equality between marginal cost and marginal revenue necessary for a firm to be in equilibrium? Is it sufficient to ensure equilibrium? Explain. *[CBSE Delhi 2015]*

[Page 244–248]

10. Explain why will a producer not be in equilibrium if the conditions of equilibrium are not met.
[Page 246, 247] *[CBSE (AI) 2015]*

11. Explain the rationale behind the conditions of equilibrium of a producer. *[CBSE (F) 2015]*

[Page 244–248]

6. NCERT Questions (With Hints to Answers)

1. The following table shows the total revenue and total cost schedules of a competitive firm. Calculate the profit at each output level. Determine also the market price of the good.

Quantity Sold	TR (₹)	TC (₹)	Profit (₹)
0	0	5	
1	5	7	
2	10	10	
3	15	12	
4	20	15	
5	25	23	
6	30	33	
7	35	40	

[**Hint:**

Quantity Sold (Q)	TR (₹)	TC (₹)	Profit (= TR – TC) (₹)	Market Price ($= \frac{TR}{Q}$) (₹)
0	0	5	–5	—
1	5	7	–2	5
2	10	10	0	5
3	15	12	3	5
4	20	15	5	5
5	25	23	2	5
6	30	33	–3	5
7	35	40	–5	5

2. The following table shows the total cost schedule of a competitive firm. It is given that the price of the good is ₹10. Calculate the profit at each output level. Find the profit maximising level of output.

Quantity Sold	0	1	2	3	4	5	6	7	8	9	10
TC (₹)	5	15	22	27	31	38	49	63	81	101	123

[**Hint:**

Quantity Sold	TC (₹)	Price (₹)	TR (₹)	Profit (= TR – TC) (₹)
0	5	10	0	–5
1	15	10	10	–5
2	22	10	20	–2
3	27	10	30	3
4	31	10	40	9
5	38	10	50	12
6	49	10	60	11
7	63	10	70	7
8	81	10	80	–1
9	101	10	90	–11
10	123	10	100	–23

Profit maximising level of output is 5 units, because here, the difference between total revenue and total cost (*i.e.*, profit) is maximum which is equal to 12.]

7. Miscellaneous Questions and Reference to the Text for Answers

A. Questions of 3 & 4 marks each

1. Explain producer's equilibrium with the help of a table.
   [Page 244, 245]
2. What is meant by producer's equilibrium? What are its main conditions?
   [Page 243, 244]
3. Explain the conditions leading to maximisation of profits by a producer. Use marginal cost and marginal revenue approach.
   [Page 244–246]
4. Explain what happens to the profits if output level is beyond the equilibrium level.
   [Page 246, 247]
5. Explain what happens to the profits if output level is below the equilibrium level.
   [Page 246, 247]

B. Questions of 6 marks each

1. What is meant by producer's equilibrium? When will a producer be in equilibrium in case of losses.
   [Page 243, 249, 253]
2. Explain the conditions of producer's equilibrium with the help of a diagram.
   [Page 244–246]
3. Show that a perfectly competitive firm maximises its profit only when price = MC.
   [Page 244–247, 249]
4. Explain the concepts of break-even point and shut-down point, using a suitable diagram.
   [Page 260]
5. Why should MC curve be rising in a situation of producer's equilibrium?
   [Page 244–246, 248]
6. Gross profits are maximised only when a firm's MC curve cuts MR curve from below. Explain diagrammatically.
   [Page 244–246]

7. Will production be ever undertaken if P < MC for a profit maximising firm under perfect competition? Give reasons in support of your answer.

[Page 246, 247, 249]

8. Why will a profit maximising firm in a competitive market never strike its equilibrium in a state when MC is falling? Explain your answer using a suitable diagram.

[Page 245, 246, 248]

9. For a firm under perfect competition, profits are not maximised even when MR > MC. Explain why.

[Page 244–247, 252]

10. A firm under perfect competition will not suspend production even when P < AC, but it will definitely do so if P < AVC. Explain the fact using a suitable diagram.

[Page 260]

DOs and DON'Ts

1. You must understand that a producer will never undertake production of a commodity if variable costs are not covered.

   During short period, the producer is facing two types of costs: (i) fixed costs, and (ii) variable costs. Fixed costs are incurred even when output = 0. Variable costs vary with output. Variable costs are zero when output is zero, and these costs increase as output increases. Thus, while the producer cannot control the fixed costs, he can definitely control the variable costs. He would never undertake production of a commodity when variable costs are not covered. A situation when even variable costs are not covered is called '**economically unviable situation**'. On the other hand, a situation when variable costs are covered is called '**economically viable situation**'.

2. Do not hold the opinion that once a producer finds his equilibrium and maximises his profit, he never changes his level of output for all time to come. A producer defines his equilibrium with respect to the given cost and revenue conditions, or with respect to a given set of MR and MC curves. Over time, his cost of production might change, leading to a shift in MC curve. Likewise, demand for his product might change, leading to a shift in MR curve. In such situations, the producer has to rediscover his point of equilibrium. Check the following diagram (Fig. 6) for an illustration:

   MC_1 is the initial marginal cost curve, and MR is the marginal revenue curve. Q_1 is the initial equilibrium. OL is the equilibrium output where profit is maximised.

   Let us assume that there is no change on the demand side. So that MR curve remains the same as before. But, the cost of inputs increases for the firm. Consequently, marginal cost curve shifts to a higher level: it shifts from MC_1 to MC_2. Now, Q_1 no longer remains the point of equilibrium. Profit will no longer be maximised at OL level of output. The equilibrium point will shift from Q_1 to Q_2. The equilibrium output will reduce from OL to OS. Thus, we conclude that equilibrium output keeps changing for the firm (or, profit maximising output keeps changing for the firm) as cost of production changes. Likewise, change in market demand for the product will also lead to a new equilibrium.

FIGURE 6

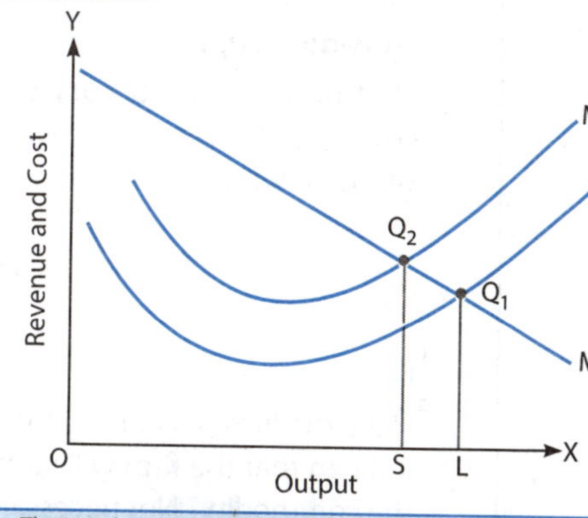

Q_1 : The initial equilibrium point.
OL : The initial equilibrium output.
MC_1 shifts to MC_2 when the cost of production increases.
Q_2 : The new equilibrium point.
OS : The new equilibrium output.

abilityZONE

The Difference between TR and TC is Maximum only when MR = MC, and MC is Rising—A Diagrammatical Presentation

Fig. 7 illustrates the situation of profit maximisation (maximum difference between TR and TC) when MR = MC, and MC is rising.

In Fig. 7, *ab* points to the maximum possible difference between TR and TC. It is when TC is increasing at increasing rate, so that MC is rising.

Tangent at point *a* is indicated by line-1. It shows the slope of TR at point *a*, which is equal to MR at point *a*.

Tangent at point *b* is indicated by line-2. It shows the slope of TC at point *b*, which is equal to MC at point *b*.

FIGURE 7

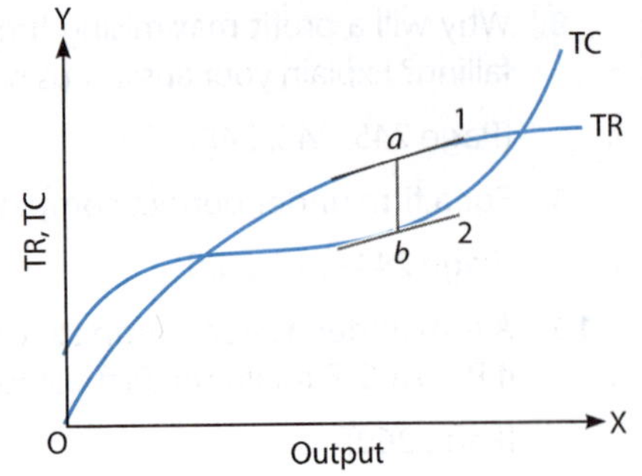

Because 1 and 2 are parallel to each other, their slopes should be equal. Accordingly, MR (at point *a*) = MC (at point *b*).

Thus, MR = MC (and MC is rising) when TR – TC is maximum (= *ab*).

Break-even Point and Shut-down Point

Break-even Point

In microeconomics, break-even is said to occur when:

$$TR = TC$$

Or, $$\frac{TR}{Q} = \frac{TC}{Q}$$

Or, $$P = AC$$

A firm is just covering all its costs.

Fig. 8 illustrates the situation of break-even point.

Break-even is struck at point Q where AR (= Price) = AC = LQ = OP. A firm is just covering its costs as price (= OP) happens to be equal to AC (average cost) = LQ.

FIGURE 8

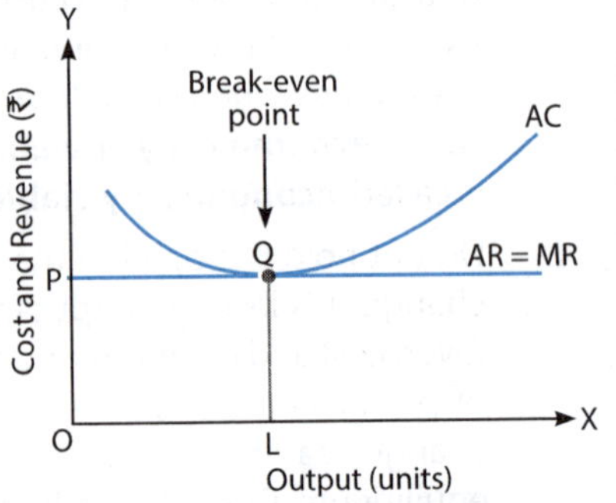

Break-even occurs at point Q. Here, AR = AC or TR = TC. The firm is just making normal profits.

Shut-down Point

Shut-down point occurs when a firm is just covering its variable costs only. Or, it is a situation when:

$$TR = TVC$$

Or, $$\frac{TR}{Q} = \frac{TVC}{Q}$$

Or, $$AR = AVC$$

Here, the firm is incurring loss of fixed cost. Does it mean that the firm will suspend production of the commodity? Not necessarily. It may continue to produce because the loss of fixed cost is to be incurred even when output is suspended.

Fig. 9 illustrates the situation of shut-down point.

FIGURE 9

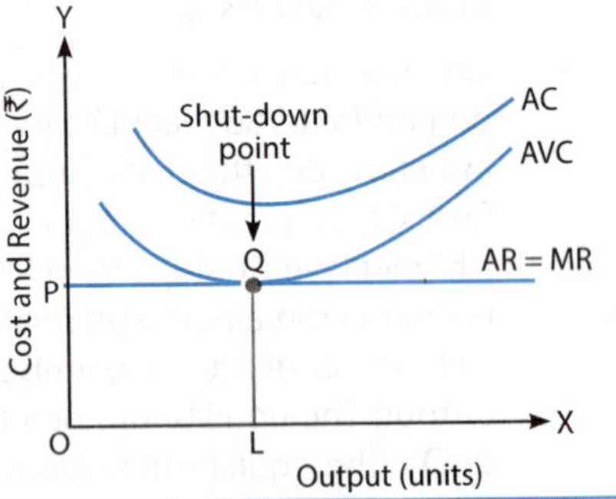

Shut-down occurs at point Q. Here, AR = AVC. The firm is incurring the loss of AFC per unit of output.
Total loss to the firm = AFC × Output
= TFC for a given level of output.

Shut-down is struck at point Q where AR (Price) = AVC = LQ = OP.

A firm is operating with a price just covering its AVC. Thus, price (or average revenue = OP) = average variable cost (= LQ). When AR = AVC, the firm is incurring the loss of AFC per unit of output. Its total loss = TFC for a given level of output.

CHAPTER 10

Theory of Supply

TODO

- Concept of Supply
- Supply Schedule
- Supply Curve and its Slope
- Supply Function (Determinants of Supply)
- Law of Supply
- Movements along a Supply Curve and Shifts in Supply Curve
- Price Elasticity of Supply: Meaning and Measurement

1. Concept of Supply

Ask a producer: how much quantity of a commodity he is willing to sell? 'Depends on price' should be his obvious reply. At higher price, he should be willing to sell more, while at a lower price, he should be willing to sell less. Accordingly, supply of a commodity refers to a table showing various amounts of a commodity that the producers are willing to sell at different possible prices of that commodity at a point of time.

Supply

Supply of a commodity refers to a schedule (or a table) showing various quantities of a commodity that the producers are willing to sell at different possible prices of the commodity at a point of time.

Supply and Stock are Different Concepts

Stock of a commodity refers to the total quantity of that commodity which at any given time is available with the firm for purpose of (present or future) sale in the market. Supply refers to that part of the stock that the firm is presently prepared to sell at a given price. Supposing, the stock of wheat with a firm is 100 tonnes and the prevailing price is ₹ 500 per quintal. If at this price, the firm is prepared to sell 10 tonnes of wheat, then the supply of wheat will be 10 tonnes only. If the price rises to ₹ 600 per quintal and the firm is prepared to sell 50 tonnes of wheat then its supply will, accordingly, be 50 tonnes.

Supply	Stock
(i) Supply refers to the quantity of a commodity offered for sale corresponding to different possible prices of the commodity.	(i) Stock refers to the total quantity of the commodity available with the producer for the present or future sale.
(ii) Supply is a flow concept. It is measured per unit of time period.	(ii) Stock is not a flow concept. It is measured at a point of time.
(iii) Supply is always related to price of the commodity.	(iii) Stock is not related to price of the commodity. It indicates 'inventory' of the firm.

Supply and Quantity Supplied are Different Concepts

There is a difference between the terms 'supply' and 'quantity supplied'. Quantity supplied refers to a specific quantity of a commodity that the producers are ready to sell at a specific price of the commodity. Supply, on the other hand, refers to entire schedule showing various quantities offered for sale at different possible prices of the commodity.

Supply and Quantity Supplied

Supply refers to the entire schedule showing various quantities of the commodity offered for sale at different possible prices of that commodity. Quantity supplied refers to a specific amount offered for sale at a specific price of the commodity.

2. Supply Schedule

Supply schedule is a table showing various quantities of a commodity offered for sale at different possible prices of that commodity. It has two aspects:

(i) Individual Supply Schedule, and (ii) Market Supply Schedule.

(i) Individual Supply Schedule

Individual supply schedule refers to supply schedule of an individual firm in the market. It shows different quantities supplied by a firm at different prices of a commodity. Table 1 is an individual supply schedule.

Table 1. Individual Supply Schedule

P_X (Price of Good-X) (₹)	Q_X (Quantity of Good-X) (Units)
5	0
10	10
15	20
20	30

It is clear from this Table that as the price rises, supply extends. At ₹ 5 per unit, the firm is not willing to sell any unit. When price is ₹ 10 per unit then supply is of 10 units and when it rises to ₹ 20 per unit, the supply also extends to 30 units.

(ii) Market Supply Schedule

Market supply schedule refers to supply schedule of all the firms in the market producing a particular commodity. Sum total of the firms producing a particular commodity is called 'Industry'. Thus, market supply schedule refers to supply schedule of the industry as a whole.

Table 2 is a market supply schedule. It is based on the assumption that there are only two firms (A and B) supplying Good-X in the market.

Table 2. Market Supply Schedule

P_X (Price of Good-X) (₹)	Q_X (Firm 'A') (Units)	Q_X (Firm 'B') (Units)	Market Supply (Units)
5	0	0	0
10	10	5	10 + 5 = 15
15	20	10	20 + 10 = 30
20	30	20	30 + 20 = 50

Table 2 shows that when price of Good-X is ₹ 5 per unit, the firms will not supply any quantity. When price increases to ₹ 10 per unit, firm 'A' supplies 10 units and firm 'B' supplies 5 units. Thus, the market supply is (10 + 5) units = 15 units. As the price rises, market supply also increases.

Individual Supply Schedule and Market Supply Schedule

Individual supply or individual supply schedule is a table showing various amounts of a commodity that an individual firm in the market is willing to sell at different possible prices of that commodity.

Market supply or market supply schedule is a table showing various amounts of a commodity that all the firms in the industry are willing to sell at different possible prices of that commodity.

3. Supply Curve

Supply curve is a graphic presentation of supply schedule, showing various quantities of a commodity offered for sale at different possible prices of that commodity. It shows the positive relationship between price of a commodity and its quantity supplied. Higher quantity is offered at higher price of the commodity. Supply curve has two aspects:

(i) Individual Supply Curve, and (ii) Market Supply Curve.

(i) Individual Supply Curve

Individual supply curve is a graphic presentation of supply schedule of an individual firm in the market. Sloping upwards, it indicates positive relationship between price of a commodity and its quantity supplied, as SS curve in Fig. 1.

FIGURE 1

Individual Supply Curve

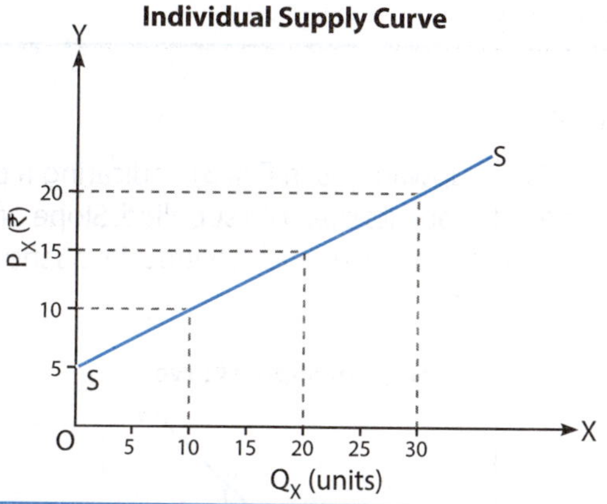

Supply curve (SS) slopes upward. It shows that more of a commodity is supplied at a higher price. It is drawn as a straight line for the sake of simplicity.

This figure is drawn on the basis of individual supply schedule of Table 1. SS curve has a positive slope, showing that quantity supplied increases in response to an increase in own price of the commodity, and it decreases in response to a decrease in own price of a commodity. Thus, if price is ₹ 5 per unit, the firm is not prepared to sell any quantity of the commodity. When price is ₹ 15 per unit, the firm is ready to sell 20 units of the commodity. And, when price is ₹ 20 per unit, the quantity supplied increases to 30 units.

(ii) Market Supply Curve

Market supply curve is a graphic presentation of market supply schedule. It is supply curve of the industry as a whole. It is derived by way of horizontal summation of supply curves of all the firms in the industry.

FIGURE 2

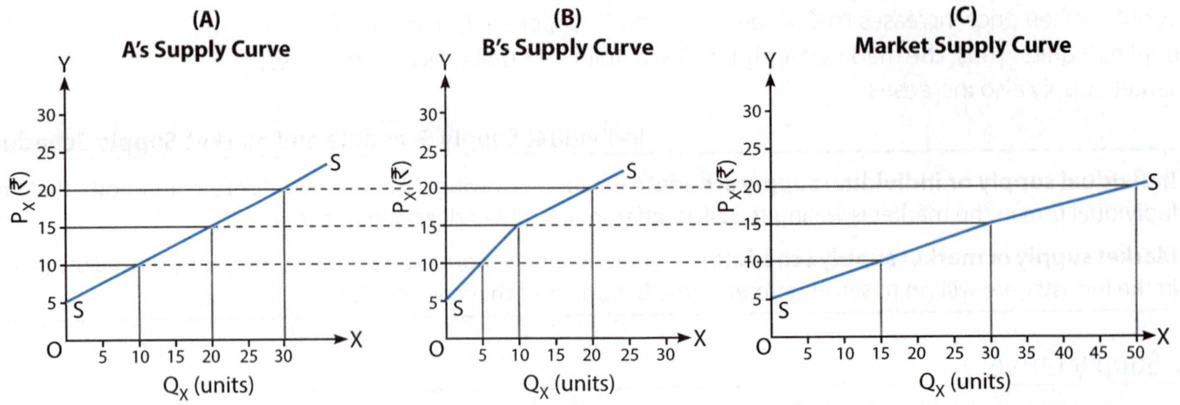

Market supply curve is a horizontal summation of individual supply curves. It shows various quantities of a commodity that all the firms in the market are ready to sell at different possible prices of that commodity.

A and B segments of Fig. 2 show individual supply curves, while segment C shows market supply curve. It shows that when price is ₹ 10 per unit, market supply is (10 + 5) units = 15 units, when price is ₹ 15 per unit, market supply is (20 + 10) units = 30 units, and when price is ₹ 20 per unit, market supply is (30 + 20) units = 50 units. Market supply curve is a horizontal summation of the individual supply curves of the various firms producing a particular commodity in the market.

HOTS

Q. What is minimum supply price of a commodity?

Ans. Minimum supply price of a commodity refers to reserve price of the commodity. It is the price below which the producers will not sell any quantity of the commodity.

Slope of Supply Curve

Supply curve normally slopes upward (as in Fig. 3), indicating a positive relationship between price of a commodity and its quantity supplied. Slope of supply curve refers to the ratio between 'change in price' and 'change in quantity supplied'. This is explained with reference to Fig. 3.

FIGURE 3

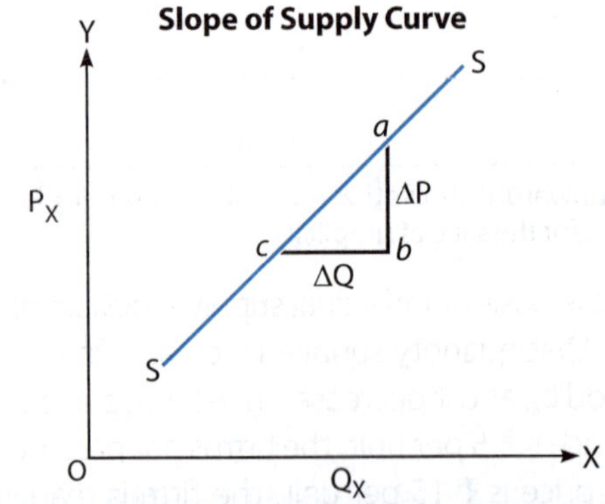

$$\text{Slope of Supply Curve} = \frac{\Delta P}{\Delta Q} = \frac{ab}{bc}$$

It is constant, because supply curve is a straight line.

Slope of supply curve is estimated as $\frac{\Delta P}{\Delta Q}$. It is equal to $\frac{ab}{bc}$ in Fig. 3. It shows the rate at which price of the commodity changes corresponding to a unit change in quantity supplied.

The ratio $\left(\frac{\Delta P}{\Delta Q}\right)$ is constant at all points of a straight line supply curve. It points to the fact that the slope of a straight line supply curve is constant. It refers to a linear relationship between price and quantity supplied.

4. Supply Function (Determinants of Supply)

Supply function studies the functional relationship between supply of a commodity and its various determinants. The supply of a commodity mainly depends on the own price of the commodity, price of related goods, goal of the firm, price of factors of production and state of technology. Thus, supply of a commodity is a function of several factors as expressed in the following equation:

$$S_X = f(P_X, P_r, N_F, G, P_F, T, E_X, G_P)$$

(Here, S_X = Supply of commodity-X; f = Functional relation; P_X = Own price of commodity-X; P_r = Price of related goods; N_F = Number of firms in the industry; G = Goal of the firm; P_F = Price of factors of production; T = State of technology; E_X = Business expectations; G_P = Government policy.)

Following is a brief description of the various determinants of supply of a commodity:

(1) **Own Price of a Commodity:** There is a direct relationship between own price of a commodity and its quantity supplied. Generally, higher the price, higher the quantity supplied, and lower the price, lower the quantity supplied.

(2) **Price of Related Goods:** Supply of a good depends upon the price of related goods. Consider a firm selling tea. If price of coffee rises in the market, the firm will be willing to sell less tea at its existing price. The same quantity of tea will be sold only at a higher price.

(3) **Number of Firms in the Industry:** Market supply of a commodity depends upon number of firms in the industry. Increase in the number of firms implies increase in market supply, and decrease in the number of firms implies decrease in market supply of a commodity.

(4) **Goal of the Firm:** If goal of the firm is to maximise profits, more quantity of the commodity will be offered only at a higher price. On the other hand, if goal of the firm is to maximise sales (or maximise output or employment) more will be supplied even at the same price.

(5) **Price of Factors of Production:** Supply of a commodity is also affected by the price of factors used for the production of the commodity. If the factor price decreases, cost of production also reduces. Accordingly, more of the commodity is supplied at its existing price. Conversely, if the factor price increases, cost of production also increases. In such a situation less of the commodity is supplied at its existing price.

(6) **State of Technology:** Improvement in the technique of production reduces cost of production. Consequently, more of the commodity is supplied at its existing price.

(7) **Business Expectations:** In situations of bullish expectations, investment tends to rise and supply starts rising. Accordingly, quantity supplied rises even when own price of the commodity remains constant. Just the opposite may happen in situations of bearish expectations.

(8) **Government Policy:** 'Taxation and subsidy' policy of the government also impacts market supply of a commodity. Increase in taxation may decrease supply, while increase in subsidies may increase it.

HOTS

Q.1. How market supply responds to improvement in technology?

Ans. Improvement in technology lowers cost per unit of output. Accordingly, output is expanded and market supply increases. Quantity supplied tends to rise even when own price of the commodity remains constant.

Q.2. What are 'bullish' and 'bearish' business expectations?

Ans. Bullish expectations refer to a situation when the producers expect high returns (profits) in the near future. Accordingly, level of investment (and therefore, the level of production activity) tends to rise in the economy. Bearish expectations, on the other hand, refer to a situation when the producers expect low returns in the near future. Accordingly, level of investment (and therefore, the level of production activity) tends to fall in the economy.

5. Law of Supply

Law of supply states that, other things remaining constant, there is a positive relationship between own price of a commodity and its quantity supplied. Thus, more is supplied at higher price and less at the lower price.

In other words, there is positive relation between own price and quantity supplied of a commodity.

The law of supply states that other things remaining constant, quantity supplied increases with increase in own price of a commodity, and *vice versa*.

[**Note:** It is a common practice to use the term 'supply' instead of 'quantity supplied'. Thus, it is commonly said that there is a positive relationship between own price and supply of a commodity. But, it must be borne in mind that the term 'supply' in relation to own price of the commodity always means 'quantity supplied'.]

Explanation

Law of supply is explained with the help of Table 3.

Table 3. Law of Supply: Positive relation between Price and Quantity Supplied of a Commodity

P_X (₹)	S_X (Units)
10	100
11	200
12	300

Table 3 shows that quantity supplied increases from 100 to 200 units when own price of the commodity increases from ₹ 10 to ₹ 11 per unit. Likewise, it increases from 200 to 300 units when price increases from ₹ 11 to ₹ 12 per unit. Implying that there is a positive relationship between own price of the commodity and its quantity supplied. Fig. 4 gives diagrammatic illustration of this relationship.

FIGURE 4

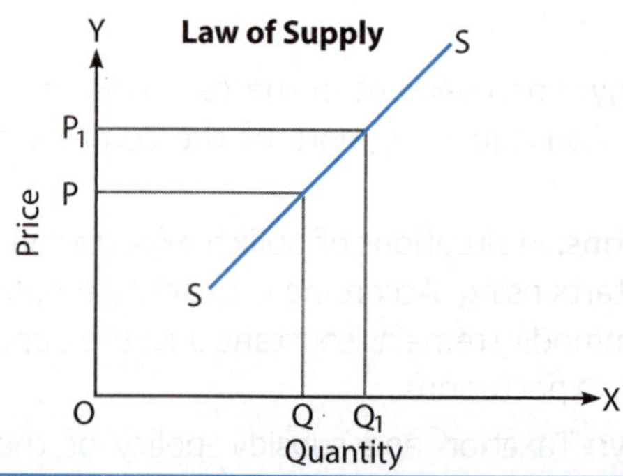

SS slopes upward from left to right. It shows positive relationship between own price of the commodity and its quantity supplied: as price rises quantity supplied also rises.

Supply curve (SS) slopes upward. It shows increase in quantity supplied in response to increase in own price of the commodity. Thus, quantity supplied increases from OQ to OQ_1, when price rises from OP to OP_1.

Assumptions of the Law of Supply

Important assumptions of the law of supply are as these:

(i) There is no change in the price of the factors of production.
(ii) There is no change in the technique of production.
(iii) There is no change in the goal of the firm.
(iv) There is no change in the price of related goods.
(v) There is no change in business expectations.
(vi) The government policy relating to price and production of the commodity does not change.

Broadly, the law of supply assumes that all other determinants of supply of a commodity, other than own price of the commodity, remain constant.

Exceptions to the Law of Supply

The positive relationship between own price and quantity supplied of a commodity may not always hold good, or may not firmly hold good in certain situations, as under:

(i) The law of supply does not apply strictly to agricultural products whose supply is governed by natural factors. If due to natural calamities, there is a fall in the production of wheat, then its supply will not increase, however high the price may be.
(ii) Supply of goods having social distinction will remain limited even if their price tends to rise.
(iii) At a given point of time, sellers may be willing to sell more of a perishable commodity even at a lower price.

6. Movements along a Supply Curve and Shifts in Supply Curve

Movements along a supply curve refer to extension or contraction of supply in response to change in own price of the commodity, other determinants of supply remaining constant. Extension of supply implies increase in quantity supplied when own price of the commodity increases. Contraction of supply implies decrease in quantity supplied when own price of the commodity decreases.

Shifts in supply curve refer to increase or decrease in quantity supplied even own price of the commodity remains constant. These are caused by factors other than own price of the commodity (or other determinants of supply, other than own price of the commodity). Increase in supply implies a forward shift in supply curve: quantity supplied increases even when own price of the commodity is constant. Decrease in supply implies a backward shift in supply curve: quantity supplied decreases even when own price of the commodity is constant. Following is a tabular and diagrammatic description of the concepts of movements along a supply curve and shifts in supply curve.

Movements along a Supply Curve: Extension and Contraction of Supply

Movements along a supply curve, caused by change in own price of the commodity are often studied as:

(i) Extension of Supply, and (ii) Contraction of Supply.

Extension of supply occurs when quantity supplied of a commodity increases due to an increase in own price of the commodity. Contraction of supply occurs when quantity supplied of a commodity decreases due to decrease in own price of the commodity. Table 4 and Fig. 5 show extension of supply. Table 5 and Fig. 6 show the contraction of supply.

Table 4. Extension of Supply

P_X (₹)	Q_X (Units)	Description
1	1	Rise in Own Price of the Commodity
		↓
5	5	Extension of Supply

FIGURE 5

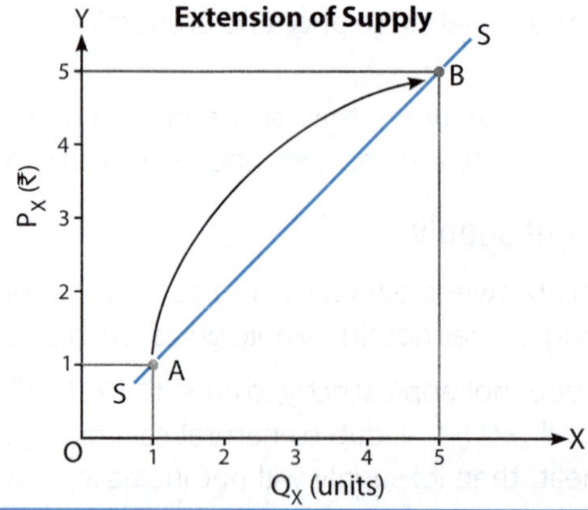

Extension of supply is indicated by a movement from point A to B on the supply curve. Quantity supplied increases in response to increase in own price of the commodity.

In Table 4, when price of the commodity-X is ₹ 1 per unit, its quantity supplied is 1 unit. When price rises to ₹ 5 per unit, supply extends to 5 units. In Fig. 5, SS is the supply curve of commodity-X. When price is ₹ 1 per unit, supply is 1 unit. When price rises to ₹ 5 per unit, supply extends to 5 units. The producer moves from point 'A' to point 'B' on the same supply curve which is why it is called movement along the supply curve.

Table 5. Contraction of Supply

P_X (₹)	Q_X (Units)	Description
5	5	Fall in Own Price of the Commodity
		↓
1	1	Contraction of Supply

FIGURE 6

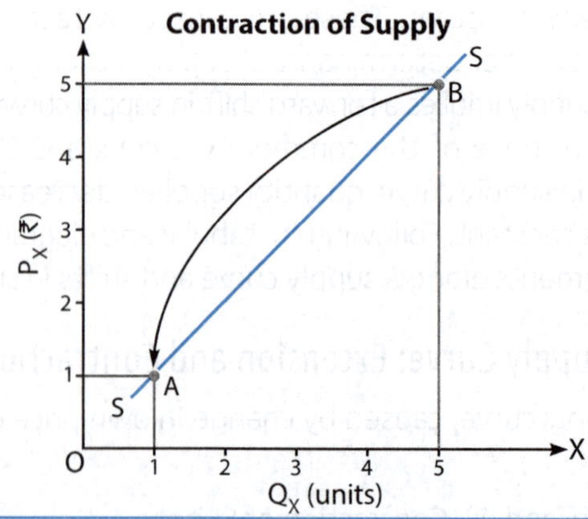

Contraction of supply is indicated by a movement from point B to A on the supply curve. Quantity supplied decreases in response to decrease in own price of the commodity.

In Table 5, when price of commodity-X is ₹ 5 per unit, quantity supplied is 5 units. When price falls to ₹ 1 per unit, quantity supplied decreases to 1 unit. In Fig. 6, SS is the supply curve of commodity-X. When price is ₹ 5 per unit, supply is 5 units. When price falls to ₹ 1 per unit, quantity supplied reduces to 1 unit. The producer moves from point 'B' to point 'A' on the same supply curve. Thus, it is a movement along the supply curve.

HOTS

Q. Why more of a commodity is offered at a higher price?

Ans. More of a commodity is offered at a higher price because of two reasons:

(i) Other things remaining constant, higher price implies higher profit. Accordingly, the producer is induced to produce more and sell more.

(ii) Increase in output (required to increase supply) occurs under the law of diminishing returns. It implies increasing MC (Marginal Cost) as output is increased. Accordingly, price must rise if more is to be produced to supply more.

Shift in Supply Curve: Increase and Decrease in Supply

Shift in supply curve refers to a situation of increase or decrease in quantity supplied of a commodity even when own price of the commodity remains constant. It is caused by factors, other than own price of the commodity. Increase in supply is indicated by a forward shift in supply curve and decrease in supply is indicated by a backward shift in supply curve.

Increase and Decrease in Supply

Increase in supply occurs when more is supplied at the existing price, while decrease in supply occurs when less is supplied at the existing price. Increase in supply is indicated by a forward shift in supply curve; decrease in supply is indicated by a backward shift in supply curve.

Increase in Supply

Table 6 and Fig. 7 illustrate the situation of increase in supply or forward shift in supply curve.

Table 6. Increase in Supply

P_X (₹)	Q_X (Units)
10	20
10	30

FIGURE 7

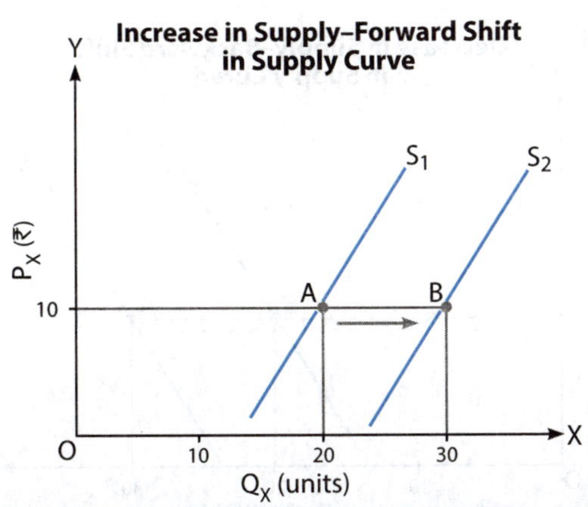

At the existing price of ₹ 10, quantity supplied increases from 20 to 30 units of the commodity. Accordingly, supply curve shifts forward from S_1 to S_2. The producer shifts from point A on the old supply curve to point B on the new supply curve.

Table 6 shows that initially 20 units of the commodity are supplied at the price of ₹10 per unit. Owing to some causes (generally related to reduction in the cost of production), firms are now willing to supply 30 units even when own price of the commodity remains to be ₹10 per unit. Diagrammatically, it implies a forward shift in supply curve (or shift to the right) as from S_1 to S_2 in Fig 7. The producer shifts from point A on the old supply curve to point B on the new supply curve.

Causes of Increase in Supply

Increase in supply may occur due to the following factors:

(i) Improvement in technology leading to a fall in cost of production.

(ii) Reduction in factor prices, causing a fall in cost of production.

(iii) Decrease in the price of a competing product. It prompts the producer to sell more at the existing price.

(iv) Increase in number of firms in the industry. It causes increase in market supply even when price of the commodity remains the same.

(v) High business expectations. It prompts the producers to increase investment. Accordingly, supply increases.

(vi) Shift in goal of the firm from profit maximisation to sales maximisation. 'Clearance Sale' often leads to higher supplies even when price remains the same.

(vii) Decrease in taxation (like excise duty) or grant of subsidy. This induces the producers to increase supplies even when price remains the same.

Decrease in Supply

Table 7 and Fig. 8 illustrate the situation of decrease in supply or backward shift in supply curve.

Table 7. Decrease in Supply

P_X (₹)	Q_X (Units)
10	30
10	20

FIGURE 8

Decrease in Supply–Backward Shift in Supply Curve

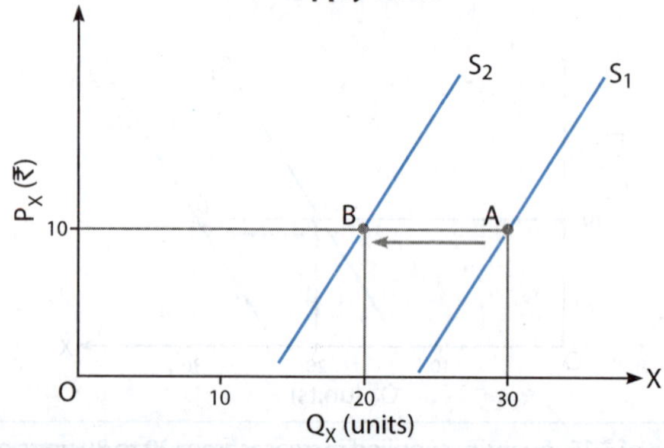

At the existing price of ₹ 10, quantity supplied decreases from 30 to 20 units of the commodity. Accordingly, supply curve shifts backward from S_1 to S_2. The producer shifts from point A on the old supply curve to point B on the new supply curve.

Table 7 shows that initially 30 units of the commodity are supplied at the price of ₹ 10 per unit. Owing to some factors (generally related to increase in the cost of production), firms are now willing to supply only 20 units even when own price of the commodity remains to be ₹ 10 per unit. Diagrammatically, it implies a backward shift in supply curve (or shift to the left) as from S_1 to S_2 in Fig. 8. The producer shifts from point A on the old supply curve to point B on the new supply curve.

Causes of Decrease in Supply

Decrease in supply occurs due to the following reasons:

(i) Use of outdated technology, causing a fall in efficiency and rise in cost of production.

(ii) Increase in factor prices, causing increase in cost of production.

(iii) Increase in price of a competing product. It prompts the producers to restrict their supplies at the prevailing price.

(iv) Decrease in number of firms in the industry. This decreases market supply of the product even when price remains constant.

(v) Low business expectations. It prompts the producers to reduce investment. Accordingly, supply reduces.

(vi) Shift in goal of the firm from sales maximisation to profit maximisation. When the focus is on profit maximisation, firms (in monopoly market) often restrict sale of their product.

(vii) Increase in taxation (like excise duty) or withdrawal of subsidy. It prompts the producers to restrict supply of their product.

How does change in Technology affect Supply Curve of a Firm?

Better technology leads to a fall in the cost of production. Accordingly, producers are willing to supply more at the existing price. This implies a forward shift in supply curve, as in Fig. 9.

FIGURE 9

Technology impacts Supply

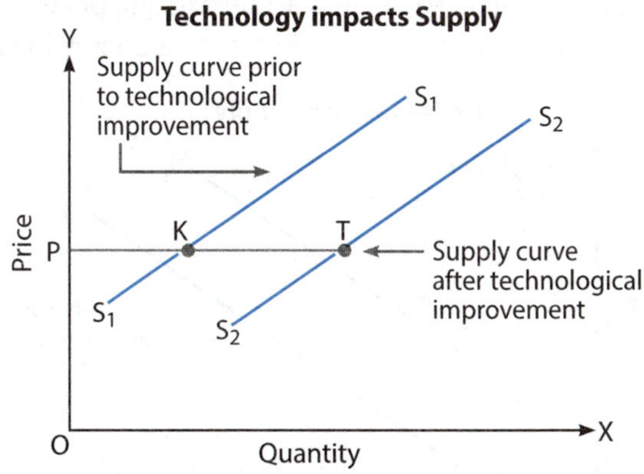

When technology improves, cost of production falls. Accordingly, producers are willing to offer higher supply of a commodity at its existing price. Thus, quantity supplied increases from PK to PT, even when price remains the same. Supply curve shifts to the right from S_1S_1 to S_2S_2.

Initially, PK quantity was supplied at price OP. After technological improvement (and the consequent reduction in cost of production), PT quantity is supplied at the same price. It is a situation of increase in supply.

How does change in Input Price affect Supply Curve?

Input price may increase or decrease. In case of increase in input price, cost of production tends to rise. Accordingly, producers will supply less of the commodity at its existing price. This implies a backward shift in supply curve or decrease in supply. On the other hand, if input price falls, cost of production will decline. Accordingly, producers will supply more of the commodity at its existing price. This implies a forward shift in supply curve or increase in supply.

Fig. 10 illustrates these situations. S_1S_1 is initial supply curve. When input price increases, supply curve shifts backward to S_3S_3, and when input price falls, supply curve shifts forward to S_2S_2.

FIGURE 10

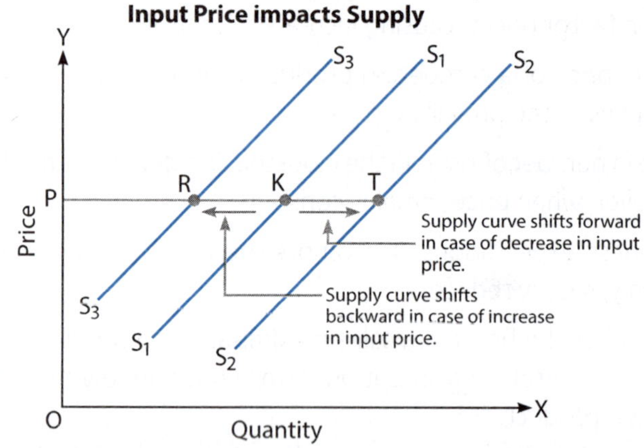

Initially, the producer is at point K. He supplies PK quantity at OP price of the commodity. Decrease in input price cause a forward shift in supply curve. Accordingly, the producer shifts from point K on S_1S_1 to point T on S_2S_2. At the existing price (OP), quantity supplied increases from PK to PT. In case of increase in input price, supply curve shifts from S_1S_1 to S_3S_3. At the existing price (OP), quantity supplied decreases from PK to PR.

Excise Tax and Supply Curve

Excise tax is a tax on the production of goods. It raises the cost of production. Accordingly, a producer is willing to sell less at the existing price. This is a situation of decrease in supply or backward shift in supply curve, as shown in Fig. 11.

FIGURE 11

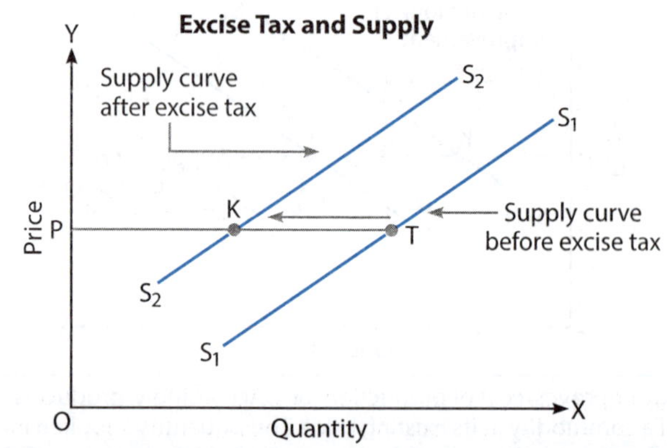

When excise tax is levied, supply curve shifts to the left, from S_1S_1 to S_2S_2. Less quantity is supplied at the existing price of the commodity.

Initially, at OP price, the producer sells PT quantity. After excise tax, he is willing to sell only PK quantity. Supply curve shifts backward from S_1S_1 to S_2S_2.

Subsidy and Supply Curve

Subsidy is offered by the producers to increase production of the commodity, when it is economically not viable for the producers to do so at the existing market price. The resultant loss to the producers (when they are required to produce more at the existing price) is compensated by way of subsidy. Thus, when subsidy is offered, supply curve of the commodity shifts to the right, as in Fig. 12.

FIGURE 12 **Subsidy and Supply**

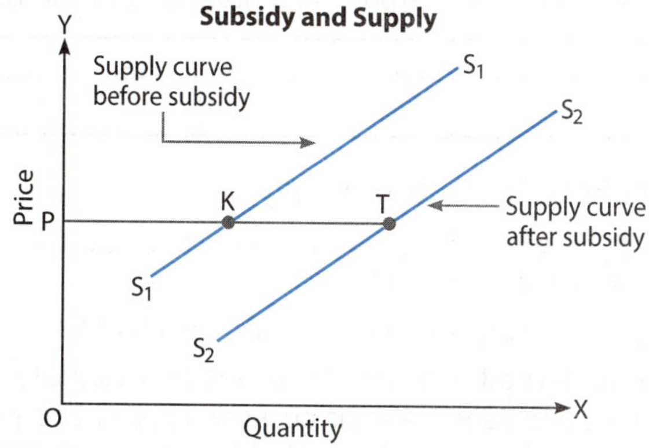

Initially, PK quantity was produced at price OP. Induced by subsidy, quantity supplied increases to PT even when own price of the commodity remains constant.

The figure shows that, initially quantity supplied was PK at OP price of the commodity. After subsidy is offered, quantity supplied increases from PK to PT even when own price of the commodity does not change.

Price of Related Product and Supply Curve

Change in price of a substitute good significantly impacts the supply of a commodity. For example, if the price of tea rises, the firms would be willing to sell less of coffee at its existing price. Implying that the supply curve (of coffee) would shift backward. On the other hand, if price of tea reduces, the producers of coffee would like to sell more of coffee at its existing price. This would lead to a forward shift in supply curve (of coffee). Fig. 13 illustrates these situations.

FIGURE 13 **Price of a Related Product and Supply: Supply of Coffee when there is a change in the Price of Tea**

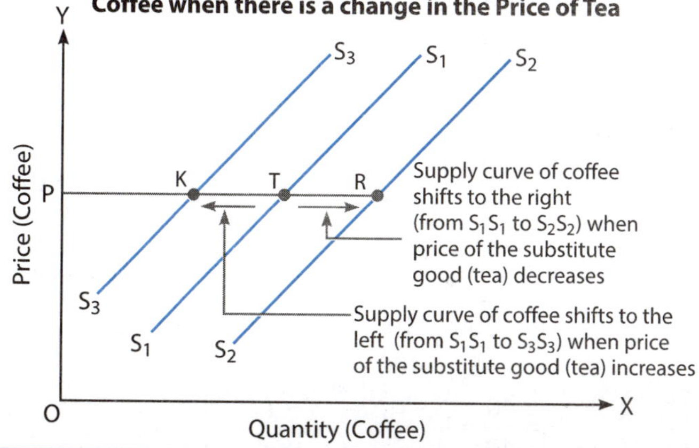

A rise in price of tea leads to a backward shift in supply curve of coffee. Because a rise in the price of tea will shift the buyers from tea to coffee. Taking advantage of this situation, the producers will be willing to sell less of coffee at the existing price. On the other hand, a fall in the price of tea leads to a forward shift in supply curve of coffee. Because a fall in the price of tea might shift the buyers from coffee to tea. Fearing the loss of the market, the producers will be willing to sell more of coffee at its existing price.

7. Price Elasticity of Supply

Price elasticity of supply measures the degree of extension and contraction of supply in response to a given change in own price of the commodity. Law of supply tells us the direction in which supply will change as a result of change in own price of the commodity: a fall in price will lead to contraction of supply and a rise in price will lead to extension of supply. But, if we want to measure the extent of extension and contraction of supply, we have to study the concept of price elasticity of supply.

> Price elasticity of supply measures the degree of extension and contraction of supply in response to a given change in own price of the commodity.

Measurement of Price Elasticity of Supply

There are two well known methods of measuring price elasticity of supply (briefly called elasticity of supply). These are:

(i) Proportionate (or Percentage) Method, and (ii) Geometric Method.

(i) Proportionate Method: According to this method, elasticity of supply (E_S) is the ratio between 'percentage change in quantity supplied' and 'percentage change in price' of the commodity.

$$E_S = \frac{\text{Percentage Change in Quantity Supplied}}{\text{Percentage Change in Price}}$$

Symbolically,

$$E_S = \frac{\frac{\Delta Q}{Q} \times 100}{\frac{\Delta P}{P} \times 100} = \frac{\Delta Q}{\Delta P} \times \frac{P}{Q}$$

Q	: Initial quantity
P	: Initial price
ΔQ	: Change in quantity supplied
ΔP	: Change in price of the commodity

Example:

A producer offers to sell 400 units of a commodity when its price is ₹10 per unit, while only 200 units are offered if the price reduces to ₹5 per unit. Find elasticity of supply.

Solution:

$$E_S = \frac{\Delta Q}{\Delta P} \times \frac{P}{Q}$$

$$= \frac{200}{5} \times \frac{10}{400} = 1$$

Q	: 400
ΔQ	: 200
P	: 10
ΔP	: 5

Alternative Approach:

$$E_S = \frac{\Delta Q}{\Delta P} \times \frac{P}{Q} = \frac{Q_1 - Q}{P_1 - P} \times \frac{P}{Q}$$

$$= \frac{200 - 400}{5 - 10} \times \frac{10}{400}$$

$$= \frac{-200}{-5} \times \frac{10}{400}$$

$$= \frac{40}{40} = 1$$

Q	: Initial quantity
Q_1	: Quantity supplied after change in price
P	: Initial price
P_1	: New price

(ii) Geometric Method: Geometrically, elasticity of supply depends on the 'origin' of the supply curve. Assuming the supply curve to be a straight line and positively sloped (sloping upward), we can specify three possible situations of elasticity of supply as in the following diagrams:

Situation 1: $E_S = 1$, when a Straight Line, Positively Sloped Supply Curve starts from the Point of Origin 'O'

FIGURE 14

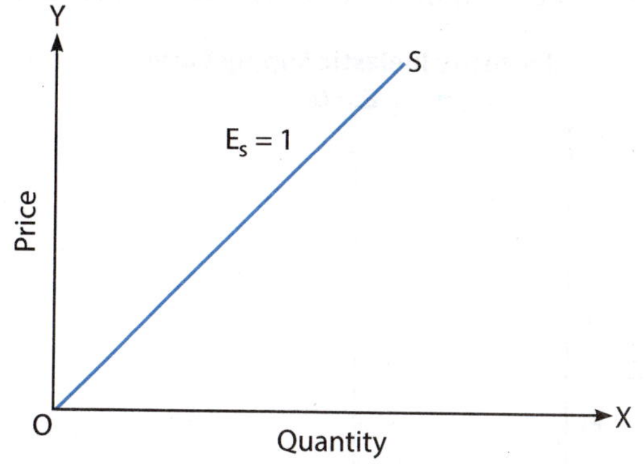

No matter what angle it makes, a straight line (upward sloping) supply curve, shooting from the origin always shows $E_S = 1$ (Refer to Ability Zone for proof).

Situation 2: $E_S > 1$, when a Straight Line, Positively Sloped Supply Curve starts from Y-axis

FIGURE 15

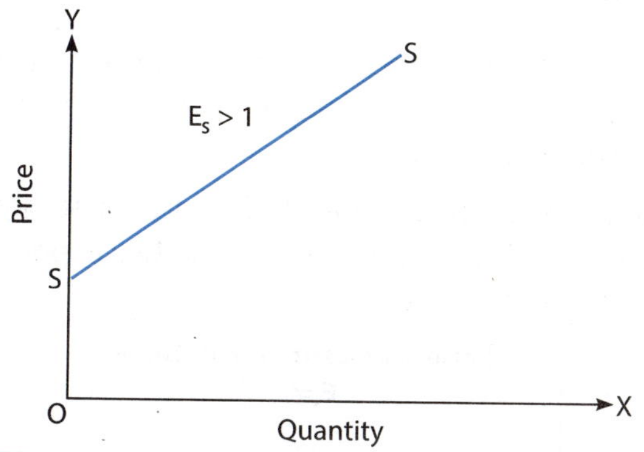

A straight line (upward sloping) supply curve, shooting from Y-axis always shows $E_S > 1$, irrespective of the angle it makes.

Situation 3: $E_S < 1$, when a Straight Line, Positively Sloped Supply Curve starts from X-axis

FIGURE 16

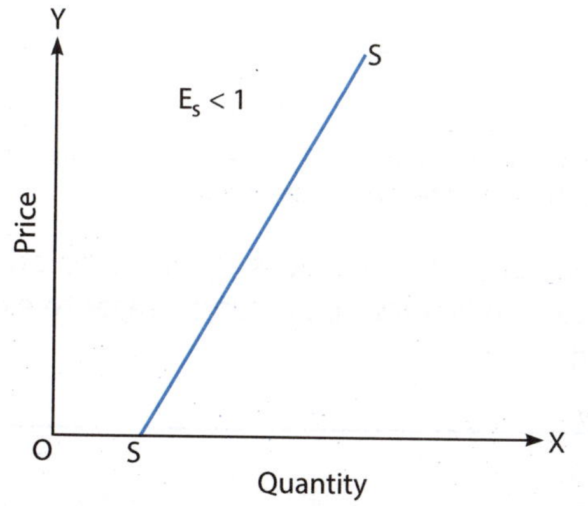

A straight line (upward sloping) supply curve, shooting from X-axis always shows $E_S < 1$, irrespective of the angle it makes.

Two Extreme Situations of E_s

(i) Zero Elasticity of Supply: It refers to a vertical straight line supply curve, showing constant supply, no matter what the price is. Fig. 17 illustrates this situation.

FIGURE 17

Perfectly Inelastic Supply Curve

$E_s = 0$

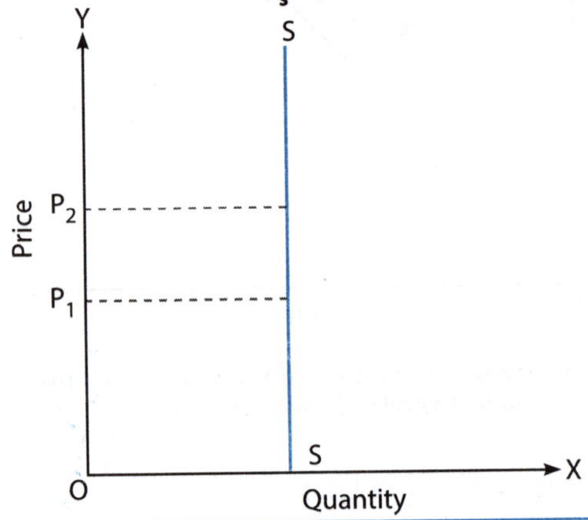

$E_s = 0$, when supply does not at all respond to change in price of the commodity. Supply is constant even at a zero price.

Fig. 17 shows that quantity supplied remains constant at OS, whether price of the commodity is OP_1 or OP_2. Vertical straight line supply curve is also called a perfectly inelastic supply curve.

(ii) Infinite Elasticity of Supply: It refers to a horizontal straight line supply curve, showing infinite supply corresponding to a particular price of the commodity. Fig. 18 illustrates this situation.

FIGURE 18

Perfectly Elastic Supply Curve

$E_s = \infty$

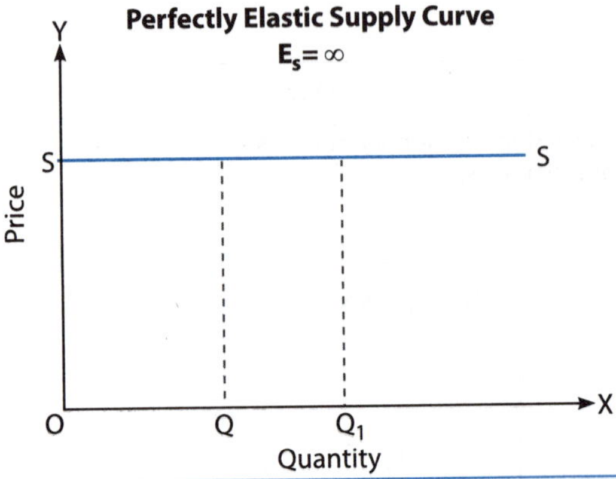

When $E_s = \infty$, even a small change in price will cause an infinite change in quantity. Thus, if price falls below OS, supply of the commodity reduces to zero.

Fig. 18 shows that quantity supplied is infinite when price of the commodity is OS. It reduces to zero (in fact supply curve ceases to exist) even when price is slightly reduced.

Elastic, Inelastic and Unitary Elastic Supply

(i) Supply is said to be elastic when $E_s > 1$.

(ii) Supply is said to be inelastic when $E_s < 1$.

(iii) Supply is unitary elastic when $E_s = 1$.

Factors Affecting Elasticity of Supply

Following factors affect the elasticity of supply of a commodity:

(1) Nature of Inputs used: The elasticity of supply depends on the nature of inputs used for the production of a commodity. If commonly available inputs are used, supply will be elastic. If inputs used are not commonly available, supply will be inelastic.

(2) Natural Constraints: The elasticity of supply is significantly influenced by the natural constraints. If we wish to produce more teak wood, it will take years of plantation before it becomes usable. Supply of teak wood will, therefore, be less elastic.

(3) Risk Taking: The elasticity of supply depends on the willingness of entrepreneurs to take production-related risk. If entrepreneurs are willing to take risk of higher output, the supply will be more elastic. On the other hand, if entrepreneurs are not willing to take risk of higher output, the supply will be inelastic.

(4) Nature of the Commodity: Perishable goods are relatively less elastic in supply than durable goods. Because perishables goods have a shorter shelf-life than the durable goods.

(5) Cost of Production: Elasticity of supply is also influenced by cost of production. Supply will be less elastic in case increase in production causes a substantial increase in the cost of production.

(6) Time Factor: Longer the time period, greater will be the elasticity of supply. Because, over a long period of time, factors are easily available and supply can be easily increased.

(7) Technique of Production: Supply will be less elastic in case production of a commodity involves the use of a complex and expensive technology. Because, change in the level of output becomes difficult.

HOTS

Q.1. What causes a downward movement along a supply curve of a commodity?

Ans. All movements along a supply curve are to be explained with reference to change in own price of the commodity. Downward movement along a supply curve happens when own price of the commodity falls. It is a situation of contraction of supply.

Q.2. The price elasticity of supply of Good-X is one and a half times the price elasticity of supply of Good-Y. 30 per cent fall in the price of X results in 18 per cent fall in its supply. If the supply of Y increases by 25 per cent, calculate the percentage rise in price of Y.

Ans. Given, Fall in price of X = (−) 30 per cent

Fall in supply of X = (−) 18 per cent

Rise in supply of Y = 25 per cent

Price elasticity of supply of Good-X = 1.5 (Price elasticity of supply of Good-Y)

$$\Rightarrow \frac{\text{Percentage fall in supply of X}}{\text{Percentage fall in price of X}} = 1.5\left(\frac{\text{Percentage rise in supply of Y}}{\text{Percentage rise in price of Y}}\right)$$

$$\frac{(-)18}{(-)30} = 1.5\left(\frac{25}{\text{Percentage rise in price of Y}}\right)$$

$$\text{Percentage rise in price of Y} = \frac{1.5 \times 25 \times (-)\,30}{(-)\,18} = 62.5\%$$

∴ Percentage rise in price of Good-Y = 62.5%.

Q.3. Price elasticity of Good-X is one and a half times the price elasticity of Good-Y. S_X rises from 125 units to 175 units due to a 16 per cent rise in P_X. Calculate the percentage fall in S_Y if P_Y reduces from ₹10 to ₹7.

Ans. Percentage change in $S_X = \frac{175 - 125}{125} \times 100 = 40$ per cent

Percentage change in P_X = 16 per cent

Percentage change in $P_Y = \frac{7 - 10}{10} \times 100 = (-)\,30$ per cent

Given, Price elasticity of Good-X $= 1\frac{1}{2}$ (Price elasticity of Good-Y)

$$\left(\frac{\text{Percentage change in } S_X}{\text{Percentage change in } P_X}\right) = 1\frac{1}{2}\left(\frac{\text{Percentage change in } S_Y}{\text{Percentage change in } P_Y}\right)$$

$$\Rightarrow \quad \frac{40}{16} = \frac{3}{2}\left(\frac{\text{Percentage change in } S_Y}{(-)\,30}\right)$$

$$\Rightarrow \quad \text{Percentage change in } S_Y = \frac{40 \times (-)\,30 \times 2}{16 \times 3} = (-)\,50\%$$

$\therefore$ Percentage fall in $S_Y = 50\%$.

POWER POINTS

- **Supply** refers to various quantities of a commodity that the producers wish to sell at different possible prices of the commodity at a point of time.
- **Quantity Supplied** refers to a specific quantity that the producer is willing to sell at a specific price of the commodity.
- **Factors affecting Supply are:**
  (i) Own price of a commodity, (ii) Price of related goods, (iii) Number of firms in the industry, (iv) Goal of the firm, (v) Price of factors of production, (vi) State of technology, (vii) Business expectations, and (viii) Government policy (relating to taxation and subsidies).
- **Law of Supply** states that the higher the price, greater the quantity supplied or lower the price, lesser the quantity supplied of a commodity, other determinants of supply (other than own price of the commodity) remaining constant.
- **Individual Supply Schedule** is a table showing different quantities of a commodity that an individual firm is ready to sell at different prices.
- **Market Supply Schedule** is a table showing different quantities of a commodity that all the firms in a market are willing to sell at different prices of that commodity at a given time.
- **Supply Curve** is a graphic presentation of supply schedule, showing positive relationship between price and quantity supplied of a commodity.
- **Market Supply Curve** is a horizontal summation of the individual supply curves.
- **Movement along a Supply Curve** refers to extension and contraction of supply of a commodity.
- **Extension of Supply** refers to increase in quantity supplied in response to increase in own price of the commodity.
- **Contraction of Supply** refers to decrease in quantity supplied in response to decrease in own price of the commodity.
- **Shift in Supply Curve** shows increase or decrease in supply of a commodity.
- **Increase in Supply** refers to shift in supply curve to the right. It is a situation when the producers are willing to sell more of a commodity at its existing price.
- **Decrease in Supply** refers to shift in supply curve to the left. It is a situation when the producers are willing to sell less of a commodity at its existing price.
- **Elasticity of Supply** measures the degree of extension and contraction of supply in response to a given change in own price of the commodity.
- **Measurement of Elasticity of Supply:** $E_s = \frac{\Delta Q}{\Delta P} \times \frac{P}{Q}$.

- Perfectly Elastic Supply is a situation of an infinite change in quantity supplied due to a very small change in price. Supply curve is a horizontal straight line, shooting from the Y-axis.
- Perfectly Inelastic Supply is a situation when supply remains constant, no matter what the price of the commodity is. Supply curve is a vertical straight line, shooting from the X-axis.
- $E_S = 1$, when a straight line (upward sloping) supply curve shoots from the origin.
- $E_S > 1$, when a straight line (upward sloping) supply curve shoots from the Y-axis.
- $E_S < 1$, when a straight line (upward sloping) supply curve shoots from the X-axis.

EXERCISE

1. Very Short Questions (Remembering & Understanding) (1 mark each)

A. Multiple Choice Questions: Choose the Correct Answer

1. **Which of the following statements is correct?**
   (a) There is difference between supply and stock
   (b) Supply does not depend on government's tax policy
   (c) Stock refers to the quantity which comes to market for sale
   (d) Stock and supply are always equal
2. **Graphical presentation of supply curve of an individual firm in the market is called:**
   (a) producer's demand curve (b) consumer's demand curve
   (c) individual supply curve (d) market supply curve
3. **The entire schedule showing various quantities offered for sale at different possible prices of the commodity is called:**
   (a) quantity supplied (b) supply
   (c) individual supply (d) none of these
4. **According to law of supply:**
   (a) there is positive relation between supply and price
   (b) there is negative relation between supply and price
   (c) there is constant relation between supply and price
   (d) there is no relation between supply and price
5. **Expansion of supply occurs due to change in:**
   (a) goal of the firm (b) own price of the commodity
   (c) number of firms (d) technique of production
6. **The law of supply does not apply to:**
   (a) agricultural products (b) industrial products
   (c) perishable commodities (d) both (a) and (c)
7. **Supply curve shifts forward due to:**
   (a) decrease in factor price (b) increase of firms in the market
   (c) high business expectations (d) all of these
8. **Movement along the supply curve occurs due to:**
   (a) increase in own price of the commodity
   (b) decrease in own price of the commodity
   (c) factors other than own price of the commodity
   (d) both (a) and (b)

9. Increase in quantity supplied due to rise in price is called:
(a) increase in supply (b) decrease in supply
(c) extension of supply (d) none of these

10. When supply falls due to factors other than own price of the commodity, it indicates:
(a) contraction of supply (b) decrease in supply
(c) extension of supply (d) none of these

11. In case of contraction of supply, we move:
(a) to right on the another supply curve (b) from lower point to upper point
(c) from upper point to lower point (d) both (b) and (c)

12. In case of increase in supply, we move:
(a) to right on another supply curve
(b) to left on another supply curve
(c) from upper point to lower point of the supply curve
(d) from lower point to upper point of the supply curve

13. Imposition of a unit tax, shifts the supply curve:
(a) to the right (b) to the left
(c) to the right as well as to the left (d) none of these

14. Subsidy on the production of a commodity causes:
(a) increase in supply (b) decrease in supply
(c) no change in supply (d) both (a) and (b)

15. When supply curve is a vertical straight line, it indicates:
(a) unitary elastic supply (b) perfectly elastic supply
(c) perfectly inelastic supply (d) relatively elastic supply

16. A straight line supply curve passing through the origin forming an angle of 60° indicates:
(a) $E_s = 0$ (b) $E_s = 1$
(c) $E_s > 1$ (d) $E_s < 1$

17. An upward sloping straight line supply curve shooting from the X-axis indicates that:
(a) elasticity of supply is equal to zero (b) elasticity of supply is equal to one
(c) elasticity of supply is greater than one (d) elasticity of supply is less than one

18. When supply curve is parallel to X-axis, elasticity of supply is:
(a) zero (b) infinity
(c) unity (d) negative

19. Supply is more elastic in case of:
(a) very short period (b) short period
(c) long period (d) both (b) and (c)

20. The supply of durable goods is usually:
(a) more elastic (b) less elastic
(c) perfectly elastic (d) perfectly inelastic

21. In case of $E_s > 1$, the supply curve is:
(a) a horizontal straight line parallel to X-axis (b) a vertical straight line parallel to Y-axis
(c) a straight line starting from Y-axis (d) a straight line starting from X-axis

22. When market supply (assuming only three sellers in the market) is 120 units, and sum total of individual supply of two sellers is 76 units, the supply of third individual seller will be:
(a) 44 units (b) 196 units
(c) 50 units (d) 200 units

23. **If 18% fall in price of the commodity causes 27% decrease in its supply, elasticity of supply will be:**

(a) 1.5 (b) 0.5

(c) 0.67 (d) 2.5

24. **When 15% increase in price of the commodity causes 10% increase in the quantity supplied, then elasticity of supply is:**

(a) elastic (b) inelastic

(c) perfectly elastic (d) perfectly inelastic

25. **If $E_s = 0.6$, and the percentage change in price = 5, then percentage change in quantity supplied is:**

(a) 8.33 (b) 4.4

(c) 5.6 (d) 3

Answers

1. (a) **2.** (c) **3.** (b) **4.** (a) **5.** (b) **6.** (d) **7.** (d) **8.** (d) **9.** (c) **10.** (b) **11.** (c) **12.** (a) **13.** (b) **14.** (a) **15.** (c) **16.** (b) **17.** (d) **18.** (b) **19.** (c) **20.** (a) **21.** (c) **22.** (a) **23.** (a) **24.** (b) **25.** (d)

B. Information & Concept-based Questions

1. **What is meant by the term supply?**

Ans. Supply of a commodity refers to a schedule showing different quantities of a commodity that the producer is willing to sell corresponding to different possible prices of the commodity at a point of time.

2. **What is meant by supply schedule?**

Ans. Supply schedule is a table showing various quantities of a commodity offered for sale corresponding to different possible prices at a point of time.

3. **Define supply curve.**

Ans. Supply curve is a graphic presentation of supply schedule, indicating positive relationship between price of a commodity and its quantity supplied.

4. **State the law of supply.**

Ans. The law of supply states that higher the price, greater the quantity supplied; the lower the price, the smaller the quantity supplied, other determinants of supply (other than own price of the commodity) remaining constant.

5. **What causes a movement along a supply curve of a good?**

Ans. Change in own price of a good causes a movement along a supply curve of a good.

6. **What is meant by extension of supply?**

Ans. When a rise in own price of a commodity leads to increase in quantity supplied of a commodity, it is called expansion/extension of supply.

7. **What is meant by contraction of supply?**

Ans. When a fall in own price of a commodity leads to decrease in quantity supplied of a commodity, it is called contraction of supply.

8. **Define increase in supply.**

Ans. When the quantity supplied increases due to factors other than own price of the concerned commodity, it is a situation of increase in supply.

9. **Define decrease in supply.**

Ans. When the quantity supplied decreases due to factors other than own price of the concerned commodity, it is a situation of decrease in supply.

10. **What is meant by price elasticity of supply?**

Ans. Price elasticity of supply is a percentage change in quantity supplied in response to a percentage change in price of the commodity.

11. When is the supply of a commodity called 'elastic'?

Ans. When percentage change in quantity supplied is greater than the percentage change in own price of commodity, supply is said to be elastic.

12. When does supply become more elastic?

Ans. Supply becomes more elastic when $E_s > 1$.

13. When does supply become less elastic?

Ans. Supply becomes less elastic or inelastic when $E_s < 1$.

14. What is meant by zero elastic supply?

Ans. When quantity supplied does not respond to any change in price, it is called zero elastic supply.

15. Draw a supply curve with unitary elasticity.

Ans. See Fig. 14 of this chapter.

16. What change in supply takes place when price remains constant at ₹10 per unit, the supply increases from 25 units to 40 units?

Ans. Increase in supply.

17. Price elasticity of supply of a good is 0.8. Is the supply 'elastic' or 'inelastic', and why?

Ans. Supply is inelastic because $E_s < 1$.

2. Reason-based Questions (Comprehension of the Subject-matter)

Read the following statements carefully. Write 'True' or 'False' with a reason.

1. Supply may remain constant even when quantity supplied changes.

Ans. True. Because, supply refers to the entire supply schedule (or supply curve) while quantity supplied refers to a specific point on the supply curve which changes with change in own price of the commodity.

2. Supply never changes unless price changes.

Ans. False. Supply can change due to factors other than own price of the concerned commodity such as technology and input prices.

3. A producer supplies more of a commodity only at a higher price.

Ans. True. More of a commodity is offered at a higher price because other things remaining constant, higher price implies higher profit. Accordingly, the producer is induced to produce more and sell more.

4. Increase in price always causes increase in sales of a commodity.

Ans. False. Increase in price only means increase in quantity supplied, only when other determinants of supply (other than price) are constant.

5. Increase in supply means more is sold because market prices tend to increase.

Ans. False. Increase in supply means more is sold at a given price.

6. Extension and contraction of supply are related to factors other than own price of the concerned commodity.

Ans. False. Extension and contraction of supply are related to own price of the concerned commodity, other factors remaining constant.

7. Supply increases in response to increase in price of the concerned commodity.

Ans. False. Supply expands in response to increase in price of the concerned commodity. It increases in response to factors other than own price of the concerned commodity.

8. Contraction of supply causes a shift in supply curve.

Ans. False. Contraction of supply causes a downward movement along a supply curve.

9. Price elasticity of supply measures the change in quantity supplied in response to a change in own price of the commodity.

Ans. True. Price elasticity of supply $= \dfrac{\text{Percentage change in quantity supplied}}{\text{Percentage change in price}}$.

10. If a straight line upward sloping supply curve shoots from the origin, elasticity of supply is always equal to one.

Ans. True. When a straight line upward sloping supply curve passes through the origin (no matter what the angle it forms), the elasticity of supply is equal to one.

11. If elasticity of supply = 0, supply curve becomes a horizontal straight line.

Ans. False. If elasticity of supply = 0, supply curve becomes a vertical straight line parallel to Y-axis.

12. At a point of intersection of two supply curves, flatter curve shows higher elasticity of supply.

Ans. True. Flatter curve shows higher elasticity of supply at the point of intersection of two supply curves. Because, corresponding to a given change in price (at the point of intersection) flatter curve shows greater change in quantity.

13. $E_S = 1$ only if supply curve forms a $\angle 45°$ at the origin. Is it true?

Ans. False. $E_S = 1$ for all straight line supply curves shooting from origin.

14. If a straight line upward sloping supply curve shoots from the Y-axis, elasticity of supply < 1.

Ans. False. When a straight line upward sloping supply curve shoots from the Y-axis, elasticity of supply (E_s) > 1.

15. If a straight line upward sloping supply curve shoots from the X-axis, elasticity of supply > 1.

Ans. False. When a straight line upward sloping supply curve shoots from the X-axis, elasticity of supply (E_s) < 1.

16. When a firm is using some rigid technology, its E_s tends to be high.

Ans. False. When a firm is using rigid technology, E_s tends to be low. Because, possibilities of variations in output are reduced.

17. In the long period, elasticity of supply tends to be lower than in the short period.

Ans. False. Longer the time period, greater will be the elasticity of supply. Because, over a long period of time, more and more factors are easily available and their input can be changed to increase (or decrease) output of the commodity.

3. HOTS & Applications

1. Firm's supply curve shows its supply function. Comment.

Ans. Yes. Firm's supply curve (showing the relation between quantity sold of a commodity and its price) is its supply function on the assumption that other determinants of supply (other than own price of the commodity) remain constant.

2. How would you explain a situation when supply of a commodity increases without any increase in price of the commodity?

Ans. When supply of a commodity increases without any increase in price of the commodity, it is known as the situation of increase in supply. Increase in supply occurs when quantity supplied increases due to determinants other than own price of the concerned commodity.

3. If there is change in any other determinant of supply (other than own price of the concerned commodity), the supply curve must shift to the right or left. Do you agree? Give reason.

Ans. Yes. Shift in the supply curve occurs due to factors other than own price of the concerned commodity. When other factors are conducive to increase in supply, the supply curve shifts to the right. When the other factors prompt a cut in supply, the supply curve shifts to the left.

4. Introduction of new technology increases marginal product. How would it affect supply curve of a firm?

Ans. Introduction of new technology increases MP (marginal product). It implies a fall in MC (marginal cost). Accordingly, supply curve of a firm shifts to the right which shows that the producers are now willing to offer more quantity of a commodity at its existing price.

5. Will the seller always be ready to sell more of a commodity at a higher price in the market?

Ans. A seller generally tends to sell more of a commodity at a higher price because higher price implies higher profit. Accordingly, the seller is induced to produce more and sell more. But, it is not always true. In a situation, when he expects a rise in the price of the commodity in the near future, he may decide to hold the stock for future sale. Accordingly, his current supply will be reduced. Thus, we state that the positive relation between price and quantity supplied of a commodity holds good only on the assumption that other determinants of supply (other than own price of the commodity) do not change.

6. Supply is more responsive to price in the long period compared to short period. Comment.

Ans. Yes. In long period, all factors are variable factors, while in the short period some factors are fixed and some are variable. Accordingly, while in the long period supply can be increased by employing more of all the factors, in the short period supply can be increased by employing more of the variable factors only.

Thus, supply can be increased to a much larger extent in the long period compared to short period. Therefore, it is more responsive to price in the long period compared to the short period.

7. When price of a good increases from ₹ 15 per unit to ₹ 19 per unit, its quantity supplied increases from 75 units to 95 units. Calculate the price elasticity of supply.

Ans. Given, P = ₹ 15; P_1 = ₹ 19; $\Delta P = P_1 - P$ = ₹ 19 – ₹ 15 = ₹ 4

$Q = 75$ units; $Q_1 = 95$ units; $\Delta Q = Q_1 - Q = (95 - 75)$ units = 20 units

$$E_s = \frac{P}{Q} \times \frac{\Delta Q}{\Delta P}$$

$$E_s = \frac{15}{75} \times \frac{20}{4}$$

$$E_s = 1$$

Price elasticity of supply = 1 (one).

8. The price elasticity of supply is 4. When its price falls from ₹ 10 to ₹ 8 per unit, its quantity supplied falls by 400 units. Calculate the new quantity at the reduced price.

Ans. Given, P = ₹ 10; P_1 = ₹ 8; $\Delta P = P_1 - P$ = ₹ 8 – ₹ 10 = (–) ₹ 2

ΔQ = (–) 400 units

$E_s = 4$

$$E_s = \frac{P}{Q} \times \frac{\Delta Q}{\Delta P}$$

$$4 = \frac{10}{Q} \times \frac{-400}{-2}$$

$$4 = \frac{2{,}000}{Q}$$

$$\Rightarrow \quad Q = 500$$

New quantity = 500 units – 400 units = 100 units.

9. The quantity supplied of a commodity at a price of ₹ 8 per unit is 50 units. Its price elasticity of supply is 1.6. Calculate the price at which its quantity supplied will be 35 units.

Ans. Given, Q = 50 units; Q_1 = 35 units; $\Delta Q = Q_1 - Q$ = (35 – 50) units = (–) 15 units

P = ₹ 8; $E_s = 1.6$

$$\text{Price elasticity of supply } (E_s) = \frac{P}{Q} \times \frac{\Delta Q}{\Delta P}$$

$$1.6 = \frac{8}{50} \times \frac{-15}{\Delta P}$$

$$1.6 = \frac{-120}{50\Delta P}$$

$$\Delta P = \frac{-120}{50 \times 1.6} = -1.5$$

New price = ₹ 8 – ₹ 1.5 = ₹ 6.5.

10. A 10 per cent rise in the price of a commodity raises its supply from 200 units to 225 units. Calculate its price elasticity of supply.

Ans. Given, percentage change in price = 10 per cent

$Q = 200$ units; $Q_1 = 225$ units; $\Delta Q = Q_1 - Q = (225 - 200)$ units = 25 units

$$\text{Percentage change in quantity supplied} = \frac{\Delta Q}{Q} \times 100$$

$$= \frac{25}{200} \times 100 = 12.5 \text{ per cent}$$

$$\text{Price elasticity of supply } (E_s) = \frac{\text{Percentage change in quantity supplied}}{\text{Percentage change in price}}$$

$$= \frac{12.5\%}{10\%} = 1.25$$

Price elasticity of supply = 1.25.

11. **Total revenue of a firm rises from ₹ 50 to ₹ 100 when the price of its product rises from ₹ 5 per unit to ₹ 10 per unit. Calculate the price elasticity of supply.**

Ans. Given, P = ₹ 5; P_1 = ₹ 10; ΔP = P_1 – P = ₹ 10 – ₹ 5 = ₹ 5

When price = ₹ 5, total revenue (P × Q) = ₹ 50

$$\text{Quantity supplied (Q)} = \frac{50}{5} = 10 \text{ units}$$

When price = ₹10, total revenue ($P_1 \times Q_1$) = ₹100

$$\text{New quantity supplied } (Q_1) = \frac{100}{10} = 10 \text{ units}$$

Q = 10 units; Q_1= 10 units; ΔQ = Q_1 – Q = (10 – 10) units = 0 unit

$$\text{Price elasticity of supply } (E_s) = \frac{P}{Q} \times \frac{\Delta Q}{\Delta P}$$

$$= \frac{5}{10} \times \frac{0}{5} = 0$$

Price elasticity of supply = 0 (zero).

12. **A fruit seller sells 56 kg per day when price of apples is ₹ 7 per kg. When price rises to ₹ 8 per kg, how much quantity of the apples will the seller sell when elasticity of supply is unitary in this case?**

Ans. Suppose the seller supplies X kg.

Here, P = ₹ 7; P_1 = ₹ 8; ΔP = P_1 – P = ₹ 8 – ₹ 7 = ₹ 1

Q = 56 kg; Q_1 = X kg; ΔQ = Q_1 – Q = (X – 56) kg

$E_s = 1$

$$\text{Elasticity of supply } (E_s) = \frac{P}{Q} \times \frac{\Delta Q}{\Delta P}$$

$$1 = \frac{7}{56} \times \frac{(X-56)}{1}$$

$$1 = \frac{X-56}{8}$$

$$X - 56 = 8$$

$$X = 8 + 56 = 64$$

New quantity supplied = 64 kg.

13. **Price elasticity of supply of Good-Y is three-fourth the price elasticity of supply of Good-X. The price of X rises from ₹ 10 to ₹ 11.50 per unit and its quantity supplied increases by 18 per cent. If price of Y falls from ₹ 11 to ₹ 9.90, find the percentage fall in its supply.**

Ans.

$$\text{Percentage change in price of X} = \frac{11.50 - 10}{10} \times 100$$

$$= \frac{1.5}{10} \times 100 = 15 \text{ per cent}$$

Percentage change in supply of X = 18 per cent

$$\text{Percentage change in price of Y} = \frac{9.90 - 11}{11} \times 100$$

$$= \frac{-1.1}{11} \times 100 = (-)\ 10 \text{ per cent}$$

Percentage change in supply of Y = ?

Given,

$$\text{Price elasticity of supply of Good-Y} = \frac{3}{4}(\text{Price elasticity of supply of Good-X})$$

$$\frac{\text{Percentage change in supply of Y}}{\text{Percentage change in price of Y}} = \frac{3}{4}\left(\frac{\text{Percentage change in supply of X}}{\text{Percentage change in price of X}}\right)$$

$$\Rightarrow \frac{\text{Percentage change in supply of Y}}{(-)10} = \frac{3}{4}\left(\frac{18}{15}\right)$$

$$\Rightarrow \text{Percentage change in supply of Y} = \frac{3 \times 18 \times (-)10}{4 \times 15}$$

$$= (-)\ 9 \text{ per cent}$$

Percentage fall in supply of Y = 9%.

14. The following headline appeared in the *Economic Times* on 26th December, 2014:

"Import duty on crude & refined edible oil up by 5%."

Use a diagram and economic theory to analyse the impact of the statement on the supply of crude and refined edible oil in the domestic market.

Ans. When import duty on crude and refined edible oil is up by 5% (other things remaining constant), it causes a rise in the cost of imports. Accordingly, producers will supply less of crude and refined edible oil at the existing price, or they will sell the same quantity only at a higher price. This implies a backward shift in supply curve or decrease in supply as in Fig. 19. S_1S_1 is the initial supply curve. When government increases import duty, supply curve shifts to the left from S_1S_1 to S_2S_2.

FIGURE 19

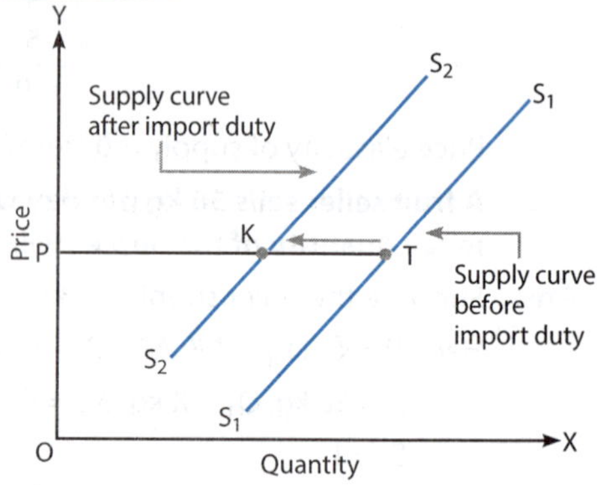

4. Evaluation (Value-based Questions)

1. Identify two such situations when elasticity of supply is low even when there is a substantial rise in price due to rise in demand for a commodity.

Ans. (i) When existing stocks of the producers/suppliers are low, and

(ii) When owing to non-availability of factor and non-factor inputs, it is difficult to increase output in a given time period.

2. Owing to political considerations, Russia has banned the import of seafood from the European Countries. How would analyse the impact of this decision (i) on the export of seafood from the Indian market, and (ii) on the domestic supplies of seafood in India?

Ans. (i) If Russia has banned the import of seafood from the European Countries, it generates an opportunity for the Indian exporters to send supplies of seafood to the Russian market. India can earn foreign exchange which it badly needs to import military hardware from Russia.

(ii) If seafood is exported to Russia, domestic supplies would definitely be reduced in India. Accordingly, price of seafood for the domestic consumers will rise. In other words, supply curve of seafood in the Indian domestic market will shift to the left.

5. CBSE Questions—Past 4 years (With Answers or Reference to the Text for Answers)

1. Explain how changes in prices of other products influence the supply of a given product. *[CBSE Delhi 2012]*
   [Page 273]
2. Explain how changes in prices of inputs influence the supply of a product. *[CBSE (AI) 2012]*
   [Page 272]
3. Explain the distinction between "change in quantity supplied" and "change in supply". Use diagram.

   Or *[CBSE (AI) 2012]*

   Explain the distinction between "movement along the supply curve" and "shift of supply curve". Use diagrams.
   [Page 267–271] *[CBSE (F) 2013]*
4. Draw supply curves showing price elasticity of supply equal to (i) zero, (ii) one, and (iii) infinity throughout.
   [Page 275, 276] *[CBSE (F) 2012]*
5. How does the change in tax on a product influence the supply of that product? Explain. *[CBSE (F) 2012]*

   Or

   How does change in per unit tax influence the supply of a good by a firm? Explain. *[CBSE (F) 2014]*

   Or

   What is 'change in supply'? Explain the effect of tax imposed on a good on the supply of the good.
   [Page 272] *[CBSE (F) 2015]*
6. When the price of a good rises from ₹ 20 per unit to ₹ 30 per unit, the revenue of the firm producing this good rises from ₹ 100 to ₹ 300. Calculate the price elasticity of supply. *[CBSE Delhi 2013]*
   [Page 396]
7. A firm's revenue rises from ₹ 400 to ₹ 500 when the price of its product rises from ₹ 20 per unit to ₹ 25 per unit. Calculate the price elasticity of supply. *[CBSE Delhi 2013]*
   [Page 397]
8. The price elasticity of supply of a good is 0.8. Its price rises by 50 per cent. Calculate the percentage increase in its supply. *[CBSE Delhi 2013]*
   [Page 397]
9. Give the meaning of market supply. *[CBSE (AI) 2013]*

   Or

   Define market supply. *[CBSE (F) 2013]*

   Or

   What is market supply of a product? *[CBSE (AI) 2014]*
   [Page 263]
10. Give one reason for an "increase" in supply of a commodity. *[CBSE (AI) 2013]*
    [Page 270]
11. Give one reason for "decrease" in supply of a commodity. *[CBSE (AI) 2013]*
    [Page 271]
12. A firm supplies 10 units of a good at a price of ₹ 5 per unit. Price elasticity of supply is 1.25. What quantity will the firm supply at a price of ₹ 7 per unit? *[CBSE (AI) 2013]*
    [Page 397]
13. The price elasticity of supply of a commodity is 2.0. A firm supplies 200 units of it at a price of ₹ 8 per unit. At what price will it supply 250 units? *[CBSE (AI) 2013]*
    [Page 397]
14. A 15 per cent rise in the price of a commodity raises its supply from 300 units to 345 units. Calculate its price elasticity of supply. *[CBSE (AI) 2013]*
    [Page 398]
15. When is supply of a good said to be inelastic? *[CBSE (F) 2013]*
    [Page 276]

16. Explain the distinction between "decrease in supply" and "contraction in supply". Use diagrams.
[Page 268–271] *[CBSE (F) 2013]*

17. Total revenue of a firm rises from ₹ 400 to ₹ 500 when the price of its product rises from ₹ 8 per unit to ₹ 10 per unit. Calculate the price elasticity of supply. *[CBSE (F) 2013]*
[Page 398]

18. A fall in the price of a firm's product results in a fall in its supply by 40 per cent. Its price elasticity of supply is 1.6. Calculate the percentage fall in its price. *[CBSE (F) 2013]*
[Page 398]

19. Price elasticity of supply of a good is 2. By what percentage should its price rise so that its supply rises by 30 per cent? *[CBSE (F) 2013]*
[Page 398]

20. Explain how technological progress is a determinant of supply of a good by a firm. *[CBSE (AI) 2014]*
[Page 265, 271]

21. Explain how input prices are a determinant of supply of a good by a firm. *[CBSE (AI) 2014]*
[Page 265, 272]

22. Define supply. *[CBSE (F) 2014]*
[Page 261]

23. How does subsidy influence the supply of a good by a firm? Explain. *[CBSE (F) 2014]*
[Page 273]

24. The measure of price elasticity of demand of a normal good carries minus sign while price elasticity of supply carries plus sign. Explain why. *[CBSE Delhi 2015]*
[Because (i) price and quantity demanded of a commodity are negatively related, and (ii) price and quantity supplied of a commodity are positively related.]

25. Explain the significance of 'minus sign' attached to the measure of price elasticity of demand in case of a normal good, as compared to the 'plus sign' attached to the measure of price elasticity of supply. *[CBSE (AI) 2015]*

Or

Why is minus sign attached to the measure of price elasticity of demand of a normal good in comparison to the plus sign attached to the measure of price elasticity of supply? Explain. *[CBSE (F) 2015]*
[Similar explanation as to Q. 24]

26. What is supply? Explain the effect of technological progress on supply of a good. *[CBSE (F) 2015]*
[Page 261, 271]

6. NCERT Questions (With Hints to Answers)

1. How does technological progress affect the supply curve of a firm?
[**Hint:** A cost saving technological progress will reduce the marginal cost of production. So the marginal cost curve shifts downward. It means supply curve shifts forward, signifying increase in supply. See Fig. 9 of this chapter.]

2. How does the imposition of a unit tax affect the supply curve of a firm?
[**Hint:** Imposition of a unit tax shifts the marginal cost curve of the firm upward. Accordingly, supply curve shifts to the left implying that less would be supplied at the same price. See Fig. 11 of this chapter.]

3. How does an increase in the price of an input affect the supply curve of a firm?
[**Hint:** Increase in input price shifts the marginal cost curve of the firm upward. Accordingly, supply curve shifts upward or to the left implying less supply at the same price. See Fig. 10 of this chapter.]

4. How does an increase in the number of firms in a market affect the market supply curve?
[**Hint:** When number of firms increases in the market, the market supply curve shifts to the right.]

5. What does the price elasticity of supply mean? How do we measure it?

[**Hint:** Price elasticity of supply is defined as the percentage change in quantity supplied caused by a given percentage change in own price of the commodity. It is measured as the ratio between percentage change in quantity supplied and percentage change in price of the commodity.]

6. What is the supply curve of a firm in the short run?

[**Hint:** The rising segment of firm's MC curve (starting from the shut-down point, when price = average variable cost) represents the firm's supply curve in the short run. Check Ability Zone for details.]

7. What is the supply curve of a firm in the long run?

[**Hint:** The rising segment of the firm's MC curve (starting from the break-even point, when price = average cost) represents the firm's supply curve in the long run. Check Ability Zone for details.]

8. Consider a market with two firms. The following table shows the supply schedules of the two firms: the SS_1 column gives the supply schedule of firm 1 and the SS_2 column gives the supply schedule of firm 2. Compute the market supply schedule.

Price (₹)	SS_1 (Units)	SS_2 (Units)
0	0	0
1	0	0
2	0	0
3	1	1
4	2	2
5	3	3
6	4	4

[**Hint:**

Market Supply Schedule

Price (₹)	SS_1 (Units)	SS_2 (Units)	Market Supply (= $SS_1 + SS_2$) (Units)
0	0	0	0
1	0	0	0
2	0	0	0
3	1	1	2
4	2	2	4
5	3	3	6
6	4	4	8

9. Consider a market with two firms. In the following table, columns labeled as SS_1 and SS_2 give the supply schedules of firm 1 and firm 2 respectively. Compute the market supply schedule.

Price (₹)	SS_1 (kg)	SS_2 (kg)
0	0	0
1	0	0
2	0	0
3	1	0
4	2	0.5
5	3	1
6	4	1.5
7	5	2
8	6	2.5

[**Hint:** **Market Supply Schedule**

Price (₹)	SS_1 (Units)	SS_2 (Units)	Market Supply (= SS_1+ SS_2) (kg)
0	0	0	0
1	0	0	0
2	0	0	0
3	1	0	1
4	2	0.5	2.5
5	3	1	4
6	4	1.5	5.5
7	5	2	7
8	6	2.5	8.5

10. There are three identical firms in a market. The following table shows the supply schedule of firm 1. Compute the market supply schedule.

Price	0	1	2	3	4	5	6	7	8
SS_1 (Units)	0	0	2	4	6	8	10	12	14

[**Hint:**

Price	SS_1 (Units)	SS_2 (Units)	SS_3 (Units)	Market Supply (= SS_1 + SS_2 +SS_3) (Units)
0	0	0	0	0
1	0	0	0	0
2	2	2	2	6
3	4	4	4	12
4	6	6	6	18
5	8	8	8	24
6	10	10	10	30
7	12	12	12	36
8	14	14	14	42

11. A firm earns a revenue of ₹ 50 when the market price of a good is ₹ 10. The market price increases to ₹ 15 and the firm now earns a revenue of ₹ 150. What is the price elasticity of the firm's supply curve?

[**Hint:** When price (P) = ₹ 10; total revenue (P × Q) = ₹ 50

∴ Quantity supplied (Q) $= \frac{50}{10} = 5$ units

When price (P_1) = ₹ 15; total revenue ($P_1 \times Q_1$) = ₹ 150

∴ New quantity supplied (Q_1) $= \frac{150}{15} = 10$ units

P = ₹ 10; P_1 = ₹ 15; $\Delta P = P_1 - P$ = ₹ 15 – ₹ 10 = ₹ 5

$Q = 5$ units; $Q_1 = 10$ units; $\Delta Q = Q_1 - Q = (10 - 5)$ units = 5 units

$$\text{Price elasticity of supply } (E_s) = \frac{P}{Q} \times \frac{\Delta Q}{\Delta P} = \frac{10}{5} \times \frac{5}{5} = 2.]$$

12. The market price of a good changes from ₹ 5 to ₹ 20. As a result, the quantity supplied by a firm increases by 15 units. The price elasticity of the firm's supply curve is 0.5. Find the initial and final output levels of the firm.

[**Hint:** Let the firm initially supply X units.

P = ₹ 5; P_1 = ₹ 20; $\Delta P = P_1 - P$ = ₹ 20 – ₹ 5 = ₹ 15

Q = X units; Q_1 = (X +15) units; ΔQ = 15 units

$E_s = 0.5$

$$E_s = \frac{P}{Q} \times \frac{\Delta Q}{\Delta P} = \frac{5}{X} \times \frac{15}{15}$$

$$\Rightarrow \quad 0.5 = \frac{5}{X} \quad \Rightarrow \quad X = \frac{5}{0.5} = 10$$

Thus, $Q = 10$ units

$Q_1 = X + 15 = 10 + 15 = 25$ units.]

13. At the market price of ₹ 10, a firm supplies 4 units of output. The market price increases to ₹ 30. The price elasticity of the firm's supply is 1.25. What quantity will the firm supply at the new price?

[**Hint:** Let the firm supply X units at the new price.

$E_s = 1.25$

$P = ₹\ 10;\ P_1 = ₹\ 30;\ \Delta P = P_1 - P = ₹\ 30 - ₹\ 10 = ₹\ 20$

$Q = 4$ units; $Q_1 = X$ units; $\Delta Q = Q_1 - Q = (X - 4)$ units

$$E_s = \frac{P}{Q} \times \frac{\Delta Q}{\Delta P} = \frac{10}{4} \times \frac{X-4}{20}$$

$$\Rightarrow \quad 1.25 = \frac{X-4}{8} \quad \Rightarrow \quad X - 4 = 10$$

$$\Rightarrow \quad X = 10 + 4 = 14 \text{ units.]}$$

7. Miscellaneous Questions and Reference to the Text for Answers

A. Questions of 3 & 4 marks each

1. Explain the concept of supply with the help of a table and figure.
   [Page 261–263]
2. List any three determinants of supply of a commodity.
   [Page 265]
3. Explain the law of supply with the help of an imaginary supply curve.
   [Page 266, 267]
4. Distinguish between 'change in supply' and 'change in quantity supplied' of a commodity. Use diagrams.

   Or

   Distinguish between movement along the supply curve and shift in supply curve with the help of suitable figures.
   [Page 267–271]
5. State the concepts of extension and contraction of supply with the help of figures.
   [Page 267–269]
6. State the concepts of increase and decrease in supply with the help of figures.
   [Page 269–271]
7. What is meant by elasticity of supply? State the formula for measuring it.
   [Page 274]
8. Define price elasticity of supply. How is it measured by geometric method? (In case of a straight line supply curve.)

   Or

   Explain the geometric method of measuring price elasticity of supply. Use diagram.
   [Page 274, 275]
9. What are the different types of elasticity of supply?
   [Page 275, 276]
10. State the factors which influence elasticity of supply.
    [Page 277]

11. Draw straight line supply curves with price elasticity of supply equal to (i) one, (ii) less than one, (iii) more than one, (iv) infinity, and (v) zero.
[Page 275, 276]
12. State the law of supply and the assumption behind it.
[Page 266, 267]
13. Explain the effect of change in technology on the supply of a good.
[Page 271]
14. Explain the effect of rise in input prices on the supply of a good.
[Page 272]
15. Government imposes a tax on production of a good. Explain its effect on supply of that good.
[Page 272]
16. Explain the effect of subsidy on the supply of a good.
[Page 273]
17. How does change in the prices of other commodities affect the supply of a good?
[Page 273]

B. Questions of 6 marks each

1. What do you mean by the term supply? Discuss the law of supply with the help of a table and diagram.
[Page 261, 266, 267]
2. What is meant by supply? Which factors do influence supply?
[Page 261, 265]
3. Distinguish between extension of supply and increase in supply with the help of diagrams.
[Page 268–270]
4. Define price elasticity of supply. Briefly explain the methods of measuring it.
[Page 274, 275]
5. Define elasticity of supply. On the basis of the value of coefficient of elasticity of supply, how many types of situations can you imagine? Represent those situations diagrammatically.
[Page 274–276]
6. Define price elasticity of supply. Draw a supply curve for each of the following situations of elasticity of supply:
(i) Elasticity of Supply > 1, (ii) Elasticity of Supply < 1,
(iii) Elasticity of Supply = 1.
[Page 275]

DOs and DON'Ts

1. Remember that it is totally illogical to say that a straight line upward sloping supply curve shooting from the origin, should form a 45° angle when $E_s = 1$. The fact is that $E_s = 1$: (i) when an upward sloping supply curve is a straight line, and (ii) when it shoots from the origin. **It does not matter what angle it forms while shooting from the origin**. See Ability Zone for a proof.
2. It is important to understand the difference between stock of a commodity and supply of a commodity. Stock refers to the total quantity of a commodity available for sale at a point of time. Supply refers to the total quantity of a commodity which the producer is ready to sell against the given price of a commodity. If the prevailing price is low, the producer may not be ready to sell any quantity of the available stock. To the contrary, if the producer expects a substantial fall in price of the commodity in the near future, he may be in a hurry to clear his entire stock at the existing price. Often the firms always keep some inventory stock so that they can cater to demand for the product on regular basis.
3. It is important to note that the slope of supply curve is different from elasticity of supply.
Elasticity of supply (E_s) is estimated as under:

$$E_s = \frac{\Delta Q}{\Delta P} \times \frac{P}{Q} \quad \left[\begin{array}{l}\text{Here, P: Price of the commodity} \\ \text{Q: Quantity supplied.}\end{array}\right]$$

$$\text{Slope of supply curve} = \frac{\Delta P}{\Delta Q}$$

Accordingly, elasticity of supply may be expressed as under:

$$E_s = \frac{1}{\text{Slope of Supply Curve}} \times \frac{P}{Q}$$

ability ZONE

A Simplified Algebraic/Geometric Presentation of Some Important Concepts Relating to the Theory of Supply

Supply Function

On the assumption that other determinants of supply remain constant (other than own price of the commodity), supply function may be expressed as under:

$$Q^s_X = c + dP_X$$

Here, Q^s_X = Quantity supplied of commodity-X; P_X = Price of commodity-X; $d = \frac{\Delta Q^s_X}{\Delta P_X}$ (change in quantity in response to a unit change in price of the commodity-X); c = Some constant (or quantity supplied corresponding to zero price).

Graphic presentation of a supply function is called supply curve.

Illustration

Consider the following data-set, showing quantity supplied corresponding to different possible prices of the commodity.

P_X (₹)	10	15	20	25	30
Q^s_X (Units)	0	10	20	30	40

Supply function for this data-set is as under:

$$Q^s_X = -20 + 2P_X$$

Thus,

If $P_X = 10$, $Q^s_X = -20 + 2 \times 10 = 0$

If $P_X = 15$, $Q^s_X = -20 + 2 \times 15 = 10$

If $P_X = 20$, $Q^s_X = -20 + 2 \times 20 = 20$

and so on.

Graphic presentation of this supply function offers the following supply curve (Fig. 20), as given alongside.

FIGURE 20

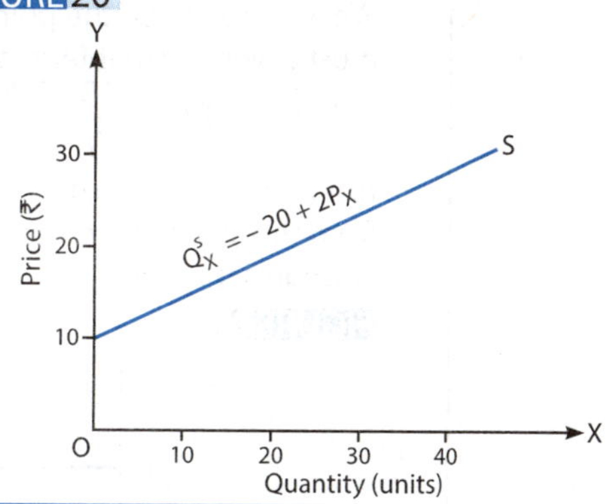

How do we get 2 as the value of *d*?

We know, $d = \frac{\Delta Q^s_X}{\Delta P_X}$.

In the data-set, when P_X changes from 10 to 15, $\Delta P_X = 5$. Correspondingly, when Q^s_X changes from 0 to 10, $\Delta Q^s_X = 10$. Accordingly, $\frac{\Delta Q^s_X}{\Delta P_X} = \frac{10}{5} = 2$. This is true for every change in P_X and the corresponding change in Q^s_X. This simply implies that if P_X changes by 1 unit, Q^s_X changes by 2 units.

How do we get –20 as the value of *c*?

We know, when $P_X = 10, Q^s_X = 0$, and we also know that if P_X changes by 1 unit, Q^s_X changes by 2 units. Now if P_X is to be zero (implying a fall of 10 units), then Q^s_X must fall by 20 units. Accordingly, when $P_X = 0$,

$$Q^s_X = -20 + 0 = -20$$

Elasticity of Supply

$E_s = 1$, if a straight line upward sloping supply curve starts from the origin.

Proof: $E_s = \frac{\Delta Q_X^s}{\Delta P_X} \times \frac{P_X}{Q_X^s}$ ...(i)

If P_1 is taken to be the initial price and S_1 as initial quantity, then

$$E_s = \frac{bc}{ac} \times \frac{OP_1}{OS_1} \quad ...(ii)$$

$$E_s = \frac{bc}{ac} \times \frac{S_1b}{OS_1} \quad ...(iii)$$

Δbca and ΔOS_1b are similar triangles. Accordingly, ratio of their sides should be equal.

Thus, $\frac{bc}{ac} = \frac{OS_1}{S_1b}$ ...(iv)

Relating equation (iv) to (iii), we get

$$E_s = \frac{OS_1}{S_1b} \times \frac{S_1b}{OS_1} = 1$$

FIGURE 21

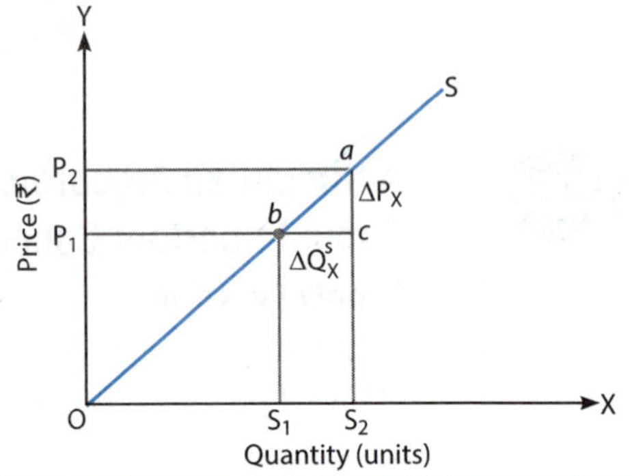

$E_s = 1$ provided
— supply curve is a straight line.
— it slopes upward.
— it shoots from the origin.
As is evident from the figure (and the proof given here), it does not matter at what angle the supply curve is drawn.

Identity between MC Curve and Supply Curve of a Firm under Perfect Competition

In chapter 9 we discussed producer's equilibrium. The central point of discussion was that a profit maximising firm strikes its equilibrium when MR = MC and MC is rising. In a state of perfect competition, price is given to a firm. Implying that, AR is constant for different levels of firm's output. Constant AR implies that AR = MR. So that the equilibrium condition that MR = MC can also be stated as P = MC. At a given P, a firm strikes its equilibrium when P = MC and MC is rising.

We also discussed the point that in the short run, a firm may suffer losses. But in any case it must cover its variable cost. So that, during the short period a firm will undertake production only if TR = TVC or $\frac{TR}{Q} = \frac{TVC}{Q}$ or AR = AVC, or P = AVC. This reveals an important fact that short run supply curve of the firm starts from its shut-down point, the point where P = AVC. Starting from this point, the firm's short run supply curve would be the same as its MC curve. Fig. 22 illustrates this point.

FIGURE 22

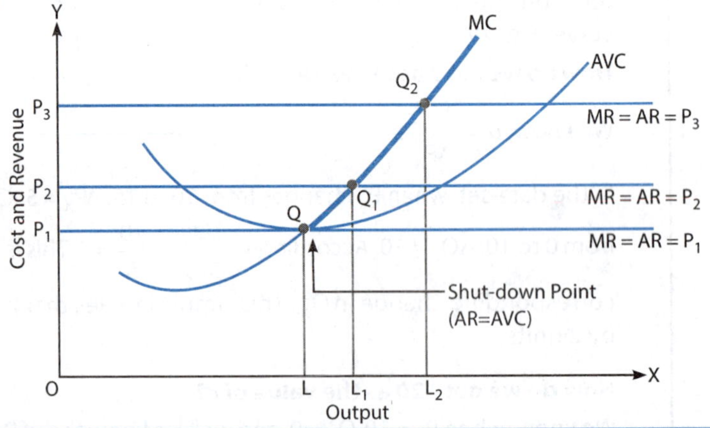

Short run supply curve of the firm : Q onward

Fig. 22 shows that if $P = P_1$, the firm strikes its equilibrium at point Q which is the starting point of its supply curve. It produces OL quantity. If $P = P_2$, the firm strikes its equilibrium at point

Q_1 (where, P = MC and MC is rising). The firm now produces OL_1 quantity. Likewise, if P = P_3, the firm strikes its equilibrium at point Q_2 (here again P = MC and MC is rising). The firm decides to produce OL_2 quantity. Note carefully, the firm's equilibrium is occurring along the rising segment of MC starting from the shut-down point Q. In other words, the rising segment of MC curve (starting from the shut-down point) shows the price-quantity relationship.

It shows how much quantity a profit maximising firm intends to produce, corresponding to different possible prices of the concerned commodity. This is what the supply curve reveals. Hence, the conclusion that, during the short run, firm's rising segment of MC curve (starting from its shut-down point) is the same as its supply curve.

> During the short run, rising segment of MC curve (starting from the shut-down point) is the same as the firm's supply curve.

In the long run, a firm must cover all its costs. Or, that P must cover AC. Otherwise, production will not be undertaken. Equality between P and AC refers to the firm's break-even point. Implying that a profit maximising firm will undertake production only from its break-even point. In other words, it means that in the long run, the firm's supply curve starts from its break-even point where P = AC. Starting from this point, the firm's supply curve would be the same as its MC curve. Fig. 23 illustrates this point.

FIGURE 23

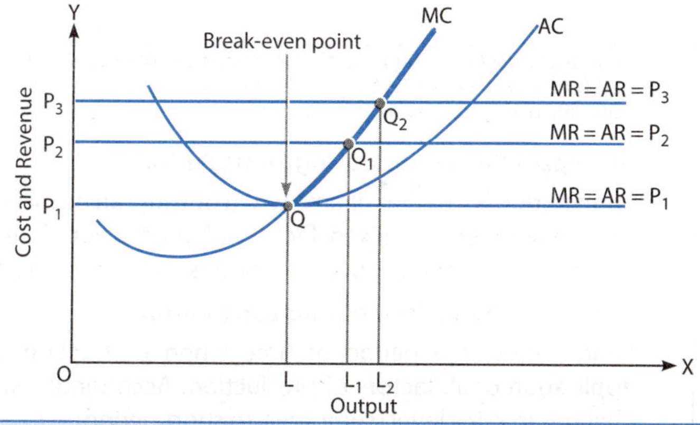

Long run supply curve of the firm : Q onward
Q : Break-even point where price = average cost

Fig. 23 shows that Q is the break-even point for the firm where P = AC. At point Q, the firm produces OL quantity of the commodity.

It just covers its total cost of production. If price happens to be lower than P_1, production will not be undertaken. When P = P_2, the firm strikes its equilibrium at point Q_1 (where P = MC and MC is rising) and OL_1 quantity is produced. Likewise, if P = P_3, equilibrium is struck at point Q_2 and OL_2 quantity is produced. Each equilibrium point (corresponding to different P levels) is located on the rising segment of MC curve (starting from the break-even point). This segment shows equilibrium quantity or the quantity that the firm intends to produce (or it intends to supply) at different levels of price of the commodity.

Hence, the fact that the rising segment of the firm's MC curve (starting from its break-even point when P = AC) is the same as the firm's supply curve in the long run.

> In the long run, the rising segment of the firm's MC curve (starting from the break-even point, when price = average cost) is the same as the firm's supply curve.

Time Period (or Time Horizon) and Supply Behaviour

Economists have broadly classified time horizon into three periods, *viz.*, (i) Very Short Period, also called Market Period, (ii) Short Period, and (iii) Long Period.

(i) Supply Behaviour during Very Short Period (or Market Period)

Very short period or market period is the period of time during which production cannot be changed at all. Accordingly, supply of the commodity can be increased only up to its existing stock.

Example: In a poultry farm, supply of eggs during the market period is just the stock of eggs lying with the farmer. Production of eggs is constant.

In fact, in case of perishable goods (goods which cannot be stocked like green vegetables), the supply during very short period is absolutely constant: it forms a vertical straight line, as in Fig. 24.

FIGURE 24

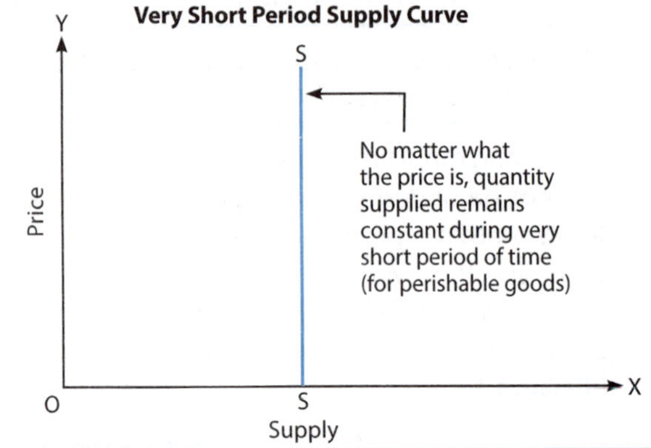

A vertical straight line supply curve (shooting from the X-axis) shows constant supply of the commodity even at the zero price. This may be true in case of perishable goods which cannot be stocked and of which production is constant during the very short period of time.

(ii) Supply Behaviour during Short Period

Short period is a period of time when output can be increased through greater application of the variable factors. Fixed factors of production (like, plant and machinery) cannot be changed. Accordingly, supply responds to changes in price, but only to a limited extent.

(iii) Supply Behaviour during Long Period

Long period is a period of time when production can be increased through greater application of all factors of production. Accordingly, supply becomes more responsive to changes in price level (compared to short period).

Fig. 25 shows supply curves of short period and long period.

FIGURE 25

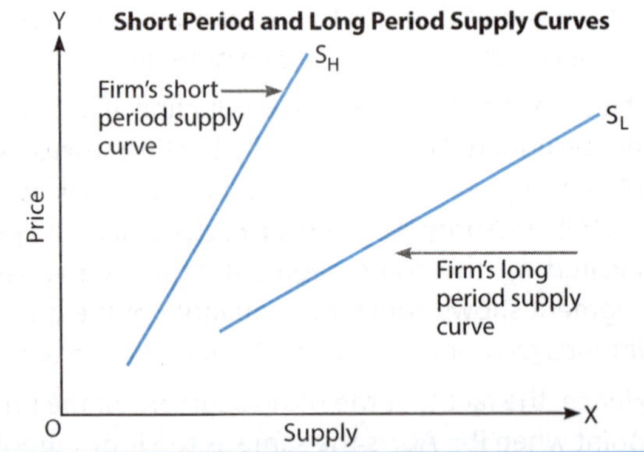

Long period supply curve is flatter than the short period supply curve. This shows that supply is more responsive to changes in price during the long period. It happens because during the long period, production can be increased (or decreased) by changing the input of all the factors of production, while during the short period, production can be increased (or decreased) by changing the input of variable factors only.

S_H (short period supply curve) is much steeper compared to S_L (long period supply curve).

Forms of Market

CHAPTER 11

TODO

- Concept of Market
- Forms of Market:
  - (i) Perfect Competition
  - (ii) Monopoly
  - (iii) Monopolistic Competition
  - (iv) Oligopoly
- Principal Basis of Market Classification

1. Concept of Market

What is market? Ordinarily, an individual would answer this question pointing to a shopping complex. But, for a student of Economics, this is not an appropriate answer. In Economics, the concept of market has a special meaning. It refers to a mechanism or an arrangement that facilitates the sale and purchase of goods. This arrangement could simply be through telephonic communication or even through electronic mail. We are all familiar with 'online marketing' which is marketing without any shopping complex.

In Economics, market does not refer to any shopping complex. It refers to a mechanism or an arrangement that facilitates contact between the buyers and sellers for the sale and purchase of goods and services.

What is Market?

> Market refers to a mechanism or an arrangement that facilitates contact between the buyers and sellers for the sale and purchase of goods and services.

In the light of this definition, size of the market is not to be viewed as the size of some geographical area where sale and purchase of goods is done. Instead, it is to be viewed in terms of the volume or value of sale and purchase of goods and services. Thus, size of the market is large when the volume or the value of the sale and purchase is large.

2. Forms of Market

Depending on the degree of competition or number of firms in the market (engaged in the sale of a particular commodity), a market is often described as one of the following forms: (i) perfect competition, (ii) monopoly, (iii) monopolistic competition, and (iv) oligopoly. Following is a brief description of these forms of the market.

Perfect Competition

Perfect competition is said to exist when there is a large number of sellers and buyers of a commodity, and no individual buyer or seller has any control over its price. Product is homogeneous and its price is determined by the forces of market supply and market demand.

Perfect competition is a form of the market where there is a large number of buyers and sellers of a commodity. Homogeneous product is sold and its price is determined by the forces of market supply and market demand. An individual buyer or a seller has no control over price.

Features of Perfect Competition and their Implications/Significance

A perfectly competitive market has the following features. Each feature is explained with reference to its implications for the buyers and sellers of a commodity.

(1) Large Number of Small Buyers and Sellers of a Commodity: The number of buyers is so large that the demand of an individual buyer is only a small fraction of the market demand for a commodity. Likewise, the number of sellers is so large that the supply of an individual seller (firm) is only a small fraction of the market supply. It implies that:

No individual buyer, by varying his demand, can influence market price of the commodity. Also, no individual seller (firm), by varying its sale, can influence market price. So that, for an individual buyer or an individual firm, market price is given. In other words, price is constant for a firm (and for a buyer). Geometrically, it is indicated by a horizontal straight line as in Fig. 1. It shows that under perfect competition, a firm can sell any amount of the commodity at the given price. Briefly, it means that a firm under perfect competition is a price taker, not a price maker.

FIGURE 1

Price Line for a Firm under Perfect Competition

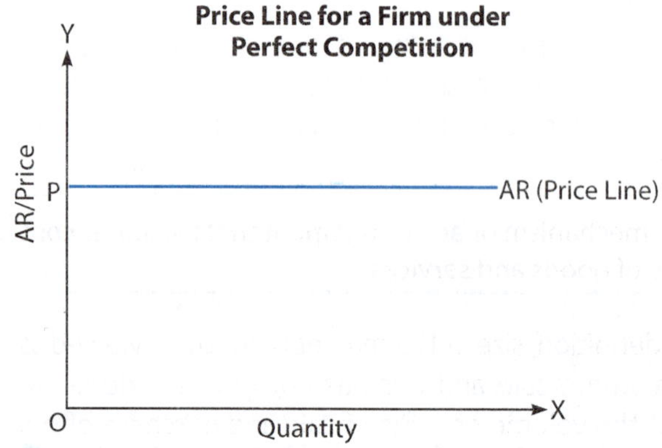

A firm can sell any amount of the commodity, at the existing price.

Implications/Significance of Large Number of Buyers and Sellers of a Commodity

These are as under:

(i) An individual seller (or a buyer) is selling (or buying) such a small fragment of the market supply (or market demand) that market price remains beyond his control. Market price is given to a firm (as well as to a buyer). A firm can sell any amount of the commodity at the given price. Also, a buyer can buy any amount of the commodity at the given price.

(ii) Firm's demand curve becomes a horizontal straight line, or perfectly elastic.

(iii) Firm is a price taker, not a price maker.

(2) Homogeneous Product: Under perfect competition, each firm (in the industry) sells an homogeneous product. A product is said to be homogeneous when each unit of it (sold in the market) is identical in size, shape, colour, weight (or in any other respect). So that, the buyers do not find any difference in the product as sold by different firms in the market. It is a situation of zero degree of product differentiation. It may also be called a situation of the market where buyers find products of different firms (in the industry) as perfect substitutes of each other.

When the product is homogeneous (and there is a zero degree of product differentiation), a firm cannot exercise any control over price. Even a slightest increase in the price by one firm will shift its buyers to other firms in the market. Also, there is no need for advertisement to promote sales of a firm. So that there are no advertisement costs or selling costs.

Implications/Significance of the Homogeneous Product

Following observations may be noted in this regard:

(i) Because of homogeneous product, uniform price prevails in the market.

(ii) It is a situation of zero degree of product differentiation. So that, products of different firms (in the industry) are perfect substitutes of each other.

(iii) Zero degree of product differentiation leads to zero degree of market control, or zero degree of monopoly control of the market. Accordingly, minimum possible price prevails in the market.

(3) Perfect Knowledge: Buyers and sellers are fully aware of the prevailing price in the market. They are also aware of the fact that homogeneous product is being sold in the market. Accordingly, producers cannot charge different prices from different buyers. Higher profit through 'price discrimination' is ruled out.

(4) Freedom of Entry and Exit: A new firm is free to enter the industry and an existing firm is free to leave it. Here, we need to understand the concepts of short period and long period. Short period, by definition, is too short for an existing firm to leave the industry, as well as too short for a new firm to join the industry. Long period is long enough for the existing firm to leave the industry, as well as long enough for the new firm to enter the industry.

Thus, entry and exit of the firms is possible only in the long period, not in the short period.

Implications/Significance of Freedom of Entry and Exit

These are as under:

(i) Because of free entry and exit, firms in the long run earn only normal profits (TR = TC or AR = AC). This is how it happens: In case extra-normal profits are earned, new firms will join the industry. Market supply will increase. Market price will fall. Extra-normal profits will be wiped out. In case of extra-normal losses, some of the existing firms will leave the industry. Market supply will decrease. Market price will increase. Extra-normal losses will be wiped out.

(ii) Because, during the short period, exit/entry is ruled out, a firm may operate under any of the following situations:

(a) normal profits (TR = TC or AR = AC),

(b) extra-normal profits (TR > TC or AR > AC), and

(c) extra-normal losses (TR < TC or AR < AC).

(5) **Independent Decision-making:** There is no agreement between different firms (in the industry) regarding quantity to be produced or, price to be charged. In other words, firms do not form 'trusts' or cartels. Accordingly, perfect competition ensures: (i) optimum level of output (the level of output where AC for each firm is the lowest), and (ii) lowest level of price (the level of price which allows only normal profits). Thus, perfect competition facilitates highest output and lowest price, compared with any other form of the market.

(6) **Perfect Mobility:** Factors of production are perfectly mobile. They will move to that industry where they get higher price. Accordingly, uniform factor price prevails in the market.

(7) **No Extra Transport Cost:** Buying a commodity from one seller, rather than the other, does not involve any extra transport cost. This further ensures that any producer is not able to charge higher price for the product. Only one price prevails in the market.

Three Vital Conclusions

Study of the features of perfect competition offers three vital conclusions, as under:

(1) A Firm under Perfect Competition is a Price Taker, not a Price Maker

Price is determined by the forces of market demand and market supply. A firm sells its output at the given price. Therefore, a firm under perfect competition is a price taker, not a price maker. This is explained with reference to three basic characteristics of perfect competition:

(i) **Large Number of Firms:** The number of firms selling a product is so large that no individual firm (by increasing or decreasing its output) can make any meaningful difference in the total market supply. Accordingly, an individual firm cannot influence the market price. A firm is to take the market price as given (or as constant).

(ii) **Homogeneous Product:** All firms in the industry produce homogeneous product. Or, products of all firms in the industry are perfect substitutes of each other. So that, if any firm fixes its price higher than the existing market price, buyers would shift to other firms. The firm will simply be driven out of the market. However, here comes an obvious question: **Why cannot a firm exercise price control by lowering its price?** Answer is simple: If a firm can sell any quantity at the existing price, it makes no sense to lower the price.

(iii) **Perfect Knowledge:** Buyers are assumed to have perfect knowledge regarding 'product-availability' and product price. Thus, a firm cannot charge its own price even on the pretext of 'buyers ignorance'.

Hence, it is concluded that under perfect competition, it is not possible for a firm to control price of the product. The firm is simply a price taker, not a price maker.

(2) Demand Curve of the Firm under Perfect Competition is Perfectly Elastic

Perfectly elastic demand curve implies that the elasticity of demand for the firm's product is equal to infinity ($E_d = \infty$). It is indicated by a horizontal straight line, as in Fig. 2. It shows that the firm can sell any amount of the commodity at the prevailing price. But, even a small increase in price would lead to zero demand.

FIGURE 2

Firm's Demand Curve Under Perfect Competition

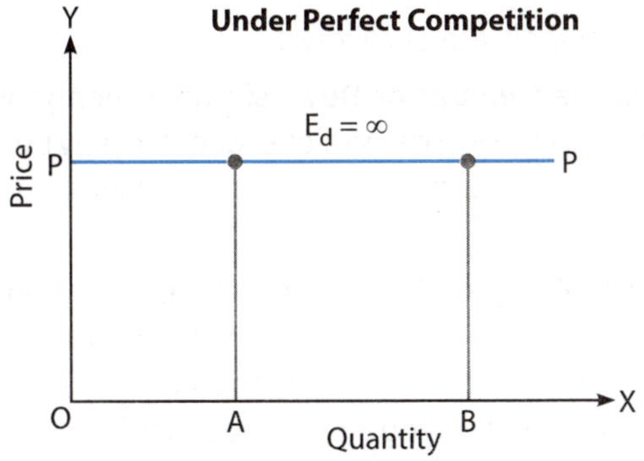

Firm's entire output is demanded at the price OP. This price is determined by the forces of market supply and market demand. An individual firm cannot change it.

Fig. 2 shows that at the given price OP, the firm can sell any quantity: OA or OB, and even more than that. But, a slightest increase in price would mean that the demand is zero.

A perfectly elastic demand curve is simply indicates that the firm has no control over price.

(3) A Firm under Perfect Competition earns only Normal Profits in the Long Run

This is owing to the fact that there is freedom of entry and exit under perfect competition. In situations of extra-normal profits, new firms will join the industry. Consequently, market supply will increase. Market price will fall. Extra-normal profits will be wiped out. In situations of extra-normal losses, some firms will leave the industry. Consequently, market supply will fall. Market price will rise. Extra-normal losses will be wiped out.

HOTS

Q.1. What prevents a perfectly competitive firm to lower the product price and capture the entire market?

Ans. Two points need to be noted in answer to this question:

(i) Why should a firm lower the price when at the existing market price it can sell any amount it wishes to sell? It makes absolutely no sense.

(ii) Under perfect competition, there is a large number of buyers and sellers of a product. Each firm produces only a small fraction of the total market supply. It has a limited production capacity. Now, if an individual firm lowers the price, all buyers in the market will rush to this firm for supplies of the product. But, by definition, the firm is so small that it cannot produce enough for all the buyers in the market. Hence, the possibility of capturing the entire market by lowering the price is ruled out.

Q.2. Differentiate between consumer's demand curve and firm's demand curve.

Ans. Demand curve shows the relationship between price and quantity demanded. In case of consumer's demand, it is the relationship between price and quantity demanded by an individual buyer. On the other hand, in case of firm's demand, it is the relationship between price and quantity demanded of firm's output by the various buyers in the market.

Quantity demanded of a firm's product, obviously, is equal to sales/output of that firm. Therefore, firm's demand curve also shows the relationship between price of the commodity and firm's sales/output.

Monopoly

It is a form of the market in which there is a single seller of a product with no close substitutes. **Example:** Railways in India are a monopoly industry of the Government of India. Since there is only one producer of a product in the market, the distinction between 'firm' and industry disappears.

[**Note:** An industry is a group of firms producing a particular product.]

Features of Monopoly

The main features of monopoly are as follows:

An Important Observation

Monopolist tries to increase his profits by restricting the supply of his product and fixing high price. Accordingly, greater the monopoly power in any market, lesser is the output and higher is the price. Thus, people get less output and have to pay high price under monopoly. Under perfect competition, on the other hand, we get maximum possible output at the minimum possible price.

(1) **One Seller and Large Number of Buyers:** Under monopoly, there is a single producer of a commodity. He may be alone, or there may be a group of partners or a joint stock company or a state. However, there is a large number of buyers of the product.

(2) **Restrictions on the Entry of New Firms:** Under monopoly, there are some restrictions on the entry of new firms into the monopoly industry. Generally, there are patent rights granted to the monopoly firm. Or, a monopoly firm has exclusive control over a technique (of production) or over the raw material needed for production.

(3) **No Close Substitutes:** A monopoly firm produces a commodity that has no close substitutes. **Example:** There is no close substitute of railways as a 'bulk carrier'.

(4) **Full Control Over Price:** Being a single seller of the product, a monopolist has full control over its price. A monopolist, thus, is a price maker. He can fix whatever price he wishes to fix for his product.

(5) **Price Discrimination:** A monopolist may charge different price from different buyers. It is called price discrimination. *"Price discrimination refers to the practice of charging different prices from different buyers for the same good."*

Monopoly is a form of the market in which there is a single seller or producer of a commodity. There are no close substitutes of the monopoly product and there are legal, technical or natural barriers to the entry of new firms in the monopoly market. A monopolist has complete control over price and can also practise price discrimination.

Demand Curve for a Monopoly Firm

Full control over price under monopoly does not mean that the monopolist can sell any amount of the commodity at any price. Once the monopolist fixes price of the commodity, quantity demanded will depend upon the buyers. Buyers will demand more if price is lowered, and demand less if price is raised. So that, there is an inverse relationship between price and quantity sold by the monopoly firm. Accordingly, demand curve for a monopoly firm slopes downward, as in Fig. 3.

D_M is the demand curve for the monopoly firm. It shows inverse relationship between price and quantity: OQ quantity is sold when price is OP. When the price is reduced from OP to OP_1, quantity sold increases from OQ to OQ_1.

FIGURE 3

D_M: Demand Curve for a Monopoly Firm

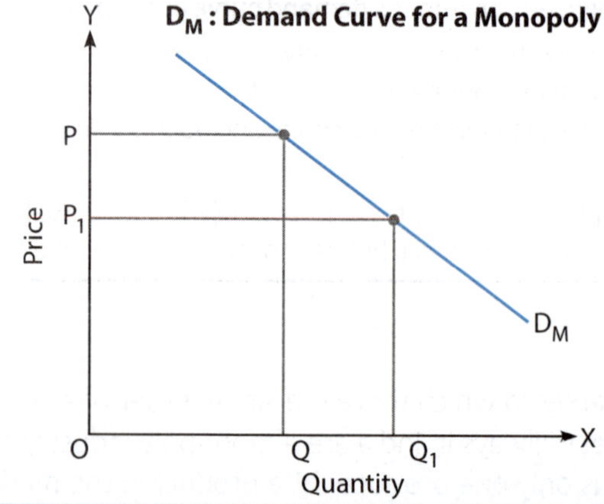

Firm's demand curve (D_M) under monopoly slopes downward, showing an inverse relationship between price and quantity. More is sold at a lower price and less is sold at a higher price.

HOTS

Q. A monopolist is a price maker. How?

Ans. A monopolist is a price maker. It means that he can fix whatever price he wishes to fix for his product. It is because of the following reasons:

(i) A monopolist is a single seller of the product in the market. There is no competition.

(ii) There are no close substitutes of the monopoly product. So that, there is no fear that the buyers would shift from one product to the other to any significant extent.

(iii) There are legal, technical or natural barriers to the entry of new firms. So that, there is no challenge to the price fixed by the monopolist.

How does a Monopoly Market Structure arise?

Monopoly market structure may arise in any of the following ways:

(1) Government Licensing/Government Control: The government may grant license for the production of a particular commodity only to one producer. Accordingly, monopoly comes into existence. Also, the government may decide to control the production of certain goods (or services) exclusively through its departmental undertakings, like Railways in India.

(2) Patent Rights: New products may secure patent rights. It amounts to monopoly rights regarding the shape, design or other characteristics of the product. Patent rights may be secured on new technology. It prohibits the use of patented technology by others. Accordingly, monopoly market structure emerges.

(3) Cartels: It refers to formation of a group by the competing firms in the market. Of course, this is possible when the number of firms is small. The group as a whole secures monopoly control of the market.

(4) Natural Occurrence: Monopoly may emerge as a gift of nature. The only spring of water in an island, for example, may be under the control of one person.

'Patent Rights' and 'Patent Life'

- **'Patent rights'** is the official recognition of the originators/ innovators of a new product or technology. No body can copy their product or technology without obtaining a license.
- **'Patent life'** refers to the number of years for which a patent right is granted.

HOTS

Q. Why are patent rights granted?

Ans. Patent rights are granted with a view to:

(i) encouraging research and development, and

(ii) encouraging new discoveries and innovations.

Monopolistic Competition

It is a form of the market in which there are many sellers of the product, but the product of each seller is different from that of the other. Thus, there are many sellers, selling a differentiated product. Product differentiation is generally promoted through trademark or brand name. **Example:** Firms producing different brands of toothpastes, *viz.*, Colgate, Close-up, Pepsodent, etc.

Monopolistic competition combines the features of monopoly and perfect competition. Trademark or brand name gives some monopoly power to the firms. Different firms often charge different price for their product. In other words, each firm tends to exercise some control over price. On the other hand, since many firms are producing a commodity (like toothpaste) there is competition in the market. No firm is able to exercise full control over price of the product. Thus, we can say that a firm under monopolistic competition exercises only a partial control over price.

HOTS

Q. What makes it possible to exercise partial control over price? Why full control over price is not possible?

Ans. It is through product differentiation that a firm under monopolistic competition exercises partial control over price. Difference in design, colour or even packaging of the product attracts buyers to buy a particular product even at a relatively higher price.

Full control over price is ruled out under monopolistic competition, because:

(i) there are many competitors in the market, and

(ii) there is a large number of close substitutes.

Features of Monopolistic Competition

The main features of monopolistic competition are as under:

(1) Large Number of Buyers and Sellers: As under perfect competition, there is a large number of buyers and sellers. Also, the size of each firm is small. Each firm has a limited share of the market.

(2) Product Differentiation: Product differentiation (briefly called 'differentiation') is a distinct feature of monopolistic competition. Differentiation implies that rival firms are selling products which are not perfect substitutes but close substitutes of each other. **Example:** Colgate toothpaste and Binaca toothpaste are close substitutes of each other, even when they may not be perfect substitutes for most buyers in the market.

Implications/Significance of Product Differentiation

The following observations highlight the implications/significance of product differentiation:

(i) It allows a firm a partial control over price of its product. It implies a partial monopoly power of a firm in the market.

(ii) It causes high elasticity of demand for the firm's product owing to the availability of a large number of close substitutes.

(iii) It offers a wide range of differentiated product to the consumers. Accordingly, consumers welfare is raised.

(iv) The product differentiation may be real or fake. In case it is fake, it leads to exploitation of the consumers through higher price.

(3) Selling Costs: Product differentiation is often supported with heavy advertisement expenditure (implying selling costs). These costs are incurred by a firm to increase its market share. Because of advertisement, buyers develop a brand loyalty. It is this 'brand loyalty' that allows partial control over price.

(4) Downward Sloping Demand Curve: Partial control over price leads to downward sloping demand curve of the firm: quantity sold increases when price is reduced. If price is raised, quantity sold tends to reduce.

Focus of Attention

Both under monopoly and monopolistic competition, firm's demand curve tends to slope downward from left to right. But, under monopolistic competition, the demand curve is much flatter than under monopoly. We know, flatter the curve, more elastic it is. So that, demand curve under monopolistic competition shows a higher degree of elasticity of demand than under monopoly. This is because a large number of close substitutes (of the product) are available in a monopolistic competitive market, whereas in monopoly market there are no close substitutes at all.

(5) Non-price Competition: Even when product differentiation allows the firms to pursue their independent price policy, they often avoid getting into price-war. Instead they focus on non-price competition.

Non-price Competition

Non-price competition is a market strategy adopted by a firm to increase its market share by promoting its product through advertisement.

Example:

— Getting the product-quality highlighted through celebrities.

— Sponsoring entertainment programmes in schools to promote brand loyalty.

— Promising better 'after-sale service' of the durable goods like AC and TV.

(6) Freedom of Entry and Exit: Firms are free to enter the industry or leave it. However, new firms have no absolute freedom of entry into industry. Products of some firms may be legally patented. New firms cannot produce identical products. **Example:** No rival firm can produce/sell a patented item like Woodland brand of shoes.

(7) Lack of Perfect Mobility: Factors of production, goods and services lack perfect mobility. Accordingly, different prices prevail for the same factor or for the same product.

(8) Lack of Perfect Knowledge: Sellers and buyers of the products (as well as owners of factors of production) lack perfect knowledge about the market. Because of product differentiation, it is not even possible to have perfect knowledge about a variety of brands in the market. This leads to consumer's exploitation by way of higher price for the low quality product.

HOTS

Q. **Differentiate between price discrimination and product differentiation.**

Ans. Price discrimination occurs when a producer charges different price from different buyers of the same product. **Example:** The only surgeon in your area may charge low fee from the poor patients and high fee from the rich patients.

This is done to maximise revenue from the sale of a good/service.

Product differentiation occurs when different producers differentiate their product in terms of its shape, size, packaging, trademark or brand name. This is done by a firm to increase its market share. Also, product differentiation allows partial control over price of the product.

Oligopoly

It is a form of the market in which there are a few big firms and a large number of buyers of a commodity. Each firm has a significant share of the market. Price and output decision of one firm significantly impacts the price and output decisions of the rival firms in the market. Accordingly, there is a high degree of interdependence among the competing firms: price and output policy of one firm depends on the price and output policy of other(s). This type of competition (involving high degree of interdependence) is called 'cut-throat competition'.

Example: There are only a few car-producers in the Indian Auto market. Toyota, Ford, GM, Audi, BMW and Volkswagen are some well known brands.

Features of Oligopoly

The principal features of oligopoly are as under:

(1) Small Number of Big Firms: Oligopoly market is the one in which a small number of big firms dominate the market for a product. Market dominance is retained through intense advertising. Advertising generates brand loyalty. Established brand loyalty enables the producer to exercise partial control over price. It makes demand for the product as relatively less elastic. Accordingly, firms are able to generate extra-normal profits.

(2) **High Degree of Interdependence:** Oligopoly market is characterised by a small number of big firms in the industry. Each firm is so big that often it has global presence. It sells its product across all parts of the world. The market share of each firm is so significant that its price and output policy leaves a significant impact on the price and output policy of the rival firms. So that, there is a very high degree of interdependence among the competing firms with regard to their price and output policy. Price and output behaviour of one firm is often not free of the reaction of other firms in the market. Thus, a firm may be reluctant to raise price of its product, fearing that the rival firms might not raise it, and the buyers would shift to the rivals. Likewise, a firm may be reluctant to lower the price of its product, fearing that the rival firms might lower it more, and the buyers would shift to the rivals. This kind of interdependence makes it very difficult to specify any precise relationship between price and demand. It is precisely because of this reason that it has not been possible to develop a generally acceptable theory that explains how an oligopolist achieves an equilibrium.

(3) **Difficult to Trace Firm's Demand Curve:** It is not possible to determine firm's demand curve under oligopoly. This is because of high degree of interdependence among the competing firms. Thus, when a firm lowers its price, demand for its product may not increase, because the rival firms may lower the price more, because of which the buyers shift to the rival firms. Implying that there is no specific response of quantity demand to change in price. This makes it impossible to draw any specific demand curve for a firm under oligopoly.

(4) **Formation of Cartels:** With a view to avoiding competition, oligopoly firms often form cartels. A cartel is a formal agreement among the firms to avoid competition. It is sort of collusion against competition. Therefore, it is often called collusive oligopoly. Under it, output and price are fixed by different firms as a group.

Sometimes, leading firm in the market is accepted by the cartel as a 'Price Leader'. All firms in the cartel choose the same price as set by the price leader.

Collusive oligopoly is like a monopoly form of the market. A cartel takes full control of the market. It makes monopoly profits.

(5) **Entry Barriers:** There are barriers to the entry of new firms. These are created largely through patent rights. Because of these barriers, the existing firms are not much worried about the entry of new firms in the market. They continue to earn extra-normal profits even in the long run.

(6) **Non-price Competition:** Under oligopoly, firms tend to avoid price competition. Instead, they focus on non-price competition. **Example:** In India both Coke and Pepsi sell their product at the same price. But, in order to increase its share of the market, each firm takes to aggressive non-price competition. Coke and Pepsi sponsor different games and sports; they also offer lucrative schemes (like of maintenance of school garden) if their product is patronised.

Collusive and Non-Collusive Oligopoly

Oligopoly is broadly classified as 'collusive oligopoly' and 'non-collusive oligopoly'.

Collusive oligopoly (also called Cooperative Oligopoly) is a form of the market in which there are few firms in the market and all decide to avoid competition through a formal agreement. They collude to form a cartel. Price and output of the member firms is fixed as a collective/cooperative decision. Sometimes a leading firm in the market is accepted by the cartel as a price leader. Members of the cartel accept the price policy as specified by the price leader.

Non-collusive oligopoly (also called Non-cooperative Oligopoly) is a form of the market in which there are few firms in the market, and each firm pursues its price and output policy independent of the rival firms. Each firm tries to increase its market share through competition. Competition is preferred to collusion as a means of profit maximisation. Because there are only a few big firms in the market, there is a cut-throat competition. Brand loyalty is developed through aggressive advertisement.

Perfect and Imperfect Oligopoly

If oligopoly firms are producing homogeneous products, it is called perfect oligopoly. On the other hand, if oligopoly firms are producing differentiated products, it is called imperfect oligopoly.

HOTS

Q.1. Why is firm's demand curve indeterminate under oligopoly?

Or

How firms are interdependent in an oligopoly market?

Ans. Firm's demand curve is indeterminate under oligopoly because there is a high degree of interdependence among the firms. Price and output policy of one firm has a significant impact on the price and output policy of the rival firms in the market. When one firm lowers its price to increase its sales, the rival firms may also lower the price to retain their sales. And, when one firm raises the price (to increase profits), the rival firms may not do it. So that, the firm which raises the price suffers the loss of market share. In such a situation, it becomes very difficult to estimate change in firm's sales caused by a change in price. A precise relationship between price and sales cannot be established. It implies that the firm's demand curve cannot be drawn.

Q. 2. What are cartels? Give an example.

Ans. A cartel is a formal 'collusive agreement' among the firms under oligopoly. Firms collude to avoid competition. They fix their output and price as decided by the cartel. Collectively the firms try to earn monopoly profits.

Example: OPEC set-up in 1960 by the world's five major oil producing countries: Iran, Iraq, Kuwait, Saudi Arabia and Venezuela.

Q. 3. Why is the number of firms small in the oligopoly market?

Or

What explains the emergence of oligopoly market?

Ans. Following factors explain the emergence of oligopoly market:

(i) **Government Licensing:** The government may grant licenses only to a few firms for the production of a commodity. **Example:** Coal mining rights in India have been offered only to a few companies.

(ii) **Patent Rights:** Some enterprises acquire patent rights on account of their innovative product or innovative technology. Such rights restrict the entry of new firms. Accordingly, a few firms dominate the market as oligopoly firms.

(iii) **Scale of Investment and Selling Costs:** Scale of investment and selling costs related to certain products may be so high that it becomes difficult for the most investors to afford it. It leads to concentration of the market in the hands of small number of big investors. Software and Auto industries may be cited as examples.

Q. 4. What form of the market it is when there are only two firms producing a commodity?

Ans. It is Duopoly. It is a distinct situation of the oligopoly form of the market.

Perfect Competition, Monopolistic Competition, Monopoly and Oligopoly–Some Differences

S. No.	Reference	Perfect Competition	Monopolistic Competition	Monopoly	Oligopoly
1.	Number of Sellers and Buyers	Large	Large	One seller, but large number of buyers	A small number of big sellers and a large number of buyers
2.	Product	Homogeneous	Product differentiation	Homogeneous or differentiated	Homogeneous or differentiated
3.	Price	Uniform	Not uniform because of product differentiation	Not uniform because of price discrimination	Not uniform because of product differentiation
4.	Entry of Firms	Free entry	Not absolute freedom	Not possible	Restricted through patent rights and related factors
5.	Knowledge of Market Conditions	Perfect knowledge	Imperfect knowledge	Imperfect knowledge	Imperfect knowledge
6.	Mobility	Perfect mobility	Imperfect mobility	Imperfect mobility	Imperfect mobility
7.	Firm's Demand Curve	Perfectly elastic	Relatively more elastic	Relatively less elastic	Cannot be specified
8.	Slope of Firm's Demand Curve	Horizontal straight line (AR = MR)	Slopes downward with high elasticity (AR > MR)	Slopes downward with low elasticity (AR > MR)	No specific relationship between price and quantity demanded
9.	Selling Costs	Not required	Very significant	Not required	Very significant
10.	Degree of Price Control	No control over price	Partial control over price	Full control over price	Partial control over price
11.	Level of Profit in the Long run	AR = AC ⇒ normal profits	AR = AC ⇒ normal profits	AR > AC ⇒ extra-normal profits	AR > AC ⇒ extra-normal profits (particularly through collusion and cartel formation)

3. Principal Basis of Market Classification

You can now sum up your understanding of different forms of the market by identifying the following factors as the principal basis of market classification:

(1) Number of Buyers and Sellers: When there is a large number of buyers and sellers of homogeneous commodity, it is a situation of perfect competition.

— When there is a large number of buyers and sellers, but the commodity is not homogeneous, it is a situation of monopolistic competition.

— When there is one seller but a large number of buyers of a commodity, it is a situation of monopoly.

(2) Nature of the Commodity: In a perfectly competitive market, the product must be homogeneous, while in monopolistic competition, the product is always differentiated. In monopoly, the product may or may not be homogeneous.

(3) Degree of Price Control: Perfect competition is said to exist when the producer has no control over price. In contrast, the monopolist has full control over price. Monopolistic competition exists when there is partial control over price.

(4) Knowledge of the Market: In case of perfect competition, buyers and sellers have perfect knowledge of the market. In other forms of the market, there is imperfect knowledge of the market.

(5) Mobility of Factors: Perfect mobility of the factors is a unique feature of perfect competition. It is not found in other forms of the market.

POWER POINTS

- Perfect Competition is a form of the market in which there is a large number of buyers and sellers of a homogeneous product. Price is determined by the forces of the market supply and market demand. An individual firm is a price taker.
- Monopoly is a form of the market in which there is a single seller of a commodity with complete control over its price.
- Monopolistic Competition is a form of the market in which there is a large number of sellers, selling differentiated product. Each firm has a partial control over price.
- Oligopoly is a form of the market in which there are a few big firms. Two important forms of oligopoly are: collusive oligopoly and non-collusive oligopoly.
  In collusive oligopoly, firms form a cartel to avoid competition. In non-collusive oligopoly, there is a cut-throat competition and a high degree of interdependence among the firms.
  Oligopoly market is also categorised as perfect oligopoly and imperfect oligopoly. Under perfect oligopoly, homogeneous product is produced, while under imperfect oligopoly, firms produce differentiated products.
- Shape of Firm's Demand Curve under Different Markets:
  — It is a horizontal straight line under perfect competition. It indicates that elasticity of demand (E_d) = ∞.
  — It slopes downward under monopoly. More can be sold only at a lower price. But it is not very elastic. This is because there are no close substitutes of the monopoly product in the market.
  — It slopes downward under monopolistic competition. But it is relatively more elastic than under monopoly. This is because there is a large number of close substitutes of a product in monopolistic competition.
  — It is indeterminate under oligopoly. This is because of a high degree of interdependence among the firms. Price and output policy of one firm significantly impacts the price and output policy of the rival firms in the market. It becomes difficult to specify any precise relationship between 'price and demand' for a firm's product.

EXERCISE

1. Very Short Questions (Remembering & Understanding) (1 mark each)

A. Multiple Choice Questions: Choose the Correct Answer

1. **In which kind of market, a firm is a price taker?**
   (a) Perfect competition (b) Monopoly
   (c) Monopolistic competition (d) Oligopoly
2. **'A firm can sell more only at the lower price.' To which market would you relate this statement?**
   (a) Perfect competition (b) Monopoly
   (c) Oligopoly (d) Duopoly
3. **In case of perfect competition:**
   (a) a firm is able to charge higher price
   (b) a firm is able to charge uniform price
   (c) a firm is able to sell any amount at the prevailing price
   (d) both (b) and (c)
4. **Firm's demand curve under monopoly shows:**
   (a) no relationship between price and demand (b) inverse relationship between price and demand
   (c) positive relationship between price and demand (d) none of these
5. **Charging different prices from different buyers for the same good is called:**
   (a) price extension (b) price contraction
   (c) price discrimination (d) price control

6. Under monopoly, a firm has:

(a) partial control over price (b) full control over price
(c) no control over price (d) none of these

7. Which market induces cartels?

(a) Perfect competition (b) Monopoly
(c) Oligopoly (d) None of these

8. In the context of monopolistic competition, which one of the following statements is correct?

(a) Firm has full control over price (b) Horizontal straight line demand curve of the firm
(c) Freedom of entry and exit (d) Selling costs do not exist

9. Which characteristic of monopolistic competition is compatible with monopoly?

(a) One seller and large number of buyers (b) Full control over price
(c) Freedom of entry and exit (d) Demand curve slopes downward

10. If the demand curve of a firm is a horizontal straight line:

(a) a firm can sell any amount at the existing price
(b) a firm can sell only a specified amount at the existing price
(c) all firms will sell equal amount of a commodity
(d) firms can differentiate their product

11. A firm can earn super normal profits even in the long run under:

(a) perfect competition (b) monopoly
(c) monopolistic competition (d) all of these

12. Compared with monopolistic competition, a firm's demand curve under monopoly is:

(a) equally elastic (b) less elastic
(c) more elastic (d) infinitely elastic

13. A market situation in which there are only two producers is called:

(a) monopoly (b) oligopoly
(c) duopoly (d) none of these

14. In monopolistic competition, the products are:

(a) homogeneous only (b) homogeneous supported with advertisement
(c) differentiated only (d) differentiated supported with advertisement

15. The AR curve and industry demand curve are the same:

(a) in case of monopoly (b) in case of oligopoly
(c) in case of perfect competition (d) none of these

16. When a monopolist resorts to price discrimination, price will be higher in the market where demand is:

(a) unitary elastic (b) elastic
(c) inelastic (d) none of these

17. In the context of oligopoly, which one of the following is incorrect?

(a) Small number of big firms (b) Perfect knowledge among the buyers
(c) Indeterminate firm's demand curve (d) Non-price competition

18. In case of perfect competition, products of all firms in the industry are:

(a) close substitutes only (b) close substitutes supported with advertisement
(c) differentiated supported with advertisement (d) perfect substitutes of each other

19. Under collusive oligopoly, price is often decided by:

(a) the industry (b) the firm
(c) price leader (d) none of these

20. **Homogeneous products are sold under:**
(a) collusive oligopoly
(b) non-collusive oligopoly
(c) perfect oligopoly
(d) imperfect oligopoly

Answers

1. (a) **2.** (b) **3.** (d) **4.** (b) **5.** (c) **6.** (b) **7.** (c) **8.** (c) **9.** (d) **10.** (a) **11.** (b) **12.** (b)
13. (c) **14.** (d) **15.** (a) **16.** (c) **17.** (b) **18.** (d) **19.** (c) **20.** (c)

B. Information & Concept-based Questions

1. **Define market for a good.**

Ans. Market refers to the mechanism of sale and purchase of goods and services.

2. **Define perfect competition.**

Ans. Perfect competition is a form of the market in which there is a large number of buyers and sellers and where homogeneous product is sold at a uniform price.

3. **What do you mean by monopoly?**

Ans. Monopoly is a market form with a single seller and many buyers of a commodity, with no close substitutes.

4. **Define monopolistic competition.**

Ans. Monopolistic competition is a form of the market with many buyers and sellers, where differentiated product is sold with a partial control over price.

5. **Define oligopoly.**

Ans. Oligopoly is a form of the market in which there is a large number of buyers, but only a few big sellers of a commodity.

6. **What is a price taker firm?**

Ans. A price taker firm means that it has to accept the price as determined by the forces of market demand and market supply.

7. **What is a price maker firm?**

Ans. A price maker firm refers to that firm which has complete control over price of the product in the market.

8. **What is the shape of firm's demand curve under perfect competition?**

Ans. Firm's demand curve under perfect competition is a horizontal straight line parallel to X-axis.

9. **Why are AR and MR equal under perfect competition?**

Ans. Under perfect competition, AR is constant for a firm. Hence, AR = MR.

10. **What is the shape of demand curve under monopolistic competition?**

Ans. Demand curve under monopolistic competition is downward sloping.

11. **In which market form are the products homogeneous?**

Ans. Under perfect competition, products are homogeneous.

12. **What will you call that market which has characteristics both of monopoly and perfect competition?**

Ans. Monopolistic competition has the characteristics both of monopoly and perfect competition.

13. **In which market form are average revenue and marginal revenue of a firm always equal?**

Ans. Under perfect competition, average revenue and marginal revenue of a firm are always equal.

14. **In which form of market there is product differentiation?**

Ans. The product is differentiated under monopolistic competition.

15. **What is patent right?**

Ans. Patent right is the official recognition of the originators/innovators of a new product or technology. No one else can use their product or technology without obtaining a license.

16. What is the motivation behind granting patent rights?

Ans. Patent rights prohibit the use of patented technology by others. These rights promote research and innovations.

17. What is cartel?

Ans. Cartel refers to collective decision making by a group of firms with a view to avoiding competition and securing monopoly control of the market.

2. Reason-based Questions (Comprehension of the Subject-matter)

Read the following statements carefully. Write 'True' or 'False' with a reason.

1. Price of the product never changes under perfect competition.

Ans. False. Under perfect competition, an individual firm cannot change the price. But market price can change owing to changes in demand and supply.

2. A firm under perfect competition has no control over price of the product.

Ans. True. Under perfect competition, there are large number of buyers and sellers of a homogeneous product. No single seller by changing his supply can influence the price.

3. There is a large number of buyers both under monopoly and monopolistic competition.

Ans. True. In case of monopoly, there is single seller and large number of buyers. Under monopolistic competition, there are large numbers of both buyers and sellers.

4. A monopoly firm is a price maker.

Ans. True. Monopolist is a price maker because he is the single seller of a commodity with no close substitutes.

5. A monopolist fixes price of his product on the basis of elasticity of demand for his product

Ans. True. Often, higher price is fixed when elasticity of demand is low. Low price is fixed when elasticity of demand is high.

6. Product differentiation allows partial control over price.

Ans. True. Because of product differentiation, each firm can decide its price policy independently. So that each firm has a partial control over price of its product.

7. A monopoly producer cannot control both price as well as quantity of his product.

Ans. True. As a single seller he can fix whatever price he wishes to fix for his product. But he can sell more only by lowering the price of his product.

8. A monopolist can exercise price discrimination.

Ans. True. A monopolist can charge different prices for the same commodity from different buyers because of no close substitutes of his product.

9. A firm under monopolistic competition cannot influence market price.

Ans. False. A firm under monopolistic competition has partial control over the price owing to product differentiation.

10. Firm's demand curve under perfect competition is a horizontal straight line.

Ans. True. Because price of the product is given to a firm under perfect competition.

11. Slope of firm's demand curve = ∞ under perfect competition.

Ans. False. Slope of firm's demand curve under perfect competition is zero, as it is a horizontal straight line.

12. Firm's demand curve shows highest elasticity in a state of monopolistic competition (in which there is a large number of close substitutes) than in a state of monopoly or perfect competition.

Ans. False. Firm's demand curve shows highest elasticity (= ∞) in state of perfect competition. Because a firm can sell whatever amount it wishes to sell at a given price, even a slightest increase in price will reduce the demand to zero.

13. Firm's demand curve under monopolistic competition is more elastic than under monopoly.

Ans. True. Firm's demand curve under monopolistic competition is more elastic than under monopoly because of availability of close substitutes under monopolistic competition.

14. Firm's demand curve is indeterminate under oligopoly.

Ans. True. Firm's demand curve is indeterminate or cannot be drawn under oligopoly because of high degree of interdependence among the firms.

15. For a perfectly competitive firm, there are only normal profits in the long run.

Ans. True. Under perfect competition, only normal profits prevail in the long run because of freedom of entry and exit of the firms in the market.

16. A firm under monopolistic competition makes only normal profits in the long run.

Ans. True. A firm makes only normal profits in the long run under monopolistic competition because of freedom of entry and exit of the firms in the market.

17. Price exceeds MC under monopoly, but not under perfect competition.

Ans. True. Because under perfect competition AR = MR, while under monopoly AR > MR. While equilibrium in both cases is struck when MR = MC.

18. There is a high degree of interdependence among firms in oligopoly form of the market.

Ans. True. Because there is only a small number of big firms in the market.

19. A firm under perfect competition gets only a break-even price in the long run.

Ans. True. A firm under perfect competition gets only a break-even price in the long run. It is a price which corresponds to normal profits in the long run.

20. There are no selling costs in perfect competition and monopoly forms of the market.

Ans. True. It is because homogeneous products are sold at a uniform price under perfect competition and because monopoly product has no close substitutes in the market.

21. A perfectly competitive firm operates at the lowest point of AC curve in the long run.

Ans. True. A perfectly competitive firm makes only normal profits (AR = AC) in the long run which happens only at the lowest point on the AC curve.

3. HOTS & Applications

1. Firm's demand curve as a horizontal straight line under perfect competition shows that an individual producer has no control over price of his product. Is it true?

Ans. Yes, it is true. Under perfect competition, demand curve of the firm is a horizontal straight line parallel to X-axis. It implies the firm will sell the product at the prevailing price which is determined by the industry. The individual firm cannot influence the price.

2. In the long period, level of output under monopoly is always less than under perfect competition, even when a monopolist earns extra normal profits. Do you agree?

Ans. Yes, it is true. In the long period, level of output under monopoly is less than under perfect competition. This is because under perfect competition, long period equilibrium is struck at the lowest point of AC. This indicates that the resources are most efficiently (optimally) utilised, offering us the highest possible output. Under monopoly, equilibrium at the lowest point (of AC) is not possible because price line slopes downward.

3. A monopoly firm can make abnormal profits in the long run, but not a firm under monopolistic competition. Do you agree?

Ans. Yes. A monopoly firm can make abnormal profits in the long run because of lack of freedom of entry and exit of firms in the market. Due to freedom of entry and exit of firms under monopolistic competition, a firm cannot earn abnormal profits in the long run.

4. Perfect competition is no competition. How?

Ans. Because a firm under perfect competition can sell whatever amount it wishes to sell at the existing price. It only has to adjust its output and supply; there is no price war or price competition in the market. Also, there is no commodity competition because all producers of a commodity are selling only homogeneous product; there is no product differentiation.

5. Does price never change under perfect competition, given the fact that a firm under perfect competition is a price taker?

Ans. A firm under perfect competition is a price taker; itself it cannot change price of the product in the market. But it does not mean that price of the product does not change in the market. Price under perfect competition is determined by the forces of market demand and market supply. Accordingly, it must change when either market supply or market demand happens to change.

6. Why a firm under perfect competition will not lower the price to increase its sales?

Ans. A perfectly competitive firm will not lower the price because of the following reasons:

(i) A firm under perfect competition can sell whatever amount it wishes to sell at the existing price. So that there is no rationality of lowering the price.

(ii) An individual firm under perfect competition is such a small supplier in the market that by lowering the price, it cannot ever cater to the entire market demand for the commodity. Accordingly, reduction in price cannot be sustained by an individual firm.

7. Do you find a situation of price rigidity under oligopoly? What does it lead to?

Ans. Yes, we do find the situation of price rigidity under oligopoly. It occurs as under:

(i) If the firm increases the price of the product, the rival firms may not increase it, leading to a loss of the market (because the buyers will shift to the rival firms).

(ii) If the firm lowers the price of the product, the rival firms may also lower it, leading to a loss of total revenue without any gain of additional buyers.

Hence, the price is neither raised nor lowered. Implying rigidity of the price. Rigidity of the price leads to non-price competition. Because of non-price competition, there are high selling costs. It keeps the market price higher than what it taught to be. Resources are not optimally utilised; social welfare is not maximised.

8. It is because of high degree of interdependence that firm's demand curve remains indeterminate under oligopoly. Comment.

Ans. Yes. Firm's demand curve is indeterminate under oligopoly because there is a high degree of interdependence among the firms. Price and output policy of one firm has a significant impact on the price and output policy of the rival firms in the market. When one firm lowers its price, the rival firms may also lower the price. And, when one firm raises the price, the rival firms may not do it. Accordingly, it becomes very difficult to estimate change in firm's sales caused by a change in price. Implying that a precise relationship between price and sales cannot be established. Or, that the firm's demand curve cannot be drawn.

9. The following headline appeared in *The Times of India,* on 28th December, 2014:

"Purchase only made-in-India gadgets."

Use economic theory to analyse the impact of the statement in terms of competition in the domestic market.

Ans. The government issued this advisory to its various departments. This is expected to offer protection to the domestic industry (producing gadgets) from foreign competition. Competition in the domestic market is likely to reduce. The market will drift more towards oligopolistic structure in which a few domestic firms dominate the market.

10. *There are different brands of cell phones sold in India, at a competitive price.*

What form of the market it is?

Ans. There are only a few well known brands dominating the cell phone market in India. Also each brand is facing a cut-throat competition. Both these characteristics point to oligopoly form of the market. Further, these oligopoly firms are engaged in a price competition. Which is why, over time cell phone prices in India have tended to decline. This points to the fact that cell phone market in India is more like non-collusive oligopoly rather that collusive oligopoly.

4. Evaluation (Value-based Questions)

1. **Is FDI (foreign direct investment) in retail trading a step towards competitive market structure? Give reason.**

Ans. FDI in retail trading is expected to promote competitive market structure. But, a market structure in which there is competition among a few. Because, only big firms can bring FDI. Once big firms enter the market, they tend to increase their control of the market through heavy advertisement. Initially, these firms may sell their product at a lower price, lower than the domestic producers. This is called 'price-cutting'. But once they achieve a strong foot-hold, they start exploiting the market by charging higher and higher price. There is a competitive market structure, but with high market concentration.

2. **What is the difference between 'perfectly competitive market structure' and 'competitive market structure under oligopoly'? Which of these two (market structures), in your opinion is more suitable for the growth and development of the Indian economy?**

Ans. Perfectly competitive market structure refers to that form of the market in which there is a large number of small producers. An individual producer exercises no control over the market. His production is only a small fragment of the total market sale. He exercises no control over price. He can sell any quantity at the given price. The producers earn only normal profits in the long run.

Competitive market structure under oligopoly refers to that form of the market in which there are a few big firms producing a commodity. Each firm has a significant share of the market. Accordingly, price and output of one firm significantly impacts the price and output policy of the rival firms. There is a high degree of interdependence among firms which leads to cut-throat competition. Each firm tries to increase its share of the market through innovative technology and by introducing innovative products in the market.

Both these market structures are suitable for the growth and development of the Indian economy. But in different areas of production activity.

Perfectly competitive market structure is most suited in the area of retail trade. In fact, already our retail trade activity is in the ambit of perfectly competitive market structure. Being dominated by a large number of small producers, retail trade in India is generating lots of employment opportunities. We understand how important it is in a country like India which is highly overpopulated and has a huge reserve of employable population.

On the other hand, there are certain areas of production which need huge investment and innovative technology. These include automobile industry, civil aviation, software engineering, defence goods industry, and the like. India lacks funds for investment as well as the innovative technology. Accordingly, we have to depend on 'multinational corporations'. These are global enterprises but a few in number. FDI (Foreign Direct Investment) by these enterprises would definitely lead to the emergence of oligopoly market structure. But this is the only way we can achieve growth in such areas of production activity which need high investment and innovative technology.

3. **How is elasticity of demand relevant to you when, as a monopolist, you are a price maker?**

Ans. Monopolist is a price maker, of course. But, he fixes price on the basis of elasticity of demand for his product. Higher the elasticity of demand, lower the price, and *vice versa*.

4. **As a student of Economics, how would you evaluate the implications of non-price competition in oligopoly form of the market?**

Ans. Non-price competition refers to a situation of the market in which oligopoly firms avoid competition by lowering price of the commodity. Instead they focus on competition through advertisements and lucrative offers for the buyers. In India, Coke and Pepsi sell their product at the same price. But in order to increase its share of the market, each firm takes to aggressive non-price competition. The firms spend heavily on the advertisements. Also, they spend heavily on event sponsorship (sponsoring games or sports) when their product is patronise.

Non-price competition leads to significant implications as under.

(i) Selling costs tend to mount up over and above the production costs.

(ii) Market price of the commodity tends to be much higher than its cost of production.

(iii) Allocation of resources becomes sub-optimum because demand is induced through advertisement rather than quality of the product.

(iv) Owing to sub-optimum allocation of resources, social welfare is not maximised.

Briefly, non-price competition leads to wasteful expenditure and the loss of social welfare.

5. Imagine yourself as a CEO of a global software company like Microsoft. How will you decide your price policy?

Ans. Global firms like Microsoft are operating in an oligopoly market structure. In such a market structure, priority is accorded to the formation of a cartel in which different firms collectively exploit the market like a monopolist. In case formation of a cartel is not possible (owing to legal restrictions), then non-price competition is the best option. It implies greater reliance on advertisement (pushing and promoting qualities of the product as well as benefits related to its purchase) rather than price-cutting. Competitive price policy is often avoided. Because, whenever product price is reduced, the rival firms may offer a higher reduction, causing a fall in profits.

5. CBSE Questions—Past 4 years (With Answers or Reference to the Text for Answers)

1. What is a price taker firm? *[CBSE Delhi 2012]*

   [Page 300, 311]

2. Explain the implication of large number of buyers in a perfectly competitive market. *[CBSE Delhi 2012; (F) 2014]*

   Or

   There are large number of buyers in a perfectly competitive market. Explain the significance of this feature. *[CBSE Delhi 2015]*

   [Page 298]

3. Explain why are firms mutually interdependent in an oligopoly market. *[CBSE Delhi 2012]*

   Or

   Why are the firms said to be interdependent in an oligopoly market? Explain. *[CBSE Delhi 2014]*

   [Page 307]

4. What is a price-maker firm? *[CBSE (AI) 2012]*

   [Page 303]

5. Explain the implications of large number of sellers in a perfectly competitive market. *[CBSE (AI) 2012]*

   Or

   There are large number of sellers in a perfectly competitive market. Explain the significance of this feature. *[CBSE Delhi 2015]*

   [Page 298]

6. Explain why there are only a few firms in an oligopoly market. *[CBSE (AI) 2012]*

   Or

   Why is the number of firms small in oligopoly? Explain. *[CBSE (AI) 2014]*

   Or

   Explain the cause of limited number of firms in an oligopoly market. *[CBSE (F) 2015]*

   [Page 307]

7. Define oligopoly. *[CBSE (F) 2012]*

   [Page 305]

8. Explain the implications of 'homogeneous product' in a perfectly competitive market. *[CBSE (F) 2012]*

Or

In a perfectly competitive market the buyers treat products of all the firms as homogeneous. Explain the significance of this feature. *[CBSE (AI) 2015]*

[Page 299]

9. Explain the implications of 'differentiated product' in monopolistic competition. *[CBSE (F) 2012]*

Or

Explain the significance of the feature 'product differentiation' in monopolistic competition. *[CBSE (F) 2015]*

[Page 304]

10. Explain "large number of buyers and sellers" feature of a perfectly competitive market. *[CBSE Delhi 2013]*

[Page 298]

11. Explain any two features of monopoly market. *[CBSE Delhi 2013]*

[Page 302]

12. Explain "freedom of entry and exit to firms in industry" feature of monopolistic competition. *[CBSE Delhi 2013]*

[Page 305]

13. A monopolist can sell any quantity he likes at a price. Is it true? Give reason for your answer. *[CBSE Delhi 2013]*

[False. A monopolist can sell more only by lowering the price of his product.]

14. Under which market form is a firm a price taker? *[CBSE (AI) 2013]*

[Page 300]

15. Why can a firm not earn abnormal profits under perfect competition in the long run? Explain. *[CBSE (AI) 2013]*

[Page 301]

16. Why is the demand curve of a firm under monopolistic competition more elastic than under monopoly? Explain. *[CBSE (AI) 2013]*

[Page 304]

17. Give the meaning of 'collusive' oligopoly. Explain any two features of oligopoly. *[CBSE (F) 2013]*

[Page 305–307]

18. What is perfect oligopoly? *[CBSE Delhi 2014]*

[Page 307]

19. What is imperfect oligopoly? *[CBSE (AI) 2014]*

[Page 307]

20. What is meant by collusive oligopoly? *[CBSE (F) 2014]*

[Page 307]

21. Explain the feature 'interdependence of firms' in an oligopoly market. *[CBSE Delhi 2015]*

[Page 306]

22. Explain the implication of non-price competition in an oligopoly market. *[CBSE (AI) 2015]*

[Page 306, 315, 316]

23. Distinguish between cooperative and non-cooperative oligopoly. *[CBSE (AI) 2015]*

[Page 307]

24. There are no barriers in the way of firms leaving or joining industry in a perfectly competitive market. Explain the significance of this feature. *[CBSE (F) 2015]*

[Page 299]

6. NCERT Questions (With Hints to Answers)

1. What are the characteristics of a perfectly competitive market?

   [**Hint:**

   (i) The number of buyers and sellers of a commodity is so large that no individual buyer or seller can influence the market price. Accordingly, a firm under perfect competition is only a price taker, not a price maker.

   (ii) All sellers sell identical units of a given product. Accordingly, even a partial control over price is not possible. A uniform price prevails in the market. Firm's demand curve (AR curve or price line) is indicated by a horizontal straight line, parallel to X-axis.

   (iii) Buyers and sellers have full knowledge regarding the prevailing market price.

   (iv) A firm can enter or leave the industry any time. Consequently, only normal profits prevail in the long run.]

2. Explain why the demand curve facing a firm under monopolistic competition is negatively sloped.

   [**Hint:** Partial control over price enables a firm to pursue its own price policy. But while it fixes the price, it cannot fix demand for its product. More can be sold only at a lower price. Implying a negatively sloped demand curve.]

3. What would be the shape of the demand curve so that the total revenue curve is a positively sloped straight line passing through the origin?

   [**Hint:** Demand curve will be a horizontal straight line parallel to X-axis so that the total revenue curve is a positively sloped straight line passing through the origin.]

4. Comment on the shape of the MR curve in case the TR curve is

   (i) a positively sloped straight line passing through the origin?

   (ii) a horizontal line?

   [**Hint:**

   (i) When TR curve is a positively sloped straight line passing through the origin, MR curve will be a horizontal straight line parallel to X-axis.

   (ii) When TR curve is a horizontal line, MR curve will touch X-axis, *i.e.,* MR will be zero (0). Because addition to TR (which is MR) will be zero in this case.]

7. Miscellaneous Questions and Reference to the Text for Answers

A. Questions of 3 & 4 marks each

1. State three features of perfect competition.
   [Page 298–300]
2. State three features of monopoly.
   [Page 302]
3. State three features of monopolistic competition.
   [Page 304, 305]
4. State three features of oligopoly.
   [Page 305, 306]
5. Explain the conditions of perfect competition. Why is the demand curve facing a firm under perfect competition perfectly elastic?
   [Page 298–301]
6. How is the demand curve under monopolistic competition different from demand curve of a firm under perfect competition?
   [Page 300, 301, 304]

7. To what extent firm under monopolistic market can influence the price of its product? On what factor does it depend?
[Page 304]
8. Distinguish between perfect competition and monopoly.
[Page 308]
9. Distinguish between perfect competition and monopolistic competition.
[Page 308]
10. Distinguish between monopoly and monopolistic competition.
[Page 308]
11. Why is the demand curve of a firm under perfect competition parallel to X-axis and negatively sloped under monopoly?
[Page 300–302]
12. Draw the average revenue curve of a firm under (i) Monopoly, and (ii) Perfect competition. Explain the difference in these curves, if any.
[Page 298, 300–302]
13. Explain the concept of cartels, giving an example of a cartel.
[Page 303, 307]

B. Questions of 6 marks each

1. Explain the basis on which different markets are defined.
[Page 308]
2. What are the characteristics of a perfectly competitive market? Explain.
[Page 298–300]
3. How is a seller under perfect competition a price taker and not a price maker? What is the relevance of the characteristic that there are "large number of sellers" in this context?
[Page 298, 300]
4. Explain the features of monopoly market.
[Page 302]
5. Explain the characteristics of monopolistic competition. Compare demand curves under monopolistic competition and monopoly.
[Page 302–305]
6. Define perfect competition. In what way does it differ from monopoly?
[Page 298, 301, 308]
7. Define monopoly. In what way does it differ from monopolistic competition?
[Page 301, 303, 308]
8. Define monopolistic competition. In what way does it differ from perfect competition?
[Page 298, 303, 308]
9. Explain the following features of perfect competition:
(i) Large number of buyers and sellers.
(ii) Homogeneous products.
[Page 298, 299]
10. Explain the following:
(i) 'Free entry and exit' feature of perfect competition.
(ii) 'Differentiated products' feature of monopolistic competition.
[Page 299, 304]

11. Explain the implications of the following:

(i) The feature 'differentiated products' under monopolistic competition.

(ii) The feature 'large number of sellers' under perfect competition.

[Page 298, 304]

12. Explain the characteristic features of oligopoly. Also distinguish between collusive and non-collusive oligopoly.

[Page 305–307]

13. Explain the following features of oligopoly:

(i) Small number of big firms.

(ii) Non-price competition.

[Page 305, 306]

DOs and DON'Ts

1. It needs to be noted with emphasis that a firm's demand curve/AR curve (also called price line) is a horizontal straight line (parallel to X-axis) when AR is constant. When AR is constant, MR = AR. Both AR and MR are indicated by the same horizontal straight line. This is a situation of a perfectly competitive market structure.

In case of monopoly and monopolistic competition, firm's demand curve slopes downward (from left to right). It indicates that more can be sold only at a lower price. Thus, as AR tends to fall, quantity demanded tends to rise. When AR falls, MR falls faster than AR.

In case of oligopoly, firm's demand curve cannot be specified. Because we cannot find any specific relationship between price and demand.

A query is sometimes raised by the readers: why discuss only the situations of (i) constant AR & MR, and (ii) declining AR & MR; why not also discuss the situation of rising AR & MR? The readers must note that such a question is absolutely irrelevant. Because, firm's demand curve (when it can be specified) is either a horizontal straight line (as under perfect competition) or a downward sloping curve (as under monopoly and monopolistic competition). Under no form of the market, firm's demand curve reflects a situation of rising AR (and MR). Studying such a situation would amount to making a ridiculous suggestion that more is sold when price is raised by a firm.

2. Do remember that, it is only under perfect competition that a firm (in the long run) strikes its equilibrium at a point where AC is the lowest. It is point Q in Fig. 4.

At point Q : (i) MR = MC, and (ii) MC is rising. Hence, the state of equilibrium.

At point Q : AR = AC. So that only normal profits are earned.

At point Q : Resources are most efficiently utilised. Because, Q indicates the lowest cost per unit of output.

Briefly, Q is a point of equilibrium when output is maximum, cost is minimum, and the producers generate only normal profits. Such an ideal situation is possible only and only under perfect competition.

FIGURE 4

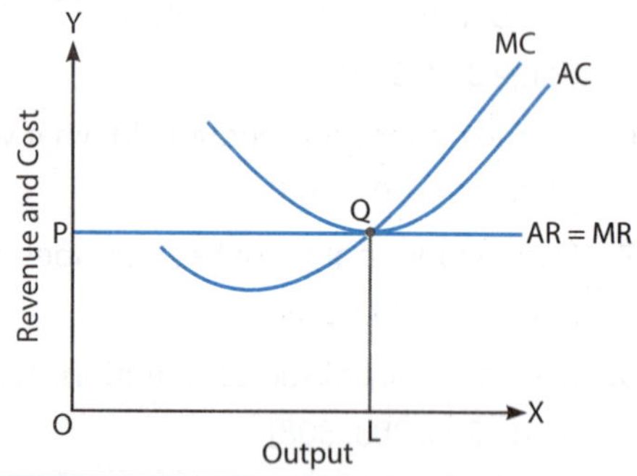

- MC cuts AC at its lowest point, Q.
- Q is the point of equilibrium. Here, (i) MR = MC, and (ii) MC is rising.
- At point Q : AC = MC = AR = MR.

ability ZONE

❑ Merits and Demerits of Monopoly

Monopoly form of the market is generally regarded as 'a dead weight' from the society's point of view. Of course, its demerits are many, yet there are few merits. Details are as under:

Merits

(i) **High Level of Skill and Efficiency:** If monopoly comes into existence through the merger of many firms, level of skill and efficiency tends to improve. Because diverse abilities of different firms are combined.

(ii) **High Level of Research and Development:** Monopoly firms, owing to their huge resources, can afford research and development in different areas of business growth. Accordingly, new techniques of production are discovered, besides new products and new uses of the existing products.

Demerits

(i) **Less Output:** Output under monopoly is always less than under perfect competition. Yes, it is true even when both under monopoly and perfect competition, firm's equilibrium is achieved when MR = MC.

This is because:

Whereas under perfect competition, a firm is to adjust its output to a given price, the monopolist tries to restrict his output with a view to raising the market price.

(ii) **High Price:** Monopoly firm always attempts to secure high price for its product with a view to maximising its profits. It achieves it by restricting its output/sale.

Geometrically, while under perfect competition, MC = MR = AR (price), under monopoly MC = MR < AR (price) because AR is always above MR. Thus, under perfect competition, price = MC while under monopoly, price > MC.

The difference between AR and MC is a measure of monopoly power, also called market power.

(iii) **Economic Concentration:** Monopoly form of the market encourages concentration of income and wealth. Unlike under perfect competition (where there is a large number of small firms producing a commodity), a monopolist is a single producer of a commodity in the market. This implies concentration of economic power through market control. This increases the gulf between the 'haves' and 'have nots'.

Briefly, while monopolies promise high level of efficiency, as their principal merit, 'restricted output' and 'high level of price' (or market control) are their principal demerits. It is with a view to discouraging market control that the government of a country (as in India) may resort to anti-trust legislations. These are the legislative measures (or legal measures) restricting the formation of such trusts which are expected to increase 'Market Control'.

[**Note:** Demerits of monopoly suggest how a perfectly competitive market is better than monopoly market. Likewise, merits of monopoly suggest how monopoly market is better than a perfectly competitive market.]

❑ Competitive Behaviour Vs Competitive Market Structure

Competitive behaviour refers to a situation when producers compete with each other for a greater market share, like Coke and Pepsi are competing across different parts of the world. Competitive market structure is where there is a large number of sellers selling a product. It is a situation like that of perfect competition where each producer can sell whatever quantity of the commodity he wishes to sell at the given market price. It is important to note that even when there is perfect competition, there is no competitive behaviour of the producers to increase their market share.

❑ A Situation of Zero Cost Monopoly

Consider a situation when there is only one spring catering to the drinking water requirement of a village in a remote area. This spring happens to be under control of one individual. It is a typical situation of zero cost monopoly. How much water would the owner of this spring sell? Obviously, till his TR is maximised. We know TR is maximised when MR = 0. Implying that a monopolist (with zero cost of production) would supply his product till MR = 0, so that TR is maximised.

FIGURE 5

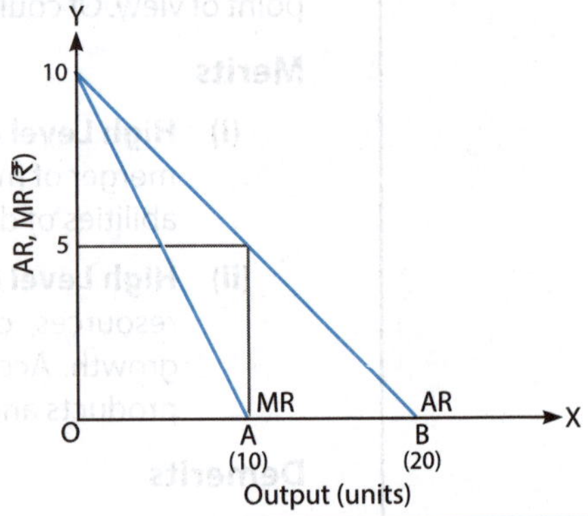

Fig. 5 shows that at zero price, demand stretches to 20 units. But the monopolist is interested in maximising his revenue which occurs when he sells 10 units (half of 20, the maximum market demand), when MR = 0, and the price = ₹ 5.

> **In a situation of zero cost of production, the monopolist maximises his TR when MR = 0. This occurs when he sells half the total output demanded at zero price.**

Market Equilibrium Under Perfect Competition and Effects of Shifts in Demand and Supply

HAPTER 12

TODO

- Concept of Market Equilibrium: Equilibrium Price and Equilibrium Quantity
- Determination of Market Equilibrium Under Perfect Competition
- Effect of Shift in Demand and Supply on Market Equilibrium: How Chain Effect Works?
- Simultaneous Change in Demand & Supply and Market Equilibrium
- Simple Applications of Tools of Demand and Supply Curves

1. Concept of Market Equilibrium: Equilibrium Price and Equilibrium Quantity

Market equilibrium is defined as a state of the market when demand for a commodity is equal to its supply, corresponding to a particular price. Thus, in a state of equilibrium, the market clears itself: market demand = market supply of a commodity ($D_X = S_X$). There is neither excess demand nor excess supply. In such a situation, the price that prevails in the market is called equilibrium price. Quantity supplied/ demanded is called equilibrium quantity.

Market equilibrium occurs when $D_X = S_X$. It leads to:

(i) equilibrium price, the price which clears the market as market demand is exactly equal to market supply ($D_X = S_X$).

(ii) equilibrium quantity, the quantity that leaves no excess demand or excess supply in the market (because $S_X = D_X$).

In fact, equilibrium price implies the situation of equilibrium quantity and equilibrium quantity implies the situation of equilibrium price.

2. Determination of Market Equilibrium Under Perfect Competition

Under perfect competition, market equilibrium is determined by the forces of (i) market demand, and (ii) market supply. Recall the concepts of market demand and market supply as discussed in chapters 4 and 10 of the book:

Market demand refers to the sum total of demand for a commodity by all the buyers in the market.

Market supply refers to the sum total of supply of a commodity by all the firms in the market.

In the context of market equilibrium when we talk of market demand and market supply, we are in fact referring to market demand schedule and market supply schedule (or market demand curve and market supply curve).

Market demand schedule (or market demand curve) shows different amounts of a commodity that the buyers are ready to buy corresponding to different possible prices of the commodity.

Market supply schedule (or market supply curve) shows different amounts of a commodity that the sellers or firms are willing to sell corresponding to different possible prices in the market.

Market equilibrium is struck when, at the prevailing price in the market, quantity demanded is equal to quantity supplied. There is no excess demand or excess supply in the market. Table 1 and Fig. 1 illustrate the situation of market equilibrium.

Table 1. Market Equilibrium Under Perfect Competition

Price of Commodity-X (₹)	Quantity Supplied of Commodity-X (Dozen)	Quantity Demanded of Commodity-X (Dozen)	
5	50	10	Excess Supply
4	40	20	
3	**30**	**30**	← Market Equilibrium
2	20	40	Excess Demand
1	10	50	

FIGURE 1

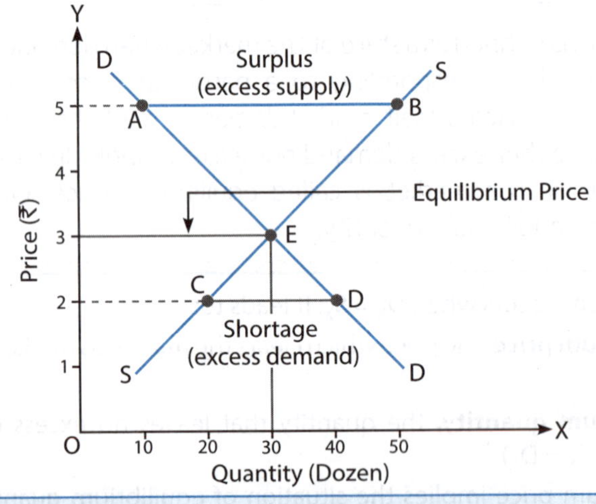

✦ Equilibrium is struck at point E.
Here, equilibrium price = ₹ 3; equilibrium quantity = 30 dozen.

✦ If price happens to be ₹ 5, there is excess supply = AB. If price happens to be ₹ 2, there is excess demand = CD.

Table 1 shows that when price of commodity-X is ₹ 5, market supply = 50 dozen and market demand = 10 dozen. It is a situation of excess supply and excess stocks. At a given price, producers are willing to sell more than what the buyers are willing to buy. Pressure of excess supply (and excess stocks) reduces the market price. Supposing, the price reduces from ₹ 5 to ₹ 4. Reduction in own price of the commodity leads to a rise in quantity demanded (in accordance with the law of demand) and a fall in quantity supplied (in accordance with the law of supply). Consequently, quantity demanded increases to 20 dozen whereas quantity supplied reduces to 40 dozen. Even at this price, market is not cleared: market demand < market supply. Pressure of excess supply still exists in the market. This will lead to further reduction in price. Supposing it reduces to ₹ 3 per dozen. Now, quantity demanded increases to 30 dozen while quantity supplied decreases to 30 dozen. Thus (when P_X = ₹ 3), quantity supplied and quantity demanded are equal to each other. The market clears itself. Accordingly, ₹ 3 is the equilibrium price; 30 dozen is the equilibrium quantity. There is no excess demand or excess supply in the market.

In Fig.1, DD is demand curve and SS is supply curve. They intersect each other at point E, where market demand = market supply. Thus, point E is the equilibrium point. This point shows that equilibrium price is ₹ 3 and equilibrium quantity is 30 dozen. If initially price (P_X) happens to be ₹ 5, then market supply (50 dozen) exceeds market demand (10 dozen). This is a situation of excess supply. This is equal to AB in Fig. 1. Pressure of excess supply leads to reduction in market price. In response to it, quantity supplied tends to fall and quantity demanded tends to rise. Fall in quantity supplied is indicated by a movement along the supply curve from B towards E. Rise in quantity demanded is indicated by a movement along the demand curve from A towards E. It is at point E, that the excess supply is finally eliminated. Now, quantity demanded = quantity supplied = 30 dozen. Corresponding to this equilibrium quantity, equilibrium price is ₹ 3. The market is cleared. Likewise, if initially P_X happens to be ₹ 2, then market supply (20 dozen) will be less than market demand (40 dozen). This is a situation of excess demand. This is equal to CD in Fig. 1. Pressure of excess demand will lead to a rise in market price. In response to it, quantity demanded tends to fall and quantity supplied tends to rise. Fall in quantity demanded is indicated by a movement along the demand curve from D towards E. Rise in quantity supplied is indicated by a movement along the supply curve from C towards E. It is at point E, that the excess demand is finally eliminated. Now quantity demanded = quantity supplied = 30 dozen, and equilibrium price is ₹ 3. The market is cleared.

Three Basic Assumptions of Market Equilibrium Under Perfect Competition

These are that:

(i) Price and quantity supplied are positively related, or that supply curve of a commodity slopes upward from left to right.

(ii) Price and quantity demanded are negatively related, or that demand curve of a commodity slopes downward from left to right.

(iii) Forces of supply and demand operate freely without any government intervention.

HOTS

Q. How are decisions taken by consumers and producers in a market co-ordinated?

Ans. The decisions of consumers in the market are expressed through market demand schedule and market demand curve. The decisions of the producers are expressed through market supply schedule and market supply curve. The decisions of consumers and producers are co-ordinated by the interaction of market demand and market supply. This is known as **price mechanism**.

3. Effect of Shift in Demand and Supply on Market Equilibrium: How Chain Effect Works?
Or
How Market Absorbs the Impact of Shift in Demand and Supply of a Commodity?

We have already studied how, under conditions of perfect competition, market (for a commodity) finds its equilibrium automatically through the free play of supply and demand forces. Let us now examine the impact (on market equilibrium) of shifts in demand and supply related to a commodity. In what follows, we study the chain effect of shift in demand and shift in supply.

Chain Effect of Shift in Demand

Shift in demand refers to increase in demand or decrease in demand. It occurs owing to change in determinants of demand, other than own price of the commodity. **Example:** Demand increases when there is increase in income of the buyers, and decreases when there is decrease in income of the buyers. We know in a situation of increase in demand, demand curve shifts to the right, while in a situation of decrease in demand, demand curve shifts to the left. Fig. 2(A) shows increase in demand, while Fig. 2(B) shows decrease in demand. The chain effect of increase/decrease in demand is described in terms of observations written below Fig. 2(A) and 2(B) respectively.

FIGURE 2

(A) Chain Effect of Increase in Demand or How Market Absorbs the Impact of Increase in Demand

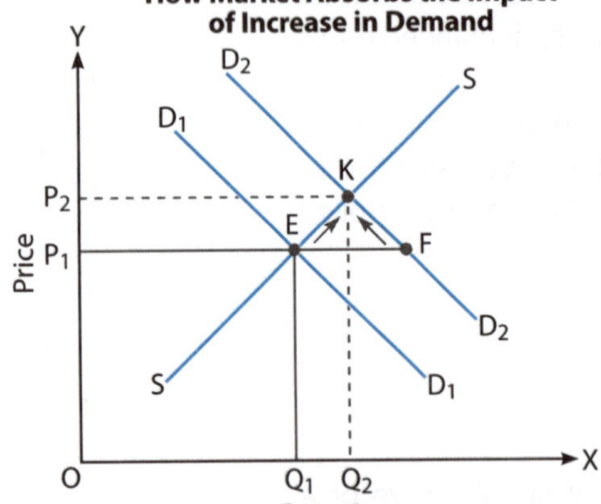

(B) Chain Effect of Decrease in Demand or How Market Absorbs the Impact of Decrease in Demand

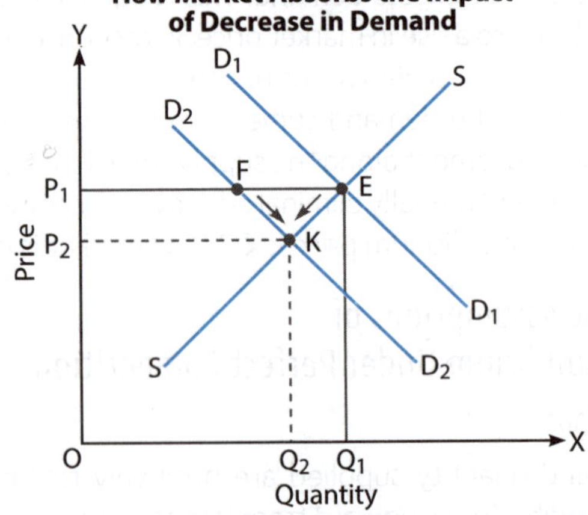

Fig. (A)
- E: The point of initial equilibrium.
- Increase in Demand: Demand curve shifts from D_1D_1 to D_2D_2. It causes excess demand.
- Excess Demand = EF. It leads to rise in price from OP_1 to OP_2.
- Rise in price causes extension of supply from E to K, and contraction of demand from F to K.
- K : The point of new equilibrium. New equilibrium price $= OP_2$; New equilibrium quantity $= OQ_2$.

Observations

(i) D_1D_1 is the initial demand curve, crossing supply curve at point E, the point of initial equilibrium.

(ii) Owing to increase in demand, demand curve shifts to the right, from D_1D_1 to D_2D_2. And, at the existing price (OP_1), quantity demanded rises from point E to point F.

Fig. (B)
- E: The point of initial equilibrium.
- Decrease in Demand: Demand curve shifts from D_1D_1 to D_2D_2. It causes excess supply.
- Excess Supply = EF. It leads to fall in price from OP_1 to OP_2.
- Fall in price causes extension of demand from F to K, and contraction of supply from E to K.
- K : The point of new equilibrium. New equilibrium price $= OP_2$; New equilibrium quantity $= OQ_2$.

Observations

(i) D_1D_1 is the initial demand curve, crossing supply curve at point E, the point of initial equilibrium.

(ii) Owing to decrease in demand, demand curve shifts to the left, from D_1D_1 to D_2D_2. And, at the existing price (OP_1), quantity demanded falls from point E to point F.

(iii) As an immediate impact of increase in demand, there is excess demand in the market. It is = EF (at the existing price).

(iv) Owing to the pressure of demand, price of the commodity tends to be higher than the equilibrium price: it rises from OP_1 to OP_2.

(v) Owing to a rise in price, quantity demanded tends to contract. Contraction of demand occurs from point F towards point K.

(vi) Owing to a rise in price, quantity supplied tends to extend. The extension of supply occurs from point E towards point K.

(vii) The process of extension of supply and contraction of demand (caused by a rise in price) continues till excess demand is fully eliminated, and the market clears itself once again.

(viii) K is the point of new equilibrium, where Supply = Demand, and the market clears itself once again.

(ix) Corresponding to the new equilibrium, quantity demanded/supplied = OQ_2, and equilibrium price = OP_2.

(x) The net effect of increase in demand is: (a) increase in equilibrium price from OP_1 to OP_2, and (b) increase in equilibrium quantity from OQ_1 to OQ_2.

(iii) As an immediate impact of decrease in demand, there is excess supply in the market. It is = EF (at the existing price).

(iv) Owing to excess supply, price of the commodity tends to be lower than the equilibrium price: it falls from OP_1 to OP_2.

(v) Owing to a fall in price, quantity demanded tends to extend. Extension of demand occurs from point F towards point K.

(vi) Owing to a fall in price, quantity supplied tends to contract. The contraction of supply occurs from point E towards point K.

(vii) The process of extension of demand and contraction of supply (caused by a fall in price) continues till excess supply is fully eliminated, and the market clears itself once again.

(viii) K is the point of new equilibrium, where Supply = Demand, and the market clears itself once again.

(ix) Corresponding to the new equilibrium, quantity demanded/supplied = OQ_2, and equilibrium price = OP_2.

(x) The net effect of decrease in demand is: (a) decrease in equilibrium price from OP_1 to OP_2, and (b) decrease in equilibrium quantity from OQ_1 to OQ_2.

Chain Effect of Shift in Supply

As in case of demand, shift in supply refers to increase in supply or decrease in supply. It occurs due to change in determinants of supply, other than own price of the commodity. **Example:** Supply increases when cost of production falls, and decreases when cost of production rises. (Supply may increase also when new firms enter the industry, and decrease when some existing firms leave the industry.) We know, in a situation of increase in supply, supply curve shifts to the right, while in a situation of decrease in supply, supply curve shifts to the left. Fig. 3(A) shows increase in supply, while Fig. 3(B) shows decrease in supply. How the market absorbs the impact of increase/decrease in supply is described in terms of the observations written below Fig. 3(A) and 3(B) respectively.

FIGURE 3

(A) Chain Effect of Increase in Supply or How Market Absorbs the Impact of Increase in Supply

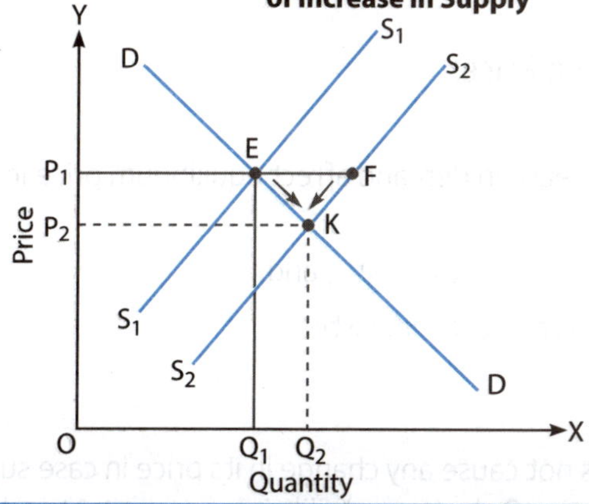

(B) Chain Effect of Decrease in Supply or How Market Absorbs the Impact of Decrease in Supply

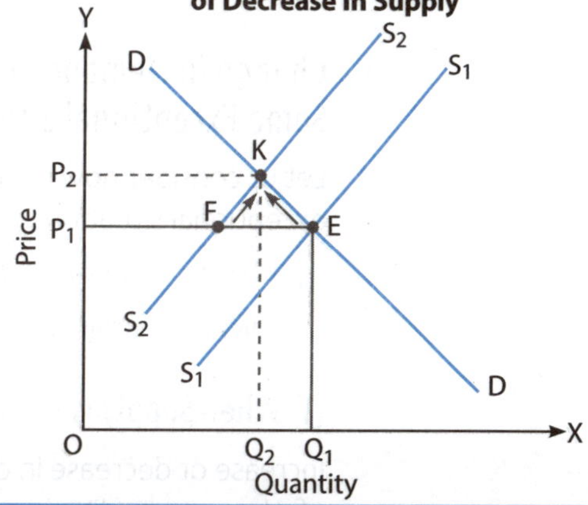

Fig. (A)
- E: The point of initial equilibrium.
- Increase in Supply: Supply curve shifts from S_1S_1 to S_2S_2.
- Excess Supply = EF. It leads to fall in price from OP_1 to OP_2.
- Fall in price causes extension of demand from E to K, and contraction of supply from F to K.
- K : The point of new equilibrium. New equilibrium price = OP_2; New equilibrium quantity = OQ_2.

Fig. (B)
- E : The point of initial equilibrium.
- Decrease in Supply: Supply curve shifts from S_1S_1 to S_2S_2.
- Excess Demand = EF. It leads to rise in price from OP_1 to OP_2.
- Rise in price causes contraction of demand from E to K, and extension of supply from F to K.
- K : The point of new equilibrium. New equilibrium price = OP_2; New equilibrium quantity = OQ_2.

Observations

(i) S_1S_1 is the initial supply curve, crossing demand curve at point E, the point of initial equilibrium.

(ii) Owing to increase in supply, supply curve shifts to the right, from S_1S_1 to S_2S_2.

(iii) As an immediate impact of increase in supply, there is excess supply = EF (at the existing price).

(iv) Owing to excess supply, price of the commodity tends to be lower than the equilibrium price: it falls from OP_1 to OP_2.

(v) Owing to a fall in price, quantity demanded tends to extend. Extension of demand occurs from point E towards point K.

(vi) Owing to a fall in price, quantity supplied tends to contract. The contraction of supply occurs from point F towards point K.

(vii) The process of extension of demand and contraction of supply (caused by a fall in price) continues till the excess supply is fully eliminated, and the market clears itself once again.

(viii) K is the point of new equilibrium where the market clears itself once again.

(ix) Corresponding to the new equilibrium, quantity demanded = quantity supplied = OQ_2. And, equilibrium price = OP_2.

(x) The net effect of increase in supply is: (a) equilibrium price reduces from OP_1 to OP_2, and (b) equilibrium quantity rises from OQ_1 to OQ_2.

Observations

(i) S_1S_1 is the initial supply curve, crossing demand curve at point E, the point of initial equilibrium.

(ii) Owing to decrease in supply, supply curve shifts to the left, from S_1S_1 to S_2S_2.

(iii) As an immediate impact of decrease in supply, there is excess demand = EF (at the existing price).

(iv) Owing to excess demand, price tends to be higher than the equilibrium price: it rises from OP_1 to OP_2.

(v) Owing to a rise in price, quantity demanded tends to contact. Contraction of demand occurs from point E towards point K.

(vi) Owing to a rise in price, quantity supplied tends to extend. Extension of supply occurs from point F towards point K.

(vii) The process of extension of supply and contraction of demand (caused by a rise in price) continues till excess demand is fully eliminated, and the market clears itself once again.

(viii) K is the point of new equilibrium, where the market clears itself once again.

(ix) Corresponding to the new equilibrium, quantity demanded = quantity supplied = OQ_2. And, equilibrium price = OP_2.

(x) The net effect of decrease in supply is: (a) equilibrium price increases from OP_1 to OP_2, and (b) equilibrium quantity decreases from OQ_1 to OQ_2.

HOTS

Q. Increase in demand always causes a rise in price. Comment.

Ans. It is only when other things remain constant that the increase in demand leads to increase in price. But if other things are not constant then this relationship may not hold good. For example, if there is an equal increase in supply, the price may not increase. In fact if the increase in the supply is more than the increase in demand, the price may fall. Also, in a situation when supply is perfectly elastic, price remains constant, no matter what the increase in demand is [see Fig. 4(A)].

Change in Demand and Equilibrium Price: Some Exceptional Situations

Let us consider how increase and decrease in demand affect equilibrium price in two exceptional situations:

(1) When supply of the commodity is perfectly elastic, and

(2) When supply of the commodity is perfectly inelastic.

(1) When Supply is Perfectly Elastic

Increase or decrease in demand does not cause any change in its price in case supply of the commodity is perfectly elastic. Only the equilibrium quantity tends to change. This is illustrated in Fig. 4(A) and 4(B).

Fig. 4(A) shows E as the point of equilibrium where perfectly elastic supply curve (SS) intersects demand curve (DD). OP is the equilibrium price. Forward shift in demand curve from DD to D_1D_1 leaves price of the commodity unchanged at OP. However, equilibrium quantity increases from OQ to OQ_1.

Likewise, backward shift in demand curve from DD to D_2D_2 [as in Fig. 4(B)] causes a decrease in equilibrium quantity from OQ to OQ_2. Price of the commodity remains unaffected at OP.

FIGURE 4

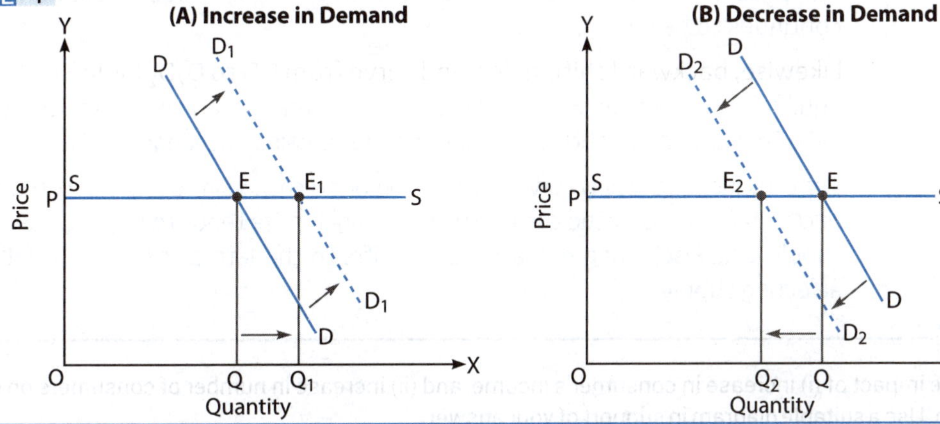

✦ Fig. 4(A) shows increase in demand when supply is perfectly elastic. Price remains unaffected. Equilibrium quantity increases from OQ to OQ_1.

✦ Fig. 4(B) shows decrease in demand when supply is perfectly elastic. Here also, price remains unaffected. Equilibrium quantity decreases from OQ to OQ_2.

HOTS

Q. Why price remains unchanged when supply curve is perfectly elastic and demand curve shifts?

Ans. Perfectly elastic supply implies a situation of infinite supply corresponding to a given price. In such a situation, if demand curve shifts to the right (implying increase in demand) it does not lead to excess demand because (at the existing price) supply is infinite. Hence, price remains constant. Likewise, if demand curve shifts to the left (implying decrease in demand) it does not lead to excess supply. Because (at the existing price) supply is infinite. Hence, price remains constant.

(2) When Supply is Perfectly Inelastic

In a situation of perfectly inelastic supply (or constant supply), increase or decrease in demand causes a change in price of the commodity. Equilibrium quantity remains constant simply because supply is perfectly inelastic. This is illustrated in Fig. 5(A) and 5(B).

FIGURE 5

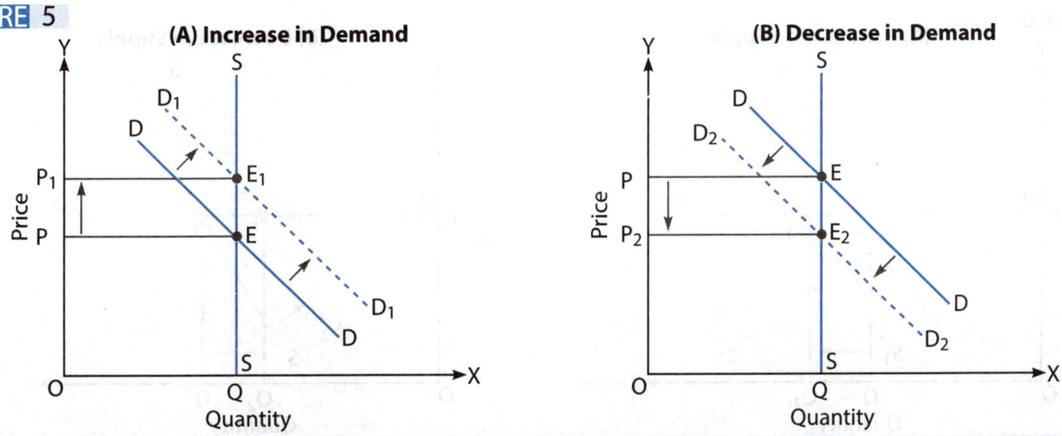

✦ Fig. 5(A) shows perfectly inelastic supply (=OQ). In such a situation, forward shift in demand curve (from DD to D_1D_1) causes an increase in price from OP to OP_1. Equilibrium quantity remains constant (=OQ).

✦ Fig. 5(B) shows perfectly inelastic supply (=OQ). Here, demand curve shifts to the left (from DD to D_2D_2). Equilibrium price reduces from OP to OP_2. Equilibrium quantity remains constant (= OQ).

Fig. 5(A) shows E as the point of equilibrium where perfectly inelastic supply curve (SS) intersects demand curve (DD). OP is the equilibrium price.

Forward shift in demand curve from DD to D_1D_1 shifts equilibrium point from E to E_1. The price of the commodity increases from OP to OP_1 but equilibrium quantity continues to be OQ.

Likewise, backward shift in demand curve from DD to D_2D_2 [as in Fig. 5(B)] shifts equilibrium point from E to E_2. This causes a decrease in equilibrium price from OP to OP_2. Equilibrium quantity of the commodity remains unchanged at OQ.

Perfectly inelastic supply curve is a situation of no change in supply, no matter what the price is. So, when demand curve shifts to the right, price tends to rise without affecting supply. Likewise, when demand curve shifts to the left, price tends to fall without affecting supply.

HOTS

Q. Analyse the impact of (i) increase in consumer's income, and (ii) increase in number of consumers on market equilibrium. Use a suitable diagram in support of your answer.

Ans. (i) When income of the consumers rises, demand curve shifts to the right [refer to Fig. 2(A) and observations below it].

(ii) When number of consumers increases, quantity demanded tends to increase at the existing price. Again, it implies a forward shift in demand curve [refer to Fig. 2(A) and observations below it].

Change in Supply and Equilibrium Price: Some Exceptional Situations

Let us consider how increase and decrease in supply affect equilibrium price in two exceptional situations:

(1) When demand for the commodity is perfectly elastic, and

(2) When demand for the commodity is perfectly inelastic.

(1) When Demand is Perfectly Elastic

Increase or decrease in supply of a commodity does not cause any change in its price in case demand for the commodity is perfectly elastic. Only the equilibrium quantity tends to change. This is illustrated in Fig. 6(A) and 6(B).

FIGURE 6

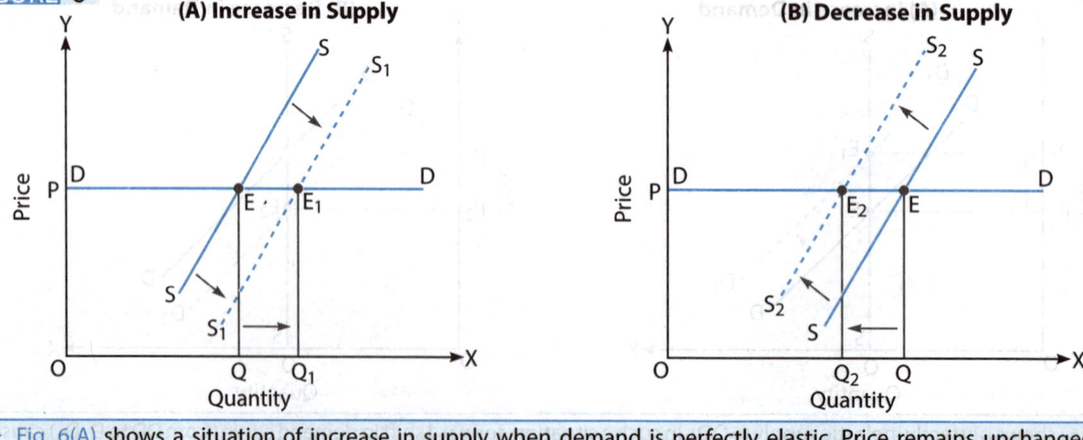

✦ Fig. 6(A) shows a situation of increase in supply when demand is perfectly elastic. Price remains unchanged at OP. Equilibrium quantity increases from OQ to OQ_1.

✦ Fig. 6(B) shows a situation of decrease in supply when demand is perfectly elastic. Price remains unchanged at OP. Equilibrium quantity decreases from OQ to OQ_2.

Fig. 6(A) shows E as the point of equilibrium where perfectly elastic demand curve (DD) intersects supply curve (SS). OP is the equilibrium price.

Increase in supply implies a shift in supply curve to the right (from SS to S_1S_1). It does not cause any change in equilibrium price. It continues to be OP. However, equilibrium quantity increases from OQ to OQ_1.

Decrease in supply implies a shift in supply curve to the left (from SS to S_2S_2). It causes a decrease in the equilibrium quantity from OQ to OQ_2. Price of the commodity remains constant at OP.

Perfectly elastic demand is a situation of infinite demand corresponding to a given price. In such a situation, increase or decrease in supply (supply curve shifting to right or left) does not cause any impact on the price. Decrease in supply will not cause excess demand and increase in supply will not cause excess supply (or deficiency of demand). Because, demand is infinite at the existing price. Accordingly, price will not change.

(2) When Demand is Perfectly Inelastic

In a situation of perfectly inelastic demand (or constant demand) increase or decrease in supply causes a full impact on price of the commodity. Of course, equilibrium quantity remains constant, simply because demand is constant. This is illustrated in Fig. 7(A) and 7(B).

FIGURE 7

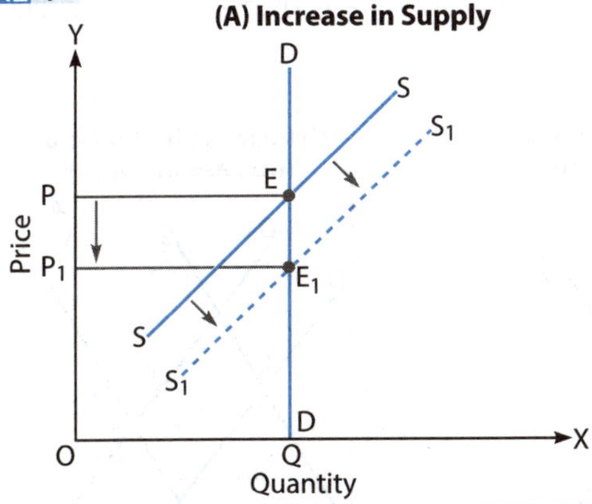

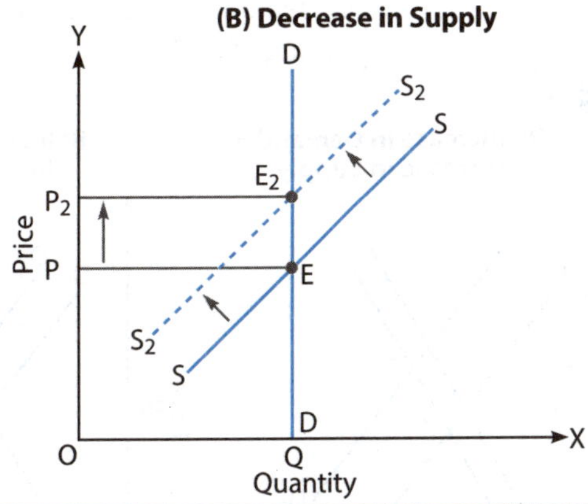

- Fig. 7(A) shows a situation of increase in supply when demand is perfectly inelastic. Equilibrium price reduces from OP to OP_1. Equilibrium quantity remains constant at OQ.
- Fig. 7(B) shows a situation of decrease in supply when demand is perfectly inelastic. Equilibrium price increases from OP to OP_2. Equilibrium quantity remains constant at OQ.

Fig. 7(A) shows E as the point of equilibrium where supply curve (SS) intersects perfectly inelastic demand curve (DD). OP is the equilibrium price. Increase in supply implies a shift in supply curve to the right from SS to S_1S_1 [as in Fig. 7(A)]. As a result, equilibrium quantity of the commodity remains unaffected. It continues to be OQ. The equilibrium price decreases from OP to OP_1.

Decrease in supply implies a shift in supply curve to the left from SS to S_2S_2 [as in Fig. 7(B)]. It causes an increase in the equilibrium price from OP to OP_2. Equilibrium quantity remains unchanged at OQ.

In a situation of perfectly inelastic demand curve, demand remains constant, no matter what the price is. Accordingly, when supply curve shifts to the right (and price tends to fall) or when it shifts to the left (and price tends to rise), demand remains constant. However, equilibrium price falls when supply increases, and it rises when supply decreases.

HOTS

Q. **Analyse the impact of (i) increase in the number of firms, and (ii) decrease in input price on the equilibrium price and equilibrium quantity. Use diagram.**

Ans. (i) When the number of firms increases, market supply of the commodity increases. Supply curve shifts to the right [refer to Fig. 3(A) and observations below it].

(ii) When input price decreases, cost of production reduces. It cases a forward shift in supply curve [refer to Fig. 3(A) and observations below it].

4. Simultaneous Change in Demand & Supply and Market Equilibrium

So far, we have studied the effect on market equilibrium of either the change in demand or the change in supply.

However, there may be simultaneous changes both in demand and supply. There may be simultaneous increase in demand and supply, or there may be simultaneous decrease in demand and supply. These situations are discussed as under:

(1) Simultaneous Increase in Demand and Supply

Simultaneous increase in demand and supply must lead to increase in equilibrium quantity of the commodity. But the change in price depends on whether: (i) Increase in demand = Increase in supply, (ii) Increase in demand > Increase in supply, and (iii) Increase in demand < Increase in supply. These situations are diagrammatically illustrated through Fig. 8.

FIGURE 8

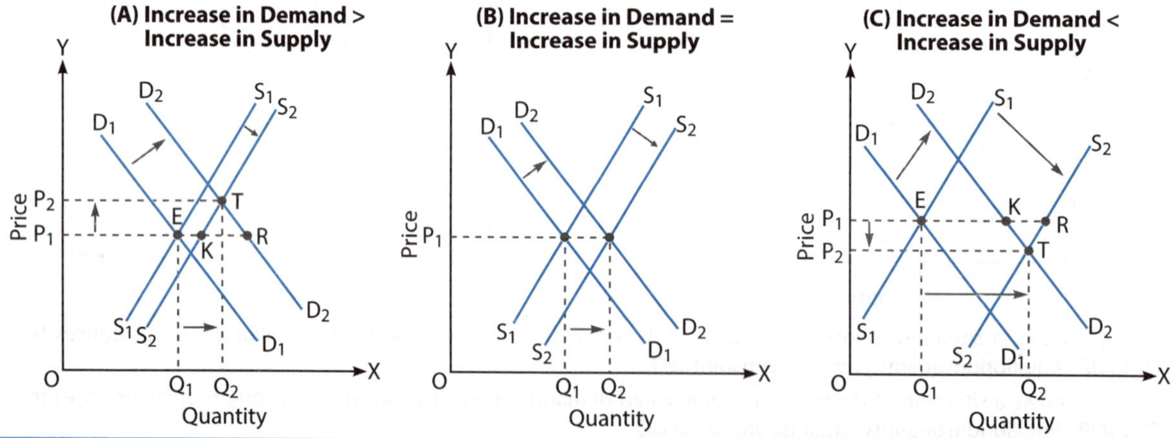

- In Fig. 8(A), increase in demand is greater than increase in supply. It causes excess demand. Accordingly, equilibrium price tends to rise from OP_1 to OP_2. Equilibrium quantity increases from OQ_1 to OQ_2.
- In Fig. 8(B), increase in demand is equal to increase in supply. It keeps supply and demand in a state of equilibrium corresponding to the same price. Accordingly, there is no change in equilibrium price. Equilibrium quantity increases from OQ_1 to OQ_2.
- In Fig. 8(C), increase in demand is less than increase in supply. It leads to excess supply. Accordingly, equilibrium price tends to fall from OP_1 to OP_2. Equilibrium quantity increases from OQ_1 to OQ_2.

(i) In Fig. 8(A), D_1D_1 is the initial demand curve and S_1S_1 is the initial supply curve. E is the point of initial equilibrium. OP_1 is equilibrium price and OQ_1 is equilibrium quantity. Due to increase in demand, D_2D_2 is the new demand curve. Due to increase in supply, S_2S_2 is the new supply curve. One can see that increase in demand (= ER) is greater than increase in supply (= EK). Excess demand = ER – EK = KR. This will cause a rise in price. Rise in price causes contraction of demand and extension of supply. Demand contracts from point R towards point T.

Supply extends from point K towards point T. New equilibrium is struck at point T. Here, S_2S_2 and D_2D_2 intersect each other. It shows that: (a) equilibrium price rises from OP_1 to OP_2, and (b) equilibrium quantity rises from OQ_1 to OQ_2.

(ii) In Fig. 8(B), increase in demand is equal to increase in supply. There does not emerge a situation of either excess demand or excess supply. Accordingly, equilibrium price remains unchanged, *i.e.*, OP_1. However, equilibrium quantity increases from OQ_1 to OQ_2. This is because both demand and supply happen to rise.

(iii) In Fig. 8(C), D_1D_1 is the initial demand curve and S_1S_1 is the initial supply curve. E is the point of initial equilibrium. OP_1 is equilibrium price and OQ_1 is the equilibrium quantity. Due to increase in demand, D_2D_2 is the new demand curve. Due to increase in supply, S_2S_2 is the new supply curve. One can see that increase in demand (= EK) is less than increase in supply (= ER). Excess supply (or deficient demand) = ER – EK = KR. This leads to fall in price. Fall in price causes extension of demand and contraction of supply. Demand extends from point K towards point T. Supply contracts from point R towards point T. Now market equilibrium is struck at point T. Here, Demand = Supply = OQ_2. The net effect is that: (a) equilibrium price reduces from OP_1 to OP_2, and (b) equilibrium quantity increases from OQ_1 to OQ_2.

(2) Simultaneous Decrease in Supply and Demand

Fig. 9 illustrates the effect of simultaneous decrease in demand and supply on price and quantity.

FIGURE 9

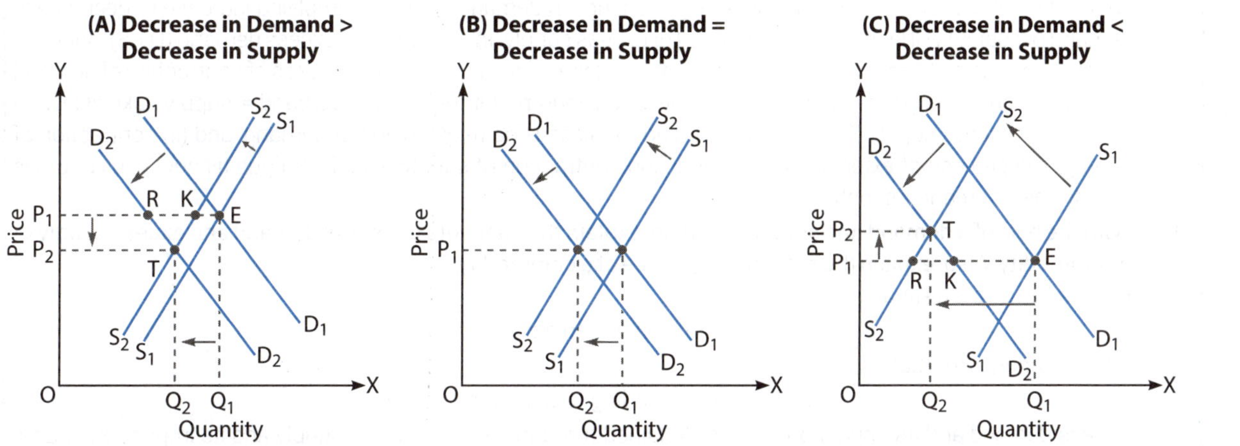

- In Fig. 9(A), decrease in demand is greater than decrease in supply. It is a situation of excess supply. Accordingly, equilibrium price tends to fall from OP_1 to OP_2. Equilibrium quantity decreases from OQ_1 to OQ_2.
- In Fig. 9(B), decrease in demand is equal to decrease in supply. It keeps supply and demand in a state of equilibrium corresponding to the same price. Accordingly, there is no change in equilibrium price. Equilibrium quantity reduces from OQ_1 to OQ_2.
- In Fig. 9(C), decrease in supply is greater than decrease in demand. It is a situation of excess demand. Accordingly, equilibrium price increases from OP_1 to OP_2. Equilibrium quantity decreases from OQ_1 to OQ_2.

(i) In Fig. 9(A), D_1D_1 is the initial demand curve and S_1S_1 the initial supply curve. E is the point of initial equilibrium. OP_1 is equilibrium price and OQ_1 is equilibrium quantity. Due to decrease in demand, D_2D_2 is the new demand curve. Due to decrease in supply, S_2S_2 is the new supply curve. In this figure, demand has decreased more than supply. It is a situation of excess supply. Excess supply = ER (fall in demand) – EK (fall in supply) = RK. Accordingly, price tends to fall. Because of a fall in price, there is extension of demand and contraction of supply.

Demand extends from point R towards point T. Supply contracts from point K towards point T. New equilibrium is struck at point T. Here, S_2S_2 and D_2D_2 intersect each other. It shows that: (a) equilibrium price falls from OP_1 to OP_2, and (ii) equilibrium quantity falls from OQ_1 to OQ_2.

(ii) In Fig. 9(B), decrease in demand is equal to decrease in supply. There does not emerge a situation of excess demand or excess supply. Accordingly, there is no change in equilibrium price (= OP_1). However, equilibrium quantity decreases from OQ_1 to OQ_2. This is because both demand and supply happen to decrease.

(iii) In Fig. 9(C), S_1S_1 is the initial supply curve and D_1D_1 is the initial demand curve. E is the point of initial equilibrium. OP_1 is equilibrium price and OQ_1 is equilibrium quantity. D_2D_2 is the new demand curve, indicating decrease in demand. S_2S_2 is the new supply curve, indicating decrease in supply. In this figure, decrease in supply is greater than decrease in demand. It is a situation of excess demand. Excess demand = ER (fall in supply) – EK (fall in demand) = RK. Accordingly, price tends to rise. Because of a rise in price, there is contraction of demand and extension of supply. Demand contracts from point K towards point T. Supply extends from point R towards point T. New equilibrium is struck at point T. Here, S_2S_2 and D_2D_2 intersect each other. It shows that: (a) equilibrium price rises from OP_1 to OP_2, and (b) equilibrium quantity falls from OQ_1 to OQ_2.

HOTS

Q.1. How is new equilibrium struck when supply or demand curve tends to shift?

Ans. When supply or demand curve tends to shift, new equilibrium is struck through the process of extension and contraction of demand and supply. Generally, a change in demand or supply (implying increase or decrease in demand or supply) will lead to excess demand or excess supply. In a situation of excess demand (D > S), price will tend to rise causing (i) contraction of demand, and (ii) extension of supply. The process of contraction of demand and extension of supply would continue till new equilibrium is struck where demand = supply. Likewise, in a situation of excess supply (S > D), price will tend to fall causing (i) extension of demand, and (ii) contraction of supply. The process of extension of demand, and contraction of supply would continue till new equilibrium is struck where demand = supply.

Q.2. With the help of a demand and supply schedule, explain the concepts of excess demand and excess supply of a commodity. Also, explain their effect on the price of a commodity.

Ans. Excess demand is a situation when:

$D_X > S_X$, corresponding to a given price of X.

Excess supply is a situation when:

$S_X > D_X$, corresponding to a given price of X.

Excess demand and its impact on price is explained through Table 2. Excess supply and its impact on price is explained through Table 3.

Table 2. **Excess Demand**

P_X (₹)	S_{X_1} (Units)	D_{X_1} (Units)	D_{X_2} (Units)
10	100	20	40
8*	80*	40	80* New Equilibrium
6*	60*	60* Initial Equilibrium	120
4	40	80	160
2	20	100	200

Initially, the equilibrium is struck when $S_{X_1} = D_{X_1} = 60$, and P_X = ₹ 6.

Let us assume that demand for the commodity increases as indicated by D_{X_2}. Now, at the equilibrium price (= ₹ 6), quantity demanded increases from 60 to 120. This causes excess demand = 120 – 60 = 60. This leads to a rise in price. Rise in price leads to extension of supply and contraction of demand. Supply extends from 60 to 80. Demand contracts from 120 to 80. New equilibrium is struck when supply = demand = 80. Now, the equilibrium price is = ₹ 8. Thus, **as a consequence of excess demand, equilibrium price increases from ₹ 6 to ₹ 8.**

Table 3. **Excess Supply**

P_X (₹)	D_{X_1} (Units)	S_{X_1} (Units)	S_{X_2} (Units)
10	20	100	200
8	40	80	160
6*	60*	60* Initial Equilibrium	120
4*	80*	40	80* New Equilibrium
2	100	20	40

Initially, the equilibrium is struck when $S_{X_1} = D_{X_1} = 60$. Equilibrium price = ₹ 6.

Assume that supply of the commodity increases, as indicated by S_{X_2}. Now, at the existing equilibrium price, quantity supplied increases from 60 to 120. This causes excess supply = 120 − 60 = 60. This leads to a fall in price. Fall in price causes extension of demand and contraction of supply. Demand extends from 60 to 80. Supply contracts from 120 to 80. Now, the equilibrium is struck when supply = demand = 80. The equilibrium price is = ₹ 4. Thus, **as a consequence of excess supply, equilibrium price decreases from ₹ 6 to ₹ 4.**

Q.3. Equilibrium price is established only when D = S. Why?

Ans. Because, if demand (D) and supply (S) are not equal, there would be either excess demand (D > S) or excess supply (S > D). In case there is excess demand, market price will tend to rise. Consequently, there will be extension of supply and contraction of demand. The process of extension and contraction would continue till market clears itself: S = D and equilibrium price is established. Similarly, if there is excess supply, market price will tend to fall, leading to extension of demand and contraction of supply. The process of extension and contraction would continue till market clears itself: S = D and equilibrium price is established.

5. Simple Applications of Tools of Demand and Supply Curves

We have studied supply-demand analysis in terms of the consumer behaviour and producer behaviour. We have also studied how equilibrium is established in a competitive market. Further we analysed how equilibrium price and equilibrium quantity are impacted by a change in demand/supply. The present section studies some simple applications of the tools of supply and demand curves. The study focuses on two cases of government intervention in the commodity market, *viz.*, (i) Price Ceiling, and (ii) Price Floor.

(1) Price Ceiling

We know, in a competitive market, prices of goods and services are determined by the forces of supply and demand.

In developing countries like India essentials of life (like food grains and life saving medicines) are often found to be extremely scarce. Consequently, their open market price(s) are often very high. These prices may be so high that the bulk of the poor population finds it difficult to buy them. It leads to under-nourishment and malnutrition. Such a situation often compels the government to introduce 'price ceiling'. It means fixing a maximum price for a commodity which is generally lower than the equilibrium market price.

Price Ceiling

Ceiling means maximum limit. Price ceiling means maximum price of a commodity that the sellers can charge from the buyers. Often, the government fixes this price lower than the equilibrium market price of a commodity, so that the poor can afford to buy it.

However, when price ceiling is introduced, supply and demand forces are impacted. Fig. 10 illustrates this impact. Let us assume that the concerned commodity is *bajra*. This is a staple food in the deserts of Rajasthan. There is a large number of buyers and sellers of *bajra* in the deserts of Rajasthan. The market for *bajra* is almost similar to that of perfect competition. Accordingly, we are assuming that the market price of *bajra* is determined by the forces of supply and demand.

FIGURE 10

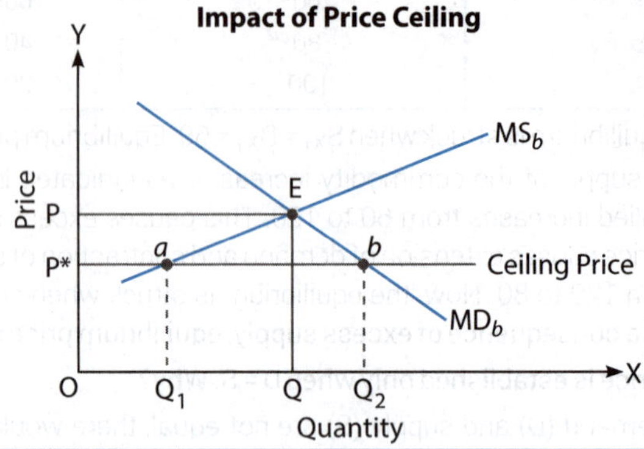

- Equilibrium Price = OP.
- Equilibrium Quantity = OQ.
- Ceiling Price = OP*.
- Excess Demand = $ab = Q_1Q_2$.

MD_b is the demand curve and MS_b is the supply curve of *bajra*. E indicates the point of market equilibrium. OP is the equilibrium price and OQ is the equilibrium quantity. Considering the fact that the poor people in the deserts of Rajasthan cannot afford to buy *bajra* at OP price, the government fixes the price ceiling at OP*. It is lower than the equilibrium price. The story does not end here. Ceiling price is likely to impact the market supply and market demand. When price reduces from OP to OP*, demand for *bajra* extends from OQ to OQ_2. On the other hand, supply contracts from OQ to OQ_1. Consequently, a gap emerges between market demand and market supply. It is a situation when $MD_b > MS_b$ or a situation of excess demand. In the diagram (Fig. 10), excess demand = $ab = Q_1Q_2$ (= $OQ_2 - OQ_1$).

Excess demand for *bajra* has its own implications. It shows that the people fail to buy *bajra* to the extent they wish to buy. Accordingly, a situation of 'partial hunger' may continue to exist. **How can this problem be tackled?** Rationing is the remedy. Each person is allocated a fixed quota of *bajra* at the ceiling price. Accordingly, everybody gets a fair amount of the commodity. The problem of hunger is addressed along with the problem of price.

But, price ceiling with rationing is not totally free from demerits. Following observations may be noted in this regard:

(i) You are to stand in long queues to get your allotted quota of the commodity. (ii) Often you are offered a low quality product. (iii) There is a pilferage from the ration shops. Rationed goods are often driven to the black market, rather than being delivered to the poor.

Black marketing compounds the problem of scarcity and keeps poorest of the poor in a state of deprivation. If a price ceiling with rationing is to succeed, the government must improve its distribution system. The government must evolve a system that ensures that what the government wants to deliver to the poor is actually delivered to them.

Price Ceiling and Black Marketing

Price ceiling often keeps the price of the commodity lower than its equilibrium price. Accordingly, its leads to:

(i) the extension of demand , and

(ii) the contraction of supply.

The net consequence is excess demand (*ab* in Fig. 10). Unfulfilled demand in the market often leads to black marketing. It happens even when the government tries to distribute the commodity through fair price shops. Black marketing defeats the very purpose of price ceiling. Price ceiling is imposed to ensure availability of the commodity at a reasonable price, particularly to poorer sections of the society. But black marketing reduces the actual availability of the commodity to this very sections of the society. It compounds the problem of economic divide.

(2) Price Floor

Floor means the lowest limit. Price floor means the minimum price fixed by the government for a commodity in the market. It seems paradoxical. But it is true that the government in most countries fixes floor price for most agricultural products, food grains in particular. The following real life situation should make this point clear.

A poor farmer in India grows wheat, partly for self-consumption and partly for sale in the market. There are so many farmers growing wheat. It is a seasonal crop. Across different farms, it is harvested almost at the same time. Holding capacity of the most farmers is extremely limited, almost nil. Most farmers, therefore, sell their produce immediately after harvest. Consequently, there is glut in the market and the price crashes. Thus, even high output generates low income. Good harvest brings poverty. Such a situation would only compel the farmer to cut his planned output of wheat. This could lead to nation-wide shortage of wheat. To avoid hardship to the farmers as well as shortage of wheat in the country, the government often resorts to the policy of floor price of wheat. A minimum price is fixed which the traders must pay the farmers in the wholesale market. Accordingly, income of the farmers is regulated and continuous production of wheat is assured.

But the traders may not buy wheat at all at the floor price. **What happens in such a situation?** Now, the government offers 'support price' to the farmers. It is a price that corresponds to the minimum price, but implies that the government would buy the entire surplus of the farmers' produce which they fail to sell in the open market at the floor price. In fact, floor price invariably implies support price as well.

Implications of floor price (and support price) are illustrated through Fig. 11.

FIGURE 11

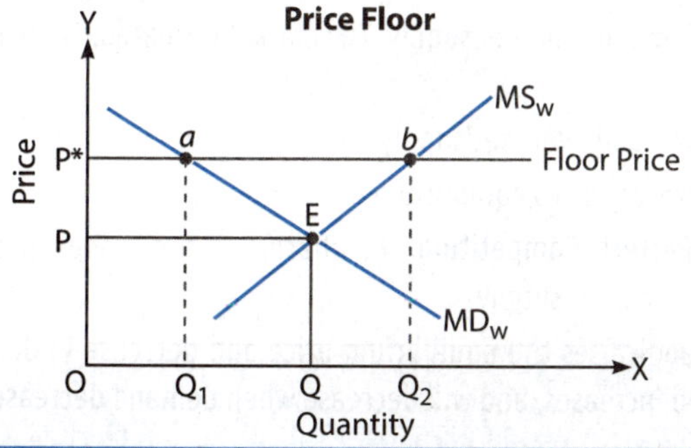

- Equilibrium Price = OP.
- Equilibrium Quantity = OQ.
- Floor Price = OP*.
- Excess Supply = $ab = Q_1Q_2$.

The diagram shows OP as the equilibrium price and OQ as equilibrium quantity of wheat. Considering the fact that the equilibrium price may be considerably low for the farmers, the government fixes OP* as the floor price.

Traders in the market are bound to pay at least OP* price for the purchase of wheat. But, a rise in price causes market demand to contract from OQ to OQ_1. On the other hand, market supply expands from OQ to OQ_2. There emerges excess supply = *ab* = Q_1Q_2 (= $OQ_2 - OQ_1$). The government buys this surplus and stores it as a buffer stock. This stock is used during the periods of scarcity (due to droughts).

Alternatively, the government could impose legal restriction on the area under wheat, so that the production of wheat is restricted and the market price of wheat rises. But, in view of the fact that most farmers in India are small farmers, restriction on acreage under wheat may cause forced fallowing of land (keeping the land idle) which again causes a cut in the farmers' income. When farmers' interest is to be safeguarded (by way of support price) the government has to bear the impact of it.

However, the cost of storage of wheat (as a buffer stock) is a major demerit of the floor price/support price policy of the government.

HOTS

Q. Do you agree with the view that buffer stock is a tool of price floor?

Ans. It is true that buffer stock is an important tool of 'price floor'. Floor price is the minimum price fixed by the government for sale of a commodity in the market. Often this is higher than the equilibrium price. Generally, it is done in case of farm-goods with a view to stabilising income of the farmers. However, floor price is often supplemented with the Support Price Policy. This implies that the government will buy the surplus stock of the farmers in case they fail to sell it in the open market at the floor price. By buying the surplus stocks of the farmers, the government creates its own buffer stock (to be used for public distribution). Thus, floor price is a tool of the buffer stock. Fig. 11 illustrates this situation.

Equilibrium Price : OP

Floor Price : OP*

(i) Excess Supply = *ab* = Q_1Q_2.

(ii) Market price would reduce to the level of equilibrium price, unless 'Support Price' is offered. At this price, the government buys the surplus product from the producers and stores it as a buffer stock. This stock is used for public distribution.

POWER POINTS

- **Market Equilibrium** is a situation when market demand = market supply. The market is cleared. There is no excess demand or excess supply in the market.
- **Equilibrium Price** is the price at which market demand = market supply.
- **Equilibrium Quantity** is that quantity which corresponds to equilibrium price.
- **Determination of Equilibrium Price Under Perfect Competition:** Equilibrium price under perfect competition is determined by the forces of market demand and market supply.
- **Effect of Change in Demand:** Increase in demand raises the equilibrium price and decrease in demand lowers it. Also, equilibrium quantity will increase when demand increases, and will decrease when demand decreases. However:
  - (i) **In case of Perfectly Elastic Supply,** increase or decrease in demand does not cause any change in equilibrium price. Only the equilibrium quantity changes.
  - (ii) **In case of Perfectly Inelastic Supply,** increase or decrease in demand does not cause any change in equilibrium quantity. Only the equilibrium price changes.

- **Effect of Change in Supply:** Increase in supply causes a fall in equilibrium price and decrease in supply causes a rise in equilibrium price. Equilibrium quantity will increase if supply increases and decrease if supply decreases. However:
  - (i) **In case of Perfectly Elastic Demand,** increase or decrease in supply does not cause any change in equilibrium price. Only the equilibrium quantity changes.
  - (ii) **In case of Perfectly Inelastic Demand,** decrease in supply results in an increase in price and increase in supply leads to a decrease in price. The equilibrium quantity remains constant.
- **Effect of a Simultaneous Change in Demand and Supply on Equilibrium Price:**
  - (i) When demand increases more than supply, equilibrium price will increase.
  - (ii) When demand and supply increase equally, equilibrium price remains constant.
  - (iii) When supply increases more than demand, equilibrium price falls.
- **Ceiling Price** refers to the maximum price of a product, as fixed by the government. Often, the ceiling price is fixed lower than the equilibrium price. Government fixes this price to ensure the availability of essential commodities to the weaker sections of the society.
- **Floor Price** is the minimum price of a commodity, as fixed by the government. Often, this is higher than the equilibrium price of the commodity. Nobody in the market can buy the product at a price lower than the floor price. Often this is equated with the support price.
- **Support Price** is the assured minimum price offered by the government to the farmers for the purchase of their output. Often, this is higher than the equilibrium price. It is offered to the farmers in order to regulate their income.

EXERCISE

1. Very Short Questions (Remembering & Understanding) (1 mark each)

A. Multiple Choice Questions: Choose the Correct Answer

1. Under perfect competition, equilibrium price of the commodity is determined by:

(a) demand for the commodity alone (b) supply of commodity alone
(c) both demand and supply (d) the government

2. In the situation of market equilibrium:

(a) market demand = market supply (b) market demand > market supply
(c) market demand < market supply (d) none of these

3. In a situation of excess supply, market price tends to

(a) rise (b) fall
(c) remain constant (d) none of these

4. If demand for a product falls, equilibrium price will:

(a) fall (b) rise
(c) either of the two (d) neither of the two

5. The market price is related to:

(a) short period (b) very short period
(c) long period (d) very long period

6. What will be the effect on equilibrium price if supply is decreased without any change in demand?

(a) No change in price (b) Price will fall
(c) Price will rise (d) None of these

7. A fall in input prices would cause:

(a) fall in equilibrium price and rise in quantity (b) rise in equilibrium price and fall in quantity
(c) fall in equilibrium price as well as quantity (d) rise in equilibrium price as well as quantity

8. Supply being perfectly inelastic, what will be the effect of increase or decrease in demand on price and equilibrium quantity?

(a) Price increases or decreases respectively
(b) No effect on equilibrium quantity
(c) Both (a) and (b)
(d) None of these

9. When will increase in supply bring down the price, leaving the quantity demanded unchanged?

(a) When demand for the commodity is perfectly elastic
(b) When demand for the commodity is perfectly inelastic
(c) When demand for the commodity is less elastic
(d) When demand for the commodity is more elastic

10. What would price ceiling lead to when the maximum price is fixed lower than the equilibrium price?

(a) Excess demand
(b) Excess supply
(c) Deficient demand
(d) None of these

11. The period of time, when supply is fully adjusted to change in demand is called:

(a) short period
(b) very short period
(c) mid period
(d) long period

12. Market supply curve of perishable goods is a vertical straight line parallel to Y-axis. It happens in which of the following periods?

(a) Long period
(b) Short period
(c) Very short period
(d) All of these

13. The minimum assured price offered by the government to the farmers for the purchase of their output is called:

(a) ceiling price
(b) equilibrium price
(c) support price
(d) market price

14. At P_X = ₹ 5, demand for Good-X is 30 units and supply of Good-X is 20 units, it is a situation of:

(a) excess demand
(b) excess supply
(c) equilibrium
(d) none of these

15. Decrease in the number of consumers causes:

(a) equilibrium price to rise
(b) equilibrium price to fall
(c) no change in equilibrium price
(d) none of these

16. Increase in the income of the buyers (in case of an inferior good) will cause:

(a) fall in equilibrium price and quantity
(b) rise in equilibrium price and quantity
(c) fall in equilibrium price and quantity to rise
(d) rise in equilibrium price and quantity to fall

17. When both the demand and supply curves shift to indicate increase in demand and supply in the same proportion:

(a) only equilibrium price remains unchanged
(b) only equilibrium quantity remains unchanged
(c) equilibrium price remains unchanged but equilibrium quantity decreases
(d) equilibrium price remains unchanged but equilibrium quantity increases

18. Which of the following statements is correct, in the case of excess demand?

(a) Market supply will be less than market demand
(b) Equilibrium price and equilibrium quantity will increase
(c) Both (a) and (b)
(d) Neither (a) nor (b)

Answers

1. (c) **2.** (a) **3.** (b) **4.** (a) **5.** (b) **6.** (c) **7.** (a) **8.** (c) **9.** (b) **10.** (a) **11.** (d) **12.** (c)
13. (c) **14.** (a) **15.** (b) **16.** (a) **17.** (d) **18.** (c)

B. Information & Concept-based Questions

1. **Define equilibrium price.**

Ans. Equilibrium price refers to that price which equates market demand for a commodity with its market supply.

2. **What is meant by equilibrium quantity?**

Ans. Equilibrium quantity is that quantity which corresponds to the equilibrium price in the market.

3. **What is meant by market equilibrium?**

Or

Define market equilibrium.

Ans. Market equilibrium is a situation when market demand is equal to market supply.

4. **What is meant by excess demand for a product?**

Ans. Excess demand refers to the situation in which market demand is more than market supply of a commodity at a given price.

5. **What is meant by excess supply of a product?**

Ans. Excess supply refers to the situation in which market supply is more than market demand of a commodity at a given price.

6. **How is price affected by increase in demand?**

Ans. In a situation of increase in demand, other things remaining constant, equilibrium price must rise.

7. **How is price affected by decrease in demand?**

Ans. When demand decreases, equilibrium price must decrease, other things remaining unchanged.

8. **How is price affected by increase in supply?**

Ans. When supply increases, equilibrium price will decrease, other things being equal.

9. **How is price affected by decrease in supply?**

Ans. When supply decreases, equilibrium price will increase, other things remaining constant.

10. **How is the price of a commodity affected when its demand increases more than supply?**

Ans. When demand increases more than supply, equilibrium price of a commodity will rise, other things remaining constant.

11. **How is the price of a commodity affected when its demand increases less than supply?**

Ans. When demand increases less than supply, equilibrium price will fall, other things remaining constant.

12. **What will be the effect on equilibrium price and quantity of an increase in equal proportion of demand and supply of a commodity?**

Ans. Other things remaining constant, when demand and supply increase in an equal proportion, there will be no change in equilibrium price. However, the equilibrium quantity will increase.

13. **Define price ceiling.**

Ans. Ceiling price refers to the maximum price of a commodity that the sellers can charge from the buyers.

14. **What is meant by price floor?**

Ans. Price floor refers to the minimum price fixed by the government for a commodity in the market. It is done with a view to stabilising income of the farmers.

2. Reason-based Questions (Comprehension of the Subject-matter)

Read the following statements carefully. Write 'True' or 'False' with a reason.

1. **Under perfect competition, equilibrium price is determined by the forces of market demand and market supply.**

Ans. True. Under perfect competition, equilibrium price is determined at the point of intersection of market demand and market supply. An individual firm cannot change it.

2. **In case of excess demand, equilibrium price must rise.**

Ans. True. Excess demand generates pressure of demand on the existing supply. As an immediate impact, market price rises. It triggers extension of supply and contraction of demand. Finally, equilibrium is reached in the market where $D_X = S_X$. But new equilibrium price happens to be higher than the initial equilibrium price.

3. **When there is no excess demand or excess supply in the market, everybody is equally satisfied (or nobody suffers any shortage).**

Ans. False. When there is no excess demand or excess supply, market is cleared. But it does not mean that everybody is equally satisfied. At the given market price, some people may not be able to buy the product, and therefore remain unsatisfied.

4. **In a situation of perfectly elastic supply price of the commodity tends to remain constant, no matter demand increases or decreases.**

Ans. True. The price will remain unchanged with perfectly elastic supply curve, as demand increases or decreases. Because supply responds proportionately to the increase or decrease in demand.

5. **Equilibrium price may not change even when market demand happens to change.**

Ans. True. Because market supply may change proportionate to market demand.

6. **Price may remain constant even when both supply and demand for a commodity tend to change.**

Ans. True. If the demand and supply of a commodity change equally, and in the same direction there will be no change in its price.

7. **Equilibrium price may fall even when market demand tends to rise.**

Ans. True. Because supply may rise proportionately greater than the rise in demand.

8. **In a situation when productivity increases owing to improvement in technology, equilibrium price tends to fall.**

Ans. True. Owing to improvement in technology supply of the good in the market will increase causing a rightward shift of the supply curve. Accordingly, equilibrium price will decrease.

9. **In a situation of war when people are fearing shortage of rice, equilibrium price of rice tends to rise.**

Ans. True. Because, fearing shortage of rice, demand curve for rice will shift forward, causing a rise in equilibrium price.

10. **In a situation when import of inputs becomes expensive, equilibrium price of the commodity tends to rise.**

Ans. True. When import of inputs become expensive, the cost of production rises, leading to a cut in supplies. The supply curve shifts to the left. Accordingly, equilibrium price of the commodity tends to rise.

11. **In a state of increasing cost of production leading to a substantial cut in production, equilibrium price will fall.**

Ans. False. With a substantial cut in production, supply curve shifts to the left and equilibrium price will increase.

12. **If population increases, supply curve remains unchanged in the context of market equilibrium.**

Ans. True. Population changes affect only the market demand, not the market supply.

13. **If consumers tend to buy more corresponding to the existing price of the commodity, supply curve should shift to the right.**

Ans. False. If consumers tend to buy more corresponding to the existing price of the commodity, demand curve should shift to the right.

14. **Market price is always equal to or greater than the support price of a commodity.**

Ans. True. In a situation of support price (which is the minimum price assured to the producers), market price ought to be equal or greater than the support price.

3. HOTS & Applications

1. A situation of excess demand or excess supply is automatically corrected under perfect competition. Do you agree? Explain the process of correction.

Ans. Yes. Under perfect competition, situations of excess demand or excess supply are automatically corrected through the free play of market forces, called price mechanism.

When there is excess supply:

—market price decreases.

—decrease in market price leads to extension of demand and contraction of supply.

—the process of extension and contraction continues till excess supply is eliminated.

—new equilibrium is established with lower price and higher quantity than before.

When there is excess demand:

—market price increases.

—increase in market price causes contraction of demand and extension of supply.

—the process of extension and contraction continues till excess demand is eliminated.

—new equilibrium is established with higher price and higher quantity than before.

2. In a situation of constant demand, equilibrium quantity does not change even when supply increases or decreases. Do you agree?

Ans. Yes. In a situation of constant demand or perfectly inelastic demand, increase or decrease in supply causes a full impact on price of the commodity but equilibrium quantity does not change.

3. If elasticity of demand = ∞, equilibrium price remain unchanged, no matter supply increases or decreases. Do you agree?

Ans. Yes, we agree with this. When demand is perfectly elastic (or elasticity of demand is infinity), equilibrium price remain unchanged with increase or decrease in supply. Because (being perfectly elastic) demand increases or decreases proportionate to the increase or decrease in supply.

4. Equilibrium price never changes in a situation of perfectly elastic supply, no matter what the demand is. Is it true? Explain diagrammatically.

Ans. Yes, it is true. Equilibrium price will remain unchanged when supply is perfectly elastic whether demand increases or decreases. See Fig. 12. Here, price remains constant at OP when demand increases to D_1D_1 and also remains constant at OP when demand decreases to D_2D_2.

FIGURE 12

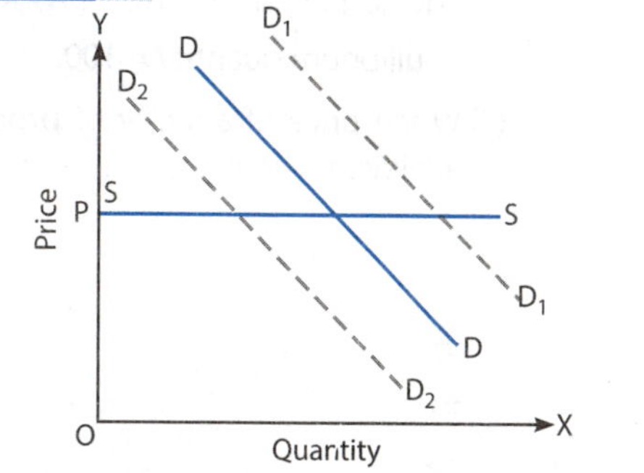

5. In case of inferior goods, a rise in income of the buyers causes a fall in equilibrium price of the commodity. Comment. Illustrate using a diagram.

Ans. Yes. The income effect for an 'inferior good' is negative. It implies that for an increase in income of its buyers, the demand for the good falls. Diagrammatically, demand curve, DD, as shown in Fig. 13 shifts leftward, *i.e.*, from DD to D_1D_1. The new equilibrium is struck at point E_1. The equilibrium price decreases from OP to OP_1.

FIGURE 13

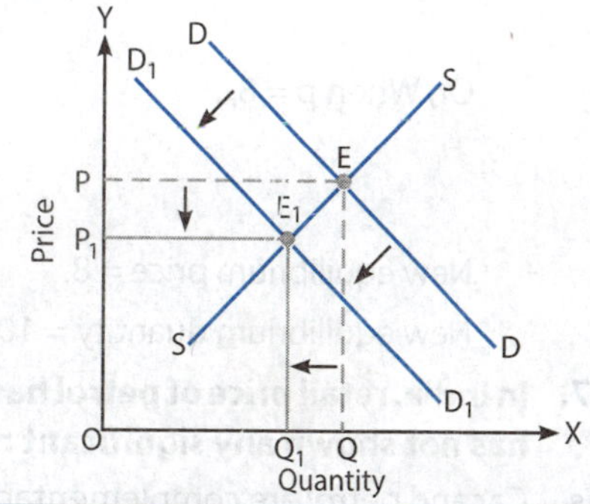

6. Suppose the demand and supply curves of a Good-X are given by the following two equations simultaneously:

$$Q_d = 120 - 2p$$
$$Q_s = 60 + 4p$$

(i) Find the equilibrium price and equilibrium quantity.

(ii) Suppose that the price of a factor of production producing the commodity has changed, resulting in the new supply curve given by the equation:

$$Q_{s'} = 72 + 4p$$

Find the new equilibrium price and new equilibrium quantity as against the original equilibrium price and equilibrium quantity.

Ans. (i) Market equilibrium is struck when:

Market Demand = Market Supply

Or, $Q_d = Q_s$

$\therefore$ $120 - 2p = 60 + 4p$

$\Rightarrow$ $4p + 2p = 120 - 60$

$\Rightarrow$ $6p = 60$

$\Rightarrow$ $p = 10$

When p = 10, $Q_d = 120 - 2p$

$= 120 - 2(10)$

$= 120 - 20 = 100$

Or, When p = 10, $Q_s = 60 + 4p$

$= 60 + 4(10)$

$= 60 + 40 = 100$

Equilibrium price = 10.

Equilibrium quantity = 100.

(ii) When price of a factor of production has changed, new equilibrium price and equilibrium quantity is achieved when:

$Q_d = Q_{s'}$

$120 - 2p = 72 + 4p$

$\Rightarrow$ $4p + 2p = 120 - 72$

$\Rightarrow$ $6p = 48$

$\Rightarrow$ $p = 8$

When p = 8, $Q_d = 120 - 2p$

$= 120 - 2(8)$

$= 120 - 16 = 104$

Or, When p = 8, $Q_s = 72 + 4p$

$= 72 + 4(8)$

$= 72 + 32 = 104$

New equilibrium price = 8.

New equilibrium quantity = 104.

7. In India, retail price of petrol has significantly fallen during the past six months. But, demand for cars has not shown any significant rise. Use your Economics to explain this fact.

Ans. Car and petrol are complementary goods. A significant fall in the price of petrol is expected to induce a rise in demand for cars. But, it did not happen. The reason is as this:

Car is expensive consumer good. Demand for cars is expected to rise only when: (i) there is a significant rise in income of the buyers, or (ii) there is a significant fall in the price of cars, or (iii) there is a significant cut in the interest rate for car loans. None of these factors has shown any positive change during the past six months. Accordingly, demand for cars has not shown any rise in response to fall in petrol price in India.

4. Evaluation (Value-based Questions)

1. Do you agree with the view that the market absorbs the impact of increase or decrease in demand only through the process of 'extension and contraction of demand and supply'? Give reason.

Ans. Yes, it is true that the market absorbs the impact of increase or decrease in demand only through the process of 'extension and contraction of demand and supply'.

Reason: When there is increase in demand, demand curve shifts to the right. Excess demand emerges in the market. Price tends to be higher than the equilibrium price. It leads to extension of supply and contraction of demand. It is through this process of extension and contraction that excess demand is eliminated and new equilibrium is established in the market.

Likewise, when there is decrease in demand, demand curve shifts to the left. Excess supply emerges in the market. Price tends to be lower than the equilibrium price. It leads to extension of demand and contraction of supply. It is through this process of extension and contraction that excess supply is eliminated and new equilibrium is established in the market.

2. What kind of supply shock do you expect in the market when the rice crop is severally damaged by the drought? How will the market adjust itself to the supply shock? What suggestions would you offer to tackle the problems arising out of the supply shock?

Ans. When a drought severally damages the rice crop, output of rice will significantly fall. It leads to supply shock in the market. The supply of rice decreases: supply curve shifts to the left, as in Fig. 14.

FIGURE 14

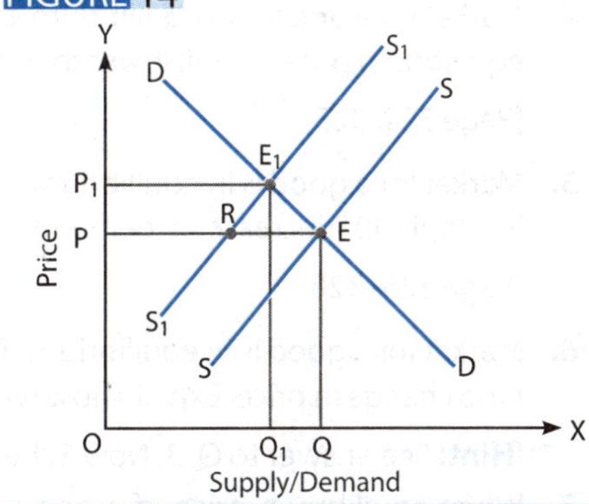

- SS : The initial supply curve.
- DD : The initial demand curve.
- E : The initial equilibrium.
- Supply Shock : SS curve shifts to the left as S_1S_1.
- E_1 : New equilibrium.
- At the new equilibrium:
  (i) equilibrium price rises from OP to OP_1, and
  (ii) equilibrium quantity falls from OQ to OQ_1.

SS is the initial supply curve, and DD the initial demand curve. E is the point of initial equilibrium. OQ is the equilibrium quantity and OP the equilibrium price. The supply shock (caused by the drought) shifts the supply curve from SS to S_1S_1: supply of rice decreases. As a result, there is deficient supply (or excess demand) = RE. The pressure of demand causes price to rise. The rise in price leads to extension of supply and contraction of demand. Supply extends from point R towards point E_1. Demand contracts from point E towards point E_1. New equilibrium is established in the market at point E_1. **The equilibrium quantity reduces from OQ to OQ_1. The equilibrium price increases from OP to OP_1.** The problem that emerges has two dimensions:

(i) high price of rice, and (ii) low supply of rice.

The problem of high price of rice can be addressed by fixing a price ceiling. The government can fix maximum price of rice in the market. Any attempt to charge higher price, higher than the ceiling price would attract a legal action.

The problem of low supply of rice can be addressed in two ways: (i) The government can release more rice from its buffer stocks, and (ii) The government can import rice from rest of the world.

3. Farmers may suffer a loss even when they reap a good harvest. Does your supply-demand analysis provide an answer to this paradox?

Ans. Owing to their poverty (and immediate need for cash) farmers are often driven to a distressed sale of their produce. But good harvest causes a glut (of supply) in the market. This causes a price-crash. The price may fall so much that the total revenue of the farmer happens to decrease despite the fact that his output/sale is more than before.

5. CBSE Questions—Past 4 years (With Answers or Reference to the Text for Answers)

1. Market for a good is in equilibrium. There is simultaneous "increase", both in demand and supply of the good. Explain its effect on market price. *[CBSE Delhi 2012]*

[Page 332, 333]

2. Market for a good is in equilibrium. There is simultaneous "decrease", both in demand and supply of the good. Explain its effect on market price. *[CBSE Delhi 2012]*

[Page 333, 334]

3. Market for a good is in equilibrium. There is simultaneous "decrease" both in demand and supply but there is no change in market price. Explain with the help of a schedule how it is possible. *[CBSE (AI) 2012]*

[**Hint:** Show S–D schedules like this:

Schedule–1			
Schedule showing Market Equilibrium			
P_X (₹)	D_X (Units)	S_X (Units)	Equilibrium
5	500	400	D > S
10	450	450	D = S (Equilibrium)
15	400	500	S > D

Schedule–2			
Schedule showing Simultaneous Decrease both in D and S and no change in Market Price			
P_X (₹)	D_X (Units)	S_X (Units)	Equilibrium
5	250	200	D > S
10	225	225	D = S (Equilibrium)
15	200	250	S > D

4. Market for a good is in equilibrium. Explain the chain of reactions in the market if the price is (i) higher than equilibrium price and (ii) lower than equilibrium price. *[CBSE (AI) 2012]*

[Page 324, 325]

5. Market for a good is in equilibrium. Explain the chain of reactions in the market when there is (i) "decrease" in supply (ii) "decrease" in demand. *[CBSE (F) 2012]*

[Page 326–328]

6. Market for a good is in equilibrium. There is simultaneous "increase" both in demand and supply but there is no change in price. Explain how is it possible. Use a schedule. *[CBSE (F) 2012]*

[**Hint:** See answer to Q. 3. Now Schedule–1 will become Schedule–2.]

7. When equilibrium price of a good is less than its market price, there will be competition among the sellers. Is it true? Give reasons for your answer. *[CBSE Delhi 2013]*

[Yes, the statement is true. Equilibrium price is that price at which there is neither excess demand nor excess supply in the market. When equilibrium price is less than market price (price that prevails in the market) it points to a situation of excess supply in the market. Implying that there are undesired stocks of the product with the sellers.

Obviously, this will lead to competition among the sellers who will like to clear their undesired stocks. Fig. 15 illustrates this situation.]

FIGURE 15

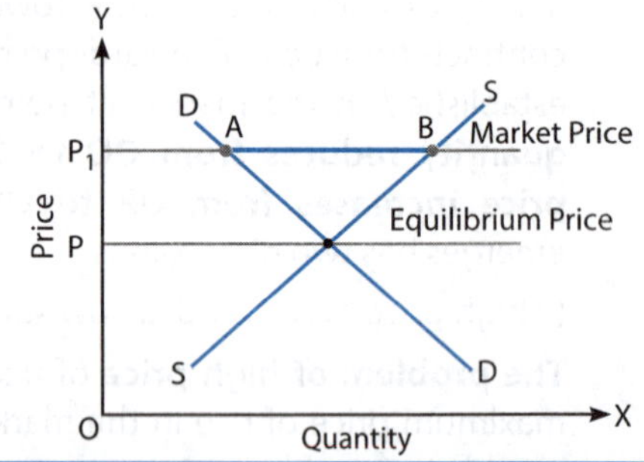

Excess Supply: AB
Consequence: Competition among sellers to clear the undesired stocks.

8. Equilibrium price of an essential medicine is too high. Explain what possible steps can be taken to bring down the equilibrium price but only through the market forces. Also explain the series of changes that will occur in the market. *[CBSE (AI) 2013]*

[Possible steps to lower the market price of an essential medicine are as these:

(i) The government can lower/abolish excise duty on the production of the medicine.

(ii) The government can offer subsidy to the producer engaged in the production of the concerned medicine.

In either situation the market supply of the product is expected to rise, leading to a shift in the supply curve to the right, as in the diagram (Fig. 16).

A shift in supply curve from S_1S_1 to S_2S_2 generates excess supply = AB. This leads to a fall in market price, triggering extension of demand and contraction of supply. Finally, new market equilibrium is struck at point E, indicating lower market price and higher equilibrium quantity (OP_2 price rather than OP_1 and OQ_2 quantity rather than OQ_1).]

FIGURE 16

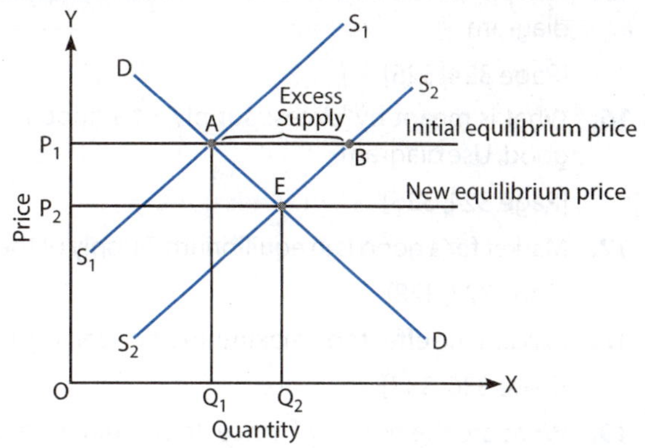

9. If equilibrium price of a good is greater than its market price, explain all the changes that will take place in the market. Use diagram. *[CBSE (AI) 2013]*

[Page 324, 325]

10. Market for a necessary good is competitive in which the existing firms are earning extra-normal profits. How can the policy of liberalisation by the government help in making the market more competitive in the interest of the consumers? Explain. *[CBSE (F) 2013]*

[Policy of liberalisation will remove certain barriers like licencing, quotas from the market. Consequently, new firms will join the industry. This will make the market more competitive, and the market supply will increase. Implying a shift in the market supply curve to the right. Other things remaining constant, a rightward shift in the market supply curve will lead to a fall in equilibrium price and a rise in equilibrium quantity. Extra-normal profits will ultimately be wiped out, and consumers are expected to enjoy larger quantity at a lower price.]

11. Explain the effect of "increase" in demand for a good on its equilibrium price and equilibrium quantity.

[Page 326, 327] *[CBSE (F) 2013]*

12. Market for a commodity is in equilibrium. Demand for the commodity 'increases'. Explain the chain of effects of this change till the market again reaches equilibrium. Use diagram. *[CBSE Delhi 2014; (AI) 2014]*

Or

Market for a good is in equilibrium. The demand for the good 'increases'. Explain the chain of effects of this change. *[CBSE Delhi 2015; (AI) 2015]*

Or

Market for a good is in equilibrium. There is 'increase' in demand for the good. Explain the chain of effects of this change. *[CBSE (F) 2015]*

[Page 326, 327]

13. Market of a commodity is in equilibrium. Demand for the commodity 'decreases'. Explain the chain of effects of this change till the market again reaches equilibrium. Use diagram. *[CBSE Delhi 2014; (AI) 2014]*

Or

Market for a good is in equilibrium. Demand for the good 'decreases'. Explain the chain of effects of this change. *[CBSE Delhi 2015; (F) 2015]*

[Page 326, 327]

14. Market for a product is in equilibrium. Supply of the product 'decreases'. Explain the chain of effects of this change till the market again reaches equilibrium. Use diagram. *[CBSE Delhi 2014]*

Or

Market for a good is in equilibrium. Supply of the good 'decreases'. Explain the chain of effects of this change on the market for the good. Use diagram. *[CBSE (F) 2014]*

Or

Market for a good is in equilibrium. The supply of good "decreases". Explain the chain of effects of this change.

[Page 327, 328] *[CBSE (AI) 2015; (F) 2015]*

15. What is 'excess demand' for a good in a market? Explain its chain of effect on the market for that good. Use diagram. [CBSE (F) 2014]
[Page 324, 325]
16. What is meant by 'excess supply' of a good in a market? Explain its chain of effects on the market for that good. Use diagram. [CBSE (F) 2014]
[Page 324, 325]
17. Market for a good is in equilibrium. Supply of the good 'increases'. Explain the chain of effects of this change.
[Page 327, 328] [CBSE Delhi 2015; (AI) 2015]
18. Explain the effects of 'maximum price ceiling' on the market of a good. Use diagram. [CBSEDelhi 2015]
[Page 336, 337]
19. What are the effects of 'price floor' (minimum price ceiling) on the market of a good? Use diagram.
[Page 337, 338] [CBSE (AI) 2015]
20. What is maximum price ceiling? On what type of goods is it normally imposed. Use diagram. [CBSE (F) 2015]
[Page 336, 337]

6. NCERT Questions (With Hints to Answers)

1. Explain market equilibrium.

   [**Hint:** Market equilibrium is a situation of zero excess demand and zero excess supply. Or, it is a situation where: market demand = market supply.]

2. When do we say there is excess demand for a commodity in the market?

   [**Hint:** When market demand exceeds market supply of a commodity at a given price there is excess demand for a commodity in the market.]

3. When do we say there is excess supply for a commodity in the market?

   [**Hint:** When market supply of a commodity is more than market demand for a commodity at the given price there is excess supply for a commodity in the market.]

4. What will happen if the price prevailing in the market is

   (i) above the equilibrium price?

   (ii) below the equilibrium price?

   [**Hint:** The equilibrium price is the price at which market demand and market supply are equal to each other.

   (i) When price prevailing in the market is above the equilibrium price, demand will be less than supply, *i.e.*, there is excess supply in the market. Excess supply will force the market price to slide down causing extension of demand and contraction of supply. The process of extension and contraction would continue till the equilibrium between supply and demand is struck. Thus, equilibrium price will be restored through the free play of market forces.

   (ii) When price prevailing in the market is below the equilibrium price, demand will be more than supply, *i.e.*, there is excess demand in the market. Pressure of excess demand will cause a rise in market price causing contraction of demand and extension of supply. The process of contraction and extension would continue till the equilibrium between supply and demand is struck. Equilibrium price will again be restored through the free play of market forces.]

5. Explain how price is determined in a perfectly competitive market with fixed number of firms.

   [**Hint:** In a perfectly competitive market, equilibrium price is determined by the forces of market demand and market supply. Market demand refers to the sum total of demand for a commodity by all the buyers in the market. Whereas market supply refers to the sum total of supply of a commodity by all the firms in the market. Considering market demand schedule (or market demand curve) on the one hand, and market supply schedule (or market supply curve) on the other, we identify equilibrium price as the one where market demand = market supply, or where market demand curve and market supply curve intersect each other. See Fig. 1 of this chapter.]

6. How are equilibrium price and quantity affected when income of the consumers (i) increase? (ii) decrease?

[**Hint:**

(i) For a normal commodity, an increase in income of the consumers means increase in its demand. Accordingly, demand curve shifts rightward and both equilibrium price and equilibrium quantity tend to increase.

(ii) For a normal commodity, a decrease in income of the consumers means decrease in its demand. Accordingly, demand curve shifts leftward and both equilibrium price and equilibrium quantity tend to decrease.]

7. How do the equilibrium price and quantity of a commodity change when price of input used in its production changes?

[**Hint:** With increase in input price, the supply curve shifts to the left. Accordingly, equilibrium price increases and equilibrium quantity reduces in the product market. Conversely, when there is decrease in input price, the supply curve shifts to the right, causing decrease in equilibrium price and increase in equilibrium quantity.]

8. Using supply and demand curves, show how an increase in the price of shoes affects the price of a pair of socks and the number of pairs of socks bought and sold.

[**Hint:** Shoes and socks are complementary goods. Accordingly, demand for socks is expected to fall with rise in the price of shoes. Thus, demand curve (for socks) shifts backward. Less will be purchased at the same price. When demand curve shifts backward, the equilibrium price and quantity will be affected as shown in Fig. 17.

FIGURE 17

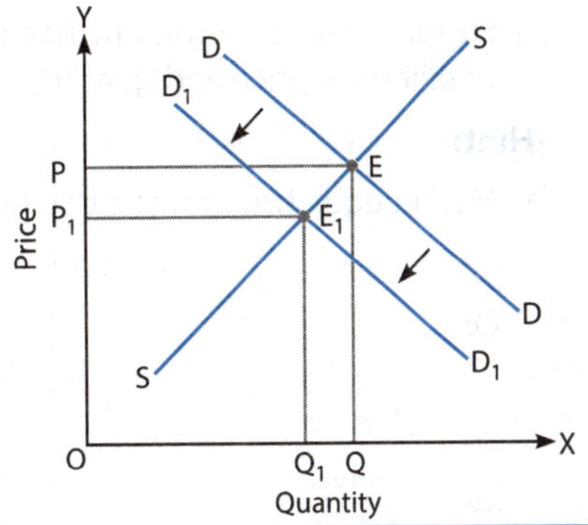

In Fig. 17, DD is the initial demand curve and SS is the initial supply curve related to socks. E is the initial equilibrium where supply and demand curves intersect each other. OP is the equilibrium price and OQ is the equilibrium quantity of socks. When the price of shoes increases, demand curve for socks shifts backward as indicated by D_1D_1. Equilibrium price (of a pair of socks) falls from OP to OP_1 and equilibrium quantity (number of pairs of socks bought and sold) falls from OQ to OQ_1.]

9. How will a change in price of coffee affect the equilibrium price of tea? Explain the effect on equilibrium quantity also through a diagram.

[**Hint:** Coffee and tea are substitute goods. Let us assume that the price of coffee increases. This will cause a shift in demand curve for tea to the right as shown in Fig. 18.

FIGURE 18

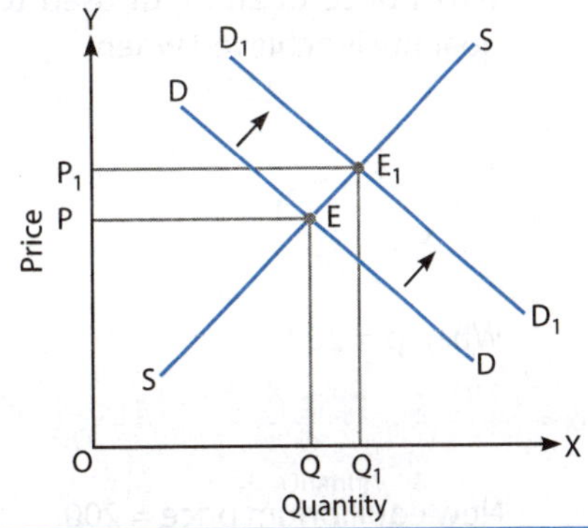

In Fig. 18, DD is the initial demand curve and SS is the initial supply curve related to tea. E is the initial equilibrium where supply and demand curves intersect each other. OP is the equilibrium price and OQ is the equilibrium quantity of tea. When the price of coffee increases, demand curve (for tea) shifts forward as indicated by D_1D_1. Consequently, Equilibrium price (of tea) increases from OP to OP_1 and equilibrium quantity increases from OQ to OQ_1.

In case price of coffee decreases, demand curve for tea would shift to the left. Consequently, new equilibrium would indicate a fall in equilibrium quantity as well as a fall in equilibrium price.]

10. If the price of a substitute(Y) of Good-X increases, what impact does it have on the equilibrium price and quantity of Good-X?

[**Hint:** With increase in the price of the substitute of Good-X, demand curve of Good-X will shifts to the right. Accordingly, equilibrium price and quantity of Good-X would tend to increase.]

11. Explain through a diagram the effect of a rightward shift of both the demand and supply curves on equilibrium price and quantity.

[**Hint:** There are three possible situations of a simultaneous rightward shift of both the demand and supply curves:

(i) When demand increases more than supply, equilibrium price and quantity both will rise. See Fig. 8(A) of this chapter.

(ii) When demand and supply increase equally, equilibrium price will remain stable and equilibrium quantity will rise. See Fig. 8(B) of this chapter.

(iii) When demand increases less than supply, equilibrium price will fall and equilibrium quantity will rise. See Fig. 8(C) of this chapter.]

12. Suppose the demand and supply curves of salt are given by:

$$Q_d = 1{,}000 - p, \quad Q_S = 700 + 2p$$

(a) Find the equilibrium price and quantity.

(b) Now suppose that the price of an input used to produce salt has increased so that the new supply curve is:

$$Q_S = 400 + 2p$$

How does the equilibrium price and quantity change? Does the change conform to your expectation?

(c) Suppose the government has imposed a tax of ₹ 3 per unit on sale of salt. How does it affect the equilibrium price and quantity?

[**Hint:**

(a) Market equilibrium is struck when:

Market Demand = Market Supply

Or, $Q_d = Q_s$

$\therefore$ $1{,}000 - p = 700 + 2p$

$\Rightarrow$ $2p + p = 1{,}000 - 700$

$\Rightarrow$ $3p = 300$

$\Rightarrow$ $p = 100$

When p = 100, $Q_d = 1{,}000 - p$

$= 1{,}000 - 100$

$= 900$

Equilibrium price = 100.

Equilibrium quantity = 900.

(b) When price of an input used to produce salt has increased, new equilibrium price and equilibrium quantity is achieved when:

$1{,}000 - p = 400 + 2p$

$\Rightarrow$ $2p + p = 1{,}000 - 400$

$\Rightarrow$ $3p = 600$

$\Rightarrow$ $p = 200$

When p = 200, $Q_d = 1{,}000 - p$

$= 1{,}000 - 200$

$= 800$

New equilibrium price = 200.

New equilibrium quantity = 800.

Owing to increase in input price, supply curve shifts backward. Consequently, equilibrium price is expected to rise and equilibrium quantity is expected to fall. In tune with this expected result, the new equilibrium price has risen from 100 to 200 and equilibrium quantity has decreased from 900 to 800.

(c) When sales tax is imposed (= ₹ 3 per unit) the supply equation changes as under:

$Q_s = 700 + 2(p - 3)$ [out of the price charged, the producer has to pay ₹ 3 to the government]

Equating supply and demand equations, the equilibrium price is achieved, as under:

$$1{,}000 - p = 700 + 2(p - 3)$$

$$\Rightarrow \quad 1{,}000 - p = 700 + 2p - 6$$

$$\Rightarrow \quad 2p + p = 1{,}000 - 700 + 6$$

$$\Rightarrow \quad 3p = 306$$

$$\Rightarrow \quad p = 102$$

Equilibrium quantity:

$$1{,}000 - 102 = 898$$

Or

$$700 + 2(102 - 3) = 700 + 198 = 898$$

After sales tax,

Equilibrium price increases from 100 to 102.

Equilibrium quantity reduces from 900 to 898.]

7. Miscellaneous Questions and Reference to the Text for Answers

A. Questions of 3 & 4 marks each

1. Explain briefly the concept of equilibrium.
   [Page 323]
2. How is price determined in the market?
   [Page 324, 325]
3. Explain equilibrium price. How is it determined?
   [Page 323–325]
4. What will be the effect of simultaneous change in demand and supply on price?
   [Page 332–334]
5. What will be the effects of a decrease in both the market demand and supply of a commodity on its price? Explain.
   [Page 333, 334]
6. How are the equilibrium price and quantity of a commodity affected when its supply rises and demand is perfectly elastic?
   [Page 330, 331]
7. Show with the help of diagrams, the effect on equilibrium price and quantity when:
   (i) demand is perfectly elastic and supply decreases.
   (ii) supply is perfectly elastic and demand increases.
   [Page (i) 330, 331 (ii) 328, 329]
8. Show with the help of diagrams, the effect on equilibrium price and quantity when:
   (i) demand is perfectly inelastic and supply decreases.
   (ii) supply is perfectly inelastic and demand increases.
   [Page (i) 331 (ii) 329, 330]

9. Define equilibrium price. Explain with the help of a diagram the effect of an increase in demand for a commodity on its equilibrium price and equilibrium quantity.
   [Page 323, 326, 327]
10. How is price of a commodity affected by change in its supply?
   [Page 327, 328]
11. "If the demand and supply of a commodity both increase, the equilibrium price may not change, may increase, may decrease." Explain using diagrams.
   [Page 332, 333]
12. What can be the effects on the equilibrium price of a commodity when its demand and supply curves both shift to the right simultaneously? Show any two of these effects on a diagram.
   [Page 332, 333]
13. How is the equilibrium price of a commodity affected by a leftward shift of the demand curve? Explain with the help of a diagram.
   [Page 326, 327]

B. Questions of 6 marks each

1. What do you understand by equilibrium price? How do the forces of demand and supply determine the equilibrium price?
   [Page 323–325]
2. Explain the effect of the following three situations:
   (i) Effect of change in demand on the equilibrium price when supply is constant.
   (ii) Effect of change in supply on the equilibrium price when demand is constant.
   (iii) Effect of simultaneous change in demand and supply on equilibrium price.
   [Page 329–333]
3. At a given price there is excess demand for a good. Explain how the equilibrium price will be reached. Use diagram.
   [Page 324, 325]
4. At the given price of a commodity, there is excess supply. What changes will establish the equilibrium price? Explain with the help of a diagram.
   [Page 324, 325]
5. How does an increase in demand for a commodity affect its equilibrium price and equilibrium quantity? Explain with the help of a diagram.
   [Page 326, 327]
6. Explain the effect of a leftward shift of demand curve for a commodity on its equilibrium price and quantity with the help of a diagram.
   [Page 326, 327]
7. Explain with the help of a diagram the effect of a rightward shift of supply curve of a commodity on its equilibrium price and quantity.
   [Page 327, 328]
8. Explain with the help of a diagram the effect of a leftward shift of supply curve of a commodity on its equilibrium price and quantity.
   [Page 327, 328]
9. Briefly discuss how is new equilibrium established when demand or supply curve happens to shift.
   [Page 334]

10. How is the equilibrium price and equilibrium quantity of a normal commodity affected by an increase in the income of its buyers? Explain with the help of a diagram.

[Page 326, 327]

11. How will an increase in the income of the buyers of an inferior good affect its equilibrium price and equilibrium quantity? Explain with the help of a diagram.

[Page 326, 327]

12. Explain how change in price of the substitute commodity-Y (related to commodity-X) would affect market equilibrium with respect to commodity-X.

[Page 326, 327]

[**Hint:** Increase in the price of the substitute commodity-Y would cause increase in the demand for X, implying a forward shift in demand curve for X. Conversely, decrease in the price of the substitute commodity-Y would cause backward shift in demand curve for X.]

13. Explain the impact of increase in the number of consumers on market equilibrium.

[Page 330]

14. How does improvement in technology and the consequent decline in production cost affect market equilibrium?

[Page 327, 328, 332]

15. Explain market equilibrium when the number of firms happens to increase or decrease in the market and only normal profits are earned.

[Page 332]

16. How does increase in consumers' income impact market equilibrium?

[Page 330]

17. Market for a good is in equilibrium. What is the effect on equilibrium price and quantity if both market demand and market supply of the good increase in the same proportion? Use diagram.

[Page 332, 333]

18. Market for a good is in equilibrium. What is the effect on equilibrium price and quantity if the proportionate increase in market demand is greater than increase in market supply? Use diagram.

[Page 332, 333]

19. Market for a good is in equilibrium. What is the effect on equilibrium price and quantity if the proportionate increase in market demand is less than increase in market supply? Use diagram.

[Page 332, 333]

20. Given market equilibrium of a good. What is the effect of simultaneous decrease in both demand and supply of that good on its equilibrium price and quantity?

[Page 333, 334]

21. Explain the chain of effects of an increase in demand for a commodity on its equilibrium price and quantity.

[Page 326, 327]

22. Explain the chain of effects of an increase in supply of a commodity on its equilibrium price and quantity.

[Page 327, 328]

DOs and DON'Ts

1. Do not ever jump to the conclusion that when equilibrium is established in the market for a commodity, then the concerned commodity becomes available to each and every user of this commodity. The equilibrium price may be so high that it may be beyond the reach of certain buyers to buy the commodity. Such a problem becomes a social problem when the high price commodity is a necessity of life, like rice or wheat. In such situations, government intervention becomes essential even in market economies where market prices are determined by the market forces of demand and supply.
2. When the equilibrium is established and the market is cleared, it should not be taken as always a situation of zero stock of the commodity with the producers. The stocks may be distinguished as 'desired stock' and 'undesired stock'. When the market is cleared, it only implies that the producers are not left with any undesired stocks (or unplanned stocks). Desired stocks are planned stocks which a producer might like to maintain to cope with future demand. Undesired stocks, on the other hand, are unplanned stocks which arise because there is a lack of demand in the market, and some output remains unsold.

ability ZONE

❑ Economically 'Viable' and 'Non-viable' Industry

An industry is said to be economically 'viable' if corresponding to the minimum price (at which it can afford to sell its product), there is some demand in the market. In other words, there is some price corresponding to which supply and demand happen to coincide.

An industry is said to be 'non-viable' if corresponding to even the minimum price (at which it can sell its product), there are no buyers in the market. In other words, there is no price corresponding to which supply and demand for the product happen to coincide.

Geometrically: (i) In case of a 'viable' industry, supply and demand curves must intersect at some point. (ii) In case of a 'non-viable' industry, supply curve is entirely above the demand curve. These curves do not meet anywhere. See Figs., 19(A) and 19(B).

FIGURE 19

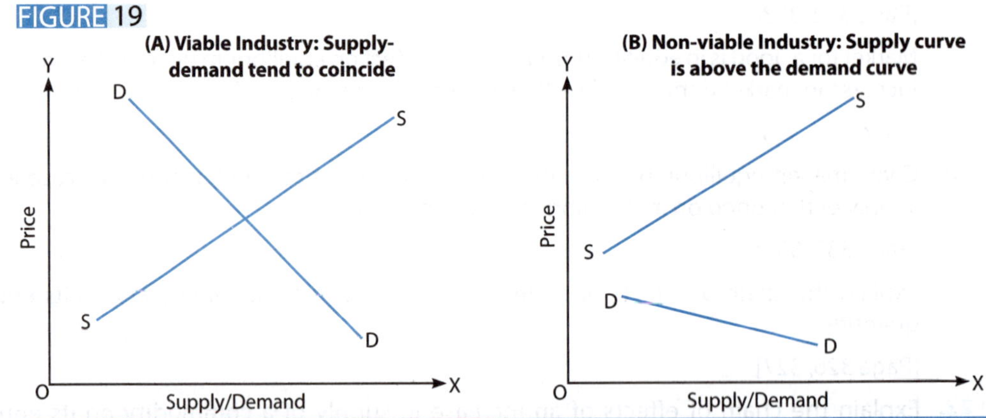

✦ Fig. 19(A) shows that there is some price where supply and demand happen to coincide. This is a situation of viable industry.

✦ Fig. 19(B) shows no such point where supply and demand happen to coincide. Entire supply curve is above the demand curve. This is a situation of non-viable industry.

micro

- Solved Numericals
- Unsolved Numericals
- CBSE Sample Question Paper, 2015–16 (Solved)

SOLVED NUMERICALS

[CBSE Exam Past 4 Years and Related Ones]

Economics, Economy and Central Problems of an Economy

1. Given the following data, draw a production possibility curve. Also find marginal opportunity cost.

Possibilities	A	B	C	D	E	F
Wheat (kg)	100	95	85	70	50	25
Rice (kg)	0	10	20	30	40	50

Sol.

Wheat (kg)	Rice (kg)	Marginal Opportunity Cost
100	0	—
95	10	$\frac{5}{10} = 0.5$
85	20	$\frac{10}{10} = 1.0$
70	30	$\frac{15}{10} = 1.5$
50	40	$\frac{20}{10} = 2.0$
25	50	$\frac{25}{10} = 2.5$

FIGURE 1

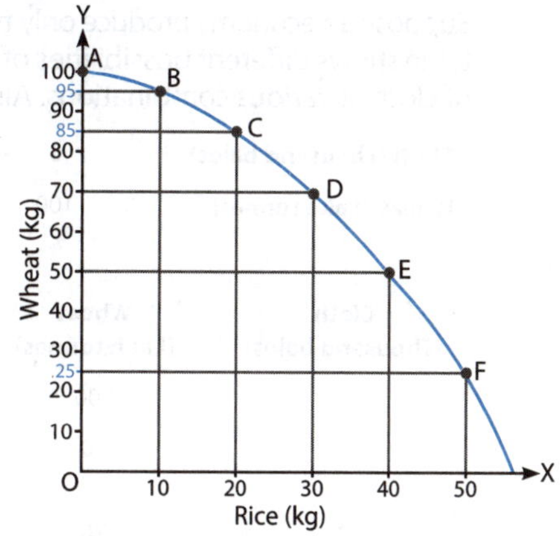

The Table shows that the marginal opportunity cost of producing more of rice in place of wheat is rising. Accordingly, production possibility curve (Fig. 1) is found to be concave to the origin.

2. Draw PPC for an economy, if production possibilities are as under. Also find marginal opportunity cost.

Shirt (Millions)	0	1	2	3	4	5
Computer (Thousands)	15	14	12	9	5	0

Sol.

Shirt (Millions)	Computer (Thousands)	Marginal Opportunity Cost
0	15	—
1	14	$\frac{1}{1} = 1$
2	12	$\frac{2}{1} = 2$
3	9	$\frac{3}{1} = 3$
4	5	$\frac{4}{1} = 4$
5	0	$\frac{5}{1} = 5$

FIGURE 2

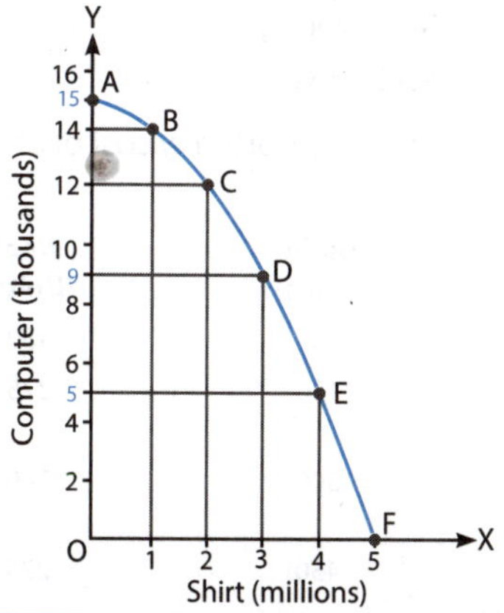

3. An economy produces two goods: watches and shoes. The following table summarises its production possibilities. Calculate the marginal opportunity cost of watches at various combinations. Give a diagrammatic presentation of production possibilities.

Watches (Millions)	0	1	2	3	4	5
Shoes (Thousands)	90,000	80,000	68,000	52,000	34,000	10,000

Sol.

Watches (Millions)	Shoes (Thousands)	Marginal Opportunity Cost
0	90,000	—
1	80,000	$\frac{10,000}{1} = 10,000$
2	68,000	$\frac{12,000}{1} = 12,000$
3	52,000	$\frac{16,000}{1} = 16,000$
4	34,000	$\frac{18,000}{1} = 18,000$
5	10,000	$\frac{24,000}{1} = 24,000$

FIGURE 3

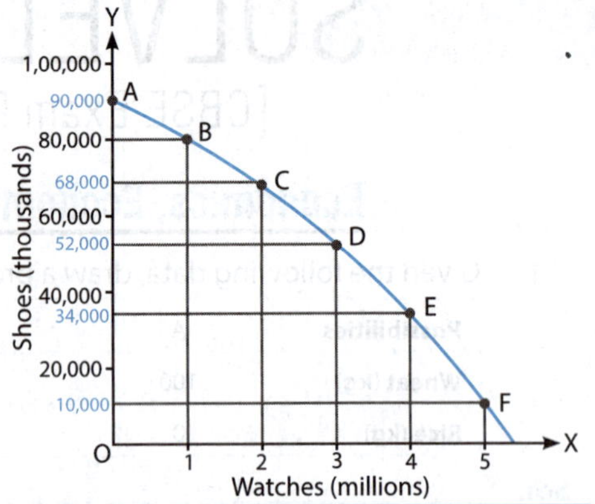

4. Suppose an economy produce only two goods, namely wheat and cloth, with its available resources. Following table shows different possibilities of production of wheat and cloth. Calculate the marginal opportunity cost of cloth at various combinations. Also draw the production possibility curve.

Cloth (Thousand bales)	0	1	2	3	4
Wheat (Lakh tonnes)	100	90	70	40	0

Sol.

Cloth (Thousand bales)	Wheat (Lakh tonnes)	Marginal Opportunity Cost
0	100	—
1	90	$\frac{10}{1} = 10$
2	70	$\frac{20}{1} = 20$
3	40	$\frac{30}{1} = 30$
4	0	$\frac{40}{1} = 40$

FIGURE 4

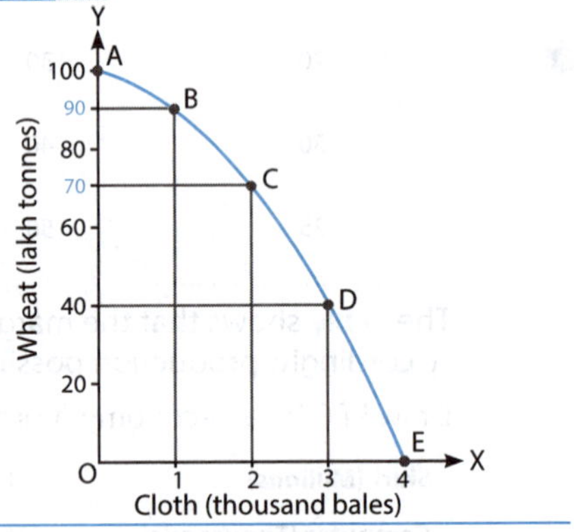

5. Citizens of a country produce two goods, garlic and wool, according to the following production possibility schedule:

Garlic (Units)	0	150	300	450	600	750	900
Wool (Units)	450	375	300	225	150	75	0

Find the opportunity cost of producing additional garlic. Is it constant or increasing? Draw a suitable diagram.

Sol.

Garlic (Units)	Wool (Units)	Marginal Opportunity Cost
0	450	—
150	375	$\frac{75}{150} = 0.5$
300	300	$\frac{75}{150} = 0.5$
450	225	$\frac{75}{150} = 0.5$
600	150	$\frac{75}{150} = 0.5$
750	75	$\frac{75}{150} = 0.5$
900	0	$\frac{75}{150} = 0.5$

FIGURE 5

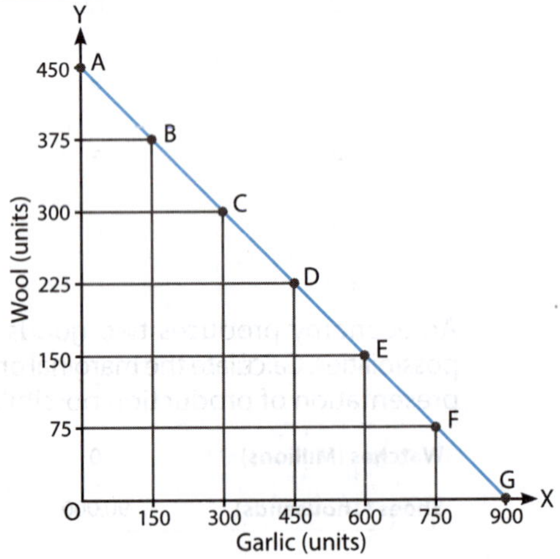

- Marginal opportunity cost $= \frac{\text{Loss of wool production}}{\text{Gain of garlic production}} = 0.5.$
- Opportunity cost of producing additional garlic remains constant, *i.e.*, 0.5.

[**Note:** Marginal opportunity cost indicates opportunity cost of producing additional garlic.]

6. Find marginal opportunity cost when shifting some resources from Use-1 to Use-2 causes a loss of output of 1,500 units in Use-1 and gain of output of ₹ 1,000 units in Use-2.

Sol. Marginal opportunity cost $= \frac{\text{Loss of output}}{\text{Gain of output}} = \frac{1{,}500}{1{,}000} = 1.5.$

7. An acre of land produces 100 bananas and zero apples, or 200 apples and zero bananas. Find marginal opportunity cost of bananas and apples.

Sol. Marginal opportunity cost of bananas $= \frac{\text{Loss of apples}}{\text{Gain of bananas}} = \frac{200}{100} = 2.$

Marginal opportunity cost of apples $= \frac{\text{Loss of bananas}}{\text{Gain of apples}} = \frac{100}{200} = 0.5.$

8. Suppose that you choose the science subjects. You had two other options: the art subjects (A) or the commerce subjects (C). If you would have chosen (A), you would have expected a career, offering you ₹ 4 lakh annually; if you would have chosen (C), you would have expected a career, giving you ₹ 5 lakh annually. What is your opportunity cost of choosing the science subjects?

Sol. Opportunities: A : Arts; Value = ₹ 4 lakh

C : Commerce; Value = ₹ 5 lakh

Opportunity cost of choosing science = ₹ 5 lakh, because opportunity cost is the loss of value of next best alternative.

9. Giving reason, comment on the shape of production possibilities curve based on the following schedule:

Good-X (Units)	0	1	2	3	4
Good-Y (Units)	10	9	7	4	0

[CBSE Delhi 2015; (AI) 2015; (F) 2015]

Sol.

Good-X (Units)	**Good-Y (Units)**	**Marginal Opportunity Cost** $\left(\frac{\Delta Y}{\Delta X}\right)$
0	10	—
1	9	$\frac{1}{1} = 1$
2	7	$\frac{2}{1} = 2$
3	4	$\frac{3}{1} = 3$
4	0	$\frac{4}{1} = 4$

The schedule shows that the marginal opportunity cost of producing more of Good-X in place of Good-Y is rising. Accordingly, production possibility curve is to be concave to the origin.

10. Giving reason, comment on the shape of production possibilities curve based on the following schedule:

Good-X (Units)	0	1	2	3	4
Good-Y (Units)	8	6	4	2	0

[CBSE Delhi 2015]

Sol.

Good-X (Units)	**Good-Y (Units)**	**Marginal Opportunity Cost**
0	8	—
1	6	$\frac{2}{1} = 2$

2	4	$\frac{2}{1}=2$
3	2	$\frac{2}{1}=2$
4	0	$\frac{2}{1}=2$

The schedule shows that the marginal opportunity cost of producing more of Good-X in place of Good-Y is constant. Accordingly, production possibility curve is to be a downward sloping straight line.

11. Giving reason, comment on the shape of production possibilities curve based on the following schedule:

Good-X (Units)	0	1	2	3	4
Good-Y (Units)	20	18	14	8	0

[CBSE Delhi 2015; (F) 2015]

Sol.

Good-X (Units)	**Good-Y (Units)**	**Marginal Opportunity Cost**
0	20	—
1	18	$\frac{2}{1}=2$
2	14	$\frac{4}{1}=4$
3	8	$\frac{6}{1}=6$
4	0	$\frac{8}{1}=8$

The schedule shows that the marginal opportunity cost of producing more of Good-X in place of Good-Y is rising. Accordingly, production possibility curve is to be concave to the origin.

12. Giving reason, comment on the shape of production possibilities curve based on the following schedule:

Good-X (Units)	0	1	2	3	4
Good-Y (Units)	30	27	21	12	0

[CBSE (AI) 2015]

Sol.

Good-X (Units)	**Good-Y (Units)**	**Marginal Rate of Transformation**
0	30	—
1	27	3Y : 1X
2	21	6Y : 1X
3	12	9Y : 1X
4	0	12Y : 1X

Since marginal rate of transformation is increasing, the production possibility curve is to be concave to the origin.

13. Giving reason, comment on the shape of production possibilities curve based on the following schedule:

Good-X (Units)	0	1	2	3	4
Good-Y (Units)	16	12	8	4	0

[CBSE (AI) 2015]

Sol.

Good-X (Units)	**Good-Y (Units)**	**Marginal Rate of Transformation**
0	16	—
1	12	4Y : 1X
2	8	4Y : 1X
3	4	4Y : 1X
4	0	4Y : 1X

Since marginal rate of transformation is constant, the production possibility curve is to be a straight line sloping downward.

14. Giving reasons, comment on the shape of production possibilities curve based on the following table:

Good-X (Units)	0	1	2	3	4
Good-Y (Units)	4	3	2	1	0

[CBSE (F) 2015]

Sol.

Good-X (Units)	Good-Y (Units)	Marginal Opportunity Cost
0	4	—
1	3	$\frac{1}{1}=1$
2	2	$\frac{1}{1}=1$
3	1	$\frac{1}{1}=1$
4	0	$\frac{1}{1}=1$

The schedule shows that the marginal opportunity cost of producing more of Good-X in place of Good-Y is constant. Accordingly, production possibility curve is to be a downward sloping straight line.

Consumer's Equilibrium—Utility Analysis

1. The total utility (TU) from 9 units of commodity-X is 20 and from 10 units is 15. Calculate the marginal utility from 10th unit.

Sol. $MU = TU_{10} - TU_9 = 15 - 20 = -5$.

2. The marginal utility from the consumption of commodity-X is given in following table:

Units of X	1	2	3	4	5
MU_X	10	9	7	3	-5

Calculate total utility for each unit of consumption of commodity-X.

Sol.

Units of X	1	2	3	4	5
MU_X	10	9	7	3	-5
TU_X	10	19	26	29	24

3. A consumer gets 50 utils of utility from the consumption of 1st unit of commodity-X. On the assumption that for every additional unit of X, he loses 10 utils of utility, how much unit (s) of X will he consume if, it was available to him at price of ₹ 5 per unit, and his marginal utility of money = 10?

Sol. We are given the following information:

Units of Commodity-X	1	2	3	4	5	6
MU_X	50	40	30	20	10	0

$P_X = ₹\ 5$ per unit

$MU_M = 10$

We know, equilibrium is struck when:

$$\frac{MU_X}{P_X} = MU_M$$

It happens when: $\frac{MU_X}{5} = 10$

Or, when $MU_X = 50$

Implying that the consumer finds his equilibrium when he consumes only one unit of the commodity-X.

4. On the consumption of 10 units of a commodity, a consumer finds that MU_X has exceeded the marginal utility of money. Should he reduce the consumption of X so that he strikes an equilibrium. Give reason in support of your answer.

Sol. Given, $\frac{MU_X}{P_X} > MU_M$, when 10 units of a commodity are consumed.

The consumer should not reduce but increase the consumption of X in order to achieve the equilibrium.

At equilibrium point, $\frac{MU_X}{P_X} = MU_M$

In order to achieve equilibrium, MU_X should reduce because price (P_X) remains constant and MU_M is also constant. This will happen only when consumption of commodity-X is increased. Because due to law of diminishing marginal utility, as he increases the consumption of a commodity, the marginal utility derived from its successive units decreases.

5. Marginal utility schedule for Good-X and Good-Y is given in the following table. Assuming price of X is ₹ 1, and price of Y is ₹ 1 and money income of the consumer is ₹ 13. Find the optimum combination of Good-X and Good-Y for maximising consumer's utility.

Q	1	2	3	4	5	6	7	8	9	10
MU_X (Utils)	28	24	21	20	16	13	9	5	3	1
MU_Y (Utils)	32	29	27	23	20	18	17	16	12	9

Sol. At equilibrium, $\frac{MU_X}{MU_Y} = \frac{P_X}{P_Y} = MU_M$

$$\frac{MU_X}{MU_Y} = 1 \quad \Rightarrow \quad MU_X = MU_Y$$

The consumer gets maximum satisfaction when he purchases 5 units of X and 8 units of Y. Because at this combination, $MU_X = MU_Y = 16$.

Consumer's Equilibrium—Indifference Curve Analysis

1. A consumer has an income of ₹ 200 per day. Price of X and Y is ₹ 2 and ₹ 5 respectively. Plot the budget line of the consumer.

Sol. We are given, P_X = ₹ 2; P_Y = ₹ 5; Income = ₹ 200

If entire income of the consumer is spent on X, then $\frac{200}{2}$ = 100 units of X can be purchased. If entire income is spent on Y, then $\frac{200}{5}$ = 40 units of Y can be purchased. Putting the combinations (100, 0) and (0, 40) in the diagram (Fig. 6), we get the budget line of the consumer.

PL is the budget line of the consumer.

FIGURE 6

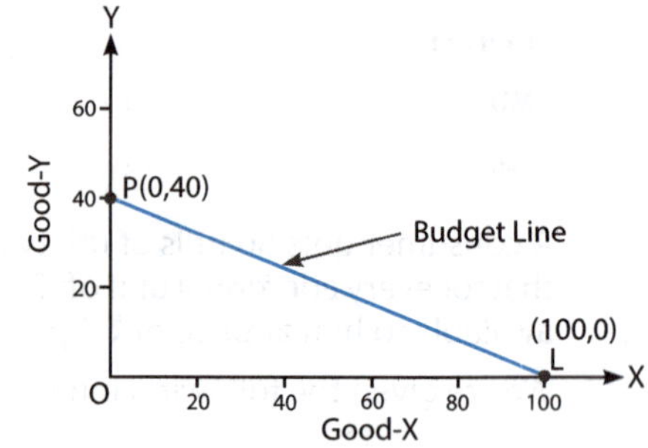

2. A consumer consumes only two goods X and Y. Her money income is ₹ 24 and the prices of Goods X and Y are ₹ 4 and ₹ 2 respectively. Answer the following questions:
   (i) Can the consumer afford a bundle 4X and 5Y? Explain
   (ii) What will be the MRS_{XY} when the consumer is in equilibrium? Explain.

Sol. (i) No, the consumer cannot afford a bundle of 4X and 5Y.

Given, money income = ₹ 24; P_X = ₹ 4 and P_Y = ₹ 2; if he purchases 4X and 5Y, then

$$4 \times 4 + 5 \times 2 = 26 > 24$$

Therefore, he is not able to buy a bundle of 4X and 5Y.

(ii) When the consumer is in equilibrium: $MRS_{XY} = \frac{P_X}{P_Y}$

The price ratio indicates that for every additional unit of Good-X, the consumer has to sacrifice 2 units of Good-Y. So that price ratio is 2 : 1. Accordingly, in a state of equilibrium, the marginal rate of substitution between Good-X and Good-Y must be equal to 2 : 1.

Theory of Demand

1. From the following table prepare demand schedule for household B, given demand schedule of household A, C and market demand schedule.

Price (₹)	Household A (Units)	Household B (Units)	Household C (Units)	Market Demand (Units)
7	6	—	11	26
6	8	—	16	36
5	12	—	22	51
4	17	—	30	71
3	24	—	42	98

Sol. **B's Demand Schedule**

Price (₹)	Quantity (Units)
7	26 – (6 + 11) = 9
6	36 – (8 + 16) = 12
5	51 – (12 + 22) = 17
4	71 – (17 + 30) = 24
3	98 – (24 + 42) = 32

2. Demand schedule for three consumers such as Mohan, Rohan and Mitu for a commodity is given below. Derive the market demand schedule.

Price (₹)	Demand Schedule of Mohan (Units)	Demand Schedule of Rohan (Units)	Demand Schedule of Mitu (Units)
1	60	55	24
2	50	40	13
3	40	25	5
4	30	10	0
5	20	0	0

Sol. **Market Demand Schedule**

Price (₹)	Quantity (Units)
1	60 + 55 + 24 = 139
2	50 + 40 + 13 = 103
3	40 + 25 + 5 = 70
4	30 + 10 + 0 = 40
5	20 + 0 + 0 = 20

3. If Mitu is dropped out of the market, what will be new market demand schedule?

Sol. If Mitu drops out from market the new market demand schedule is as follows:

New Market Demand Schedule

Price (₹)	Quantity (Units)
1	60 + 55 = 115
2	50 + 40 = 90
3	40 + 25 = 65
4	30 + 10 = 40
5	20 + 0 = 20

4. There are four consumers of a fruit called smile. They are: Isla, Ifraah, Ila and Ibema. Their demand curves for smile are given below. Derive the market demand curve.

Price (₹)	Quantity Demanded by Isla (Units)	Quantity Demanded by Ifraah (Units)	Quantity Demanded by Ila (Units)	Quantity Demanded by Ibema (Units)
1	16	7	15	8
2	11	6	12	6
3	7	5	9	4
4	4	4	6	2
5	2	3	3	0
6	1	2	0	0

Sol. In order to draw a market demand curve, we must first derive a market demand schedule, as under:

Market Demand Schedule

Price (₹)	Quantity (Units)
1	16 + 7 + 15 + 8 = 46
2	11 + 6 + 12 + 6 = 35
3	7 + 5 + 9 + 4 = 25
4	4 + 4 + 6 + 2 = 16
5	2 + 3 + 3 + 0 = 8
6	1 + 2 + 0 + 0 = 3

FIGURE 7

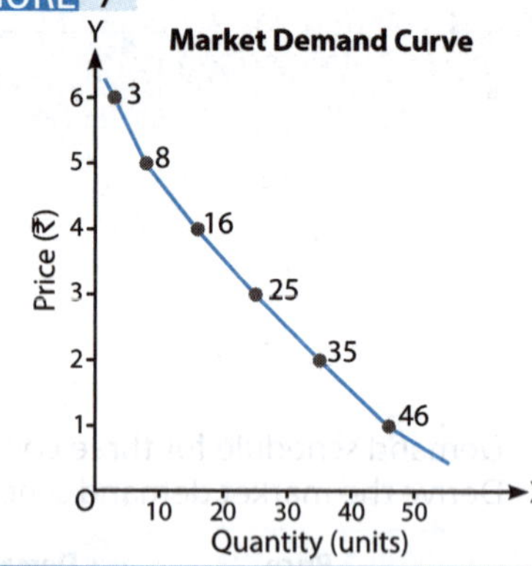

Market demand curve as based on the given market demand schedule.

[**Note:** Market demand curve is a horizontal summation of individual demand curves.]

5. Demand schedule for commodity-X of individual A and B is given in the following table. Derive the market demand schedule and market demand curve.

Price of Commodity-X (₹)	Demand of A (Units)	Demand of B (Units)
1	9	7
2	7	6
3	6	5
4	4	4
5	3	3

Sol. Market demand schedule for commodity-X is the sum of individual demand schedule of A and B.

Market Demand Schedule

Price of Commodity-X (₹)	Quantity (Units)
1	9 + 7 = 16
2	7 + 6 = 13
3	6 + 5 = 11
4	4 + 4 = 8
5	3 + 3 = 6

FIGURE 8

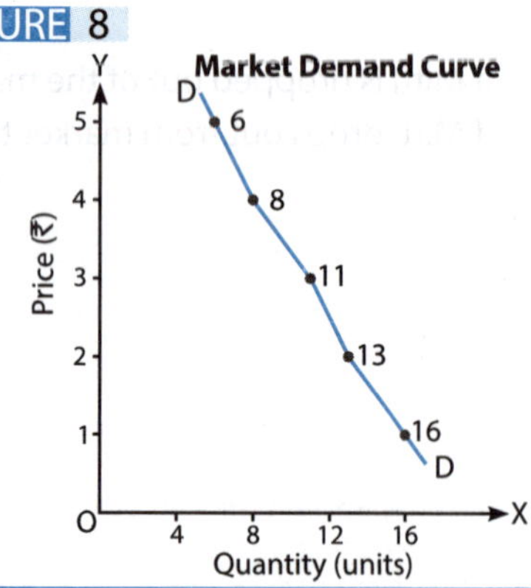

6. Following diagram shows the demand curve of Ragini for chocolate. Find quantity demanded of chocolate at price of ₹ 5, ₹ 8 and ₹ 10.

FIGURE 9

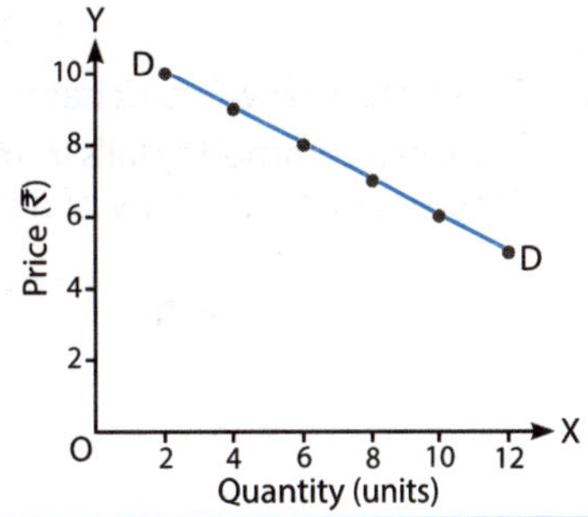

Sol. As per the demand curve DD, price and quantity combinations are:

(2, 10); (4, 9); (6, 8); (8, 7); (10, 6) and (12, 5)

Thus, at price of ₹ 5, ₹ 8 and ₹ 10 per unit of chocolate, quantity demanded are 12, 6 and 2 units respectively.

Price Elasticity of Demand

1. (i) Price of the commodity-X falls from ₹ 5 per kg to ₹ 4 per kg and the demand of consumer A for it rises from 4 kg to 6 kg. Express your opinion regarding the nature of elasticity of demand of commodity-X.
   (ii) If there is no change in the quantity demanded of commodity-X, what will be the nature of the price elasticity of demand?

Sol. (i) $E_d = (-)\frac{P}{Q} \times \frac{\Delta Q}{\Delta P}$

Here, $P = 5; P_1 = 4 \quad \therefore \quad \Delta P = 4 - 5 = -1$

$Q = 4;\ Q_1 = 6 \quad \therefore \quad \Delta Q = 6 - 4 = 2$

Price elasticity of demand $(E_d) = (-)\frac{5}{4} \times \frac{2}{-1} = \frac{10}{4}$

$= 2.5$ (greater than unity)

Ans. (i) Elasticity of demand is greater than unity.

(ii) Price elasticity of demand will be zero. Implying a situation of perfectly inelastic demand.

2. Supposing the initial demand was 100 units. With the rise in price by ₹ 5, the quantity demanded decreases by 5 units. Elasticity of demand is 1.2. Find out the price before the change in demand.

Sol. Supposing the price (P) before change = X

$E_d = (-)\frac{P}{Q} \times \frac{\Delta Q}{\Delta P}$

Here, $\Delta P = 5; \Delta Q = (-)\ 5$

$P = X; Q = 100$ and $E_d = 1.2$

Price elasticity of demand $(E_d) = (-)\frac{P}{Q} \times \frac{\Delta Q}{\Delta P} = 1.2$

Or, $(-)\frac{X}{100} \times \frac{-5}{5} = 1.2$ or $\frac{X}{100} = 1.2$

Or, $X = 1.2 \times 100 = 120$

Ans. Price before change in demand = ₹ 120.

3. A consumer buys 100 units of Good-Y at ₹ 5 per unit. The price elasticity of demand for the good is 2. At what price will he be willing to buy 140 units of Good-Y?

Sol. Suppose consumer buys 140 units at price of ₹ X per unit.

$E_d = (-)\frac{P}{Q} \times \frac{\Delta Q}{\Delta P}$

Here, $E_d = 2; P = ₹\ 5; P_1 = ₹\ X; \Delta P = ₹\ (X - 5)$

$Q = 100$ units; $Q_1 = 140$ units; $\Delta Q = Q_1 - Q = (140 - 100)$ units $= 40$ units

Price elasticity of demand $(E_d) = (-)\frac{P}{Q} \times \frac{\Delta Q}{\Delta P}$

$2 = (-)\frac{5}{100} \times \frac{40}{(X - 5)} = (-)\frac{2}{X - 5}$

$$2 \times (X - 5) = -2 \text{ or } 2X - 10 = -2$$
$$2X = -2 + 10 = 8$$
$$X = 4$$

Ans. The consumer will purchase 140 units of Good-Y at the price of ₹ 4.

4. Price of a commodity falls from ₹ 4 to ₹ 3 per unit. As a result total expenditure on it rises from ₹ 200 to ₹ 300. Find out price elasticity of demand by percentage method.

Sol.

Price (₹)	Total Expenditure (₹)	Quantity Demanded (Units)
4	200	$\frac{200}{4} = 50$
3	300	$\frac{300}{3} = 100$

Change in Price	Percentage Change in Price	Change in Demand	Percentage Change in Demand
₹ 4 to ₹ 3	$\frac{3-4}{4} \times 100$ $= -25\%$	50 units to 100 units	$\frac{100-50}{50} \times 100$ $= 100\%$

$$\text{Price elasticity of demand } (E_d) = (-)\frac{\text{Percentage change in quantity demanded}}{\text{Percentage change in price}}$$
$$= (-)\frac{100\%}{-25\%} = 4$$

Ans. Price elasticity of demand = 4.

5. The demand by a consumer for a commodity declines by 10 per cent when its price increases from ₹ 5 to ₹ 6 per unit. What is the price elasticity of demand of the commodity?

Sol. Percentage change in price $= \frac{\Delta P}{P} \times 100 = \frac{6-5}{5} \times 100 = \frac{1}{5} \times 100 = 20\%$

Percentage change in quantity demanded = (–) 10%

$$\text{Price elasticity of demand } (E_d) = (-)\frac{\text{Percentage change in quantity demanded}}{\text{Percentage change in price}}$$
$$= (-)\frac{-10\%}{20\%} = 0.5$$

Ans. Price elasticity of demand = 0.5.

6. The price elasticity of demand for commodity-X is known to be twice that of commodity-Y. Price of X falls by 5 per cent while that of commodity-Y rises by 5 per cent. What is the percentage change in quantities of X and Y?

Sol. If $E_d = 1$ for commodity-Y.
$E_d = 2$ for commodity-X.

∴ 5 per cent rise in price of Y should mean 5 per cent decrease in quantity of Y and 5 per cent fall in price of X should mean 10 per cent increase in quantity of X.

Ans. Quantity of X will increase by 10 per cent, and quantity of Y will decrease by 5 per cent.

7. The consumer buys 160 units of a good at a price of ₹ 8 per unit. Price falls to ₹ 6 per unit. How much quantity will the consumer buy at the new price if price elasticity of demand is (–) 2?

Sol. As in the above numerical, elasticity of demand has been specified with a negative sign. Accordingly, we need not use '–' sign as a prefix to the formula of measuring elasticity of demand. Thus,

$$E_d = \frac{P}{Q} \times \frac{\Delta Q}{\Delta P}$$

Here, $E_d = (-)2; P = 8; P_1 = 6; \Delta P = P_1 - P = 6 - 8 = (-)2$

$Q = 160; Q_1 = X; \Delta Q = Q_1 - Q = X - 160$

Thus, $$(-)\,2 = \frac{8}{160} \times \frac{X-160}{-2} = \frac{X-160}{-40}$$
$$X - 160 = 80$$
$$X = 80 + 160 = 240$$

Ans. The consumer will buy 240 units at the new price.

8. There is 50 per cent fall in price of the commodity. But quantity demanded remains to be 150 units. Find elasticity of demand.

Sol. Here, elasticity of demand is zero because in response to decrease in price of the commodity, the quantity demanded remains the same, *i.e.*, 150 units.

9. For a commodity, $\Delta P/P = -0.2$, and elasticity of demand = −0.3. Find percentage change in quantity demanded.

Sol. Percentage change in price $= \frac{\Delta P}{P} \times 100 = -0.2 \times 100 = (-)\ 20\%$

$$\text{Elasticity of demand } (E_d) = \frac{\text{Percentage change in quantity demanded}}{\text{Percentage change in price}}$$

$$-0.3 = \frac{\text{Percentage change in quantity demanded}}{-20\%}$$

$\therefore$ Percentage change in quantity demanded = −0.3 × −20 per cent = 6 per cent

Ans. Percentage change in quantity demanded = 6%.

10. For a commodity, $\Delta P/P = -0.2$, and elasticity of demand = −0.5. Find quantity demanded after a fall in price when initially it was 60 units.

Sol. Given, $\frac{\Delta P}{P} = (-)\ 0.2;\ E_d = -0.5$

Initial quantity demanded (Q) = 60 units

$$\text{Elasticity of demand } (E_d) = \frac{P}{Q} \times \frac{\Delta Q}{\Delta P} = \frac{\Delta Q}{Q} \times \frac{P}{\Delta P}$$

$$-0.5 = \frac{\Delta Q}{60} \times \frac{1}{-0.2}$$

$$0.5 = \frac{\Delta Q}{12}$$

$$\Delta Q = 6$$

$$Q_1 = Q + \Delta Q = 60 + 6 = 66$$

Ans. New quantity = 66 units.

11. If $E_d = -\ 0.2$ and $\frac{\Delta P}{P} = 0.6$, find new expenditure if initially it was ₹ 1,000.

Sol. $E_d = (-)\ 0.2$

Percentage change in price $= \frac{\Delta P}{P} \times 100 = 0.6 \times 100 = 60\%$

Percentage change in quantity demanded = (–) 0.2 × 60 per cent = (–) 12%

Let the initial price = ₹ 100 and initial quantity = 100 units

When price increases by 60 per cent, P_1 = ₹ 100 + ₹ 60 = ₹ 160

When quantity demanded reduces by 12 per cent, Q_1 = (100 – 12) units = 88 units

Thus:

Assumed initial expenditure = 100 × 100 = ₹ 10,000

New expenditure (if initial expenditure = 10,000) = 88 × 160 = ₹ 14,080

New expenditure (if initial expenditure = 1,000) = $14{,}080 \times \frac{1{,}000}{10{,}000} = 1{,}408$

Ans. New expenditure = ₹ 1,408.

12. Price of the commodity increases from ₹ 10 to ₹ 12 per unit and expenditure on the commodity increases by 20 per cent. Find elasticity of demand. Give a logical support to your answer.

Sol. (Using percentage method):

Given that initial price = ₹ 10, new price = ₹ 12, and increase in expenditure = 20 per cent, let us assume that initial quantity = 100. Accordingly, initial expenditure = 10 × 100 = ₹ 1,000, new expenditure

$= 1{,}000 + 20\%$ of $1{,}000 = ₹\,1{,}200$. New quantity $= \frac{1{,}200}{12} = 100$. Thus, quantity demanded remains constant, even when price rises from ₹ 10 to ₹ 12 (or by 20%). Implying that elasticity of demand = 0.

13. Draw a diagram showing increase in expenditure in response to increase in price, when $E_d = 0$.

Sol. The diagram (Fig. 10) shows increase in expenditure in response to increase in price when quantity demanded is constant ($E_d = 0$).

FIGURE 10

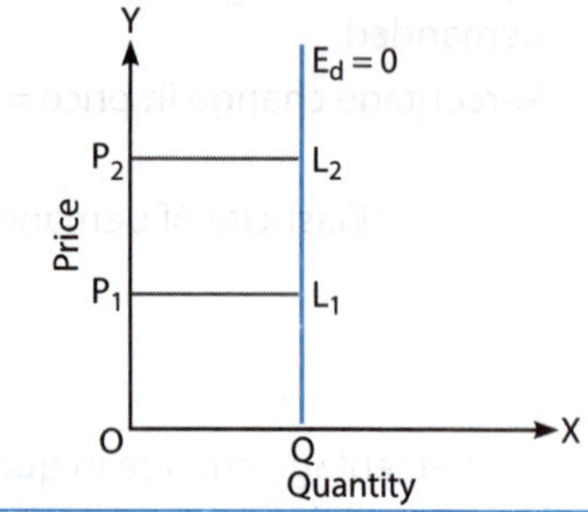

14. What is elasticity of demand in a situation when percentage change in quantity is infinite in response to a finite change in price? Draw a diagram, and support your answer logically.

Sol. In this situation, elasticity of demand is infinity. Because a finite change in price causes infinite change in quantity demanded.

The diagram (Fig. 11) shows that even a slightest increase in price would cause the quantity demanded to reduce to zero. Implying a situation of perfectly elastic demand ($E_d = \infty$).

FIGURE 11

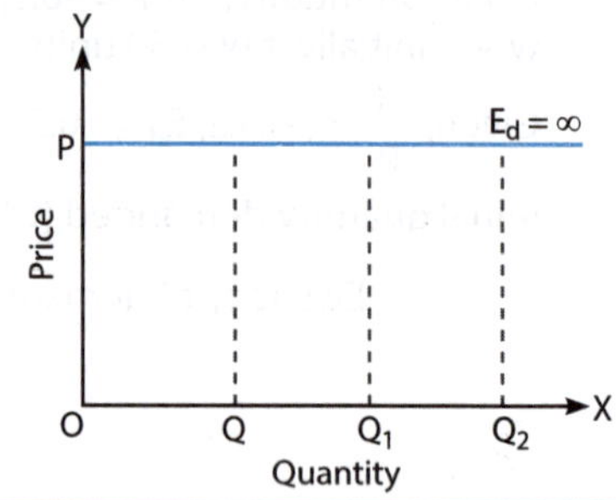

15. Price elasticity of demand is estimated to be 2. Price of the commodity happens to increase by 10 per cent. Find the change in quantity demanded when initially he was buying 120 units of the commodity.

Sol. Percentage change in price = 10 per cent

Or, $\frac{\Delta P}{P} = 0.1; Q = 120; E_d = 2$

We know,

$$\text{Price elasticity of demand } (E_d) = (-)\frac{\Delta Q}{Q} \times \frac{P}{\Delta P}$$

$$2 = (-)\frac{\Delta Q}{120} \times \frac{1}{0.1} \quad \Rightarrow \quad 2 = (-)\frac{\Delta Q}{12}$$

$$\Delta Q = -24$$

$$Q_1 = Q + \Delta Q = 120 + (-)\,24 = 96$$

Ans. New quantity = 96 units.

16. Given a straight line downward sloping demand curve, how will you find that elasticity of demand is 'zero' when it is touching the X-axis, and 'infinity' when it is touching the Y-axis. Use a diagram.

FIGURE 12

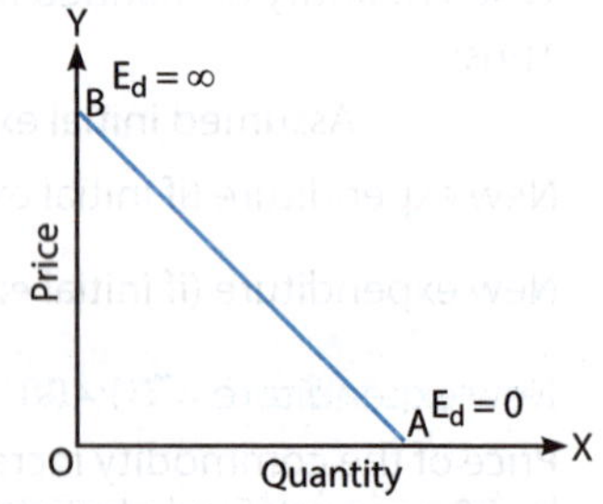

Sol. We know, $E_d = \frac{\text{Lower segment}}{\text{Upper segment}}$

At point A (when demand curve touches the X-axis), lower segment = 0.

$\therefore \quad E_d = \frac{0}{AB} = 0$

At point B (when demand curve touches the Y-axis), upper segment = 0.

$\therefore \quad E_d = \frac{AB}{0} = \infty.$

17. A consumer buys a certain quantity of a good at a price of ₹ 10 per unit. When price falls to ₹ 8 per unit, she buys 40 per cent more quantity. Calculate price elasticity of demand.

Sol. Suppose the consumer initially buys 100 units of the good.

New quantity = 100 + 40 per cent of 100 = 140

$P = 10; P_1 = 8; \Delta P = P_1 - P = 8 - 10 = (-)\ 2$

$Q = 100; Q_1 = 140; \Delta Q = Q_1 - Q = 140 - 100 = 40$

$$\text{Price elasticity of demand } (E_d) = (-)\frac{P}{Q} \times \frac{\Delta Q}{\Delta P}$$

$$= (-)\frac{10}{100} \times \frac{40}{-2} = 2$$

Alternative Approach:

$$\text{Percentage change in price} = \frac{\Delta P}{P} \times 100$$

$$= \frac{8-10}{10} \times 100 = \frac{-2}{10} \times 100 = (-)\ 20\%$$

$$\text{Price elasticity of demand } (E_d) = (-)\frac{\text{Percentage change in quantity demanded}}{\text{Percentage change in price}}$$

$$= (-)\frac{40\%}{(-)20\%} = 2$$

Ans. Price elasticity of demand = 2.

18. When price of a good is ₹ 7 per unit a consumer buys 12 units. When price falls to ₹ 6 per unit he spends ₹ 72 on the good. Calculate price elasticity of demand by using the percentage method. Comment on the likely shape of demand curve based on this measure of elasticity. *[CBSE Delhi 2012]*

Sol. Given, $P = ₹\ 7; P_1 = ₹\ 6; \Delta P = P_1 - P = ₹\ 6 - ₹\ 7 = (-)\ ₹\ 1$

$Q = 12 \text{ units}; Q_1 = \frac{72}{6} = 12 \text{ units}; \Delta Q = Q_1 - Q = (12 - 12) \text{ units} = 0 \text{ unit}$

$$\text{Price elasticity of demand } (E_d) = (-)\frac{P}{Q} \times \frac{\Delta Q}{\Delta P}$$

$$= (-)\frac{7}{12} \times \frac{0}{-1} = 0$$

Ans. Price elasticity of demand = 0 (zero).

Demand curve in this case will be a vertical straight line parallel to Y-axis. Because, no matter what the change in price is, there is no change in quantity demanded of the commodity.

19. A consumer buys 10 units of a good at a price of ₹ 9 per unit. At price ₹ 10 per unit he buys 9 units. What is price elasticity of demand? Use expenditure approach. Comment on the likely shape of demand curve on the basis of this measure of elasticity. *[CBSE Delhi 2012]*

Sol.

Price (₹)	Demand (Units)	Total Expenditure (₹)
9	10	90
10	9	90

Since, total expenditure remains constant, price elasticity of demand is equal to unity.

Ans. Price elasticity of demand = 1.

Demand curve will be a rectangular hyperbola, provided total expenditure remains constant at all levels of price of the commodity.

20. A consumer buys 20 units of a good at a price of ₹ 5 per unit. He incurs an expenditure of ₹ 120 when he buys 24 units. Calculate price elasticity of demand using the percentage method. Comment upon the likely shape of demand curve based on this information. *[CBSE Delhi 2012]*

Sol. Given, $P = ₹\ 5; P_1 = \frac{120}{24} = ₹\ 5; \Delta P = P_1 - P = ₹\ 5 - ₹\ 5 = 0$

$Q = 20 \text{ units}; Q_1 = 24 \text{ units}; \Delta Q = Q_1 - Q = (24 - 20) \text{ units} = 4 \text{ units}$

$$\text{Price elasticity of demand } (E_d) = (-)\frac{P}{Q}\times\frac{\Delta Q}{\Delta P}$$

$$= (-)\frac{5}{20}\times\frac{4}{0} = \frac{20}{0} = \infty$$

Ans. Price elasticity of demand = ∞ (infinity).

Demand curve in this case will be a horizontal straight line parallel to X-axis, provided there is an infinite demand corresponding to a given price of the commodity.

21. A consumer buys 10 units of a commodity at a price of ₹ 10 per unit. He incurs an expenditure of ₹ 200 on buying 20 units. Calculate price elasticity of demand by the percentage method. Comment upon the shape of demand curve based on this information. *[CBSE (AI) 2012]*

Sol. Given, $P = ₹\,10;\ P_1 = \frac{200}{20} = ₹\,10;\ \Delta P = P_1 - P = ₹\,10 - ₹\,10 = 0$

$Q = 10$ units; $Q_1 = 20$ units; $\Delta Q = Q_1 - Q = (20 - 10)$ units $= 10$ units

$$\text{Price elasticity of demand } (E_d) = (-)\frac{P}{Q}\times\frac{\Delta Q}{\Delta P}$$

$$= (-)\frac{10}{10}\times\frac{10}{0} = \frac{100}{0} = \infty$$

Ans. Price elasticity of demand = ∞ (infinity).

Demand curve in this case will be a horizontal straight line parallel to X-axis provided that the demand is infinite corresponding to a given price of the commodity.

22. A consumer buys 14 units of a good at a price of ₹ 8 per unit. At price ₹ 7 per unit he spends ₹ 98 on the good. Calculate price elasticity of demand by the percentage method. Comment upon the shape of demand curve based on this information. *[CBSE (AI) 2012]*

Sol. Given, $P = ₹\,8;\ P_1 = ₹\,7;\ \Delta P = P_1 - P = ₹\,7 - ₹\,8 = (-)\,1$

$Q = 14$ units; $Q_1 = \frac{98}{7} = 14$ units; $\Delta Q = Q_1 - Q = (14 - 14)$ units $= 0$ unit

$$\text{Price elasticity of demand } (E_d) = (-)\frac{P}{Q}\times\frac{\Delta Q}{\Delta P}$$

$$= (-)\frac{8}{14}\times\frac{0}{-1} = \frac{0}{-14} = 0$$

Ans. Price elasticity of demand = 0 (zero).

Demand curve will be a vertical straight line parallel to Y-axis, provided quantity demanded remains constant at all levels of price of the commodity.

23. A consumer buys 8 units of a good at a price of ₹ 7 per unit. When price rises to ₹ 8 per unit he buys 7 units. Calculate price electricity of demand through the expenditure approach. Comment upon the shape of demand curve based on this information. *[CBSE (AI) 2012]*

Sol.

Price (₹)	Demand (Units)	Total Expenditure (₹)
7	8	56
8	7	56

Since, total expenditure remains constant, price elasticity of demand is equal to unity.

Ans. Price elasticity of demand = 1.

Demand curve will be a rectangular hyperbola, if total expenditure remains constant at all levels of price of the commodity.

24. A consumer buys 13 units of a good at a price of ₹ 11 per unit. When price rises to ₹ 13 per unit he buys 11 units. Use expenditure approach to find price elasticity of demand. Also comment on the shape of the demand curve based on this information. *[CBSE (F) 2012]*

Sol.

Price (₹)	Demand (Units)	Total Expenditure (₹)
11	13	143
13	11	143

Since, total expenditure remains constant, price elasticity of demand is equal to unity.

Ans. Price elasticity of demand = 1.

Demand curve will be a rectangular hyperbola in case total expenditure on the commodity remains constant at all levels of price of the commodity.

25. A consumer buys 11 units of a good at a price of ₹ 10 per unit. He can buy 13 units of the same by incurring an expenditure of ₹ 130. Calculate price elasticity of demand by the percentage method. Also comment on the shape of the demand curve based on this information. *[CBSE (F) 2012]*

Sol. Given, $P = ₹\ 10;\ P_1 = \frac{130}{13} = ₹\ 10;\ \Delta P = P_1 - P = ₹\ 10 - ₹\ 10 = 0$

$$Q = 11 \text{ units};\ Q_1 = 13 \text{ units};\ \Delta Q = Q_1 - Q = (13 - 11) \text{ units} = 2 \text{ units}$$

$$\text{Price elasticity of demand } (E_d) = (-)\frac{P}{Q} \times \frac{\Delta Q}{\Delta P} = (-)\frac{10}{11} \times \frac{2}{0} = \frac{20}{0} = \infty$$

Ans. Price elasticity of demand = ∞ (infinity).

Demand curve will be a horizontal straight line parallel to X-axis, provided that the demand is infinite corresponding to a given price of the commodity.

26. A consumer buys 10 units of a good at a price of ₹ 11 per unit. When the price falls to ₹ 9 per unit, he spends ₹ 90 on the good. Calculate price elasticity of demand using the percentage method. Also comment upon the shape of demand curve based on this information. *[CBSE (F) 2012]*

Sol. Given, $P = ₹\ 11;\ P_1 = ₹\ 9;\ \Delta P = P_1 - P = ₹\ 9 - ₹\ 11 = (-)₹\ 2$

$$Q = 10 \text{ units};\ Q_1 = \frac{90}{9} = 10 \text{ units};\ \Delta Q = Q_1 - Q = (10 - 10) \text{ units} = 0 \text{ unit}$$

$$\text{Price elasticity of demand } (E_d) = (-)\frac{P}{Q} \times \frac{\Delta Q}{\Delta P} = (-)\frac{11}{10} \times \frac{0}{-2} = \frac{0}{20} = 0$$

Ans. Price elasticity of demand = 0 (zero).

Demand curve will be a vertical straight line parallel to Y-axis, provided there is no change in quantity demanded at all levels of price of the commodity.

27. Price elasticity of demand for flowers and toys are respectively (–) 0.9 and (–) 0.5. Demand for which one is more elastic and Why? *[CBSE Sample Paper 2013]*

Sol. Demand for flowers will be more elastic than toys because percentage change in quantity demanded is more responsive to a given percentage change in price in the case of flowers than in the case of toys. Negative sign as a prefix to the elasticity of demand only signifies the inverse relationship between price and quantity demanded of a commodity.

28. The price elasticity of demand for a good is –0.4. If its price increases by 5 per cent, by what percentage will its demand fall? Calculate. *[CBSE Delhi 2013]*

Sol. Given, $E_d = -0.4$

Percentage change in price = 5%

$$\text{Price elasticity of demand } (E_d) = \frac{\text{Percentage change in quantity demanded}}{\text{Percentage change in price}}$$

$$-0.4 = \frac{\text{Percentage change in quantity demanded}}{5\%}$$

Percentage change in quantity demanded = –0.4 × 5 per cent = –2 per cent

Ans. Percentage fall in quantity demanded = 2%.

29. The demand for good rises by 20 per cent as a result of fall in its price. Its price elasticity of demand is (–) 0.8. Calculate the percentage fall in price. *[CBSE Delhi 2013]*

Sol. Given, $E_d = -0.8$

Percentage change in quantity demanded = 20%

$$\text{Price elasticity of demand } (E_d) = \frac{\text{Percentage change in quantity demanded}}{\text{Percentage change in price}}$$

$$-0.8 = \frac{20\%}{\text{Percentage change in price}}$$

$$\text{Percentage change in price} = \frac{20\%}{-0.8}$$

$$\text{Percentage change in price} = -25\%$$

Ans. Percentage fall in price = 25%.

30. A 5 per cent fall in the price of a good raises its demand from 300 units to 318 units. Calculate its price elasticity of demand. [CBSE (AI) 2013]

Sol. Given, percentage change in price = (–) 5%

$$Q = 300 \text{ units}; Q_1 = 318 \text{ units}; \Delta Q = Q_1 - Q = (318 - 300) \text{ units} = 18 \text{ units}$$

$$\text{Percentage change in quantity demanded} = \frac{18}{300} \times 100 = 6\%$$

$$\text{Price elasticity of demand } (E_d) = (-)\frac{\text{Percentage change in quantity demanded}}{\text{Percentage change in price}}$$

$$= (-)\frac{6\%}{(-)5\%}$$

$$= 1.2$$

Ans. Price elasticity of demand = 1.2.

31. When the price of a commodity falls by 20 per cent, its demand rises from 400 units to 500 units. Calculate its price elasticity of demand. [CBSE (AI) 2013]

Sol. Given, percentage change in price = (–)20%

$$Q = 400 \text{ units}; Q_1 = 500 \text{ units}; \Delta Q = Q_1 - Q = (500 - 400) \text{ units} = 100 \text{ units}$$

$$\text{Percentage change in quantity demanded} = \frac{100}{400} \times 100 = 25\%$$

$$\text{Price elasticity of demand } (E_d) = (-)\frac{\text{Percentage change in quantity demanded}}{\text{Percentage change in price}}$$

$$= (-)\frac{25\%}{(-)20\%}$$

$$= 1.25$$

Ans. Price elasticity of demand = 1.25.

32. Price elasticity of demand of a good is – 0.75. Calculate the percentage fall in its price that will result in 15 per cent rise in its demand. [CBSE (AI) 2013]

Sol. Given, $E_d = -0.75$

$$\text{Percentage change in quantity demanded} = 15\%$$

$$\text{Price elasticity of demand } (E_d) = \frac{\text{Percentage change in quantity demanded}}{\text{Percentage change in price}}$$

$$-0.75 = \frac{15\%}{\text{Percentage change in price}}$$

$$\text{Percentage change in price} = \frac{15\%}{-0.75}$$

$$\text{Percentage change in price} = -20\%$$

Ans. Percentage fall in price = 20%.

33. A 20 per cent fall in the price of a good, raises its demand from 600 units to 750 units. Calculate its price elasticity of demand. [CBSE (F) 2013]

Sol. Given, percentage change in price = (–) 20%

$$Q = 600 \text{ units}; Q_1 = 750 \text{ units}; \Delta Q = Q_1 - Q = (750 - 600) \text{ units} = 150 \text{ units}$$

$$\text{Percentage change in quantity demanded} = \frac{150}{600} \times 100 = 25\%$$

$$\text{Price elasticity of demand } (E_d) = (-)\frac{\text{Percentage change in quantity demanded}}{\text{Percentage change in price}}$$

$$= (-)\frac{25\%}{(-)20\%} = 1.25$$

Ans. Price elasticity of demand = 1.25.

34. A consumer buys 18 units of a good at a price of ₹ 9 per unit. The price elasticity of demand for the good is (–) 1. How many units the consumer will buy at a price of ₹ 10 per unit? Calculate. *[CBSE Delhi 2014]*

Sol. Given, $P = ₹\ 9; P_1 = ₹\ 10; \Delta P = P_1 - P = ₹\ 10 - ₹\ 9 = ₹\ 1$

$Q = 18$ units; $Q_1 = ?$

$E_d = -1$

$$\text{Price elasticity of demand } (E_d) = \frac{P}{Q} \times \frac{\Delta Q}{\Delta P}$$

$$-1 = \frac{9}{18} \times \frac{\Delta Q}{1}$$

$$\Delta Q = -2$$

Now, $\Delta Q = Q_1 - 18$

$\Rightarrow$ $-2 = Q_1 - 18$

$Q_1 = 18 - 2 = 16$

Ans. Consumer will buy 16 units at a price of ₹ 10 per unit.

35. Price elasticity of demand of a good is (–) 1. When its price per unit falls by one rupee, its demand rises from 16 to 18 units. Calculate the price before change. *[CBSE Delhi 2014]*

Sol. Given, $P = ?; \Delta P = ₹\ 1$

$Q = 16$ units; $Q_1 = 18$ units; $\Delta Q = Q_1 - Q = (18 - 16)$ units $= 2$ units

$E_d = -1$

$$\text{Price elasticity of demand } (E_d) = \frac{P}{Q} \times \frac{\Delta Q}{\Delta P}$$

$$-1 = \frac{P}{16} \times \frac{2}{-1}$$

$$-8 = -P$$

Thus, $P = 8$

Ans. Price before change = ₹ 8.

36. A consumer buys 30 units of a good at a price of ₹ 10 per unit. Price elasticity of demand for the good is (–) 1. How many units the consumer will buy at a price of ₹ 9 per unit? Calculate. *[CBSE Delhi 2014]*

Sol. Given, $P = ₹\ 10; P_1 = ₹\ 9; \Delta P = P_1 - P = ₹\ 9 - ₹\ 10 = (-)₹\ 1$

$Q = 30$ units; $Q_1 = ?$

$E_d = -1$

$$\text{Price elasticity of demand } (E_d) = \frac{P}{Q} \times \frac{\Delta Q}{\Delta P}$$

$$-1 = \frac{10}{30} \times \frac{\Delta Q}{-1}$$

$$\Delta Q = 3$$

Now, $\Delta Q = Q_1 - 30$

$3 = Q_1 - 30$

$Q_1 = 30 + 3$

$= 33$

Ans. Consumer will buy 33 units at a price of ₹ 9 per unit.

37. When the price of a good falls from ₹ 10 to ₹ 8 per unit, its demand rises from 20 units to 24 units. What can you say about price elasticity of demand of the good through the 'expenditure approach'? [CBSE (AI) 2014]

Sol.

Price (₹)	Quantity Demanded (Units)	Total Expenditure (₹)
10	20	200
8	24	192

Here, total expenditure decreases with a fall in price; hence, price elasticity of demand of the good is less than unity. It is a situation of inelastic demand.

Ans. Price elasticity of demand < 1.

38. When the price of a good rises from ₹ 10 to ₹ 12 per unit, its demand falls from 25 units to 20 units. What can you say about price elasticity of demand of the good through the 'expenditure approach'? [CBSE (AI) 2014]

Sol.

Price (₹)	Quantity Demanded (Units)	Total Expenditure (₹)
10	25	250
12	20	240

Here, total expenditure decreases with a rise in price; hence, price elasticity of demand of the good is more than unity. It is a situation of elastic demand.

Ans. Price elasticity of demand > 1.

39. A consumer buys 27 units of a good at a price of ₹ 10 per unit. When the price falls to ₹ 9 per unit, the demand rises to 30 units. What can you say about price elasticity of demand of the good through the 'expenditure approach'? [CBSE (AI) 2014]

Sol.

Price (₹)	Quantity Demanded (Units)	Total Expenditure (₹)
10	27	270
9	30	270

Here, total expenditure remains constant with a fall in price; hence, price elasticity of demand of the good is equal to unity. Demand curve is a rectangular hyperbola in the case when expenditure remains constant at all levels of price of the concerned good.

Ans. Price elasticity of demand = 1.

40. When price of a good falls from ₹ 15 per unit to ₹ 12 per unit, its demand rises by 25 per cent. Calculate price elasticity of demand. [CBSE (F) 2014]

Sol. Given, P = ₹ 15; P_1 = ₹ 12; $\Delta P = P_1 - P$ = ₹ 12 − ₹ 15 = (−) ₹ 3

$$\text{Percentage change in price} = \frac{\Delta P}{P} \times 100 = \frac{-3}{15} \times 100 = (-)\ 20\%$$

Percentage change in quantity demanded = 25 per cent

$$\text{Price elasticity of demand } (E_d) = (-)\frac{\text{Percentage change in quantity demanded}}{\text{Percentage change in price}}$$

$$E_d = (-)\frac{25\%}{(-)20\%}$$

$$E_d = 1.25$$

Ans. Price elasticity of demand = 1.25.

41. Price elasticity of demand of a good is (−) 1. Calculate the percentage change in price that will raise the demand from 20 units to 30 units. [CBSE (F) 2014]

Sol. Given, $E_d = -1$

Q = 20 units; Q_1 = 30 units; $\Delta Q = Q_1 - Q$ = (30 − 20) units = 10 units

Percentage change in quantity demanded $= \frac{\Delta Q}{Q} \times 100 = \frac{10}{20} \times 100 = 50\%$

$$\text{Price elasticity of demand } (E_d) = \frac{\text{Percentage change in quantity demanded}}{\text{Percentage change in price}}$$

$$-1 = \frac{50\%}{\text{Percentage change in price}}$$

∴ Percentage change in price = (–) 50%

Ans. Percentage change in price = (–) 50%.

42. Price elasticity of demand of two goods A and B is (–) 3 and (–) 4 respectively. Which of the two goods has higher elasticity and why? *[CBSE (F) 2014]*

Sol. Given,

Price elasticity of demand (E_d) of Good-A = (–) 3

Price elasticity of demand (E_d) of Good-B = (–) 4

Price elasticity of Good-B is higher as compared to Good-A. This is because the negative sign just indicates the inverse relationship between price and demand. It does not relate to the value of elasticity of demand. Accordingly, in terms of elasticity of demand (–) 4 is to be treated as higher than (–) 3.

Ans. Good-B has higher elasticity of demand.

43. A consumer spends ₹ 1,000 on a good priced at ₹ 8 per unit. When price rises by 25 per cent, the consumer continues to spend ₹ 1,000 on the good. Calculate price elasticity of demand by percentage method. *[CBSE Delhi 2015]*

Sol. Initial price (P) = ₹ 8

Rise in price by 25 per cent $= 8 \times \frac{25}{100} =$ ₹ 2

New price (P_1) = ₹ 8 + ₹ 2 = ₹ 10

Given, P = ₹ 8; P_1 = ₹ 10; $\Delta P = P_1 - P$ = ₹ 10 – ₹ 8 = ₹ 2

$Q = \frac{1{,}000}{8} = 125$ units; $Q_1 = \frac{1{,}000}{10} = 100$ units; $\Delta Q = Q_1 - Q = (100 - 125)$ units = (–) 25 units

$$\text{Price elasticity of demand } (E_d) = (-)\frac{P}{Q} \times \frac{\Delta Q}{\Delta P}$$

$$= (-)\frac{8}{125} \times \frac{-25}{2}$$

$$= \frac{4}{5} = 0.8$$

Ans. Price elasticity of demand = 0.8.

44. A consumer spends ₹ 60 on a good priced at ₹ 5 per unit. When price falls by 20 per cent, the consumer continues to spend ₹ 60 on the good. Calculate price elasticity of demand by percentage method. *[CBSE Delhi 2015]*

Sol. Initial price (P) = ₹ 5

Fall in price by 20 per cent $= 5 \times \frac{20}{100} =$ ₹ 1

New price (P_1) = ₹ 5 – ₹ 1 = ₹ 4

Given, P = ₹ 5; P_1 = ₹ 4; $\Delta P = P_1 - P$ = ₹ 4 – ₹ 5 = (–) ₹ 1

$Q = \frac{60}{5} = 12$ units; $Q_1 = \frac{60}{4} = 15$ units; $\Delta Q = Q_1 - Q = (15 - 12)$ units = 3 units

$$\text{Price elasticity of demand } (E_d) = (-)\frac{P}{Q} \times \frac{\Delta Q}{\Delta P}$$

$$= (-)\frac{5}{12} \times \frac{3}{-1}$$

$$= \frac{5}{4} = 1.25$$

Ans. Price elasticity of demand = 1.25.

45. A consumer spends ₹ 100 on a good priced at ₹ 4 per unit. When price falls by 50 per cent, the consumer continues to spend ₹ 100 on the good. Calculate price elasticity of demand by percentage method. *[CBSE Delhi 2015]*

Sol. Initial price (P) = ₹ 4

Fall in price by 50 per cent = $4 \times \frac{50}{100}$ = ₹ 2

New price (P_1) = ₹ 4 – ₹ 2 = ₹ 2

Given, P = ₹ 4; P_1 = ₹ 2; $\Delta P = P_1 - P$ = ₹ 2 – ₹ 4 = (–) ₹ 2

$$Q = \frac{100}{4} = 25 \text{ units}; Q_1 = \frac{100}{2} = 50 \text{ units}; \Delta Q = Q_1 - Q = (50 - 25) \text{ units} = 25 \text{ units}$$

$$\text{Price elasticity of demand } (E_d) = (-)\frac{P}{Q} \times \frac{\Delta Q}{\Delta P}$$

$$= (-)\frac{4}{25} \times \frac{25}{-2}$$

$$= 2$$

Ans. Price elasticity of demand = 2.

46. A consumer spends ₹ 1,000 on a good priced at ₹ 10 per unit. When its price falls by 20 per cent, the consumer spends ₹ 800 on the good. Calculate the price elasticity of demand by the percentage method. *[CBSE (AI) 2015]*

Sol. Initial price (P) = ₹ 10

Fall in price by 20 per cent = $10 \times \frac{20}{100}$ = ₹ 2

New price (P_1) = ₹ 10 – ₹ 2 = ₹ 8

Price (₹)	Expenditure (₹)	Quantity Demanded (Units)
10	1,000	$\frac{1,000}{10} = 100$
8	800	$\frac{800}{8} = 100$

$$\text{Percentage change in quantity demanded} = \frac{\Delta Q}{Q} \times 100 = \frac{100 - 100}{100} \times 100 = \frac{0}{100} \times 100 = 0$$

$$\text{Price elasticity of demand } (E_d) = (-)\frac{\text{Percentage change in quantity demanded}}{\text{Percentage change in price}}$$

$$= (-)\frac{0}{-20\%}$$

$$= 0$$

Ans. Price elasticity of demand = 0 (zero).

47. A consumer spends ₹ 100 on a good priced at ₹ 4 per unit. When its price falls by 25 per cent, the consumer spends ₹ 75 on the good. Calculate the price elasticity of demand by the percentage method. *[CBSE (AI) 2015]*

Sol. Initial price (P) = ₹ 4

Fall in price by 25 per cent = $4 \times \frac{25}{100}$ = ₹ 1

New price (P_1) = ₹ 4 – ₹ 1 = ₹ 3

Price (₹)	**Expenditure (₹)**	**Quantity Demanded (Units)**
4	100	$\frac{100}{4} = 25$
3	75	$\frac{75}{3} = 25$

Percentage change in quantity demanded $= \frac{\Delta Q}{Q} \times 100 = \frac{25-25}{25} \times 100 = \frac{0}{25} \times 100 = 0$

$$\text{Price elasticity of demand } (E_d) = (-)\frac{\text{Percentage change in quantity demanded}}{\text{Percentage change in price}}$$

$$= (-)\frac{0}{-25\%}$$

$$= 0$$

Ans. Price elasticity of demand = 0 (zero).

48. A consumer spends ₹ 400 on a good priced at ₹ 8 per unit. When its price rises by 25 per cent, the consumer spends ₹ 500 on the good. Calculate the price elasticity of demand by the percentage method. *[CBSE (AI) 2015]*

Sol. Initial price (P) = ₹ 8

Rise in price by 25 per cent $= 8 \times \frac{25}{100}$ = ₹ 2

New price (P_1) = ₹ 8 + ₹ 2 = ₹ 10

Price (₹)	**Expenditure (₹)**	**Quantity Demanded (Units)**
8	400	$\frac{400}{8} = 50$
10	500	$\frac{500}{10} = 50$

Percentage change in quantity demanded $= \frac{\Delta Q}{Q} \times 100 = \frac{50-50}{50} \times 100 = \frac{0}{50} \times 100 = 0$

$$\text{Price elasticity of demand } (E_d) = (-)\frac{\text{Percentage change in quantity demanded}}{\text{Percentage change in price}}$$

$$= (-)\frac{0}{25\%}$$

$$= 0$$

Ans. Price elasticity of demand = 0 (zero).

49. A consumer spends ₹ 400 on a good priced at ₹ 4 per unit. When the price rises by 25 per cent, the consumer continues to spend ₹ 400. Calculate the price elasticity of demand by percentage method. *[CBSE (F) 2015]*

Sol. Initial price (P) = ₹ 4

Rise in price by 25 per cent $= 4 \times \frac{25}{100}$ = ₹ 1

New price (P_1) = ₹ 4 + ₹ 1 = ₹ 5

Given, P = ₹ 4; P_1 = ₹ 5; $\Delta P = P_1 - P$ = ₹ 5 – ₹ 4 = ₹ 1

$Q = \frac{400}{4} = 100$ units; $Q_1 = \frac{400}{5} = 80$ units; $\Delta Q = Q_1 - Q = (80 - 100)$ units = (–) 20 units

$$\text{Price elasticity of demand } (E_d) = (-)\frac{P}{Q} \times \frac{\Delta Q}{\Delta P}$$

$$= (-)\frac{4}{100} \times \frac{-20}{1}$$

$$= \frac{4}{5} = 0.8$$

Ans. Price elasticity of demand = 0.8.

50. A consumer spends ₹ 200 on a good priced at ₹ 5 per unit. When the price falls by 20 per cent, he continues to spend ₹ 200. Find the price elasticity of demand by percentage method. *[CBSE (F) 2015]*

Sol. Initial price (P) = ₹ 5

Fall in price by 20 per cent $= 5 \times \frac{20}{100} =$ ₹ 1

New price (P_1) = ₹ 5 – ₹ 1 = ₹ 4

Given, P = ₹ 5; P_1 = ₹ 4; $\Delta P = P_1 - P$ = ₹ 4 – ₹ 5 = (–) ₹ 1

$$Q = \frac{200}{5} = 40 \text{ units};\ Q_1 = \frac{200}{4} = 50 \text{ units};\ \Delta Q = Q_1 - Q = (50 - 40) \text{ units} = 10 \text{ units}$$

$$\text{Price elasticity of demand } (E_d) = (-)\frac{P}{Q} \times \frac{\Delta Q}{\Delta P}$$

$$= (-)\frac{5}{40} \times \frac{10}{-1}$$

$$= \frac{5}{4} = 1.25$$

Ans. Price elasticity of demand = 1.25.

51. A consumer spends ₹ 60 on a good priced at ₹ 1 per unit. When the price rises by 100 per cent, he continues to spend ₹ 60 on the good. Calculate the price elasticity of demand by percentage method. *[CBSE (F) 2015]*

Sol. Initial price (P) = ₹ 1

Rise in price by 100 per cent $= 1 \times \frac{100}{100} =$ ₹ 1

New price (P_1) = ₹ 1 + ₹ 1 = ₹ 2

Given, P = ₹ 1; P_1 = ₹ 2; $\Delta P = P_1 - P$ = ₹ 2 – ₹ 1 = ₹ 1

$$Q = \frac{60}{1} = 60 \text{ units};\ Q_1 = \frac{60}{2} = 30 \text{ units};\ \Delta Q = Q_1 - Q = (30 - 60) \text{ units} = (-)\ 30 \text{ units}$$

$$\text{Price elasticity of demand } (E_d) = (-)\frac{P}{Q} \times \frac{\Delta Q}{\Delta P}$$

$$= (-)\frac{1}{60} \times \frac{-30}{1}$$

$$= \frac{1}{2} = 0.5$$

Ans. Price elasticity of demand = 0.5.

Production Function and Returns to a Factor

1. Complete the following table, on the assumption that for additional unit of the variable factor, marginal product decreases by 5 units of output.

Units of Labour	TP	AP	MP
—	—	—	—
—	—	—	—
—	—	—	—
—	—	—	–5

Sol.

Units of Labour	TP	AP	MP
1	10	10	10
2	15	7.5	5
3	15	5	0
4	10	2.5	–5

2. Given the following information about a firm, identify the stages of production.

Units of Labour	1	2	3	4	5	6	7	8
Units of Output	4	12	24	32	36	36	28	16

Sol.

Units of Labour	Units of Output (TP)	MP	Stages
1	4	4	Increasing returns to a factor
2	12	8	
3	24	12	
4	32	8	Diminishing returns to a factor
5	36	4	
6	36	0	
7	28	–8	Negative returns to a factor
8	16	–12	

3. Calculate average physical product and marginal physical product, given the following information about total physical product of a firm.

Employment of Variable Factor (Units)	Employment of Fixed Factor (Units)	Total Physical Product (Units)
0	5	0
1	5	10
2	5	24
3	5	40
4	5	56
5	5	70
6	5	80
7	5	84

Sol.

Employment of Variable Factor (Units)	TPP (Units)	APP (Units)	MPP (Units)
0	0	0	0
1	10	10	10
2	24	12	14
3	40	13.33	16
4	56	14	16
5	70	14	14
6	80	13.33	10
7	84	12	4

4. Complete the following table. Identify the phase of production which is relevant from the viewpoint of producer's equilibrium.

Units of Labour	TP	AP	MP
1	4	—	—
2	12	—	—
3	24	—	—
4	32	—	—
5	36	—	—
6	36	—	—
7	28	—	—
8	16	—	—

Sol.

Units of Labour	TP	AP	MP	
1	4	4	4	
2	12	6	8	
3	24	8	12	Relevant phase for Producer's Equilibrium: Phase of diminishing returns to a factor which is a phase of rising MC. (MP 12 to 0)
4	32	8	8	
5	36	7.2	4	
6	36	6	0	
7	28	4	–8	
8	16	2	–12	

5. From the information given in the table, identify different stages of production and state the related law.

Units of Labour	0	1	2	3	4	5	6	7	8	9
Units of Output	0	4	12	24	32	36	36	28	16	2

Sol.

Units of Labour	Units of Output	MP_L	Stages
0	0	0	
1	4	4	
2	12	8	Increasing returns to a factor (MP 0 to 12)
3	24	12	
4	32	8	
5	36	4	Diminishing returns to a factor (MP 12 to 0)
6	36	0	
7	28	–8	
8	16	–12	Negative returns to a factor (MP 0 to –14)
9	2	–14	

The law of variable proportions is associated with this case.

6. Using the following productions figures of a firm derive the relationship between total product and marginal product.

Units of Land	1	1	1	1	1	1	1	1	1
Units of Labour	0	1	2	3	4	5	6	7	8
TP	0	4	11	25	37	41	43	43	41

Sol.

Units of Land	1	1	1	1	1	1	1	1	1
Units of Labour	0	1	2	3	4	5	6	7	8
TP	0	4	11	25	37	41	43	43	41
MP	—	4	7	14	12	4	2	0	-2

Relation between Total Product (TP) and Marginal Product (MP):

(i) Up to 3rd unit of labour employment, MP increases and TP increases at increasing rate.

(ii) From 4th unit to 6th unit of labour employment, MP decreases and TP increases at diminishing rate.

(iii) At 7th unit of labour employment, MP is zero and TP is maximum.

(iv) At 8th unit of labour employment, MP is negative and TP start declining.

7. In the following table, identify the different phases of the law of variable proportions and also explain the causes.

Variable Input (Units)	1	2	3	4	5	6
Total Product (Units)	10	22	32	40	40	35

Sol.

Variable Input (Units)	Total Product (Units)	Marginal Product (Units)	Phases
1	10	10	**Phase-I**
2	22	12	Increasing returns to a factor
3	32	10	**Phase-II**
4	40	8	Diminishing returns to a factor
5	40	0	**Phase-III**
6	35	–5	Negative returns to a factor

Causes of Increasing Returns:

(i) Greater application of the variable factor facilitates better division of labour.

(ii) Greater application of the variable factor improves coordination between the factors.

(iii) Greater application of the variable factor ensures better utilisation of the fixed factor.

Causes of Diminishing Returns:

(i) **Fixity of the Factors:** As more and more units of a variable factor are combined with the fixed factor, the latter gets over utilised. Hence, the diminishing returns.

(ii) Factors of production are imperfect substitutes of each other.

(iii) The coordination between factors gets distorted so that marginal product of the variable factor declines.]

8. Complete the following table: *[CBSE Delhi 2013]*

Units of Labour	Average Product (Units)	Marginal Product (Units)
1	8	—
2	10	—
3	—	10
4	9	—
5	—	4
6	7	—

Sol.

Units of Labour	Average Product (Units)	Marginal Product (Units)	Total Product (Units)
1	8	8	8
2	10	12	20
3	10	10	30
4	9	6	36
5	8	4	40
6	7	2	42

9. Complete the following table: *[CBSE Delhi 2013]*

Units of Labour	Average Product (Units)	Marginal Product (Units)
1	16	—
2	20	—
3	—	20
4	18	—
5	—	8
6	14	—

Sol.

Units of Labour	Average Product (Units)	Marginal Product (Units)	Total Product (Units)
1	16	16	16
2	20	24	40
3	20	20	60
4	18	12	72
5	16	8	80
6	14	4	84

Concepts of Cost

1. From the data calculate:
(i) average fixed cost, (ii) average variable cost, (iii) marginal cost.

Output (kg)	0	1	2	3	4	5
Total Cost (₹)	40	100	120	130	150	190

Sol.

Output (kg)	Total Cost (₹)	Total Fixed Cost (₹)	Average Fixed Cost (₹)	Total Variable Cost (₹)	Average Variable Cost (₹)	Marginal Cost (₹)
0	40	40	∞	—	—	—
1	100	40	40	60	60	60
2	120	40	20	80	40	20
3	130	40	13.3	90	30	10
4	150	40	10	110	27.5	20
5	190	40	8	150	30	40

2. Given below is the cost schedule of a firm. Its total fixed cost is ₹ 100. Calculate average variable cost and marginal cost at each given level of output.

Output (Units)	1	2	3	4
Total Cost (₹)	350	450	610	820

Sol.

Output (Units)	TC (₹)	TFC (₹)	TVC (₹)	AVC (₹)	MC (₹)
1	350	100	250	250	250
2	450	100	350	175	100
3	610	100	510	170	160
4	820	100	720	180	210

3. Complete the following table:

Output (Units)	Total Cost (₹)	Total Variable Cost (₹)	Marginal Cost (₹)
0	12		
1	18		
2	21		

Sol.

Output (Units)	Total Cost (₹)	Total Variable Cost (₹)	Marginal Cost (₹)
0	12	—	—
1	18	18 – 12 = 6	18 – 12 = 6
2	21	21 – 12 = 9	21 – 18 = 3

[**Hint:** The fixed cost is to be incurred even when output is zero. Thus, in the above example, ₹ 12 is fixed cost. The variable cost is the difference between total cost and fixed cost.]

4. Following information is given about a firm:

Output (Units)	0	1	2	3	4	5	6
Total Cost (₹)	150	300	420	600	790	1,000	1,260

From this information, find out:

(i) AFC of producing 3 units,
(ii) AVC of producing 4 units,
(iii) Least AC level of output,
(iv) MC of producing 5th unit, and
(v) TVC of producing 6 units.

Sol.

Output (Units)	Total Cost (₹)	Total Fixed Cost (₹)	Average Fixed Cost (₹)	Total Variable Cost (₹)	Average Variable Cost (₹)	Marginal Cost (₹)	Average Cost (₹)
0	150	150	∞	—	—	—	∞
1	300	150	150	150	150	150	300
2	420	150	75	270	135	120	210
3	600	150	50	450	150	180	200
4	790	150	37.5	640	160	190	197.5
5	1,000	150	30	850	170	210	200
6	1,260	150	25	1,110	185	260	210

Ans. (i) AFC of producing 3 units = ₹ 50.
(ii) AVC of producing 4 units = ₹ 160.
(iii) Least AC level of output = 4 units.
(iv) MC of producing 5th unit = ₹ 210.
(v) TVC of producing 6 units = ₹ 1,110.

5. Complete the following table:

Output (Units)	Total Cost (₹)	Average Variable Cost (₹)	Marginal Cost (₹)
0	60	—	—
1	140	—	—
2	190	—	—
3	240	—	—
4	300	—	—

Sol.

Output (Units)	TC (₹)	TFC (₹)	TVC (₹)	AVC (₹)	MC (₹)
0	60	60	0	0	—
1	140	60	80	80	80
2	190	60	130	65	50
3	240	60	180	60	50
4	300	60	240	60	60

6. Complete the following table:

Output (Units)	AFC (₹)	TFC (₹)	TVC (₹)	MC (₹)
0	—	50	—	—
1	—	—	—	10
2	—	—	18	—
3	—	—	—	6
4	—	—	20	—

Sol.

Output (Units)	AFC (₹)	TFC (₹)	TVC (₹)	MC (₹)
0	∞	50	—	—
1	50	50	10	10
2	25	50	18	8
3	16.67	50	24	6
4	12.5	50	20	–4

7. Calculate MC, given the following information. Also find AFC.

Output (Units)	Total Variable Cost (₹)	Total Fixed Cost (₹)
0	—	500
1	400	—
5	1,600	—

Sol.

Output (Units)	TVC (₹)	TFC (₹)	MC (₹)	AFC (₹)
0	—	500	—	∞
1	400	500	400	500
5	1,600	500	$\frac{1,600-400}{5-1}=\frac{1,200}{4}=300$	100

8. What should the firm's fixed cost of production, when average variable cost is ₹ 50 per unit, total cost of production is ₹ 500, and only 2 units of output are produced?

Sol. TC = ₹ 500; AVC = ₹ 50; Output = 2 units

TVC = AVC × Output

= ₹ 50 × 2 = ₹ 100

Fixed Cost = TC – TVC

= ₹ 500 – ₹ 100 = ₹ 400

Ans. Fixed cost = ₹ 400.

9. From the following table calculate AVC of each given level of output:

Output (Units)	1	2	3	4	5	6
Marginal Cost (₹)	20	16	18	19	21	24

Sol.

Output (Units)	MC (₹)	TVC (₹)	AVC (₹)
1	20	20	20
2	16	36	18
3	18	54	18
4	19	73	18.25
5	21	94	18.8
6	24	118	19.67

10. Complete the following table:

Output (Units)	Total Variable Cost (₹)	Average Variable Cost (₹)	Marginal Cost (₹)
1	10	—	—
—	—	8	6
3	27	—	—
—	—	10	13

Sol.

Output (Units)	Total Variable Cost (₹)	Average Variable Cost (₹)	Marginal Cost (₹)
1	10	10	10
2	16	8	6
3	27	9	11
4	40	10	13

11. Complete the following table:

Output (Units)	Total Variable Cost (₹)	Average Variable Cost (₹)	Marginal Cost (₹)
1	—	12	—
2	20	—	—
—	—	10	10
4	40	—	—

Sol.

Output (Units)	Total Variable Cost (₹)	Average Variable Cost (₹)	Marginal Cost (₹)
1	12	12	12
2	20	10	8
3	30	10	10
4	40	10	10

12. Find out (a) explicit cost, and (b) implicit cost from the following:

		(₹ in thousand)
(i)	Investment in fixed assets	2,000
(ii)	Borrowings at 12% interest per annum	1,500
(iii)	Wages paid during the year	120
(iv)	Annual rental value of the owner's factory building	180
(v)	Annual depreciation	100
(vi)	Estimated annual value of the management services of the owner	240

[CBSE Sample Paper 2013]

Sol. (a) Explicit Cost = Interest on borrowing + Wages paid during the year + Annual depreciation

= ₹ 180 thousand + ₹ 120 thousand+ ₹ 100 thousand

= ₹ 400 thousand

(b) *Implicit Cost = Imputed interest on own investment + Annual rental value + Estimated annual value of the management services

= ₹ 60 thousand + ₹ 180 thousand+ ₹ 240 thousand

= ₹ 480 thousand

Ans. (a) Explicit cost = ₹ 400 thousand.

(b) Implicit cost = ₹ 480 thousand.

**We assume that the investor has withdrawn ₹ 500 thousand (₹ 2,000 thousand – ₹ 1,500 thousand) from his bank thereby losing 12% interest (i.e., 12% of ₹ 500 thousand = ₹ 60 thousand).*

13. Complete the following table: *[CBSE Delhi 2013]*

Output (Units)	Average Cost (₹)	Marginal Cost (₹)
1	12	—
2	10	—
3	—	10
4	10.5	—
5	11	—
6	—	17

Sol.

Output (Units)	Average Cost (₹)	Marginal Cost (₹)	Total Cost (₹)
1	12	12	12
2	10	8	20
3	10	10	30
4	10.5	12	42
5	11	13	55
6	12	17	72

Concept of Revenue

1. A jeweller sells 3 diamond-rings at ₹ 12,000 per ring. If he sells 4 rings, his marginal revenue of 4th ring will be ₹ 10,500. At what price will he sell four rings?

Sol. (i) Total revenue of 3 rings = ₹ 12,000 × 3 = ₹ 36,000

(ii) Marginal revenue of 4th ring = ₹ 10,500

(iii) Total revenue of 4 rings = ₹ 36,000 + ₹ 10,500 = ₹ 46,500

(iv) Average revenue or price of 4 rings = ₹ 46,500 ÷ 4 = ₹ 11,625

Ans. Price = ₹ 11,625.

2. Calculate marginal revenue using following information:

Price (₹)	10	9
Sale/Demand (Units)	100	110

Sol.

Price (₹)	Sale/Demand (Units)	Total Revenue (₹)
10	100	1,000
9	110	990

$$MR = \frac{\Delta TR}{\Delta Sale} = \frac{990 - 1{,}000}{110 - 100} = \frac{-10}{10} = -1$$

Ans. Marginal revenue = –1.

3. Find out the average revenue and marginal revenue on the basis of the following data:

Units of Production	Total Revenue (₹)	Average Revenue (₹)	Marginal Revenue (₹)
1	20		
2	36		
3	48		
4	56		
5	60		
6	60		
7	56		

Sol.

Units of Production	Total Revenue (₹)	Average Revenue (₹)	Marginal Revenue (₹)
1	20	20	20
2	36	18	16
3	48	16	12
4	56	14	8
5	60	12	4
6	60	10	0
7	56	8	–4

4. From the table given below, calculate total revenue, average revenue, and marginal revenue.

Units Sold	Price (₹)	Total Revenue (₹)	Marginal Revenue (₹)
5	6		
4	7		
3	8		

Sol. Rewrite the table as follows.

Units Sold	Average Revenue or Price (₹)	Total Revenue (₹)	Marginal Revenue (₹)
3	8	24	—
4	7	28	4
5	6	30	2

5. On the basis of information given below, calculate AR and MR and explain their mutual relationship.

Units of a Good	1	2	3	4	5	6
TR (₹)	4	7	9	10	10	9

Sol.

Units of a Good	TR (₹)	AR (₹)	MR (₹)
1	4	4 (= 4 ÷ 1)	4
2	7	3.5 (= 7 ÷ 2)	3 (= 7 – 4)
3	9	3 (= 9 ÷ 3)	2 (= 9 – 7)
4	10	2.5 (= 10 ÷ 4)	1 (= 10 – 9)
5	10	2 (= 10 ÷ 5)	0 (= 10 – 10)
6	9	1.5 (= 9 ÷ 6)	–1 (= 9 – 10)

Relationship between TR, MR and AR:

(i) When MR is positive, TR rises up to 4th units.

(ii) When MR = 0, TR is maximum at 5th unit.

(iii) When MR is negative, TR starts falling, *i.e.*, after 5th unit.

(iv) When AR and MR both are falling, MR falls at a faster rate than AR (*i.e.*, MR curve lies below AR curve).

6. Complete the following table:

Output (Units)	Average Revenue (₹)	Marginal Revenue (₹)	Total Revenue (₹)
1	—	15	—
2	—	—	26
3	11	—	—
4	—	3	—

Sol.

Output (Units)	Average Revenue (₹)	Marginal Revenue (₹)	Total Revenue (₹)
1	15	15	15
2	13	11	26
3	11	7	33
4	9	3	36

7. Complete the following table:

Output (Units)	Price (₹)	Marginal Revenue (₹)	Total Revenue (₹)
1	—	30	—
2	—	—	52
3	22	—	—
4	—	6	—

Sol.

Output (Units)	Price (₹)	Marginal Revenue (₹)	Total Revenue (₹)
1	30	30	30
2	26	22	52
3	22	14	66
4	18	6	72

8. Complete the following table:

Output (Units)	Price (₹)	Total Revenue (₹)	Marginal Revenue (₹)
1	—	6	—
2	—	—	2
3	—	—	–2
4	—	—	–2

Sol.

Output (Units)	Price (₹)	Total Revenue (₹)	Marginal Revenue (₹)
1	6	6	6
2	4	8	2
3	2	6	–2
4	1	4	–2

9. Complete the following table:

Output (Units)	Price (₹)	Total Revenue (₹)	Marginal Revenue (₹)
—	10	—	10
—	7	—	4
—	5	—	1
—	3	—	–3

Sol.

Output (Units)	Price (₹)	Total Revenue (₹)	Marginal Revenue (₹)
1	10	10	10
2	7	14	4
3	5	15	1
4	3	12	–3

10. Find MR when TR increases from ₹ 1,500 to ₹ 2,000, and output increases from 100 units to 150 units.

Sol. $MR = \frac{\Delta TR}{\Delta Q} = \frac{2{,}000 - 1{,}500}{150 - 100} = \frac{500}{50} = 10$

Ans. MR = ₹ 10.

11. Show that AR = Price.

Sol. $AR = \frac{TR}{Q} = \frac{P \times Q}{Q}$ [where P is price, and Q is output]

$= P = \text{Price}$

12. At what rate TR of the firm will increase if it is facing a perfectly elastic demand curve, and price of the product happens to be ₹ 10 per unit. Give logical reasoning.

Sol. MR is rate of change in TR.

When demand is perfectly elastic

AR = MR = Price

∴ MR = ₹ 10

Implying that TR will increase by ₹ 10 for every additional unit of output.

Ans. TR will increase by ₹ 10.

13. A perfectly competitive firm faces the market price of ₹ 20 per unit. Derive its TR schedule for a range of output from 1 to 10 units. What will happen to market price if the firm decides to suspend its production for the time being?

Sol.

Output (Units)	1	2	3	4	5	6	7	8	9	10
Price (₹)	20	20	20	20	20	20	20	20	20	20
Total Revenue (₹)	20	40	60	80	100	120	140	160	180	200

If the firm decides to suspend its production for the time being, the market price will not change. Because the supply of a single seller cannot influence the market supply in a perfectly competitive market.

14. Complete the following table:

Price (₹)	Output (Units)	Total Revenue (₹)	Marginal Revenue (₹)
7	—	7	—
—	2	10	—
—	3	—	–1
1	—	—	–5

Sol.

Price (₹)	Output (Units)	Total Revenue (₹)	Marginal Revenue (₹)
7	1	7	7
5	2	10	3
3	3	9	–1
1	4	4	–5

15. Complete the following table:

Units of Output	Total Revenue (₹)	Average Revenue (₹)	Marginal Revenue (₹)
1	—	10	—
2	—	8	—
3	—	6	—

Sol.

Units of Output	Total Revenue (₹)	Average Revenue (₹)	Marginal Revenue (₹)
1	10	10	10
2	16	8	6
3	18	6	2

Producer's Equilibrium

1. Find producer's equilibrium, from the following. Give logical reason.

Quantity Sold (Units)	Total Revenue (₹)	Total Cost (₹)
5	15	18
6	20	22
7	25	26
8	30	27
9	35	32
10	40	38

Sol.

Quantity Sold (Units)	Total Revenue (TR) (₹)	Total Cost (TC) (₹)	Marginal Revenue (MR) (₹)	Marginal Cost (MC) (₹)	Profit (π = TR – TC) (₹)
5	15	18	—	—	–3
6	20	22	5	4	–2
7	25	26	5	4	–1
8	30	27	5	1	3
9	35	32	5	5	3
10	40	38	5	6	2

Producer is in equilibrium at 9th unit of output.

Reason: At output levels 8th and 9th unit, the difference between TR and TC, *i.e.*, profit is maximum, which is equal to 3 in both the cases. But the producer is in equilibrium at 9th unit only where MR = MC (= 5), and MC is rising.

Ans. Producer's equilibrium is struck when output level is 9 units.

2. Find out the profit from the following:

Quantity Sold (Units)	Price (₹ per unit)	Average Cost (₹)
1	15	15
2	16	12
3	17	10
4	18	12
5	19	14

Sol.

Quantity Sold (Units)	Price (₹ per unit)	AC (₹)	TR (₹)	TC (₹)	Profit (π = TR – TC) (₹)
1	15	15	15	15	0
2	16	12	32	24	8
3	17	10	51	30	21
4	18	12	72	48	24
5	19	14	95	70	25

3. Find the profit maximising level of output.

Quantity Sold (Units)	Total Revenue (₹)	Marginal Cost (₹)
1	12	15
2	26	9
3	34	6
4	40	2
5	42	3

Sol.

Quantity Sold (Units)	Total Revenue (₹)	Marginal Cost (₹)	Total Cost (₹)	Profit (π = TR – TC) (₹)
1	12	15	15	–3
2	26	9	24	2
3	34	6	30	4
4	40	2	32	8
5	42	3	35	7

Profit is maximised when the output level is 4 units because here, profit is maximum, *i.e.*, 8 and after this starts declining.

Ans. Profit is maximum at 4th unit.

4. What should the firm's profit, when average variable cost is ₹ 20 per unit, average fixed cost is ₹ 10 per unit, price of the output is ₹ 25 per unit and only 8 units of the output are produced?

Sol. AVC = ₹ 20; AFC = ₹ 10; Price = ₹ 25 and Output = 8 units

TVC = AVC × Output = ₹ 20 × 8 = ₹ 160

TFC = AFC × Output = ₹ 10 × 8 = ₹ 80

TC = TFC + TVC = ₹ 80 + ₹ 160 = ₹ 240

TR = Price × Output = ₹ 25 × 8 = ₹ 200

Profit = TR – TC = ₹ 200 – ₹ 240 = (–) ₹ 40

In this case, firm is incurring loss of ₹ 40 because TC > TR.

Ans. Profit = (–) ₹ 40 (loss).

5. From the following table, find out the level of output at which the producer will be in equilibrium. Give reasons for your answer. *[CBSE (AI) 2013]*

Output (Units)	Marginal Revenue (₹)	Marginal Cost (₹)
1	8	10
2	8	8
3	8	7
4	8	8
5	8	9

Sol.

Output (Units)	Marginal Revenue (₹)	Marginal Cost (₹)
1	8	10
2	8	8
3	8	7
4	8	8
5	8	9

Producer's equilibrium is struck when output level is 4 units.

Reason: At output levels 2nd and 4th unit, MR and MC (= 8). But the producer is in equilibrium when 4 units of output are produced. Because, it is here only that: (i) MR = MC, and (ii) MC is rising.

Ans. The producer is in equilibrium when output level = 4 units.

6. From the following table find out the level of output at which the producer is in equilibrium. Give reasons for your answer. (Use marginal cost–marginal revenue method.) *[CBSE (F) 2013]*

Output (Units)	Marginal Cost (₹)	Total Revenue (₹)
1	12	10
2	10	20
3	8	30
4	10	40
5	12	50

Sol.

Output (Units)	Marginal Cost (MC) (₹)	Total Revenue (TR) (₹)	Total Cost (TC) (₹)	Marginal Revenue (MR) (₹)	Profit (π = TR – TC) (₹)
1	12	10	12	10	–2
2	10	20	22	10	–2
3	8	30	30	10	0
4	10	40	40	10	0
5	12	50	52	10	–2

Producer's equilibrium is struck when output level is 4 units.

Reason: At output levels 2nd and 4th unit both MR and MC are equal which is 10 in this case. But the producer is in equilibrium at 4th unit only where MR = MC (= 10) and MC is rising.

Ans. The producer is in equilibrium when 4 units of output are produced.

7. From the following information about a firm, find the firm's equilibrium output in terms of marginal cost and marginal revenue. Give reasons. Also find profit at this output. *[CBSE Delhi 2014]*

Output (Units)	Total Revenue (₹)	Total Cost (₹)
1	7	8
2	14	15
3	21	21
4	28	28
5	35	36

Sol.

Output (Units)	Total Revenue (₹)	Marginal Revenue (₹)	Total Cost (₹)	Marginal Cost (₹)
1	7	7	8	8
2	14	7	15	7
3	21	7	21	6
4	28	7	28	7
5	35	7	36	8

In the above table, MR = MC in two situations: (i) when 2 units of output are produced, and (ii) when 4 units of output are produced. However, in situation 1, when output is 2 units, MC is falling, whereas in situation 2, when output is 4 units, MC is rising. A producer strikes equilibrium when two conditions are satisfied:

(i) MR = MC, and (ii) MC is rising

This means that the equilibrium will be struck when 4 units of output are produced and not when 2 units of output are produced.

When 4 units of output are produced, TR = ₹ 28 and TC = ₹ 28

Profit = TR – TC

Profit = ₹ 28 – ₹ 28 = 0

Ans. The producer is earning only normal profits at the point of equilibrium. Normal profits are a part of TC.

8. From the following information about a firm, find the firm's equilibrium output in terms of marginal cost and marginal revenue. Give reasons. Also find profit at this output. *[CBSE (AI) 2014]*

Output (Units)	Total Revenue (₹)	Total Cost (₹)
1	6	7
2	12	13
3	18	17
4	24	23
5	30	31

Sol.

Output (Units)	Total Revenue (₹)	Marginal Revenue (₹)	Total Cost (₹)	Marginal Cost (₹)
1	6	6	7	7
2	12	6	13	6
3	18	6	17	4
4	24	6	23	6
5	30	6	31	8

In the above table, MR = MC in two situations: (i) when 2 units of output are produced, and (ii) when 4 units of output are produced. However, in situation 1, when output is 2 units, MC is falling, whereas in situation 2, when output is 4 units, MC is rising. A producer strikes equilibrium when two conditions are satisfied:

(i) MR = MC, and (ii) MC is rising

This means that the equilibrium will be struck when 4 units of output are produced and not when 2 units of output are produced.

When 4 units of output are produced, TR = ₹ 24 and TC = ₹ 23

Profit = TR – TC

Profit = ₹ 24 – ₹ 23 = ₹ 1

Ans. The producer is earning supernormal profit of ₹ 1 at the point of equilibrium.

9. From the following information about a firm, find the firm's equilibrium output in terms of marginal cost and marginal revenue. Give reasons. Also calculate profit at this output. *[CBSE (F) 2014]*

Output (Units)	Total Revenue (₹)	Total Cost (₹)
1	8	10
2	16	18
3	24	23
4	32	31
5	40	41

Sol.

Output (Units)	Total Revenue (₹)	Marginal Revenue (₹)	Total Cost (₹)	Marginal Cost (₹)
1	8	8	10	10
2	16	8	18	8
3	24	8	23	5
4	32	8	31	8
5	40	8	41	10

In the above table, MR = MC in two situations: (i) when 2 units of output are produced, and (ii) when 4 units of output are produced. However, in situation 1, when output is 2 units, MC is falling, whereas in situation 2, when output is 4 units, MC is rising. A producer strikes equilibrium when two conditions are satisfied: (i) MR = MC, (ii) MC is rising

This means that in the above scenario, equilibrium will be struck when 4 units of output are produced and not when 2 units of output are produced.

When 4 units of output are produced, TR = ₹ 32 and TC = ₹ 31

$$\text{Profit} = TR - TC$$

$$\text{Profit} = ₹\,32 - ₹\,31 = ₹\,1$$

Ans. The producer is earning supernormal profit of ₹ 1 at the point of equilibrium.

Theory of Supply

1. When the price of a doll is ₹ 4 per doll, a doll maker supplies 8 dolls per day. If the price rises to ₹ 5 per doll, he is willing to supply 10 dolls per day. Calculate the price elasticity of supply of dolls.

Sol. Price elasticity of supply $= \frac{P}{Q} \times \frac{\Delta Q}{\Delta P}$

$P = ₹\,4;\ P_1 = ₹\,5;\ \Delta P = P_1 - P = ₹\,5 - ₹\,4 = ₹\,1$

$Q = 8$ dolls; $Q_1 = 10$ dolls; $\Delta Q = Q_1 - Q = (10 - 8)$ dolls $= 2$ dolls

$$\text{Price elasticity of supply } (E_s) = \frac{4}{8} \times \frac{2}{1} = 1 \text{ (unity)}$$

Ans. The price elasticity of supply is equal to unity.

2. The price elasticity of supply of a commodity is 2.5. At a price of ₹ 5 per unit, its quantity supplied is 300 units. Calculate its quantity supplied at a price of ₹ 4 per unit.

Sol. Suppose, quantity supplied (when price = ₹ 4 per unit) = M units.

$$\text{Price elasticity of supply } (E_s) = \frac{P}{Q} \times \frac{\Delta Q}{\Delta P}$$

$P = ₹\,5;\ P_1 = ₹\,4;\ \Delta P = P_1 - P = ₹\,4 - ₹\,5 = (-)\,₹\,1$

$Q = 300$ units; $Q_1 = M$ units; $\Delta Q = Q_1 - Q = (M - 300)$ units

$E_s = 2.5$

$$\text{Price elasticity of supply } (E_s) = \frac{5}{300} \times \frac{M - 300}{-1}$$

$$2.5 = \frac{1}{60} \times \frac{M - 300}{-1} \quad \Rightarrow \quad 150 = \frac{M - 300}{-1}$$

$$-150 = M - 300 \quad \Rightarrow \quad M = -150 + 300 = 150$$

Ans. Quantity supplied = 150 units.

3. Following schedule shows cases A and B of change in quantity supplied in response to change in price.

Price (₹)	Quantity Supplied (A)	Quantity Supplied (B)
1	20	0
2	40	20
3	60	40
4	80	60
5	100	80

(i) Calculate elasticity of supply when price rises from ₹ 2 to ₹ 3 both in case A and case B.

(ii) Why do supply elasticity differ in two cases even though absolute change in quantity supplied is 20 units in both the cases?

Sol. (i) **Case A:** $P = ₹\,2; P_1 = ₹\,3; \Delta P = P_1 - P = ₹\,3 - ₹\,2 = ₹\,1$

$Q = 40; Q_1 = 60; \Delta Q = Q_1 - Q = 60 - 40 = 20$

$$\text{Elasticity of supply } (E_s) = \frac{P}{Q} \times \frac{\Delta Q}{\Delta P} = \frac{2}{40} \times \frac{20}{1} = 1 \text{ (unity)}$$

Case B: $P = ₹\,2; P_1 = ₹\,3; \Delta P = P_1 - P = ₹\,3 - ₹\,2 = ₹\,1$

$Q = 20; Q_1 = 40; \Delta Q = Q_1 - Q = 40 - 20 = 20$

$$\text{Elasticity of supply } (E_s) = \frac{P}{Q} \times \frac{\Delta Q}{\Delta P} = \frac{2}{20} \times \frac{20}{1} = 2 \text{ (greater than unity)}$$

Ans. (i) Elasticity of supply is equal to unity in case 'A'.

Elasticity of supply is greater than unity in case 'B'.

(ii) The elasticity of supply differs in both the cases due to the difference in the percentage change in the quantity supplied which is $\frac{20}{40} \times 100 = 50$ per cent in case A, and $\frac{20}{20} \times 100 = 100$ per cent in case B.

4. At a price of ₹ 8 per unit, the quantity supplied of a commodity is 200 units. Its price elasticity of supply is 1.5. If its price rises to ₹ 10 per unit, calculate the quantity supplied at the new price.

Sol. Suppose, M units of the commodity are supplied at the new price.

$$\text{Price elasticity of supply } (E_s) = \frac{P}{Q} \times \frac{\Delta Q}{\Delta P}$$

$P = ₹\,8; P_1 = ₹\,10; \ \Delta P = P_1 - P = ₹\,10 - ₹\,8 = ₹\,2$

$Q = 200$ units; $Q_1 = M$ units; $\Delta Q = Q_1 - Q = (M - 200)$ units

$E_s = 1.5$

$$1.5 = \frac{8}{200} \times \frac{M - 200}{2} \quad \text{or} \quad 1.5 = \frac{M - 200}{50}$$

Or, $75 = M - 200$ or $M = 75 + 200$

Or, $M = 275$

Ans. The quantity supplied = 275 units.

5. Even if a straight line upward sloping supply curve is not making a 45° angle, elasticity of supply is found to be = 1, when the supply curve shoots from the origin. Use a diagram and prove this point.

Sol. Let P_1 be the initial price and Q_1 the initial quantity on the supply curve OS which is short of making a 45° angle (OS* makes a 45° angle).

FIGURE 13

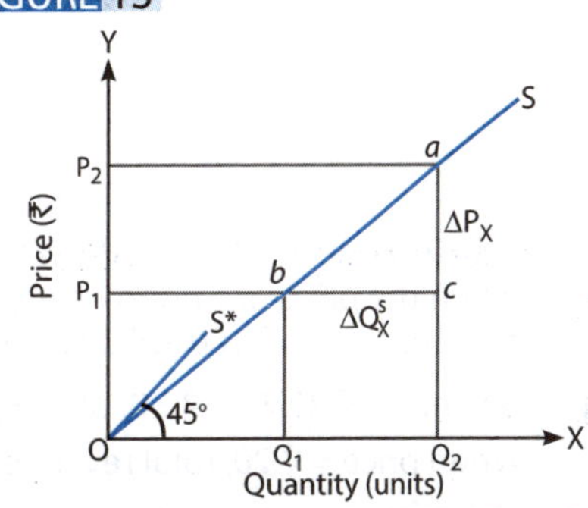

Note:
OS* is a supply curve making a 45° angle.
OS is a supply curve short of making a 45° angle.
We are proving that $E_s = 1$ even on OS line.

$$E_s = \frac{\Delta Q^s_X}{\Delta P_X} \times \frac{P_X}{Q^s_X} \quad \text{...(i)}$$

$$\Rightarrow \quad E_s = \frac{bc}{ac} \times \frac{OP_1}{OQ_1} \quad \text{...(ii)}$$

$$\Rightarrow \quad E_s = \frac{bc}{ac} \times \frac{Q_1 b}{OQ_1} \quad \text{...(iii)}$$

Δbca and $\Delta OQ_1 b$ are similar triangles.

Accordingly, ratio of their sides should be equal.

$$\text{Thus,} \quad \frac{bc}{ac} = \frac{OQ_1}{Q_1 b} \quad \text{...(iv)}$$

Relating (iv) to (iii), we get

$$E_s = \frac{OQ_1}{Q_1 b} \times \frac{Q_1 b}{OQ_1} = 1$$

Thus, any upward sloping supply curve that shoots from the point of origin (and is a straight line), has elasticity of supply equal to 1.

6. Find elasticity of supply when price increases by 20 per cent and quantity increases from 100 to 250 units of the commodity.

Sol. Percentage change in price = 20 per cent

$$\text{Percentage change in quantity supplied} = \frac{\Delta Q}{Q} \times 100$$

$$= \frac{250 - 100}{100} \times 100 = \frac{150}{100} \times 100 = 150\%$$

$$\text{Elasticity of supply } (E_s) = \frac{\text{Percentage change in quantity supplied}}{\text{Percentage change in price}}$$

$$= \frac{150\%}{20\%} = 7.5 \text{ (elastic)}$$

Ans. Elasticity of supply = 7.5.

7. Elasticity of supply is found to be = 2. Quantity supplied happens to increase by 20 per cent in response to increase in price. Find the new price when the initial price happens to be ₹ 20 per unit.

Sol. Given, $E_s = 2; P = 20; \frac{\Delta Q}{Q} = 0.2$

We know, $\text{Elasticity of supply } (E_s) = \frac{\Delta Q}{\Delta P} \times \frac{P}{Q} \text{ or } \frac{\Delta Q}{Q} \times \frac{P}{\Delta P}$

$$2 = 0.2 \times \frac{20}{\Delta P} \quad \Rightarrow \quad 2 = \frac{4}{\Delta P}$$

$$\Rightarrow \quad \Delta P = \frac{4}{2} = 2$$

$$P_1 = P + \Delta P$$

$$= 20 + 2 = 22$$

Ans. New price = ₹ 22.

8. Price elasticity of supply for a commodity is 5. When price of the commodity rises from ₹ 9 per unit to ₹ 10 per unit, supply rises by 25 units. Calculate quantity supplied at ₹ 9 per unit. *[CBSE Sample Paper 2013]*

Sol. Let us assume that initially quantity supplied = M units.

Given, $P = ₹ 9; P_1 = ₹ 10; \Delta P = P_1 - P = ₹ 10 - ₹ 9 = ₹ 1$

$Q = M$ units; $\Delta Q = 25$ units

$E_s = 5$

$$\text{Price elasticity of supply } (E_s) = \frac{P}{Q} \times \frac{\Delta Q}{\Delta P}$$

$$5 = \frac{9}{M} \times \frac{25}{1} \quad \Rightarrow \quad 5M = 225$$

Or, $M = 45$

Ans. Quantity supplied at ₹ 9 per unit = 45 units.

9. When the price of a good rises from ₹ 20 per unit to ₹ 30 per unit, the revenue of the firm producing this good rises from ₹ 100 to ₹ 300. Calculate the price elasticity of supply. *[CBSE Delhi 2013]*

Sol. Given, $P = ₹ 20; P_1 = ₹ 30; \Delta P = P_1 - P = ₹ 30 - ₹ 20 = ₹ 10$

When price = ₹ 20, total revenue $(P \times Q)$ = ₹ 100

$$\therefore \quad \text{Quantity supplied } (Q) = \frac{100}{20} = 5 \text{ units}$$

When, price = ₹ 30, total revenue $(P_1 \times Q_1)$ = ₹ 300

$$\therefore \quad \text{New quantity supplied } (Q_1) = \frac{300}{30} = 10 \text{ units}$$

$Q = 5$ units; $Q_1 = 10$ units; $\Delta Q = Q_1 - Q = (10 - 5)$ units $= 5$ units

$$\text{Price elasticity of supply } (E_s) = \frac{P}{Q} \times \frac{\Delta Q}{\Delta P} = \frac{20}{5} \times \frac{5}{10} = 2$$

Ans. Price elasticity of supply = 2.

10. A firm's revenue rises from ₹ 400 to ₹ 500 when the price of its product rises from ₹ 20 per unit to ₹ 25 per unit. Calculate the price elasticity of supply. *[CBSE Delhi 2013]*

Sol. Given, P = ₹ 20; P_1 = ₹ 25; $\Delta P = P_1 - P$ = ₹ 25 – ₹ 20 = ₹ 5

When price = ₹ 20, total revenue (P × Q) = ₹ 400

$$\therefore \quad \text{Quantity supplied (Q)} = \frac{400}{20} = 20 \text{ units}$$

When, price = 25, total revenue $(P_1 \times Q_1) = 500$

$$\therefore \quad \text{New quantity supplied } (Q_1) = \frac{500}{25} = 20 \text{ units}$$

Q = 20 units; Q_1 = 20 units; $\Delta Q = Q_1 - Q$ = (20 – 20) units = 0 unit

$$\text{Price elasticity of supply } (E_s) = \frac{P}{Q} \times \frac{\Delta Q}{\Delta P} = \frac{20}{20} \times \frac{0}{5} = 0$$

Ans. Price elasticity of supply = 0 (zero).

11. The price elasticity of supply of a good is 0.8. Its price rises by 50 per cent. Calculate the percentage increase in its supply. *[CBSE Delhi 2013]*

Sol. Given, $E_d = 0.8$

Percentage change in price = 50%

$$\text{Price elasticity of supply } (E_s) = \frac{\text{Percentage change in quantity supplied}}{\text{Percentage change in price}}$$

$$0.8 = \frac{\text{Percentage change in quantity supplied}}{50\%}$$

Percentage change in quantity supplied = 50 × 0.8 = 40%

Ans. Percentage change in quantity supplied = 40%.

12. A firm supplies 10 units of a good at a price of ₹ 5 per unit. Price elasticity of supply is 1.25. What quantity will the firm supply at a price of ₹ 7 per unit? *[CBSE (AI) 2013]*

Sol. Let the quantity supplied after change be M units.

Given, P = ₹ 5; P_1 = ₹ 7; $\Delta P = P_1 - P$ = ₹ 7 – ₹ 5 = ₹ 2

Q = 10 units; Q_1 = M units; $\Delta Q = Q_1 - Q$ = (M – 10) units

$E_s = 1.25$

$$\text{Price elasticity of supply } (E_s) = \frac{P}{Q} \times \frac{\Delta Q}{\Delta P}$$

$$1.25 = \frac{5}{10} \times \frac{M-10}{2} \quad \Rightarrow \quad 1.25 = \frac{M-10}{4}$$

$$\Rightarrow \quad M - 10 = 5 \quad \Rightarrow \quad M = 5 + 10 = 15$$

Ans. New quantity = 15 units.

13. The price elasticity of supply of a commodity is 2.0. A firm supplies 200 units of it at a price of ₹ 8 per unit. At what price will it supply 250 units? *[CBSE (AI) 2013]*

Sol. Given, P = ₹ 8; P_1 = X; $\Delta P = P_1 - P$ = (X – 8)

Q = 200 units; Q_1 = 250 units; $\Delta Q = Q_1 - Q$ = (250 – 200) units = 50 units

$E_s = 2$

$$\text{Price elasticity of supply } (E_s) = \frac{P}{Q} \times \frac{\Delta Q}{\Delta P}$$

$$2 = \frac{8}{200} \times \frac{50}{X-8}$$

$$\Rightarrow \quad 2 = \frac{2}{X-8} \quad \Rightarrow \quad X - 8 = 1$$

$$\Rightarrow \quad X = 1 + 8 = 9$$

Ans. New price = ₹ 9.

14. A 15 per cent rise in the price of a commodity raises its supply from 300 units to 345 units. Calculate its price elasticity of supply. *[CBSE (AI) 2013]*

Sol. Given, percentage change in price = 15%

$Q = 300$ units; $Q_1 = 345$ units; $\Delta Q = Q_1 - Q = (345 - 300)$ units = 45 units

$$\text{Percentage change in quantity supplied} = \frac{45}{300} \times 100 = 15\%$$

$$\text{Price elasticity of supply } (E_s) = \frac{\text{Percentage change in quantity supplied}}{\text{Percentage change in price}}$$

$$= \frac{15\%}{15\%} = 1$$

Ans. Price elasticity of supply = 1.

15. Total revenue of a firm rises from ₹ 400 to ₹ 500 when the price of its product rises from ₹ 8 per unit to ₹ 10 per unit. Calculate the price elasticity of supply. *[CBSE (F) 2013]*

Sol. Given, P = ₹ 8; P_1 = ₹ 10; $\Delta P = P_1 - P$ = ₹ 10 − ₹ 8 = ₹ 2

When price = ₹ 8, total revenue ($P \times Q$) = ₹ 400

$$\therefore \quad \text{Quantity supplied } (Q) = \frac{400}{8} = 50 \text{ units}$$

When, price = ₹10, total revenue ($P_1 \times Q_1$) = ₹ 500

$$\therefore \quad \text{New quantity supplied } (Q_1) = \frac{500}{10} = 50 \text{ units}$$

$Q = 50$ units; $Q_1 = 50$ units; $\Delta Q = Q_1 - Q = (50 - 50)$ units = 0 unit

$$\text{Price elasticity of supply } (E_s) = \frac{P}{Q} \times \frac{\Delta Q}{\Delta P} = \frac{8}{50} \times \frac{0}{2} = 0$$

Ans. Price elasticity of supply = 0 (zero).

16. A fall in the price of a firm's product results in a fall in its supply by 40 per cent. Its price elasticity of supply is 1.6. Calculate the percentage fall in its price. *[CBSE (F) 2013]*

Sol. Given, $E_s = 1.6$

Percentage change in quantity supplied = (–) 40%

$$\text{Price elasticity of supply } (E_s) = \frac{\text{Percentage change in quantity supplied}}{\text{Percentage change in price}}$$

$$1.6 = \frac{-40\%}{\text{Percentage change in price}}$$

$$\text{Percentage change in price} = \frac{-40\%}{1.6}$$

$$\text{Percentage change in price} = -25\%$$

Ans. Percentage fall in price = 25%.

17. Price elasticity of supply of a good is 2. By what percentage should its price rise so that its supply rises by 30 per cent? *[CBSE (F) 2013]*

Sol. Given, $E_s = 2$

Percentage change in quantity supplied = 30%

$$\text{Price elasticity of supply } (E_s) = \frac{\text{Percentage change in quantity supplied}}{\text{Percentage change in price}}$$

$$2 = \frac{30\%}{\text{Percentage change in price}}$$

$$\text{Percentage change in price} = \frac{30\%}{2}$$

$$\text{Percentage change in price} = 15\%$$

Ans. Percentage rise in price = 15%.

UNSOLVED NUMERICALS

Economics, Economy and Central Problems of an Economy

1. You have ₹ 1,000 as your pocket money. You can deposit this money in a bank and get ₹ 1,100 after an year. However, you have two other choices:
   (i) lend this money to your friend who is ready to pay you ₹ 1,050 after an year, or
   (ii) keep the money with you as cash in hand.
   What is opportunity cost of keeping the money as cash in hand?
   [**Ans.** Opportunity cost = ₹ 100]

2. If the slope of PPC remains constant (or does not change) with an increase in the production of Good-X (on horizontal axis) at the cost of Good-Y (on vertical axis), what is the shape of PPC? Draw the PPC.
   [**Ans.** Downward sloping straight line touches X-axis and Y-axis. See Fig. 1.]

FIGURE 1

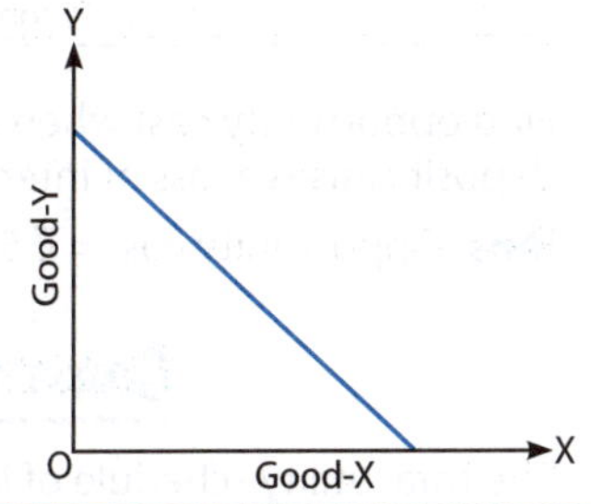

3. An economy produces two goods: wheat and rice. These could be produced in only two combinations.
   Combination A: Wheat: 20,000 tonnes; Rice: 5,000 tonnes
   Combination B: Wheat: 10,000 tonnes; Rice: 9,000 tonnes
   What is the marginal opportunity cost of producing an extra tonne of rice at the cost of wheat? (Compare combination A with combination B.)
   [**Ans.** Marginal opportunity cost = 2.5 tonnes of wheat per tonne of rice]

4. Calculate the marginal opportunity cost for the various combinations of Good-X and Good-Y in the following table:

Combination	Good-X	Good-Y
A	0	95
B	10	85
C	20	73
D	30	58
E	40	41
F	50	22
G	60	0

   [**Ans.** Marginal opportunity cost = —, 1, 1.2, 1.5, 1.7, 1.9, 2.2]

5. Draw PPC for the following PPC schedule. Also, calculate the marginal opportunity cost for different combinations:

Combination	Rice ('000 tonnes)	Maize ('000 tonnes)
A	0	120
B	25	100
C	50	75
D	75	45
E	100	0

[**Ans.** Marginal opportunity cost = —, 0.8, 1, 1.2, 1.8; See Fig. 2 also.]

FIGURE 2

Production Possibility Curve (PPC)

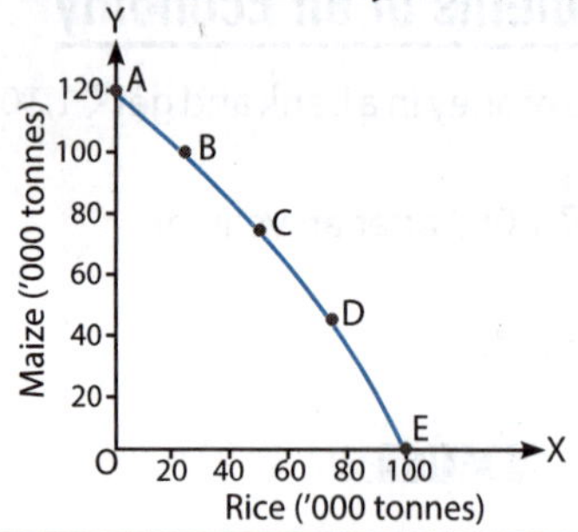

6. Find opportunity cost when investment of ₹ 50,000 in the stock market, by way of withdrawal of demand deposit causes a loss of interest income of ₹ 5,000 per annum. Give logical reasoning.

   [**Ans.** Opportunity cost = ₹ 55,000]

Consumer's Equilibrium—Utility Analysis

1. The total utility schedule of individual 'A' is given below. Derive the marginal utility schedule.

Units Consumed	0	1	2	3	4	5
Total Utility	0	15	27	38	48	55

   [**Ans.** Marginal utility schedule: —, 15, 12, 11, 10, 7]

2. Calculate total utility for the various units of commodity-X, given the following information:

Units of Commodity-X	1	2	3	4	5	6	7	8
MU_X (Utils)	20	16	12	9	8	3	0	–5

   [**Ans.** Total utility: 20, 36, 48, 57, 65, 68, 68, 63]

3. When the consumer is in equilibrium, MU of commodity-X is 45 and price of commodity-X is ₹ 9. Calculate the marginal utility of money. (Assuming marginal utility of money for the consumer is constant in equilibrium.)

   [**Ans.** Marginal utility of money (MU_M) = 5]

4. Following is the total utility schedule of Mr. X:

Units of Commodity-X	1	2	3	4	5	6	7
TU_X (Utils)	20	37	51	61	66	66	64

   (i) Derive MU schedule.

   (ii) Find out the level of consumption at which Mr. X reaches the saturation point.

   (iii) How many units should the consumer purchase to maximise satisfaction when the price of the commodity is ₹ 5? (Assume that utility is expressed in utils and 1 util = ₹ 2). Give reasons for your answer.

   [**Ans.** (i) Marginal utility: 20, 17, 14, 10, 5, 0, – 2; (ii) Mr. X reaches the saturation point when 6 units of the commodity are consumed, and MU = 0; (iii) 4 units]

5. Suppose, price of commodity-Y (P_Y) is ₹ 10 per unit. Also, assume that marginal utility of money (MU_M) is 8 (and constant). Using the following marginal utility schedule of the consumer, find out equilibrium level of consumption and total expenditure on commodity-Y.

Units Consumed	1	2	3	4	5	6
Marginal Utility	170	130	110	80	30	0

   [**Ans.** Equilibrium level of consumption = 4 units of commodity-Y;
   Total expenditure on commodity-Y = ₹ 40]

6. Summit has ₹ 90 with him. He intends to purchase goods X and Y with his money. The market price of X and Y per unit is ₹10. The marginal utility schedule of goods X and Y is given below. Find out how many units of X and Y should Summit purchase so that he gets maximum satisfaction.

Units of Commodity	1	2	3	4	5	6	7	8	9	10
MU of X	80	72	64	56	48	40	32	24	16	8
MU of Y	40	32	24	20	16	12	8	4	0	0

[**Ans.** 7 units of commodity-X; 2 units of commodity-Y]

Theory of Demand

1. Suppose the price of a touch-screen mobile is ₹ 15,000. How would you expect its demand curve to be affected with a favourable shift in tastes and preferences of the consumers, price remaining unchanged?
[**Ans.** Demand curve will shift forward, to the right]

2. Following table represents the demand schedule of households, A, B and C. Derive market demand.

Price (₹)	Household A (Units)	Household B (Units)	Household C (Units)
8	6	12	22
7	7	13	23
6	8	14	24
5	9	15	25
4	10	16	26

[**Ans.** Market demand: 40, 43, 46, 49, 52]

3. Following table represents the market demand schedule and demand schedule of Ram, Sohan and Mohan:

Price (₹)	Ram (Units)	Sohan (Units)	Mohan (Units)	Market Demand (Units)
3	7	(i)	8	20
4	6	4	(ii)	16
5	4	3	3	(iii)
6	(iv)	2	1	5

(**Assumption:** Market includes three buyers.) Calculate the missing entries.
[**Ans.** (i) 5, (ii) 6, (iii) 10, (iv) 2]

4. Calculate the demand schedule of Raju, using following table. (Assuming Market includes four buyers.)

Price (₹)	Ramesh (Units)	Raju (Units)	Rahim (Units)	Rina (Units)	Market Demand (Units)
5	19	—	7	6	32
4	20	—	10	9	44
3	21	—	12	11	51
2	22	—	14	15	61
1	23	—	18	19	74

[**Ans.** Demand (by Raju): 0, 5, 7, 10, 14]

5. Individual demand schedules of Rakesh and Mohit for ice cream is given below. Derive market demand schedule for ice cream from the following:

Price of Ice Cream (₹ per unit)	Demand of Rakesh (Units)	Demand of Mohit (Units)
10	1	2
9	2	3
8	3	4
7	4	5
6	5	6

[**Ans.** Market demand: 3, 5, 7, 9, 11]

6. Given below are the individual demand schedules of Maggi and Pasta. Derive market demand schedule and market demand curve (assuming market includes two buyers, Maggi and Pasta) from the following:

Price (₹ per unit)	Maggi (Units)	Pasta (Units)
5	4	6
4	5	7
3	6	8
2	7	9
1	8	10

[**Ans.** Market demand: 10, 12, 14, 16, 18; See Fig. 3 also.]

FIGURE 3

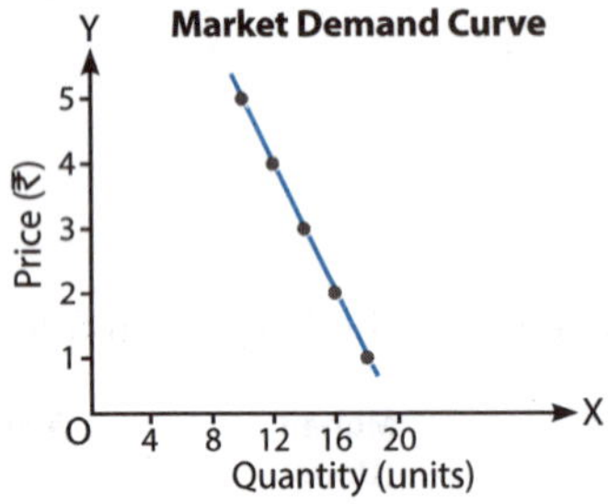

Price Elasticity of Demand

1. Find out elasticity of demand given the following information:

Price per unit (₹)	Quantity Demanded (kg)
10	20
9	25

[**Ans.** $E_d = 2.5$]

2. A consumer purchased 10 units of a commodity when its price was ₹ 5 per unit. He purchased 12 units of the commodity when its price falls to ₹ 4 per unit. What is the price elasticity of demand for the commodity at that price?
[**Ans.** $E_d = 1$ (unitary elastic demand)]

3. As a result of 10 per cent fall in price of a good, its demand rises from 100 units to 120 units. Find out the price elasticity of demand.
[**Ans.** $E_d = 2$ (greater than unity)]

4. A certain quantity of the commodity is purchased when its price is ₹ 10 per unit. Quantity demanded increases by 50 per cent in response to a fall in price by ₹ 2 per unit. Find elasticity of demand.
[**Ans.** $E_d = 2.5$]

5. A consumer buys 80 units of a good at a price of ₹ 4 per unit. When the price falls, he buys 100 units. If price elasticity of demand is (–)1, find out the new price.
[**Ans.** New price = ₹ 3]

6. When the price is ₹ 5 per unit a consumer buys 40 units of a commodity and his price elasticity of demand is (–) 1.5. How much will he buy if the price is reduced to ₹ 4 per unit?
[**Ans.** New quantity = 52 units]

7. Price elasticity of demand of a good is (–) 1. At a price the consumer buys 60 units of the good. How many units will the consumer buy if the price falls by 10 per cent?
[**Ans.** New quantity = 66 units]

8. At a given market price of a good a consumer buys 120 units. When price falls by 50 per cent he buys 150 units. Calculate price elasticity of demand.
[**Ans.** $E_d = 0.5$]

9. Price elasticity of demand is found to be (–) 2. Price falls from ₹ 10 per unit to ₹ 8 per unit. Find the percentage change in quantity demanded.
[**Ans.** 40%]

10. A commodity shows $E_d = (-)\ 2$. Quantity demanded reduces from 300 units to 150 units in response to increase in price. Find the increased price when initially it was ₹ 20 per unit.
[**Ans.** Increased price = ₹ 25]

11. For a commodity, $\frac{\Delta P}{P} = -0.2$, and elasticity of demand is – 0.5. Find quantity demanded after a fall in price when initially it was 60 units.
[**Ans.** New quantity = 66 units]

12. A consumer buys 80 units of a good at a price of ₹ 5 per unit. Suppose price elasticity of demand is (–) 2. At what price will he buy 64 units?
[**Ans.** New price = ₹ 5.5]

13. When price of the commodity reduces from ₹ 5 per unit to ₹ 4 per unit, expenditure on the commodity reduces from ₹ 60 to ₹ 48. Find price elasticity of demand.
[**Ans.** $E_d = 0$ (zero)]

14. When price of a good rises from ₹ 5 per unit to ₹ 6 per unit, its demand falls from 20 units to 10 units. Compare expenditures on the good to determine whether demand is elastic or inelastic.
[**Ans.** Demand is elastic, as it is greater than unity]

15. When price of a good falls from ₹ 10 per unit to ₹ 9 per unit, its demand rises from 9 units to 10 units. Compare expenditures on the good to find price elasticity of demand.
[**Ans.** $E_d = 1$]

Production Function and Returns to a Factor

1. Calculate the average and marginal product from the following:

Units of Labour	1	2	3	4	5
Total Product	18	38	50	60	72

[**Ans.** AP: 18, 19,16.67, 15, 14.4; MP: 18, 20, 12, 10, 12]

2. Complete the following table:

Units of Labour	Total Product	Average Product	Marginal Product
1	40	—	—
2	—	—	60
3	—	—	50
4	180	—	—
5	—	36	—
6	—	—	–18

[**Ans.** TP: 40, 100,150, 180, 180, 162; AP: 40, 50, 50, 45, 36, 27; MP: 40, 60, 50, 30, 0, –18]

3. Calculate the total and marginal product from the following:

Units of Labour	1	2	3	4	5
Average Product	4	5	5	4	3

[**Ans.** TP: 4, 10, 15, 16, 15; MP: 4, 6, 5, 1, –1]

4. Complete the following table:

Input (Units)	Total Product	Average Product	Marginal Product
1	20	—	—
2	—	—	18
3	—	—	16
4	—	—	14
5	—	—	12
6	—	—	10

[**Ans.** TP: 20, 38, 54, 68, 80, 90; AP: 20, 19, 18, 17, 16, 15]

5. Following is known about a firm:

Units of Labour (Input)	1	2	3	4	5	6
Total Output	50	110	150	180	180	150

State and explain the law underlying the change in output as input is changed. Also identify the various stages (or phases) in total product.

[**Ans.** Find MP and identify the stages of production as (i) stage of increasing returns when MP increasing, (ii) stage of diminishing returns when MP is diminishing, and (iii) stage of negative returns when MP is negative.

Note: The end of stage-1 marks the beginning of stage-2, and the end of stage-2 marks the beginning of stage-3.]

6. Identify the different output levels which makes the different phases/stages of the operation of the law of variable proportions from the following data:

Variable Input	0	1	2	3	4	5
Total Product	0	8	20	28	28	26

[**Ans.** Find MP and identify the stages of production as (i) stage of increasing returns when MP increasing, (ii) stage of diminishing returns when MP is diminishing, and (iii) stage of negative returns when MP is negative.

Note: The end of stage-1 marks the beginning of stage-2, and the end of stage-2 marks the beginning of stage-3.]

Concepts of Cost

1. From the following data on the cost of production of a firm calculate TFC, AFC, TVC, AVC and MC:

Output (kg)	0	1	2	3	4	5	6
TC (₹)	60	80	100	111	116	130	150

[**Ans.** TFC: ₹ 60 (at each level); AFC: ∞, 60, 30, 20, 15, 12, 10;
TVC: —, 20, 40, 51, 56, 70, 90; AVC: —, 20, 20, 17, 14, 14, 15;
MC : —, 20, 20, 11, 5, 14, 20]

2. From the following data regarding cost of a firm, calculate:
(i) average fixed cost and (ii) average variable cost.

Output (Units)	0	1	2	3	4	5	6
Total Cost (₹)	60	78	90	102	112	120	126

[**Ans.** AFC: ∞, 60, 30, 20, 15, 12, 10; AVC: —, 18, 15, 14, 13, 12, 11]

3. Calculate TVC and AVC with the help of the following data:

Output (Units)	1	2	3
MC (₹)	20	16	12

[**Ans.** TVC: 20, 36, 48; AVC: 20, 18, 16]

4. Calculate total variable cost and total cost from the following cost schedule of a firm whose fixed costs are ₹ 10.

Output (Units)	1	2	3	4
Marginal Cost (₹)	6	5	4	6

[**Ans.** TVC: 6, 11, 15, 21; TC: 16, 21, 25, 31]

5. From the following data on the cost of production of a firm calculate (i) average fixed cost, and (ii) average variable cost of producing four units and the marginal cost of the fourth unit:

Output (kg)	0	1	2	3	4
Total Cost (₹)	80	102	122	140	156

[**Ans.** (i) AFC (of fourth unit) = ₹ 20;
(ii) AVC (of fourth unit) = ₹ 19; Marginal cost (of fourth unit) = ₹ 16]

6. From the following table, calculate average variable cost of each given level of output:

Output (Units)	1	2	3	4
Marginal Cost (₹)	40	30	35	39

[**Ans.** AVC: 40, 35, 35, 36]

7. Complete the following table:

Output (Units)	**Total Cost (₹)**	**Average Fixed Cost (₹)**	**Average Cost (₹)**	**Variable Cost (₹)**
1	20	6		
2	26	3		
3	39	2		

[**Ans.** AC: 20, 13, 13; VC: 14, 20, 33]

8. Complete the following table:

Output (Units)	**Total Variable Cost (₹)**	**Average Variable Cost (₹)**	**Marginal Cost (₹)**
1	20	—	—
—	—	16	12
3	54	—	—
—	—	20	26

[**Ans.** Output: 1, 2, 3, 4; TVC: 20, 32, 54, 80; AVC: 20, 16, 18, 20; MC: 20, 12, 22, 26]

Concept of Revenue

1. Find out total revenue, average revenue and marginal revenue:

Price (₹)	1	2	3	4	5	6	7
Demand (Units)	10	9	8	7	6	5	4

[**Ans.** TR: 10, 18, 24, 28, 30, 30, 28; AR: 1, 2, 3, 4, 5, 6, 7; MR: 10, 8, 6, 4, 2, 0, –2]

2. From the table given below, calculate total revenue and marginal revenue:

Units Sold	Average Revenue (₹)	Total Revenue (₹)	Marginal Revenue (₹)
3	8		
4	7		
5	6		

[**Hint:** Average Revenue = Price]

[**Ans.** TR: 24, 28, 30; MR: —, 4 , 2]

3. Find average revenue and marginal revenue from the following data:

Units Sold	Total Revenue (₹)	Average Revenue (₹)	Marginal Revenue (₹)
1	10		
2	24		
3	33		
4	40		
5	40		
6	36		
7	28		

[**Ans.** AR: 10, 12, 11, 10, 8, 6, 4; MR: 10, 14, 9, 7, 0, –4, –8]

4. Find marginal revenue on the basis of the following data:

Units Sold	Total Revenue (₹)	Marginal Revenue (₹)
1	10	
2	18	
3	24	
4	28	
5	30	

[**Ans.** MR: 10, 8, 6, 4, 2]

5. Complete the following table:

Output (Units)	Price (₹)	Total Revenue (₹)	Marginal Revenue (₹)
1	7	—	—
2	6	—	—
3	4	—	—
4	2	—	—

[**Ans.** TR: 7, 12, 12, 8; MR: 7, 5, 0, –4]

6. Complete the following table:

Output (Units)	Total Revenue (₹)	Marginal Revenue (₹)	Average Revenue (₹)
1	14	—	—
2	24	—	—
3	24	—	—
4	16	—	—

[**Ans.** MR: 14, 10, 0, –8; AR: 14, 12, 8, 4]

7. Complete the following table:

Output (Units)	Marginal Revenue (₹)	Total Revenue (₹)	Average Revenue (₹)
1	10	—	—
2	8	—	—
3	0	—	—
4	– 2	—	—

[**Ans.** TR: 10, 18, 18, 16; AR: 10, 9, 6, 4]

8. Complete the following table:

Units Sold	Total Revenue (₹)	Average Revenue (₹)	Marginal Revenue (₹)
1	20	—	—
2	—	18	—
3	—	—	12
4	56	—	—
5	—	—	4
6	—	—	0

[**Ans.** TR: 20, 36, 48, 56, 60, 60; AR: 20, 18, 16, 14, 12, 10; MR: 20, 16, 12, 8, 4, 0]

Producer's Equilibrium

1. Find out profit of the producer, when total revenue is ₹ 400, total variable cost is ₹ 270, average fixed cost is ₹ 25 per unit and 4 units of output are produced.
[**Ans.** Profit = ₹ 30]

2. Calculate the profit from the following:

Output (Units)	Marginal Revenue (₹)	Total Cost (₹)
1	7	8
2	5	10
3	4	12
4	2	15
5	1	16

[**Ans.** Profit = –1, 2, 4, 3, 3]

3. Complete the following table:

Output (Units)	Total Revenue (₹)	Total Cost (₹)	Profit (₹)
1	6	8	—
2	—	9	–1
3	10	—	0
4	12	11	—
5	14	8	—

[**Ans.** TR: 6, 8, 10, 12, 14; TC: 8, 9, 10, 11, 8; Profit: –2, –1, 0, 1, 6]

4. Find the profit maximising level of output.

Quantity Sold (Units)	Total Revenue (₹)	Marginal Cost (₹)
1	14	15
2	30	12
3	44	9
4	48	5
5	52	6

[**Ans.** Profit is maximum when output level= 3 units are produced, as it is here that the difference between TR and TVC is maximised. TVC = ΣMC]

5. Find producer's equilibrium from the following table given below:

Quantity Sold (Units)	Total Revenue (₹)	Marginal Cost (₹)
1	9	15
2	18	8
3	27	9
4	36	10
5	45	11

[**Ans.** Producer is in equilibrium when 3 units of output are produced, as it is here that MR = MC, and MC is rising]

6. Given below is a cost and revenue schedule of a producer. At what level of output is the producer in equilibrium? Give reasons for your answer.

Quantity Sold (Units)	Price (₹ per unit)	Total Cost (₹)
1	15	14
2	16	24
3	17	30
4	18	51
5	19	75

[**Ans.** The producer is in equilibrium when 4 units of output are produced. It is here that the difference between TR and TC is maximum, along with the fact that MR = MC, and MC is rising]

Theory of Supply

1. Price of a commodity increases from ₹ 10 to ₹ 12. As a result, its supply rises from 35 units to 42 units. Find out elasticity of supply.

   [**Ans.** $E_s = 1$]

2. As a result of 15 per cent rise in the price of a commodity, its supply increases from 25 to 30 units. Calculate elasticity of supply.

   [**Ans.** $E_s = 1.33$]

3. The price of a commodity is ₹ 12 per unit and its quantity supplied is 500 units. When its price rises to ₹ 15 per unit, its quantity supplied rises to 650 units. Calculate its price elasticity of supply. Is supply elastic?

   [**Ans.** $E_s = 1.2$; Yes, Supply is elastic]

4. Price elasticity of supply for a product is 'unity'. A firm supplies 25 units of this product at a price of ₹ 5 per unit. If the price of product rises to ₹ 6 per unit, how much quantity of the product will be supplied by the firm?

   [**Ans.** New quantity = 30 units]

5. When the price of a commodity falls from ₹10 per unit to ₹ 9 per unit, its quantity supplied falls by 20 per cent. Calculate its price elasticity of supply. Is its supply elastic?

   [**Ans.** $E_s = 2$; Yes, Supply is elastic]

6. The quantity supplied of a commodity at a price of ₹ 8 per unit is 400 units. Its price elasticity of supply is 2. Calculate the price at which its quantity supplied will be 600 units.

   [**Ans.** New price = ₹10]

7. When the price of a commodity rises from ₹ 10 to ₹ 11 per unit, its quantity supplied rises by 100 units. Its price elasticity of supply is 2. Calculate its quantity supplied at the increased price.

   [**Ans.** Quantity supplied = 600 units]

8. The price elasticity of supply of a commodity is 2. When its price falls from ₹ 10 to ₹ 8 per unit, its quantity supplied falls by 500 units. Calculate the quantity supplied at the reduced price.

   [**Ans.** Quantity supplied = 750 units]

9. For a commodity, if $E_s = 1.4$ and $\frac{\Delta P}{P} = 0.6$, find the percentage change in quantity supplied.

   [**Ans.** 84%]

10. The market price of a good changes from ₹ 5 to ₹ 20. As a result, the quantity supplied by the firm increases by 15 units. The price elasticity of supply is 0.5. Find the initial and final output levels of the firm.

    [**Ans.** 10 units and 25 units]

CBSE Sample Question Paper, 2015-16

INTRODUCTORY MICROECONOMICS

Time Allowed: 1½ Hours **Maximum Marks: 50**

General Instructions:

(i) *All questions are compulsory. However, there is internal choice in some questions.*

(ii) *Marks for questions are indicated against each question.*

(iii) *Question No. 1-5 are very short answer questions carrying 1 mark each. They are required to be answered in one sentence.*

(iv) *Question No. 6-8 are short answer questions carrying 3 marks each. Answers to them should not normally exceed 60 words each.*

(v) *Question No. 9-11 are also short answer questions carrying 4 marks each. Answers to them should not normally exceed 70 words each.*

(vi) *Question No. 12-15 are long answer questions carrying 6 marks each. Answers to them should not normally exceed 100 words each.*

(vii) *Answers should be brief and to the point and the above word limit be adhered to as far as possible.*

1. If it is given that the total variable cost for producing 15 units of output is ₹3,000 and for 16 units is ₹3,500. Find the value of marginal cost. **(1)**

Ans.

$$MC = TVC_{16} - TVC_{15}$$
$$= ₹\,3{,}500 - ₹\,3{,}000$$
$$= ₹\,500$$

Value of marginal cost = ₹ 500.

2. Ceteris Paribus, if the government provides subsidies on electricity bills, what would be the likely change in the market demand of desert coolers? **(1)**

Ans. Market demand of desert coolers will increase because electricity and desert coolers are complementary goods and subsidies lead to the fall in price of electricity.

3. Which of these can be referred to as 'point of satiety'? **(1)**

(i) Marginal Utility is negative

(ii) Marginal utility is zero

(iii) Total Utility is rising

(iv) Total Utility is falling

Ans. (ii)

4. Which of the following is an assumption of Production Possibility Frontier? **(1)**

(i) Resources are not fully employed

(ii) Resources are not equally efficient for production of the two goods

(iii) Resources are not efficiently employed

(iv) Resources available are not fixed

Ans. (ii)

5. State any two central problems under 'problem of allocation of resources'. **(1)**

Ans. (i) What to produce, and

(ii) How to produce.

6. 'Supply curve is the rising portion of marginal cost curve over and above the minimum of average variable cost curve'. Do you agree? Support your answer with valid reason. **(3)**

Ans. Yes, we do agree with the given statement that supply curve (short run) is the rising portion of marginal cost over and above the minimum of average variable cost curve.

At a given price, a firm strikes its equilibrium when P (price) = MC (because AR is constant under perfect competition) and MC is rising.

In the short run, a firm must cover its variable cost. So that, it will undertake production only if TR = TVC or $\frac{TR}{Q} = \frac{TVC}{Q}$ or AR = AVC, or P = AVC. Therefore, short run supply curve of the firm starts from its shut-down point, the point where P = AVC. Starting from this point, the firm's short run supply curve would be the same as its MC curve (because the firm's equilibrium is occurring along the rising segment of MC). Fig. 1 illustrates this point.

FIGURE 1

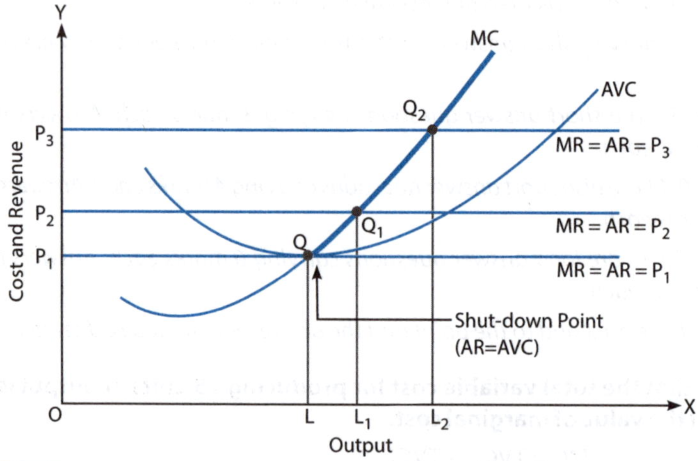

7. Explain 'black marketing' as a direct consequence of price ceiling. **(3)**

Ans. Black marketing is the direct consequence of price ceiling. Price ceiling refers to the maximum price of a commodity that the sellers can charge from the buyers. Often, the government fixes this price lower than the equilibrium market price so that the concerned commodity remains within the reach of the poorer sections of the society. When ceiling price is lower than the equilibrium price, there is likely to be excess demand in the market, leading to shortage of the commodity which in turn leads to black marketing. Fig. 2 illustrates this situation.

FIGURE 2

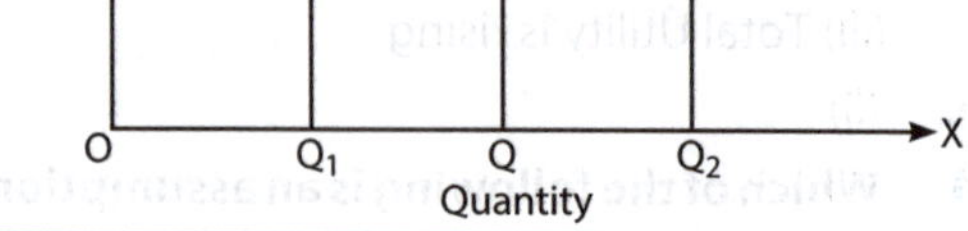

Equilibrium Price : OP

Ceiling Price : OP*

(i) Excess Demand = AB = Q_1Q_2.

(ii) Black marketing (related to excess demand).

Or

Explain the concept of 'buffer stock' as a tool of price floor. **(3)**

Ans. Buffer stock is an important tool of 'price floor'. Floor price is the minimum price fixed by the government for sale of a commodity in the market. Often this is higher than the equilibrium price. Generally, it is done in case of farm-goods with a view to stabilising income of the farmers. However, floor price is often supplemented with the Support Price Policy. This implies that the government will buy the surplus stock of the farmers in case they fail to sell it in the open market at the floor price. By buying the surplus stocks of the farmers, the government creates its own buffer stock (to be used for public distribution). Thus, floor price is a tool of the buffer stock. Fig. 3 illustrates this situation.

FIGURE 3

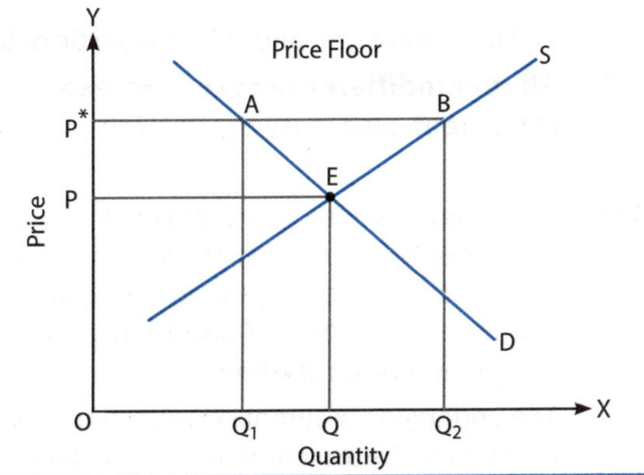

Equilibrium Price : OP

Floor Price : OP*

(i) Excess Supply = AB = Q_1Q_2.

(ii) Market price would reduce to the level of equilibrium price, unless 'Support Price' is offered. At this price, the government buys the surplus product (lower than the equilibrium price) from the producer and stores it as a buffer stock. This stock is used for public distribution.

8. Explain any two sources of restricted entry under monopoly. **(3)**

Ans. Two sources of restricted entry under monopoly are as under:

(i) Government Licensing/Government Control: The government may grant license for the production of a particular commodity only to one producer. Accordingly, monopoly comes into existence. Also, the government may decide to control the production of certain goods (or services) exclusively through its departmental undertakings, like Railways in India.

(ii) Patent Rights: Patent rights is the most important form of entry-barrier. Patent rights is the official recognition of the originators of a new product or technology. No one else can use their technology without obtaining a license.

9. Comment upon the degree of elasticity of demand for Good-X, in the following given situations, if the price of the commodity rises from 5 per unit to 7 per unit and the quantity demanded falls from 20 units to 16 units:

(i) Using the total household expenditure method.

(ii) Using proportionate method. **(4)**

Ans. **(i) Expenditure Method:**

Price (₹)	Demand (Units)	Total Expenditure (₹)
5	20	100
7	16	112

With increase in price, total expenditure on Good-X has tended to rise. Accordingly, elasticity of demand should be less than unity ($E_d < 1$).

Elasticity of demand < 1 (inelastic or less elastic demand).

(ii) Proportionate Method:

Given, $P = ₹\,5$; $P_1 = ₹\,7$; $\Delta P = P_1 - P = ₹\,7 - ₹\,5 = ₹\,2$

$Q = 20$ units; $Q_1 = 16$ units; $\Delta Q = Q_1 - Q = (16 - 20)$ units $= (-)\,4$ units

$$\text{Elasticity of demand } (E_d) = (-)\frac{\Delta Q}{\Delta P} \times \frac{P}{Q}$$

$$= (-)\frac{-4}{2} \times \frac{5}{20} = 0.5$$

Elasticity of demand = 0.5 (inelastic or less elastic demand).

10. 'Higher indifference curve represents higher level of satisfaction to the consumer'. Explain the statement, also state the underlying assumption related to this property of indifference curve. **(4)**

Ans. Higher indifference curve represents higher level of satisfaction. In indifference map, higher indifference curve represents those combinations which yield higher level of satisfaction than the combinations on the lower indifference curve. In other words, each point on a higher indifference curve shows that for a given level of consumption of Good-Y, the consumption of Good-X tends to be more than before. This implies higher level of satisfaction.

The underlying assumption related to this property of indifference curve is monotonic preferences of the consumer. The assumption reveals that more of one commodity (with no less of the other) yields higher level of satisfaction.

Or

A consumer consumes two goods X and Y. Explain what will happen if $\frac{MU_X}{P_X}$ is greater than $\frac{MU_Y}{P_Y}$? **(4)**

Ans. Equilibrium of the consumer in case of two commodities occurs when:

$$\frac{MU_X}{P_X} = \frac{MU_Y}{P_Y}$$

Given, $\frac{MU_X}{P_X} > \frac{MU_Y}{P_Y}$.

The consumer would increase the consumption of X in place of Y, because rupee worth of satisfaction in case of X $\left(=\frac{MU_X}{P_X}\right)$ is greater than in case of Y $\left(=\frac{MU_Y}{P_Y}\right)$. As consumption of Y is reduced, MU_Y would start rising. Likewise, increase in the consumption of X would cause a fall in MU_X. The process of substituting X for Y would continue till $\frac{MU_X}{P_X} = \frac{MU_Y}{P_Y}$ and the equilibrium is achieved, when the consumer maximises his satisfaction.

11. Define marginal opportunity cost. Explain the concept with a hypothetical numerical example. **(4)**

Ans. Marginal opportunity cost (or marginal rate of transformation) is the rate at which output of Good-Y is to be sacrificed for a unit more of Good-X, when the given resources are fully and efficiently utilised in the production of goods X and Y, and the technology remains constant. It refers to the slope of PPC (production possibility curve). It is also called the opportunity cost of producing a unit more of Good-X in terms of the loss of output of Good-Y.

Example:	Output of Y	Output of X
	10	10
	7	11

When some resources are shifted from Use-Y to Use-X, there is a loss of output of 3 units of Y for a unit more of Good-X. MOC $= \frac{\Delta Y}{\Delta X} = \frac{3}{1} = 3$. [Here, ΔY refers to loss of output of Good-Y. ΔX refers to loss of output of Good-X.]

12. (a) What is meant by price rigidity, under oligopoly? **(2)**

(b) Elaborate the implication of the conditions of equilibrium of a firm. **(4)**

Ans. (a) Price rigidity means that firms under oligopoly would not like to change the price of the commodity. The reason is like this:

(i) If the firm increases the price of the product, the rival firms may not increase leading to a loss of the market (the buyers will shift to the rival firms).

(ii) If the firm lowers the price of the product, the rival firms may also lower the price leading to a loss of total revenue without any gain of additional buyers.

(b) The implications of the conditions of equilibrium of a firm (producer) is explained with the help of Fig. 4.

A firm is said to be in equilibrium when (i) MR = MC, and (ii) MC is rising.

(i) When MR is not equal to MC, we have two situations: (1) MR > MC, and (2) MR < MC.

(1) When MR > MC (as at K-level of output), every additional unit of output contributes greater revenue than cost. Increase in output in such a situation would increase the level of profits.

FIGURE 4

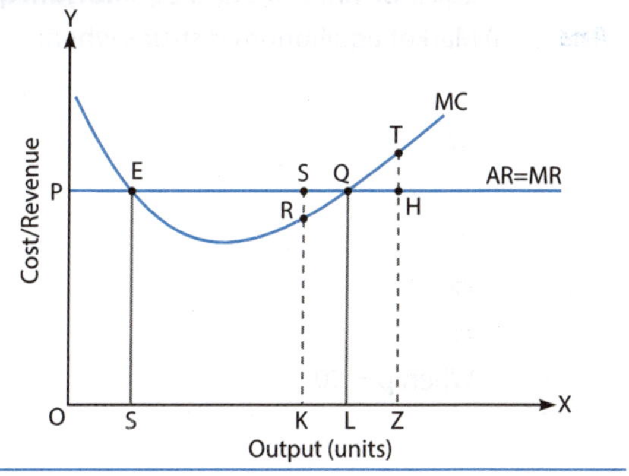

(2) When MR < MC (as at Z-level of output), every additional unit of output causes greater cost than revenue. A cut in the level of output in such a situation would increase the level of profits.

Thus, MR must be equal to MC for a firm to be in equilibrium.

(ii) When MC is not rising at the point where MR = MC. Instead it is falling (as at point E). In that case, the firm will be able to generate more profits by producing more because (MR – MC) would be increasing.

Hence, the conclusion that the firm is in equilibrium only when: (i) MR = MC, and (ii) MC is rising.

13. (a) Distinguish between stock and supply.

(b) Complete the following schedule: **(2+4)**

Units Produced	TPP (in ₹)	APP (in ₹)	MPP (in ₹)
1	100	—	—
2	—	—	140
3	—	140	—
4	480	—	—

Ans. (a) (i) Supply means the quantity of a commodity offered for sale at a given price in the market. Stock of a commodity refers to the quantity of a commodity available in the market for present as well as future sale.

(ii) Supply is always studied with reference to price, stock is NOT.

(b)

Units Produced	TPP (in ₹)	APP (in ₹)	MPP (in ₹)
1	100	100	100
2	240	120	140
3	420	140	180
4	480	120	60

14. Suppose the demand and supply curves of a commodity-X are given by the following two equations simultaneously:

$$Q_d = 200 - p \qquad Q_s = 50 + 2p$$

(i) Find the equilibrium price and equilibrium quantity.

(ii) Suppose that the price of a factor of production producing the commodity has changed, resulting in the new supply curve given by the equation:

$$Qs' = 80 + 2p$$

Analyse the new equilibrium price and new equilibrium quantity as against the original equilibrium price and equilibrium quantity. (3+3)

Ans. (i) Market equilibrium is struck when:

Market Demand = Market Supply

Or, $Q_d = Q_s$

$\therefore$ $200 - p = 50 + 2p$

$\Rightarrow$ $2p + p = 200 - 50$

$\Rightarrow$ $3p = 150$

$\Rightarrow$ $p = 50$

When p = 50, $Q_d = 200 - p$

$= 200 - 50$

$= 150$

Equilibrium price = 50.

Equilibrium quantity = 150.

(ii) When price of a factor of production has changed, new equilibrium price and equilibrium quantity is achieved when:

$Q_d = Q'_s$

$\therefore$ $200 - p = 80 + 2p$

$\Rightarrow$ $2p + p = 200 - 80$

$\Rightarrow$ $3p = 120$

$\Rightarrow$ $p = 40$

When p = 40, $Q_d = 200 - p$

$= 200 - 40$

$= 160$

New equilibrium price = 40.

New equilibrium quantity = 160.

15. Show diagrammatically the conditions for consumer's equilibrium, in Hicksian analysis of demand. (6)

Ans. Consumer's equilibrium refers to a situation when a consumer maximises his satisfaction spending his given income across different goods and services.

In terms of Hicksian analysis of demand (or IC analysis) a consumer attains equilibrium when:

(i) IC and price line are tangent to each other.

or

When slope of IC and slope of price line are equal to each other.

and (ii) IC is convex to the origin, at the point of equilibrium.

FIGURE 5

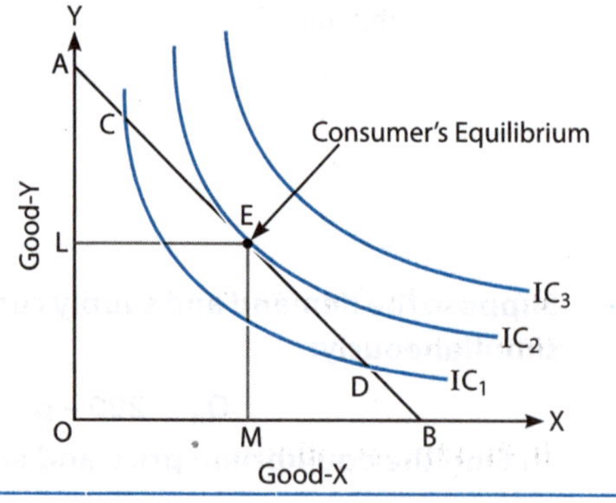

In Fig. 5, AB is the budget or price line. IC_1, IC_2 and IC_3 are indifference curves. A consumer can buy any of the combinations, A, B, C, D and E of Good-X and Good-Y shown on the price line AB. He cannot get any combination on IC_3 as it is away from price line AB. He can buy those combinations which are not only on price line AB but also coincide with the highest indifference curve which is IC_2 in this case. Out of A, B, C, D and E combinations, the consumer will be in equilibrium at combination 'E', because at this point price line (AB) is tangent to the highest indifference curve IC_2. No doubt, the consumer can buy 'C' or 'D' combinations as well but these will not give him maximum satisfaction being situated on lower indifference curve IC_1. It means consumer's equilibrium point is the point of tangency of price line and indifference curve. At equilibrium,

$$\text{Slope of Indifference Curve} = \text{Slope of Budget or Price Line or } MRS_{XY} = \frac{P_X}{P_Y}$$

Also, at point E, IC_2 is convex to the origin. Accordingly, equilibrium is stable. If IC_2 was not convex at the point of equilibrium, we shall never have stable equilibrium.

In a state of equilibrium, the consumer is buying OL amount of Good-Y and OM amount of Good-X. It is here that he is maximising his satisfaction. Any departure from this point would only mean lesser satisfaction.